TRADITIONAL FOLK SONG IN MODERN JAPAN

TRADITIONAL FOLK SONG

IN

MODERN JAPAN

SOURCES, SENTIMENT AND SOCIETY

David W. Hughes

SOAS, UNIVERSITY OF LONDON

GLOBAL
ORIENTAL

TRADITIONAL FOLK SONG IN MODERN JAPAN
SOURCES, SENTIMENT AND SOCIETY
David W. Hughes

First published 2008 by
GLOBAL ORIENTAL LTD
PO Box 219
Folkestone
Kent CT20 2WP
UK

www.globaloriental.co.uk

ISBN 978-1-905246-65-6

British Library Cataloguing in Publication Data
A CIP catalogue entry for this book is available from the British Library

The Publishers and author wish to thank the Great Britain-Sasakawa Foundation
and SOAS, University of London, for their generous support in the
making of this book.

Set in Garamond 11.5 on 13pt by IDSUK (Data Connection) Ltd.
Printed and bound in England by Antony Rowe Ltd., Chippenham, Wiltshire

to Gina,

to Sue and Jerry Hughes,

and

to all 'the folk' of Japan

CONTENTS

□

4.   The modern urban folk song world

5.   The modern countryside and the performing arts

LIST OF MUSICAL
EXAMPLES

◰

LIST OF FIGURES

�«□»

LIST OF TABLES

◩

Table 0.1 Provinces and prefectures of Japan

Provincial system (645–1871) No. (in Figure 0.1)	Prefectural system (1871–present) No. (in Figure 0.2)	Provincial system (645–1871) No. (in Figure 0.1)	Prefectural system (1871–present) No. (in Figure 0.2)
A Mutsu (divided in 1868 into):		47 YAMATO =	47 NARA
		48 Kii ~	48 Wakayama
1 Mutsu ~	1 Aomori	49 Izumi	
2 Rikuchū ~	2 Iwate	50 Kawachi	52 Ōsaka
3 Rikuzen ~	3 Miyagi	51 Settsu	
4 Iwaki		53 Yamashiro	
5 Iwashiro	8 Fukushima	54 Tango	56 Kyōto
		55 Tanba	
B Dewa (divided in 1868 into):		57 Tajima	
		58 Harima	60 Hyōgo
6 Ugo ~	6 Akita	59 Awaji	
7 Uzen ~	7 Yamagata	61 Awa =	61 Tokushima
		62 Tosa =	62 Kōchi
9 Sado		63 Iyo =	63 Ehime
10 Echigo	11 Niigata	64 Sanuki =	64 Kagawa
12 Etchū =	12 Toyama	65 Bizen	
13 Noto		66 Bitchū	68 Okayama
14 Kaga	15 Ishikawa	67 Mimasaka	
16 Echizen		69 Inaba	
17 Wakasa	18 Fukui	70 Hoki	71 Tottori
19 Hitachi ~	19 Ibaragi	72 Oki	
20 Shimotsuke =	20 Tochigi	73 Izumo	75 Shimane
21 Kōzuke =	21 Gumma	74 Iwami	
22 Shimo'osa		76 Bingo	
23 Kazusa	25 Chiba	77 Aki	78 Hiroshima
24 Awa		79 Suō	
26 Musashi		80 Nagato	81 Yamaguchi
	27 Saitama	82 Chikuzen	
	28 Tōkyō	83 Chikugo	85 Fukuoka
29 Sagami =	29 Kanagawa	84 Buzen	
30 Kai =	30 Yamanashi	86 Bungo ~	87 Ōita
31 Shinano =	31 Nagano	88 Hyūga =	88 Miyazaki
32 Hida		89 Ōsumi	
33 Mino	34 Gifu	90 Satsuma	91 Kagoshima
35 Izu		92 Higo =	92 Kumamoto
36 Suruga	38 Shizuoka	93 Hizen ~	94 Saga
37 Totomi		96 Iki	
39 Mikawa		97 Tsushima	95 Nagasaki
40 Owari	41 Aichi		
42 Ōmi =	42 Shiga		
43 Iga			
44 Ise	46 Mie		
45 Shima			

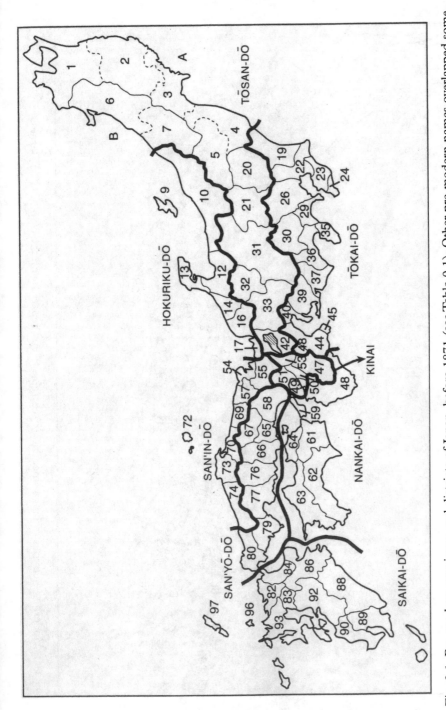

Fig. 0.1 Pre-modern provinces and districts of Japan, before 1871 (see Table 0.1). Other pre-modern names overlapped some of these, e.g. Tsugaru (modern Aomori and northern Iwate) and Nanbu (modern southern Iwate). Prepared with the help of Gina Barnes.

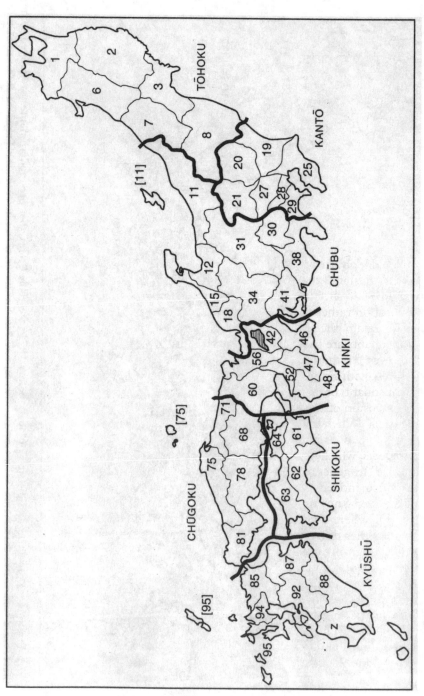

Fig. 0.2 Modern prefectures of Japan since 1871 (see Table 0.1). Prepared with the help of Gina Barnes.

STYLISTIC CONVENTIONS

Modified Hepburn romanization is used for Japanese words. The five vowels of standard Japanese, romanized *a i u e o*, are pronounced roughly as in Spanish, but with lips unrounded for *u*; a macron indicates a doubled duration rather than any change in the quality of the vowel. Vowels in sequence retain their original sound (thus, *-ei-* in *geisha* rhymes with 'day'). Consonants are basically as in English, but *y* is always a semivowel (as in English 'yes') rather than a vowel (as in English 'tying'), so that *kyū* rhymes closely with English 'cue'. An *n* at the end of a word, or followed by another consonant or an apostrophe, is pronounced as a syllable-length nasalized extension of the immediately preceding vowel – what linguists call a 'syllabic nasal'. When followed by *m, b* or *p* this syllabic nasal is pronounced *m*. The *r* is 'flapped' as in Spanish *pero*.

Local dialects, which occur in many song lyrics, vary in ways too complex to summarize. In general, I have romanized lyrics as if they were standard Japanese, since indeed most people sing them with that pronunciation. Many of the best-known songs are from the northeast, with its distinctive 'zūzū' dialect, where standard *shi* and *ji* come out more like *su* amd *zu*, among many other differences; singers from elsewhere, however, never imitate this (although my attempts to do so always draw smiles). Japanese is a pitch-accent language rather than stress-accented (like English) or tonal (like Chinese), but pitch patterns differ locally and have surprisingly little effect on melody (see further §1.6).

Japanese poetic metre is counted in terms of what linguists call moras instead of syllables. Thus a long vowel, which in some contexts functions as one syllable, almost always counts as two moras – two beats – of a line, since it is in effect a double vowel. Similarly the syllabic nasal *n* counts as one beat. The word *min'yō* 'folk song' thus takes up four counts of a seven-'syllable' line: *mi-n-yo-o*. However, since long vowels are often ignored in folk song, my use of macrons is perhaps inconsistent when romanizing lyrics. Otherwise, long vowels are marked except in the common place names Tokyo, Kyoto and Osaka.

With no accepted standard practice for the hyphenation and word division of romanized Japanese, I have done whatever I felt would help the reader.

All Japanese terms appearing in running text are italicized, except for widely recognized words (samurai, geisha, shamisen, koto, shakuhachi, Kabuki, Noh, Bunraku, Bon, etc).

Japanese personal names, when cited in full in running text, are given in Japanese order, surname first. This order is also maintained in the bibliography, but there a comma has been inserted after the surname.

All translations are mine unless otherwise stated. In translating song texts, I have tried to preserve the original order of images line by line – a necessary compromise in a situation where space does not permit the inclusion of both word-by-word and fully literary translations. Thus a bit of poetic flow is sacrificed for a bit of structure. I do this partly for consistency with the principles I use in translating Japanese 'classical' music lyrics, where the individual images are often closely linked with musical gestures. In strophic folk song, however, there is little relationship between semantic content and melody or other aspects of expression. Within translated or quoted text, material between square brackets has been added or adjusted by myself.

I have tried to cite English references even if the information is ultimately from a Japanese source, as long as the English source guides the reader to the Japanese original. For information on Japanese music in general, consult the Japan sections of the *New Grove Dictionary of Music and Musicians* (Grove Sadie & Tyrrell 2001) and the *Garland Encyclopedia of World Music: East Asia* (Provine et al. 2001), plus Malm 2000, Wade 2005 and Tokita & Hughes 2007. When the same information occurs in different works of one author, I generally cite only the source where I first encountered it, unless another source is deemed much more accessible.

References to the accompanying compact disc are given as 'CD' plus track number. References to the Audio-Videography are in the form R + number.

Interviews and personal communications are cited as follows. Any time an individual is cited as a source of information without further reference, it can be assumed to have been a personal communication from some time between 1977 and the present. I have only added the words 'pers. comm.' and a date when confusion about the source seemed possible or when the timing of the comment seemed important to its proper significance. I accept that best practice would have given dates for all such information, but this was impracticable.

Brief cross-references abound, generally to a chapter section (shown as §, or in plural as §§) rather than to a specific page. The General Index provides further guidance. Terms that are used often are defined in the Glossary of Selected Terms.

FOREWORD

■

This Foreword is intended to give the reader two things: a strategy for approaching the reading of this book, and, in the self-reflexive mode, some information about my research experiences.

This book is an extensive revision and expansion of my doctoral dissertation, whose subtitle has become this book's title (University of Michigan, 1985; published by UMI, 1986). All old sections have been revised and many new ones added. The number of musical examples has been increased, photos have been added, and – most crucially – a compact disk now allows a taste of the range of Japanese folk song.

Each chapter but the last ends with a section summarizing its contents. Reading these summary sections first may help establish the overall framework in the reader's mind. With that much background, the reader should survive the rather threatening sea of terminology in Chapter 1 without giving up altogether.

Appendix 1 contains translations of several dozen 'new folk songs' as well as of popular songs linked in some way to folk song. I have included these in preference to extensive translations of more traditional folk songs, because there are already several books available containing the latter (some cited in note 3 of Chapter 2). But numerous translations of traditional verses are found in Chapter 2 in particular.

The general reader can safely ignore all endnotes.

Steven Feld noted in the preface to the second edition of *Sound and Sentiment* (1990) that several major new theoretical models or emphases had impacted on ethnomusicology since his first edition, and that he would have both researched and written differently now. The same is true for this book. In the years since the 'first edition' (the dissertation) appeared, we have had, in no particular order, Benedict Anderson and imagined communities, Appadurai and globalization, more from Said on orientalism and 'the Other', the new ethnography and reflexivity, a stronger emphasis on gender, Bourdieu, Giddens, space and place, phenomenology and hermeneutics, studies of nostalgia and Japaneseness in Japan, and others. Taking any of these fully on board would have meant a major rewrite at the expense of expanding the ethnographic data. Several of these approaches do find their way briefly into these pages, but given that we still have no good history or ethnography of Japanese folk song's development in the modern period, I have chosen to concentrate on Japan and on data and interpretation, rather than on comparisons with elsewhere or on testing or developing a theoretical model. I have tried to pack in as much data as possible, again to fill the gap. This does not make for a zippy read; for a more compact introduction to Japan's folk music, start with Hughes 2007, Koizumi & Hughes 2001 and Groemer 2001.

As to my research experiences: I lived, researched and worked in Japan from 1977 to 1981, during the peak of a folk song 'boom', and was fortunate to become involved in both the professional and the amateur folk song worlds. As foreigners have rarely entered these worlds, I had a curiosity value which ultimately proved very convenient for opening doors. Solely by virtue of being a foreigner with modest relevant skills and knowledge, I was asked (astonishingly, even paid) to perform frequently in public, on stage, television and radio; to serve as judge at folk song contests; to act as master of ceremonies for a recital by folk artists licensed to CBS-Sony; to 'star' in a 'folk song musical' partly inspired by myself and my fieldwork (*Ushioi no Sato* by Katō Toshio, 1981); even to record, with my teacher, a commercial album of Japanese folk songs. (The record company laboured under the misapprehension that an album of Japanese folk songs half of which were badly sung by an American – with backing from some of his American friends – would sell well in the United States; I merely laboured under apprehension, but went ahead with the project because my teacher wished it and in order to get a first-hand taste of the recording industry's approach to folk song.) As a result of such exposure and surprising attention, I was invited to visit several communities around Japan to study the local songs.

Shorter follow-up visits to Japan were made in 1984, 1988, 1989, 1993, 1998, 1999, 2000, 2003, 2006 and 2007, allowing me to add detail, fill in gaps and – most importantly – observe Japan's 'folk song world' after the boom around 1980 had cooled down (*sameta*) to a low flame (*teika*), as my friend Takahashi Yūjirō put it.

After much thought, I have followed the practice of my dissertation and taken the entire period from 1977 to the present as my 'ethnographic present'. This is because the 'folk song world' has changed remarkably little during these thirty years. When significant changes have occurred, I discuss them explicitly and cite dates.

Much of my research consisted of participant observation, at many levels and in many contexts of the *min'yō* world. To indicate the diversity of my experience, here are a few examples to add to my LP and my '*min'yō* musical'. I sometimes was invited to join in the live singing or drumming for village ancestral Bon dances (joining in the dancing was, of course, taken for granted). I took formal singing lessons primarily with two contrasting teachers: a full-time professional with a recording contract and hundreds of pupils, and an amateur who taught only a handful of neighbours. In 1979, my wife Gina Barnes and I were guest artists on an old-style folk song tour of northern Japan (see Fig. 3.2): the troupe would steam into a town in our tour bus, loudspeaker blaring an announcement of our concert at the local gymnasium or town hall, then present three hours of variegated folk songs and dances. Our co-artists on that tour (including such major figures as Asari Miki, Izumo Ainosuke II and Sasaki Motoharu, whose various careers span the decades from 1930 to the present) taught us more than can be conveyed in this book. And I often visited with the members of local folk song preservation societies, who were mostly elderly amateurs whose musical tastes and experiences were frozen in the headlights of modernizing, Westernizing Japan.

Nor were these folk song activities hermetically sealed off from other musics. Here is the musical reality of today's Japan. One night around 1980 I went along to play shamisen for a friend (Dezaki Tayo II; see §4.4.2) who was teaching a folk song class at a Tokyo community centre. Perhaps surprisingly, many of her students, mostly middle-aged or elderly women clad in kimono, stayed on to take part in the class that followed immediately in the same room: 'social dancing' – fox-trot, waltz, cha-cha-cha and the like. The women were at first eager to dance with me, since as a Westerner I was presumed to be a master trotter; they soon learned why I had taken up folk song rather than ballroom dancing. And the same Katō who landed me in the '*min'yō* musical' also forced the same long-suffering populace of Kitakami, Iwate Prefecture, to sit through 'A Musical Evening with David Hughes' ('Debito Hyūzu Ongaku no Yūbe'). Katō's production had me sharing the stage with several local professionals, with the wonderful 'folk song granny' Itō Moyo (see Index) – and with the local jazz trombonist and his wife the opera singer, the city's most renowned professional Western-style musicians. These two Japanese from contrasting Western musical spheres, and myself from yet a different Japanese one, somehow had to find some common ground for one number (neither jazz nor opera being counted among my talents). I suggested something like 'St. Louis Blues', with me on guitar. Hubby instantly produced a lead sheet in Western notation for his wife, then put on a recording of Bessie Smith's rendition. Consulting the notation, his wife was shocked: 'But she's not singing this melody at all!' Never mind, just fake it, he suggested helpfully, but faking is not a skill vouchsafed to divas. On the night, she sang it note for note from the lead sheet, in rampant *bel canto*.

In return trips since 1981, I have largely managed to maintain a low profile and avoid being drawn into the more outrageous types of event. But in those prime research years, when Westerners interested in traditional music were like extraterrestrials, it was difficult to avoid involvement even when I wanted to. I did manage to firmly reject doing a vitamin commercial for television, one which would have joined my Tsugaru-jamisen plucking to the shakuhachi of fellow American John Neptune and the vocals of Kanazawa Akiko, then Japan's leading folk song star. ('Don't you at least want to know the fee?')

Through such experiences, I was frequently in the presence of performers, and they responded congenially to my constant questioning despite generally having much better things to do. (In 2000, the singer Hikage Yūko recalled with a laugh my first visit to her father's folk song bar Hideko in 1979: 'You were always asking, "What does that mean? What does that mean?"') One reason that I was treated so kindly was that many self-defined 'modern' Japanese consider *min'yō* unworthy of serious attention in today's world and indeed may denigrate the people involved in it as old-fashioned, country bumpkins, or even of loose morals; thus folk song fans are always delighted to welcome a sympathetic newcomer to their ranks. Since the status of 'Western academic with beard' is a relatively prestigious one in Japan (even wearing jeans), my presence was also often used by those who wished to borrow some of that misplaced prestige to increase respect for traditional folk song; I hope they were successful. Upon hearing me sing on television or radio, listeners often phoned or wrote to say how embarrassed they were that, despite being native Japanese, they could not sing their own folk songs as well as the foreigner (doubtless because they had never tried!), and that henceforth they would pay more attention and respect to their musical heritage; I hope they have.

Does all this performing activity indicate that I have mastered Japanese folk singing? I suppose that a journalist from *Action Comics* (sic!), appropriately reviewing my LP, put it best, if somewhat tactlessly: in terms of vocal technique, *maa, heta desu* – 'Well, he's pretty bad.' He did go on to grant me what constitutes a compliment among traditionalists at least: my singing was *tsuchikusai* – it 'smelled of the earth'. I could, literally, have hoped for no greater praise (although I did begin to use a mouthwash).

In November 2000, I updated the final paragraphs of my final chapter, based on a moving visit to a *min'yō* bar in Osaka a few days earlier. On that evening I had listened to a six-year-old girl singing with gusto and incipient talent, accompanied by her parents and grandparents, cheered by an appreciative crowd. I had heard her at age three, and now I also watched her one-year-old sister 'sing' while held up to the microphone by a relative (Fig. 7.2). Six years later, I updated again to describe their continuing love for *min'yō* and their burgeoning talents.

I can never recall that incident without choking up. I love this music. It is wonderful to see tiny children developing that same love. In the three decades since I first tasted *min'yō*, the fan base for this genre has plummeted precipitously. Most younger Japanese seem able to appreciate *min'yō* only if arranged in some rock-based quasi-'World Music' package; even then they have little regard for the lyrics and the world they paint. Educational policy-makers have shamefully abandoned traditional music, leaving their children adrift from their own parents and grandparents.

Doubtless most ethnomusicologists have experienced such emotions. We expect and accept that the musics we have come to love will keep evolving as they always have – that they must do this if they are to remain alive and relevant. We know that tastes change, that performers will turn to other per-formance modes or to other genres. And I know that this music, *min'yō*, 'belongs' first and foremost to the Japanese, not to me. But I cannot suppress the feeling that modern Japanese are losing something of value. Musical change is not value-free.

I will be pleased if this book suggests (among other things) that folk song, far from being irrelevant to modern Japan, may also be, in some small measure, instrumental in creating a more humane society. I am hoping that the folk song teacher Otowa Jun'ichirō was right when he said: 'Folk song builds people.'

ACKNOWLEDGEMENTS

The road to Japanese folk song (although I did not realize it then) began at Yale University, where I studied Japanese language and linguistics. It was Professor Samuel Martin who inspired me to tackle the language and also, with others in the Linguistics Department, forced me to hone my critical and analytical powers. It was the most serendipitous of coincidences that my first teaching job – in linguistics – took me to the University of Michigan where Professor William Malm was presiding over an active Japanese music performing group. His combination of enthusiasm and insight was irresistible, and he proved a conscientious supervisor for the doctoral thesis that formed the kernel of this book.

At Michigan, among many other contributory friends and teachers, Professor Richard Beardsley gave generous guidance in the early stages of my research. Professors Judith Becker, Norma Diamond and Aram Yengoyan, as examiners of my doctoral thesis, also provided valuable comments.

So many people and institutions aided my research in Japan that I must run the risk of seeming ungrateful by offering only a partial list. Professors Kikkawa Eishi and Kishibe Shigeo helped me make initial contacts. At the Performing Arts Division of the Tokyo National Cultural Properties Research Institute, Messrs Misumi Haruo and Kakinoki Gorō during my initial years, and later Misumi's successor Ms Nakamura Shigeko, made themselves readily available to me. This office became the scene of a monthly folk song research gathering of performers, scholars and producers, whose discussions were always extremely valuable. Professor Koizumi Fumio was my adviser during my stay at Tokyo University of Fine Arts and Music from 1979 to 1981. The staff at these last two institutions have continued to be uniformly helpful.

Among folk musicians in Japan, amateur or professional, there were so many who took the time to answer my questions and demonstrate their art that I can only offer a giant 'arigatō' to them as a group. Many of them are named in the body of this publication. In terms of formal teaching, I spent the most time with Tanaka Yoshio of Osaka and his family, with Takahashi Yūjirō of Tokyo and Sugita Akiko of Nara; I cannot begin to express my indebtedness to these three teachers, especially to Tanaka Sensei (see Figures 0.3, 4.2). My fellow students under these three masters also have provided many insights and fond memories.

Particularly for the years 1977–81, let me also thank collectively: the members of the Traditional Performing Arts production division at NHK Television; the staff at Japan Columbia Records, Japan Victor/JVC Records and CBS-Sony Records (particularly the former for allowing me to become a 'recording artist' myself); the staff of the monthly magazine *Min'yō Bunka*; the staff of the National Theatre; and all the other members of the broadcast and recording industry who provided opportunities to experience the world of professional folk song from the inside.

Through friends at NHK I met Katō Toshio of Kitakami City, Iwate Prefecture, who opened his home to me for several months in 1980, providing a base for my research into the folk performing arts of that area. He introduced me to many fascinating people, all of them extremely kind and patient, and he himself produced a flood of trenchant observations on the 'folk scene'. On subsequent visits to Iwate, aside from Katō-san, the folklorist Professor Kadoya Mitsuaki of Iwasaki similarly offered lodging, introductions, guidance and much more of his time than his busy schedule should have allowed. To all the people of southern Iwate, I owe an enormous debt of gratitude and affection.

To the amateur performers (often members of local folk music preservation societies) in villages throughout Japan, I express my gratitude for having been allowed into their communities. Of these visits I preserve the warmest of memories.

Three years of preparation at the University of Michigan, before going into the field, were supported by National Defense Foreign Language fellowships awarded through the Center for Japanese Studies. The staff at the Center provided a comforting human environment throughout my Michigan years.

From 1978 to 1980 my field research was funded by the Japanese Ministry of Education and by the JDR 3rd Fund. A brief return visit in 1984 was supported by Clare Hall, Cambridge University, where I held a Research Fellowship. The Japan Foundation funded three months' research during summer 1988 and a six-month stay in 2000 (primarily for research on Okinawan folk song). The British Academy enabled me to present papers related to this book at the 1988 Melbourne meeting of the International Musicological Society, at Hokkaido University of Education, Sapporo in July 1989 (combined with a quick bit of research), and at the Society for Ethnomusicology meeting in Toronto in November 1996. Finally, the Japan

Foundation Endowment Committee funded short, multi-purpose visits in 1999 and 2006. All publications under my name in the Bibliography can be said to have benefitted from those trips.

So many friends and colleagues have contributed comments and insights over the three decades of my *min'yō* life that I truly can only thank them collectively. Many have written works that are cited in the body of this book.

Sadly, during the three decades and more of my involvement with *min'yō*, many of the people named in this book have passed away. I have avoided the expression 'late', because truly these people are still with me.

I fear the time has come to take credit for any errors of omission or commission, and to absolve my myriad interlocutors in Japan of blame if I have misunderstood or misrepresented any of their remarks.

The traditional final word goes to the long-suffering spouse, in this case Gina Barnes (Figs 0.3, 3.1). Suffice it to say that she did everything I could have hoped for and then far more in order to help me complete this project, despite the pressures of her own career. She took part in many of my *min'yō* adventures, and still does so today. We have both found many years of joy and stimulation in the world of Japanese folk song.

DWH
London, June 2007

CHAPTER 1

FOLK SONG IN JAPAN: THE BACKGROUND

1.1 Introduction: The heart's home town

Min'yō wa kokoro no furusato.
Folk song is the heart's home town.

One hears or reads this expression frequently in discussions of folk song in Japan. Among enthusiasts it has somewhat the aura of a religious pronouncement. Of uncertain origin, the phrase spread through its use in the introductory announcement on the weekly Japan Broadcasting Corporation radio show *Min'yō o tazunete* (*In search of folk song*), launched in 1950 (Asano 1966: 204; Maruyama 1981: 25). Occasionally, the expression is inverted: instead of 'Folk song is the heart's home town', we hear 'Folk song is the home town's heart' (*Min'yō wa furusato no kokoro*).

'Home town' is perhaps the most natural English translation of *furusato*; 'old village' is more literal, and 'home community' or 'native place' is often more accurate since the *furusato* may now be anything from a tiny hamlet to the megavillage called Tokyo. But given the term's strong rural resonances, '(my) old country home' may be best. To many Japanese, the *furusato* is an ongoing source of identity, nostalgia and solace. Even second-generation Tokyoites occasionally identify their native place not as Tokyo but as the rural village or country town where their grandparents were raised, where their cousins may still live, a place they may see only during the annual summer ancestral Bon festival while visiting family graves, or at New Year. It is a constant in a shifting world, a comfort when the urban pace is too trying.

For those Japanese who cannot visit their *furusato* as often as they would like, they can send their hearts, at least, through folk song. Japanese folk songs are inextricably linked to local places, often to specific *furusato*. For people who have no *furusato* aside from the big city, folk song can help them imagine one – because Japanese folk song has come to the city.

Folk song's close links with 'place', with specific locations on the land-scape of Japan, make it a powerful tool for both evoking and satisfying feelings of nostalgia. Nostalgia requires separation, loss, absence: as the mythical American country song says, 'How can I miss you if you won't go away?'[1] So rural-to-urban migrants become aware of, and potentially miss, their native place in a way that non-migrants cannot. But those who remain in their birth community might nonetheless yearn for the life-style of an ear-lier time – a way of life that they may never have experienced, that indeed may never have existed and is thus only imagined, and that in any case may only relate to a different place. Thus, the separation that triggers nostalgia may be spatial, temporal, ideological or all of these.[2]

Folk song therefore, is, also inevitably implicated in events at a national level. There is a tension between the need for Japanese today to function as citizens of a modern nation-state, on the one hand, and the desire for the benefits of belonging to a smaller-scale community on the other. Benedict Anderson's term 'imagined community' (1983) was meant to apply only to the former, the nation-state, an artificial entity partially constructed through the mobilization of symbols; in Japan, however, even the local community may now have to be 'imagined' and constructed, so that people can be 're-embedded' (Giddens 1990), relocated in a comfortable and comforting 'place'. Folk song has a role to play in these processes, in the construction of community and identity at all levels, and this is a recurring theme of the present book.[3]

Folk song is implicated nationally partly through the impact of Appadu-rai's new 'scapes' (1996): mediascape, technoscape, ethnoscape, finanscape, ideoscape. These same scapes ensure also that Japan's universe does not stop at its shores: it is an island only in a geographical sense. In most other ways it is a part of the world at large, and ever more firmly so through the processes of globalization.[4]

However, *min'yō* – Japanese folk song – has been little affected by transna-tional forces, and its sphere of performance is still largely confined within geographical Japan. Performance tours abroad are infrequent compared with other traditional music genres. Moreover, those Japanese most likely to go abroad for more than a brief holiday are also the ones least likely to count themselves among *min'yō* fans (see e.g. §4.2); accordingly, the solace and identity urban migrants find in songs from the *furusato* are less often sought by modern-day Japanese overseas.[5] Also, Japanese folk song has so far played but a miniscule part in the 'World Music' phenomenon.

For most of this book, then, it is events within Japan that concern us, with the global context impinging only occasionally. Moreover, we will be more concerned with modernization than with post-modernism. My central pur-pose is to provide an overview of the world of Japanese traditional folk song and its role in the ever-changing, ever-expanding universe that is modern Japan. Urbanization, industrialization, Westernization, the growth of mass media – all often grouped as aspects of modernization – have affected both the music itself and the values and social structures surrounding musical behaviour. One aim of my research has been to determine which features of the folk song world have changed in the face of modernization and which have remained constant, and why. Topics covered, aside from the music itself, include professionalization and recruitment to the profession, standardization, song contests, urban–rural tensions, preservation societies, the media, the concept of *furusato* and many others.

No full-length study of such socio-cultural matters exists. In Japan, aspects of these topics have been addressed briefly in several books and in frequent articles. Early and typical examples are Asano 1966: Ch. 9 and Takeuchi 1973: Ch. 7, with later works adding little in the way of new perspectives on these particular issues. The most relevant works are referenced at appropriate places below.

This is not to say that the literature on *min'yō* has not grown in the past few decades. My bibliography lists twenty-four full-length books by the incomparable Takeuchi Tsutomu alone, every one of which is of value and interest. (He has also been the leading radio broadcaster of *min'yō* programmes and an important record producer.) However, most of these deal either with the purely traditional side, historical aspects, song collecting, or more recently (in the *Min'yō no kokoro* series aimed at today's aficionados rather than at scholars) with learning to sing and to compete in contests. His 1985 book on these contests does indeed relate closely to the modern context, and indeed has proven so attractive to competitors that it was re-issued in 1996. Kojima Tomiko, another highly productive scholar, has produced some useful small-scale studies of particular aspects of the modern period, such as changes in transmission and the creation of 'new folk songs' (e.g. 1970, 1991, 1992).

There is also the mountain of publications resulting from the nationwide Emergency Folk Song Survey (Min'yō Kinkyū Chōsa). From 1979 to 1990, under the auspices of the Cultural Affairs Agency of the Ministry of Education, each of the forty-seven prefectures made field recordings and published a report (some exceeding 500 pages). The reports, however, are primarily song lyric collections, often with background on individual songs and a few statements concerning the current state of folk song life in a particular region. Only some reports contain musical notation; a couple have dance notation. This project's field recordings are being catalogued and eventually digitized by a team under Kojima Tomiko at the National Museum of Japanese History. (See also §7.6, end.)[6]

The website www.1134.com/min-you/99bib1.shtml lists several hundred twentieth-century Japanese-language books on *min'yō*, only partially overlapping with those in my Bibliography. From their titles, none appear to deal with the sort of sociocultural issues metioned above. The twentieth century emphasized collecting, of both tunes and texts. Recent decades have seen some excellent work on tune families, while research on lyrics has concentrated on tracing connections between folk songs of different regions or eras or between folk song and other vocal genres. However, 2007 saw the launching of a four-year large-team research project on *min'yō*, led by Hosokawa Shūhei at the International Research Centre for Japanese Studies ('Nichibunken') and including myself; its themes closely parallel those of this book, and the resulting publications should expand on issues raised here.[7]

Western-language sources on any aspects of Japanese folk song are still few. Short and concise overall introductions are Hughes 2008, Koizumi & Hughes 2001 and Groemer 2001, any of which might usefully be read at this stage. Isaku 1973 and 1981 address different issues from the ones treated in the present study and were based on a very restricted fieldwork experience, but are still useful. The introduction to Groemer 1999 gives an excellent view of one significant corner of this world, and the rest of the book translates the autobiography of one important musician. Peluse 2005 and Johnson 2006 lead a growing number of studies on the Tsugaru-jamisen phenomenon, which, along with *wadaiko* drumming, is one of the few traditional or 'roots' genres catching the interest of the younger generation.

The terms 'traditional' and 'modern' in my title need a few words of justification at this point. These terms, in their various forms, have been characterized so variously by scholars that one hesitates to choose any one formulation or to offer a new one. For 'tradition' in relation to music in particular, Timothy Rice offered one solution to this problem in his study of Bulgarian music: he provided four distinct 'senses' (1994: 12–15), frequently problematizing each of these in elegant discussions. Thus there is a thorough analysis of the irony that it is only in post-traditional, 'modern' times that most people become aware of tradition as a concept to be cognized and manipulated within their own culture. (Again, separation heightens awareness.) Still, Rice managed such analysis without feeling the need to offer hard definitions, and a central or basic default meaning was taken for granted and used throughout the book in phrases such as 'traditional costume', 'village traditions' and 'learning in the traditional manner'.

In Japan too, modern-day discussions about folk song often trigger debates about tradition (*dentō*) – as well as authenticity and similar concepts – although usually only in rather formal and artificial contexts; examples emerge below. For most of this book, though, the word refers simply to features of Japan as it stood before about 1868. That date marks the beginning of the Meiji period (1868–1912), when a new Japanese government encouraged modernization and Westernization in almost all spheres of culture. Despite 140 years of modernization, many aspects of present-day Japanese culture retain much of their pre-Meiji character, and these aspects will also be called 'traditional'. This is why I write of 'traditional folk song in modern Japan'. However, this usage based on chronology and content must be distinguished from Hobsbawm's valuable if often criticized concept of 'invented traditions' (1983). We shall see that many Japanese too apply the word 'traditional' to phenomena they know to be recent creations, occasionally with devious intent but usually simply because they do not consider a hoary time depth to be relevant to the notion. We return to this concept in §5.7.

What about 'modern'? 'Modernization' is, as implied above, a broad category embracing several discrete though often interrelated processes. Definitions have referred to criteria as diverse as the increased utilization of inanimate sources of energy on the one hand, and the universalization of privileges and expectations on the other. It is, in any case, a *process* resulting in cultural change. One can distinguish modernization from 'modernity', which in Giddens' sense (1990) is more a state of mind or of society than a process. But the distinction is fuzzy, and Rice (1994: 322) uses 'modernity' in preference to 'change' as an antonym to 'tradition'.

Tradition may also be viewed as a process, though usually considered largely homeostatic – that is, it attempts to maintain or re-establish equilibrium, resisting cultural change or channelling it within relatively narrow limits. Even 'invented traditions' ultimately have the same purpose.

This characterization falters somewhat when, for example, Japan is said to be 'traditionally a borrowing culture', well before globalization made us all into avid borrowers. Does this mean that modernization – in part at least a type of acculturation or borrowing – is actually part of Japanese tradition? Once we accept the view that both tradition and modernization admit cultural change, then we have the problem of determining which changes result from modernization and which are a logical extension of tradition. Another way of phrasing this problem is, Can we distinguish indigenously generated from externally motivated change? And when traditional cultural elements and patterns seem to survive unchanged, we must ask whether this survival is, in the words of Bennett, 'a lag phenomenon, or whether it represents a stable adaptation to the new . . . Japan' (1967: 449).

Our focus, however, is not on modernization *per se* but on one genre of traditional music in a modernizing context. Bruno Nettl, in several publications (most prominently 1983: 172–86, 345–54 and 1985: 3–29, 149–66), restated and refined a typology of responses of non-Western music systems to Western music in the twentieth century, which I still find useful. (In this he drew also on scholars such as Blacking 1977 and Kartomi 1981.) Among these are abandonment, exaggeration, preservation, syncretism, Westernization and modernization. Syncretism, Nettl says, results when the 'central traits' of the two music systems are compatible and are merged into a new system. He defines Westernization as the incorporation of central but non-compatible elements of Western music with the intention of making the non-Western system a part of the Western system. Modernization, by contrast, involves the borrowing of non-central but compatible elements of Western music in such a way as to preserve the essence of the non-Western system. (Defining 'central elements', of course, is contentious.)

Thus, Nettl sees modernization as a way to guarantee the survival of a tradition in living form, as opposed to mere preservation or to the loss of its essence via Westernization. In this schema, the replacement of a traditional bowed instrument by a Western violin does not of itself constitute Westernization of the *system* but simply the adoption of a single Western trait which may not replace any of the central features of the system. UNESCO's Intangible Cultural Heritage programme and the Japanese systems that helped inspire it must, of course, wrestle with similar issues.

Because urbanization has been accelerated by the industrial and communication revolutions, it is often difficult to distinguish its effects from those of Westernization and modernization. Urbanization, even in pre-modern times, created its own environment for change: large concentrations of population, usually a greater ethnic mix than found in a village or small town, often a more adventuresome and younger population than in rural areas, greater cash expenditure on leisure activities, and so forth. When combined with modernization, the city can extend its impact rapidly via the media. The modern urban musical culture is often characterized by increased opportunities for patronage, by professionalization, commercialization (via e.g. the recording industry) and in general by ease of access to foreign musical elements. Thus the city should have a distinctive impact on the trajectory of musical development. We return to Nettl's ideas in Chapter 7.

The present study deals with a consciously and indigenously identified 'folk' music as it developed a dual identity (both urban and rural) in adapting to modernity. I have tried to demonstrate that, while the urbanized and rural traditions are related, they have developed along unique paths in response to (1) the differing needs of urban and rural residents and (2) the differential effects of the environments (natural, human, institutional) which condition these needs. These differences survive despite the ever-shrinking separation of urban and rural via absorption, the media, travel, national education and so forth. In both settings, a significant segment of the populace assigns positive value to folk song and its cultural role – which was not true in the cities a century ago.

Developments in Japan are often parallelled by those in other countries. Georgina Boyes (1993) describes in chilling detail the ideological currents, the hegemonic power plays, the urban–rural and class tensions lurking beneath the surface of the English Folk Revival. As the concept of 'the Folk' began to settle in England and in that other class-conscious island nation, Japan, at approximately the same moment in the latter nineteenth century, comparing subsequent developments should prove rewarding, but that is a task for another publication.

Still, Japan is Japan. Some of the factors which, taken together, set Japan apart as an interesting case study in musical change are as follows.

(1) As an early and successful modernizer and industrializer, twentieth-century Japan followed a path unlike that of China or the countries of Southeast Asia.

(2) As a country with a striking degree of ethnic and cultural unity,[8] where ninety per cent of the people consider themselves middle-class,[9] Japan has confronted different problems than, say, India, Turkey, Iran or the countries of Africa and Latin America.

(3) The stylistic distance between traditional folk music and the international popular music of the twentieth century is far greater than in most Western European countries, with implications for the interaction of those styles.

(4) Certain phenomena of modern-day folk song transmission shed light on important aspects of the interaction of cultural values and modernization. I have in mind features such as the *iemoto* ('headmaster/househead') system, the Japanese-style folk song bar, and local folk song preservation societies, all discussed in this book.

(5) The very fact that the Japanese have, during the past hundred years and under Western influence, developed a major and flourishing cultural category which they call 'folk song' (*min'yō*) sets Japan apart from many other non-Western cultures. Interesting comparisons can be drawn with countries like England and the United States, whose folk song 'revivals' can be placed next to Japan's *min'yō* 'booms', and with Korea and China, which have been influenced both by the West and by Japan in consciously developing their own 'folk song' cultures (see Howard 1999; Tuohy 1999).

(6) Japan shows a high degree of native activity in research and documentation of traditional folk song. In particular, Japanese researchers have generally paid more attention than those in China and Korea (see Schimmelpenninck 1997: 11; Maliangkay 1999) to producing accurate music transcriptions of actual performances. The years 1979–80 saw the completion, in its fourth decade, of a mammoth project of folk song documentation and transcription by the Japan Broadcasting Corporation (the nine-volume *Nihon min'yō taikan*, subsequently re-issued with CDs of field recordings; see NMT in Bibliography) as well as the launching of the Emergency Folk Song Survey described above. Non-governmental concern with folk song is also impressive in scope.

Folk song in Japan today forms a fairly distinct category conveniently designated by the term *min'yō* – literally 'folk song'.[10] Scholars use another term, *minzoku geinō*, to designate the larger category of folk performing arts. A study of *minzoku geinō* would generate relatively more insights about religion, ritual, symbolism, gender, changes in traditional village organization and so forth, while studying *min'yō* reveals relatively more about musical change, urban–rural interaction, the birth of new social organs, commercialism, and traditional values in flux. In short, the *min'yō* world, more sensitive to social currents, gives greater insight into ongoing social and musical processes than would a study of the ultra-conservative world of *minzoku geinō*. (But see Thornbury 1997 and Lancashire 1998 for studies of change in the latter.) For such reasons, among others, I chose to focus on *min'yō*. However, folk song is partially embedded in the category *minzoku geinō*, and often it seemed appropriate to shift the focus to the larger picture. Let me state clearly that the decision to focus on the genre *min'yō* does not imply that the boundaries of this indigenous category can be consistently drawn, nor that it is independent of other types of music. But despite its imprecision, the concept of *min'yō* is very real and important to the Japanese.

Since modernization with regard to folk song can safely be considered to have begun in the mid-Meiji period, this study will focus on the events of the past hundred years or so. My most intense fieldwork was conducted between 1977 and 1981, but with ten shorter visits since then. Given that the basics of the 'folk song world' have changed very little between 1977 and today, my 'ethnographic present' is in effect the last three decades. (Publicity for a *min'yō* concert in Tokyo in 2006 (*Hōgaku Jānaru* July 2006: 14) named eight singers and one *shamisen* lute player – all of whom were already major stars in 1981.) Significant changes during this period are noted at various points, especially in Chapter 7. Chapter 2 deals with 'traditional' Japan, an obviously fictitious entity whose temporal limits are discussed in §2.1.

Of course, 'the West' is not the only source of influence on other music systems. But the influence of Asia or Africa on recent Japanese music life pales into insignificance compared to that of 'the West' (despite the occasional djembe, didgeridoo, cajón or kanūn accompanying *min'yō*). Thus, in this particular study we are justified in concentrating on Westernization and modernization. We shall touch on these matters again in Chapter 7.

1.2 The word *min'yō* and its changing meaning

In the West, scholarly attempts to establish an agreed definition of 'folk song' or 'folk music' have proven futile, simply because there is no isolable unified phenomenon to which such a concept could be wed – even in our own culture, let alone universally. Even in establishing a Weberian ideal type, there is little agreement on the constituent features: Must folk songs be anonymously composed? Rural? Transmitted only via aural/oral tradition? Must performers be amateurs? Must there be a communal orientation? Each of these criteria poses problems – so much so that Bohlman, in his book

The Study of Folk Music in the Modern World, decided not to offer a single definition at all (1988: xviii). In general, ethnomusicologists seem to be shying away from offering etic definitions, focusing instead on native usage, as we will do.

Nonetheless, heated and revealing discussions on the topic are frequent among fans, performers and scholars. Debate rages over the nature and definition of folk song, its place in the modern world, the correct or preferred performance practice, the cultural value of folk performance, the very existence of the folk, and so forth.[11] Similar discussions, equally revealing, are in fact frequently encountered in twentieth-century Japan. Indeed, they occur also in China (Tuohy 1999), Korea (Howard 1999) and other countries where the Western Romantic concept of 'the folk' has taken root.

The term for folk song most commonly used in Japanese scholarly and public discourse is *min'yō* (民謡),[12] and an investigation of its scope and meaning provides a useful starting point for the chapters to follow. It will also be helpful to discuss now the evolution and semantics of certain other Japanese terms which crop up later. Although this chapter necessarily throws the reader into a sea of terminology, it will be convenient for reference later on.

Early terms for village song, some from as far back as the eighth century, included *hinaburi, hinauta, inaka-uta, kuniburi, kunibushi* (all compounds of native Japanese morphemes meaning roughly 'country song/style') and *fuzoku(-uta)*, *fuzoku* being a compound of Chinese origin used in the sense of '(rural) customs'. (For others from pre-modern times, see Ōnuki 1989, Nakai et al. 1972: 3, NOD 1989: 46.) There is little hint of a concept of 'folk'. Nor do any of these terms seem to have been current among mostly non-literate villagers themselves, who in any case would have little reason to refer to their songs as 'country' songs. The simple term *uta* was available to describe all vocal music including courtly poems, which were indeed sung and still sometimes are.

The word *min'yō* – literally 'folk song' – is a compound of Chinese origin, encountered in Chinese sources already by the fifth century (Asano 1983: 3). Its earliest known usage in Japan is a single occurrence in a dynastic history published in 901 (NKD 1972: 18.704). Although the combination of the elements *min* 'folk, the people' and *yō* 'song' was perfectly logical, the term occurs only sporadically thereafter until the late nineteenth century. Its modern use stems not from Chinese influence but from a re-emergence around 1890, amid the Westernizing trend of the Meiji period, as a natural and direct loan-translation of the German word *Volkslied*.[13] Credit is usually assigned to the writer Mori Ōgai, who used the term in 1891 in translating the title of Meyer's *Griechische Volkslieder*, or his friend Ueda Bin; both had recently studied in Europe (Machida 1971: 289; Asano 1966: 32, 1983: 3; NOD 1989: 46). However, its presence in an 1891 dictionary (see below) suggests that the term was 'in the air', as in other countries falling under the Romantic spell. Indeed, just as the term's modern currency stems from a German word, so the German Romantic view of folk song crucially influenced Japanese scholars' approaches.

The term *min'yō* did not, however, immediately win the day (see Nakamura 1991). At first, several terms were used with little discrimination by scholars of that period. An entry in the 1891 edition of Ōtsuki's dictionary *Genkai* reads:

> *Zokuyō* [popular/commoner songs]: A type of *hayariuta*. [Synonyms:] *Zokka. Zokkyoku. Min'yō. Riyō.*

Min'yō itself did not merit a separate entry; we can only guess at the reasons. *Hayariuta* is from two native Japanese elements, our old friend *uta* 'song' and the verb *hayaru* 'be popular, faddish; spread'. All of the other terms listed, however, are pseudo-Chinese compounds of the type favoured by scholars but less heard among the traditional lay populace. The elements *-ka* and *-yō* mean 'song'; *-kyoku* 'melody'; *min-* 'the people'; *ri-* 'country, rural'; *zok(u)-* 'common, popular, vulgar'.

I say 'pseudo-Chinese' because such compounds are not necessarily borrowed from Chinese. Just as English makes new compounds from Latin or Greek elements (e.g. 'microcomputer'), so the Japanese often coin words by combining pairs of Chinese characters, as the Chinese themselves do, and pronouncing them in Japanized Chinese.[14] In both cases – Latinate English and 'Sinate' Japanese – the results have a scientific, scholarly ring. The proliferation of Sinate terms in the sphere of folk song during the late nineteenth century is an indication of the sudden increase in interest on the topic among the intelligentsia.

During the early twentieth century, the term *min'yō* gradually dislodged the other challengers from its semantic area. However, this word born among literati was slow to catch on with the wider public. One small bit of evidence is provided by the first known recordings of Japanese music, made in 1900 while the Kawakami Otojirō Troupe was performing at the Paris Exhibition; these were recently rediscovered and issued as R35 (see Audio-Videography). Two selections are songs now known as *min'yō*: 'Yoneyama Jinku' and 'Oiwake Bushi'. But in the notes left by the troupe, while many others among the twenty-eight tracks are identified by genre (*nagauta, hauta* etc.), these two are not. A few years later, they would surely have been called *riyō* or *min'yō* by the members of this relatively urbanized troupe.

The stages by which the word *min'yō* has come into general use reflect the changing economic and musical relations between town and countryside. Its spread is also our best evidence for the spread of the concept itself, as the 'folk' first began to believe that they were singing a special type of song.

Despite its urban origins, the word long lacked currency even in the cities. Country songs began to pour into Tokyo at the end of the nineteenth century, as industrialization and improvements in transportation accelerated urbanization (see Chapter 3). For several decades, however, these imported songs were called by many different terms such as those given above. It was possibly in 1920 that the word *min'yō* was first used in reference to a public performance, when a '*min'yō* concert' was advertised in Tokyo. According to the organizer's testimony, the unfamiliar word caused some confusion. Some people bought tickets thinking they would be hearing the music of the Noh theatre, since the character used for -*yō* is the same as that for Noh singing (*utai*); others, notably the Tokyo police who looked on with suspicion, took the element *min-* in the sense which it was given by the growing left-wing movement, anticipating a leftist rally singing 'people's songs' (Kikuchi 1980: 43). Still, most ticket-buyers seem to have known what they were getting.

Another urban understanding of the term is described by Kurata (1979: 338). In 1929, a well-known music critic wrote to a newspaper to complain about the *min'yō* 'Tōkyō Kōshinkyoku' [Tokyo March]. This was not a traditional rural song but a Western-influenced tune, written for a film soundtrack; its lyrics are full of recent borrowings from English, such as 'jazz' and 'rush hour'. Thus, the term *min'yō* was often earlier understood in three distinct senses, all etymologically reasonable and with distinct English equivalents: 'folk song', 'people's song' and (as here) 'popular song'. Both conceptualization and terminology regarding folk song were still unsettled.

In rural areas, meanwhile, the term was virtually unknown: people simply called their local songs *uta*, the general and ancient word for song. This was true of many rural residents as late as the 1960s.[15] More specific terms such as *taue-uta* 'rice-planting song(s)' could be used when precision was necessary. Lively entertainment songs, usually of urban origin, sometimes made their way into the village with wandering performers or with travellers who had learned them at drinking parties, in the theatres or in pleasure houses. These might be referred to as *hayariuta* 'popular [in the sense of "spreading among the populace"] songs', but eventually they would just be considered *uta*, on a par with other songs. Work songs brought in by a seasonal or permanent migrant worker, perhaps in conjunction with the introduction of a new technology such as *sake* or noodle manufacture, were not considered *hayariuta* but fell into the general *uta* category, to be referred to specifically when necessary as, e.g., *sake*-barrel-cleaning songs, *sake*-mash-stirring songs, etc. Actually, specificity was rarely needed, since most work songs were sung only in one context.[16]

By the late 1920s, though, the word *min'yō* had reached many rural areas, perhaps particularly through the 'new folk song' (*shin-min'yō*) movement spearheaded by urban-based poets and composers (§3.4.3). These 'new *min'yō*' were often commissioned by local chambers of commerce and the like to attract tourists, taking advantage of increased domestic travel since the turn of the century. One such song, 'Chakkiri Bushi', composed in 1927, is currently the only well-known *min'yō* from Shizuoka Prefecture, and few people would now call it a 'new' *min'yō* at all.

The first quarter of the twentieth century also saw the spread of certain local songs of the type that once would have been called *hayariuta* but were now increasingly called *min'yō*: songs such as 'Esashi Oiwake', 'Iso Bushi' and 'Yasugi Bushi' (§3.4.1). Each of these (and others like them) had a place-name – a specific town or village – as the first part of its title, reflecting the strong tendency in traditional Japan to identify cultural artifacts (from songs to food to clothing) with specific places. Country folk could hear these songs on commercial recordings after around 1905 and on radio after 1925, but at first few could afford the equipment. More commonly they would hear them performed by itinerant professionals or, if they had occasion to travel, by the female entertainers in teahouses or inns.

The word *min'yō* was thus first experienced by most people in connection with songs from *outside* their area, in effect establishing a contrast between *uta* and *min'yō*: local versus intrusive folk songs. I found even in the late 1970s that some elderly countryfolk, asked for a '*min'yō* from your village', would offer a widely popular folk song such as 'Hanagasa Ondo', even while realiz-ing that this song was associated with another region altogether. This shows that *min'yō*, a term indeed introduced from outside, was often perceived as describing extra-community songs, having no applicability to locally rooted songs. At this first stage, therefore, *min'yō* seems to have come to mean some-thing like 'folk songs from outside known to us'. Furthermore, these outside songs were usually heard sung by polished performers with relatively elabo-rate accompaniments. Takeuchi (1981: 9) recognizes the existence of this stage suggesting that to most people the term implied something like:

> Songs [presumably with rural associations] sung by the type of people with good voices, who appear on television and radio accompanied by shamisen [3-string banjo-like instrument], shakuhachi [end-blown bamboo flute], etc. . . . sung by good-looking men and women wearing fancy-patterned kimono . . . who learned them in the city.

At the next stage, the concept apparently broadened to include 'folk songs from our area known to outsiders'. For example, some Shizuoka residents who accepted the above-mentioned 'new' folk song 'Chakkiri Bushi' as a fully-fledged local *min'yō* would not grant that designation to more tradi-tional work songs connected with tea-growing, seemingly because the latter were not known in the cities and were neither heard on the radio nor recorded by professional folk singers. Similarly, residents of Nara Prefecture are wont to claim that there are no *min'yō* from Nara – even though they should be aware of the existence of some of the hundreds of work, dance and ceremonial songs collected there even in recent decades, none widely known outside the circle of serious folk song fans (and some local residents). At this second stage, then, to be called a *min'yō*, a song had to be known outside of its home area. What these two usages share is the requirement that a song be widely known: *min'yō* was being interpreted in its *'popular* song' sense, the concept of 'folk' still being little known. Presumably, a rural origin for such a song was taken for granted.

Despite these examples, since the 1970s *min'yō* has become widely (though not universally) accepted as referring to *all* Japanese folk songs. This is particularly due to the influence of television and radio *min'yō* programmes, which have since the 1970s devoted much more time to little-known local work and dance songs – and called them *min'yō*. At the same time, with the increased intellectualization concerning folk song in recent decades, accompanied by a new respect for rural lifeways as people gain the economic security to complain about the human and natural environment in the cities, there is a counter-trend which romanticizes the true rural song and its context and excludes from the *min'yō* category arranged versions by urban folk singers. Consequently, it is common to hear purists say, 'There aren't any real *min'yō* anymore,' or 'Any song performed on stage is not a *min'yō*,' or 'The only true *min'yō* are the work songs.' In other words, the gradually broadened category is being subdivided or narrowed anew by some speakers.[17]

Such purists aside, the basic outlines of the current concept of *min'yō* are relatively clear, though the limits remain inexact. People are occasionally unsure whether a particular song should be considered a *min'yō*, a *shin-min'yō*, a *hayariuta*, or maybe a non-*min'yō* geisha-party song (*sawagi-uta, zokkyoku,* etc.).[18] But they have, in any case, come to recognize the existence of a type of song called *min'yō*, with its own associated activity spheres and personalities – what is often called the *min'yōkai* ('folk song world').

A Japanese website (www.worldfolksong.com/songbook/sokkuri/a005.htm) called the song 'Akatonbo' (Red Dragonfly) a *min'yō*. Yet the author accepted the opinion that the tune, composed by Yamada Kōsaku in 1921, was influenced by Schumann's *Introduction and Allegro Concertante in D minor,* Op. 134 (1853): the first fourteen notes are identical. (Yamada had lived in Europe for several years.) Although some Japanese have told me they actually thought this was a traditional folk song and thus would call it a *min'yō*, the website author knew the truth but presumably chose the word because the song is known and loved throughout Japan and has some folk flavour (e.g. a pentatonic scale, bucolic lyrics). If challenged, perhaps s/he would have accepted the alternative terms *shin-min'yō* or *dōyō* (composed songs for children).

Very few non-scholars, of course, know the history of the word *min'yō*. Even professional folk singers may not have had occasion to garner this information. Thus the singer Yamamoto Kenji from Aomori Prefecture (b. 1943) says he heard somewhere that the term was coined by the famous *min'yō* teacher Gotō Tōsui (1880–1960), who likened folk song to the voice of the cicada: *min, min* – hence *min'yō* (pers. comm., 1984).

It must be stressed that the term 'folk' (*min-*) is not perceived as a pejorative by those in Japan to whom it might be applied, nor particularly used to maintain a class system. Certainly those who dislike *min'yō* may use the term with a bit of a sneer, but the same could be said of the word 'opera' in English – or in Japanese! Thus we may ignore those Western left-wing scholars who feel that the term 'folk' is insulting and should be avoided at all costs.

1.3 Scholars' definitions of *min'yō*

In the previous section we looked at the concept of *min'yō* from the viewpoint of the typical Japanese, who until recent years were rarely concerned with the niceties of terminological distinctions. This term, of course, came to them from the scholarly community. That community itself, however, has been striving unsuccessfully to reach a consensus on both a definition of *min'yō* itself and the word's usage in opposition to various other terms ever since it was introduced. Let us consider a few representative definitions from the literature, which have influenced non-specialist thought to varying degrees.

The song-text historian Asano Kenji, while recognizing that specialists in each field would probably have their own interpretations, felt that the following definition should be adequate for textologists like himself and also reflected the condition of 'current *min'yō*':

> [*Min'yō* are] songs which were originally born *naturally* within *local* folk *communities* and, as they have been *transmitted*, [have continued to] reflect *naively* the sentiments of daily life. (Asano 1966: 43; emphasis added)

The five italicized English words are central to this definition (see ibid.: 41–3): 'Naturally' (*shizen ni*) implies that *min'yō* are not the product of specialist lyricists or composers, that they spring up, says Asano, 'like nameless flowers that bloom in the fields'. 'Local' (*kyōdo*) signifies that local colour inheres somewhere within every *min'yō*; if it is lost, the song 'has fallen into the lowest class of popular song (*hayariuta*)'. (Note the highly evaluative use of the word 'fallen'.) The word 'communities' (*shūdan*) alerts us to the communal nature of *min'yō* as a 'group product': most folk songs, Asano says, have had the individual idiosyncrasies of their maker removed over time so that only sentiments held in common remain. *Min'yō* are 'transmitted' aurally and thus inevitably undergo unconscious and unintentional alterations (as well as conscious and intentional ones). The word Asano uses – *denshō* – implies specifically aural or folk transmission, as opposed to written transmission. 'Naively' (*soboku ni*) is a compliment, for Asano feels that 'in naïveté lies the essence of *min'yō*'. Note that, as in almost all definitions of *min'yō*, musical features as such are referred to barely or not at all. This is still true in a more recent restatement by Asano (1983: 3); he merely adds that a song may lose its naïveté with the addition of instrumental accompaniment (even on traditional instruments) or the 'refining' of the melody.

I do not know to what extent Asano was familiar with Western attempts at defining folk music. In 1907 Cecil Sharp had opined:

> folk-song [or] folk-music . . . is not the composition of an individual . . . but a *communal* and *racial* product, the expression . . . of aims and ideals that are primarily *national* in character. (Sharp 1907: x; italics added)

In common with others of his time, he saw folk song as a communal product and possession reflecting national, not local, character. In 1955 the International Folk Music Council (with a few Japanese members even then) made an advance on Sharp-like definitions, giving a clearer role to the individual and to orality:

> Folk music is the product of a musical tradition that has been evolved through the process of oral transmission. The factors that shape the tradition are: (i) *continuity* which links the present with the past; (ii) *variation* which springs from the creative impulse of the individual or the group; and (iii) *selection* by the *community*. . . . (IFMC 1955: 23; italics added)

The concept of oral/aural transmission (*kōtō denshō*) as a process distinct from written transmission was European, unknown in Japan until the Meiji period: since virtually *all* traditional Japanese musics had been transmitted primarily through the aural channel, this process did not attract special concern. Its presence in Asano's definition quite likely derives from the West.

Whatever the Western influences, some aspects of Asano's definition seem to reflect specifically Japanese attitudes toward folk song. In particular, the stress on its 'local' nature relates to the importance attached by the Japanese to the concept of the *furusato* or native place: like most people, folk songs have a *furusato*. When Western scholars write of 'place' in this connection, they are generally thinking of the regional or even the national level (cf. Bohlman 1988: 53); Japanese, both scholars and tradition-bearers, mostly focus more narrowly, on a community or a province. We will frequently return to this question of place in Japan, noting a certain tension between the local and the national.

Machida Kashō (1888–1981), the acknowledged dean of folk song research, accepted his friend Asano's definition but wished to discriminate more precisely between 'real', 'authentic' folk songs and others. He defined his terms variously in different publications; this characterization – in which he distinguished between 'natural' and 'composed' songs – is typical (translated from Machida and Asano 1960: 409):

Min'yō in the broad sense

A. *kyōdo* (local) *min'yō*
   1. *shizen* (natural) *min'yō*
      a. *riyō* (rural/village songs): songs made and sung by naive farmers
         for themselves
      b. *zokuyō* (vulgar/popular songs): *riyō* which have been arranged by
         urban musical specialists [i.e. with instrumental accompaniment
         and vocal virtuosity added]
      c. *odori-uta* (dance songs): rain dances, Bon festival dances, etc.;
         festival dance songs
   2. *sōsaku* (composed) *min'yō*
      a. in the broad sense: not limited to a particular region [i.e. most of
         the later 'new folk songs' discussed in §6.4]
      b. in the narrow sense: composed with a particular region in mind
         [i.e. most of the early 'new folk songs' discussed in §3.4.3]
B. *warabeuta* (children's songs)
   1. *shizen* (natural): passed on through oral tradition
   2. *sōsaku* (composed): new works by specialist lyricists and composers
      [e.g. Meiji-period songs for schoolchildren; see Eppstein 1994]
C. *hayariuta* (popular songs)
   1. *shizen* (natural): an everyday/usual/normal [?] song (*futsū no kayō*)
      which spreads with the support of the masses
   2. *sōsaku* (composed): created as a product by record companies

Asano (1966: 57) notes some of the ambiguities of this schema, such as
the anomalous nature of the category *odori-uta* (A.1.c), whose members
could presumably equally well fall under A.1.a. Note also that one and the
same song, in different performance settings or at different stages of its
history, will qualify under several headings. Remember, though, that such a
schema is primarily a tool of scholars: the average fan or performer is rarely
concerned with this level of specificity. Asano also notes correctly that what
most present-day scholars consider *min'yō* (judging by what songs they
research) are mainly 'natural *min'yō*' (A.1 above) and 'composed *min'yō* in
the narrow sense' (A.2.b). It is not quite clear where the 'new folk songs' of
the 1920s and 1930s would fit: most were 'composed with a particular
region in mind' (A.2.b), but often at the behest of a profit-oriented record
company (C.2). A deeper discussion would reveal other anomalies.

In another publication, Machida takes a different approach (1971: 289).
Min'yō in the broad sense, he writes, includes three types (in my paraphrase):

1. primary *min'yō*, or *riyō*: the original forms as found in the countryside; not intended as performances for an audience [=A.1.a (and c?)
   above]

2. secondary *min'yō*, or *zokuyō*: versions of primary *min'yō* 'vulgarized' or popularized (*zokka*) through the addition of accompaniment on traditional instruments [=A.1.b above]
3. tertiary *min'yō*: mainly post-war; accompanied by Western instruments; really a type of popular song (*ryūkōka*)

He thus proposes to contrast three terms which in the *Genkai* dictionary definition of 1891 seemed to be treated as synonyms: *riyō, zokuyō* and *min'yō*. There is some logic to this, perhaps: the elements *ri-, zoku-* and *min-* represent respectively place, aesthetic (or moral) judgement and people. Machida implies that, while all *min'yō* are popular principally among the common folk (*min = tami*) – hence the suitability of this Western-derived term – only primary, original folk songs (*riyō*) have strong links with life in the village (*ri = sato*); as for *zoku*, see §1.5 below.[19]

Oddly, the chart accompanying Machida's explanation, which lists several dozen *min'yō*, labels them according to yet a different system (my paraphrase):

1. *min'yō* of the period of the primary economy (songs relating to agriculture, fishing, etc.); mostly work and celebration songs
2. *min'yō* of the period of the secondary economy (processing and manufacturing)
3. *min'yō* of the period of the tertiary (service) economy: leisure *min'yō*, stage *min'yō*

These two tripartite schemata are not equivalent, using different definitional criteria altogether. The former relies on distinctions based on performance practice (accompaniment style, etc.), while the latter is based loosely on economic considerations. Thus an unaccompanied weaving song would be type 1 in the first schema but type 2 in the second. His discussions in this article and in a somewhat revised version in another encyclopedia (Machida 1976a) continually confuse these two schemata – and hence the reader.

Almost all recent typologies of *min'yō* look back to the pioneering writings on folk song by the 'father of Japanese folklore', Yanagita Kunio (1875–1962).[20] He greatly influenced Japanese scholarly thinking about folk song (as well as other fields such as ethnography) with his romantic vision of the peasant as the repository of the true and original Japanese culture or ethos. According to his view, the 'true' folk song is the work song.[21] The 'vulgarization' of such pure and unselfconscious songs to *zokuyō* status is seen as a degenerative step: the addition of instruments, increased complexity of vocal technique, and the consciousness of separate roles for performer and audience, all mark a movement away from a bucolic ideal. Yanagita bridled when poets of the 1920s began producing pseudo-folk poems and calling them *min'yō* (§3.4.3); even the designation *shin-min'yō*, he felt, distinguished insufficiently between true folk products (worthy of the folklorist's attention) and professional works (see Yanagita 1940; Takeuchi 1981: 11). His attitudes strongly affected Machida.[22]

There is an incipient sense of economic and class analysis in the approach of Yanagita and his successors. He was familiar with European social economic theory (see Kawada 1993; Makita 1973; Shibusawa 1958: 66–75). Of course, Japan had long been a highly class-conscious society, but the phraseology of Machida's second and third schemata clearly shows the influence of European approaches. The Marxist social historian Matsumoto Shinhachirō (1965: 278) was upset that the word *min'yō* – 'people's song' – had come to be associated particularly with songs accompanied by the shamisen in the style of geisha parlour songs. He wanted this term reserved for the true work songs of the people: 'optimistic, rich in humour, expressive of some struggle or other'.[23]

Finally, many researchers take a less social-scientific approach and simply categorize songs by function or context. Takahashi Hideo (1989) provided a schema intended to classify all the songs collected in the nationwide Emergency Folk Song Survey (see §1.1), which intentionally excluded 'new folk songs' and stage versions. He listed seven headings: work songs, festival/-celebration songs, dance songs, party songs, narrative/auspicious songs, lullabies, children's songs. There are fifteen sub-headings and fifty-three specific sub-categories often followed by 'etcetera' – the list could never be exhaustive.

The above discussion shows that there are any number of definitional schemata for folk song in Japan, often based on different criteria. Given this variety, it is always necessary, when trying to follow an argument about the nature of folk song, to determine how the particular participants are using their terms. We can in fact largely disregard definitional niceties for the remainder of the present work. The main reason for giving such detail here was to show how the Japanese think about folk song, what criteria come into consideration, what features are deemed important.[24]

This is as good a time as any to discuss the role of the geisha, who come up repeatedly throughout this book. Simply meaning 'artistic person', during the Edo period the term came to indicate female entertainers who were indentured or voluntarily working in teahouses, specialist geisha houses, or outright brothels (cf. Foreman in press; Dalby 1983; Teruoka 1989). Many teenage girls were sold to geisha houses by impoverished parents, though a few saw glamour in the profession and sought it of their own accord. It was a reasonably honourable outlet for young women with musical talent and aspirations. The higher class of geisha were first and foremost artists – of music, conversation, poetry improvisation, and perhaps sex. Patronage by men of wealth was one factor raising the geisha's status (and was also their major escape route); another was the recognition of the well-disciplined training undergone by apprentice geisha. Geisha sang a wide range of short shamisen-accompanied song genres such as *kouta, hauta* and *zokkyoku* (and often longer songs from the Kabuki world) as well as arranged folk songs. Two of the most famous folk-singing geisha (Ichimaru and Akasaka Koume, both born in 1906) chose that profession because it would allow them to sing for a living (NMMM: 200–1). Had they been raised in northern Japan rather than in Nagano and Fukuoka, they might have become professional folk singers instead of geisha.

The profession is still alive, barely and voluntarily. The geisha's impact on modern *min'yō* has been immense. A prize-winning 1999 novel by Nakanishi Rei, made into a hit film in 2000, is named after the local song 'Nagasaki Burabura Bushi'. This fictionalized biography tells the story of the real Nagasaki geisha Aihachi and her involvement with a local historian. During the 1920s the two of them travelled about the region collecting village songs, some of which Aihachi arranged for shamisen and recorded (re-released as R65).

1.4 *Min'yō* and *minzoku geinō*

Min'yō is closely linked with another class of phenomena called *minzoku geinō*, perhaps best translated as 'folk performing arts'. Nishitsunoi estimated in 1976 that there were some 20,000 *minzoku geinō*. To most Japanese today, *min'yō* implies song first and foremost, sometimes associated with group dancing, while the term *minzoku geinō* does not immediately evoke the image of a song-centred event but suggests a festive performance, generally calendrical, with colourful costumes and props. *Min'yō* is associated ever more in the public mind with the cities and with stage performances, while the term *minzoku geinō* maintains strong rural, or at least regional, resonances.

The concept of a unified class of folk performing arts dates from the 1920s. The most common term used in those days was *kyōdo geinō* 'rural performing arts'. The public use of the term *minzoku geinō* apparently dates only from 1958 (Nishitsunoi 1976), but it is now the standard term. (Note the replacement of a geographical designation by a 'class' one, parallel to the eventual triumph of *min'yō* over *riyō*; Western influence is apparent here too.) The pre-eminent codifier of the concept is Honda Yasuji (b. 1906), and present-day researchers overwhelmingly follow his terminology and classificatory schema.[25]

Unlike *min'yō*, which as a category could be characterized musically fairly consistently, the musical features of *minzoku geinō* are tremendously diverse. Hence definitions of *minzoku geinō* rest largely on non-musical criteria. Reviewing both scholarly and lay opinions suggests a consensus which, allowing for numerous exceptions, would accept features such as these as typical:

(1) *Minzoku geinō* are usually connected with religion in the broad sense (Shintō, Buddhism, others), which accounts for several other features listed.

(2) They are communal events, closely linked with particular local communities.
(3) Performances are held at fixed times and places, on traditionally sanctioned occasions within the yearly cycle of festivals and observances.
(4) Participation is often required or restricted by criteria such as residence, family, age, class and gender.
(5) Performers may undergo elaborate ritual purification before performing.
(6) There is a strong feeling that the performance must be presented exactly as it 'always' has been.
(7) And yet, practice sessions are held only during the few weeks immediately preceding the event, virtually guaranteeing alterations over the years.
(8) Aesthetic considerations are secondary to correctness of performance.
(9) Ties with the past are maintained through tangible, physical items: costumes or instruments (often clearly dated), scrolls, genealogies, etc.
(10) The performers have local links.
(11) The performers are amateurs.[26]

Exceptions to all of these features, common even in traditional times, have increased even more in recent decades (see Chapter 4).

Although *min'yō* is often treated as a subclass of *minzoku geinō*, the majority of what are today called *min'yō* lack most of these ten traits. Much debate arises precisely on the degree to which *min'yō* performance and transmission *should* maintain such features. But both categories encompass such a diverse set of phenomena that any such debate is futile.

1.5 The concept of *zoku* in Japanese music

Researching Japanese folk song, one frequently meets words containing the element *zoku* (俗), a Chinese loan-morph with shades of meaning such as 'vulgar, common, popular, secular'. (This is not to be confused with a homophonous morpheme written 族 discussed below.) This element, encountered above in words such as *zokuyō* and *minzoku geinō*, has a history of association with heavily value-laden concepts. It generally carried negative significance until the early twentieth century, when usage became less consistent. (For a similar discussion of the evolution of the concept of 'popular' in England, see Middleton 1981.)

In early China, the concept *zoku* (pronounced *su* in modern Mandarin) was opposed to *ga* (*ya* in Mandarin), 'elegant' or 'refined'. Nakano (1989: 126–7) writes that in the *Shijing* (*Book of songs*) *zoku* was opposed to the compound *fūga* (Mand. *fengya*) implying 'aesthetic elegance and refinement', specifically with reference to literature: the classics were *ga*, while any innovations were 'considered inferior and pejoratively termed *zoku*'.

A typical early occurrence of *zoku* in Japan was in a Buddhist context, to mean 'secular, worldly' – which from a Buddhist viewpoint was effectively a pejorative. Thus we find the word *zokugaku* 'secular music' in a seventh-century manuscript known in Japan, opposed to two words meaning 'religious music'.[27] Presumably the scope of *zokugaku* in this usage would have included most of the Chinese-derived court music.

The court, predictably, saw it differently. In court circles, music for palace and government functions was respectfully called *gagaku* 'elegant/refined music'; other more popular music was called *zokugaku*. The terms *zokugaku* and *gagaku*, as well as a third term *seigaku* ('correct music'), were all borrowed from Chinese. They are pronounced *suyue*, *yayue* and *shengyue* respectively in modern Mandarin. *Suyue* and *shengyue* were in use in China by the Zhou period (1027–221 BC), and *yayue* appeared by the Tang period (AD 618–906) (cf. ODJ 3.1375). The terms were also early imported into Korea, where today they are pronounced *sogak*, *aak* and *chŏng'ak* (Song 1980a: passim).

The Confucian-influenced courtier considered music an important element in a well-ordered world, capable of influencing the behaviour of both nature and humankind. From the *Liqi* and other early Chinese Confucian documents, the Edo-period Neo-Confucianists adopted beliefs such as the one that 'since each note of the scale had an affinity with a particular grade of the social hierarchy, harmonious music was a way of producing social harmony by sympathetic induction' (Dore 1965: 48). Kumazawa Banzan wrote in 1672 that music was 'valuable for producing rain in time of drought', and further noted: 'Music exercises control over the spirit. A spirit which is calm will be liberal and inclined to the good' (quoted in Dore 1965: 48, 56).

But not all music would have such beneficial effects. The rapid development of urban popular music forms early in the Edo period (1603–1868) triggered repeated written attacks by Confucian scholars. A typical opinion is that of the Kyushu-based scholar Shōji Kōgi, writing in 1833 (quoted in Dore 1965: 48):

> An ignorant farmer about to start a fight would calm down at the sound of *gagaku* . . . and goodness would grow in his heart, but the sound of samisen [shamisen] is enough to put lewd thoughts into the mind of a saintly priest with years of Zen meditation behind him.

The shamisen (samisen), a three-string banjo-like lute, was the Edo-period *zokugaku* instrument *par excellence*. It accompanied the romantic and erotic songs of the geisha and the Kabuki theatre; appealing to samurai, merchant and peasant alike, it was potentially a threat to the rigid Confucian social hierarchy. Dazai Shundai opined in 1747 (1976: 274–5):

> Generally speaking, in *gagaku* the tempo is slow and the strings and winds play sparsely. By *gagaku* we mean correct music (*seigaku*). Lewd music (*ingaku*) is called 'busy', for it plays many notes . . . .

The *kusakari-fue* ['grass-cut flute', presumably the transverse bamboo flute common in folk music], shakuhachi and *hitoyogiri* [end-blown notched flutes] are all instruments of *zokugaku* and play busily. Yet they are less provocative than the shamisen.[28]

In 1802, a government official, Moriyama Takamori, noted that during the 1740s–60s many samurai sons had become addicted to shamisen, even performing amateur Kabuki in their mansions, but that this 'depravity' was eliminated in the reforms of the 1790s, 'and society returned to normal' (quoted in Gerstle 1989: 40).

This same treatise by Dazai refers to the 13-string koto zither, originally a *gagaku* instrument, as 'falling' (*ochiru*) to the level of *zokugaku* (ibid.: 275). And *jōruri*, shamisen-accompanied narrative music, is said to have become more *zoku*, being performed in a vulgar, obscene way – even daring to deal with the love lives of humble commoners (ibid.: 274).

Such passages confirm *zoku*'s pejorative flavour and link it with the lower classes (*sensha*). During the Edo period there was a clearly defined class hierarchy (at least in theory): emperor, nobles, samurai, farmers, artisans, merchants and outcasts, in descending order. Conscious intellectualization about music, and the use of terms such as *gagaku* and *zokugaku*, would have been encountered almost exclusively among courtiers (including court officials) and the more intellectually-inclined samurai. From their perspective, the farmers and urban classes were rarely distinguished in practice: both were 'humble commoners' drenched in *zoku*. Consider the views of Gion Nankai (1676–1751; quoted in Nakano 1989: 127):

> *[Ga]* is a concept used by aristocrats, scholars and gentlemen. It has nothing to do with the lower classes. . . . *Zoku* originally referred to the popular, common things in society. Among such things, there are the good and the bad, and we do not have to despise everything common. . . . all the vulgar, coarse, low [OK, we get the point!] language and jokes in popular stories, the crass language of commerce and everyday life, the crude language of farmers and housewives, prostitutes and actors are all *zoku*.

Around the time Nankai was writing, *zoku* had in fact made a minor incursion into the world of *ga*, but only when transformed into *ga*. The poet Bashō suggested that skilful use of *zoku* elements could raise them to the level of *ga*; indeed, through his influence the writing of *haiku* spread widely across class barriers, until one neo-Confucianist poet moaned: 'The writing of the whole country has fallen into the hands of the common people' (Nakano 1989: 129). Similar sentiments lay behind the 'new folk song' movement of the early twentieth century (§3.4.3): poets used the form of folk song, but strove to create new lyrics more elegant than those of the villagers.

Although Nankai tars merchants and farmers with the same brush, through most of recorded history the elite classes were more tolerant of rural music than of urban popular song. The repertoires of the court vocal genres *saibara* and *fuzoku*, which flourished during the Heian period, are thought to consist of arrangements, or perhaps imitations, of country songs. The theatrical genres Noh and *kyōgen* developed out of folk roots to become elite entertainment, then frequently returned to the countryside in their plots, depicting warriors, court nobles or priests interacting with rural folk in bucolic settings. The Edo-period pejorative sense of *zoku* was directed rather at the new urban shamisen music genres, since these – and the women and men who performed them – often drove the samurai to distraction and degeneracy. Thus Dazai objected more to the 'provocative' shamisen than to the folk flute.

In the late nineteenth century, Japan passed through a period of intense Westernization in emulation of the countries that had prised open her long-closed doors. Japan had to admit the obvious military and economic superiority of the West, and the still potent neo-Confucian belief in the power of music to influence society can be interpreted as suggesting that these stemmed in part from the superiority of Western music. In establishing a national school system for the first time, the government therefore paid close attention to selecting the 'correct' musics for pedagogical purposes. Western or Westernized music formed the core, mixed with certain approved elements of traditional music (see Eppstein 1994; Malm 1971; Signell 1976).[29] The prejudices of Edo-period scholars were confirmed by many foreigners' negative attitudes toward the urban pleasure quarters. The often erotic shamisen-accompanied vocal musics of the geisha houses and theatres, long regarded as immoral and vulgar, were now additionally considered a hindrance to Japan's spiritual modernization. During this period, the terms *zokkyoku*, *zokugaku* and *zokuyō* all were used to refer to such music, mostly disparagingly.

Zokkyoku was the term heard most commonly with the widest range of meanings. For some speakers, *zokkyoku* meant all music outside of the imperial court tradition – including koto music and Noh; others restricted it only to the shorter types of shamisen songs; a few gave it its even narrower modern meaning: the informally transmitted party songs of the geisha and their customers. Some of the latter were *zokuyō* in Machida's sense of arranged folk songs.

Folk song impinged less on the consciousness of the urban intelligentsia, being geographically distant, but when referred to it was typically seen as vulgar, bawdy, a music of manual labourers and prostitutes (see Asano 1983: 3). Folk songs were considered, along with *zokugaku*, morally quite unsuitable for use in school education. European folk songs, on the other hand, were frequently given Japanese moralistic lyrics and included in school songbooks of the Meiji period (see Eppstein 1994; May 1963; Berger 1991).

By the 1890s, however, Japan's growing economic and military might was restoring her self-respect and confidence in her own 'native' culture (see

Shively 1971). Victory in the Sino-Japanese War (1894–5) and Russo-Japanese War (1904–5) stimulated cultural nationalism. After the turn of the century many public figures and scholars came out in support of traditional Japanese values – and music.

This nativist resurgence in cultural confidence included a renewed respect for agricultural village lifeways as the source of Japanese values. In a movement launched in 1904, many poets who had been writing in the somewhat elitist *waka* and *haiku* genres now started writing what they called *riyō*, using the common folk song poetic metre of 7-7-7-5 syllables (Nakamura 1991: 272–4; see further §3.4.3). The effects of Western democratic thought also eliminated some of the disdain in which *zoku* music was held; certainly European Romanticism had a salubrious effect.[30]

Still, ambivalence remained. Even some who praised rural values and lifeways had doubts about the overly *zoku* typical folk lyrics. In 1910 the poet Noguchi Ujō (1882–1945) opined that such lyrics, 'the poems of the people', tended to be 'wild and vulgar', whereas the works of contemporary urban poets tended toward a precious style far removed from 'the sentiments of the people'. He sought a middle ground via what he named 'colloquial poems' (*kōgo-shi*), which aimed to evoke a pastoral atmosphere without vulgarity. (From Nakamura 1991: 278.) Noguchi called folk songs in general *zokuyō* and seemed appalled by their crudity, yet his recognition of the importance of Japan's rural heritage led him to write thousands of verses in overall folk style.

In 1905, Nakamura tells us (1991: 275), 'the Ministry of Education ordered the governors of every prefecture to research those *zokuyō* being sung in their districts'. The results were published by the Ministry in 1914 as the *Riyōshū* (Collection of *riyō*), the first great compilation of folk lyrics. The Ministry's shift of terms from *zokuyō* to the more affectively neutral *riyō* during those nine years presumably reflects a growing respect for these rural products.

In 1907, a Japanese Music Study Group was founded at Tokyo School of Music. In an address commemorating the occasion, Superintendent Tomiogi spoke up for the much-maligned *zokugaku* as representing the essence of Japaneseness and being the most 'advanced' (*hattatsu*) of all Japanese musics (Tateyama 1910: 691f.; Komiya 1956). In this period, however, there was still a lingering shame that much of Japan's non-court music had been performed and transmitted by geisha and blind musicians. In general the attitude towards shamisen vocal genres *as music* was now favourable, while the social context of their performance – geisha houses, brothels, theatre teahouses – was still viewed dimly (even by some who privately visited such places). However, there were also those who objected that the music itself and the romantic texts of many shamisen genres could have a debilitating effect on the warrior spirit of any man who suffered prolonged exposure to them.

A somewhat different meaning of *zoku* emerged about this same period, through its use in the word *minzokugaku*, 'folklore' (*minzoku* 民俗 'customs, folkways'; *gaku* 学 'study').[31] The discipline of folklore developed in Japan under the aegis of Yanagita Kunio (§1.2), for whom the essence and roots of Japanese culture lay in the customs of the 'folk'. In the word *minzoku* 'folklore', then, *zoku* has a positive valuation.

Still, Yanagita and his followers continued to use the prefix *zoku-* as a mild pejorative in the word *zokuyō*. Interestingly, though, they contrast *zoku-* with *min-* 'people's' or *ri-* 'rural' (as in *min'yō*, *riyō*) rather than with *ga-* 'elegant' or *sei-* 'correct' as the Edo neo-Confucians did. From the Machida–Asano viewpoint, true folk songs 'fall' to the status of *zokuyō* as they are popularized beyond the local area, performed by professionals, and arranged in a less 'authentic' (*seichō*) style. They 'fall' just as Dazai felt that koto music had 'fallen' from *gagaku* to *zokugaku*. Although scholars thus distinguish between pure rural songs and their more popularized *zoku* versions, the practitioner of Japanese or Western-style classical[32] music in Japan tends to consider *all* folk songs *zoku* in the sense of 'vulgar'.

Although Machida's writings evince his preference for 'authentic' *riyō* over 'arranged' *zokuyō*, he was not himself a musical purist. In fact, he wrote several *shin-min'yō* ('new folk songs'; category A.2.b in his 1960 schema) with melodies and accompaniments unlike anything heard in his idealized country village (§3.4.3). From childhood he had been trained in various urban classical shamisen vocal genres – *nagauta*, *tokiwazu*, *utazawa*, etc. – and he continued to research them throughout his life (Takeuchi 1974). Besides *shin-min'yō*, he composed several shamisen songs that might be considered *kouta* or *hauta* – types of urban party songs on the borderline between folk and classical. Nevertheless, the abiding influence of Yanagita apparently led Machida to value the independence of the *riyō* category from these other short popular songs.

Folk song scholars in Japan give their attention to many forms of *min'yō* in its broadest sense, both *zokuyō* and *riyō* as well as some *shin-min'yō*. They recognize both that music inevitably changes and that the 'folk' themselves cannot be bound by categories. The chapters that follow often take us into other genres of music which, however defined, have a relationship of give-and-take with *min'yō*. Still, folk song occupies a special and important place in the Japanese consciousness, distinct from other genres.

One other phenomenon of the same period surely impacted on attitudes to folk song. This was the birth of the Folk Craft (*mingei*) movement in the late 1920s, under the leadership of Yanagi Sōetsu (1889–1961). In his romantic view of the value of folk products, he was a kindred spirit to Yanagita Kunio. The birth of *min'yō* and *minzokugaku* (folklore), and later of *mingei*, gradually brought the 'folk' into being as a category, and one deserving of respect.[33]

1.6 Musical features of traditional *min'yō*

To understand how folk song performance style has changed in the modern period, we first need to reconstruct traditional practice as a baseline. This section concentrates on specifically musical features: scale and mode, metre and rhythm, ornamentation, polyphony, vocal quality, text setting, instrumentation. Chapter 2 will try to shed light on traditional performance contexts, transmission, lyrics and so forth. We are dealing here with specifically rural contexts, and with what eventually came to be called *min'yō*.

Our sources for this endeavour include recordings (from as early as 1900), oral testimony, drawings and paintings, travellers' accounts and so forth. I cannot describe all the variation in practice over time, space and context. The aim here is to give an overall picture sufficient to our current purposes, rather than a carefully documented in-depth portrait. Keep in mind that there is virtually no verbalized 'folk' music theory with regard to traditional folk song, unlike most other genres of Japanese music. Since what I am identifying as 'traditional' practice often survives today, I use the present tense where possible. (Besides the CD with this book, hear also the field recordings of amateur singers on R17-19, 31–3, 59, 63–4, 67; all but the last three have English notes.)

Singing can be solo or group, and used for self-delectation, dance accompaniment, to set the pace for work, to distract one's mind from the labour at hand, and so forth. Obviously such variables affect many of the musical parameters under discussion. Composers and lyricists are traditionally not known. Some of this will emerge more clearly in Chapter 2.

1.6.1 Metre and rhythm

Traditional *min'yō* can be metric or in 'free rhythm', lacking a regular pulse. Koizumi Fumio proposed naming these two categories respectively ' "Yagi Bushi" style' and ' "Oiwake" style', after two famous songs (1984b: 126–61; in English, see Koizumi & Hughes 2001; Groemer 1999: 76). He considered these as styles or types because the two metrical categories tend to co-vary with other features. Thus non-metric songs, he claimed, tend to be solo, highly melismatic and with a greater range than metric ones. Despite these tendencies, I find these terms and their definitions somewhat misleading. For example, ironically both 'Yagi Bushi' (**CD track 1**) and 'Esashi Oiwake' (for which Koizumi named ' "Oiwake" style'; **CD2**) have a range of a twelfth in most performances. And there are plenty of highly melismatic metric songs.

Metre is virtually always duple, either simple (2/4) or compound (6/8). There are no traditional terms for distinguishing metres, although the verb *hazumu* seems sometimes to have implied 6/8, and perhaps is best translated 'swing', as in jazz terminology.

Ex. 1.1 'Sado Okesa', excerpt: vocal (*top*), *shinobue* (*bottom*; mordents omitted) (transcribed from CD3)

'Swing' would be appropriate particularly because a bar of 6/8 is mostly realized as the sequence eighth-note, sixteenth-note, eighth-note, sixteenth-note (i.e. long-short-long-short) rather than as a sequence of sixteenth-notes. This can be heard in 'Sado Okesa' (Ex. 1.1, **CD3**), where as usual this long-short alternation is clearer in the instruments (here, *shinobue* flute, shamisen, koto, drums) than in the vocal, where ornamentation resists the tendency somewhat. In effect, Japanese 6/8 is a sort of 2/4 with the first and third eighth-notes doubled in duration. Such a view is supported by the fact that some tunes are performed in either 2/4 or 6/8, distinguished simply by doubling the duration in this way for 6/8 (e.g. 'Akita Daikoku Mai').

But Japanese durational values are not as regular as the above might imply. In many 2/4 pieces the first of a pair of eighth-notes may give a tiny portion of its length to the second, although not so precisely or consistently that we can confidently notate this by careful use of dots and ties. (In *nagauta* shamisen music the term *tsumema*, 'compressed duration', sometimes indicates this phenomenon.) In other cases the situation is reversed: the second of a pair of notes is slightly shorter. The *min'yō* shamisen teacher Fujimoto Hideo has suggested that there are differences in the ratios of duration of two-note pairs in shamisen accompaniments of various folk songs; he gives examples of ratios 1:1, 3:2, 2:1, 4:1, 5:1 and so forth (MB 1979.10: 30–1; §4.5.1). His model, while suggestive, is misleadingly precise and certainly does not represent what is in the head of the typical performer.[34]

A well-known instance of irregular ratios – as well as a possible candidate for triple metre – is the partly improvised shamisen accompaniment to 'Tsugaru Yosare Bushi' **(CD4)** and certain other Tsugaru folk songs, in which each bar contains three beats of unequal duration, often with agogic and/or dynamic accent on an off-beat (e.g. beat 2 lengthened, beat 3 louder). In this it recalls the Viennese waltz or the Norwegian *springar*. However, the ratios are more consistent within each of these two genres as a whole, whereas for 'Tsugaru Yosare Bushi' the exact timing depends on the player and the specific motif being played. Oddly, though, the drum accompaniment (used only between vocal sections) maintains – usually! – a steady though syncopated 2/4. Meanwhile, the solo dance that can accompany this song involves a rising onto the toes on beat 3 followed by a return to flat-footedness on beat 1. (See Kojima 1983 for measurements of durational values in Tsugaru-jamisen music, and Groemer 1999: 76ff. for further remarks.)

In general, shamisen accompaniments keep a regular rhythm and pulse (whatever the precise ratio of durations in a bar), while the vocal often diverges from this rhythm, arriving early or late on the same melody pitches. This feature is shared with the classical shamisen and koto genres as well.

Metrical groupings above the level of the individual bar are usually weak: phrases do not necessarily fall into standard lengths of, say, four bars. Moreover, in dance songs, the phrase lengths of dance and music generally do not match. Consider two typical songs for the ancestral festival *o-bon*. Each verse of the song 'Yatchiku' from Gujō Hachiman, Gifu Prefecture (R15), occupies 17 bars of 2/4, while the associated group dance takes 10 bars (one step per bar). 'Kiso Bushi' (Nagano Pref.; **CD5**) has a 12-bar dance (audible via the clapping), but the song alternates verses of 17 and 16 bars depending on number of syllables.

Free rhythm is common in *min'yō* as in many genres of Japanese music, although there is no traditional term for it in the former. (Scholars sometimes use the term *muhaku*, 'without a beat'.) Obviously some contexts suit non-metric singing better than others: it is least appropriate for accompanying dance or rhythmic work, and is less suited to group singing. (The movements of folk dance are virtually all metrically organized, unlike some classical dance.) The durational values of non-metric songs are not linked closely to those of normal speech, where there tends to be a regular pulse – syllables of equal duration – in most dialects. Durational values in free-rhythm songs are quite flexible, particularly in the longer-held notes, whose length can vary considerably between singers and in different performances by one singer (perhaps depending on tiredness, audience enthusiasm and so forth; see §4.8.1 for an example influenced by the demands of television).

Distinguishing fixed and free rhythm is sometimes difficult. There are borderline cases, such as the famous lullabye 'Itsuki no Komoriuta', known throughout Japan in a Western-influenced, instrumentally accompanied 3/4 version. Back in its home region, unaccompanied, it seems to be basically non-metric but with passages where a pulse is discernible **(CD6)**. Due to lack of appropriate indigenous terminology, it is difficult to discuss with performers whether they feel a 'beat' or not; those familiar with Western terminology may in a sense have been 'contaminated'.

1.6.2 Instrumentation

Here it is safest to use the past tense because, as §3.4.2 describes, instrumentation has been standardized for modern *min'yō* during recent decades. I am trying to depict the 'traditional' situation.

Traditional song was often unaccompanied, either because the context was unsuited to the use of instruments (as in most work songs) or because no instruments or performers were available. Rowing a boat while playing shamisen is not recommended. A group activity such as barley threshing or house-foundation pounding (earth-tamping) might be more enjoyable if instrumentalists accompanied the singing labourers, but this almost never happened. An exception is found in, for example, the rice transplanting ritual songs of Hiroshima and Okayama (sometimes called 'Hayashida'): a dozen or more village men play drums and flutes while the women plant and sing **(CD7**; see Uchida 1978). But this music is perhaps intended to encourage the rice plants rather than the workers, and is only played as a ritual, not for day-to-day transplanting. An example is shown in the last scene of Kurosawa's film *The Seven Samurai*.

Accompaniment was common for dance and party songs, and for performances by professionals such as geisha or itinerant musicians. For Bon dancing, the minimum accompaniment was hand-clapping, but commonly one would hear a large tacked-head barrel drum (*taiko*, a generic term for stick drums). Often a transverse bamboo flute (or several in unison) and a hand-gong (*kane*) were added (Fig. 1.1). The flute was called *fue, shinobue* or *takebue* (*shino/take*, bamboo; *-bue* < *fue*).[35]

Shamisen might be added to these for Bon dancing, especially in or near urban areas, but players could be in short supply, and the instrument might be inaudible over the sounds of dancing, gossiping, etc. But shamisen was favoured for almost all metric songs if available. In a party situation, it could be joined by a smaller laced-head stick drum, *shimedaiko*.

The shakuhachi, an end-blown bamboo notched flute, was uncommon in villages until fairly recently; in any case, it was formerly associated more with specific non-*min'yō* uses (see §3.3.2). When available, it suited quieter settings and smaller gatherings. Looking ahead, we find that by the mid-twentieth century it was the standard and generally the only accompanying instrument for free-rhythm songs in particular, where it shadows the voice a split-second late. A few free-rhythm songs might be accompanied by shamisen, especially when performed by geisha: the most common geisha songs were metric, but their customers often asked to be accompanied as they sang free-rhythm folk songs, and almost no geisha played shakuhachi. By whatever avenue, a few songs today are in free metre but against a metric and quite bouncy shamisen and drum part, including 'Akita Nikata Bushi' **(CD8)**, 'Honjō Oiwake' and 'Awa Yoshikono' ('Awa Odori').

The *narimono* – drums and other percussion – were originally played by whoever was free at the time. Likewise, backing vocals or choral responses were also originally sung by anyone available.

Aside from shamisen, flute, shakuhachi and percussion, other instruments were rarely used because rarely available. For some reason, the three-string *kokyū* spike-fiddle (a sort of bowed, upright mini-shamisen) was often found accompanying songs from around Toyama Prefecture, such as 'Etchū Owara' **(CD9)** and 'Mugiya Bushi'. Similarly, at some point and for some reason the two hand-drums of the Noh and Kabuki theatres, *ōtsuzumi* and *kotsuzumi*, came to be used to accompany 'Yasugi Bushi' but virtually no other folk songs. (Aside from these, all other rural drums were stick-drums – *taiko*.) In rural communities the koto was restricted to the elite; it appears rarely in commercial recordings of appropriate *min'yō* such as 'Kuroda Bushi', which derives its melody from the court music piece 'Etenraku'. It is heard, unusally, in the recording of 'Sado Okesa' on **CD3**, though without the original liner notes this would be hard to recognize. The various percussion instruments of Buddhism were used only in temples. Two types of idiophone onomatopoeically called *sasara* – a scraper (*suri-zasara*) and a set of concussion plaques (*bin-zasara*) – were found in Shintō ritual music in particular and occasionally in *min'yō*.

1.6.3 Polyphony

When several vocalists participate, they sing either in unison or in leader-chorus mode, and very rarely in antiphony. Unison may accompany some Bon dances (where all dancers may sing), some kinds of work, certain party or banquet songs (e.g. **CD10**) and so forth. The unison is far looser than the ideal for a well-trained Western chorus. (**CD11** is sung in even looser unison – a true heterophony – by two *goze*, blind itinerant female musicians.)

More often, one person sings the main part of a verse, with any or all others present providing a unison choral response. The response is often called *hayashi*(*-kotoba*), '(words of) encouragement', although *hayashi* alone can also refer to instrumental accompaniment since this too 'encourages' the singer. (To avoid ambiguity, the term *utabayashi*, 'sung *hayashi*', is now sometimes used.) Some responses are melodic; others are spoken or shouted either at fixed places or spontaneously, the shortest of these commonly being called *kakegoe* – 'calls'. Leader and chorus rarely overlap, but if they do, a sort of unintentional polyphony may occur briefly.

When instruments are added, varying relationships between parts are possible. A shakuhachi will follow the voice closely. A shamisen may also do this but will generally diverge into looser heterophony, mostly because of idiomatic differences due to the fast decay of a plucked note. While the shamisen sets a regular beat, the voice may diverge from that beat both for artistic reasons (as discussed later with regard to Fig. 4.9) and perhaps so the lyrics can be heard better.

Sometimes the shamisen provides a sort of isorhythmic quasi-drone, playing a short recurring motif (e.g. **CD12**). This is a much easier style to play and was presumably more common in the past. The bamboo transverse flute (*shinobue*) may likewise play a shortish passage that repeats throughout the tune while the vocal goes off on its own; this is quite common in Bon dance songs, where several flutists may play at once (as also in Shintō ritual music). 'Sado Okesa' (Ex. 1.1, **CD3**) combines three different though metrically linked melodic lines at once (see §1.6.8 below).

Aside from heterophony and short repeated motifs independent of the vocal, true countermelodies occur very rarely. In the renowned 'Yasugi Bushi' **(CD13)** and some of its relatives, two shamisen improvise independent parts between vocal sections. Such instrumental countermelodies are common in classical shamisen and koto genres, again mostly in non-vocal sections.

1.6.4 Ornamentation

In place of elaboration in the vertical dimension, as it were, through Western-style polyphony, instead the folk singer elaborates horizontally, ornamenting the vocal melody line to a far greater extent than in Western classical music. Polyphony and ornamentation often stand in an inverse relationship cross-culturally: too much of one tends to inhibit the other. Further, by using a relatively 'straight' tone as their point of departure – rather than a constant *bel canto* vibrato – Japanese singers can bring their melodic twists and turns into greater prominence.

The general term for ornamentation is *kobushi*, 'little melodies', though the term *goro* is also common, especially in the northeast. There are a very few terms for specific ornaments, but these are not consistently applied across Japan. (More specific terms are found in other genres such as Buddhist chant and Noh.) Some details are given in the discussion of notation in §4.5.2, and Examples 4.1 and 4.2 and Fig. 4.9 attempt to capture some sense of the detail of typical *min'yō* ornamentation.

Traditionally, ornamentation was not standardized but depended on a singer's taste and ability. No clear line separates main melody notes and ornamentation, but some idea can be had by listening to a singer who can do *kobushi* well and one who cannot. The accompanying CD gives an idea of the range of ornamental styles and abilities, omitting only the least ornamented end of the spectrum.

As Japanese singers are very proud of this element of their art, the topic arises frequently in conversation with foreigners, who are told that Western folk song has no *kobushi* and thus is rather insipid. Certain songs feature single highly ornamented breath-phrases of over twenty-five seconds (e.g. 'Etchū Owara Bushi', 'Esashi Oiwake'). But one must use ornamentation appropriately, as *min'yō* teacher Matsukawa Seiichirō (b. ca. 1920) explained in 1980: for the more naive (*soboku*) songs still rich in rural flavour, such as 'Nanbu Ushioi Uta' or 'Tsugaru Yamauta', one must not overdo the orna-ments (*mawashisugiru*) but instead sing directly (*suratto*) and freshly (*assari*). If you rely overly on technique (*gikō ni tayorisugiru*), a general audience may be impressed, but experts will know better.

1.6.5 Voice quality

There is no absolute preference for a particular tessitura or range. Most spe-cialist singers past and present do tend to prefer the higher end (cf. **CD9**), but many admired village singers choose a mid-range. A loud voice is also favoured in general, especially in appropriate contexts such as working at sea, or singing a Bon dance song while hundreds dance around you. In conversa-tions around 1980, older singers were generally proud that they did not need to rely on amplification to be heard (although having no choice anyhow).

Timbre is, of course, hard to describe in words. It seems to be common for Westerners to decry Asian cultures' singing as 'nasal', and I have heard this said of Japanese singing, but I would dispute that. A tense throat does seem to be a characteristic (see also Chapter 2, Note 12). Certainly the quality of a folk song voice is not the *bel canto* singer's pear-shaped tone.[36] Also, Western influence on *min'yō* timbre has been minimal: Western vocal styles are so far from *min'yō* that there is little mixing but rather 'compartmentalization' or 'peaceful co-existence' (in the terms of Nettl 1985 and Kartomi 1981).

In sum, suffice it to say that one can generally distinguish a folk song voice from that for other genres such as Noh, *gidayū, nagauta* or *enka*. But there is a fair amount of variety. It is the style of ornamentation more than the voice quality *per se* that characterizes *min'yō*.

In aesthetic evaluation of *min'yō* performance, the term used overwhelm-ingly is *aji*, 'flavour': this person's voice has *aji*, that way of ornamenting that song has no *aji*, etc.

1.6.6 Lyrics

Lyrical content is exemplified copiously in Chapter 2. Here we discuss other aspects of the lyrics.

Obviously, most people sang in their local dialect – they could rarely speak any other. The dialects of 'mainland' Japan (i.e. excluding Okinawa and Amami) are largely mutually intelligible, albeit with considerable difficulty in certain cases. (See further §4.6.1.)

Japanese folk songs are nearly all strophic (barring a handful of quasi-exceptions). The most common pattern of syllables per line is 7–7–7–5, a total of 26 syllables per verse, often called '*dodoitsu* metre' as it predominates in a popular song genre of that name.[37] But many other patterns exist, and in any case the syllable count is not inviolable. This poetic metre is often obscured in performance by repetitions of lines, or by interpolations and refrains of meaningful or nonsensical text.

We can follow Western folk song scholarship in distinguishing between story-songs or ballads (Jap. *kudoki*) and what Wilgus called a 'folk-lyric', a song of indeterminate length lacking a coherent, developed narrative (1959: 432; no Japanese term). The favoured subjects of *kudoki* are all tragic. Their very length (sometimes over an hour) meant that they were performed only occasionally, often by itinerant specialists (§§2.2.4, 2.4.6). In the era before the film, recording and broadcast industries, and before widespread literacy, these ballads were immensely popular.

The average villager at work or play was much more likely to sing a folk-lyric, a generally shorter song whose verses were mostly independent of each other in content and thus could be sung in any order and in any number, depending on one's powers of memory and/or improvisation. The predominance of 7–7–7–5 poetic metre, especially since the seventeenth century, allowed easy transfer of verses between different melodies. But these 26 syllables might then be repeated in whole or part, perhaps more than once, with various 'nonsense' syllables in between, so that a single verse might last for over a minute (as in 'Sasa Odori', **CD14**).

Given the ease with which verses 'float' from one song to another, and the lack of fixed lyrics for most songs, it is not easy to define what constitutes a 'song' (*uta*). This brings up the matter of song titles, which will be relevant at various places below and well exemplified in Chapter 2. In traditional times, a song was often merely referred to by the first word(s) of its standard first verse. Thus a song from Iwasaki in southern Iwate **(CD10)** is often called 'Medeta' by the locals because it begins with the lyrics *medeta ureshi ya*. Sometimes they would tack on the word *bushi* meaning 'tune': 'Medeta Bushi'. At this point, perhaps, we could say that it has become a title rather than merely a form of reference. But the locals said it is also called 'Sakamori Uta' – drinking party song: at such parties, this congratulatory song *must* be sung. Many work and dance songs are also referred to this way, by their function or context: if only one song is regularly associated with paddy-field ploughing in a particular community, then it can simply be called 'Takaki Uta' – 'Ploughing Song'. Some ballads, songs with a consistent subject matter, will be called by their theme, perhaps a pair of lovers: 'O-Natsu Seijūrō'.

Finally, songs imported from elsewhere might be known partly by the name of the place of origin: 'Yamanaka Bushi' **(CD15)** might be brought back by visitors to Yamanaka hot-spring resort – where it originally had a different name since the locals already knew where they were! As domestic travel increased in the late nineteenth century, such names became ever more common. A song from Oiwake in central Japan spread widely under the name 'Oiwake'; a localized version that developed in the northern town of Esashi then became widely famous under the double-barrelled place-name title: 'Esashi Oiwake' **(CD2**; §3.3.1); other versions in other communities likewise prefix the place-name, such as 'Honjō Oiwake'. Today, the titles of most well-known *min'yō* begin with the name of the community or, more commonly, the prefecture or pre-modern province of origin; this may be followed by an old-style name based on lyrics, function or theme. Thus: 'Tsugaru Aiya Bushi', 'Tsugaru [Province] melody [that begins with the nonsense word] *aiya*'. As that last example illustrates, many songs are named after their *hayashi(-kotoba)*, those usually nonsensical interpolations: 'Nonnoko Bushi', 'Sansa Odori' etc.

Some *hayashi*, usually in rhythmic solo heightened speech, tell mini-stories having no relation to any part of the content of the verses **(CD12)**. A famous example from 'Aizu Bandai-san' (Fukushima Pref.):

Ohara Shōsuke-san / nan de shinshō tsubushita / asane asazake / asayu ga daisuki de / sore de shinshō tsubushita / ā mottomo da, mottomo da

   Ohara Shōsuke / how did he squander his wealth? / Morning lie-ins, morning *sake*, / morning baths – he loved these; / that's how he squandered his wealth / ah, of course, of course.

One function of such *hayashi*, according to Tsugaru-jamisen legend Takahashi Chikuzan, was to give the lead singer a break during a long song (Groemer 1999: 211, with further examples).

1.6.7 Text setting

Since Japanese is a pitch accent rather than stress accent language, there is no need to set accented syllables to strong beats as in most Western music. Linguistic pitch too is far less crucial to comprehension than the tones of Chinese, for example, and it is only minimally reflected melodically in Japanese vocal music. (For weak counterclaims, see Kindaichi 1967 and Koizumi 1968.) This means that almost any text can be set to any melody as long as the number of syllables (more correctly, moras) fits. Even this is not crucial: in a metric song, as in most Western musics, it is possible simply to jam in extra syllables, or sustain a syllable or two to cover a shortage, without altering the beat; in a free-rhythm song, the melody can be sustained or shortened as needed.

1.6.8 Scale and mode

An understanding of this topic is crucial to appreciating the changes in Japanese modal sense over time, especially under Westernization. In discussing and analysing scale and mode in Japanese music, most researchers employ the schema outlined by Koizumi in any of several works (e.g. 1958, 1965, 1973, 1977, stimulated by Lachmann 1929). His model works well, but far from flawlessly, for almost all genres of traditional music. The following discussion is based largely on his formulation but is keyed particularly to folk song. I will ignore the less influential rival schemata (see Hughes 1993: 350–2), the most important of which is that of Shibata (1978) and its adaptation by Tokumaru (see Tokita 1996: 7–8). There is no 'folk' theory of scale or mode for *min'yō*, unlike certain other Japanese genres: the analysis and terminology below is entirely of scholarly origin.

The overwhelming majority of traditional folk songs are pentatonic. It is usually enlightening, however, to analyse a Japanese octave species into two disjunct three-note tetrachords of identical interval structure. Koizumi identifies four such structures as important in Japanese music; the names shown apply both to the tetrachord and to the resultant octave species or scale type (Table 1.1).

(Pitches shown are relative: there is no concept of exact pitch in traditional folk song. As in Western music, these scales can be extended upwards or downwards, but see comments below.) The names of these structures are varied in origin but are *not* used by folk musicians, nor even by present-day professionals with rare exceptions. The Ryūkyū or Okinawa scale occurs only in that region of Japan and thus will not concern us again until §7.3. *Ritsu* is a term borrowed from court music theory, but this scale type is common in folk music as well. *In* and *yō* are the Japanese pronunciations of the Chinese philosophical concepts *yin* and *yang*; the names reflect the perception by some scholars that these two scales are respectively 'dark' and 'light' in mood, although this contention is hard to demonstrate. The alternative names preferred by Koizumi are more enlightening: *miyako-bushi*, 'urban/Capital melody' is indeed most common in the urban musics of the seventeenth century and after, whereas folk song more often uses the scale appropriately

Table 1.1. Koizumi's four scale types

Ryūkyū / Okinawa	C	e	F + G	b	C
inaka-bushi / min'yō / yō	C	e-flat	F + G	b-flat	C
ritsu	C	d	F + G	a	C
miyako-bushi / in	C	d-flat	F + G	a-flat	C

named *inaka-bushi*, 'rural melody', or *min'yō*. For a reason explained later, I will use his term *miyako-bushi* but will prefer *yō* to its alternatives.

In all of these tetrachords, it is the notes a fourth apart, the extremes (shown here in upper case), that form the framework. Koizumi called these the **nuclear tones** (*kakuon*, after Lachmann's term *Kernton*); the note in between (lower case here) could be called the filler tone or infix. In the resulting scales, the nuclear tones play the central melodic function, with the infixes serving most often a subsidiary role – as leading tones, upper or lower auxiliaries, etc. Overwhelmingly, it will be one of the nuclear tones that ends a melodic section.

Notice that the *ritsu* and *yō* scales are intervallically identical: both are the 'anhemitonic pentatonic', common worldwide. Let us write them as in Table 1.2, with potential nuclear tones underlined and upper-cased, and using 1 2 3 . . . to represent *do, re, mi* . . .

It can be seen now that these two scales differ at the level not of intervallic structure but of tonal function, in that different scale degrees become tonal centres. It is this, plus the overall patterns of melodic movement, that distinguish *yō* from *ritsu*. Thus Koizumi treats them as two distinct **modes** (*senpō*) which share the same tonal material or **scale** (*onkai*); the *miyako-bushi* mode employs a different scale. Other scholars are often less scrupulous about distinguishing scale and mode. (The notes to the accompanying CD indicate the mode of each song.)

The common structure shared by all of these modes can be abstracted as C x F + G y C, where the filler tones x and y are the same distance above C and G respectively. In practice, the nuclear tones tend to be very stable in pitch (for competent singers), giving relatively firm intervals of a (perfect) fourth, fifth and octave between them (C–F, C–G, C–C, etc.). The filler tones, however, are often quite unstable, as perhaps befits their subsidiary status: variation up to around 50 cents (a quarter-tone) may occur in a single performance – which can make it difficult to distinguish between two neighbouring scales in Table 1.1. In particular, *yō* may shade into *ritsu* by lowering its infixes, and *ritsu* may shade into *miyako-bushi* (or vice versa) as their infixes are respectively lowered or raised.

Such shading usually takes place unconsciously among amateur or older professional performers: the singers of the barley-threshing song 'Bouchi Uta' from Kanagawa Prefecture (§5.4.4; **CD16**) were certainly unaware, not to

Table 1.2. The identity of the *yō* and *ritsu* scales

yō		A	c	D	+	E	g	A
ritsu	G	a	C	+	D	e	G	
	5	6	1	2		3	5	6

mention unconcerned, that in the analyst's terms they seemed to be mixing *ritsu* and *miyako-bushi* modes and various shades in between. In **CD3**, a revered recording of 'Sado Okesa' from the 1930s, with the exception of the lowest vocal pitch the intervals are consistent and precise, but we find a surprising, often simultaneous mixing of tetrachord types between voice, *shinobue* flute and strings (shamisen and koto) (see Ex. 1.1). All parts agree on the nuclear tones C, F and G, but the infixes differ for each of the three parts. The flute, with its fixed pitches, plays *ritsu* throughout in a one-octave range: C d F + G a C. It is hard to hear the string parts clearly, but I seem to hear C d/e-flat F + G a/b-flat C, so that both tetrachords alternate between *ritsu* and *min'yō*. The singer, the famous Murata Bunzō, uses the pitches A (sometimes slightly flat) C D F G A-flat. These would be analysed as three tetrachords, two partial: [G] a C + C d F + G a-flat [C], the bracketed pitches non-occurring but implied structurally. The upper tetrachord is *miyako-bushi*, sometimes sung simultaneously with a *ritsu* passage on flute and a *min'yō* passage on strings; the middle tetrachord is *ritsu*; and the lower tetrachord is somewhere between *ritsu* and *miyako-bushi*, due to the inconsistency of the pitch A. (In recent decades, performances by professionals use the *miyako-bushi* mode throughout, in all parts.)

In other words, for many performers certain differences in pitch that would catch an analyst's attention are not phonemic, not relevant to their concept of the song. All such theorizing was alien to the traditional singer. In any case, in a pentatonic genre, the distance between pitches is much greater than in, say, Western chromatic music, so even considerable latitude in intonation does not imperil the recognition or identity of a melody.

Many researchers ignore the deviations from Western chromatic intervals, forcing all songs into one of the recognized types in their transcriptions and analyses. Some do this wittingly, justifying it by reference to the non-phonemic nature of such 'deviations' for many singers; others do so unconsciously, slaves to their orientation to the essentially identical chromatic scales of Japanese court music theory and Western theory. It may, however, also be due partly to the influence of urban shamisen vocal genres such as *kouta, hauta* and *nagauta*: these deviate little from chromatic intervals except on some ornaments and when slightly flattening the downward half-step leading tones of the *miyako-bushi* mode (the reverse of the Western violinist's slight sharpening of the upward leading tone). Even for modern professional folk singers themselves, the combined effect of contact with genres like *kouta* and with Western music is such that few of these singers deviate from the intervals of the Western chromatic scale to an extent that would pain an inflexible Western listener. Still, as regards traditional singers the Koizumi model is only an approximation or idealization.

When we actually examine a large range of Japanese folk songs, we find that any note in the anhemitonic *yō/ritsu* scale may assume importance (e.g. by serving as finalis) in a certain number of songs. For various reasons it turns out to be hard to distinguish *yō* and *ritsu* in practice in certain cases. For our present purposes in this book, let us adopt the following terminology. We shall speak of the anhemitonic pentatonic as the '*yō* scale' and label its pitches numerically:

C D E G A (for example) = do re mi sol la = 1 2 3 5 6

We will classify pieces in *yō* into five modes named after the finalis: '*yō* on 1, on 2,' etc. (*Yō* on 5 or 1 could be a *ritsu* mode, depending on overall tonal functions; '*yō* on 2' could be either a true *yō* mode or a *ritsu* mode, depending on the prominence of other tones. One is reminded of indigenous debates over the modes of the *sléndro* tuning of central Javanese gamelan.) The same can be done with the *miyako-bushi* scale:

E F A B C (for example) = mi fa la si do = 3 4 6 7 1

Since the nuclear tones tend to assume melodic prominence, certain of these modes are much more common than others (see statistics compiled in Kubo 1960, conveniently quoted in Kitahara 1966: 280–2). *Yō* on 6 (6 123 5) is by far the most common folk mode; the other most common modes are *yō* on 2, *miyako-bushi* on 7 and *miyako-bushi* on 3. Pitches 4 and 1 in *miyako-bushi* tend to function as downward leading tones and therefore virtually never appear as finalis; *yō* on 1 is also rare.[38]

Four important qualifications must now be added. First, unlike European church modes, assignment of mode and finalis has no implications for the overall range of a piece. If we speak of '*yō* on 6', the actual range may be anywhere from about a major sixth to two octaves, and the finalis 6 may fall anywhere in the range. A song in *miyako-bushi* on 3 may use exactly the same tonal material and have the same range as a song in *miyako-bushi* on 7, differing only in finalis.

Second, in some pieces one of the nuclear tones serves as finalis for the verse and another for the tutti refrain. In *miyako-bushi*, for example, one section may end on 3 and the other on 7. In counting the number of pieces ending on each finalis (as in Kubo 1960), cases such as this are awkward.

Third, unlike, say, the Western major scale, a Japanese octave species does not necessarily replicate itself throughout the range of a piece. Occasionally *yō* on 6 has the following form (with A=6):

E	G	A	*c*	d	e	g	a	*b*	d'
3	5	6	*1*	2	3	5	6	7	2

The tonal material consists of three *yō* tetrachords (E–G–A, A–c–d, e–g–a) with a *ritsu* tetrachord (a–b–d') on top. The fourth between nuclear tones A and D is filled by C in the lower range and B in the upper range (the two italicized tones). This may arise partly from the latter's function as an upper auxiliary to a nuclear tone; whatever the reason, such situations are frequent. (Shibata's 1978 model, mentioned above, may capture this better than Koizumi's.) Thus, Appendix 1 refers to the mode of some songs as being '*yō* on 6 with upper neighbour 7'.

By its very nature, of course, tetrachord-based music is in some degree of tension with the octave principle. Certain genres of Japanese music, especially Buddhist vocal music (*shōmyō*) and genres such as Noh which are influenced strongly by it, regularly violate octave replication, working rather with overlapping or unlike tetrachords or pentachords; others use nuclear tones as pivot points for mid-piece modulation, so that the piece as a whole is far from pentatonic. Such niceties are only rarely relevant in folk song, so we shall not pursue them further.

Fourth, sometimes a piece uses different tonal material in ascending and descending passages, like the Western melodic minor. This is most common in a variant of the *miyako-bushi* mode that (in Koizumi's terms) uses *miyako-bushi* tetrachords in descent but substitutes a *yō* tetrachord for one or more of these in ascent:

E	F (or G)	A	B	d	e;	e	c	B	A	F	E
3	4 (or 5)	6	7	2	3;	3	1	7	6	4	3

(This mode often adds D as lower auxiliary to the lowest E.) This type of substitution is of a different nature than the unconscious shading of pitches mentioned above. (Shibata's 1978 model captures such modal aspects well.)

Given these last two points, it is clear that some songs are not strictly speaking pentatonic. We might have to speak of a particular song as being 'hexatonic (or heptatonic) with a pentatonic core'. (I have taken to calling such structures 'pentacentric'.) Taken together with the flexibility of intonation noted above, we must keep firmly in mind that pentatonicism is only a scholar's model, albeit a useful one in this case.

1.7 Folk song, *fōku songu* and *enka*

It will be helpful to introduce here two other named categories of song linked to *min'yō*. One, despite its name, is actually totally distinct and quite distant from *min'yō*, while the other has significant points of overlap.

1.7.1 Fōku songu

Fōku songu (from the English 'folk song'), like *min'yō*, is a category concept borrowed from the West, although much later. It derives directly from the American folk boom which began around 1958 with Pete Seeger and the

Kingston Trio and spread to Japan primarily through recordings by performers such as Bob Dylan, Joan Baez, and Peter, Paul and Mary. It is the music of guitars, of self-conscious introspection and protest, often of hopeless romanticism – in short, of Japanese university students. The repertoire embraces both songs from the West (in English or in translation) and, mainly, compositions by native Japanese.

Ironically, *fōku songu* are totally distinct from *min'yō* both musically and socially. Very rarely a *min'yō* – almost always a simple lullaby or children's song – is adopted and arranged by the *fōku songu* crowd (§7.3), but otherwise there is virtually no cross-influence between the genres. As evidence, consider folk singer (*fōku shingā*) Nagira Ken'ichi's 1995 book *Nihon fōku shiteki taizen*, which reviews the movement's history and major personalities from the inside. First, the word *min'yō* does not even occur in its twelve-page index. Second, skimming carefully through its 373 pages, I only ran across the word on six occasions. Even these few occurrences shed light on the considerable gulf between these two types of 'folk' song:

- On p. 32 the group (*gurūpu*) Natasha Seven, said to be skilled at 'American traditional folk' (*amerika no toradishonaru fōku*), 'old tyme style' (*ōrudo taimii sutairu*) and 'bluegrass style' (pp. 28, 31), are revealed to also have some *nihon* [Japanese] *min'yō* in their repertoire, thus proving that they are an unusually versatile and skilful (*kiyō*) group. In treating sixteen major performers or groups, plus all their various incarnations and combinations, this is the only occasion in which a *fōku* artist is said to perform *min'yō*.
- On p. 269, the author says of the singer Tomokawa Kazuki: 'I get the feeling that he's somehow grounded in *min'yō*' (*min'yō no ue ni naritatte iru*). This judgement seems to rest on nothing more than that Tomokawa sings in the distinctive and 'folksy' dialect of his home prefecture of Akita, a renowned treasure house of *min'yō*. The idea is not developed further. Only standard Japanese plus the colloquial urban dialects of Tokyo and Osaka (and frequent English loan words!) are likely to be heard from the lips of a *fōku shingā*, or of a pop singer. Dialect signals *min'yō*.
- On p. 298 he attempts to define clearly what *fōku songu* means, throwing around terms like 'campus folk', 'message folk' and 'underground folk'. In passing, he notes: 'This "*fōku songu*" is an English word, but if we translate it directly it becomes *min'yō*. However, *fōku* is different from what we call *min'yō* in Japan.' He does not elaborate: the statement is patently true for his readers.
- On p. 311 he tells how, around 1968 when he was about sixteen, in the midst of the turmoil of riots in the universities, his 'modern folk' (*modan fō ku*) group yielded to the anti-war sentiments of the time and rebuilt their repertoire around protest songs, thus becoming an 'underground' (*angura*) folk group. Concomitantly they changed their name from 'Champs Élysées'

(a name adopted for no particular reason except to sound less American than their rivals!) to the slightly more cumbersome Shin Minzoku Heiwa Min'yōshugi Ha Shūdan "Kokoro no Uta" – which I struggle to translate as The True People's Peace *Min'yō*-ist Faction Collective "Songs of the Heart". Nagira can give no concrete reason for the choice of this peppy name: 'We just lined up a bunch of likely-sounding (*sore rashii*) words.' Why was *min'yō* among them, and why was it suffixed with *shugi*, '-ism'? My guess is that, in an era of leftist-influenced 'isms', this word *min'yōshugi* was chosen partly as a sort of play on *minshushugi*, 'democracy', which differed in only one character; the combination *fōku-songu-shugi* would have been linguistically awkward, disrupting the appropriately Chinese-looking flow of Sino-Japanese characters. Also, the element *min-* could be taken not only in the sense of 'folk' but also in the more specifically leftist sense of 'the people' (as noted in §1.2), whereas the English loan word *fōku* obviously could not. At any rate, the group's repertoire remained *fōku songu*, not *min'yō*: linguistic flexibility did not entail breaching stylistic barriers.

• Finally, on pp. 35 and 53 we learn that the 'god of folk' (*fōku no kamisama*) Okabayashi Nobuyasu (b. 1946), after exposure to the Korean folk percussion ensemble SamulNori in 1986–87, turned somewhat towards *min'yō*. SamulNori is a professional folk-derived group whose dynamic but lyric-free music (also now called *samulnori*) had around that time been taken up by student protestors in Korea for various symbolic reasons; the connections to political activism may have provided a link to the Japanese *fōku* movement in Okabayashi's eyes. At any rate, this exposure led him to doubts about his musical choices: in Nagira's paraphrase, 'Wasn't Japanese [*fōku*] music basically just a copy of foreign music? What then is original [Japanese music]? What music is wedded indelibly to the Japanese language? With that, [Okabayashi] began to seek out [what he called] *en'ya-totto*, the rhythm of Japanese *min'yō*' (p. 53). *En'yatotto* is the macho chanted chorus of a boat-rowing song from northern Japan, 'Saitara Bushi', familiar to every Japanese; this one song, of course, could hardly represent the range of rhythms in traditional folk song, but it suited Okabayashi. He briefly shelved his performing career to work as a rice farmer, then, having learned to empathize with the peasantry, returned to the stage with 'my own musical style, *en'yatotto*' (ibid.). What he then sang and recorded were self-composed songs, still sung in a Western-style *fōku* voice, accompanied by the usual *fōku* instruments – but now often in pentatonic scales, perhaps also using *min'yō* instruments, invariably having a *min'yō*-style chorus, with *min'yō*-flavoured lyrics in traditional lines of 7 or 5 syllables. We shall touch on Okabayashi's output again in §7.4.4; what is important here is Nagira's reaction to Okabayashi's change of direction (pp. 53–4):

Lately I often hear people saying, 'I'd like to see the old Okabayashi.' *En'yatotto* isn't bad by any means. But [for performer and audience] to be able to enjoy

themselves together, a certain degree of consensus is needed. . . . I can't seem
to see this sort of consensus in Okabayashi these days. He's stuck in *en'yatotto*,
but we [typical *fōku* fans] don't get it.

This is an overstatement, since Okabayashi is still popular (among *fōku songu*
rather than *min'yō* fans), but it does reflect accurately the difficulty of bridging the gap between the two genres.

In referring to older traditional American folk songs (including some composed songs such as Foster's), Japanese often use the phrase *amerika (no)
min'yō*, restricting the term *fōku songu*, as they do in Japan, to recent compositions by the post-Kingston Trio generation. In the United States, both of
these phenomena are called 'folk song', and in fact the two types of song are
sung by the same performers or on the same stage. The same voice quality
may be used for both types; even the choice of instruments is often the same,
with guitars at the centre. This overlap can trigger disappointment at 'folk'
festivals, since fans of the older songs may not appreciate the newer ones and
vice versa. In Japan, the linguistic separation of the terms *min'yō* and *fōku
songu* obviates any confusion, and the two almost never appear in the same
concert. In any case, the two are clearly separated by vocal style; nor is the
typical shamisen plucker equally proficient on guitar, or vice versa.

Some observers suggest that, since *min'yō* is largely a closed category with
lyrics no longer relevant to modern life, it is *fōku songu* which are the living
min'yō of today, sociologically speaking. That conclusion is far too facile.
The myriad traditional functions of *min'yō* are fulfilled today by several kinds
of music (karaoke, muzak, rock music, 'taiko drumming' (*wadaiko*), etc.) and
also by some non-musical phenomena such as television – as well as by
min'yō itself. (See also Frith's claim (1981: 159) that rock music is 'the folk
music of our time'.)

I will henceforth have hardly any need to refer to *fōku songu* in this book.
Thus we can safely use the English phrase 'folk song' without confusion as
an equivalent of *min'yō*.

1.7.2 Enka

The term *enka* has a diverse history, starting with Meiji-period songs of
social protest (see Yano 2002; Tansman 1996; Nakamura 1991; Soeda 1967;
Sonobe 1962; Katō 1975; Komiya 1956; Malm 1971). As it arises in every
chapter, let us introduce it here.

As a category, *enka* are not easily described. We can say safely that they are
a hybrid of traditional and Western musical elements. However, especially
during recent decades, the genre has broadened out in style in much the same
way as American 'country music', in similar response to the modernistic
diversification of its audience and their tastes. Still, the 'classic' *enka*, those
probably considered most typical of the style, date from perhaps the 1930s to

the 1960s. Such songs from the earlier part of the period are now often called *natsumero*, 'nostalgic melodies' (abbreviated from <u>natsukashii</u> <u>merodii</u>).

A revealing alternative name for *enka* of that period – a product of the recording industry like many such terms worldwide – is *nihon-chō kayōkyoku*, 'Japanese-mode popular music'. Such songs, and even the broader stylistic range of songs covered by the term *enka* today, are considered much more 'Japanese' than other popular songs (*kayōkyoku*).

Terminology for types of Western-influenced or Western-derived popular song is somewhat fluid, as are the categories themselves. A 1971 survey of musical tastes (§4.2, Table 4.1) distinguished four categories of popular song (not counting traditional genres): '*enka* and Japanese-style *kayōkyoku*', 'Western-style *kayōkyoku*', 'other *kayōkyoku* (e.g. *fōku songu*-style)', and 'popular/chanson/latin/tango, etc.' (this last group all written phonetically: *popyurā*, etc.). A similar 1978 survey (Table 4.2) uses slightly different categories, partially reflecting changing perceptions: '*enka*-style *kayōkyoku*', 'Western-style *kayōkyoku*', 'popular [*popyurā*] music [chansons etc.]', and 'rock and other "New Music"'. *Fōku songu* seems to have been superseded by the category called 'New Music' (*nyū myūjikku*), born around 1975 as an outgrowth of *fōku songu* but lacking any pretence of social protest (see Nagira 1995: 303–6). In the 1970s the word 'pops' (*poppusu*) also gained currency to refer to teen-oriented Western-style pop music; thus a 1999 publication (Geinō 1999: 136 et seq.) divides the world of 'popular music' (*popyurā ongaku*) into 'jazz', 'chanson', 'rock', 'New Music', '*fōku*', 'pops', '*kayō-kyoku/enka*' – and '*min'yō*'. (The element *zoku* (§1.4) is not used in reference to Western-influenced 'popular' musics.)

Whether we call them *enka*, Japanese-style *kayōkyoku* or *enka*-style *kayōkyoku*, their typical musical features are as follows (see also Okada 1991; S. Gamō 1986; Koizumi 1984a):

- Two musical modes dominate, both hybrids of traditional pentatonicism with a Western harmonic orientation. Scholars call these the *yonanuki tan'onkai* and *yonanuki chōonkai*, which I translate as 'pentatonic minor' and 'pentatonic major'; in terms of our modal categories above, they are *miyako-bushi* on 6 and *yō* on 1, but with different implications for tonal function. Pending a fuller discussion in §3.4.3 on 'new folk songs', let us note here only that, while these two modes are very rare in traditional music, they are the two traditional modes closest to the Western minor and major modes respectively, hence the easiest to harmonize. This is one hybrid feature that made such songs instantly appealing to a populace still well familiar with, and often emotionally wedded to, traditional music yet increasingly exposed to Western music through the education system and the media.
- Instrumentation is typically a medium-size jazz dance-band with electric guitar and bass. However, this is often supplemented by shamisen, *taiko*,

shakuhachi, *shinobue* flute or some other traditional instrument, especially when the lyrics make reference to traditional themes, nostalgia for one's rural home, and so forth.

- And the lyrics do often make such references. Here lies an important clue to the nature of *enka*'s popularity. Up until the 1980s, the most typical texts are set in the first person, from the viewpoint of an urbanite, often one who has recently moved to the big city, is still missing home and mother, and is confronted with the problems of finding employment and romance. Loneliness, economic difficulties and failed love are major themes. Three main solutions are offered to these problems: *sake*, going home to one's *furusato*, or travelling on. Problems such as these most often affect people from their mid-1920s to their late 1940s, after which one's lifestyle has probably achieved some sort of stability; not surprisingly, *enka* has its peak popularity in this age range (§4.2). Fans also tend to be from the lower half of the economic scale.
- *Enka* vocals are highly ornamented – closer in style to *min'yō* than to Western popular song (excluding perhaps 'soul' style of recent decades). One distinctive feature is a very wide vibrato which appears particularly at phrase ends and accelerates gradually.
- *Enka* vocal timbre is quite distinctive. It is generally rich in overtones, resembling genres such as Buddhist chanting and *naniwa bushi* but very different from Western-style popular song and from *fōku songu*. Some *min'yō* singers, however, use a similar vocal quality.

Thus, there are points of stylistic overlap between *enka* and *min'yō*, much more than between *min'yō* and *fōku songu*. It is not surprising, then, that some *min'yō* artists also perform and record *enka*. For some this is primarily a commercial decision, for others a labour of love. Mihashi Michiya in the early 1950s was the first major figure of this type, followed since around 1980 by his *min'yō* student Hosokawa Takashi and many others. In the 1990s Nagayama Yōko won success in the *min'yō* world already by age twenty, then moved into Western-style pop, then to *enka*, then back to *min'yō*, and now mixes all styles in her stage shows (Takahashi Yūjirō, pers. comm., 1998). The reverse is also true: certain *enka* singers, particularly those with strong rural roots, may attempt folk songs in their performances. Around 1980 the two main exemplars were probably Kitajima Saburō and Sen Masao; suffice to say that *min'yō* singers admired both of them as *enka* singers. They could be distinguished from true *min'yō* singers (including Hosokawa Takashi) both by their lower vocal ranges and by their *enka*-style ornamentation. Mixing these two genres in one performer or performance is still the exception rather than the rule.

Both *enka* and *min'yō* have clear links in the Japanese mind to the *furusato*, the old home town (see Yano 1994, 2002). For *min'yō* the link is established in a number of ways: the association of nearly every song with a particular locality; the generally rural and traditional content of lyrics; contexts and functions, which again link to small-scale community life; and of course via the well-known saying that heads this chapter. For *enka* the link is different. *Enka* are predominantly urban songs, but, as noted, their lyrics often refer to 'home', sometimes to specific places. They often do this, though, by mentioning a local folk song, which might then even be quoted or imitated in the *enka*. Several examples of lyrics of this type of *enka* are found in Appendix 1, section 3, from song F onwards. See also §6.2.

1.8 Summary

This book describes developments in the Japanese folk song world since the onset of significant Westernization and modernization in the latter nineteenth century. Since that time, the concept of a genre of music called *min'yō* ('folk song') has spread gradually throughout Japan, and *min'yō* has become a distinct and respected genre. Though spurred by European Romantic influences, this development also depended on indigenous factors including urbanization, renewed national self-confidence, respect for agriculture, and improved transportation and communication. It is possible that factors such as these might have resulted in the emergence in the twentieth century of a recognized genre of 'rural/folk music' even in the absence of a European model.

We examined several scholarly definitions of *min'yō* as well as describing the development of the lay view of *min'yō*. It was noted that the concept of *min'yō* changed gradually among the populace: at first it designated only widely popular songs of rural origin, mostly performed by professionals, but eventually it came to encompass little-known local songs as well. The distinction between *min'yō* ('folk song') and *minzoku geinō* ('folk performing arts') was also discussed. In this connection, the meaning of the term *zoku* was traced through the centuries, providing some insight into changes in attitudes towards traditional popular music during the past century in particular. The important if often derided role of the geisha was noted.

We also became familiar with the basic musical parameters of *min'yō*: instrumentation, musical features, etc. Finally, *min'yō* were distinguished from two other genres of vocal music: *fōku songu* and *enka*.

NOTES

1. What was just a title in the oral tradition led to a song recorded by Dan Hicks & His Hot Licks in the 1980s.
2. Matters of nostalgia, national identity, the 'folk' and class hegemony in Japan are well covered in Marilyn Ivy's *Discourses of the Vanishing* (1995) and in numerous chapters of *Mirror of Modernity*, edited by Stephen Vlastos (1998). Space precludes introducing these here.

3. For a detailed discussion of *furusato* and the phenomenon of *furusato-zukuri* ('old village'-making), see §§6.2-3. For a view beyond Japan, Stokes 1994 is useful.

4. Japanese are often seen, even by themselves, as possessing an insular mentality (*shimaguni konjō*). This is true, though ever less so, and yet still perhaps more so than, say, for most English or Irish.

5. In the recent past, *min'yō* brought comfort to emigrés in Hawaii and South America or to troops abroad during the Second World War (§3.5).

6. Reports are typically (but with variation) edited and published by the prefectural Board of Education and entitled *[Prefecture name] no min'yō*, with a subtitle including the phrase *Min'yō Kinkyū Chōsa Hōkoku*.

7. As for pre-twentieth-century sources, a general review is found in Asano 1966: Ch. 4. See also my Chapter 2 Note 9, and the note at the head of the Bibliography.

8. The principal partly unassimilated ethnic groups, Japan-born, are the Okinawans (population ca. 1,200,000), Ainu (a few tens of thousands, depending on definition) and Koreans (ca. 600,000). Large segments of each of these groups do identify themselves with the majority culture and share its values, despite lingering exclusion from full participation. Their musical traditions are not treated here, having had virtually no effect on the hegemonic culture's folk song (but see §7.2 concerning Okinawa).

9. This is consistently revealed in surveys since the 1970s. The Marxist scholar Rob Steven, however, claimed that in the 1970s less than 10% of the work force were objectively middle-class (1983: 140 et seq.).

10. The terms 'folk', 'classical' and 'popular' will be used frequently in this work despite the problems in giving them meaningful definitions.

11. Aside from definitions of 'folk song' to be found in standard dictionaries of music or folklore, interesting viewpoints are found in Seeger 1966; Wilgus 1959: 58–60, 120, 223ff; Karpeles 1973: ch.1, 2, 10; Wiora 1972; Elbourne 1975, 1980: 90ff; and in several articles in the first issue of the journal *Popular Music* (e.g. Middleton 1981).

12. Chinese characters for certain important terms are given on first occurrence. When characters are not given in the text, the reader may consult the Index. A homophonous word *min'yō* (民踊), written with a different second character and meaning 'folk dance', has gained currency in recent decades. Several monthly magazines aimed at the folk song and dance market have played on this homophony by writing *min'yō* in a semantically neutral (non-ideographic) phonetic syllabary (*hiragana*), to appeal to readers interested in either song or dance.

13. Concerning the European use of the word *Volkslied*, coined by Herder around 1775, see Suppan 1976: 117ff. The common Chinese word for folk song today is *min'ge* (pronounced *minka* in Japanese; see Tuohy 1999), but this compound has rarely been used in Japan – one proof of the lack of Chinese influence in this sphere. The Japanese term was introduced into Korea a century ago, where it is pronounced *minyo* and is the standard and widely used term; see Howard 1999.

14. Japanese and Chinese are not related languages and have vastly different syntax and phonology, although Japanese has borrowed heavily from Chinese vocabulary.

15. Oral testimony from several areas of Japan. In a 1981 '*min'yō* musical' set in the unspecified recent past (see Foreword), a folk song researcher from America informed a group of country folk that he had come to study their local *min'yō*, to which an elderly farmer was made to reply: 'What, *min'yō*? Oh, d'you mean *uta*?'

American country singer Jimmy Driftwood (1917–98), raised in rural Arkansas, 'recalled that in his boyhood in the Ozarks, he never heard the term 'folk music'. But, he added, 'we sure played a lot of it' (obituary by Tony Russell, *Guardian* (UK) 22 July 1998).

16. Sugita Akiko, pers. comm. (1979) concerning her village in Tochigi Prefecture around 1940; confirmed by several other Japanese. For the format used to cite personal communications, see the introductory section 'Stylistic Conventions'.

17. The situation is somewhat different in Okinawa, Japan's southernmost prefecture, and in the Amami archipelago to Okinawa's immediate north. Their cultures and musical styles are sufficiently distinct from the rest of Japan to require separate treatment. See, for example, Thompson 2001, 2008; Gillan 2004; Potter 2003; Ogawa 1979, 1984; Uchida 1983.

18. Record companies have always been inconsistent in labelling folk-related materials – both cause and result of public confusion. Maruyama 1981 gives several examples from the earlier days of the industry. Today, the term World Music causes similar problems.

19. His 'tertiary *min'yō*' do not correspond easily to anything in his 1960 schema, probably because such Western-accompanied performances were only becoming common in the 1950s, particularly through the performances of Mihashi Michiya.

20. English-language discussions of Yanagita's work include Kawada 1993; Koschmann et al. 1985; Makita 1973; Morse 1990.

21. Anthropologist John Embree, working in Japan in the 1930s, came to a different conclusion: 'The songs sung at parties are [equally] true folk songs inasmuch as they are anonymous, known to all the singers, and frequently added to or varied to suit the situation' (1939: 106; cf. also 1944: 2).

22. Machida also felt that the word *min'yō* was being applied to such a heterogeneous range of phenomena that it was of little value (Maruyama 1981: 25). Like Yanagita, he wanted to distinguish true folk products from others; thus he continued to use the word *riyō* long after most others had abandoned it. Alas, even the word *riyō* was not pure. A Bon-dance song composed in the 1930s by professionals and recorded with orchestral backing was labelled a *riyō* by the record company (ibid.: 22–3), perhaps because it was intended as a 'local pride' song for a particular village. See also Nakamura 1991: 272–4 and §3.4.3 below.

23. For further typologies and discussion, see Kojima 1967: 13–4; Asano 1966: 46–7; Groemer 1994: 203–4.

24. Another example of fluid terminology is Niijima's quixotic collection of lyrics pertaining to buckwheat (1968). He distinguishes *min'yō* (in a narrow sense equivalent to Machida's *riyō*), *zokuyō* (*min'yō* not linked with a particular location) and *dōyō* ('children's songs'; he uses this scholarly term as if equivalent to the everyday word *warabeuta*, but most scholars restrict it to pseudo-children's songs by literati). However, among his *zokuyō* he includes texts from the Noh and Kabuki theatres!

25. A clear exposition in English of his schema, with bibliographic references to his works, is Hoff 1978: 142–50; an abbreviated description by Hoff is in EOJ: 2.296–8. Useful encyclopaedias include Hoshina & Yoshika 2006; Nakai et al. 1981; NMGJ 1976.

26. Performers may be rewarded, but the seasonal nature of most *minzoku geinō* renders full-time specialization uneconomical. One quasi-exception is *Edo sato-kagura*, a Tokyo-area shrine masque genre, long perpetuated by semi-professionals (see Fujie

1986); and now local groups increasingly stage performances for profit and/or prestige for tourists and others, often far from home (see Lancashire 1998). Some professional groups, often urban-based (e.g. Tokyo's Kiku no Kai), have learned *minzoku geinō* from several parts of Japan. Some are based in rural areas renowned for *minzoku geinō* – e.g. the Warabiza in Akita Prefecture (§6.4) or Ondekoza and its descendant Kodō on Sado Island in Niigata Prefecture (§7.2). Residents of the source communities, although usually flattered, often have a low opinion of such efforts, sometimes clearly out of possessive jealousy (§5.5).

27. From the *Hokke-gisho* (early seventh century); cited under the entry for *zoku-gaku* in the dictionary *Nihon kokugo daijiten* (see Bibliography, under NKD).

28. Thanks to Robert Rann for this reference and for letting me adapt his working translation. See also Kirby 1900.

29. Malm notes (1971: 259) that Western school, church and military musics were adopted not for their own sakes (e.g. on aesthetic grounds) but 'as necessary parts of a Western-derived table of organization for the particular institution in question'. While true, this picture must be combined with the Confucianist influence mentioned above.

30. Examples abound of the links between nationalism and Romanticism in general. A reawakened patriotism in Austria at the beginning of the nineteenth century is seen by Suppan (1976: 119–20) as the cause of an upsurge of interest in folk culture there.

31. Another word *minzoku* (民族), 'race, people, ethnos', is written with a different Chinese character for *zoku* and also distinguished by accent. It is the first element in expressions such as *minzokugaku* 'ethnology' and *minzoku ongaku* 'ethnomusicology'.

32. This term is no easier to define universally than is 'folk song'. There is no imputation of value in my use of the term. George Herzog proposed the term 'cultivated music' as a more neutral designation, but that phrase raises other questions, as would 'art music'.

33. Although Yanagi and Yanagita appear to have moved in different worlds, Yanagi must have been aware, in formulating his *mingei* notions, of the concepts of *min'yō* and *minzokugaku*. Several *mingei* scholars I have spoken with seem reluctant to accept this, for unclear reasons, but see Y. Kikuchi 2004.

34. In the case of 6/8 melodies, published Western-style notations might show a *dotted* 8th followed by a 16th note, but actual performance would be much closer to an 8th and a 16th. It has become a common (if rarely acknowledged) practice in native notation of *min'yō* to use dotted rhythms for 6/8 pieces, which can mislead the foreigner in the absence of a recording. Again, this is common in jazz as well.

35. For individual instruments, see the *New Grove Dictionary of Musical Instruments* (1984); for shamisen and shakuhachi, start with Malm & Hughes 2001a and Berger & Hughes 2001.

36. See comments regarding the recording of 'Suzaka Kouta' (§3.4.3) and a Japanese opera singer's appearance on a *min'yō* television show (§4.8.1).

37. Poetic metre is, strictly speaking, counted in terms of what linguists call moras instead of syllables; see the preface on 'Stylistic Conventions'.

38. Kubo's tabulation omits songs from southern Kyushu and in general seems biased against less familiar songs. In a more scrupulous compilation, *yō* on 3 and the *ritsu* sub-modes (*yō* on 5 and 2) would become less unusual (listen to, e.g. R63). But the four most common sub-modes would probably remain as above.

CHAPTER 2

SONG AND MUSIC IN THE TRADITIONAL VILLAGE

▫

2.1 Introduction: the hamlet as primary social unit

Our task now is to reconstruct the place of *min'yō* in traditional village life. Since folk song in pre-war Japan was principally a rural phenomenon, we focus first on the traditional Japanese peasant's primary social group above the family level: the *buraku*. Usually translated 'hamlet', the *buraku* would include about 60 to 200 people in a few dozen households. This was the maximal face-to-face social unit, in which everybody knew everyone else. Until the Meiji period the *buraku* maintained a high degree of social integration and independence.[1]

Trade and irrigation matters, the principal reasons for interaction between hamlets, triggered social ties, and a festival in a nearby hamlet was always an excuse to visit. Wives often, and husbands sometimes, came from other hamlets. Economic matters also occasionally took the farmer, fisher or forest worker into the nearest town.

Since the late nineteenth century, improvements in transportation and communication, along with increasing centralization of government functions, have reduced hamlet isolation. This is reflected in the gradually shifting scope of the term *mura* (usually translated 'village'; *son* in Sino-Japanese). Originally designating the hamlet, in the early twentieth century it came to signify a grouping of several hamlets with a population of a few thousand; now it may indicate a primarily rural political unit with a population of over 10,000.[2] The number of social organizations cross-cutting hamlet lines has increased greatly, and much of the rural male populace now work outside the home hamlet (§5.2).

Yet even today the old hamlets, the maximal face-to-face units, often maintain their identity – particularly those geographically circumscribed by natural features such as rivers or hills. Rural population has remained fairly steady over the last hundred years – in fact, it increased only slowly during the preceding few centuries. Therefore, a 'rural sprawl', obliterating the spaces between hamlet centres, has rarely occurred. Hamlets near urban centres, however, have increasingly become suburbs or been absorbed into an expanding city, largely losing their identities. Much of the outer ring of modern Tokyo consisted of independent fishing or farming hamlets until the early twentieth century. Even after the Second World War, Takeuchi could record hundreds of songs from the more rural districts of the Tokyo Metropolitan Area (Tōkyō-to; recording R22). A barley-threshing song from a hamlet now solidly ensconced within southwest Tokyo (Senzoku, Ōta Ward) includes these lyrics, expressive of the time when the city was still only a nearby magnet – or a threatening cloud:[3]

> mina tomodachi wa / Edo Edo to / Edo da tote / karegi ni hana wa / saku mai
> All my friends / keep talking about Edo. / It may be Edo, but / surely flowers don't bloom / on a withered tree. ('Senzoku Mugiuchi Uta')

This chapter considers music life in the traditional countryside. 'Traditional' here (following from §1.1) refers to the situation prior to full integration into a modern national culture characterized by near-universal literacy, access to print and broadcast media, widespread mechanization, ease of travel and so forth. Particular villages, and even individuals, attained each of these features at different times. Mechanization of agriculture still proceeds, long having been hindered by the small size of paddy plots, and many elderly people have still never strayed far from their home village. But in general we can say that the lifeways described below faded slowly after the Meiji Restoration (1868) and rapidly between about 1930 and 1960. As these lifeways are largely a thing of the past, I tend to use the past tense in this chapter. The approximate period for which the statements below are most accurate is the eighteenth to mid-nineteenth centuries.

Sources for this chapter include: song texts, most clearly dating from the Edo period; interviews with people who have lived within 'traditional' society; and secondary sources, many including information gleaned from similar interviews. Some of my characterizations are clearly speculative, but I believe that the overall picture is accurate.

2.2 Class divisions and music in the traditional village

2.2.1 Traditional rural class relations

I use the term 'peasant' loosely, yet technically rather than evaluatively, to indicate in a common-sense way the entire body of rural manual labourers of pre-modern Japan – farmers and fishers mostly, but also crafts workers, lumberjacks and other mountain workers. 'Villagers' or 'countryfolk' would

be more neutral terms, but we need to distinguish between the village elite –
landlords, owners of *sake* breweries or fishing boats – and the working class,
even though the distinction is not always viable. We focus on farming villages
as the most typical case.[4]

Class relations in rural Japan have taken various forms across the centuries. We pick up the story in the early nineteenth century. By then, the
samurai who had once wielded power in many villages had long since with-
drawn from the land to regional castle towns (Beardsley 1965: 86). Almost
all remaining families were involved in grain farming. The possible role-types
were primarily four: landlord, independent cultivator, tenant or labourer.
However, these distinctions generated surprisingly little active class conflict
or animosity in most villages, for two main structural reasons. First, status
lines were blurred by the multiple roles fulfilled by most households. Landlords
might work some of their own land; independent cultivators might farm some
additional land as tenants; and tenants often worked as seasonal labourers.
Second, these role distinctions were crosscut by numerous clearly defined
socio-economic relationships. Many of these were highly particularistic and
paternalistic, generally of a 'para-kinship' nature and involving frequent face-
to-face affective interaction across status lines. Potential for class conflict was
lessened also by joint participation in village affairs such as irrigation control
and funerals. All this might increase class consciousness, but it reduced class
conflict.[5]

Ideological factors also played a role. Clearly many peasants, without bit-
terness or reflection, accepted class divisions as natural simply through the
force of tradition: there had 'always' been landlords and tenants, rich and
poor, governors and governed. (See Asari Miki's remarks in the next section.)
A second factor was the fatalism permeating most Japanese Buddhist sects:
even the more reflective peasants might accept their lot as foreordained by
karma (*inga*). Many a verse has the same first line as the following work song:

> nan no inga de / kaigara-kogi narota / iro wa kuro naru / mi wa yaseru
>   By what karma / have I become a shellfish gatherer? / My complexion
> darkens / and my body grows thin. ('Kaigara Bushi')

Most nineteenth-century landlords were active participants in village life,
and the landlord-tenant relationship itself was highly affective. Absentee
landlords were rare; landlords might lower rents after poor harvests; the
wealthier often invested in village improvement projects and created employment opportunities (Waswo 1977: 29–32). Richer residents served as 'god-
parents' (*oyakata*) to less well-off villagers.[6] Under such circumstances,
poorer households might find reason to be glad when prosperity visited the
richer families. Consider the Akita folk song 'Chōja no Yama' (The Rich
Man's Mountain), in which the finding of gold in the mountain promises to
benefit the entire populace:

sakaru sakaru to / chōja no yama sakaru / sakaru chōja no yama / sue nagaku
　　Flourishing, flourishing, / the rich man's mountain is flourishing. / May the rich man's mountain / flourish evermore.

Or it might be the region's feudal lord who financed the establishment of local industry, as reflected in this pottery-making song (*rokuro uta*) from Okayama Prefecture (Katō 1980: 2.456):

Bizen tonosama / o-erai okata / tono no okage de / kama sakae / kama ga sakaerya / mura morotomo ni / itsu no yo made mo / Oizu-gawa
　　The lord of Bizen / is a great and noble man; / thanks to our lord, / the kiln flourishes. / When the kiln flourishes, / so does the whole village; / for countless ages to come, / the Oizu ('Never-growing-old') River.

Not that everyone was happy: over 2,500 peasant rebellions were recorded during the Edo period (EOJ: 3.249). But until the late eighteenth century these rarely sprang from direct conflicts among different hamlet strata. More often they were led by hamlet officers (generally richer peasants) representing the whole hamlet, and directed against the domainal authorities in the castle town. The issues were mainly high taxes and forced labour, and the protests were small-scale, relatively orderly and non-violent (ibid.: 249–50).

However, starting in the early nineteenth century (far earlier in some regions near large cities) came a gradual growth of rural capitalist enterprise – textile mills, *sake* and soy sauce factories, etc. By the 1850s, many wealthy farmers had taken an interest in such industries, and there were one or two businessmen 'in almost every village [*buraku*] outside of the backwoods areas' (Crawcour 1963: 201). Households of lesser wealth might also participate in smaller-scale cottage industry, silk production and processing, cash cropping, etc; to the degree that this enticed them to cut back on subsistence farming, it rendered them more vulnerable to the vagaries of the spreading money economy.

Increasingly, these new rural industrialists withdrew from village life, contributing less to the general welfare, participating less in village dances and so forth. Sometimes they shifted their residence, or at least their orientation, to the nearest town, becoming absentee landlords and no longer farming themselves.[7] The expressive ties between rich and poor diminished, as did traditional concessions such as lowering rents during famines. Peasant uprisings of this period were now often directed against 'merchants and other privileged segments of rural communities' (EOJ: 3.250), usually involved well-organized groups from several villages, and might be partly political (demanding democratic access to local offices). These populist rebellions, while often achieving their aims, never led to a nationwide movement: once local demands were satisfied, the peasants desisted (ibid.).

This pattern of increasing absenteeism and commercial involvement by local landlords continued into the twentieth century (Waswo 1983: ch.4). Peasant protests also continued, but on a smaller scale (ibid.: ch.5).

In sum, most traditional landlords had been active participants in a hierarchical community whose inequalities were largely tolerated because of what was perceived as (1) a relatively benevolent paternalism and (2) a lack of alternatives. Paternalism faded little by little with the encroachment of commerce and industry into the countryside. But old attitudes died hard, surviving in many areas until the Second World War (and sometimes even today). The following sections describe musical behaviour under traditional conditions.

2.2.2 Elite music and community music

In most farming, fishing or mountain communities, the vast majority of musical occasions involved either folk song or what we now call *minzoku geinō* (§1.4). Folk song was 'community music' in that it belonged in principle to all residents without restriction. It was also usually communal, performed by any or all present; this was true for most work songs, Bon dance songs, children's songs and many party songs.

Certain types of *minzoku geinō* were limited to a subset of residents. Sometimes participation was by ascription, as when only males from the hamlet's founding households could participate in a rite at the village shrine (§2.5.1). Participation might also be open to all who joined a certain voluntary society such as a *nenbutsu-kō* (a type of Buddhist association, whose membership could cross-cut status divisions and whose devotional dance songs were ancestral to many Bon dance songs). In either case, performances may or may not have been witnessed by other residents.

There were certain types of music, however, whose performance and appreciation were almost always restricted to the wealthier families. The two chief examples are: the refined urban parlour music (*sankyoku*) played on the koto (13-string long zither) and shamisen, later with shakuhachi; and *utai*, unaccompanied singing of passages from the Noh theatre. *Sankyoku*-style koto and shamisen music gradually came to be considered standard 'accomplishments' for young women of upwardly mobile families. The shakuhachi, a man's instrument, also possessed a repertoire of solo pieces (*honkyoku*) linked with a Zen sect whose members were originally former samurai but later included men from less exalted backgrounds who often came to be seen as mere beggars.

Sankyoku developed as part of the burgeoning bourgeois (*chōnin*) culture after the seventeenth century. Newly prosperous urban merchants, attempting to escape their position at the bottom of the Neo-Confucian four-tiered class system, adopted some elements of samurai culture to which their wealth gave them access, such as Noh and the tea ceremony; but they also fostered a distinctive new culture more in tune with their own character, giving us Kabuki, Bunraku puppet theatre and the woodblock print as well as *sankyoku*.

As wealthier villagers increased their social contact with the outside world through mercantile undertakings, they met representatives of urban *chōnin* culture. The fact that the culture had become a meeting-ground for samurai and townspeople lent it a cachet of respectability above and beyond any consideration of aesthetic appeal. Soon the village elite had begun to study koto, *utai*, poetry writing, tea ceremony and so forth.[8]

This culture did not come free. There was a right and a wrong way to play the koto or to make tea; one needed a teacher, who, with rare exceptions, had to be paid. Also, one needed leisure time, available only at certain times of the year if at all. Finally, a set of tea-making paraphernalia or a koto was not cheap. A praise-song from Iwami, sung by itinerant musicians, invoked the koto along with the *tsuzumi* hand-drum (associated with Noh) as symbols of prosperity:

kore no o-yakata / hanjō nasaru / oku wa koto no ne / naka no ma wa tsuzumi
   This mansion / is prosperous: / from the inner parlour, a koto sounds, / from the middle parlour, a tsuzumi. (Sanga 1772: 332)

Nor would poorer villagers see their 'betters' perform. These arts were, after all, to be appreciated in a refined, private setting – a parlour or garden, say – and one did not invite one's tenants into the parlour.

Conversely, though, well-off families usually still participated in the annual Bon dance, being expected to join in as equals (but also to contribute a larger share towards communal expenses). But to the degree that the family could afford the time and money to indulge in the urban arts, they were less likely to be working any land or participating in cooperative village projects, meaning they also lost access to communal work songs. Thus the elite gradually became estranged from some types of song.

Since the elite households' retreat into such private activities generally paralleled their abdication of the spirit of *noblesse oblige*, other villagers rarely looked kindly on those pursuits. A 1922 study of landlord-tenant disputes cited as one cause of tenant resentment the landlords' indulgence in tea ceremony at the expense of agricultural improvement (Waswo 1977: 107n).

These patterns of elite versus community musical behaviour continued in some isolated hamlets into the 1950s or later, until poorer farmers gained access to prestige culture through economic and communication developments. Some villages never developed a significant elite-community distinction in musical behaviour in the first place. Here are two reminiscences.

Asari Miki (b. 1920), a renowned professional folk singer, was raised in a poor farming family in Aomori Prefecture. Her village around 1930 had a few wealthy households, but she never thought of comparing their condition with hers: they were simply in a 'separate category' (*bekkaku*). The rich were obviously innately superior anyway, for even in school they always excelled. But they were not isolated from village affairs, and 'at the Bon dance season, all were equal'. The only koto player, the daughter of a wealthy household, never played in public. Two or three of the wealthier men played classical shakuhachi. The shamisen was not used for parlour music in her area (perhaps because of its connections in the north with blind itinerant mendicants; see §2.4.6). But each village was sure to have one or two 'life-of-the-party' types who had acquired a cheap shamisen for accompanying folk songs; 'they were always invited to parties – and they always came'. They never seemed to be able to tune their instruments, nor to do more than strum the strings rhythmically, but in those last days before the flood of professional troupes, recordings and radio, even this was highly appreciated.

Sasaki Kaneshige (b. 1914) lived in the isolated hamlet of Ōtsugunai in the mountains of Iwate. Since the late nineteenth century, semi-professional troupes of Ōtsugunai farmers have used the agricultural off-season to tour surrounding villages performing a type of masked dance-drama known as *yamabushi kagura* (see Honda 1974), formerly performed by ascetic 'mountain priests' (*yamabushi*) until the latter were forbidden from practising in the Meiji period. Kaneshige was the troupe's leader when we met in 1980. These tours were an important source of by-income. Membership was restricted to certain families to minimize competition, but economic status was not a factor in selection. The rich-poor spread in Ōtsugunai was modest, he said, but in any case urban teachers of the elite arts could hardly have visited this isolated community regularly.

Sasaki lived for eight years in Japanese-occupied Manchuria, repatriating after the war; there he learned to play shakuhachi, both folk and *sankyoku* style. Returning home, he found those skills of no use: there were no *sankyoku* performers, nor had shakuhachi-accompanied folk song yet caught on there.

2.2.3 Regional variation

The degree of penetration of urban arts into the countryside depended on local circumstances of geography, economy and history. In some areas, urban influence was so pervasive or class divisions so scarce as to eliminate any elitist tinge to such arts. This was most commonly true, not of isolated 'pure' music such as *utai* (basically Noh stripped of instruments, dance and costumes) or *sankyoku*, but of full-fledged dramatic forms such as Noh, Kabuki and Bunraku puppet theatre. Urban professional Kabuki and puppet troupes often toured the countryside, and villagers might pool resources to hire a teacher or build a Kabuki-style revolving stage for use both by the professionals and by themselves. Clearly, one reason (aside from expense) that only the village elite studied *utai* and *sankyoku* was that the average peasant found them dull; such was emphatically not the case with Kabuki and Bunraku.

Proximity to a city could stimulate artistic activity. Near Kyoto and Osaka, townspeople often combined with prosperous farmers in cultural societies or 'circles'. Around 1700 the headman of one urbanizing village near Osaka arranged for the teaching of Noh music and dance to villagers rich and poor. They performed frequently in nearby towns (Harada 1963: 243). A quirk of history might lead to such urban arts flourishing even in communities quite remote from the major urban centres, such as Kurokawa (Yamagata Pref.).

That the strength of such village performing traditions might rise and fall in tune with local economic conditions is suggested by this passage from the historical novel *Rōdō* by Kinoshita Naoe (1869–1937). The time is the 1890s, the location an actual village near Tokyo which was dying due to industrial pollution from a copper refinery.

> Yanaka used to be a rich village. Young men had had plenty of free time and money for lessons. Some played the *samisen* [shamisen] and sang ballads; some learned dancing and even appeared in village theatres. In their slack season, they even went on tour with their [Kabuki] plays. [translated in Aoki & Dardess 1981: 293]

Policies toward the arts varied in different feudal domains (*han*) and at different periods. Certain lords encouraged the arts, whether out of personal interest or to keep the peasants too pre-occupied to revolt; others saw such indulgence as reducing domainal production figures and tax revenue. At one point during the Edo period, the lord of Date (modern Miyagi Pref.) forbade any but the richest residents to study Kabuki or to dance during the transplanting and harvest seasons (Seshaiah 1980: 67). Meanwhile, in Yamaguchi Prefecture during the eighteenth century, the lord granted one village the exclusive right to perform Kabuki within the domain, apparently excusing the villagers from any agricultural obligations (Nishiyama 1964: 197).

Thus the general correlation between musical behaviour and economic status in the traditional village might be overridden by factors such as local economic conditions, urban influence and the lord's predilections. Not only major cities but even lesser 'castle towns' (and their modern successors) exerted influence on the surrounding hinterland.

2.2.4 *Folk song and social protest*

Given the harsh conditions of peasant life, as well as the thousands of peasant rebellions, it is interesting that we rarely encounter, either in printed collections or in modern performance, folk songs expressing overt social or political protest. We find complaints about backs sore from weeding or weaving, expressions of loneliness by indentured servants, and other generalized grumbling – but virtually no attempt to assign systemic responsibility for these conditions. Verses antagonistic to one's immediate superior are rare. Is this an artifact of collection bias and modern tastes, or does it reflect the actual frequency of such verses in traditional Japan?[9]

Possible explanations for this paucity vary in plausibility. First, as noted, peasants generally accepted their lot with fatalistic resignation due both to Buddhist influence and to the reasonable perception that little could be done about the situation – that in fact it could be worse without paternalism. Under this explanation, protest songs are rare because feelings of protest were rare. We might then expect class consciousness to be expressed freely and frequently in lyrics but class antagonism to be muted.

Second, even peasants with concrete grievances may have feared to express them: it was dangerous to complain even in song (Matsumoto 1965: *passim*). Much safer to leave the singing of such sentiments to the travelling minstrels and song-sheet sellers, or the storytellers and playwrights of the big cities, who occasionally drew their material from tragic tales of peasant rebellions. These performers and authors, of course, were no safer: an Edo storyteller, Komamonoya Bunzō, was beheaded in 1758 for selling printed copies of a tale of peasant protest (Matsumoto 1965: 202).[10] Given this situation, we would need to look beneath the surface of the lyrics for implied criticism. Examples of texts are given below.[11]

Third, villagers may have refrained from singing such verses to collectors because they were felt inappropriate for the occasion. A folk-song scholar's visit was generally a memorable occasion, not to be dimmed by parading angry sentiments, in keeping with Japanese etiquette.

Fourth, pre-modern political songs may have been as ephemeral as the short-lived peasant uprisings. Greenway claimed this as a characteristic of protest songs in general (1953: 6). Had we been present during an uprising, we might have 'caught' a song or two. A few such songs have indeed been documented for the nineteenth century, in the period leading to the Meiji Restoration. The surviving examples, at least, seem to have been marching songs, distinguished by tempo. rhythm and vocal style from *min'yō*, but often based on children's songs for familiarity.[12]

This said, here are several examples of verses of social protest actually sung in the villages. Direct reference to peasant uprisings is virtually absent. The most prominent exceptions are long ballads (*kudoki* or *kudoki bushi*) performed by itinerant singers, who might also sell printed copies of the text. Such ballads often derived from Kabuki or puppet theatre stories, and occasionally vice versa. The favoured subjects were tragic: lovers' suicides, children maltreated by step-parents, and – very rarely – a peasant leader executed (e.g. the story of Sakura Sōgorō; see Kuramitsu 1976: 41; Matsumoto 1965: 239). But the length of such *kudoki* (often over an hour) made their performance uncommon. Their social criticism was more implicit than direct: no blatant moral was drawn, no call to rebellion offered, no references to one's own village included, but it was clear where sympathies lay.[13]

Villagers at work or play usually sang shorter 'folk-lyrics' whose independent verses could be sung in any order. These could easily absorb an occasional verse of protest or complaint, whether improvised or traditional. The examples in this section are all of this type:

> Komura Tanosuke / jūku de shotai / nijūichi-go wa / ki no sora ni
> Komura Tanosuke, / at nineteen, had a family, / at twenty-one, / hung up in a tree. (transplanting song; Matsumoto 1965: 233)

> Fukuchi no tonosama / onbo no yaku yo / shinin horiagete / kubi o kiru
> The lord of Fukuchi / is the cremator, / digging up a corpse / and cutting off its head. (Matsumoto 1965: 234)

Komura Tanosuke led a 1642 revolt near the castle town of Takamatsu (Kagawa Pref.) and was crucified. The corpse which the lord of Fukuchi treated so unkindly was that of the leader of a major uprising in Fukuchiyama (Hyōgo Pref.) during the Kyōhō era (1716–36).

Certain other verses may contain veiled references to uprisings. The veil is often heavy. For example, none of the standard folk-song dictionaries (Kodera 1935; Nakai et al. 1972; Asano 1983) mentions the theory that the following verse expresses the sentiments of a departing band of peasant rebels. Most scholars assume that this verse, like its close relatives throughout Japan, refers to a lovers' parting.

> Gujō no Hachiman / dete yuku toki wa / ame no furanu ni / sode shiboru
> Hachiman Town in Gujō, / when I leave it, / though no rain is falling, / my sleeve is wringing wet [i.e. with tears]. ('Gujō Bushi' = 'Gujō Kawasaki')

But Matsumoto (1965: 234) claims the reference is to an anti-tax uprising in the 1750s and that the protesters expected never to return alive. Gujō Hachiman is the site of one of the major shrines to the god of war, and Matsumoto guesses that the rebels had come there to pray.[14]

This points up the problem of interpreting the intended sentiment of the creator of a text. Such discussions tell us more about the discussants themselves than about Edo-period peasants. As another example, consider these two verses from a rowing song from Hokkaido.

> yamase ni ame dara / nishin wa tairyō da / oyakata yorokobu / yanshu wa tsukareru
> When the mountain wind brings rain, / we can catch lots of herring; / the net-boss is delighted, / the boatmen are exhausted.
> Sutsutsu ni dashi aru / yama ni wa yuki aru / oki ni wa nami aru / oyakata kane aru
> Sutsutsu has an east wind, / the mountains have snow, / the ocean has waves, / the net-boss has money. ('Funakogi Nagashi Uta')

Nakai (MB: 31.16–7) follows his standard-language translation of verse 1 with this elucidation: 'But after all, it was a great catch, and the boss is

delighted, so ours is a happy exhaustion.' He comments: 'They are not envy-
ing the net boss; rather, they are celebrating the fact that their own labours
have brought money to the boss too.' Such a touching concern for the net-
boss's welfare would have been unlikely even in feudal times. Nakai does not
advance the slightly more believable claim that the boatmen's reaction is one
of self-interest – that a happy boss will be kinder to them. Nor does he see
in the parallelism of the third and fourth lines an ironic contrasting of the
respective situations of boss and workers. After verse 2, Nakai adds a paren-
thetical '(laughter)', defusing any sense of strong emotions. But the laughter
might have been bitter. Compare the following verse from another Hokkaido
fishermen's song, which is at least resentful if not antagonistic:

oyakata tairyō de / umai sake nonde / oretachi himojute / cha mo nomenu
　　The boss, after a big catch, / drinks delicious *sake*; / we-all go hungry / and
can't even drink tea. ('Sōran Bushi')

The following verse, found in several songs in the Sawauchi region of
Iwate, contains two potential puns. The word *o-yone*, 'rice', in line 2 is also a
common female given name; *mi* in line 4 can mean 'winnow' or 'body'. The
latter interpretations are invoked in telling the tale of a maiden named O-Yone,
offered by her parents to the local lord in lieu of taxes. Such incidents were
not uncommon, but did this particular incident actually take place, or was
this simply an irresistable pun? Whatever the original truth, the linkage with
O-Yone does seem to have been made by the locals rather than scholars.

Sawauchi sanzengoku / o-yone no dedoko / masu de hakarane de / mi de hakaru
　　Sawauchi, a 15,000-bushel fief, / famous for producing rice/O-Yone / measured not with a pint-box / but with a winnow/one's body. ('Sawauchi Jinku')

Real people do appear in song texts from time to time in censorious
contexts. Tarobei, a landlord and village headman in Shimane Prefecture,
neglected his duties to visit the brothels of the nearest town. Although the following verse again resembles a typical love song, locals claim that the reference is to the occasion when Tarobei's mansion burned down as he slept in a
brothel: he was awakened to see the distant glow, not of dawn but of fire. This
incident brought his dereliction to the attention of the domainal authorities,
who exiled him (pers. comm., Sanko Bushi Preservation Society).

okite inasare / Mochida no Tarobei / yoakegarasu ga / nakanu ma ni
　　Wake up, / Tarobei of Mochida, / before the dawn crow / cries. ('Sanko Bushi')

The verse below from Tokushima Prefecture is more direct. Although collected as part of the urban Bon dance song 'Yoshikono Bushi' ('Awa Odori'),
it was presumably first sung by indigo workers at the workplace, feeling

insufficiently rewarded by the local entrepreneur who marketed their product (Misumi Haruo, pers. comm.):

> Awa no daijin / jigoku no oni yo / ai o shiborazu / chi o shiboru
> The tycoon of Awa / is a devil from hell: / he doesn't extract indigo dye, / he extracts blood.

Songs of protest against 'the system' as a whole, based on principle, are even rarer than songs of specific criticism. Perhaps one can see a generalized plaint in this text (featuring a pun on the word *torotoro*):

> hyakushō wa nezumi ja / shōyadono wa neko ja / hyakushō megakete / torotoro [= torō, torō] to
> The peasant is a mouse; / the squire is a cat, / his eyes on the peasant / drowsily [= thinking 'I'll catch him']. (Awaji 1825: no.97)

The same source, an 1825 collection of peasant song lyrics from Awaji Island (Hyōgo Pref.), contains several other anti-squire verses – presumably not sung in the squire's presence.[15] Somewhat more common are complaints about parental interference in matrimonial matters. In the general case:

> omoi omoware / sou no wa en yo / oya no sowasu wa / en ja nai
> Loving and being loved, / going together: that's marriage; / forced together by parents: / that's no marriage. (Matsuhara 1927: 224)

In a specific case of maltreatment of a bride by her parents-in-law, the villagers are said to have made up a song of criticism even as the situation continued. The place was Kizukuri Village, Tsugaru, the year 1808. Typical verses are:

> muri da oyashu ni / tsukawarete / tō no yubiko kara / chiko nagasu
> Her unreasonable parents-in-law / made her work so hard that / from her ten fingers / blood streamed.
> koko no oyatach'ya / mina oni da / koko sa kuru yome / mina baka da
> The parents here [in this village] / are all devils; / the brides who come here / must all be idiots. ('Yasaburō Bushi')

As a final example of songs of complaint, consider the following verses from two lullabies in Kyushu, southern Japan:

> odoma kanjin kanjin / an futotach'ya yoka shu / yoka shu yoka obi / yoka kimon
> I'm just a beggar, a beggar; / they're fine folk, / fine folk with fine sashes / and fine kimono. ('Itsuki no Komori Uta')

> goryō yoku kike / danna mo kike yo / omori waru surya / ko ni ataru
> Mistress, listen well; / master, listen too: / if you mistreat the nursemaid, / the child will suffer too. ('Hakata Komori Uta')

Traditional nursemaids were often teenage girls from poor families, sent as indentured servants to wealthy households in nearby villages. They might only visit home once a year, for the ancestral O-Bon festival. The verse from 'Itsuki no Komori Uta' (especially in the context of the entire song) exudes self-pity, self-deprecation and resignation. The second song is more aggressive and includes several other verses insulting the baby's parents, although it is unlikely they ever heard these.

In sum, while the Japanese peasantry had plenty to complain about, *min'yō* did not commonly serve as vehicles for systemic criticisms or rebellious calls to arms. But given the frequently veiled nature of such references as well as the ideologically charged approaches to interpretation, more research is needed.[16]

2.3 The folk song repertoire in the traditional village

To get an idea of folk song life in the traditional *buraku*, one could start by listing all the songs *of any type*, folk or otherwise, known in a single hamlet. However, no such surveys have been done. Even community-specific surveys of *min'yō* alone have only come to be done after the Second World War, generally under the auspices of village Boards of Education (*kyōiku iinkai*), which treat as a unit the several *buraku* constituting the village.[17] It is nevertheless clear that the repertoire was much smaller in the days before the diffusion of recording and broadcasting. Asari Miki, a professional folk singer who now knows several hundred songs, recalls that in her village in the 1930s, when radios and phonographs were scarce, she heard at most a few dozen adult songs.

An interesting pre-war survey is that by ethnologists John and Ella Embree in Suye village in southern Japan during 1935–36 (Embree 1944). The survey's value is compounded by their excellent ethnography of the same village (Embree 1939). Suye at that period had some 1,663 people in seventeen hamlets (ibid.: 19, 24), and not all of the songs collected were known in every hamlet – or, of course, by any single resident. In those days, when radios and record players were still rare, 'the [Westernized] popular songs of the city [were] almost unknown in the village', but the songs of the geisha houses (*kouta, zokkyoku*, etc.) would occasionally slip into the repertoire (Embree 1944: 4). Embree (ibid.: 10) feels that his collection,

> while probably not complete, at least presents a fair proportion of the popular songs regarded by the people of Suye as local. . . . These . . . include a few which in actual fact are not local . . . and omit a few which might be regarded as local to [this region] by people of another part of the county.

If he indeed recorded 'a fair proportion' of the village's songs, then the repertoire of Suye village as a whole was somewhat in excess of the following:

1. 'Banquet songs': some fifteen tunes with over seventy-five total verses. (Embree does not give the tunes nor always state which verses are sung to the same tune.)
2. 'Hamlet dance songs': four songs of several verses each, to accompany dances on certain ceremonial occasions (to end a drought, celebrate the completion of a building or bridge, etc.). These are supposedly hamlet-specific.
3. 'Seasonal songs': five short songs: three seasonal festival songs, one wedding song (weddings being seasonal in traditional Japan), and one paddy-weeding song. These were hardly sung at all by 1935.
4. 'Foundation pounding songs' are not found in Suye but exist in the neighbouring village. Embree thinks that equivalents probably existed in Suye, going uncollected because they were not needed during his stay. Seven songs; two are very short, while two are ballads (*kudoki*) well over 100 lines long.
5. 'Children's game songs': nineteen songs of varying length.
6. 'Lullabies': four songs.
7. 'Miscellaneous songs': one two-line song given.
8. Songs known to be from outside the area: three songs (fifteen verses) given, but other outside songs are also heard 'from time to time' (Embree 1944: 86).

The Embrees thus collected some thirty adult songs and nineteen children's songs from the village, not counting the seven potentially present foundation pounding songs. They surely missed some songs and have also intentionally omitted 'a few' imported from other areas. But even if the Embrees only heard half the songs known in the village, the total figure still would have been little more than a hundred songs. This rough estimate at least gives an idea of the repertoire's order of magnitude, permitting comparison with the present-day situation in Chapter 4.

Suye in the 1930s stood somewhere between tradition and modernity, between the village of 200 years ago and that of today. Cross-cutting forces of consolidation had reduced but not eliminated hamlet identity and independence (Embree 1939: 59ff.). Less than a tenth of marriages were hamlet-endogamous, and over 70 per cent of wives came from outside Suye village (ibid.: 72–3). The machine age had begun to affect agriculture, transportation and clothes-making, but anyone over thirty could still recall a time before machines (ibid.: 45f). There were twenty phonographs and five radios among over 1,600 people (ibid.: 48), but their effect was negligible. A *sankyoku* club met once a week: eight or nine upper-class villagers gathered to pick up some 'culture' from a teacher who commuted from the county seat, forty-five minutes away by bus. This sort of 'club' was a recent innovation under urban influence (ibid.: 165–6). At school, children learned a body of somewhat Westernized composed songs which were being taught in every school in Japan using government-issue songbooks (see Eppstein 1994). Embree omits these from his collection 'with one or two exceptions' (1944: 66).

I am unaware of any systematic studies of either the size or the sources of the repertoire of an individual singer in a traditional Japanese village.[18] We can assume that the 'best' singers (i.e. those who knew the most songs; Embree 1939: 102) could sing almost all songs heard in the hamlet, as well as some picked up elsewhere. As an example, consider the repertoire of Itō Moyo, the 'best' singer in her village since before the Second World War.

Itō (1901–2002) was born to a poor farming family in Susumago, near Kitakami City in southern Iwate. She found one advantage in poverty: 'I've never had anything, so I've never lost anything!' Marrying at eighteen, she moved to the adjacent hamlet of Ezuriko. Enjoying singing from early childhood, she would willingly volunteer to join any communal work group in order to learn the songs associated with each type of work. These work teams (*yui*) carried out agricultural tasks on each member household's land in turn. She also sought out songs connected with non-communal work. In this way she learned several work songs in both her own and her husband's hamlet (which shared much of their repertoire): one song each for paddy ploughing (*takaki*), transplanting (*taue*), weeding (*ta no kusatori*), rice hulling (*momisuri*), millet pounding (*hietsuki*) and foundation pounding (*dozuki*; **CD17**).[19] She could also sing the song associated with a transplanting dance in her natal hamlet.

The work teams especially enjoyed offering their services to the wealthy farmers, who would both pay well and throw them a feast afterwards. At such parties, work songs were never sung, she said: they belonged to the work situation.[20] There was a separate class of party songs, chief of which was the lively dance-song 'Nanbu Sakata'. As the acknowledged local master of this song, Moyo was sure to be invited to any local party. As is usual, she was often 'paid' with small gifts of food or occasionally cash. Various popular songs (*hayariuta*) of urban origin were also heard at parties. These included some *min'yō* from other areas, such as the ubiquitous 'Sado Okesa', as well as commercially produced popular songs.[21] She learned many of these as well, especially once radio became commonly available.

There were also semi-ceremonial songs for wedding receptions and other celebrations. Most villages had only one such song, often treated as a sort of standard closing number; her village had two. Moyo could also sing the song used in wedding processions. There is, in addition, a very short excerpt of Noh singing, a celebratory passage from the play *Takasago*, commonly sung at weddings throughout Japan; this universality has nearly but not quite relieved it of all class associations. She did not consider herself able to perform it, possibly because *utai* is locally considered to be a male art.

She could sing the Bon dance song 'Sansa Odori' (popular throughout south-central Iwate), several children's songs and a few Buddhist hymns (*goeika*). The hymns were known by only a few villagers, some of whom liked them as much for their musical characteristics as for their religious significance.

Moyo had learned these songs already during the pre-war years. Between the war and our interviews in 1980, she also learned several dozen popular *min'yō* via radio, friends and cassette tapes, which she would sing frequently at parties. She also admitted to a passive knowledge of many recent popular songs – which, however, she rarely had occasion or desire to try to sing.

Making a precise and complete listing of Moyo's *min'yō* repertoire would have been impossible, but its size in the 1930s was probably comparable to the tentative figures derived from Embree's study. Very few rural people in traditional Japan would have known as many as a hundred songs of any type.

Listing one community's total repertoire is not, of course, the same as counting that of one person. Itō Moyo was exceptional in her zeal to learn, which was the reason I chose her for this particular research. A potentially rather different situation emerges from Kojima Tomiko's 1992 article on folk song in Tairadate Village in the Tsugaru region of Aomori Prefecture, fifty minutes by train from Aomori City. When Kojima visited between 1986 and 1991, its nine hamlets had a declining population of just over 3,000. Since Tsugaru has produced some of Japan's most renowned *min'yō*, Kojima expected that Tairadate would have a large repertoire. But in fact, interviewing seventeen people born between 1903 and 1925, she discovered only about thirty-five songs in total for all hamlets, and only one person claimed to know more than seven songs. The figure included several children's songs, Buddhist hymns, and simple recited work-song choruses as well as full-fledged *min'yō*. Moreover, about a third of these songs were from other prefectures, and many others originated elsewhere in Aomori. She concluded that local songs were dying out rapidly, due mainly to loss of original context or competition from songs from outside.

This reminds us of the difficulty of generalizing. *Min'yō* researchers tend to focus on older villagers (such as Itō Moyo) to get a sense of the rich past when many more songs had a role in village life. But younger residents of Tairadate might well know more *min'yō* in total, perhaps being more likely to commute to the city for formal lessons, learn from recordings and so forth. Repertoire expansion and changing modes of transmission are discussed in subsequent chapters.

2.4 Folk song life in the traditional hamlet

With the concrete example of Suye as a reference point, let us paint a picture of folk song life in a 'typical' traditional hamlet. This idealized picture is sufficiently representative to serve as a launching-pad for the discussion in subsequent chapters.

Life in traditional rural Japan followed seasonal rhythms. In farming areas, the year was in effect divided into the farming season and the off-season. Fishing villages or families followed a less simple but equally regular pattern, dependent on the migrations of various species of fish. Each type of work and play had its season and its associated songs.[22]

Wet-rice agriculture was the predominant village livelihood in traditional Japan. The agricultural season extended from paddy ploughing around March to the harvest around October. (Double-cropping areas of southern Japan had a different pattern.) Major festivals and events such as weddings were concentrated in the off-season.[23] This was also the period for migrant work in lumber and fishing camps, textile mills, *sake* breweries, etc., and for tasks within the hamlet such as house construction and net mending.

It will be convenient to distinguish several performance contexts, for two reasons. First, the nature of musical performance itself often varies sharply with the setting. Second, we shall see later that a song's traditional context and function have much to do with its fate in modern Japan. Sections 2.4.2–5 treat, respectively, the nature of songs in association with calendrical community observances, in the workplace, in party situations, and as performed by itinerant musicians. In the course of the discussion, we also focus on some significant features of performance and transmission of the folk performing arts. First, however, we must consider gender.

2.4.1 Gender roles in Japanese music life

In traditional Japan, gender roles were highly stereotyped. In the traditional classical performing arts, many restrictions, formal or otherwise, are placed on female participation in certain genres (much less so on males). Even today, many shakuhachi teachers refuse to teach women (though women are increasingly asking). The majority of amateur students of Noh singing and dance (*utai* and *shimai*) are women – indeed, their fees are economically crucial to the teachers (Johnson 1982) – but there are almost no professional female performers. While women predominate as both teachers and pupils of classical dance (*nihon buyō*), which has close links with the Kabuki theatre, an actual performance featuring female actors is not considered true Kabuki but will need to be qualified by some adjective or special term. While men play all parts in Noh and Kabuki, a sort of compensation is provided by the renowned Takarazuka company (founded in 1913), performing gaudy musicals where all roles are taken by women.

In the folk sphere, we must distinguish *minzoku geinō* from *min'yō* for a start. Many folk performing arts of a ritual nature are restricted to either male or (less often) female participation, just as they may also be restricted by age, lineage, residence or other factors. In recent years, rural depopulation and competing activities have forced many villages to make exceptions in order to assemble sufficient performers.

But in the world of *min'yō*, both traditionally and today, gender restrictions among singers are very weak. In theory, either a man or a woman could sing any song. In reality, though, in the traditional village, since certain types of work were commonly performed by one or the other gender, the associated songs were sung by that gender. (This does not pertain to modern stage performances; see §4.4.1.) Dance or party songs could be sung by anyone. All instruments could be played by either gender as well, with the apparent exception of the shakuhachi. Thus the folk song world was and is less fettered by gender distinctions than most other spheres of Japanese performing arts.

2.4.2 Song as part of 'calendrical observances'

Every hamlet, during the year, would have several large-scale events which were at least partly religious and partly musical. The common term for these is *matsuri*, 'festival', though scholars may call them *nenjū gyōji*, 'calendrical observances' or even just *minzoku geinō*, 'folk performing arts'. These categories might, however, include totally secular events as well.[24]

A festival could last several days. On the eve (*yoimiya*) of the official part, a public, secular song contest might well be held; after the official part, a secular banquet (often called *naorai*) might involve more song and dance. Ritual song cycles themselves also commonly included popular songs which had reached the village and taken on ritual significance in their new context, as Hoff showed for a cycle of rice-transplanting songs (1971: 18ff). Let us consider chiefly three representative examples of religion-linked annual events involving public song: *ta-asobi, taue* and *bon odori*.

The agricultural ritual cycle in the typical rice-growing hamlet began shortly after the lunar New Year (late January or early February).[25] Then, a ritual known by such names as *ta-asobi* or *haru-tauchi* was held in the forecourt of the hamlet Shintō shrine, a specially sacralized paddy or another specified location. The successive stages of the rice cycle – ploughing, sowing, weeding, harvesting, storing – were enacted in varying degrees of abstractness in a single performance lasting several hours, to increase the chances that the year's agricultural activities would proceed successfully.

Most *ta-asobi* songs functioned as what scholars call *yoshuku*, 'celebration in advance'. The lyrics describe an ideal situation, a desired result, as if the mere act of describing it would bring it about. The power of language to affect the course of events is expressed in the word *kotodama*, 'word soul'. Belief in this power is seen already in Japan's earliest written sources (eighteenth century). A typical *ta-asobi* lyric is this one from Tokumaru, now in Itabashi Ward, Tokyo:

chōchō o kazoesōrō / higashi no chō ni ichiman-chō / minami no chō ni ichiman-chō / nishi no chō ni ichiman-chō / kita no chō ni ichiman-chō / naka no

chō ni ichiman-chō / naka no chō no / yokisōrō tokoro o / Tenjin Daimyōjin no / naeshiro-dokoro to / uchihajime moshisōrō
   Count the hectares [of seedbed]: / to the east, 10,000 hectares; / to the south, 10,000 hectares; / to the west, 10,000 hectares; / to the north, 10,000 hectares; / in the middle, 10,000 hectares. / In the middle, / in a good spot, / the Great God Tenjin's / seedbed / we shall begin to prepare. (Itabashi-ku 1971: 13)

This text paints an image of great abundance. Japanese ritual songs never state the situation negatively. There are songs throughout the country beginning with the line, 'This is a bumper year,' but none beginning, 'The harvest was a disaster.' Disasters must be approached positively, as in the 'Smallpox Dance' ('Hōsō Odori') from southern Kyushu, which survived in many villages well into the twentieth century (NMT: 9.409):

kotosh'ya yoi toshi / o-hoso hayaru / o-hoso no kamisama / odori suki de gozaru / odori odoreba / o-hoso ga karui . . .
   This is a good [*sic!*] year: / smallpox is rampant. / The god of smallpox / likes dancing. / If we dance [for him], / the smallpox will be light . . .

The belief in *kotodama* supported the ritual importance of precise performance of transmitted lyrics and music. Nevertheless, changes occurred. Even closely related rituals from neighbouring hamlets invariably diverge considerably. Thus the *ta-asobi* of Tokumaru now differs greatly in text and melody from that of the adjacent hamlet, Shimo-Akatsuka. Such splitting of a single performance type into diverse descendants was common for several reasons. First, songs were mostly passed on orally. Sometimes ritual song texts would be recorded in writing by a village official or other local literate, to be referred to if necessary when rehearsing, but this was uncommon.[26] Also, musical notation was rare in villages. The nature of the textual divergences suggests strongly that many are unintentional.

   Another factor hindering exact transmission was seasonality. *Ta-asobi* and most other 'calendrical observances' occurred only once a year, allowing plenty of time to forget. Some rituals were even less frequent, such as the Onbashira festival of Nagano Prefecture, held every six years! Furthermore, performers were not professionals but just ordinary villagers stealing time from daily chores. There would be rehearsals before each performance – perhaps nightly for several weeks – but that still might leave eleven to seventy months with no reinforcement of learning. Until recently it was generally considered wrong to rehearse or perform such rituals out of season.

   Not only were performers non-professional, they could change from year to year. Participants were often selected by age. The Daimokutate of eastern Nara Prefecture (Kami-Fukagawa Hamlet, Tsuge Village), a long ballad accompanied by dance, is offered before the hamlet shrine each October. It was traditionally performed compulsorily by boys of age seventeen, when they were considered to become adults (pers. comm. from participants, 1977;

Nakai et al. 1981: 261). Thus performers obviously lacked experience, despite being taught by conscientious elders. In 1977 the boys' ages varied, as not enough seventeen-year-olds were available; and some concealed small lyrics sheets in their hands.

Of course, one could also hypothesize that differences between neighbouring hamlets were intentionally created or maintained to mark social boundaries. Not having investigated this hypothesis, I can only observe that differences are often treasured today.

In short, while ritual correctness was highly valued, a combination of factors prevented the exact re-creation of the performance each year. This did not lessen the importance of such occasions in community life: many residents turned out to watch, for such performances of course had entertainment as well as ritual value. The gods themselves like to be entertained.

On the other hand, rarely did a song from a ritual sequence such as *ta-asobi* escape the bounds of its immediate situation and become popular as, say, a party song. Besides their close association with the original context, there are at least four other reasons why they seldom spread.

(1) Ritual propriety often restricted the content of the lyrics to themes of little interest in other settings (as seen in the sample quoted above).

(2) Emphasis on correct performance often destroyed the spontaneity and verve necessary to make the music come alive.

(3) Due to the stress on invariance, both language and melody failed to change in step with the times and were soon perceived as outmoded and archaic.

(4) The short rehearsal time often meant that the performance was technically and artistically wanting, hence unlikely to tempt secular imitators.

Clearly *ta-asobi* is a *minzoku geinō*, and its constituent songs are not *min'yō* as commonly defined (§1.2). The situation differed somewhat with the only other stage of the rice cycle commonly marked by a large-scale, formal group performance. This is *taue*, the transplanting of seedlings into the main paddies in May or June. In most areas, the young women, as symbols of fertility, did the actual transplanting while the men provided music on flutes and percussion. Such performances were usually done in only one or two sacralized paddies, then non-ritualized transplanting continued without the aid of music.

In western Japan, rice-transplanting songs can be seen as constituting a suite (see Hoff 1971; Uchida 1978). Within this are songs clearly derived from the quasi-learned, quasi-urban 'popular song' repertoire, whose texts have at best a tangential relevance to rice-planting (Hoff 1971: 18–21). *Taue* songs thus are much less homogeneous than the *ta-asobi* songs of most areas, which appear predominantly to have been created expressly for use in the ritual. Many *taue* songs may continue to be heard outside of their adopted ritual context, leading one scholar to state unequivocally of one such song: 'This is completely and quintessentially a *min'yō*, so much so that one cannot [*sic!*] call it a rice-planting ritual song (*taue-uta*)' (Miyao 1976: 128). This evokes again the notion of *min'yō* as separate from ritual, thus opposed to typical *minzoku geinō*.

Still, just as popular songs and 'regular' folk songs were drawn into some ritual suites, so ritual songs could on occasion overcome the above obstacles and cross over to other settings. Although tracing such developments is difficult, there is no shortage of suggestive examples. Let us consider just one, the case of so-called 'seasonal songs'.

Throughout Japan, a frequent feature of ritual performance of the type called *kagura* is a song text beginning with the phrase *X kureba*, 'when X comes', X being the name of a season. One text from Nagano Prefecture is as follows (Misumi 1976: 114):

aki kureba / minabito-goto ni / ine o koku / ujiko wa yoki to / inoriowasu
When autumn comes, / each and every person / strips the rice grains from the stalks; / the shrine parishioners / pray that the crop is good.

The following text, related to the above verse, was recorded in Akita Prefecture, functioning as both a work song and a party song but not as a ritual song (ibid.; Machida 1964: no. 1):

haru kureba / uzura mo hibari mo / ko o daku shi / ora mo dakitai / jushichihachi
When spring comes, / both quail and skylark / embrace their young; / I'd like to embrace a young thing too – / about age 17 or 18.

The archaic diction of the first text places it earlier in time than the secularized version. Yet even the latter possesses a degree of ritual power: as late as the 1940s, it was believed that singing it in the wrong season would bring disaster (Machida 1964: 8). Clearly 'secular' is a relative concept.

Many other examples show the quasi-magical power of folk song in certain contexts. 'The Rich Man's Mountain' (§2.2.1) is still often sung at wedding feasts because of its auspicious lyrics. It is said that a certain man re-married against the wishes of his relatives; angry, they refused to sing this song at the feast, and the marriage soon collapsed (Ikeda & Miyao 1961: vol. 1).

Two further examples both concern rain. Two elderly gentlemen in Yamagata Prefecture told Takeuchi that their local 'rain song' (not performed since 1939) had never failed to end a drought (Takeuchi 1978: 270–1). This is not surprising, since they also said that the villagers sang it daily until the rains came. And in July 1980, at Gonshōji temple in Ōmori on the western edge of Tokyo, I attended a performance of the 'Water-stopping Dance' ('Mizudome no Mai'). This dance was reportedly created in the fourteenth century by a Buddhist priest – to halt the torrential downpour brought on by a rain dance he himself had created. Today this dance is performed on a fixed date each year, and the present head priest assured me of its efficacy: there are always clear skies on that day. When I tactlessly pointed out that it had been raining since early morning, he replied, 'Ah, but it will definitely clear up later.'

Another annual occasion for traditional village song puts us more squarely in the realm of *min'yō*: the Bon (ancestral festival) dance (*bon odori*). The O-Bon festival itself, traditionally centred around the full-moon night of the seventh month, is nominally Buddhist.[27] In many a Japanese village the Bon dance was the apogee of the annual social calendar, a chance for young folk to see potential partners in their finest finery. As a widespread 'floating verse' notes:

> odori odoraba / shina yoku odore / shina no yoi no o / yome ni toru
> If you're going to dance, / dance with style: / the most stylish / will become my bride. ('Sasa Odori', **CD14**)

Many Bon dances and songs grew out of the *nenbutsu odori* tradition (Ōhashi 1974), a populist religious practice spread by itinerant priests by the thirteenth century, in which a group of believers did a simple circle or processional dance while striking gongs and singing or chanting the praises of Amitabha Buddha. By the Edo period, however, while O-Bon remained a religious festival, the Bon dance itself had been largely secularized; the songs had much more in common with drinking-party songs than with ritual music in terms of lyrics and overall mood.[28]

A Bon dance with lyrics rich in Buddhist sentiments survives in Tokyo harbour, on Tsukuda Island (**CD18**; NMT: vol.1); aside from the *nenbutsu* phrase 'Hail Amitabha', one verse notes that 'people, grasses, trees, all turn to earth' after death, recalling the impermanence of life. Evidence that this dance is still perceived as strongly Buddhist was the chilly reply I got from a priest at Tsukuda's Shintō shrine when I asked for directions to the dance: 'This is a Shintō shrine, not a Buddhist temple.' (Most Japanese happily relate to both Shintō and Buddhism.)

In most hamlets, residents danced in a circle in the local temple courtyard. Young folk from neighbouring hamlets might come to join in (and court) if their own dance was held on a different night. The majority of Bon dance songs had alternating parts for a lead singer and the entire assembly. The solo lines would be sung either by a person perched on a platform or tower in the middle of a circle (perhaps with instrumentalists; Figs 1.1, 4.3) or by whichever of the dancers started singing the next verse first. Sometimes there was no soloist, and all present sang in unison. Other hamlets preserved an apparently older form: a procession of a small subset of residents (usually young) who danced door-to-door, giving special attention to households where a death had occurred since the previous O-Bon.[29]

Particularly in the circle dance form, the role of lead singer (*ondo-tori*) was crucial. Since dancing might continue all night, this role generally alternated among several individuals. A lead singer needed: a voice powerful enough (in the pre-amplification era) to be heard over the hubbub of conversation, handclaps, and accompanying instruments such as drums, gongs and flutes; a memory for song texts; often a facility for improvising new verses; and a pleasing and skilful voice. This last was somewhat less important than the first two factors, for a beautiful voice was useless if one could not be heard nor think of any lyrics! Still, the preference was for a mellifluous voice which could execute the *kobushi* ornaments.

These requirements differ from those for singers in a ritual performance such as *ta-asobi*. In the latter case, although many villagers would come to watch, the performance was first and foremost for the Shintō deities, who valued correctness above all. Whether there were several singers in unison, as for *ta-asobi*, or only one at a time as for many *kagura*, two primary characteristics were demanded: correct performance and freedom from personal pollution.[30]

As these various types of calendrical observance differed in what was expected of performers, the method of selecting performers also differed (§2.2.2). *Ta-asobi* was a Shintō rite, linked to the hamlet shrine, and participation was limited to parishioners (*ujiko*) of the shrine.[31] In Tokumaru, a dozen or so adult males, after ritual purification, were entrusted with learning the performance for that year (pers. comm. from participants, 1979). For the 1979 performance, some participants read from lyric-books, while others muddled through without, occasionally forgetting their lines. Given this difficulty in recalling the lyrics, it is doubtful whether any other villagers knew any of the songs of the cycle.

In the large-scale *taue* rites of western Japan, the important role of ritual leader (*sanbai, sage*) was occupied by a part-time but highly committed specialist, but the roles of singer–transplanter (for women) and musician (for men) were accessible to any villagers willing to learn and to undergo purification. The number of participants could be quite large compared to *ta-asobi*. One reason was that *taue* songs were often widely known, unlike those of *ta-asobi*: one researcher, apparently referring to the 1920s, estimated that some forty-eight verses from one village's cycle were known by 'everyone' in the village (quoted in Hoff 1971: 171).

In the case of *bon odori*, the role of lead singer (*ondo-tori*) could be filled successively by any number of people, the only requirements being the largely aesthetic criteria listed above. Lead singers were predominantly male. The *ondo-tori* had the ambiguous status associated with musicians in many cultures. He was highly valued in the sense that the dance could not proceed without him. And he was attractive to women: in the licentious atmosphere prevailing in many regions at Bon, a good singer could often have his pick of the young women for a night's pleasure (see Narita 1978: 162). However, anyone who had taken the time to become a good singer (and a sex object) had quite possibly been spending too much time singing and carousing when others worked. Such amusements must not interfere with daily life:

odori odoru mo / konnichi kagiri / asu wa yamayama / kusatori ni
  We can dance / only today; / tomorrow, it's to the hills / to cut grass.
('Torajo-sama'; Honda 1998, CD R15)

Thus a good singer risked being called a *dōrakumono*, a pleasure-bent carouser.

Surely few singers of *ta-asobi* could project such charisma, due to the nature of the music, the group unison singing and the overall performance situation. But some of the quasi-ritual folk theatricals known as *kagura* gave the performers sufficient scope to show off their abilities and charms. A man from Okayama, on a performing tour of a neighbouring prefecture early in the twentieth century, danced a particular *kagura* dance so well that a local woman followed him home – to his great distress (Ochiai 1980: 1009).

Entertainment being paramount in *bon odori*, some villages offered prizes to the best singer, which might even attract contestants from the next province. In some cases singers were ranked according to the terminology of *sumō* wrestling, and the best singers might hire themselves out at nominal rates (Kodera 1935, entries 'Banzuke Odori' and 'Banshū Ondo').

In Okuda Village, Ōshima Island, Tokyo Prefecture, each 15 January, all the songs that had entered the village in the previous year would be 'offered' – sung – to the Shintō tutelary deity by the young men of the village (Takeuchi 1980: 151). This rare custom has presumably lapsed in the age of broadcasting and recording!

This is only a rough overview of the nature of song linked with calendrical religious activities. We have seen that there is usually no clear separation of sacred and secular in texts or melodies. The boundary between festival songs and the so-called work songs discussed next is itself often fuzzy. However, the former usually had instrumental accompaniment while the latter did not – clearly an artifact of context. And it was rarely necessary to practise or to purify oneself before singing a work song. Further differences emerge below.

2.4.3 Work songs

Many Japanese today feel that work songs (*shigoto-uta*, *rōsaku-uta*) are the purest, most authentic or most representative folk songs. As a peasant's life revolved around work, it is easy to imagine that the workplace was a frequent setting for singing. The dozens of types of work song might also lead us to believe that the peasant's day was one long songfest.[32] The matter is less simple. Indeed, the very question of what constitutes a 'work song' is fraught; let us consider three reasons.

First, work songs often contain verses borrowed from other song types, especially from popular songs (*hayariuta*) originating in cities or the pleasure quarters of harbour and post towns. Borrowing was facilitated by the predominance of the 7-7-7-5 poetic metre in both folk and popular strophic songs (§1.6.6–7). Since most work songs were 'folk-lyrics', with verses mostly independent in content, verses from other songs were easily incorporated on the spur of the moment. Such borrowing, perhaps with some reworking of lyrics to suit local conditions, was much more common than outright improvisation of new verses (§2.5.3). At any rate, one is left wondering in what sense such composite songs can be called 'pure' or 'authentic' compared to dance or party songs. Also, work song lyrics were not restricted to subjects relating to the associated work; indeed, such lyrics were in the minority.[33]

Second, aside from such borrowing of verses into a work song, the labourers might sing entire *hayariuta* or other non-work songs. Thus the workplace was a good place to learn the latest 'hit', such as 'Shonga Bushi', which spread throughout Japan in the Edo period:

> narota narota yo / Shonga Bushi narota / kyonen Tsukue no / fushinba de
>   I learned it! I learned it! / I learned 'Shonga Bushi' / last year, in Tsukue, / at
>   the construction site. (Awaji 1825: no.44)

These could gradually come to be considered work songs, as tempo and text changed to meet the needs of the workplace. Asari Miki recalls her mother singing dance songs such as 'Tsugaru Sansagari' and *hayariuta* such as 'Sanosa' while weeding in the paddy in the 1930s; in her village there were no specialized weeding songs. This well-known phenomenon again challenges the notion of the purity of work songs. Another example, fictional but clearly based on fact, occurs in Nagatsuka's semi-autobiographic 1912 novel *The Soil* (*Tsuchi*; Nagatsuka 1989: 64): the peasant Kanji would sing, while working in the fields, the song which the itinerant sweets-seller (§2.4.6) sang as she passed daily through the village.

Third, not all 'work songs' were actually sung while working. Poor peasants could hardly afford to keep interrupting work to sing. Moreover, when a task involved hard labour, it was nearly impossible to sing at all:

> utae utae to / semekakerarete / uta wa de mo sezu / ase ga deta
>   'Sing! Sing!' / they kept urging me, / but a song wouldn't come out, / only
>   sweat. (foundation-pounding song; Machida 1964: no.248)

Thus, many so-called work songs were sung only during a break.

Let us now consider the role of song in, or near, the workplace. Motegi (1999; recording R59) provides an excellent starting point: a study of singing in the *sake*-making industry of Niigata Prefecture. In winter, the agricultural off-season, this industry is the major income source in several Japanese communities, and much of it is still non-mechanized. In a given community, a dozen or two songs may be specifically linked with *sake*-making. They may be sung while working or separately for relaxation or celebration.

Motegi asked nearly a hundred workers from various communities why they sing on the job, given the arduous nature of the work (bitter cold, little sleep, heavy labour). She groups the answers into seven categories in descending order of frequency of mention (1999: 52–7). (1) To keep up spirits in the face of the conditions. (2) To time the duration of certain stages of the process (e.g. stirring the fermenting mixture) – so many verses per stage. (See also NHK 1979: 76; Machida 1964: 42.)[34] (3) To keep track of the number of buckets of water being poured in – one verse per bucket. (4) To coordinate group labour rhythmically. (5) To ensure that actions are performed in correct order. (6) For amusement and relaxation when a task is done. (7) To re-affirm their pride in their identity as a highly specialized professional group who also possess a certain body of specialist songs. Reasons 2 to 5 are directly functional in the context of this profession and relate clearly to the success of the labour. Reasons 1, 6 and 7, though still important, relate less specifically to the content of the work. Similar reasons lie behind most singing at the workplace. And where both sexes are involved (*sake*-making is usually a male profession), courting and flirting also come into play.

True 'work songs', those sung while actually working, were most necessary with tasks requiring rhythmic group coordination: barley threshing, net hauling, rowing, etc. (Some would consider these the *only* true work songs.) The following rowing song makes the point:

> ano saki koereba / mata saki dete kuru / hayashi o soroete / kaisaki soroete
> After we pass that promontory, / there's another one coming up. / Keep the chorus aligned; / keep the oar-tips aligned. ('Funakogi Nagashi Uta')

When coordination was needed but the labourers were too tired to sing, they might simply keep time with short yells (*kakegoe*) (see Machida 1964: no. 249, 120). For some strenuous tasks – rowing, foundation pounding – the job of singing was assigned to a song-leader (*ondo-tori*) who might not actually be involved in the hard part of the work. (Nice work if you can get it!)

As for non-rhythmic but generally communal tasks like ploughing and weeding, singing was simply a way to pass the time and forget or overcome one's physical exhaustion:

> uta wa utaitote / utau ja nai ga / uta wa shigoto no / magiregusa
> It's not because I like to sing / that I'm singing, / but the song helps / to distract me from my work. ('old song'; Ochiai 1980: 939)

> shigoto ku ni shite / naku yor'ya utae / uta wa yoibana / ki no harete
> If you're suffering at work, / instead of crying, sing. / If the song is good, / you'll cheer up. (rice-pounding song; Machida 1964: no.87)

Singing certainly could be distracting. Asari Miki recalls that when her mother burst into song in the paddy, the other workers straightened up from their weeding to listen or sing along.

ine no naka kara / kouta ga moreru / kouta kikitaya / kao mitaya
   From among the rice-plants / comes a little ditty. / I want to hear the song / and see the [singer's] face. (weeding song; Machida 1964: no.52)

A good singer could attract attention even from a greater distance:

iki na kouta de / kuwa tsumu nushi no / o-kao mitasa ni / mawarimichi
   The man singing that charming ditty / while picking mulberries: / to see his face / I'll take a detour. (mulberry-picking song; Machida 1964: no.179)

Of course, it was more enjoyable if everyone joined in – indeed, not singing was considered unusual:

haru no no ni dete / utawanu hito wa / hara ni yango no / arige na
   Going into the fields in spring / and not singing – / she must have a baby / in her belly. (mulberry-picking song; Machida 1964: no.179)

Itō Moyo emphasized that singers were not judged by singing skill: it only mattered that someone or other could add another song to pass the time (*jikan-tsubushi*). You'd sing and work all day, then be surprised at how far you'd got with the work: 'Hey, the sun's set already!'

uta no go-sensei ga / ohitori yori mo / heta na tsurebush'ya / omoshiroi
   Rather than a song expert / singing alone, / an off-key group song / is more fun. (foundation-pounding song; Ochiai 1980: 960)

Several types of ritual or congratulatory song are today called work songs though actually sung only before or after the associated task. For example, before putting axe to tree in clearing a field, farmers in the Shiiba area (Miyazaki Pref.) sang to the mountain god (*yama no kami*) to request safety and ask forgiveness for killing a living thing (**CD19**; Takeuchi 1981: 119ff). This song resembles those of calendrical observances in that its music and lyrics are treated as inviolate. The whalers of Taiji (Wakayama Pref.) celebrated a successful hunt with a powerful dance based loosely on work movements (see Nakai et al. 1972: 119). The lyrics of the accompanying song are not obviously religious, unlike the mountain god song, perhaps because it is being sung after, rather than before, the desired goal has been attained: the boatmen can relax somewhat.

The seasonality of most work meant that a given song might only be heard for a couple of months each year; thus work songs were subject to the same risk of forgotten lyrics as with yearly ritual songs. The difference is that there was little concern if lyrics from a non-ritual work song were forgotten.

In most work songs, as indeed in most dance and many party songs, a single singer would begin each verse, being answered or joined by others.

When particular tasks were commonly performed by men or women only, the associated songs were of course usually transmitted by that gender alone. But such restrictions in transmission were usually unintentional epiphenomena. In rice-planting rites of western Japan, the fact that women do the planting is important as a symbol of fertility, but the lyrics they sing are not significantly different from those of the male leader.

Finally, a word about 'industrial song' in Japan. This category of song received much scholarly attention in the West, where the Industrial Revolution arrived somewhat earlier (see Lloyd 1967: ch.5; Watson 1983; Greenway 1953). Japan reveals no musical or textual justification for distinguishing such a category. Perhaps five principal industrial settings gave rise to work songs: large textile factories, which employed excess young women from surrounding farming villages; crab- and fish-canning factories of northern Japan, also staffed mainly by women; coal mines; *sake* factories; and laying and maintaining railroad tracks (R31 track 8; see also Hashimoto 1985). Their lyrical themes seem little different from agricultural songs. They are no more likely to express complaints about the 'bosses' than are other work songs. Section 3.4.3 describes some attempts by factory owners and professional songwriters in the 1920s to provide 'new folk songs' for workers; these seem to have proven largely unsuccessful.[35]

Since field recordings of work songs are hard to obtain today, further examples are included on the CD **(CD20–22)**. Most of those on R1, 17–18, 31, 59, 63–4 and 67 were recorded outside the work situation. The videotape set of twenty-nine work songs from Ōita Prefecture (R38), recorded in 1995–6, could only partially succeed in its aim of illustrating their original contexts.[36]

2.4.4 Party songs

Wedding and New Year's banquets, roofbeam-raising ceremonies, celebrations after planting or harvest, goodbye parties, even the occasional spur-of-the-moment gathering around a bottle of *sake*: these were important settings for singing in traditional Japan and still are today.[37] Most party songs have the spontaneity of work songs, their lyrics unconstrained by ritual correctness. Nor is participation restricted. Unlike work songs, on the other hand, party songs often featured instrumental accompaniment, or at least hand-clapping. The shamisen, rare in ritual music, came into its own at parties.[38] Its function in this context was quite different from its elitist role in the urban-style chamber music favoured by upwardly-mobile villagers (§2.2.2). Extempore solo or group dancing was also frequent and influenced party song rhythms just as work rhythms affected work songs.

We noted in §2.3 that work songs were not readily transferred to a party setting. Still, it happened often enough that variants of a melody might be heard in both settings. It could happen, for example, when a party situation demanded that each person offer a song: after the standard 'party songs', people would sing whatever they could – most likely work songs (see Takeuchi 1980: 312). Of course, one normally chose the most melodic and textually interesting work songs, not a simple *kakegoe*.

The most common terms for traditional songs suitable for parties are *(o)zashiki-uta* ('parlour songs') and *sakamori-uta* ('drinking songs'). Although not all such parties were held in the 'parlour', there was always *sake* present. A subset of party songs is *iwai-uta* ('celebration songs'), which are specifically congratulatory and may be treated as quasi-ritual; 'The Rich Man's Mountain', whose omission destroyed a marriage (§2.4.2), is an example.[39]

The term *ozashiki-uta* actually covers a wide range of song types. Most often it designates quiet, refined solo songs such as 'Yamanaka Bushi' **(CD15)**, which were linked both thematically and in reality with the urban pleasure quarters and the women who worked there. Yamanaka was a small rural spa town in Ishikawa Prefecture which flourished during the Edo period:

omae misometa / kyonen no gogatsu / shikamo ayame no / yu no naka de
I fell for you / last year, in May, / in an iris-scented / hot bathing pool.

A song like this might be brought home by a resident returning from a spa visit. The small-town geisha, if generally less talented musically than her big-city counterpart, did play shamisen and could often 'sell' a song by force of personality (aided by the boozy ambience and sexual energy of the context). And in a way she *was* literally selling the song. Many a peasant spent more than he could afford on visits to such women – and much of their time together might be spent singing the latest popular song (*hayariuta*).

Kamigōri Bushi o / kōte mo narae / shirihane-goe ni / odayaka ni
'Kamigōri Bushi' – / learn it even if you have to buy it, / with its vocal offglides, / smooth and calm. (Awaji 1825: no.53)

The geisha also entertained customers with a livelier type of *ozashiki-uta*, frequently called *sawagi-uta* ('boisterous songs'). An example is the comical song from Kumamoto Prefecture, 'Otemoyan' **(CD23)**, laden with local dialect and suggestive yet obscure puns.

Otemoyan, / anta kono goro / yomeiri shita de wa nai kai na / yomeiri shita kot'a shita batten / goteidon ga gujappe daru ken / mada sakazuk'ya senjatta . . .
'Otemoyan, / the other day / you got married, didn't you?' / 'I did get married, but / my husband has a pockmarked face, so / we haven't made it official yet . . .'

Drums, hand-gongs and flutes could be added to such a song, and improvised dancing of a comical and/or licentious nature was sure to occur.

Frequent in such songs is a rhythmically spoken *hayashi* interlude or postlude
(see §1.6.7). These are usually humorous, nonsensical and/or licentious and,
lacking melody, can be performed even by those who lack confidence in their
singing, like 'rap' **(CD12)**.

Wedding songs are not officially part of the ceremony but rather of the
celebration that follows. Such a party may well, aided by alcohol, slide into
extreme boisterousness and licentiousness, but each community has certain
songs that must be sung. Certain auspicious verses are likely to crop up in
such songs throughout Japan. Here are three verses sung by a group of elderly
women to local melodies, during a celebration at the house of Chida Minosuke
in Iwasaki, Iwate Prefecture, on New Year's Day 1979. (Pine, tortoise and crane
are symbols of longevity.)

> omae ya hyaku made / wash'ya kujūku made / tomo ni shirage no / haeru
> made
>   You [will live] to a hundred, / and I to ninety-nine, / until our hair / has grown
> white together.
>   medeta medeta no / wakamatsu-sama yo / eda mo sakaete / ha mo shigeru
>   Auspicious, auspicious, / the young pine: / its branches flourish / and its
> leaves [needles] proliferate.
>   kono ya zashiki wa / medetai zashiki / naka ni tsuru-kame / mai-asobu
>   The parlour of this house / is an auspicous parlour: / inside, the crane and
> tortoise / dance and sport together.

Next an old man performed a solo passage of Noh singing, leading into yet
another congratulatory folk song, then to yet another which repeated one of
the above verses. Then a woman in her thirties offered an *enka*, and a girl
aged around five sang a Japanese translation of the 1876 American song 'My
Grandfather's Clock'. These last two songs are not auspicious by nature –
unless we see a *kotodama*-like reference to longevity in the lines, 'A hundred
years without stopping, together with grandpa, tick-tock (*chiku-taku*).' In
earlier centuries as today, no doubt, wedding parties accommodated such
popular songs along with the quasi-compulsory, quasi-ritual congratulatory
ones.

2.4.5 Bawdy songs

In Japanese folk song, verses about sexual intercourse, sleeping together and
genitalia are common enough that one song claims (hyperbolically):

> uta no monku wa / kazukazu aredo / shikijō no hairanu / uta wa nai
>   Song texts / are countless, but / a song without sexual content / cannot be
> found. (Ochiai 1980: 939)

There is no single Japanese term for such songs, though *bareuta* is perhaps the most common; the adjective *hiwai*, close to the English word 'bawdy', is also often used. These terms can embrace the full range from mild *double-entendres* to hard-core verbal pornography, but implies most readily a sort of middle range of explicitness. There is a term *shunka*, literally 'spring song', 'spring' being a common euphemism for sex. *Shunka*, however, embraces any and all bawdy songs, whether *min'yō* or otherwise (as in Soeda 1966, the major work on the phenomenon).[40]

Such lyrics, however, are rarely heard in public anymore. In the past, bawdy lyrics surfaced in various situations. They could enliven the work-place, distracting from arduous labour. And they were expected during any alcohol-fuelled party, accompanied perhaps by blatantly sexual comical dancing with various objects representing genitalia.

In agricultural ritual songs, sexual lyrics often perform a more serious function. Thus in the rice transplanting song cycle translated by Hoff (1971; §2.4.2), references to sex and procreation function as a sort of sympathetic magic to increase crop fertility.

Sex was not a taboo topic in rural Japan, at least if approached with humour. Embree notes (1939: 195): 'While the actual sex act is very private, jokes about it and imitations of it in dances are both free and frequent. Young children, especially boys, often play at sex games, jokingly chasing girls and exposing themselves.' By the time Embree was writing, school education had reduced the sexual openness of younger women in particular (ibid.: 194), but older women and men could still enliven a party or a workplace with earthy banter and songs. This example uses a humorous term for a woman's genitals:

yucha s'man batten / uchi no kaka unago / kesa mo hagama de / bobo aruta
  I beg your pardon, but / my wife is a lady: / even this morning, in a rice kettle / her *bobo* she washed. (Embree 1939: 109; re-translated)

Traditional Japanese were not, obviously, without modesty: it is said that those who danced and sang 'Echigo Odori' (Niigata Pref.) wore towels to hide their faces so as to feel free to sing bawdy verses.[41] The following was apparently one of the less explicit verses:

nushi no aru hana / otte koso otoko / nushi no nai hana / dare mo oru
  A flower with a husband, / pluck it and you're a real man. / A flower without a husband, / anyone could pluck.

The range of sexual expression ran the gamut from subtle to blatant, from heartfelt to teasing. Most sexual verses are from the male viewpoint (regardless of the singer's gender). There are, however, many lyrics written from the viewpoint of the women of the pleasure quarters, who are now generally called *geisha*. Most traditional geisha were either raised in the pleasure quarters or, more often, sold into legal servitude by impoverished peasant parents. Their main hope of liberation lay in marriage to a wealthy patron. As such hopes were most often dashed, geisha lyrics often deal with the fickleness of men and the impossibility of establishing a lasting relationship. Many of these songs were written by the women themselves to sing with shamisen. In musical and textual style they often resemble (and some may even be considered) *kouta* or *hauta*, or their livelier relatives *zokkyoku* and *dodoitsu*. The lyrics tend to be poignant rather than humorous, and much more allusive and elusive than those of village origin. Typical verses of this style:

> semete hitoyo sa karine ni mo / tsuma to ichigon iwaretara / kono ichinen mo harubeki ni / doshita inga de kataomoi / iyagarashansu kao mireba / watash'ya guchi yue nao kawai
> Sleeping together a single night, / could I but hear the single word 'wife', / this yearning would be dispelled. / What karma makes me love in vain? / Seeing the face that doesn't care for me, / fool that I am, I love it all the more.
> ('Okamoto Shinnai')

> anata wa goten no yaezakura / watash'ya kakine no asagao yo / ikura hodo yoku saita tote / goten no sakura ni todokanai
> You are the cherry tree of the mansion; / I am the morning glory on the fence. / However well I may blossom, / I cannot attain the cherry tree of the mansion.
> ('Mamurogawa Ondo')

The latter verse in particular expresses the gulf in social status separating the singer from her wealthier patrons.

As elsewhere, Japanese folk song collections rarely reflect the frequency with which sexually explicit lyrics were actually sung. Only the less direct verses were likely to be collected and published.[42] Machida Kashō gave some insights into the reasons (3 June 1980). Recording material for the early volumes of the *Nihon min'yō taikan*, he and his colleagues were concerned with 'sound, not words': the tunes were the important element, so they neither sought bawdy (*hiwai*) lyrics nor printed them if offered. Besides, he said, 'those weren't the important lyrics'. (I failed to ask why.) Moreover, the singers would stop performing such lyrics as soon as the microphone was set up.

At an afternoon tea session with several elderly village women in Iwasaki, Iwate in 1988, one verse caused the group to dissolve in laughter. The combination of the singer's missing dentures, local dialect and, possibly, elusive *double-entendre* left me perplexed. Could they perhaps explain to me what I had missed? Alas, while elderly women in particular enjoy singing such lyrics, it is another matter to get them to *explain* them, especially to a younger male foreign academic. So we agreed that one woman would later explain to her daughter, who would explain to her husband, who would explain to me. (I never did get the answer.)

On other occasions, generally in festive settings, I did collect several bawdy verses from elderly women, and from men of all ages but mostly over forty. I never once actually asked for bawdy lyrics (no, really): they always arose naturally.

To suggest the range of bawdiness, here, without comment, are typical specimens from across the spectrum. Singers receive the anonymity they would almost certainly desire.

kawaigararete / neta yo mo gozaru / naite akashita / yo mo gozaru
   Being loved and adored / I've spent many a night. / Awake all night crying – / I've had nights like that, too. ('Shinodayama Inekari Uta'; rice-reaping song)

arisō de nasasō de / nasasō de arisō de / arisō de nai no wa / mara no hone
   Seems to be there, then it isn't; / seems not to be there, then it is. / What seems to be there but isn't / is the bone in a penis. ('Sōran Bushi'; fishing song)

ora 'e no nēchan to / tonari no anchan to / hatake no sumako de / ippatsu yarakashita / fuku kami motane de / kabocha no happa de / kururiitto fuitaba / mikka mo itekatta
   My older sister / and the guy next door / went to a corner of the field / for a quickie. / No paper to wipe with, so / using a pumpkin leaf / they wiped themselves – / and were sore for three days. ('Akita Ondo'; Bon/party song)

hito no kaka surya / isogashi mon da to kita mon da / yumoji himo toku / fundoshi hazusu / ireru moch'ageru / yogaru ki o yaru / kami dasu nuku fuku / atari mimawasu / geta mekkeru yara / nigeru yara
   If you're gonna do it with someone's wife, / you'll be busy: / untie her slip, / take off your loincloth, / stick it in, get it on, / satisfy yourself, / take out paper, pull out, wipe off, / take a look around, / find your sandals, / make your getaway. ('Akita Ondo')

hitoyo nete mite / nehada ga yokerya / tsuma to nasaryō yo / matsudai made mo
   Let's try sleeping together one night – / if our skins feel good together, / you'll be my wife / until the end of time. (Gifu Pref.; NMZ: 3.262)

Ono no machi no / Horokuya no musume / bobo ni ke ga nai to / azana o sasare / kuma no kawa nara / te no hira hodo hoshiya / naka kiriakete / nikawa de tsukete / ima koso haeta ni / nazete miyo
   In Ono Town, / the daughter at Horokuya Inn / hasn't got any pubic hair, / so they say. / Wish I had some bearskin, / about a hand's width worth. / I'd slice it down the middle, / stick it on with glue, / [and say] 'You've just grown some – / think I'll give it a rub.' (Gifu Pref.; NMZ: 3.261)

nēsan wa / Sanzu no kawa no watashibune / shinikuru hito o / minna noseru / watashi mo shi ni kita / nosete tabe
   She is / the ferry-boat across the River Sanzu [Buddhist equivalent of the Styx]: / all the people who have died, / she gives them a ride. / I too have 'died' [homonym: come to 'do it']; / give me a ride. (rice-hulling song; Machida 1964: no.89)

2.4.6 Songs of itinerant musicians

The three preceding sections dealt with songs which, whatever their origin, had come to be performed by villagers in our 'typical' hamlet. In addition, all but the most isolated hamlets would be visited by some of the several types of professional performers who roamed the countryside. These itinerants often performed a difficult repertoire to a standard which the locals could not hope to match. Many of their songs were long ballads (*kudoki*) sometimes lasting an hour or more. Still, some villagers did attempt to learn.[43]

Visits often followed a regular and eagerly anticipated schedule. At the New Year's season, performers of genres such as *manzai*, *daikoku-mai* and *harukoma* visited at least the wealthier houses to offer a song and dance of good luck for the year to come. Typically there were two performers, who might also play drum and/or shamisen. Songs about Daikoku, god of wealth, have passed into the village tradition in many areas **(CD24, 25)**:

> ake no hō kara Fuku-Daikoku / maikonda. . .
> From the east Daikoku the Wealthy / has come dancing in. . . ('Akita Daikoku Mai')

Like English wassailers or west African praise singers, the Japanese artists sang nothing but good of their potential patrons:

> kono ya no dannasama / o-kokoro yoshi de / shōbai hanjō de / mōkedashita
> The master of this house / is a good-hearted man. / Success and prosperity / have been his. ('Daikoku Mai', Yamagata Pref.)

The recipients of the performance were expected to express their gratitude in offerings of rice or other consumables, or in cash. And as in west Africa, if no payment was forthcoming, insults might replace praise (Groemer 1999: 209–10).

Sweets vendors (*ameuri*) made the rounds of northern Japan in particular, in ones or twos, playing an instrument (gong, flute, shamisen), singing and dancing to attract customers (Takeuchi 1973b: 202–28; Groemer 1999: 207–8, 217–8). These colourful performer-merchants made quite an impression on villagers, who often tried to learn their long ballads (Takeuchi 1976: 26).

Many other artists made the rounds, either performing *al fresco* or being invited into a home. Shadow-play masters (*kagee-shi*) roamed western Japan (Takeuchi 1973b: 135–50). *Yomiuri*, sellers of song-sheets, fanned out from the cities, singing from their printed ballad-sheets (*kawaraban*), which they then sold to literate locals (ibid.: 88–100; Groemer 1994b, 1995). These were the equivalent of the English broadside ballads: generally of urban authorship, but in a quasi-folk idiom. The main difference is that the Japanese song-sheets did not tell which tune to use. The song-seller or his customers could set the lyrics to any convenient melody. (See also Mitamura 1926; Ono 1960: 322.)

The long *kudoki* sung by many itinerants drew their themes from a common fund of stories, shared with the Kabuki and puppet theatres and other popular Edo-period performance genres. Among dozens of themes, the most popular were the tragic love stories: Suzuki Mondo, O-Natsu and Seijūrō, Shirai Gonpachi, Yaoya O-Shichi, Oguri Hangan. This emphasis reflects the extent of the impediments to romantic love in traditional Japan.

Performance of *kudoki* was largely left to specialists, mainly due to length. Among *kudoki* printed in Narita 1978, the longest runs to 603 lines of twelve to fourteen syllables; one of the three specimens translated by Hearn (1894) takes twenty-six pages of English. Thus, until printed versions could be had (and read), the villagers largely settled for looking forward to visits by professionals. That the villagers did learn some ballads from song-sheets is clear from the striking similarity of variants of many surviving *kudoki*, especially in western Japan (Takeuchi 1973b: 100). Also, sometimes a group such as the village Young Men's Association (§2.5.1) would hire a professional to stay awhile and teach them a *kudoki* (Takeuchi 1976: 28–9). A *kudoki* which took root in a village was likely to become a Bon-dance song or occasionally a foundation-pounding song, since these activities could accommodate long ballads sung by a song-leader. Even for these occasions, *kudoki* singing was often entrusted to a specialist from a nearby village (§2.4.2).

The most significant of the itinerants from the viewpoint of modern *min'yō* may have been the *goze*, blind female balladeers. In traditional Japan, music was one of the few professions open to the blind. Although the origins of the *goze* are uncertain, during the Edo period they played a major role in spreading folk and popular songs. They evolved a rigid social code for the transmission of their art and the control of performance rights. The best-documented are the *goze* of Echigo (modern Niigata Prefecture) whose tradition survives vestigially to the present day. (See Groemer 2007; Saito 1975; Ichikawa 1969; Oyama 1977: 299f.; Fritsch 1992, 1996; R8, 9).

References to *goze* abound in nineteenth-century literature and art. In the 1830s the woodblock artist Hiroshige depicted a trio, their shamisen on their backs, along the highway linking Edo and Kyoto (Fig. 2.1). In 1825, the writer Takizawa Bakin reported that the Echigo *goze* had started visiting the villages of Musashino, north of Tokyo, each winter (Asano 1983: 81). These Echigo *goze* travelled northwards, too, even into Hokkaido.

Sugimoto Kikue (1898–1983), the 'last' of the traditional Echigo *goze*, was the principal informant for most recent researchers. Her early career seems similar to that of the *goze* of Hiroshige and Bakin's day. (The following information is mainly from Oyama 1977.) Blind from age five, she was adopted into a *goze* house a year later. Progressing rapidly, she soon was sent out with a team of six or seven women (including a sighted 'guide') to cover routes decided at the annual meeting of the local *goze* guild. Each village they visited had at least one large house which acted as a '*goze* lodging' (*goze-yado*).[44] During the day, in groups of two or three, they performed door-to-door throughout the village. In the evening, the villagers gathered at the *goze-yado* for a full performance.

The *goze*'s repertoire was large and varied. Most popular were the *danmono* – ballads so long that they were divided into sections (*dan*; **CD11**). Only the shorter ballads were officially called *kudoki*. In addition, the *goze* had to know the latest popular songs (*hayariuta*) and other miscellaneous ditties. Sugimoto Kikue could sing some ten *danmono*, ten *kudoki* and dozens of shorter songs (Oyama 1977: 292). Among the shorter songs, in her case, are several 'new *min'yō*' from the 1920s and 1930s, especially those dealing with her home prefecture, Niigata (such as 'Tōkamachi Kouta'). 'Sendō Kouta', one of the first of the 'folk-song-style popular songs' (§3.4.3), was added to her repertoire in 1922, the same year it appeared on 78 rpm – like her nineteenth-century forebears, she was quick to learn the latest *hayariuta*. In the same year she learned 'Kago no Tori', another popular song which used a folk-like scale but a very untraditional 3/4 metre. She also performed New Year's items such as 'Harukoma' when necessary. Comic and/or bawdy songs were also highly appreciated by her audiences. One such is 'Hesoana Kudoki' ('Ballad of the Bellybutton'), a parody of a love-suicide *kudoki*:

> aware sae naru ka na / Hesoana Kudoki / kuni wa doko yo to / tazunete kikeba / kuni wa Uchimata / Fundoshi-gōri . . .
>   Oh how tragic, / the Ballad of the Bellybutton! / In what province, / you ask? / It's Crotch Province, / Loincloth County . . . (Oyama 1977: 298)

As professionals dependent on public patronage, the *goze* would try to sing whatever the audience wanted. They were 'singers', not 'folk singers'; they sang *uta*, not *min'yō*. Aratake Tami (b. 1911), a *goze* from Kagoshima in Kyūshū, stressed that she would sing 'anything – popular songs, army songs, children's songs, "new folk songs" and so forth' (pers. comm., 1979).

In 1901, there were eighty-nine *goze* based in the town of Takada, one of two large *goze* centres in Niigata; by the 1930s there were only twenty-three (Ichikawa 1969: 25). Sugimoto Kikue and her two companions, the last survivors, made their final trek in 1964 – about the time she was 'discovered' by *min'yō* researchers. She was designated a Living National Treasure in 1971.

There were also blind male itinerants, whose repertoire and lives resembled those of the *goze* but who were not organized into 'houses'. It was from such men that the flashy, powerful Tsugaru-jamisen style emerged in the Tsugaru region of Aomori Prefecture in the late 1800s (§§2.5.3, 4.6.1, 7.2; Suda et al. 1998). The most famous Tsugaru-jamisen artist of the twentieth century was Takahashi Chikuzan (1910–98); his life is described in his autobiography (Takahashi 1975, translated in Groemer 1999) and in Kuramitsu 1976. This genre is popular today with many young Japanese who do not otherwise care for *min'yō*.

The seemingly romantic life-style of such itinerants captured the public imagination, spawning two award-winning feature-length films in 1977: *Chikuzan Hitori-tabi* (*The Lonely Travels of Chikuzan*, released in the West as *The Life of Chikuzan*), based on his autobiography; and *Hanare-goze O-Rin* (*The Ostracized Goze O-Rin*; English version called *Melody in Grey*), set in 1918.

Most itinerant performers were treated with ambivalence: highly appreciated though their visits were, they were accorded very low social status. The blind performers of the north were often disparagingly called beggars (*kojiki*, *hoido*); the males might be called, or call themselves, 'priests' (*bosama*), which in this case was just a slightly more polite term for beggars. The Daikoku dance seen by Hearn in Shimane in 1891 was being transmitted within an outcast village (Hearn 1894: 285f.). Takahashi Chikuzan relates that in the 1920s in Aomori City, 'people who went around begging all used to live together', whether in special flophouses or in a graveyard. This included 'umbrella repairmen, guys who made leather drumheads, dog butchers . . ., reciters of *Naniwa bushi, shakuhachi* players. All kinds of *geinin* [performers] were there' (Groemer 1999: 207). Perhaps this disparagement of *geinin*, especially blind ones, was why Chikuzan preferred to list himself in the Tokyo telephone directory as a masseur rather than a musician as late as the early 1970s (Nishitsunoi Masahiro, pers. comm. 1980).

This brings us to the wandering mendicant shakuhachi players known as *komusō* ('priests of nothingness'). Originally and officially, they were members of the Fuke sect of Zen, playing solo shakuhachi as a spiritual exercise, not primarily a musical or economic one. Their meditative solo music held little attraction for most villagers. The instrument itself, however, was eventually to become a major factor in modern folk song.[45]

2.4.7 *The villager travels*

Song migration did not depend only on itinerant musicians. Visits to festivals or to regional market towns led to interaction with people from nearby villages. And country folk did occasionally have opportunities to travel far from home, even before modern advances in transport. Migrant labour provided the chief example. There were full-time workers such as pack-horse drivers and sailors, and seasonal labourers such as fishermen, textile workers and *sake* brewers. They might take with them a work song from home to adapt for use in the new situation: Hokkaido's famous fishnet-hauling song 'Sōran Bushi' was a modification of a boat-loading song from Aomori (Hughes 2000). They often returned home with songs learned at the workplace or from the singing girls who catered to the workers. Several examples of such song migration have been given above. Trips to the big city or to nearby administrative 'castle towns' were rarer but occasionally necessary, as when paying taxes. Indeed, the court song genres *saibara* and *fuzoku*, which flourished in the Heian period (794–1198), are commonly held to be adaptations of country songs brought to the capital by tax-bearing peasants.

Religious pilgrimages provided one of the few other socially sanctioned excuses for long-distance travel during the Edo period.[46] The Ise shrines in Mie Prefecture have long been the national focus of Japan's most popular pilgrimage. Villagers often formed associations called *kō* in order to accumulate funds to send representatives to Ise or other celebrated sacred spots.[47] Failing that, one could simply slip out of the village and make one's way to Ise, for pilgrims were often given free lodging and food. In addition to its religious significance, the pilgrimage provided much-needed relief from the pressures of village life. In certain years the pilgrimage urge would sweep the country: over 2 million people visited Ise during four months in 1771, and almost 5 million in the spring of 1830 (Matsumoto 1965: 172–8). Male travellers in particular spent much time and money in the teahouses of Ise.

From the teahouse women or from other pilgrims, travellers would learn some version of the song 'Ise Ondo'. Originally sung by the lumberjacks who hauled trees for the periodic rebuilding of the shrine, it became the representative song of Ise. Variants are found in every corner of Japan, as dance, work or party songs; they are most immediately recognized by a refrain beginning something like *yātokose yoiyana* and ending *nan de mo se*. Even the isolated village of Shiiba in the mountains of Miyazaki uses a version as a foundation-pounding song (**CD26**).

A traveller might hear new songs whatever the purpose of the journey. As opportunities to travel increased after Meiji, so did the chances to learn songs. Hot-spring resorts had their associated songs, praising the curative powers of local waters and/or women. Not only 'folk songs' were acquired. For example, Buddhist pilgrims might learn the folk-style hymns known as *goeika*, often relating to specific temples on popular pilgrimage circuits.

2.5 Folk song performance and transmission

2.5.1 Institutionalized transmission

Traditional rural songs tended to be learned casually rather than through formal, systematized teaching. Performance situations too were predominantly informal. It was seldom necessary to make a conscious effort to learn a work or party song of the 'folk-lyric' type: verses were short and could be remembered after a few hearings, and anyhow there was freedom to omit, add or alter verses almost at will. One would simply listen to various performances, select (consciously or unconsciously) favourite passages of melody or lyrics and assemble one's own version. (See Etchūya's comments in §3.3.3 below.) Even in the case of Itō Moyo (§2.3), who consciously set out to learn as many songs as possible, her main *modus operandi* was simply to join in every work and party situation in order to pick up more verses. Occasionally she would use her free time to ask a favourite singer to sing a song over to her a few times, but 'these weren't lessons (*okeiko*) or anything like that, it was just for fun'.[48] Sasaki Motoharu of Hokkaido (b. 1926) recalls that his grandfather, an amateur singer known far and wide for his skill during the early twentieth century, was often visited by other singers who would ask for his evaluation of their performances; no payment was involved.

More formal lessons were possible for certain types of song. To learn geisha songs, for example, one could become a customer (see §2.4.4). Once the customer had paid for her company, the geisha would happily teach the latest *hayariuta* or *kouta*. This was how Murata Yaroku (1851–1926) learned the song 'Oiwake Bushi' in the 1870s (§3.3.1). In such cases, literate students might have used a printed *hayariuta* lyrics collection. The development of formal teaching of the newly recognized genre of *min'yō* itself is discussed in Chapter 3.

Conscious effort was also needed to learn a long *kudoki* ballad. This could be done by paying an itinerant singer, by requesting guidance from a villager who knew one, or by referring to a printed broadside (§2.4.6).

Until perhaps the late 1960s, a person who devoted too much time to singing and learning songs risked being labelled a *dōrakumono*, a pleasure-bent carouser. Certainly some of the best village singers managed to learn so many songs so well only by shirking work, spending money on drink and on travel to consult experts, and otherwise being less than responsible members of the community. They were viewed with the same ambivalence as the itinerant musicians. If a child showed too much interest in singing, its parents were likely to admonish it: 'Don't act like a *goze*/beggar/*dōrakumono*.' Sasaki Motoharu said of his grandfather (mentioned above): 'He loved to sing – he was a *dōrakumono*, so life was very difficult for my grandmother.'

Some songs and instrumental music were considered too important to village life to leave to chance. The principal examples were ritual music and certain work songs important to the timing of the work, such as *sake*-making songs (§2.4.3). Due to their importance, the latter were not only sung while making *sake* but also practised at other times.

We noted (§2.4.2) that the music and dance for village rituals was often taught intensively for a few weeks just prior to the ritual. This might apply also to Bon dance songs, although these were usually more widely known already. In ensuring the success of such performances, two types of village institution played a major role: Young Men's Associations and *miyaza*.

Young Men's Associations (*wakamonogumi*, *wakashū* etc.) varied greatly in both form and functions (Varner 1977; Norbeck 1953). Members were typically all the hamlet's men from about age fifteen to forty. The Association often played the major role in organizing internal hamlet affairs, from members' moral education to arranging their marriages, from discipline and communal labour to festival preparations. At festival time, members would perform in plays or ritual dances, carry portable shrines, arrange and compete in quasi-ritual wrestling matches and so forth; participation was usually compulsory. They were often responsible for providing music for the Bon dance, whether this meant learning the music themselves or hiring outside musicians. This is still often true today, although the associations themselves have changed in character and name (§5.2).

Miyaza ('shrine guild') is the cover term for a type of institution which has been characterized as a 'socio-religious monopoly' (Davis 1976: 25). In origin it was a hereditary organization of (male) heads of a hamlet's elite households, usually the most senior settlers, which exercised exclusive control over access to the hamlet deities in order to legitimize its members' political, social and economic dominance. Such dominance weakened during the Edo period, and by Meiji non-exclusivist hamlet-wide parishes were common, with all or most village households as parishioners (*ujiko*) of the tutelary deity.

Most performance events controlled by *miyaza* (or similar institutions) would be *minzoku geinō* rather than *min'yō*.[49] Takeuchi, however, located a useful example of the latter (1978: 183ff.). Visiting Tarao Hamlet (Shiga Pref.) in 1965, he found that all male residents became eligible at age fifteen for *miyaza* membership. Until the early twentieth century, their induction ceremony featured a congratulatory song by senior members. The song, 'Goshaku Tenugui', descends from a seventeenth-century *hayariuta* whose traces linger throughout Japan. Here it had become associated with *miyaza* ceremonials and was supposedly excluded from other settings. Thus an elderly woman, asked whether she knew the song, responded in the negative: 'I'm a woman, you know, and besides, I wasn't born in this village' (ibid.: 185). Since only men belonged to the *miyaza*, women rarely heard the song.

Incidentally, children's songs (*warabe-uta*) form a separate repertoire with fairly recognizable features: regular rhythm, syllabic text setting, etc. (Koizumi 1969; Berger 1969; Koizumi & Hughes 2000; Machida & Asano 1968). Many are linked with specific games or movements. They are largely transmitted from child to child without adult intervention. (A different category of songs is taught in schools; see §2.3.) Children may, of course, sing adult songs as well; most of today's professional folk singers started doing so in early childhood.

2.5.2 *Owning and stealing songs*

The above example of a song sung only by members of a *miyaza* suggests a question: Was there in traditional Japan anything approximating song ownership as found in many other cultures? Consider three disparate examples.

Among Australian aborigines, songs were owned by communities or kin groups and are not to be given to outsiders (Clunies Ross & Wild 1984). By contrast, Navajo curing chants are owned by individual ceremonialists who are theoretically free to 'give' them away (David McAllester, pers. comm. 1974). Finally, in twentieth-century England, the rural folk who used to gather to sing at a pub in Blaxhall, Suffolk, recognized a limited type of ownership: for any song of which a particular person had become the acknowledged master, it was considered wrong for anyone else to sing that song in the master's presence. The 'owner' could also pass the song on to someone else (Carole Pegg, pers. comm.; see also Dunn 1980).

In Japan, certainly some *minzoku geinō* and *min'yō* have been jealously guarded by a hamlet or a common-interest group, although I have never heard this described as 'ownership'. The motivations for such protectionism were diverse. Ritual performances could lose efficacy if transmitted to (or even watched by) outsiders. On the other hand, local pride might be the operative factor: I have heard performers from Okinawa to Iwate express the desire to prevent neighbouring hamlets from stealing the most admired features of their favourite *minzoku geinō*. This attitude has actually been sharpened in recent decades because of competition for prizes at concours and for government recognition (discussed later).

A variant of this attitude characterized the Kichiseikai in Kichijōji (Tokyo) around 1980. The members were construction workers and volunteer firemen; traditionally these two professions were filled by the same people. A song type known as *kiyari* has long been one of the badges of membership in these professions, but few modern workers can sing them. The Kichiseikai was formed to correct this situation, and its members (fewer than twenty) met frequently to study *kiyari*. Although they strove to spread these songs among their co-workers, I got the definite impression that they wanted these songs to remain exclusive to their profession. This seems true of many s-pecialist songs today, such as those of our Niigata *sake* brewers (§2.4.3).

In Japanese performing arts in general, especially among professionals, features of music, dance or acting are often 'owned' and transmitted selectively. Such monopolization is one way of protecting one's livelihood, one's 'trade secrets'. In the imperial court in the 1840s, a court musician who had to play an instrument officially assigned to another family had to apply for a 'one-day licence' to perform; in 1147, a court musician who failed to get permission before playing a piece belonging to another family was castigated and forbidden to do so again (Nishiyama 1971: 271, 263). Many genres have 'secret pieces' (*hikyoku*), taught only to selected successors. (The *iemoto* system is discussed in §4.5.1.)

In conflict with this is a learning philosophy espoused frequently in many types of traditional performing arts: one 'steals the art' (*gei o nusumu*) of the best performers. This is often said with a twinkle in the eye. I have heard the phrase often from the older professional folk musicians of northeast Japan, who often travelled with *min'yō* troupes before the Second World War. Many a song or a shamisen riff was learned on such tours, for one could hear someone perform the same piece day after day for months on end. Performers such as Tsugaruya Suwako II (b. 1913) have assured me that 'stealing the art' has been the standard form of folk song transmission 'since ancient times' (*mukashi kara*). The very word 'steal', however, implies a degree of possession, if not ownership, by the 'victim', as well as a degree of value inhering in the object stolen. Thus, although the phrase is used widely today by *min'yō* enthusiasts, it may indeed have once been most appropriate in a context of competition such as might exist among professionals.

The two attitudes, ownership and theft, seldom clashed in the traditional village unless ritual efficacy or economic gain was at stake. If Itō Moyo wanted to sing 'Nanbu Sakata' exactly as another villager had, nobody was likely to object. If, however, a song was linked with a formalized competition of some sort, possessiveness might surface. In Yatsuo Town (Toyama Pref.), during an annual festival, representatives from different neighbourhoods compete in singing 'Etchū Owara' (**CD9**; R62). Through exposure at the festival, certain singers come to be considered masters (*meijin*) whose interpretations of the melody become models for others (Asano 1983: 84). Takami, interviewing performers around 1980, affirmed that the song is commonly transmitted through 'stealing', but also reported: 'it is difficult, they say, to assimilate good melodies of others since they . . . belong to the respective performers' (1981: 25, 21). It is not clear what sort of possession is implied. However, it is not a case of a particular *song* being owned, just a particular *version*, one person's approach to melody, rhythm and ornamentation. The expression *gei o nusumu* refers to stealing someone's *gei*, their 'art' – i.e. their interpretation. Thus the type of 'ownership' in Yatsuo differs from that in the Suffolk pub mentioned above.

2.5.3 Improvisation and composition

It is a truism among scholars that improvisation is rare in Japanese music. If 'improvisation' refers to the intentional introduction of a significant degree of unpredictable and unpremeditated melodic, textual or rhythmic material into a performance, then this is indeed true for all classical genres. The traditional folk world allowed relatively more freedom, but we need to specify what sorts of unpredictable events could occur.[50]

Traditional villagers rarely distinguished between improvisation and composition. Even the classical genres had no 'cult of the composer'. No examples parallel the author-identifying final verse ('If anyone asks you who wrote this song . . .') of some American folk songs. Nonetheless, novelty was prized in non-ritual song. A singer was valued partly for an ability to command a large stock of verses, whether via memorization, premeditated composition or improvisation. Occasionally singers might alter a melody or lyrics, or create new verses to the extent that the song would be identified with them. During Meiji, an Akita woodworker named Emazō did just that to a local party song; the resulting version was often called 'Emazō Jinku', 'Emazō's Song' (Asano 1983: 363; Nakai et al. 1972: 244), though anyone could sing it.

Let us focus first on lyrics. There is no record in recent times of the simultaneous complete improvisation (as opposed to alteration) of words and tune: the melody was always pre-selected.[51] One might distinguish four varieties of textual improvisation. First, a singer simply selected from the pre-existing fund of possible verses for a given song. This was by far the most common type, occurring with almost every performance of a party or work song. The 'fund' was vast: due to the dominance of 7–7–7–5 poetic metre and to the fragmented nature in 'folk-lyric' texts, most verses could be used in most songs. Such use was largely unconstrained by melodic considerations, for there is almost no relation between speech accent and melodic movement in Japanese folk song. There were few restrictions on the choice of verses. Even if the poetic metre differed, the melody could usually be adapted easily.[52] On rare occasions certain words were avoided as inauspicious; at a wedding party, for example, singing (or even saying) the word *kiru* ('cut') might jeopardize the new marital bond. A good singer was one who, besides ideally having a pleasing voice, was never at a loss for an appropriate verse.

In Iwasaki, Iwate Prefecture, in 1988, I attended an *ocha-kai* afternoon 'tea party': people who could not work the fields due to age or inclement weather would gather in someone's house to drink tea, sing and even dance. On this day several elderly women and one old man were present (Fig. 2.2). I asked them, between songs, whether they ever made up new verses. Oh no, said the ladies, somewhat horrified at the idea: we always sing the verses just as they have been passed on 'by generations of ancestors' (*senzo daidai*). Not true, said the old man, Chūichi: he often made up new verses. He then offered a version of a well-known local song with his self-composed verse. This verse, however, was one that occurs in many other songs around Japan, a common 'floating verse'. This struck me not as intentional deception but rather a matter of semantics; had I asked him directly, he might have acknowledged that he had adopted or adapted the verse from elsewhere. The women were expressing an ideology of respect for tradition and ancestors; the man was expressing a creative, risk-taking attitude more common among men than women in rural Japan.

This type of verse selection/adaptation might be referred to as *tsukuri-uta* or 'made-up song', but is also described with the word *sokkyō* – as are all cases of improvisation. Even quite elderly people use this Sino-Japanese word.

A second type of textual improvisation involved adapting the content of pre-existing verses to new situations. The name of a person, place or profession could be altered, as in this text family from the Chūgoku region: 'By what karma have I become a miner/wire maker/paper maker/raftsman/shellfish gatherer/wax-berry gatherer/cotton pounder/weaver?' In this case the rest of the verse also changed to match the profession: 'Spending my best years in a hole/Spending my best years in a reed hut/Working in water from early in the morning/Setting out, lunch in hand, from early in the morning . . .' etc. (**CD27**; Asano 1983: entries 163, 231, 521, 1816, 1872, 1898, 1934; R1, song 193). Surely this type of alteration generally resulted from a period of private ratiocination rather than emerging on the spot in public.

The third type is the improvisation of an entire verse. A good description of this process was elicited by Kawachi (1979: 206) from a man, born in Tsugaru around 1900, who commuted to the herring fisheries in the Kuril Islands every year from about 1925 to 1940: 'In those days, what sort of songs did you sing?' 'Let's see . . . Well, all kinds. Whatever we happened to see, we made a song and sang it. For example, "Over there they've put the kettle on . . ." and so on.' The aforementioned Akita carpenter, Emazō, reportedly improvised the following verse one evening when a pretty girl passed his door: 'Hey, girl, where are you going all alone? The sun is just setting; you'd better not go too far' (Asano 1983: 363). Verses such as these two would be unlikely to survive long on literary merit alone, but many currently popular verses surely arose in just this way.

In the 'tea party' session in Iwasaki described above, Chūichi described a situation in which anyone might safely risk a bit of creativity. Foundation tamping (*dozuki*) and pile driving (*monki-zuki*) involved up to a dozen men and women pulling on ropes in coordination, to repeatedly raise and drop a heavy pounding stone or log, daily for up to a week. Songs kept everyone in time. But the strenuous work made singing difficult, so the melodies were fairly simple, and the lyrics could be largely nonsense syllables – anything so long as the timing was kept. Here in Iwasaki, no outside specialist *ondo-tori* was hired: the villagers provided their own singing. A tired singer would look around to see whose face was least red from exertion, and then call on that person to continue. Then the new singers would have to *monku o koshiraeru* – 'make the lyrics'. These must not be too complex or serious, they must keep the mood lively to distract everyone from the hard labour. He sang the following humorous example:

kore kara sanchō da / nan tara sonata wa *ē ya'arē* / koshitsuke mita zo ya / go-kagetsu da ka
    Starting now, pull three times. / Hey, you over there, / I've seen your waist-line: / Five months [pregnant], are you?

Or he might sing, 'Last night I stole a fish from my neighbour's fishpond.' Such 'nonsensical verses' (*mudauta*) could be freely invented, the rules of poetic metre safely disregarded in the heat of the moment. Each line is followed by a meaningless *hayashi-kotoba* that helps keep the beat: variants of *ē yara yarē*. Did he ever sing one of the long *kudoki* that are sometimes sung by professionals in such situations? No, he just 'looked at everyone's faces' and sang whatever came to mind. The women agreed: more polished creativity was neither possible nor necessary under such conditions.

In a singing session in Shiiba village, Miyazaki Pref., in 1994 (captured on recording R63, disc 1, track 24; p. 22 of notes by Kojima Tomiko), as verses to a grass-cutting song were being sung by several people in turn, the last singer could not dredge up an existing verse and so created one:

> minna gama dase *yo* / ano hi ga ireba / tsurete modorite / daite neru
> Every one be patient: / when the sun sets / we'll all take someone home / and sleep with them.

Such creativity was rare enough that the singers laughingly discussed it afterwards.

Improvisation of this type is traced back to courting rites known as *utagaki*, mentioned in Japan's earliest written works of the eighth and ninth centuries (see Asano 1983: 73). On certain nights, scholars believe, young people would gather to sing, dance, eat and make love. A man sang (improvised?) part of a verse, and if a woman could not complete it she had to be his 'wife for a night'. In recent centuries such song 'duels', with or without sexual overtones, were often held in shrines or temples on the eve of a major festival, lasting until dawn. Ossified relics, shorn of improvisation, survive in several places (see Asano 1983: entries 296, 541, 2353).

The only living example preserving the improvisational element to any extent is the *kakeuta* tradition of Akita Prefecture (NMZ: 2.152–3; Miyazaki 1999a, b, c). All-night singing sessions were long held at certain temples and shrines as a religious offering, though the lyrics were secular. (The same sometimes occurred at hot springs.) Pairs of singers, perhaps originally man and woman, exchanged partly improvised verses on a range of subjects. *Kakeuta* survives through conscious preservation in the form of two judged contests (with prizes) in August and September, one being held at Kanazawa Hachimangū shrine. Lyrics are sung, mostly in 7–7–7–5 metre, to a single tune, 'Senboku Nikata Bushi', a local song whose melody moves slowly enough to allow time to construct a reply; the accompanying shakuhachi also plays a brief interlude between verses, for the same reason. Current competitors are mostly quite elderly. Singers are judged both on their voices and on the quality of their lyrics. Akita-born musician Takahashi Yūjirō (pers. comm.) has heard that the improvised lyrics were often quite bawdy and mocking, but twentieth-century collections of actual lyrics, as usual, show none of the seriously bawdy examples, and even the mocking of one's opponent has been toned down or indeed replaced by mutual praise – all in keeping with post-war concepts of public behaviour as well as the attempt to upgrade the image of *min'yō*. Here is a typical sequence of verses from a contest in 1974 (NMZ: 2.152–3):

A: omae no nodo no sono utsukushisa / aba no horeta mo muri ga nai

Your voice (lit.: throat) is so beautiful, it's no wonder your wife fell in love with you.

B: horeta hareta wa mukashi no hanashi / ima wa binbō de nodo kareta

Falling in love and celebrating our wedding – that was long ago; now I'm poor and my voice has withered.

A: nodo ga kareta to kenson suru na / anna yoi ie dar'ya tateta

Your voice has withered? Don't be so modest. That fine house of yours, who built that?

B: ie wa tateta ga shakkin shotte / aba no koshimaki shichi oita

I built the house, all right, but I'm buried in debt; even the wife's underskirt has gone to the pawnshop.

Some textual themes are set. Also, since around 1965 reference to current events and incidents have been encouraged, so that the 1998 contests featured verses about a poisoned can of curry on a supermarket shelf, political corruption, and so forth (Miyazaki 1999b, c). Advance preparation is obviously possible, and verses (originally improvised or not) often recur. In the mid-twentieth century, one *haiku* scholar was known to write potential verses and teach them to good singers (Miyazaki 1999a: 46). Still, on-the-spot improvisation is frequent, since one must respond to one's opponent. Here is an exchange from 1998 (Miyazaki 1999b, c):

A: fukyō tsuzukeba jiken mo ōi / Nikata utatte fukyō tobasō

Recession continues, incidents abound. Let's sing 'Nikata Bushi' and fly them away.

B: utatte tobu yō na fukyō ja nai yo / ginkō mondai kaiketsu saki yo

You can't fly this recession away with singing: first, solve the banking problems.

A: tonde kuru no wa Kita-Chōsen no misairu dake de / watash'ya iranai hoshiku nai

The only thing flying is North Korean missiles; I don't need or want them.

One verse referred to the fact that the contest was being videotaped at the behest of the Ministry of Education, who planned to distribute copies nationwide:

Monbushō no bideo ba Kokkai ni motte iki / misete okure yo kono sakebi

Take this Ministry of Education video to the Diet and let them see the uproar [among the competitors, about the dire situation of the Japanese economy].

The fourth type of improvisation is of long narrative songs. The work of Parry and Lord on Yugoslav epic singers and the Homeric tradition has attuned us to the question of formulaic 'recomposition' in oral tradition (see

Lord 1960). The closest analogy to this phenomenon in Japan was in the *danmono* of the blind *goze* (§2.4.5). However, the *goze*'s *danmono* were much shorter than the Yugoslav epics – rarely over an hour – and had more the nature of memorized than re-created texts. Comparison of song melody, shamisen part and lyrics of performances by Sugimoto Kikue twenty or more years apart reveals an occasional line or small group of lines added or missing, several alterations in modifiers or grammatical particles, moderate changes in musical detail, but no large-scale reworking.[53]

This leads us to vocal melodic improvisation. Clear examples are difficult to find. In singing, there is little evidence for a conscious aesthetic of intentional novelty (except among Tsugaru singers, discussed below). Villagers singing together were more likely to comment on textual divergences in their performances than on melodic variation, even though the latter might seem more prominent to us.[54] (A typical example of heterophonic melodic divergence with textual near-unity is heard in the 'unison' singing of three *goze* on **CD11**.)

Variation by a single individual in successive renditions seems to have gone largely unnoticed; it was usually unconscious and not termed improvisation. An anecdote: In 1981 I was asked by Iwate Broadcasting Company to co-host live television coverage of the Chaguchagu Umakko festival in Morioka, which involves praying for the health of work-horses. I was also asked to sing the pack-horse driver's song linked with the festival, which I had heard but never studied. Since I was about to leave Japan and had no time to learn it, the director agreed that I could instead sing another local song. Arriving in Morioka the evening before the early-morning broadcast, I was introduced to eighty-year-old Kikuchi Kantarō, acknowledged master of the festival song (Fig. 2.3). He insisted that I must sing only the official festival song. Assuring me that I would be able to learn it in a matter of minutes, he immediately sang me the first half of the verse, some thirty seconds of music. I imitated it, not very precisely, I thought, but he was satisfied and immediately began to sing the second half. I interrupted to ask whether he could sing the first part again, since I hadn't 'quite' memorized it (to put it mildly). He repeated it, but the melody seemed rather different from the previous time, at least on my scale of measurement. He sang it a third time, and there still seemed to be more variation than I could deal with. By now I had activated my cassette recorder and managed to 'capture' a single version to learn in my room that night. I asked him whether he always sang the song the same, every time, and whether I should also strive to do so; the answer was yes to both. In fact, he said, he was singing the song 'exactly like I used to when I was a pack-horse driver,' back in the early 1930s. Similar remarks, in the presence of similar variation, were made by 83-year-old Senda Kanbei of Matsue (Shimane Pref.) as he taught me the dance song 'Sanko Bushi' in 1979: I should try 'as much as possible' to follow his rhythm and melodic ornamentation exactly.

It must be remembered, however, that each of these men was the principal bearer of a song whose survival had recently become a matter of local concern. We shall learn in subsequent chapters of the activities of folk song 'preservation societies', and of other factors promoting the view of a single 'correct' version of a song. Even these two men were surely affected by these trends, so we cannot assume that they would have placed so much stress on 'correctness' fifty years before. Some variation was inevitable anyway in an oral, secular folk tradition maintained by amateurs.

There is one major folk instrumental tradition where improvisation is highly valued – where, indeed, it is the lifeblood of the music. This is Tsugaru-jamisen, the solo shamisen tradition of the Tsugaru region of modern Aomori Prefecture. It is a comparatively young style, emerging gradually from the late nineteenth century (Groemer 1999: 35ff.; Suda et al. 1998; Peluse 2006). It was born among the blind male itinerants of whom Takahashi Chikuzan (§2.4.5) was the most famous recent exemplar. It developed independently of the modernizing atmosphere of Meiji Japan and – until recently – owed nothing to Western concepts. It did, however, develop rapidly in the hothouse atmosphere of the early professional troupes. It has always been a specialist art, demanding a level of technique far beyond the typical village strummer.

Tsugaru-jamisen originated basically as accompaniment for Tsugaru *min'yō*, which itself once allowed – nay, demanded – considerable melodic freedom, especially from professionals. Consider these comments from Asari Miki and another great Tsugaru singer, Harada Eijirō (b. 1912), talking about their days touring with the famed shamisen player Kida Rinshōei (1911–78) (cited with references in Groemer 1999: 57):

> *Harada:* One thing that's great about Tsugaru songs is that everyone does them differently. You, Kon Jūzō, and I all sing melodies in a different way . . . .
>   *Asari:* [And yet] no matter what you came up with, [Kida] wouldn't mess it up . . . .
>   *Harada:* He was also great at adding shouts. Today's *shamisen* players don't do that well.

Kida used to boast happily of stealing Tsugaru-jamisen 'riffs' from Shirakawa Gunpachirō (1909–61). The two were friendly rivals as members of the same troupe during the 1930s. During a typical show, each of these players would perform a *kyoku-biki* – a 'virtuoso solo' of several minutes' duration. These were considered to be improvised, but in fact each player would have spent hours each week trying out new riffs to work into an improvisation. In the emerging aesthetic of Tsugaru-jamisen performance, novelty was prized: the audience would react enthusiastically to surprising passages. Kida would tell the blind Shirakawa that he was going to take a bath; Shirakawa would then feel free to try out some of his newest ideas, certain that Kida could not steal them. In fact, Kida would be eavesdropping nearby. The next day, if Kida appeared on stage first, he would use Shirakawa's best ideas, hoping to capture the crowd's favour and unnerve his rival (NMMM: 100).[55]

Tsugaru folk song itself has been absorbed into the modern *min'yō* world as just another – although surely the most admired – regional style. In the mouths of some singers it still retains traces of its former quasi-improvisatory nature. The arts of Tsugaru are mentioned frequently in subsequent chapters, but a general book such as this one cannot give them the special treatment they deserve. Fortunately, Groemer has now done so (1999).

2.6 Summary

This chapter was intended to give the reader a feeling for the nature and context of musical performance in the traditional village, in the days when *min'yō* were still *uta* and the professional folk singer was a *rara avis*.

The nineteenth century saw a rise in the number of wealthy local landlords and entrepreneurs, who increasingly became involved with a 'higher' culture of urban origin. This led to a distinction within most hamlets between elitist music (represented for example by *sankyoku* and Noh music) and 'community' music (work songs, communal festival music and so forth).

Min'yō lyric collections contain very few verses expressing class antagonism or dealing with sex. It is suggested that antagonistic verses were in fact uncommon but that verses with sexual content were abundant in traditional song.

Among rural folk, the word *uta* was a cover term for 'song'; until the spread of scholarly terms such as *min'yō*, little terminological distinction was made among types of song. In the days before the diffusion of radio and the phonograph, few peasants could have been exposed to as many as a hundred songs, let alone sing them.

We distinguished four principal types of song performance in the hamlet: calendrical or festival songs, work songs, party songs and songs by itinerant professionals. Songs in these categories differed on several parameters, including: method of transmission; invariance; difficulty; length and structure of texts; instrumentation; number of performers; function; intended audience.

A skilled village performer was often viewed ambivalently: appreciated as a performer, but perhaps also considered a *dōrakumono* who devoted too much time to amusement. Such a person risked identification with itinerant professionals, who were of the lowest social status. Even today's professional performers may suffer from these traditional attitudes. The itinerants, however, were crucial to the development and spread of folk songs.

Only elite music and ceremonial music were transmitted formally. Teaching and performance of ceremonial music often fell to hamlet organizations such as the Young Men's Association or the Shrine Guild.

Certain long ballads were sometimes learned from printed broadsides. Most hamlet songs were, however, learned through informal imitation and 'stealing'. Textual improvisation of various types was frequent in non-ritual songs, conscious musical improvisation less so; unconscious textual and musical changes were however common.

The state of affairs described above faded gradually from the 1890s to the 1950s, giving way first to a 'folk song world' (*min'yō-kai*) and finally to a fully-fledged national industry. The next chapter follows folk song on its path from tradition to modernity.

NOTES

1. The word *buraku* was coined in the Meiji period; the equivalent unit was earlier called by names such as *mura, agata, sato* (as in *furusato*) and *hora* (see Johnson 1967: 153–4). More recently, *buraku* was often understood in a quite different sense: as a euphemism for communities of 'untouchables' (*eta* or *burakumin*). In that sense it abbreviates terms such as *hisabetsu-buraku* and *tokushu buraku*.

2. In 1940, there were 9,614 *mura/son*, by 1976 only 635 (EOJ: 8.176). Kalland (1980: 6) describes the progressive political amalgamation of one specific hamlet into *mura* of increasing scope, culminating in its redefinition as a district within a town (*machi*). Amalgamation occurs on various levels. Thus, amidst a nationwide surge of such mergers in the past few years (see Rausch 2006), the island of Sado (Niigata Pref.) became a single city (*shi*), replacing seven distinct cities, towns and villages (*shi-chō-son*). Political merging does not guarantee social merging, as Sado islanders' protests demonstrate.

3. Song titles (if any) are given after the verse(s) unless stated in the text. For lyrics in English, see R37, R17–19, Berger 1972, Hattori 1966, 1974, Migita 1970, Britton 1969, Matsuhara 1927, plus a few in Bock 1948, 1949, Isaku 1973, 1981, Groemer various. Lafcadio Hearn's works also often contain folk lyrics. In French, there is Bonneau 1933. Lyrics also appear increasingly on the web.

4. For English-language ethographies of traditional Japanese farming villages, see Beardsley et al. 1959, Embree 1939, Cornell & Smith 1956; for fishing villages, Norbeck 1954, Kalland 1981, Yanagita 1954a; for mountain villages, Yanagita 1954b, Cornell & Smith 1956. Most villages did of course have a mixed economy.

5. Socio-economic relations took many forms depending on local factors such as productivity of the region, availability of land and proximity to alternative urban employment opportunities. Only certain households generally had access to village office-holding, common lands, participation in village shrine rituals etc. High status derived not only from wealth but often from factors such as length of residence and kinship relations. The extensive English ethnographic literature on this subject includes e.g. Gamo 1981, Smith 1959, Nakane 1967, Yoshida 1964, Ishino 1953, Cornell 1964, Brown 1966, Nagai & Bennett 1953.

6. See Kitano 1959. Formal patron-client relations often survived right up until the post-war land reform. In the village described by Yoshida (1964), as late as 1943, 70% of the ninety-two households were either patrons or clients – or both!

7. Full tenancy increased steadily from 27% in 1868 to 45% in 1908 (EOJ: 8.3); in 1887, two-thirds of all farming households were tenants or tenant-owners (EOJ: 4.363).

8. An 1811 listing of 520 active members of one school of *kyōka* (a poetic genre) revealed that *chōnin* constituted the largest class of members, samurai were half as numerous, and farmers were next, followed by *sake* brewers, doctors, priests, etc. (Nishiyama 1997: 98). Presumably most of those farmers were of the village elite.

9. I examined thousands of printed verses and discussed the issue with singers and researchers. Among collections scanned were: *Taue-zōshi* (?sixteenth century; transl. Hoff 1971); *Sabishiki za no nagusami* (1676; printed in Takano 1928); *Enkyō gonen kouta shōga shu* (1748; printed in Asano 1961); *Sanga chōchūka* (1772; printed in Sasano 1956); *Hina no hitofushi* (1809; printed in Sugae 1967); *Awaji nōka* (1825; printed in Asano 1961); *Shōryō odoriuta* (compiled 1890s; printed in Takano 1928); Hara 1976; Machida 1964; Matsuhara 1927; Mikado 1977; Narita 1978; Ochiai 1980; and Takano 1929. I also utilized Matsumoto 1965, Hara 1971, 1976 – all written by Marxists – and Nishio & Yazawa 1974 and Aoki 1974; the latter two focus precisely on protest songs, mainly in the context of mass movements.

10. The comical plays called *kyōgen*, mostly of folk origin, are often cited as expressions of thinly veiled hostility towards local lords. But *kyōgen* lampoon both rich and poor, and rarely adopt a tone likely to inspire anger. More overtly critical were the *niwaka* plays of Hakata (modern Fukuoka), which developed in the seventeenth century as townsfolk vented their displeasure with the Kuroda clan overlords. The actors hid their identities behind masks. The Kurodas deemed the plays a harmless way to keep apprised of the grievances of their subjects. See Dizer 1951.

11. Tanaka (1969: 86, cited in Hoff 1981: n. 49) claims, without examples, that there are many transplanting songs expressing overt antagonism and resentment towards the landowner. Whether these were sung in the latter's presence is not clear. Consider also Lloyd's opinion (1967: 18) that, until recently, the English working people 'have generally hidden their most precious cultural possessions from the master, the squire, the parson' – out of shyness, fear or class hostility. Lloyd was referring to political and erotic songs, among others.

12. Matsumoto (1965: 241) mentions three examples associated with particular uprisings. One was based on a ball-bouncing song, the other two on counting songs. Matsumoto felt that Edo-period folk songs in general were not suited to use in mass movements precisely because of their highly melismatic nature and tense-throated vocal production, which he sees as the products of alienation caused by rapid urbanization (ibid: 277–8, 244). This view is dubious: field recordings reveal that the same style existed even in isolated hamlets far from the effects of urbanization.

13. Narita (1978: 225ff.) lists 199 *kudoki* stories, classified by subject matter. Only eight are said to be 'primarily' songs dealing with uprisings, peasant or otherwise. Of these, at least three are said elsewhere in the book to have been made *after* the Edo period; one dates from 1955!

14. In the event, the rebels succeeded and a cruel local lord was deposed. 'It is said' (NHK 1979: 62) that the Gujō Bon dance was started at the urging of the tyrant's successor, to overcome social divisions and promote amity. The source of this common claim is never given.

15. See, for example, verses 94 and 96. The metaphor of the peasants as rats, joining forces to do battle with the cat/landlord, frequently featured in tales of professional storytellers such as *taiheiki-yomi* and *otogi-shū*, particularly during the general unrest of the sixteenth and early seventeenth centuries (Matsumoto 1965: 231, 197f.).

16. A.L. Lloyd, early in his career as a leftist ethnomusicologist, concluded from an examination of English folk song that protest songs were rare (Lloyd 1944: 30); later, however, he disavowed this opinion (Lloyd 1967: 18 and *passim*). Obviously, even sympathetic scholars cannot always tell when a negative emotion is being expressed. For current attempts to interpret folk texts as anti-authoritarian statements, see §6.5. Three further examples of verses of complaint are translated in Bock 1949: 208–9.

17. Careful study of the publications of the Emergency Folk Song Survey (§1.1) might yield such information, but a cursory examination of thirty-seven of the volumes found none. Kojima 1992 makes reference to such surveys in Aomori and indeed provides a small-scale survey of one village there.

18. Hayakawa (1924) collected nearly 400 'verses' from one woman from Ishikawa Prefecture, but many are rhythmic recitations and children's songs, and it is not clear how many melodies are represented. He gives no significant biographical information. Kawachi (1979) has written a poetic narrative concerning one woman (born around 1900), her songs and their social context. Although she obviously has a large repertoire, it is not described systematically or in full. Usefully, a companion long-playing record with the same title was issued by CBS/Sony.

19. The ploughing, transplanting and foundation-pounding songs are recorded in Machida 1964 as songs 32, 21 and 242.

20. Itō qualified this statement with 'very rarely' when I expressed some surprise. Still, this was largely true – with many exceptions – of work songs throughout the archipelago. In Amami Ōshima in 1980, 86-year-old Yamada Taka searched her memory to recall for me a field song of her youth. She had not sung it in several decades, since she stopped working in the fields. No, she said, she never thought of singing it at a party: it was a work song.

21. The distinction between *hayariuta* and *min'yō* was not always clear (§1.2), especially during Itō's younger days, which overlap with the period of Embree's research.

22. For detailed examples of songs linked with particular work, see Takeuchi 1969; for links between songs and seasons, see Katō 1980. The seasonal work pattern is detailed in the English works in note 4. The yearly ritual cycle is described in some of these and in Bernier 1975.

23. In the cities, of course, the agricultural cycle is of less moment; in fact, the most important urban festivals take place in late spring and summer.

24. The impressive multi-CD set R15 is devoted to the music of *minzoku geinō* from all over Japan. Various examples also occur on R33. See also Hoshino & Yoshika 2006.

25. The lunar calendar in Japan lags behind the Western calendar by an average of about one month. Hereinafter I use Western month names in giving Western dates, and Japanese-style numbering of months ('the first month', etc.) for lunar dates.

26. However, a cycle of rice transplanting songs from western Japan was written down for mnemonic purposes perhaps as early as the sixteenth century (Hoff 1971), as was, apparently, the text of the shrine theatrical from Nara Prefecture known as Daimokutate, described below (Makino 1964: 56). Many of the works of Honda Yasuji, a pioneer in *minzoku geinō* research, reproduce ritual texts which have surfaced in villages across Japan.

27. Bon is most formally called *urabon* (from ancient Indian *ullambana*). Generally the festival period is called O-Bon (adding an 'honorific' prefix) and the dances *bon odori*.

28. Examining nearly 400 Bon-dance verses in *Sanga chōchūka* (1772), Bock (1949: 213) deemed 60% love songs, 20% 'congratulatory' and the rest 'miscellaneous'.

29. E.g.: Takeuchi 1969: 235; Nakai et al. 1981: 412; Narita 1978: 24; Bernier 1975; R63 track 1.25. A collection of texts for this purpose is *Shōryō odoriuta*, in Takano 1928.

30. Before addressing the gods in song, participants would undergo one or more types of ritual purification, such as eating food cooked over a special separate hearth, abstaining from sex, etc. For a similar example, see Blacker 1975: 256–7.

31. In most hamlets all residents were *ujiko* by ascription; elsewhere there were other requirements such as ancestry, age of one's household or length of residence.

32. Some fifty-three types of work song are listed (in English) in Isaku 1981: 50–3. Machida 1964 contains recorded samples of almost 300 work songs, classified by type. A similar classification is used for each prefecture in the volumes of NMT.

33. This is common worldwide. Collinson (1966: 76) notes that only one of forty-one Hebridean waulking songs in a certain collection refers to the task of waulking.

34. This was also sometimes true of the Hebridean waulking songs mentioned in note 33: so many songs per piece of cloth (Collinson 1966: 73).

35. Coal-mining and *sake*-making songs have frequently been collected and are among the best-known *min'yō*. Songs relating to female labourers (*jokō*) are also occasionally collected, e.g. NMT: 9.485–6, 436; Asano 1983: 406; Mikado 1977: 2.105; Nakai et al. 1972: 194.

36. Not yet seen. Miyata Shigeyuki (National Research Institute for Cultural Properties, Tokyo) says that perhaps five prefectures made such videos during 1995–6 under his urging (the others being Yamagata, Saitama, Chiba and Mie) (pers. comm. 4 June 1907).

37. Embree (1939) describes typical lively rural parties and their songs (99–111), as well as a party of a more formal, 'serious' nature (197–201).

38. Two reasons why the shamisen was rare in ritual contexts: it is a relatively 'young' instrument (dating from the sixteenth century), and it quickly developed unwholesome associations with blind professionals and the pleasure quarters. It still attracted the village elite, so long as the 'correct' kind of music was played.

39. Not all congratulatory party music would qualify as *min'yō*. Aside from occasional bits of Noh chanting, today one might hear Western-style popular songs as well. John Nathan's documentary film *Farm Song* (1978) has a marvellous scene of a New Year's party in a village in Miyagi, in which the assembled relatives take turns singing a wide variety of song types.

40. Maring and Maring (1997) shed some light on *shunka* in general today, but their paper is marred by misromanization of lyrics, mistranslation, misleading terminology, inadequate fieldwork, failure to consult important sources, and inadequate citation of sources.

41. This is according to an elderly local woman interviewed on a television special called 'Hokkai Bon Uta', NHK-TV, 5 June 1981. She also sang the verse given just below, which she had learned in her youth from the 'old granny' next door.

42. An exception is Soeda 1966, which is not limited to folk song; but his book is devoted precisely to such bawdy lyrics, reflecting the tendency to isolate them rather than include them as 'normal' verses. Embree 1944, printed in the United States, is another exception, since he strove to record every verse that he heard. Also, bawdy

verses did find their way into some collections: the 1822 *hayariuta* collection *Ukaregusa* included (typically, isolated at the end of the volume) a section containing some forty verses of 'bawdy songs' (*bareuta*; Asano 1983: 421).

43. Groemer has recently shed extensive light on these matters and on the urban–rural interface (1994b, 1996, 1999, 2007, 2008). Summaries of types of wandering performer are given in Takeuchi 1976: 26ff and Groemer 1999: 13–9, 30–1, 207–12. Most types mentioned survived into the twentieth century in some form; recordings with detailed documentation are in Ozawa 1999/R14 and to a lesser extent Honda 1998/R15.

44. Likewise, the shadow-play performers of Tottori in the late nineteenth century would often contact the head of the village Young Men's Association for help in locating a wealthy household to sponsor and lodge them (Takeuchi 1973b: 137).

45. A serialized biography of Kikuchi Tansui, one of the twentieth century's leading folk shakuhachi players, touches on his experiences as an itinerant, which he undertook for spiritual as much as musical reasons; see Shiiba 1978.

46. See Reader 1987, Foard 1982, Reader & Walter 1993. On pilgrimage and folk song in particular, see Takeuchi 1969: 22–32 and the Kinki volume of NMT (under 'Ise Ondo').

47. See Blacker 1975: 280ff. Even in the 1940s, one village of 484 people on Sado Island (Niigata Pref.), far from Ise, had eight *Ise-kō* as well as four similar organizations for pilgrimages to a famous Buddhist temple (Yoshida 1964: 230).

48. Itō claimed to have been functionally illiterate during her prime learning years. The general rise in literacy and the increased availability of printed *min'yō* lyric collections have gradually altered methods of transmission, as discussed in subsequent chapters.

49. NMGJ lists several hundred *minzoku geinō*, giving some information about the institution(s) or individuals currently performing them. Many are still transmitted in family lines. For example, the roles in the many folk theatricals included in the Kannon Festival of Nishiure (Shizuoka Pref.) were traditionally handed down within particular households; in recent decades at least, certain other houses contribute performers if necessary (NMGJ: 331–2; cf. also EOJ: 2.297).

50. Many sorts of unintentional or unavoidable variation, and intentional rationalizations of obscure or locally incompatible lyrics, occur in Japan as elsewhere. Improvisation of poetry was a standard feature of Japanese literary and social activity in the cultivated and courtly tradition; the novel *Tale of Genji* (ca. A.D. 1000) contains many examples.

51. In the short urban shamisen songs known as *dodoitsu*, which flourished in the latter nineteenth century but linger today, singers might improvise lyrics and also alter the skeletal tune considerably; the accompanist must follow as closely as possible, but divergence is inevitable. A good musical description of *dodoitsu* remains to be written.

52. For example, 'Esashi Oiwake' can be sung to a verse of either four or five lines of text; the first two lines in the latter case are sung to the same musical phrase as the first line of the former, by changing syllables more frequently, with no resulting change in the melody. The song 'Etchū Owara Bushi', on the other hand, adapts to the same situation by adding a musical phrase at the beginning to accommodate the additional line of text (cf. Takami 1981).

53. Compare 'Kuzunoha Kowakare' in Oyama 1977: 293; R8, record 2, side A; and R9, record 1, side A. The two recordings, each ending at the same point about

one-third through, are respectively 23:47 and 25:25 in length. Part of another version, from R21, is reproduced as **CD11**. The recording dates of the versions are 1973, 1971 and apparently 1970. Yamamoto (1988) analyses the textual differences among three renditions of 'Sanshōdayū'; Groemer compares both text and music of 'Kuzunoha Kowakare' performed in 1954 and 1974 (2007: 352ff, 408ff, mus. exx. 14.18–20).

54. This was a familiar situation in England too. Ian Russell reports (pers. comm.) the case of two traditional singers near Sheffield in the 1970s who sang one song together for the first time, having learned it from the same person. Afterwards they bemoaned the fact that their lyrics occasionally diverged – but failed to comment on what to Ian was an equally significant degree of melodic divergence.

55. Osabe's short story 'Tsugaru Yosare Bushi' (1974) describes a similar rivalry. Recall also the theft of a lyric by an inferior competitor in the song contest in Wagner's *Mastersingers of Nuremberg*.

CHAPTER 3

FOLK SONG

IN TRANSITION

◨

3.1 Introduction

The term *min'yō* has rural resonances. To most Japanese the true folk song is a 'country' song, made by the rural working class for its own amusement, transmitted across the generations by untutored singers. Yet all accept that *min'yō* encompasses much more than this. The Edo period had its *hayari-uta*, urban popular songs which spread to the rural areas. Then there are *zokuyō*, rural songs which were re-formed, nurtured and propagated in the urban amusement areas – and then often recirculated in the countryside as *hayariuta*. The twentieth century brought *shin-min'yō*, 'new folk songs' mostly written by urban lyricists and tunesmiths motivated by considerations quite other than those which spawned the 'true' rural songs. Not only do many *min'yō* thus have urban connections, but the cities now take the lead in *min'yō* performance and transmission. The development of the broadcasting and recording industries, coupled with a national prosperity which has brought the products of those industries within the reach of every Japanese, has allowed the urban centres to influence (some say dictate hegemonically) the tastes of the whole populace. Scholars working at urban institutions have had a powerful impact on both the performance of folk song and the ideology surrounding it. Even more importantly, Japan, 90 per cent rural a century ago, is now predominantly urban (80 per cent by some definitions).

Chapter 2 focused on the ideal-typical traditional village as the primary locus of pre-modern folk song. The present chapter charts the birth of the modern *min'yō* world, an event in which the smaller towns often acted as midwife. In Chapter 4, the focus will shift to the modern urban centre. In Chapter 5 we consider folk song activity in the modern countryside, which can no longer be viewed even in relative isolation from the influences of the city. The impact of globalization will receive separate attention at various points.

3.2 The emergence of urban folk song: enabling factors

The cities of Japan, ancient and modern alike, naturally drew much of their population from the countryside. Only in the twentieth century, however, was the influx of rural residents accompanied by the emergence of folk song as a discrete and significant form of urban musical activity. This development can be seen as the result of the combined workings of several interrelated factors, varying in importance and in the period of effectiveness.

(1) **The tremendous population shift from rural to urban** is obviously a consideration, although its precise effects on musical behaviour are less intuitively obvious. During the century preceding the Meiji Restoration of 1868, Japan's population held steady at around 30 million, of whom some 10 per cent are estimated to have lived in cities of over 10,000 people. Edo's population may have surpassed 1 million, while Osaka and Kyoto held 3–400,000 and Kanazawa and Nagoya around 100,000 (Hall 1970: 210). Since then, the urban population has grown steadily while rural figures remain practically constant. Today, over 80 per cent of 130 million Japanese are 'living in cities' (EOJ: 8.176). This urban growth resulted largely from migration from the countryside: throughout the twentieth century a goodly proportion of Japan's urbanites were country-born.[1] The growth is also increasingly attributable to the urbanization of rural settlements themselves, as farming or fishing villages grow into towns.

One might expect such a large rural influx to result in a major role for rural music in the city. But Japanese cities have always had a solid rural segment: an estimated two-thirds of Edo residents were born elsewhere (EOJ: 1.302). So other factors must be invoked to account for the modern urban *min'yō* boom. The rural origin of much of the urban populace was merely an enabling factor, not a sufficient condition.

(2) **The image of the peasant has been gradually upgraded** since the Meiji Restoration. In the preceding Edo period, the official ideology of social class was a modified Confucian four-tiered system: samurai, farmer, artisan, merchant in descending order. (Outside this system were the emperor and nobility above and various outcastes below.) In theory, the peasant (again, using this term in a non-pejorative sense) was ranked above the urban craftspeople and merchants. In reality, members of the latter two classes generally received more prestige. This was partly because of the relative wealth and resultant influence of the merchants in particular, but also because the city was perceived as the centre of culture and the peasants as boors and bumpkins. After all, it was in the city that one could rub shoulders with samurai – perhaps even gain a financial advantage over an improvident warrior. In the city a new and attractive popular culture had developed: Kabuki for the merchant and samurai, koto and tea lessons for their wives and daughters, woodblock printing and so forth (see Moriya 1984; Nishiyama 1964, 1997). The merchant class also gradually acquired access to much of samurai culture,

including performing arts such as Noh. The urban dweller felt superior, the rural dweller inferior, for in the villages only the local elite could access prestige culture (§2.2.2). In such an atmosphere, migrants to the city would likely have been attracted to the townsman's culture, and also inclined to try to disguise their rural origins. They may have found solace in the old country songs in private, but there was no impetus for the establishment of regular occasions for performing them.[2]

Since the Meiji Restoration, several developments have combined to improve city folks' image of peasants and their life-style. First, the Meiji government, even in its rush to industrialize, recognized the fundamental economic importance of the agrarian sector and stressed the value of the peasant and the simple virtues of rural life. This agrarianist doctrine was known as *nō-honshugi* (see Dore 1959: 56–85). In itself, however, it had no more concrete effect than did the peasant's putative high status in the class system. Second, the influence of the German Romantic view of the peasantry – and their songs – was felt in Japan after 1890, partly due to the return from Europe of literati such as Mori Ōgai (§1.2). Third, post-Second World War land reform and general prosperity contributed to a dramatic rise in rural living standards: the 'peasant' had become a 'farmer'. This leads us to the next major factor.

(3) **The distance between rural and urban Japan has lessened** both physically and conceptually. Universal education gave countryfolk potentially equal access to national print media as well as invalidating their image (never wholly accurate) as illiterates. The Meiji-period Democratic Rights Movement (*minken undō*) also improved centre-periphery links, having led to the establishment of a National Assembly. Later, the broadcast and recording industries increased the extent to which city and country shared a national popular culture – of which *min'yō* is now a part. Improvements in transportation and the growth of domestic tourism have also increased urban–rural interaction. Finally, with the post-war urban expansion, former rural outposts now often find themselves adjacent to or actually absorbed by the expanding cities. The result of all this is that rural dwellers today (especially the younger ones) have the knowledge and experience to deal with city folk more nearly as equals. Increased confidence in their self-worth also may lead to new respect for aspects of traditional rural culture such as music.

(4) **In the city, rural regional distinctions weakened** as in-migrants from various regions were united by a common sense of alienation from bourgeois culture. This development effectively created a sizeable common audience for the emerging category of music of rural origin. Such alienation existed until very recently despite the countervailing effects of factors 2 and 3: only in the past few decades might most rural-to-urban migrants hope to avoid mockery for their accents and unsophistication.

(5) **The gradual loosening of the connection between a song and its social context** left country songs free to find new contexts: city stages and city bars. In traditional Japan, although songs frequently migrated and

changed function, at any given moment a song tended to be identified closely with a particular use. A barley-threshing song rarely graced a wedding celebration.

This attitude has largely vanished today, both in town and country. One reason is that the original contexts themselves have often vanished. Thus mechanization has virtually eliminated the manual harvesting of rice. Such loss of context might be expected to have killed off the associated songs, as indeed often happened. As early as 1918, an observer in Okayama Prefecture bewailed the death of most local work songs (transplanting, weeding, fishing, etc.) through mechanization (cited in Asano 1966: 40). However, the gradual disappearance of group manual labour at least weakens the overall tendency to associate songs with particular situations. Those which do survive are perforce freed from their original contextual restrictions.

Other factors contributed to this separation of song and context. Again there was the influence of Romanticism, with its idealized image of peasant life and song. Romantic poets and composers saw a song as an object in itself. More importantly, after the First World War, poets like Kitahara Hakushū (1885–1942) wrote 'new folk songs' (*shin-min'yō*; §3.4.2) and 'children's songs' (*dōyō*; see Kojima 2004) of a folk-like but relatively elevated nature, which had no pre-existing contexts at all.

The ultimate context loosener, the one that completed the process, was the development of the mass media, both the print media and the recording and broadcast industries. Literacy in Japan, estimated at over 40 per cent among males even in the 1860s (Dore 1965), was over 90 per cent by 1900 (EOJ: 5.11). The rate has always been highest in urban areas. Thus almost the entire urban populace could have access to the popular collections of folk song texts which appeared with increasing frequency after the turn of the century. Collections with musical notation also are a twentieth-century phenomenon.[3] Radio broadcasts of folk song, commencing in 1926, and sales of recordings, which began in earnest around 1910, further fostered a sense of the song as a discrete item or event and engendered schizophonia, composer Murray Schafer's word for the split between an original sound and its electroacoustic reproduction (Schafer 1968).

As such factors contributed to loss of original context, the most salient feature of rural song gradually came to be the very fact of its rural 'folk' nature, rather than any more specific functions. Today, in theory, *any* rural work, dance or party song could be performed at a *min'yō* gathering or at a company New Year's party. The dominant selective criteria now seem to be a) the beauty of melody and lyrics, and b) the absence of overtly bawdy lyrics. Even these factors can be overridden by c) the need to sing *some* local song, however aesthetically dull, d) the curiosity value of a new song, and e) a positive desire for bawdy lyrics in certain contexts.[4]

(6) Another crucial factor fostering the establishment of an urban folk song culture has been **the steady growth** since the 1960s **of both leisure**

time and leisure-related expenditure.[5] The so-called leisure boom (*rejā būmu*) led to a tremendous increase in time spent taking lessons of various sorts. Although this rise may be most marked in categories like piano and golf, even traditional subjects such as Noh singing have benefited. In this atmosphere, it is not surprising that *min'yō* can now be studied as an organized leisure activity.

Many of the above factors were operative by the early twentieth century – about the time that the lineaments of the modern 'folk song world' (*min'yō-kai*) began to appear. The emergence of this 'world' as a distinct, acknowledged sphere of activity involved a number of trends and themes. Although these are described in detail later, we can introduce them in a few phrases: the shift to the city as the centre of activity; the predominance of musicians from northeastern Japan (Tōhoku); professionalization; formalization of teaching and transmission; standardization of performance; preservationism; government assistance and encouragement, mostly in the interests of tourism; ever-increasing media involvement; tension between local and national identity; and an attempt at dignification, upgrading the image of folk song as a form of music. Rather than trying to describe all these elements in a vacuum, let us start by following the course of a single song as it is 'modernized'. This song, 'Esashi Oiwake', exemplifies all of the themes mentioned and, by common consensus among scholars, is the song which played the most significant role in the birth of the *min'yō-kai*. Thus it is both an exemplar of the phenomenon and, in some ways, its agent.

3.3 The first modern folk song: 'Esashi Oiwake'

3.3.1 From 'Oiwake Bushi' to 'Esashi Oiwake'

Esashi is a small town of about 10,000 people on the southwest coast of Hokkaido, some two hours by train from the ferry-port to the main island of Japan.[6] Today it is a slightly somnolent port town, supported by squid-fishing and lumbering. But there was a time when the harbour was choked with ships from the main island, when the town rang with the voices of merchants and sailors, when the music from the geisha houses spilled into the streets. The visitors were drawn partly by trade but chiefly by the herring catch. In 1717, its population 20,000, Esashi was Hokkaido's principal harbour, port of call for 3,000 herring boats and 700 trading vessels (MB 1979.9: 3). Major Kabuki troupes and other avatars of urban culture often visited this distant port. Also converging on Esashi at the height of the season were pack-horse drivers and wagoners, prostitutes and entertainers. Coming and going, the visitors carried with them the lightest baggage of all: their favourite songs. Among the songs brought to Esashi was one known as 'Oiwake Bushi'.

Exactly when, how and in what form this song reached Esashi is unclear, but it seems to have come from the little post-town of Oiwake (hence its name) on the Nakasendō highway in Shinano (modern Nagano), carried by travellers both overland and by sea. By the early nineteenth century it was a favourite song over much of southern Hokkaido. Performance style varied considerably with context. On the one hand, 'Oiwake Bushi' was sung by pack-horse drivers and wagoners on the trail, unaccompanied and open-throated. (Its ancestor from Shinano was similarly sung by the pack-horse drivers passing through Oiwake.) Meanwhile, the geisha of the Esashi tea-houses and inns, skilled at urban shamisen genres such as *shinnai* and *toki-wazu*, performed the same song with shamisen, using a more 'refined', less full-bodied vocal style – just as their sisters in the inns of Oiwake had done. Presumably in both localities the women were creating a suitable parlour (*ozashiki*) version of a song familiar to many of their customers. This is a process by which many a work song was transmuted into what scholars often call a *zokuyō*, an arranged, urbanized folk song (§1.3).[7]

Mid-Meiji Esashi was a medium-size but booming rural town. As in other such towns as well as the farming villages of Chapter 2, the local elite aspired to the trappings of the prestigious and increasingly accessible urban culture. Rich Esashi merchants often spent the slow winter season in Osaka or Tokyo, developing their taste for the arts of tea, flower arranging, poetry and music (Kiuchi 1979: 87). Many became *tsūjin*, men-about-town who strove to be connoisseurs (*tsū*) and perhaps skilled practitioners of a wide range of artis-tic pursuits. Perhaps a prominent businessman or official, in any case a *tsūjin* needed sufficient wealth to frequent the more expensive pleasure quarters and dally with singing girls, learning the latest shamisen ditties, composing his own *kouta* lyrics and so forth (see Komiya 1956: 382–4; Teruoka 1989; Nakano 1989). Such a person was unlikely to be interested in the songs of 'crude' labourers unless they were given a touch of elegance (*iki, sui*) by the geisha.

During this period, Hokkaido was gradually joining the mainstream of Japanese economic and political life, and increasing numbers of important visitors came to Esashi, including several cabinet ministers (Esashi 1982: 71–2). They too were often *tsūjin* and would be entertained by the geisha. Many delighted especially in the distinctive local song, occasionally even composing new verses for the geisha.

It was partly to please such patrons that geisha throughout Japan would dress up a local song in urban clothing. Just as pieces from Kabuki music genres such as *nagauta* might contain a section in folk song style, for atmos-phere (e.g. the *hamauta* of 'Echigo-jishi'), so geisha often performed 'Oiwake Bushi' with a section in *shinnai* style sandwiched midway through a verse.[8]

Approaching 1900, then, there were in the Esashi area two distinct per-formance styles for 'Oiwake Bushi': geisha style and pack-horse drivers' style. The former came to be called 'Shinchi Bushi', since the better class of geisha houses were in Esashi's Shinchi district; the latter was sometimes known as 'Zumikishi Bushi', after the section of town where the horse drivers congregated. There was yet a third recognized version. While ship captains tarried in Shinchi, their crew found amusement with the less expensive (and less talented) ladies who worked in temporary huts (*hamagoya*) along the beachfront. Their version came to be called 'Hamagoya Bushi'. Thus various types of 'Oiwake Bushi' existed here, in loose correlation with profession or social status. Still, the boundaries between these types were largely obscured by individual variation. People talked less in terms of types than of particular renowned singers' versions.

Thus 'Oiwake Bushi', whatever its origins, had established itself as an identifiable and cherished local specialty, so much so that after around 1900 it was increasingly called 'ESASHI Oiwake' or 'ESASHI Oiwake Bushi' to distinguish it from versions elsewhere. (Those other versions too gradually added local identification: 'Shinano Oiwake', 'Echigo Oiwake', etc.) Some singers treated it very seriously indeed, more like an art song than a packhorse song. Thus Murata Yaroku (1851–1926), while working as a merchant's clerk in 1876, took up the study of 'Oiwake Bushi' with two geisha in the *hamagoya*. By his own testimony, he spent over two years working on a single verse – barely two minutes of music (Yokota 1920; Esashi 1982: 174, 260). His later fame suggests that his slow progress was not due (solely) to lack of ability. This sort of thoroughness and attention to detail, characteristic of the classical arts, occasionally spread into the world of *hayariuta* and thence eventually into *min'yō*; the geisha were among the principal intermediaries.

3.3.2 'Esashi Oiwake' greets the twentieth century

During the decade straddling the turn of the century, several developments spelled a new era for Esashi. During the 1890s the herring catch declined so suddenly and completely that the fishing industry was virtually dead after 1900. Then in 1904 the national railroad network reached Hokkaido's ferry port of Hakodate – but did not connect with Esashi until 1936. Nearly overnight, rail freight competition deprived the once booming port of its function as Hokkaido's principal shipping terminal.

Facing economic decline, Esashi responded variously. One solution on an individual level was to migrate to Tokyo to find work. Town officials took a more positive approach: they decided to try to lure back some of the lost visitors by capitalizing on the growth of domestic tourism. The new railroad could bring tourists at least as far as Hakodate. A major element in the publicity campaign was to be 'Esashi Oiwake'.

For 'Esashi Oiwake' was gaining fame elsewhere. The song was carried to various parts of the country by returning migrant workers, by the *tsūjin* mentioned above, and – ironically – by some of the residents (including geisha) forced to out-migrate by economic circumstances. At least one former Esashi geisha achieved popularity in Tokyo by around 1908 through singing the song (Esashi 1982: 74; Kurata 1979: 128). Meanwhile, the German researcher Erwin Walter captured several recordings of versions of 'Oiwake' (without further place-name modifier) from Niigata City, far from Esashi, in 1911–13 (R66, tracks 10–19). Although the song had probably established itself there independently earlier, many of Walter's versions are clearly linked with Hokkaido by their lyrics. In any case, by the 1920s Esashi's version was dominant.[9]

The song's spreading renown provided solace and a ray of optimism for the declining town. Around 1905, Esashi newspapers proudly began to note the popularity of the song and its accompanying dance even in Tokyo, where picture postcards of the dance were selling well (Esashi 1982: 74).[10]

The song's popularity, while modest by today's pop-chart standards, was such that in 1906 the classical shakuhachi player Gotō Tōsui (1880–1960) could open a successful 'Oiwake Bushi' classroom in Tokyo (Esashi 1982: 74; Takeuchi 1974: 68). Gotō, from Miyagi Prefecture, had begun studying shakuhachi in his early teens expressly to learn 'Oiwake'. His teacher consented to give him a single lesson on 'Oiwake' before turning exclusively to the classical repertoire (NMMM: 58; Kikuchi 1980: 40–1). The very fact that his teacher could play the song at all by 1892 reflects its growing popularity far from Esashi, as well as the shakuhachi's increasing links with folk song.[11] Moreover, for the dignified Gotō, who had come to Tokyo with prospects of becoming a physician or government official, to become instead a teacher of 'Esashi Oiwake' says much about both the status of the song itself and the increasing respectability of folk song in general. Remember that by this time the concept of *min'yō* had been 'invented', and certain of the literati had begun to accept folk song as a worthy genre of music (§1.2). Throughout the developments described in this chapter, and despite the variation in terminology, one thing is clear: nobody attempted to deny that 'Esashi Oiwake' and songs like it originated among the rural labouring class.

'Esashi Oiwake' benefited not only from the new respectability of folk song, but from a general resurgence of interest in traditional Japanese arts by 1900. Rushing to catch up with the Western powers who had forced open Japan's doors in the 1850s, the Meiji government had pursued a policy of unabashed Westernization. Traditional culture was neglected or even discouraged, particularly music (§1.5). By about 1890, however, Japan could take pride in the success of her modernization in the political, economic and military spheres and begin to re-assert the value of her traditional culture. This led to a sudden revival of concern for tradition (Kosaka 1958: 188, 218; Hall 1970: 291–3). In response to neglect and decay, the word 'preservation' (*hozon*) was very much in the air after 1890 (§5.4). In 1897 the government enacted the first law protecting art treasures, the Old Shrine and Temple Preservation Law (Koshaji Hozon Hō; see Bunkachō 1972: 13). Several shrine and temple 'preservation societies' (*hozonkai*) quickly sprang up – sometimes with governmental financial aid (Tateyama 1910: 691f.).

Traditional music also sought and gradually attained renewed respect. In 1891, a priest at Kyoto's Kiyomizu Temple petitioned the Imperial Household Ministry (Kunaishō) for aid in 'preserving' a certain temple song (N.B. just one song; Ongaku Zasshi 1891: 19). Other musicians and musicologists similarly urged government encouragement and preservation of traditional music (see Hughes 1981a: 32–3; Tateyama 1910: 679f., 702).

Finally, as Japan was winning a war with Russia in 1904–5, four significant events occurred. Superintendent Tomiogi of Tokyo School of Music, Japan's leading Western music conservatoire, stated that his school should no longer scorn Japanese music but should foster 'scientific' research and study of the popular *zokugaku* genres in particular (§1.5). At the same time, the musical acoustician Tanaka Shōhei, after fifteen years studying in Germany, began in earnest the detailed transcription into staff notation of several genres of traditional music, especially shamisen genres; he also helped develop the *bunka-fu* teaching notation for shamisen with its Western-inspired three-line staff (Komiya 1956: 367, 387; Kikkawa 1965: 372). (Transcriptions and modernized notation were among the devices Tomiogi would have considered 'scientific'.) Meanwhile Ueda Bin, a respected poet and translator of European literature, urged Japan's musicians to set about collecting and preserving rural songs, to provide material for the creation of a new national music (Asano 1966: 140); this attitude surely reflected his experience of nationalist trends in European classical music. Finally, back in Esashi, in December 1905 the local newspaper asked the following question (Esashi 1982: 74):

> Esashi's famous 'Oiwake' has gained renown in the main islands [of Japan], and now it has even appeared in a picture postcard, but are there no local residents who will help to prepare the road to preservation?

Here was a song which was more popular than ever in the Esashi region, which had begun to spread throughout Japan, yet voices proclaiming the urgent need for preservation (*hozon*) were increasingly heard (ibid.: 73–4). Two factors may have contributed to this situation. First, as noted above, the word 'preservation' had suddenly become common in the context of traditional music. Second, the existence of several variants of 'Esashi Oiwake', formerly seen as a positively-valued or neutral feature, now increasingly evoked concern or embarrassment – again for two possible reasons. First, many locals felt that this folk song which was to serve as ambassador for the town should be polished up and given the prestige associated with cultivated music. It was unthinkable that ten people should sing ten significantly different versions of, say, a *nagauta* or *shinnai* piece, hence 'Esashi Oiwake' should be treated similarly. Second, increasing contact with Western music and its prescriptive notation seems to have led Japanese in general to feel that there must be a single, immutable 'correct' version of any song. This feeling apparently extended even to folk song: there was only one 'Annie Laurie', it was thought, so why should there be more than one 'Esashi Oiwake'?

In striving for respect, 'Esashi Oiwake' – along with traditional urban music in general – had to contend with yet one more hurdle: the increasing disapproval directed towards the pleasure quarters (§1.5). The long-standing negative attitudes of the Edo government were reinforced by several new forces during Meiji. For one thing, Westerners tended (publicly at least) to look down on both prostitution and the eroticism of much Japanese music and dance, an opinion which influenced Japanese attitudes. The movement to upgrade the position of women, supported by such writers as Fukuzawa Yukichi and Higuchi Ichiyō, also had an effect on attitudes. Then, during the period of the Sino-Japanese and Russo-Japanese wars, the officially encouraged martial spirit had two consequences: men were not to waste their time in dissipation with the women of the quarters; nor should they be subjected to the songs of these women, songs of helpless love and emotional wallowing, hardly conducive to the spirit of soldierly dedication and self-sacrifice. It was an awkward period for *tsūjin*: to be thought modern (and many were in professions where they would aspire to this), they must join in the general condemnation of their old haunts, whatever their true feelings. Many singers and patrons of 'Esashi Oiwake' were caught in this bind: having learned the song from the geisha, they were being pressed indirectly to disavow their musical roots.

3.3.3 Standardization and after

Against this background, an unprecedented event took place in 1909 which has had repercussions in the *min'yō* world ever since. A dozen or so of the best singers of 'Esashi Oiwake' gathered in Esashi to produce a unified, correct (*seichō*) version of the song for dissemination (*fukyū*) and publicity (*senden*), in the interests of local pride and, ultimately, tourism (Esashi 1982: 75). This summit conference was arranged at the behest of the district governor, the local Shinto priest and other local 'intelligentsia', for the good of the town (ibid.: 75, 177, 221–3).[12] Several further meetings were needed to reach agreement (Tate 1989: 169). The chronology is uncertain, but within a few years of the 1909 meeting the following developments occurred, more or less as an extension of the decisions taken at the meeting.

(1) **Standardization**: A standard version was indeed adopted or created. Apparently the pack-horsemen's Zumikishi style was preferred to geisha-ized Shinchi.[13] Henceforth, it was agreed to insist on certain immutable features in performance; most notably, each verse must be sung in only seven breaths – a challenge, since a verse lasted over two minutes!

The stress on invariance led to historical revisionism: it was now believed that 'Esashi Oiwake' had indeed, until a recent period of decay, existed in a single form. The town newspaper claimed in 1912 (Esashi 1982: 76):

Even 'Esashi Oiwake', anciently sung as a famous local specialty, fell into great confusion and disorder (ōi ni midare) melodically as the region declined. Most people sang it arbitrarily, as they pleased.

Of course, nobody could remember when it was that there had been only one version, but it was agreed that such a golden age must have existed. One thinks again of Hobsbawm's (1983) concept of 'invented traditions'. More likely the situation had always been as the singer Etchūya Shisaburō (1875–1961) recalled it from his teens: singers developed a personal version by selecting their favourite bits and pieces from the total range of individual variants known to them (Esashi 1982: 221).

(2) **Organization**: 1909 saw the formation of a new organization, the 'Authentic Esashi Oiwake Bushi' Research Society (Seichō Esashi Oiwake Bushi Kenkyūkai; ibid.: 75). Most of the singers at the summit conference were members, and their aim was to spread the correct version of the song. The use of the word kenkyū (study, research) reflects the modernizing spirit of Meiji, with its emphasis on self-betterment through diligent study. The spontaneous formation of common-interest associations (kai) by groups of ordinary citizens was also an outgrowth of late-Meiji democratization (Yanagita 1957: 99f.). Kenkyūkai sprang up in many performing arts genres after 1890. In general, in dialogue concerning this newly recognized and respectable object of study called min'yō, we increasingly encounter scholarly-sounding Sino-Japanese compound words of a type formerly little heard in the countryside: 'research' (kenkyū), 'authentic' (seichō), 'preservation' (hozon), 'dissemination' (fukyū), and of course min'yō itself. Folk song was well on its way to objectification.[14]

(3) **Notation**: The first musical notations for the song began to appear (Esashi 1982: 102ff., 76). These were of a distinctive type, apparently owing something to certain Buddhist chant notations. Despite surface diversity and considerable evolution, all existing notations clearly derive from a common original, possibly Aimono Hisajirō's of 1909 (or 1903; MB: 15.14). This and other notations of this song are considered in §4.5.2.

(4) **Contests**: The first 'Esashi Oiwake' competitions were held in Esashi starting around 1910 (Esashi 1982: 76, 222; Takeuchi 1969: 10). There had been a few concerts consisting solely of Hokkaido versions of 'Oiwake Bushi' during the first decade of the century, and dance and music competitions were not a new idea. But these Esashi competitions belonged to a new breed, partly influenced by the classical music concours of Europe – indeed, such contests are often called by the French loan-word konkūru. The chief difference from a European contest was that every competitor sang *the same song!*

(5) **Dignification**: The winner at the 1911 Esashi concours, Hirano Genzaburō (1869–1918), sang in full formal dress (haori-hakama) – the only competitor to do so (Takeuchi 1969: 10). The following year, recommended by a Hokkaido representative to the National Diet, Hirano was invited to

give a recital in Tokyo; he met with such acclaim that he stayed for a year to teach and demonstrate 'Esashi Oiwake' (Esashi 1982: 171). A Tokyo newspaper praised his singing: the trend in the capital had recently been to sing 'Esashi Oiwake' at as 'absurdly' high a pitch as possible, but Hirano's deep-throated rendition seemed to reverberate with the elegantly lonely (*sabi no aru*) sound of the waves pounding the shore (ibid.: 77). *Sabi* is a concept commonly associated with the aesthetics of tea ceremony and many other classical arts, but until then rarely with folk song.

Hirano's dress, vocal style and demeanour all exemplified the dignity which the Esashi intelligentsia now desired for their local song. Thenceforth formal dress gradually became *de rigueur* for public performances of 'Esashi Oiwake'. Further, from this time onwards we find frequent references to the importance of 'attitude' (*kokorogamae*) in singing 'Esashi Oiwake' (see MB: 15.15): one must approach this song seriously, for it is no mere parlour plaything.

Significantly, Hirano shared the stage on one occasion with performers of the classical shamisen genres *nagauta* and *utazawa* (Esashi 1982: 77). *Utazawa* developed in the mid-nineteenth century as a slower, more elegant and dignified version of *hauta*, the popular ditties of the geisha. Renowned 'Esashi Oiwake' singer Hamada Kiichi I (1917–85) offered the analogy that, just as *utazawa* represented a conscious attempt to escape from the vulgarity (*yahisei*) of *hauta*, so 'Esashi Oiwake', in the late nineteenth century, 'began its struggle toward perfection' (R12, liner notes). Hamada also saw the song as having attained *hin'i* and *kakuchō* – refinement, nobility, 'class'. Indeed, the purveyors of this song achieved their aim of 'dignification' with startling rapidity.

An additional element in this process was the increasing choice of shakuhachi as sole accompaniment. This bamboo flute, once the specialty of itinerant samurai-monks, had in the Meiji period become more and more a tool of the literati. As the song was taken out of the hands of the geisha, so the shamisen, with its intimations of disreputability, gradually gave way to the more masculine and dignified shakuhachi. Shamisen accompaniment is rare today.[15]

(6) **Dissemination**: Other singers also now began to range out from Esashi, conducting classes, establishing 'Esashi Oiwake' clubs, etc. From this time the formal teaching of the song increased rapidly in both geographic spread and number of teachers. This was a critical step in the establishment of a new profession: the 'folk song teacher'. The teachers were now less often geisha, due to the attitudinal shifts mentioned above. By 1916 Murata Yaroku had moved his one-man classroom from Esashi to Tokyo and thence to Kōbe in western Japan, and twenty-one of the best performers were touring the country as the 'Oiwake Bushi' Publicity Troupe (Esashi 1982: 80–1). Significantly, such travelling singers performed and taught almost exclusively in urban areas at first. Whether one sought prestige, publicity or financial gain, it was urban Japan that offered the greatest possibilities.

Here again we see an attempt to reassert local control over a cherished –
and valuable – local product, reflecting the ever-increasing sense of folk
songs as 'belonging' to particular regions. (In Machida's vocabulary
described in §1.3, it was hoped to make the *zokuyō* 'Esashi Oiwake' into a
riyō once again.) The best 'Esashi Oiwake' teachers, local performers
claimed, must perforce hail from Esashi. To quote renowned singer Etchūya
Shisaburō (ibid.: 78–9):

> If you're not born and raised in Esashi, you can't do the true 'Oiwake Bushi'
> melody and ornaments. . . . If you examine [their singing] carefully, there
> are quite a number of differences between an Esashi singer's sound and that
> of an outsider. . . . There are people who moved to Esashi thirty or forty years
> ago, . . . but they can never completely lose their accents, so the tune of their
> 'Esashi Oiwake Bushi' always sounds wrong in places.

This is still a widespread view of folk song even today. Neither then
nor now, however, has this discouraged the transmission of folk songs to
'outsiders'.[16]

(7) **Recordings**: The first commercial recordings of 'Esashi Oiwake' were
issued within a few years of the establishment of the first domestic recording companies in 1907. Several early 78-rpm discs have been reissued in
various collections (R11, R12). All surviving recordings date from *after* the
1909 Esashi summit conference.

The above developments might be expected to have resulted in a rapid and
substantial degree of standardization, eliminating earlier variants. This did
not happen. Early recordings show significant individual variation even
among those singers who attended the summit conference. For example, the
stricture that the song should be sung in only seven breaths was ignored even
by such a respected singer as Hirano. This fact led Takeuchi (1980: 73,
208–10) to conclude that no such stricture could have been agreed upon at
the 1909 meeting – for how could Hirano have flown in the face of a decision taken at the urging of the regional governor? However, testimony from
a participant at the meeting (Esashi 1982: 222) suggests that such a decision
was indeed taken. Apparently these early singers did not feel strictly bound
by any decisions forced on them at the conference (Tate, pers. comm. 1988);
anyhow, some were probably incapable of going without breathing, given the
typical early singer's fondness for alcohol and tobacco.

One factor contributing to ongoing variation was the continuing rivalry
between pre-1909 factions (*ha*), primarily between the purveyors of the
'Zumikishi' and 'Shinchi' versions. If the summit conference had any unifying organizational effect, it was short-lived. By 1914 some fifty members of
the Zumikishi-ha had formed an association (*kai*) excluding Shinchi propo-
nents; they called their version the 'authentic' (*seichō*) one (Esashi 1982:

176). Meanwhile Murata Yaroku, sole surviving teacher of the Hamagoya style, formed his own *kai* and by 1920 had over 300 students in various parts of Japan; the aim of his group was to 'preserve the pure (*junsui*) "Esashi Oiwake"' (Yokota 1920: 8; Esashi 1982: 79). The Shinchi-ha, led by the prosperous restaurateur Takano Kojirō (ca. 1870–1938), also claimed to be the sole possessor of the *seichō* version. (Transcriptions of versions by Takano, Hirano and Etchūya are found in NMT 9.472–6.)

The precise causes of these rivalries remain unknown. In the traditional classical arts, which are mostly organized according to the so-called house-head system (*iemoto seido*), new schools are frequently formed by disaffected pupils, usually for a combination of artistic, personality and financial reasons. It appears that the first two factors dominated in the case of 'Esashi Oiwake', because testimony is nearly universal that teaching the song for financial gain in Esashi itself was considered improper in those days.[17]

On both artistic and personal grounds, then, the dominant Shinchi and Zumikishi factions refused to share the stage for recitals or to reach any organizational accommodation. In 1926, the Esashi Seichō Oiwake Kai Honbu ('Esashi Authentic Oiwake' Association Headquarters, i.e. the Zumikishi-ha) erected a commemorative stone at a local temple, listing the names of its supporters. It took the rival Esashi Oiwake Kai Honbu (the Shinchi-ha) six years to raise the funds to erect its own stone at another temple, with its own members' names inscribed. Both organizations, with their slightly different names, preferred to imagine that the other did not exist (Esashi 1982: 291–2). Rivalries continued until an official reconciliation was effected in 1935 and all parties were brought together in the Esashi Oiwake Kai, with the mayor as *ex officio* chairman (ibid.: 118, 186f., 227–8; Takeuchi 1980: 84–5). Once again, only the influence of powerful figures such as the mayor could overcome the differences among groups. From this time, with the waning influence of the pre-1909 generation of singers and the continuing stress on the need for invariance, it seems that the present-day standard version finally came to the fore.

In the cities, meanwhile, 'Esashi Oiwake' continued to gain popularity throughout the pre-war period. Recordings were issued with increasing frequency. Shakuhachi player Gotō Tōsui, mentioned above, continued to organize 'Oiwake' *taikai* (meets) in Tokyo; the 1917 one, with several guest singers from Esashi, attracted over 3,000 spectators (Kikuchi 1980: 42). Significantly, in 1920 Gotō's annual gathering was renamed *min'yō taikai*, as a wider range of folk songs came to be sung in the city (ibid.; Takeuchi 1974: 69 gives the date, apparently erroneously, as 1922). But 'Esashi Oiwake' held the throne: even in the late 1930s a *min'yō taikai* in Tokyo was likely to be 90 per cent 'Esashi Oiwake' (Kiuchi 1979: 257). When shamisenist Minemura Toshiko (1896–1978) came to Tokyo from Niigata in 1932, she found that other folk songs were considered merely *hamono* or *yokyō* (trifling side-amusements), mainly sung by geisha (MB 1978.9). Indeed, even today 'Esashi Oiwake' is often considered the acme of Japanese folk song.

The changes in the transmission and performance of 'Esashi Oiwake' discussed above can be seen as resulting from the interaction of traditional elements with new influences from abroad. For example, of the seven developments enumerated in this section, all but the last represent the intensification, or the transference to new spheres, of traditional musical or ideological elements rather than the simple imposition of foreign elements. Even the creation of the independent genre *min'yō* is not attributable solely to European influence: a category of country song *was* weakly recognized in court and city in earlier times, as expressed in such terms as *kuniburi, hinauta* and *fuzoku* (§1.2). As rural Japan was increasingly drawn into a modern national culture during the Meiji period, it was possibly inevitable that rural song would come to be seen as a distinct and significant type of music. Western influence may simply have accelerated the process.

'Esashi Oiwake' will reappear often below, especially in §5.5. Several other elements of its story, of less general relevance to the history of modern *min'yō*, are only touched on here. For example, even by the time of Walter's recordings in 1911 and 1913, 'Oiwake' in some regions had acquired a 'foresong' and 'aftersong' (*maeuta* and *atouta*), either or both of which may be added to the 'main song' (*hon'uta*). These derive from a different melodic source (Takeuchi 1980: ch. 10, 11) but are similar to the *hon'uta* in style, though less melismatic. At the annual 'Esashi Oiwake' National Contest held in Esashi since 1963 (§5.5), contestants sing only the main song, although guest artists may sing the full suite. As Sasaki Motoharu told me (vii.88), 'In the *hon'uta* you bring the melody to life; in the *maeuta* it's the lyrics' (*Hon'uta wa fushi o ikasu, maeuta wa kashi o ikasu*).

Also important to modern performance is the *soikake*, the person who yells *soi!* between lines of the main song as the singer takes a breath (see Takeuchi 1980: ch.8). CD2 is the standard current version as sung by Esashi native and former national contest winner Aosaka Mitsuru, an amateur when he won but later a leading local professional who also teaches tourists; CD28 is by the renowned professional Sasaki Motoharu from Hakodate (two hours by train from Esashi), who has been a judge at the contest and here strives to sing the 'correct' version.

3.4 The pre-war folk song world

3.4.1 The first 'folk songs' and their diffusion

'Esashi Oiwake' was the most prominent of the songs that came to be called *min'yō* in the pre-war period, but many other rural songs similarly made their way to the big cities and thence to all corners of Japan. Most of these songs followed a course of development roughly similar to that of 'Esashi Oiwake', whether under its influence or independently. Dignification, the formation of associations, organized teaching, bitter rivalries, government interference, recording, publicity, local pride and/or jealousy – all these became common in the *min'yō-kai*. (For overviews of this period, see Takeuchi 1981: 247; Kikuchi 1980: ch.2.) Diffusion from centre back to periphery was accomplished mainly via recordings and the movement of individual artists at first, strengthened by the emergence of radio and professional folk song troupes in the 1920s. The first songs diffused were almost exclusively dance and party/parlour (*ozashiki*) songs. These were joined by publicity-oriented 'new folk songs' starting in the 1920s. Work and ceremonial songs rarely reached the cities in the first place, mainly because dance and party songs were as a whole more suitable for public entertainment. Ceremonial songs, burdened by conservatism, were often 'old-fashioned'; work songs were sung unaccompanied, sometimes stressing rhythm at the expense of melody and lyrics. Dance and party songs, however, were usually accompanied by instruments and intended to be heard by an attentive (human) audience: they were pre-adapted to become popular *min'yō*.

The first wave of *min'yō* diffusion came during the latter Meiji period, as a score or so of local songs became well-known far from home. Without exception they were accompanied by shamisen, having passed through the hands of the geisha. In fact, most of the early recording artists were geisha.

Between the late 1890s and 1913, songs such as the following – all now familiar *min'yō* – were recorded: 'Oiwake Bushi', 'Sansa Shigure', 'Yoneyama Jinku', 'Sangai Bushi', 'Iso Bushi', 'Nagoya Jinku', 'Ise Ondo', 'Miyazu Bushi', 'Yasugi Bushi' and 'Hakata Bushi' (see Kikuchi 1980: 44, Itō 1912: 500–80, recordings R35, R61, R66). This sampling, listed in approximate north-south order, shows that songs from all parts of Japan were being filtered through Tokyo and redistributed to the provinces; there is as yet no sign of the later domination of the *min'yō* repertoire by songs from the north.[18]

Even before recordings were widely available (commercial sales having begun in 1904), local songs had shown a remarkable ability to migrate, albeit sporadically. Kobayashi Jōfū (b. 1895) recalled that 'Yoneyama Jinku', a recently popularized song from Niigata Prefecture, was known in his little farming village in Saga Prefecture in Kyushu by 1908; on the other hand, he could not recall having heard 'Esashi Oiwake' until at least the late 1920s (pers. comm., 1980). The 'Haiya Bushi' tune family has been traced all over the Japanese islands (as demonstrated in the record set R3), travelling principally by sea. The Ise pilgrimage songs (§2.4.7) spread primarily by land.[19]

Terminology was unsettled in the pre-war years (§§1.2–3). Eventually the term *min'yō* would encompass all of the above songs. Since they were all accompanied by shamisen (with the growing exception of 'Esashi Oiwake'), they were also often called *zokuyō*. An early record catalogue (Itō 1912) lumps them under the heading *kouta*, using it as a kind of catch-all for brief shamisen songs. Since most of these songs had titles identifying their town of origin, many people also considered them *riyō* (literally, 'village songs'), despite this term's usually rural implications. Some record companies in particular began to use this term on their labels, since the mystique of the rural image was becoming a useful selling point. This is not merely a terminological quibble, since the choice of term reflects for most users an ideological stance with regard to the nature and value of this kind of music.

At this early stage, however, it was not yet usual to stress the local nature of the material as a marketing strategy. For example, although the titles may have included place-names, an additional prefectural identification was normally missing from record labels – whereas today we more often find: 'Honjō Oiwake (Akita Pref.)'.

During the Taishō period (1912–26), several of these songs came to be performed on stage in the big cities. Aside from the occasional contest, the most common setting was the *yose*, a type of vaudeville or variety theatre. At a *yose*, these incipient *min'yō* would share the stage with women's *gidayū* (puppet theatre chanting), *naniwa-bushi*, *rakugo* comic storytelling, traditional popular shamisen songs of the type called *zokkyoku*, *enka*-style popular songs, and other urban-bred populist entertainments. (The recordings in R61, made in 1903, capture these various styles but without mention of the word *min'yō*; R66 includes a *zokkyoku* from 1909 and several folk songs from 1911–13.)

National radio broadcasts after 1925 contributed greatly to expanding the audience for folk song. Also, the regular use of the words *min'yō* and *riyō* on radio was crucial in spreading those terms.[20]

The early days of folk song broadcasting are well described in Takeuchi's biography of Machida Kashō, producer of the first such programmes (1974: 55f.). Most items broadcast were dance or *ozashiki* songs; work songs were heard much less often. Unaccompanied performances were likewise rare: shamisen and/or shakuhachi had already become the standard *min'yō* accompaniment, along with percussion. (Indeed, Machida told me in 1978 that he used to receive critical telephone calls if he played unaccompanied work songs too often: most preferred the arranged, urbanized *zokuyō* to the *riyō*.) This was, however, more true in the *yose* than on radio, because the *yose* were commercial concerns existing purely to sell entertainment, whereas the radio was non-commercial and exercised an educational function as well. Thus Machida did occasionally broadcast performances that went against the trend towards 'arranged', accompanied folk song.[21]

The pull of radio was such that Machida frequently received letters or phone calls from singers volunteering to perform without pay – fortunately, since the station had almost no funds for fees. Groups of local singers came from the prefectures near Tokyo at their own expense (Takeuchi 1974: 60–1). Already by this time we encounter a dichotomy which characterizes *min'yō* performance to this day. On the one hand, local groups of amateurs would sing songs from their native place; on the other, serious enthusiasts, often incipient professionals, would, like the geisha, sing songs from anywhere (one such being Mishima Issei; ibid.: 62–3).

A further source of encouragement for *min'yō* performance was the growth of contests. Some were village affairs, often held on the eve of a festival as in traditional times (§2.4.2). More and more, however, they were sponsored by the media, particularly local newspapers. The role of the newspapers in support of *min'yō* reflects a combination of public-mindedness and profit-seeking: then as now, the publicity accruing from such contests was seen as a potential boost to circulation. Many early professionals launched their careers through success in public competitions (see NMMM: 90). Perhaps the single most influential contest was sponsored by the Tō-ō Nippō newspaper in Aomori City from 1934; such renowned Tsugaru singers as Asari Miki and Kon Jūzō were successful there during the 1930s. The winners would then often join professional troupes to tour throughout northern Japan, reaching the same audience served by the blind itinerants. In fact, some of the latter, including Takahashi Chikuzan, also eventually joined troupes. (See also Groemer 1999: index entry 'competition(s)'.)

3.4.2 *Standardization of accompanying instruments*

In connection with the various developments mentioned above, instrumental accompaniment for *min'yō* was becoming standardized during the early decades of the twentieth century. (See §1.6.2 for the earlier situation.) Already by the 1920s, in the various new performance contexts of the folk song world – recordings, broadcasts, contests, concerts – unaccompanied song was virtually unthinkable.

Accompaniment depended on the type of song. For free-rhythm songs such as 'Esashi Oiwake', the shakuhachi became standard, lagging a split second behind the solo voice and providing interludes; such songs are therefore now called *takemono* – 'bamboo pieces'. For these metreless songs, shamisen was rarely added and is almost never used today.[22] Metred songs, conversely, were invariably accompanied by shamisen; in recent decades shakuhachi is increasingly added to shadow the voice or shamisen; and especially for dance songs, the transverse bamboo flute *shinobue/takebue* might join or replace the shakuhachi since it is commonly used in village dance music. Stick-drums (*taiko*) of various types, possibly joined by a small hand-gong (*kane*), are used mostly for dance songs and livelier parlour songs. For 'stage' folk song, the standard drum set uses only two drums: the laced-head *shimedaiko*, and a shallow tacked-head drum called *hiradaiko* ('flat drum') which is played on its top head and provides a good portable substitute for the larger barrel-drums used for Bon dance accompaniment. Figures 3.1 and 4.2 show typical ensembles. (Large drum ensembles as typified by Kodō are not found in *min'yō*, but see §7.3.)

Shamisen and shakuhachi players tended, like singers, to be specialists. But the *narimono* – drums and other percussion – were originally played by whoever was free at the time; only from the late 1940s did full-time *narimono* specialists begin to appear. The backing vocals – *hayashi(-kotoba)* or '(words of) encouragement' – were also originally sung by anyone, but this too began to become a specialist skill from perhaps the 1960s (§§4.4.1–2).

This standard lineup has changed very little to the present day. So 'Sōran Bushi', the renowned fishnet-hauling song which was originally unaccompanied, now almost always uses shamisen, *taiko, kane,* and shakuhachi and/or *shinobue* when heard at a *min'yō* event **(CD20, 29)**. A few additional refinements might be heard: for a pack-horse song, a belt of horse-bells shaken to provide atmosphere, but in a regular rhythm unlike what would be expected had the bells been attached to a horse; for 'Ondo no Funauta' and some other rowing songs, occasionally a small device that imitates the creaking of an oar; for 'Kokiriko Bushi', the thin bamboo concussion sticks that give the song its title; similarly, wooden 'bird-scarer' concussion plaques (*naruko*) for the *shin-min'yō* 'Yosakoi Naruko Odori'; *kotsuzumi* and *ōtsuzumi* hand-drums for 'Yasugi Bushi'; *kokyū* fiddle for 'Etchū Owara Bushi', 'Mugiya Bushi' and a few others from the same region. An artistically inclined record producer or concert organizer might come up with other possibilities for special occasions – a koto perhaps for 'Kuroda Bushi' **(CD30)**, since this Fukuoka folk song derives its melody from the court music composition 'Etenraku'. (See §7.4 for mention of a low-register shamisen.) But even today, such divergences from the norm are very rare.

With Japan's continuing absorption of Western music, recordings of *min'yō* accompanied by Western instruments, often mixed with traditional ones, are not uncommon (as discussed later). Most professionals have made such recordings, to expand their audience. Similarly, jazz bands might add a *min'yō* or two to their repertoire, resulting in recordings such as 'Sōran Rhumba', an instrumental version of 'Sōran Bushi' (Hughes 2000). Such Western accompaniment quickly became, and remains, *de rigueur* for *shin-min'yō* – the 'new folk songs' to which we now turn.

3.4.3 *The first folk song 'boom': the New Folk Song Movement*[23]

3.4.3.1 Introduction
In §1.5 we saw that the turn of the twentieth century was a period of cultural nationalism which stimulated an interest in and respect for village life. In parallel with this nationalism, a different sort of concern for the masses emerged in the Taishō period (1912–26). This was a time of particularly rapid urbanization and industrialization as well as agricultural hardship. Domestic factors combined with international influences such as the Russian Revolution and the effects of a manufacturing boom and subsequent bust triggered by the first World War. These and other factors spurred the growth of 'Taishō democracy', as expressed in rice-price riots and the beginnings of a labour movement. In this atmosphere, the imported Romanticism of the late nineteenth century (§1.2) began to develop into a more direct concern with the masses.

Let us begin in 1904, during the fervour of the Russo-Japanese War, when the nationalist newspaper *Yorozu Chōhō* launched a song lyric contest (details from Nakamura 1991: 272–4). Lyrics were specifically to be in the common folk song metre of 7-7-7-5 syllables (§1.5). The editor, the novelist and translator Kuroiwa Ruikō, asked why poems in this metre, 'loved and sung by the people', were ignored or despised by the intelligentsia despite the existence of many excellent lyrics. Also, since the general word for Japanese poetry was *uta*, 'song', was it not folk song that maintained the true nature of *sung* poetry, whereas *haiku* and *waka* were now only read, not sung? So Kuroiwa asked readers to send in 26-syllable *uta*: 'These we will call *riyō seichō* [authentic folk song]. The best of those works . . ., those that most embody the spirit of the "authentic folk song", will then be chosen for publication, and prizes sent to the authors' (ibid.: 273).

Given the spirit of the times, entries flooded in. The first winning lyric translates roughly as follows: 'With a sword for my pillow / in the front line camp, / the tactless fire of the enemy / snuffs out my dream like a lamp.' Kuroiwa's colleague, song researcher Yuasa Chikusanjin, later explained (quoted in ibid.: 273): '*Riyō seichō* was truly a new song form born out of the war, a new folk song born of the nation's age of growth.' A judge praised it as a 'superior' and 'elevated' poem.

Predictably, rival newspapers raced to start their own contests. But in the frenzy, Yuasa reports, 'people lost sight of Mr Kuroiwa's idea of authenticity. Immature youths from the country[-side] were . . . sending in a *riyō* poem.'

Notice the ironies. First, Yuasa and Kuroiwa sought 'authentic' 'elevated' lyrics, not something by 'immature youths from the country'. Why the gratuitous phrase 'from the country'? So much for respecting the folk. Second, there is no evidence that any of these 'authentic folk songs' were ever sung. So much for restoring the essence of *uta*. Third, the winning *riyō* – 'village song' – has no village flavour at all, aside from its metre. We will return to the problem of 'authenticity' in §5.7. Here we pursue the development of the conscious creation of new 'folk' lyrics by non-'folk', even as research on true traditional song continued separately in parallel.

By about 1915, a group of Japanese poets had emerged who devoted much of their energy to writing new 'children's songs' (*dōyō*)[24] and 'folk songs' (*min'yō*); their efforts turned gradually from a focus on artistic merit to a concern with what they perceived to be the needs of the people. With regard to folk song, the dimensions of the phenomenon were such that people began to speak of a 'movement' – what was soon to be dubbed the New Folk Song Movement (*shin-min'yō undō*).[25]

Initially the focus was on lyrics: the first *shin-min'yō* were made to be read, not sung, and were published in collections without musical notation. Dozens of magazines printed newly-written texts. But soon the poets came to feel that their lyrics needed melodies. By about 1920, the main magazine for children's songs (*dōyō*) began to publish in each issue a few melodies sent in by readers (Nakamura 1991: 277). Let us focus, though, on *shin-min'yō*.

The dominant lyricist of the movement, its first great figure, was Kitahara Hakushū (1885–1942; see Fukasawa 1993: 83ff.). A researcher and ideologue as well as a poet, he collected and published many traditional children's songs (*warabeuta*) and showed an active interest in folk song as well. In 1927 he wrote, echoing his own earlier statements: 'Japanese folk songs, once the voice of the people and the land, have since the Meiji period largely lost their local colour and pastoral flavour (*yachō*). . . . Authentic (*seichō*) folk songs which still preserve their original dignity are extremely rare' (Kitahara 1927: preface p.3–4). This, he said, is why such as he had emerged from among the people, striving both to keep alive the traditional songs and to create new ones, for both children and adults (ibid.). Hakushū and his colleagues rarely used the term *shin-min'yō* in describing their output: to them, both old and new songs were simply *min'yō*. Folklorists such as Yanagita Kunio, however, resented the confusion of the two categories and insisted on the prefix *shin-* 'new' for the new, literary songs; this view eventually prevailed generally.

Hakushū did indeed hope to see his songs performed, but the vast majority of his output was never set to music. This was true both for the poems he considered *min'yō* and for other lyric poems intended as traditional-style popular or parlour songs. Thus in 1923 we find him pleading with regard to one poem intended as a *kouta* (a 'little song' of the type favoured by geisha and their clients): 'I wish someone would set this to shamisen accompaniment.'[26]

It is unclear to what extent his earliest works were actually sung. I have found little independent evidence on this point, and Hakushū's own written comments are generally vague. In 1920 he tells us, concerning a long lyric penned in 1913: 'I tried making a song [text] for [the men who pulled] the floats', the decorated wheeled carts of the festival in the village west of Tokyo where he was then living (Kitahara 1987: 29.48). But there was already such a song in the village; he does not say whether *his* lyrics were indeed adopted in addition to the pre-existing ones. Three years later he had moved to a village on the eastern edge of Tokyo. Of a set of poems written there, he says (ibid.: 116): 'Most of these were written for the young men of the village. Around that time they would come to me nearly every night to receive the texts I had written for them. Then they would walk around singing them as they pleased (*omoi-omoi ni*).' It is not clear what melodies may have been adopted, nor how long such songs survived.

Hakushū's poetic peer, Noguchi Ujō (1882–1945), stressed that these new children's and folk 'songs' should indeed be written in a 'singable' metre, and he often improvised evanescent melodies for his own poems, but merely as a device to help him write the poetry (Nakamura 1991: 278).

The eventual addition of specific new melodies to 'folk' texts of Hakushū, Ujō and similar poets resulted largely from direct requests from paying patrons. An early example occurred in 1921, when Hakushū and composer Hirota Ryōtarō were commissioned by a textile factory owner in Gunma Prefecture to produce some 'new folk songs' for the women workers to sing (Kojima 1970: 5, 16; Machida 1933: 218). From about this time, with increasing numbers of young women leaving home to work in such light industries as textiles, the question of the welfare of these woman workers (*jokō*) was attracting considerable attention. The owner apparently hoped to supply his workers with some morally suitable recreation, and it is interesting that he chose 'new folk songs' as the appropriate genre. The texts of Hakushū's efforts in this cause can be found in Kitahara 1941: 308–14.

Writers and composers had high hopes for *shin-min'yō* at this time: it was felt that suitable new songs could help alleviate social problems. Noguchi strove to replace the original 'vulgar' lyrics of the folk with something more modern and morally uplifting (§1.5). The composer Fujii Kiyomi (1889–1944) travelled the length and breadth of Japan with missionary zeal to perform his compositions, occasionally holding teaching sessions afterwards (Kojima 1970: 12). Some of his songs were intended to be traditional in style and purpose (e.g. foundation-pounding songs); others were meant to serve in an 'urban, modern' context – for Fujii also wrote songs for the factory girls (ibid.: 14). I have found no accounts of the effects or acceptance of these new work songs; at any rate, virtually none are heard today.

Another step in attempting to give song back to the people was the formation in 1928 of the Nihon Min'yō Kyōkai (Japan Folk Song Association). Among its members were all the major figures in the *shin-min'yō* movement. From that same year the association began to hold annnual prize concerts for new folk songs and dances. The offerings were quite varied: some had the feel of traditional folk song, some were more like art songs or *Lieder* (Kojima 1970: 16). Most of the singers were Western-trained (perhaps less for aesthetic reasons than that they often needed to sing from notation).

These various efforts at providing *Gebrauchsmusik* for the masses attracted little attention from the record companies. Songs of this type apparently were not catching on as their creators had hoped. The New Folk Song Movement might have faded away quietly had it not been for the sudden unprecedented success of 'Suzaka Kouta' (**CD31**; Appendix 1.1A).

This was yet another song for textile mill women. In this case, the owner of the mill in Suzaka (Nagano Pref.) was appalled to hear the bawdy lyrics sung by the women as they worked. Hoping to provide them with more uplifting fare, in 1921 he asked Noguchi Ujō and local-born composer Nakayama Shinpei (1887–1952) to create a new song. By 1924 the song was ready and a dance had been choreographed. A hundred workers were selected to learn the song and dance to present it before their co-workers. That its reception was better than that of the Gunma factory songs may have been due to the presence at the launching not only of the composers but of a famous popular songstress from Tokyo (Takeuchi 1981: 12). In any case, it proved a resounding success, spreading nationwide just like a traditional *hayariuta*, without even the aid of a recording at first. (This account is from Machida 1933.)

Although 'Suzaka Kouta' was intended merely as a healthy diversion for the workers, its astonishing success alerted all of Japan to the potential publicity value of a folk song. Conscious use of local songs to entice visitors had so far been exploited only to a limited degree. We have discussed 'Esashi Oiwake' at length in this regard. 'Kiso Bushi' was a more surprising case **(CD5)**. A relatively simple, unaccompanied Bon dance song from a small lumber-producing town isolated in the mountains of Nagano, central Japan, it was recorded in 1916 after the mayor had persuaded a sympathetic recording company executive to record it in its original, unadorned form – that is the surprising bit – as a form of folkloric publicity (Morigaki 1960: 127–9). Prior to the birth of the recording industry, songs from traditional tourist spots (hot springs, pilgrimage centres and the like) often contained verses of self-praise which became free advertising when carried home by visitors. A more activist example: it is claimed, on what evidence I know not, that Sōma Province (in modern Fukushima Pref.), its population decimated by famine and plague in 1785 and 1834, aggressively used local folk songs to attract in-migrants (NMZ: 2.238). But the effect in the pre-recording, pre-radio era was much less potent.

Whatever the historical precedents among traditional *min'yō*, the decade following the success of 'Suzaka Kouta' saw the creation of hundreds of *shin-min'yō* touting the textiles of Tōkamachi, the hot springs of Iizaka, the scenery of Tenryū Gorge, the tea of Shizuoka. The titles of most of these songs consisted of the local place-name followed by 'Kouta' ('little song') or 'Ondo' (implying a dance song). The use of the word *kouta* implies the perception of similarities of mood and style to that geisha parlour song genre. However, songs of the genre *kouta* itself never used this word in their titles.

Such songs came to be called *gotōchi songu* – 'local praise songs'. (Use of the English loan-word *songu* perhaps suggests that this category was perceived as non-traditional in function.) The vast majority were commissioned, although some lyrics resulted from local competitions.[27] The lyricists, however, were still at heart poets first and employees second: many of these songs contain surprisingly little overt advertising and are nearly indistinguishable from traditional folk song.

The New Folk Song Movement flourished for approximately a decade, spurred on by competition among communities throughout Japan, by the growth of folklorism, by the poets' desire to provide moral fare to replace more 'vulgar' popular songs, and – even at this early stage of modernization – by a nostalgia for fading folkways. Indeed, in some ways the 'old home village' had become almost exotic for urban residents. Yanagita Kunio's book *Tales of Tōno* (*Tōno Monogatari*, 1910), which collected folk tales from an isolated village in Iwate, was a huge best-seller and was re-issued frequently, in large part because such stories already had a feel of romantic distance for most readers. Hosokawa (2000: 15–6) quotes extensively from the critic Kobayashi Hideo's 1933 article 'The literature which has lost its *furusato*' ('Furusato o ushinatta bungaku'). Kobayashi, though Tokyo-born, does not feel Tokyo to be his *furusato* because the city has changed too far too fast; indeed, he has no *furusato*, no place where he has built up memories. All he meets in Tokyo are 'abstract people called urbanites who were born nowhere'. However, Kobayashi also feels that the resulting nostalgic yearning for an idealized *furusato* is futile and false – not because Westernization had already destroyed the former harmony of village life, but because such a harmony had never existed. It seemed to him that literature, including *shin-min'yō*, might thus fill a gap by providing an ideal home better than any that had actually been experienced.

Whatever the reasons, a large-scale 1931 survey found that 34 per cent of respondents enjoyed listening to *shin-min'yō*. A few of the songs did take root successfully and were accepted as local songs. A very few of these are heard today at concerts of 'traditional' *min'yō*, including 'Chakkiri Bushi' and 'Tōkamachi Kouta' (described below), now treated as indigenous to Shizuoka and Niigata Prefectures respectively. 'Iizaka Kouta' (**CD32**; Appendix 1.1.E; notation in Hughes 1991: 45), a song written around 1930 to advertise Iizaka Spa in Fukushima Prefecture, is one of several *shin-min'yō* to make its way into the repertoire of the *goze* blind itinerant female musicians. This song must have appealed to their clientele, since the few surviving Niigata *goze* could still sing it in the 1970s. (The folk process had taken hold, as they had adapted the mode, melody and lyrics considerably.)[28] Another sign of the interest in *shin-min'yō* is the appearance of books such as *How to make folk songs* by the poet Nishikawa Rinnosuke (1934). Nishikawa offers a brief history of folk song, a prescriptive guide to making lyrics, a critical analysis of pseudo-folk lyrics by various poets – but no mention of music.

Then the movement ground to a halt. Of several proffered explanations for this demise, three seem likely. First, growing militarism put a damper on several forms of popular amusement, including folk music and dance in general. The government pressed artists to put themselves at their country's service. Kitahara Hakushū devoted his talents increasingly to the writing of 'citizens' songs' (*kokumin kayō*); in his 1941 collection of his works, 140 pages are given over to the reprinting of fifty-two such songs, with titles like 'Banzai Hitlerjügend' and 'Navy March' (1941: 8.259–398).

Second and most important, both the artists and the potential audience for *shin-min'yō* were increasingly being drawn off into the world of popular song (*kayōkyoku*). Songwriters like Noguchi and Nakayama had from the beginning been writing in more than one style. While producing 'folk songs' with strong local roots (as expressed in their titles), they also created songs on more general themes and with less folk-like melodies, freed from the ideological burden of having to serve as 'folk songs'. There were also many hybrids of these two types. As the non-folklike songs gained popularity at the expense of *shin-min'yō*, record companies pressured their writers and singers to focus on the former. The local praise songs may have yielded the publicity sought by local officials, but they could not rival *kayōkyoku* in record sales.

Third, once several hundred quite similar *shin-min'yō* had appeared, the publicity value of any new song would have been greatly diminished.

Still, the phenomenon did not die out completely. *Shin-min'yō* of the above type continued to be produced here and there throughout the wartime and early post-war decades. In some cases, particularly since the 1970s, they have been produced to give identity and pride to a suburban 'new town' or an urban neighbourhood (§6.3). A rather different trend, however, is the predominance especially since the 1970s of a newer type of *shin-min'yō* which seeks to identify with 'modern Japan' rather than with local communities, and whose lyrics and music are strikingly different from most of the locally focused *shin-min'yō*. We shall tell the story of these 'new "new folk songs"' in §6.4. Here we examine the characteristics of the lyrics and music of the early 'new folk songs'.

3.4.3.2 Lyrics

For the early period we can focus on Kitahara Hakushū as a representative and influential lyricist. While he strove throughout to imitate the artlessness of folk poetry, Hakushū's lyrics evolved gradually from somewhat precious pastoral poems which seem more suitable for reading than for singing, to lyrics in a style much closer to traditional folk song. The same can be said of folk-minded contemporaries such as Noguchi Ujō and Saijō Yaso (1892–1970). In most of these early poems, sentiments, subjects and imagery felt traditional, despite an occasional sense that these were indeed pseudo-folk products by self-conscious career poets. Once the texts actually began to be set to music, they were often elaborated by the addition of folk-like refrains, or by repetition of parts of each verse in a way similar to that found in many traditional *min'yō*. (Composers of these early *shin-min'yō* also aimed to fashion melodies in a style close to the traditional one, as we shall see.)

However much the poets of the New Folk Song Movement sympathized or empathized with 'the people', however much their activities can be said to have been inspired in part by democratizing and revolutionary trends, they were not revolutionaries. Their lyrics show a continuing pastoralism tinged with sentimentalism and nostalgia. Consider the second verse of Nagai Hakubi's 'Tōkamachi Kouta' (1929; Appendix 1.1D):

> How do young girls pass the height of their youth? / Buried in snow, sitting at their looms, / Still half a year before they flower.

This comes across less as a criticism of dehumanization in the weaving industry than as a sentimental evocation of local lifeways – particularly considering the context of verses 1 and 3. More overtly activist songs did appear from time to time; some of these were in the *shin-min'yō* stylistic mould, while others made use of widely popular folk melodies such as 'Yasugi Bushi' (Hattori 1959: 206–7). More commonly, however, leftist music of this period identified with internationalist styles and concerns (see Malm 1984), which is quite the opposite philosophy to that of *min'yō*.

Turning from content to form of lyrics, let us note another common compositional device in *shin-min'yō* borrowed from traditional folk song, especially dance songs: the insertion of *hayashi-kotoba*, refrains often consisting of vocables or onomatopoeia (along the lines of English 'falala') or meaningful but hardly relevant words (English 'blow the man down'). These were sometimes added by the lyricist, sometimes by the composer. The composer's setting could also call for repetitions of part of the verse, again a traditional feature. Another common feature in imitation of many *min'yō* is an introductory drawn-out *haa* or similar vocable.

Thus many features of traditional folk textual style and structure were copied in *shin-min'yō*. There were only three minor stylistic differences. First, the new songs tended to be somewhat wordier – slightly longer verses, more syllables per minute.[29] Second, whereas the textual repetitions in traditional *min'yō* are almost always exact, those in *shin-min'yō* often show some variation; compare the third and fourth lines of each verse of 'Chakkiri Bushi' (Appendix 1.1.C).[30] Finally, due to their frequent function as local publicity songs, *shin-min'yō* texts had to mention the area and its charms quite specifically. (On the other hand, many traditional songs already did this.) 'Chakkiri Bushi', commissioned for a tea-growing district, is replete with local references, mainly to tea but also to the famous Robin Hood figure Jirōchō. Still, aside from the inexact repetitions, the verses could easily be mistaken for traditional ones.

A slightly special case that forms a sort of bridge to the 'new folk songs' of the 1970s is 'Tōkyō Ondo', whose story is well told by Hosokawa (2000). In 1932, a *shin-min'yō* titled 'Marunouchi Ondo' was composed by Nakayama Shinpei with lyrics by Saijō Yaso (recording R58). Like a local praise song, it was commissioned with the aim of grabbing attention and building local pride – except that the locale, Marunouchi, was a district in the centre of Tokyo, containing both the imperial palace and the main rail station. At the time, nearby Ginza was the fashionable district of Tokyo, but Marunouchi hoped to usurp that status. The organizers plotted well. From the beginning they intended this as a dance song (hence the word 'Ondo' in the title), and in July 1932 a weeklong Bon dance was held. Dancers were required to wear a specific *yukata* robe, with 'Marunouchi' on its back, available only from a local department store. On the musicians' tower were two popular folk singers of the period. The lyrics were rich in imperial and local references, often embedded in traditional-style verses but with a modern twist. Thus:

kumo wa kokonoe / miizu wa sora ni / ondo toru ko wa / mannaka ni
   The clouds are nine-layered, / His Majesty's august virtue soars above, / and
the singer / is in the middle [of the dance plaza].
   sorota sorota yo / odoriko no teburi / biru no mado hodo / yō sorota
They're all lined up, / the dancers' hand movements, / just as well as the
windows of the buildings / they're lined up.

Other verses referred to places and events associated with the district.
   The seven-day event was a huge success. As a result, a year later the organizers broadened their sights to all of Tokyo. The new version of the song was
called 'Tōkyō Ondo' (also on R58) and is still vaguely familiar to most
Japanese.

3.4.3.3 Music

In attempting, consciously or otherwise, to create new folk songs, composers
fastened on scale structure and metre as two of the prime identifiers of folk
style. In §1.6.8 we saw that such songs overwhelmingly use one of two basically pentatonic scales, the anhemitonic *yō* (including its subtype, *ritsu*) and
the hemitonic *miyako-bushi*. In usage, as described by Koizumi, each of these
is based around a framework of nuclear tones of fairly precise intonation,
with infixed pitches of more variable intonation in between.

   Recently, however, influence from certain traditional Japanese classical
genres and latterly from Western music have led professional folk singers, as
well as judges at folk song contests, to place great store in consistency of
intonation.[31] Scholars with their transcriptions, as well as composers (if not
always performers) of *shin-min'yō*, both follow and contribute to this new
trend, adhering closely to 'Western' intervals. Thus the problems of modal
assignment mentioned in §1.6.8, arising from variably pitched infixes, do not
apply to 'new folk songs' nor, by and large, to modern professional singers'
performances of traditional songs.

   Discussing 'new folk songs' here and in §§6.3–4, we may safely use
my simplified version of Koizumi's model, with *ritsu* subsumed under *yō*.
(This is particularly so because 'new folk song' composers have virtually
never used *ritsu*.) In §1.6.8 we noted that the most common traditional folk
song mode by far is *yō* on 6 (6 123 5), followed by *yō* on 2, *in* on 7 and *in*
on 3.

   How did the early *shin-min'yō* composers deal with these modal tendencies
of traditional song? Examining fifty-one *shin-min'yō* by the genre's most pro-
lific and successful composer, Nakayama Shinpei (1887–1952), reveals that
all fifty-one end on one of the four most common traditional final pitches
listed above.[32] Of these, thirty-one are *miyako-bushi* on 7 and/or 3 (verse and
chorus may differ in finalis); sixteen are *yō* on 6; and four are *yō* on 2.

   Metrically, Nakayama and other composers stuck without exception to
the duple metres (including 6/8) which characterized the vast majority of

traditional Bon and party dance songs. Free rhythm, though common in traditional non-dance folk song, is virtually absent from *shin-min'yō*, mainly because most have been intended as dance songs, partly because free-rhythm songs are uncommon in Western music, and perhaps also partly because they are perceived to lack the steady pulse of modernity. Meanwhile, 3/4 metre was eschewed simply because it does not occur in traditional *min'yō* (with a few remarkable exceptions). The more complex rhythms of traditional songs like 'Tsugaru Yosare Bushi' (§1.6.1, **CD4**), which cannot be notated easily, were indeed too complicated to provide a model for the composers.

Thus in terms of both mode and metre, *shin-min'yō* actually show less diversity than do traditional folk songs. The quest for authenticity acted as a restraint.

Like most of the principal early 'new folk song' composers, Nakayama was a graduate of a Western-style music conservatoire, Tokyo School of Music, and he wrote many other works – marches, theatre and film songs and so forth – which did not use these common folk modes and metres. Thus it is clear that he had in his mind a precise, apparently conscious model for composing folk songs. He wrote in 1930 that it was necessary to eschew Western musical models and write in folk style 'so that we can give the people songs which will easily become familiar to them *(najimi no ii kayō)*' (quoted in Kojima 1970: 4). For a nation whose musical tastes were in transition, Nakayama and similar tunesmiths provided something for everyone.

Was the relative lack of diversity in comparison to 'real' folk songs a result of Nakayama's insufficient familiarity with the true folk style? It is instructive to consider the remarks of Machida Kashō, that pioneering folk song researcher who also wrote many *shin-min'yō* and could not have been accused of insufficient knowledge of traditional song style. People often complained, he wrote (1933: 217), that 'all *shin-min'yō* sound alike', but this was unavoidable because the patrons all wanted the same sort of simple, easy-to-sing songs that had previously been successful. In particular, he claimed, it was necessary to write in the traditional pentatonic modes because they were easier to sing for people with little or no (Western-style) music education. Other composers obviously agreed with this assessment. The irony is that Machida's most popular composition, indeed virtually the only one which has been accepted into the *min'yō* repertoire of today, is 'Chakkiri Bushi', which has a relatively complex melody involving modulation between *yō* and *miyako-bushi* (Ex. 3.1).

Still, it can be said that Machida's overall output shows greater adherence to true folk song style than does Nakayama's. For example, 75 per cent of a sample of twenty-four of Machida's melodies (taken from Machida 1933) are in the *yō* scale, as opposed to only 41 per cent of Nakayama's. Nakayama's overreliance on *miyako-bushi*, despite its relative infrequency in village song, may well reflect a personal preference for traditional urban

Ex. 3.1 'Chakkiri Bushi', excerpt (transcribed from recording R6)

popular song genres such as *kouta*. Further, while Machida's melodies flow in folklike lines, Nakayama's often move in mysterious ways. For example, many of his songs contain melodic passages which seem to reflect Western triadic thinking. In a traditional *yō* on 6 (A̲ C D E G), a passage like A-c-e or e-c-A would be unusual: the nuclear tone d would very likely make an appearance. Nakayama's use of such passages (e.g. in 'Jōshū Kouta' on R58) may arise from an unconscious syncretism with a minor triad. Another case is shown in Example 3.2, the first line of 'Kamogawa Kouta'; the mode is *miyako-bushi* on 7 (E F A B̲ C). Measures 3 and 4 contain the melodic sequence A-c-A, with c on the strong beat. Such a passage would be very unlikely to occur in a traditional piece unless the gesture resolved onto the nuclear tone B on a strong beat: A-c-A | B. In this piece the resolution is onto A, giving the sense that we are in the Western key of A minor. Such unusual leaps occur often in Nakayama's songs. Such subtle compositional distinctions differentiate Nakayama and other conservatoire-trained composers not only from Machida but from others with a folk background who occasionally composed *shin-min'yō* (e.g. Gotō Tōsui, who claimed to have gotten the idea for his 'Hachinohe Kouta' from the vaguely similar Akita folk song 'Obonai Bushi').

Nakayama's *yō* songs on 6 usually add the upper auxiliary 7, which we noted in §1.6.8 as a frequent trait of traditional *min'yō* as well. If anything, Nakayama uses this feature too often by comparison with the traditional repertoire. Still, his usage of this additional pitch is generally quite idiomatic, as with the F# of 'Suzaka Kouta' (**CD31**, Ex. 3.3).

Let us now consider the arranging and recording of these early 'new folk songs'. A preference was shown for singers who could add traditional-style

Ex. 3.2 'Kamogawa Kouta', opening vocal (transcribed from recording R57)

Ex. 3.3 'Suzaka Kouta', verse 1 (transcribed from recording R58)

ornaments (*kobushi*) on the spot, 'naturally' – for voice quality and vocal style were also perceived as critical elements in defining *min'yō*. In practice, the performers were often geisha (hear recording of 'Iizaka Kouta' on R58) but sometimes were conservatoire-trained singers making vain attempts to sound like folk singers (hear 'Suzaka Kouta', with *bel canto* vibrato throughout).

Village song was often unaccompanied or featured transverse bamboo flutes and percussion; the shamisen made an occasional appearance. In the evolving 'concert folk song' style, traditional songs were accompanied by at least shakuhachi and, for metred songs, shamisen (§3.4.2). By contrast, *shin-min'yō* recordings employed a small ensemble of Western instruments (most crucially piano and string bass), often supplemented by a few Japanese instruments such as shamisen, transverse flute and percussion; exactly these instruments were used in the original recording of 'Suzaka Kouta'. The 1933 recording of 'Tōkyō Ondo' supplemented traditional instruments with xylophone, clarinet, piano, string bass and (judging by a photo of the session) tuba and saxophone (Hosokawa 2000: 12, 18).

It was not the instrumentation so much as the harmonization that set *shin-min'yō* accompaniments apart.[33] Traditional accompaniments were basically of two types: heterophonic imitations of the vocal melody; and short repeated patterns unrelated to the vocal melody, serving as a sort of rhythmic/countermelodic drone. While still using these two types of accompaniment, the early 'new folk song' arrangers generally added a third type: chordal harmony of a sketchy sort. The original recording of 'Suzaka Kouta' is a perfect example. A shamisen follows the vocal melody in close heterophony; a bamboo flute plays a short repeated three-note motif using pitches B, D and E – but cadencing on D as against the E of the melody, as might well happen in a traditional performance; the bass plays the notes shown above the staff in Example 3.3 on the first beat of each bar; and the piano occasionally plays triads or open fifths based on those bass notes but equally often plays snatches of the vocal melody. Thus both traditional and Western elements appear.

An interesting evolution in harmonic style occurred in these early years, from a slavish insertion of the occasional major triad to what we might call 'pentatonic harmony'. As a typical harmonization of the 'slavish insertion' period, consider Example 3.4, the instrumental introduction to Nakayama's 'Kamogawa Kouta'. The mode is *miyako-bushi* ending on 7 with some cadences on 3 (3 4 6 7 1 = E F A B C). The final note of each of the two melodic phrases shown, the B, is harmonized with an arpeggio on a B-major chord. Since it was standard practice to harmonize the finalis (almost always the tonic) of a Western composition with a triad having that note as its root, the arranger here followed the same procedure. This, however, results in a chord two of whose pitches (D# and F#) are not even part of the tonal material of the mode in question, not even as secondary 'exchange tones'. A cadential passage from 'Iizaka Kouta' ends identically in harmonic terms (**CD32**). Similarly, the E which concludes 'Suzaka Kouta' is accompanied by an E-major triad on piano, even though G# occurs nowhere in the melody. In such cases it seems fair to suggest that the arrangers were motivated not by any appropriate musical logic but merely by the desire to emulate the prestigious Western harmonic language.

Ex. 3.4 'Kamogawa Kouta', instrumental introduction (transcribed from recording R57)

Remember now that both 7 and 3 (B and E in the above examples) serve as common nuclear tones in *miyako-bushi*; indeed, either is an acceptable finalis for a major melodic unit within one and the same piece. Moreover, these two degrees of the *miyako-bushi* mode were apparently equivalent harmonically from a traditional Japanese perspective: they constitute either ends of a fifth, and it would sound quite natural to play this fifth on a shamisen to accompany a cadence on either one. The *shin-min'yō* arrangers of the above examples, however, harmonized them differentially due to a Westernized perspective, in violation of this traditional harmonic identity.

That the Japanese themselves sensed something unsatisfactory about this style of harmonization can be inferred by its gradual abandonment in favour of a style arguably more appropriate to pentatonic music: a melody was harmonized with triads consisting only of pitches which actually occurred in the scale in question. We might call these 'pentatonic chords'. In the new style, the common way to harmonize the B of Example 3.4 is to use (in Western parlance) a triad on E with an unresolved suspended 4th (E A B = 3 6 7). The same chord could be used when the finalis was E = 3. That B and E can thus be harmonized identically suits their traditional harmonic equivalence as described in the previous paragraph. It also suits, however, the likely perception of a listener trained in Western functional harmony – i.e. the typical arranger of these songs – that these melodies end on an implied dominant chord. Thus Western harmonic perceptions seem to be in partial agreement with the much less developed Japanese harmonic sense in this particular case. The three pitches of this chord are, incidentally, the primary pitches of the mode. But there are other types of 'pentatonic chord'. Example 3.5, in *yō* on 6, is accompanied throughout by a reiterated triad using degrees 3, 5 and 6.[34]

It was noted above that many *shin-min'yō* composers and lyricists also wrote popular songs (*kayōkyoku*). Partly because of this overlap in personnel, *kayō kyoku* often showed apparent influence from *shin-min'yō*. This can be seen, for example, in the inclusion of the word 'Kouta' in their titles – e.g. 'Gion Kouta' (text: Appendix 1.1.I), 'Sendō Kouta' (Ex. 3.6, text: Appendix 1.3.A). Indeed, the writers often considered songs such as these to be '*min'yō*-style popular

Ex. 3.5 'Yama no Uta', pentatonic harmonization (excerpt, transcribed from recording R57)

songs'. Starting perhaps with 'Shima no Musume' in 1932 (Ex. 3.7; text: Appendix. 1.3.D), many songs of this style begin with a long-held vocable as in many *min'yō*. But the new popular songs were often more urban-oriented and 'modern' in their content and style than the *shin-min'yō*. 'Gion Kouta' was set in Kyoto, 'Naniwa Kouta' in Osaka. In general, the texts are quite different in feeling from *min'yō* (see Appendix 1.3, songs A-E).

Ex. 3.6 'Sendō Kouta', excerpt (adapted from Osada 1976a: 93)

Ex. 3.7 'Shima no Musume', opening (adapted from Osada 1976a: 110)

Nakayama Shinpei composed prolifically in both categories. In doing so, he maintained certain stylistic differences. For example, we have seen that his 'new folk songs' generally used the most common folk modes: *yō* on 6 and *miyako-bushi* on 3 or 7. When we look at two of his most successful popular songs, however, we find that 'Sendō Kouta' (Ex. 3.6) and 'Habu no Minato' are both written in *miyako-bushi* on 6. This mode occurs with exceeding rarity in *min'yō*, but it is the pentatonic mode most closely resembling the Western minor mode. Since a certain degree of similarity is a prerequisite for syncretism, this mode was ideal for serving as a bridge between traditional and Western music. Scholars now call this the *yonanuki tan'onkai* – the 'minor scale with 4th and 7th degrees missing' (A B C – E F – A) – or in English the 'pentatonic minor' for short.

There is also a so-called 'pentatonic major' (*yona-nuki chōonkai*): *yō* on 1 (C D E – G A – C), which is the traditional mode closest to the Western major. This is almost as rare in folk song as *in* on 6, but its syncretic possibilities have made it the most widely used *kayōkyoku* scale after the pentatonic minor. Its acceptance was eased by the adoption into Meiji-period school songbooks of Scots folk melodies in the same mode (which were chosen precisely because of their pentatonic nature). Despite its frequent occurrence in school and military songs, this mode did not become common until after the Second World War. Nonetheless, the pentatonic minor and major became the most frequently used modes in the *enka* category of popular music. (An excellent English-language study on scale syncretism in Japanese popular music is Kitahara 1966.)

The *yō* mode on 6 is also frequent in *kayōkyoku*, as it was in *min'yō* and *shin-min'yō*. However, in both *yō* and *miyako-bushi*, there is a tendency for *kayōkyoku* to diverge from the traditional form occasionally. There may be only one or two notes in the melody that violate the traditional modal structure (e.g. 'Gion Kouta' antepenultimate note), but that may have been just the degree of novelty sought by the public in an increasingly syncretic age. When Nakayama wrote of eschewing Western models in order to create songs which would 'easily become familiar', was he aware that these syncretic popular songs would outsell and outlive his 'new folk songs'? (I am not suggesting that the tunes alone were responsible for this.) Popular songs representing this style and period are now called *natsumero*, 'nostalgic melodies'.

The New Folk Song Movement is usually considered the first '*min'yō* boom'. Certainly, in terms of the number of songs produced and records sold, it was an impressive phenomenon. Another index of the popularity of these songs is that several were adopted into the repertoire of the Echigo *goze*, as noted above. The movement's long-term effects, however, were less impressive. Its activities had relatively little interaction with the 'real', traditional *min'yō* world, which was making its own way towards urbanization and professionalization. Also, of several hundred 'new folk songs' written during those years, perhaps twenty or less are still sung occasionally at *min'yō* events. Satō noted even in 1946 that the vast majority had already faded from the scene (1946: 150). (Rather more survive to be played over the loudspeakers in local train stations or Bon dances.) As a whole, they have never attracted as large an audience or as many performers as traditional folk song, and they were not quite urban enough to compete in the popular song market.

Despite the death of the movement, *shin-min'yō* are in fact still produced in large quantities today, if not on the scale of the 1920s and 1930s. We return to this topic in §§6.3–4 and elsewhere.

3.4.4 The first min'yō professionals

By the 1920s, then, *min'yō* was an established genre of music; commercial recordings were being issued; folk song contests were becoming frequent;

min'yō were to be heard in theatres, in incipient 'concert' settings; radio broadcasts contributed to the popularity of folk songs; and local towns, factories and spas had begun to finance the composition and recording of 'new folk songs'. The time was ripe for the appearance of a new profession, the 'folk singer' (*min'yō kashu*), and its allied profession, the folk song teacher.

The species *min'yō kashu* did not appear overnight but evolved gradually in response to increasing possibilities for patronage. Among its antecedents were the *goze* and other blind itinerants, the geisha, and the village *ondo-tori* (§2.4.2). However, the *goze* and geisha, although full-time professional entertainers, were not perceived as folk singers at first, even though their repertoires included many songs that would now be called *min'yō*. The first recordings by geisha included *kouta*, *hauta* and *min'yō* with little discrimination: all were simply 'songs' popular at geisha parties. By the 1930s, geisha like Kouta Katsutarō, who attained nationwide fame with her recordings of such *min'yō* as 'Sado Okesa' and 'Aizu Bandai-san', were sometimes identified in the public mind as *min'yō kashu* as well as geisha. But the geisha, despite their important role, have remained a minority element in the folk song world. We are concerned with those performers who were identified *primarily* as folk musicians.

These first *min'yō kashu* found themselves classed as *geinin*, professional performers who had chosen their careers of their own volition. Actors and *naniwa-bushi* reciters were other examples of *geinin*. Defining 'volition' is problematic, but my intention is to exclude those who became performers due to blindness (such as the *goze*) or caste (such as the Daikoku dancers of §2.4.6). Poverty was a frequent contributory factor but too widespread to be determinant.

The pioneer professionals often suffered under a severe image problem – particularly in the north, where most were raised. This was partly because performing folk material for a living was traditionally associated principally with blind itinerants, geisha and certain outcast communities. These were all low-status categories (with the occasional exception of geisha). Also, the 1920s and 1930s were lean years in Japan, especially in the north; the censorious label *dōrakumono* was quickly attached to anyone who devoted too much time and money to music, dance and the inevitable drinking that accompanied them.

Since the first professional folk song troupes consisted almost by definition of people who were spending more time on music than on 'productive' labour, the *dōraku* image transferred readily to these groups. Many of the early *geinin* were indeed heavy drinkers, which often shortened their careers. They also exerted an attraction on the young folk of the village that was feared by the parents and contributed further to the bad reputation of the troupes. Still, when a *min'yō* troupe arrived in the village, everyone would turn out to watch (Fig. 3.2).

Thus it is not surprising that would-be performers encountered parental resistance. In the 1930s Kon Jūzō of Aomori (1907–94) was told by his parents: 'Even if we were dead, we wouldn't want to see you become a *geinin*' (NMMM: 159). Those who became professionals in spite of this prejudice often strove to deny its correctness and to dignify the endeavour. Thus Tsugaru's Kawayama Chidori, leader of one of the earliest travelling troupes in the 1920s, continually stressed etiquette, decorum and the value of folk song for building character; one of her watchwords was: 'Character is 60 per cent, art is 40 per cent.' Nevertheless, she discouraged her son from following in her footsteps, apprenticing him instead to a tofu maker. He became a *geinin* anyway (ibid.: 161–2). A few performing parents were more supportive: Mihashi Michiya (1930–96), a folk singer who also succeeded as an *enka* artist, joined a troupe in his teens at the instigation of his mother, who was a member. Hamada Kiichi I of Esashi (1917–85) and his siblings were also led into performing careers by their father, an avid exponent of 'Esashi Oiwake'.

With or without parental support, professional troupes did form. They fanned out all through northern Japan, timing their visits to coincide with large gatherings of migrant workers or with gaps in the agricultural or fishing schedule. Temporary stages were built for the 'shows'. Diversity of entertainment was prized: the favourites were artists like Tsugaru's Kase no Momo ('Momo from Kase [Village]'; 1886–1931). Momo, like the early U.S. vaudevillians, was a jack-of-all-skills: song, shamisen, storytelling, dance, juggling, magic and improvisation of lyrics. A *geinin* to the last, Momo drank himself to death (NMMM: 108; see also Suda et al. 1998, Groemer 1999).

Touring troupes in recent years are usually assembled *ad hoc*, like the one I toured with in 1979 (Fig. 3.2; see Foreword). *Min'yō* and dance were supplemented by some humour, through the suggestive quasi-*min'yō* comic songs of Ōgata Hachirō and my own singing of one *min'yō* translated into English.

To these performers, songs were not items of folklore. According to the *min'yō kashu* Saitō Kyōko (b. 1936), both of whose parents travelled with such troupes, 'the early pros never cared about the background of a song, they just sang it'. Only recently, she feels, has the influence of scholars caused singers to feel pressure to 'understand' the history and function of *min'yō*. Thus, although the early troupers tended to focus on songs from the north, their native 'culture sphere', it was not out of any sense of duty to tradition or scholarship: they were simply singing the songs with which they were most familiar. When the audience wanted other songs, they sang other songs. If a lyric had become stale, they made another lyric.

Other early *min'yō kashu* strove to place themselves among the literati or otherwise distance themselves from the low status of the professional. This often meant that they did adopt a more scholarly, sometimes preservationist attitude towards local songs. Many adopted, or received from teachers, personal 'artist's names' (*geimei*) of the type borne by poets and scholars: Gotō

Seizaburō became Gotō Tōsui, the early 'Esashi Oiwake' teacher; Narita Takezō became Narita Unchiku. Narita (1888–1974), when not busy serving on the local police force, developed his love for the songs of his native Tsugaru. Like Gotō, he 'discovered' and arranged traditional songs (often excising bawdy passages), taught them to others, and composed 'new folk songs' in the local style (see Asano 1983: 373; Takeuchi 1974: 71–3; NMMM: 94; Groemer 1999). Narita eventually left the police to make his living as a *min'yō* teacher and performer in northern Japan. Attempting to avoid being linked with the blind beggars, he – as well as Gotō Tōsui – ignored the standard repertoire of Tsugaru itinerant musicians, the 'Three Songs of Tsugaru' (*Tsugaru no mitsumono*), and sought out traditional songs without such invidious associations.[35]

Gotō, who had launched the first public folk song competitions in Tokyo, returned to his native village near Sendai (Miyagi Pref.) after an earthquake devastated Tokyo in 1923.[36] He turned his attention to local songs – 'excavating' them, tidying up tunes and lyrics, then teaching them to students from Miyagi and surrounding prefectures. When the Sendai branch of NHK radio opened in 1928, Gotō was put in charge of *min'yō* programmes.[37] From that power base, aided by connections formed in Tokyo and by his strength of personality, Gotō made contact with many of the best singers from throughout the north, bringing them together for concerts and broadcasts. Those researching *min'yō* of that region were sure to visit Gotō for help. He is often called the 'father' or 'foster parent' (*sodate no oya*) of Japanese folk song.

A terrible singer himself, Gotō taught melodies via his shakuhachi. He also brought to *min'yō* teaching the same discipline he had learned in studying classical shakuhachi. He spoke of the 'way (*dō*; Chinese *tao/dao*) of folk song', as one speaks of the way of tea, of the warrior, etc. To him, folk song was a form of ascetic training. Although other professionals were trying to raise folk song to a 'discipline' in the literal sense, none was stricter than Gotō.

It may be surprising to learn that Gotō, despite a highly refined sensibility and a firm belief in decorum and etiquette, also showed a strong preference for unaccompanied work songs. Although he favoured shakuhachi accompaniment for 'Esashi Oiwake', he made his students sing the medley of Miyagi fishermen's songs known as 'Tairyō Utaikomi' *a capella*. He even had them imitate the action of, for example, boat-rowing in order to get the correct feeling and tempo. The dominance of northerners on the urban *min'yō* scene to this day is partly a product of Gotō's determination – plus the happy chance that the first head of Sendai Broadcasting was a childhood friend.

Elsewhere in Tōhoku, teachers and performers were emerging who shared the attitudes of Aomori's Narita and Miyagi's Gotō: respect for the identity of local songs (see Takeuchi 1981: 250–1). Thus Gotō, despite his catalytic role, must be seen as a product of the times. As to why northern Japan produced so many professional *min'yō* singers and teachers, several arguments have been advanced (e.g. ibid.: 251ff.). All can be countered, however, except for Gotō's role and the claim that Tōhoku's relative isolation from the centres of modernization helped traditional folk song maintain its important role in daily life.

Finally, let us consider some of the reasons why people left their villages to adopt such a low-status profession. First, as noted, some were 'stage children', born into the business or at least into a family that encouraged them to become performers.

Second, poverty could be a goad, if other conditions were right. Consider Asari Miki (b. 1920; see §2.2.2). The youngest of seven children of a poor Tsugaru farming family, she was adopted into a neighbouring household at age eight to serve as a nursemaid (and to reduce the burden on her own family to feed her). But she was a child prodigy, who learned her songs without a teacher, and singing eventually proved her economic salvation. At age seven she had already performed on the stage of a nearby hot-spring bathhouse (a common venue for early folk singers).[38] At age twelve she made her first recording. Finally she left home at fifteen, having taken second prize in the annual Tō-ō Nippō folk song contest (§3.4.1), to travel the countryside with a troupe. Her only goal, she said, was 'to put a smile on my mother's face' by bringing home her earnings. She had intended to retire from the business after marriage, she says, but her husband was killed in the Second World War within a year of their wedding, leaving her with a son to support. Asari has been one of Japan's most revered folk singers ever since. (In April 1998, in her late seventies, she appeared as a guest star at the first national Tsugaru-jamisen contest in Tokyo.)

Poverty was also the initial stimulus that sent many blind children to teachers of shamisen or *biwa* and thence onto the open road. Among these were the recent cult figure, the Tsugaru shamisen player Takahashi Chikuzan (§2.4.6).

Third, the most common traditional inheritance pattern, by which a single child (usually the eldest son) succeeded to the family headship and all or most of the property, meant that excess children had to make a living elsewhere. Pressure on them to remain in the village as farmers was meaningless if they had no land. Lacking a statistical study, I will only hypothesize that most males who chose a musician's career were 'excess' sons. Those who abandoned their destined role as successor to headship to become professionals seem to have experienced particularly acute guilt which they strove to justify by, for example, noting how their parents in later life finally accepted their careers with pride (see for example MB: 78.15).

The fourth reason is the simplest and most important: they loved to perform, and they were good at it. Although some professionals hated life on the road, very few, even the 'stage children', seem to have disliked performing. Most of them took naturally to the life of a *dōrakumono*.

3.5 The war years and after

Folk song activity declined precipitously during the war years, particularly after the late 1930s, in both the professional and the amateur spheres. Hamada Kiichi I had to disband his troupe in 1941 when most male members were drafted (NMMM: 81). *Shin-min'yō* writers were pressed into creating stirring martial, patriotic songs, quite unlike their folk-style works. In the villages, the exodus of males into the armed forces meant that many performance events and festivals could not take place. The remaining professionals found themselves performing principally for the troops or for wartime workers. 'Consolation troupes' (*imondan*) consisting of folk singers and/or popular musicians were sent to Taiwan, Manchuria and other outposts of empire to entertain the emperor's subjects. (The government was slightly ambivalent about *min'yō*: the fighting men must be comforted but not made homesick, and folk songs did tend to make one think of home.)

The 'folk song world' recovered rapidly after the war. This was partly because folk song was seen as a potentially important source of solace in the difficult post-war years, just as it had been during the war. Tanii Hōdō founded the Iso Bushi Preservation Society in Ibaragi Prefecture in 1947, believing that the singing and study of that song could contribute to the recovery of the Japanese spirit (§5.4.4). He was not alone in such a belief.

A major contributor to the renaissance of *min'yō* was NHK, the semi-governmental radio company (soon to add television). In 1948 NHK created the 'National Singing Competition' (*Nodojiman zenkoku konkūru*), with a *zokkyoku* division which included folk song.[39] Preliminary regional heats were held throughout Japan, many also broadcast. NHK also began in 1950 the weekly show *Min'yō o tazunete* ('In Search of Folk Song'), which often broadcast directly from local communities, focusing on their local songs. In order to rally the depressed workers in the primary sector, entertainment programmes were also aimed specifically at farmers and coal miners; not surprisingly, *min'yō* loomed large in these shows. Several songs from mining communities thus spread throughout Japan via the radio, including the internationally known dance tune 'Tankō Bushi' from Fukuoka Prefecture (Asano 1983: 158). Commercial radio also began in 1951–2. Radio Tokyo (now TBS) was very active in the *min'yō* field, sponsoring its own concours from 1954 on. Many new regional stations also sprang up, often relying on *min'yō* broadcasts to establish links with the populace (Takeuchi 1974: 369).

Takeuchi Tsutomu, with his usual perspicacity, focused on two programmes which both displayed and determined post-war trends in *min'yō*. The NHK concours underwent a gradual change in the nature of the songs heard in the *zokkyoku* division (Takeuchi 1981: 258–64). Of six finalists in 1948, three sang 'Esashi Oiwake' (under some title or other), two sang 'Hakata Bushi', and the northeast Japan (Tōhoku) representative from Yamagata sang a local pack-horse-driving song. All but the last were not *zokkyoku* in the narrow modern sense of party songs of the geisha (§1.5) but *zokuyō*, i.e. 'arranged' *riyō*, semi-classicized, with accompaniment added. More significant, perhaps, 'Esashi Oiwake', a Hokkaido song, was sung by a person from Kagoshima at the other end of Japan, while Kyushu's 'Hakata Bushi' was sung by a person from distant Yokohama. This continued the trend apparent since the beginning of the century (§3.4.1): local songs in parlour arrangements spread far and wide. The situation in the concours remained like this for the next three years, with the occasional actual *zokkyoku* – geisha party song – creeping in as well. The organizers of the programme, however, had actually expected that contestants would choose songs with local colour, namely local folk songs. The number of participants singing selections from their home districts increased gradually thereafter, and in 1956 the division was renamed the *min'yō* division. (However, the winners of this and other *min'yō* contests were almost always northerners singing northern songs, a legacy of the early professionalization described above.)

It is surprisingly difficult to erect reasonable hypotheses for why regional songs began to gain respect from this time. Clearly many people in the media and in the scholarly community felt that stressing local identity would help rebuild Japan; and wartime destruction of the cities had temporarily sent much of the populace back to the countryside, where their regional consciousness may have been recharged. We must surely give major credit to the various radio shows which, in broadcasting local *min'yō*, tended to lay a certain amount of emphasis on the local significance of each song as an important cultural element. This attitude counteracted the equally plausible levelling trend which one might have expected to emerge from the spread of nationwide mass media.

The other programme which Takeuchi found especially significant (1969: 19–20) was Radio Tokyo's *Min'yō okuni jiman* ('Folk Song, Pride of the Province'), launched in 1952. This weekly show offered songs from all over Japan, striving to provide reasonably balanced geographic coverage. The performers, however, were almost all Tokyo-based. Machida Kashō, the show's resident scholar, relied largely upon the shamisen player Fujimoto Hideo for locating singers and accompanists.[40] Fujimoto (like Machida) was trained from childhood in *nagauta, kouta* and other urban shamisen genres, coming to folk song gradually as job opportunities arose. He had a major effect on the course of modern *min'yō* performance, as discussed in Chapter 4. Much of his influence grew out of this radio show.

Machida and his staff would locate local songs, often quite unknown outside of the immediate area; many were unaccompanied or had only rudimentary shamisen parts. Having found from past experience that it was difficult to interest people in 'unprocessed' local songs (§3.4.1), Machida asked Fujimoto to create or polish the accompaniments. Several years of this resulted in several hundred shamisen arrangements in a relatively homogeneous style tinged with classical shamisen music flavours; many of these are now published in Fujimoto 1962–, today the standard source for *min'yō* shamisen notation.

Fujimoto also selected most of the performers. Many were or became his students. He encouraged the use of a vocal style quite unlike that of village folk song, again showing the influence of urban shamisen styles. (See further §4.5.1.)

Like the NHK concours, this Radio Tokyo/TBS show had a tremendous impact in acquainting the general public with *min'yō* from all over. It had somewhat the opposite effect from the NHK show, however, downplaying rather than celebrating regional stylistic differences.

Let us briefly cite three other developments of the early post-war years. The Nihon Min'yō Kyōkai (Japan Folk Song Association; Nichimin for short) was formed in 1950 as an organization of professional teachers and their students, as well as scholars, composers and interested dignitaries.[41] Through the combined strength of its member schools (*kai*) as well as through its own concours, it soon became the single most important organizational force in the modern folk song world. Its impressive range of activities leads to frequent mention in subsequent chapters (especially §7.2). A dissident faction split off in 1961 to form the Nihon Kyōdo Min'yō Kyōkai (Japan Local Folk Song Association; Kyōmin for short). In 1980 at the peak of a *min'yō* 'boom', Nichimin had 40,965 members, about half living within commuting distance of Tokyo, while Kyōmin had 37,136. Even in 2007, when the boom had cooled, Nichimin had 56 regional associations with some 900 member groups (*kai*) and over 40,000 members, while Kyōmin's 35 regional associations had over 600 *kai*, though membership had shrunk to 16,000; both now have branches in the USA and Brazil (almost all members being of Japanese descent). But these two associations have now been joined by many smaller umbrella organizations, some regional (e.g. Nihon Min'yō Suishin Kyōkai, covering the Kansai region) and some national (e.g. Zenkoku Min'yō Renmei, Zenkoku Min'yō Kyōkai). Adding such groups, the total membership would surely surpass the 1980 total of the original two.

'Folk song bars' (*min'yō sakaba*) emerged in the early 1950s. Since their birth they have provided an important place for future professionals to train and for amateurs to sing before an audience. Details are in §4.7.

Finally, the countryside saw the rapid proliferation of preservation societies (*hozonkai*) for local performing arts. This is discussed further in §5.4.

This brings us up to the doorstep of the present-day situation. Developments in the past several decades have followed the paths laid out in the early post-war years. Before going ahead, however, let us examine a new body of data for an overview of changes in musical tastes during the twentieth century.

3.6 Musical tastes in transition

In seeking patterns of musical preferences, we have access since the 1920s to increasing numbers of public opinion surveys conducted by both private and public organizations. Despite difficulties in comparing surveys whose categories, methodologies and sample populations are different, we can elucidate certain trends in musical tastes over the years.[42]

Two large-scale surveys were conducted in 1931 and 1932, with reference to twenty-five and twenty musical categories respectively (Masui 1980: 140–1). Respondents were asked to indicate any genres which they enjoyed listening to. In each case the seven most popular genres were of traditional, 'pure' Japanese music. In both surveys the favourite genre by far was *naniwa-bushi*, a narrative shamisen genre often classified as drama rather than as music. 'Folk song' (*chihō-riyō*) appears only in the 1931 survey; it ranked seventh, with 45 per cent of the respondents saying that they enjoyed listening to it. The separate category of 'new folk song' (*shin-min'yō*), by comparison, scored only 34 per cent. Only the 1932 survey was tabulated by age classes, as shown in Table 3.1.

The fact that the 1932 survey omitted the category *min'yō* confirms that the concept was still not fully established. The newish category of *kayōkyoku* ('popular song'; also called *ryūkōka*) was absent from both surveys. Machida Kashō recalled that in 1925 there was as yet no genre of popular song, 'just

Table 3.1. Musical preferences and age, 1932

	nat'l total	men 16–	26–	36–	46–	56+	women 16–	26–	36–	46–	56+
naniwa-bushi	58	49	54	60	73	85	39	50	59	73	82
biwa	40	35	40	44	44	43	33	40	43	42	41
gidayū	33	12	23	36	48	62	16	29	44	59	75
nagauta	28	13	23	28	32	34	24	32	38	44	48
Noh/*kyōgen*	15	9	15	20	24	26	9	11	14	16	17
shin-nihon-ongaku	24	26	26	24	19	16	31	28	24	20	17
mixed Jap.-West.	33	43	36	28	23	19	44	35	30	26	22
wind bands	23	40	29	19	12	8	32	21	14	9	6
symph. orch.	23	39	30	18	11	8	33	21	14	9	6
opera	24	34	24	18	12	9	43	26	18	12	9
jazz	17	32	23	13	7	4	27	15	9	5	4

Respondents were asked which of twenty categories of music they enjoyed listening to; eleven are shown here. Multiple answers were permitted; mean score per genre was 24%. The heading 16– means age 16–25, and so forth; 56+ includes all respondents age 56 or over. SOURCE: Data from Masui 1980: 141, which was based on a survey by NHK.

koto, *nagauta*, piano, etc.', so *min'yō* was a breath of fresh air for the masses (quoted in Takeuchi 1974: 117).

In ten of the eleven categories of 'pure Japanese' music (only five are shown in Table 3.1), the rate of preference increased steadily with age; in all seven genres of Western music (four shown in Table 3.1), it decreased with age. Two genres which combine Japanese and Western elements followed the latter preference pattern. One of these was New Japanese Music (*shin-nihon-ongaku*), a recently named genre of compositions for Japanese instruments but using such Western musical elements as harmony, triple rhythm, arpeggiated bass, etc.; Miyagi Michio was the best-known exponent. The other genre has no official name and is simply called 'mixed Japanese-Western'; it might be intended to include popular tunes of Western or Japanese origin played by mixed ensembles, or it could be meant to designate a more Western-influenced offshoot of New Japanese Music (see Komiya 1956: 415–8, 374–7). The skewing in preferences by age class results from the effects of Western-oriented music education in the schools and increasing participation of young people in the international cultural community.

We can continue to trace these Westernizing effects in subsequent surveys. In 1937 the most popular Japanese classical (*hōgaku*) genres still outpolled all Western genres – but the gap was closing (Masui 1980: 143). By 1949 and 1950 the Western genres had edged ahead (ibid.: 144–5). Both Japanese and Western classical musics, however, were losing ground rapidly to the genre of syncretic popular song (*kayōkyoku*), which first appeared in the 1937 survey and immediately joined *naniwa-bushi* at the top of the popularity list. *Min'yō*, meanwhile, held steady. Throughout these developments, the correlation of preference with age showed the same trend as in 1932 (with *kayōkyoku* following the pattern of the Western genres). By 1949, *min'yō* had become the favourite genre among people over age fifty – and remained so at least until the 1980s, after which surveys fail to provide sufficient detail.[43]

These same trends continue to the present, confused only by a proliferation of sub-genres of popular song. The differential correlations of Western and Japanese classical musics with age class were reconfirmed in surveys from 1971 and 1978, but both have shrunk in absolute terms *vis-à-vis* pop song and folk song (ibid.: 166, 169; see also Tables 4.1 and 4.2 in the next chapter).

Min'yō itself has held its audience share remarkably well over the decades. Comparing representative surveys from 1931, 1937, 1949, 1953, 1968 and 1971, each asking respondents to indicate any genres of music which they enjoy listening to, the percentage naming *min'yō* was 45, 49, 47, 64, 49 and 44 respectively (ibid.: 140, 143–4, 146, 173, 166).[44]

The 1953 survey also gives details on geographical preferences, tabulating its respondents by three residence classes: the six largest cities; other cities; and towns and villages (ibid.: 146). All Western genres were much more popular in the cities, as were those Japanese musics linked with Kabuki. The most popular genres showing the highest skewing towards the countryside were *naniwa-bushi* (80 per cent rural vs. 64 per cent urban) and folk song (67 per cent rural vs. 60 per cent urban).

In sum, we can say that the audience for traditional folk song held steady throughout the twentieth century in the face of a general trend toward musical Westernization, and in spite of the increasing popularity of syncretic popular song. It has continued to be most popular among the elderly and among rural residents. Another observation must remain conjectural due to the difficulty of comparing the various surveys, but is supported by my own experience. Namely, it appears that *min'yō* has been losing ground among those at the lower end of the age scale, but holding steady or gaining slightly among the elderly. In any case, folk song today can claim a sizeable and loyal fan base. In 1978, fully 24 per cent of the adult population (age sixteen and above) named *min'yō* as their single favourite type of music (ibid.: 166–7). Later surveys do not offer directly comparable information, but despite a clear decline in the numbers, *min'yō* is still a genre of major importance in twenty-first-century Japan.

The growth of the recording and broadcast industries after 1925 bears a symbiotic relationship with that of the popular song industry (see Nakamura 1991). The new word *kayōkyoku* – meaning literally merely 'sung melody' – was adopted to refer to commercial popular songs. It is said that the radio station staff chose this term in preference to the words *hayariuta* and *ryūkōka* (both meaning 'popular song') since it was assumed that not all songs broadcast would become 'popular' (ODJ 1982, entry on *kayōkyoku*). Musically, we can distinguish two main streams of *kayōkyoku*: those using pentatonic scales and traditional Japanese vocal ornamentation (yet with predominantly Western instrumentation), and those written in the style of Euro-American popular music. Koga Masao (1904–78) was the most renowned composer in the former style, while Hattori Ryōichi (1907–93) pioneered and exemplified the latter. With the American Occupation, the Western-flavoured style expanded its audience share. However, 'Japanese-style popular songs' (*nihon-chō kayōkyoku*) continue to be successful. Another word with approximately the same meaning as *nihon-chō kayōkyoku* is *enka*; indeed, these two are lumped together in the 1971 survey reported in Table 4.1 below. *Enka* are discussed further in §§1.7.2, 4.2 and 6.2.

3.7 Summary

In this chapter we have traced the beginnings of the modern folk song world (*min'yō-kai*), focusing on a single representative song, 'Esashi Oiwake'. Since the end of the nineteenth century, local rural songs have gradually made their way to the cities and to other areas of rural Japan. In time, *min'yō* became a genre of music with a dual identity. While villagers continued their traditional performance practice, urban-based professionals performed some of the same material in highly arranged versions accompanied by skilled instrumentalists.

Among the more important factors enabling folk song to move to the city were: the tremendous population shift to the cities; the upgrading of the image of the peasant; reduction of the physical and conceptual distance between city and country; weakening of rural regional distinctions among urban migrants; loosening of songs from their social contexts; and the steady growth of leisure time and expenditure.

'Esashi Oiwake', once a pack-horse drivers' song, is a typical if singularly influential example of a local song which became a *min'yō* known through-out Japan. As the region was drawn into the national culture, connections between local geisha and wealthy male patrons from Tokyo facilitated the transmission of this song from the periphery to the centre of Japan. It was also employed as a form of advertising in an attempt to capitalize on the growing domestic tourist market. The geisha, and later the artists of the urban variety theatres, contributed to the influence of traditional classical music (*hōgaku*) on 'Esashi Oiwake'. Even as it was being 'classicized', this song was becoming known as a 'folk song' (*min'yō* or *riyō*).

Subsequent developments in Esashi highlighted themes which have permeated the *min'yō* world ever since. Among the more significant are: standardization, including the designation of a 'correct', 'authentic' version of the song; stress on 'research'; formation of organizations for transmission; preservationism; dignification (expressed, e.g., in costume and demeanor of performers); use of notation; professionalization of performance (including formal concerts); professionalization of teaching; use in local publicity; local possessiveness even as attempts were made to disseminate the song; inter-ference from influential local figures; holding of competitions, often under media sponsorship (and often involving only one song!); commercial record-ing; and standardization of accompanying instruments. We can see these developments as a whole as owing something to an admiration for Western ideas; mainly, however, they represent the extension of traditional elements (adopted, e.g., from *hōgaku*) or the result of more neutral forces such as urbanization, mechanization, improvements in communication etc.

Most of the early popular *min'yō* were dance and party songs, being as a whole more suitable, through pre-adaptation, for public entertainment than were work and ceremonial songs. During the 1920s, Romanticism and 'Taishō democracy' spurred the writing of 'new folk songs' for 'the people' by professional poets and composers. These songs were often intended to help overcome social problems such as those caused by industrialization, but more and more they were simply used to attract tourism. (In using local folk song as its model, this movement took the opposite approach to the consciously internationalist leftist song movement.) Straddling the stylistic fence between traditional folk song and more Westernized popular song, these 'new folk songs' eventually lost out to both; few survive in the performing repertoire.

Professional *min'yō* troupes became common in the 1930s, especially in the north. Performers continued to struggle against the image of the debauching *dōrakumono*.

Surveys of musical preference from 1932 onwards reveal three important trends: (1) On the whole, Western-style music has gradually overtaken Japanese traditional music in popularity. (2) Western-style music is always more popular with the young than with the old. (3) The percentage of *min'yō* fans has changed very little over the decades.

Chapters 2 and 3 have traced the development of *min'yō* from the Edo period to the present. In the next few chapters, our focus narrows to the post-war period and particularly to the years since 1977 – a date chosen because it marks the onset of the most recent '*min'yō* boom'.

NOTES

1. In Tokyo, for example, the proportion of residents born elsewhere was 47% in 1920, 49% in 1930 and 38% in 1950; figures are even higher when outlying rural districts of greater Tokyo are excluded (Dore 1958: 18). Most migrants came from rural areas, not from other cities. (The drop in 1950 largely reflects temporary reverse migration due to the wartime destruction of Tokyo.)

2. This is not to say that all peasants saw the city as a sort of mecca: see the verse cited in §2.1 from a barley-threshing song from an area near Edo. Nor were urbanites totally immune to the joys of folk music. Various country songs and dances achieved brief popularity in the cities, sometimes leaving their mark on urban performing arts such as Kabuki and *rakugo*. Hoff 1981 provides one viewpoint on the attitudes toward each other of city and country.

3. Numerous popular song collections were published even during the Edo period, some being collections of specifically village song (including some of the works cited in Chapter 2 note 9). More often, Edo-period collections mixed folk songs with what today would be considered separate genres of urban popular songs.

4. We are not dealing here with ritual songs such as those associated with shrine ceremonies: these would not be considered *min'yō* (§§1.4, 2.4.1). Those that survive are still relatively context-bound, although 'folkloric' urban stage performances are becoming frequent. In the latter context, there is often some attempt to replicate the original village setting: perhaps a roped-off sacred space, an altar, etc.

5. Average weekday free time per person increased from 5 hours in 1960 to nearly 6.5 hours in 1975; leisure expenditure more than trebled between 1965 and 1975 (EOJ: 4.383). This trend continues.

6. The following description is based primarily on Tate 1989, Esashi 1982 and Satō 1987, supplemented by Takeuchi 1969: 9–12, Takeuchi 1980, Kiuchi 1979, on my own visit, and on interviews in 1988 with Tate Kazuo and Tatsuki Kumao. I have not yet read through the 572-page Takeuchi 2003, but it does go beyond his earlier works.

7. For details and other theories about the song's development, see Esashi 1982: ch.1, Tate 1989: ch. 2, Takeuchi 2003, 1980.

8. The embedding of urban-style passages, or occasionally even passages from another folk song, into a *min'yō* is known as *anko-iri*, 'filling with sweet bean-paste'.

It is not uncommon in modern performance. 'Esashi Oiwake' with *shinnai* 'filling' is heard in selections 2, 4 and 10 of the cassette tape included with Esashi 1982. 'Yoneyama Jinku' is already so 'filled' in the 1903 versions on R61.

9. The first recording of any version of 'Oiwake' dates from 1900 (R35, track 27). Nogaki Seiichi, accompanying himself on shamisen, was with the Kawakami Troupe that performed at the 1900 Paris Exposition. He called the piece simply 'Oiwake Bushi'. Again, links with Hokkaido are apparent in the lyrics, but musically we may be closer to Niigata.

10. The dance may have been choreographed in the 1860s by a Kabuki actor from Hakodate. The female group dance mimed the rowing of fishing boats and the flight of seagulls, thus emphasizing Esashi's fishing heritage rather than on the song's pack-horse history. By 1905 the costumes were of Ainu pattern; Esashi had little connec-tion with Hokkaido's Ainu culture, but the costumes impressed outsiders. (Cf. Esashi 1982: 74, 76, 82ff.)

11. Tsukitani Tsuneko has seen many shakuhachi notation books from northeast Japan from the 1910s–30s containing both classical pieces and *min'yō*, without dis-tinction. She has also heard the unprovable opinion that the greater ornamentation in Kinko-school classical shakuhachi when compared with the more Zen-linked Fuke style may result from folk song influence (pers. comm. 14 May 2007).

12. Takeuchi 1980: 70–1 offers an alternative description, rendered unlikely by the testimony of one of those present at the meeting (Esashi 1982: 221–2).

13. Wakasa Hōsaku (a.k.a. Wakasa Shōroku; ca.1870–1947) claimed that his own version was selected, as it was believed to reproduce faithfully that of a renowned singer of the 1880s; no other evidence supports this claim.

14. Other typically modern Meiji terms, often translating Western concepts, include: *bunka* 'culture'; *bunmei* 'civilization'; *hattatsu* 'progress'; *gendai* 'modern'; *jiyū* 'free-dom'; and *minken* 'people's rights'. Williams 1983 describes the development of these Western concepts themselves amid the social and industrial revolutions of the eighteenth and nineteenth centuries in Europe.

15. Kōji Toyotarō reportedly pioneered the use of shakuhachi for this song in the 1890s (Tsukitani 2006).

16. Note that Etchūya seems to be assuming that one's dialect affects the way one sings a melody (as opposed to mere pronunciation of the lyrics). This too is a com-monly held belief today, although it has never been demonstrated. See further §4.6.1.

17. See, e.g., Satō 1987: 65. The son of the renowned teacher Ōmi Hassei (1903–66) recalls that his father's fee was a stick of firewood per lesson; there was no real need for anyone to charge fees in those days, since 'fish was dirt-cheap' (Kiuchi 1979: 48–9).

18. Komiya 1956: 441–8 and Nakamura 1991 are English-language surveys of the early days of Japan's recording industry. Kurata 1979 and Morigaki 1960 are more comprehensive.

19. Tune family research, a major feature of Western folk song research, is also com-mon in Japan.

20. The percentage of the populace living in households with radios grew from 6% in 1930 to 39% in 1940, 55% in 1950 and 78% in 1955 (Kato 1959: 219). Actual coverage was higher in the early days since extension speakers could serve several households with one receiver.

21. We should also mention the annual performances of *minzoku geinō* from all over Japan, held at the Nihon Seinenkan hall in Tokyo from 1925. These were of great value to specialist researchers but had little impact on the general public.

22. But as noted in §1.6, a few songs in free metre are set against a metric shamisen and drum part; e.g. 'Honjō Oiwake', 'Awa Yoshikono' ('Awa Odori').

23. This section and §6.3 are an expansion, revision and re-arrangement of Hughes 1991.

24. *Dōyō*, like *min'yō*, is a 'Sinate' Sino-Japanese term of literati creation. *Dōyō* were often considered a subtype of *min'yō*.

25. Numerous 'new folk songs' of this period are translated in Appendix 1.1. Kojima 1970 provides an excellent discussion of these early *shin-min'yō*, including treatment of the text settings. Tunes and texts of many of the works are in Machida 1933. For a list of several hundred *shin-min'yō* from the 1920s to the 1970s, see NMZ 5.247–59. Examples of *dōyō* are given in Sanbe 1974 (in Japanese) and Berger 1991 and Uyehara 1949 (in English).

26. This statement is included in his notes to his poem collection *Ashi no ha* (1923); I quote it from the more accessible recent compendium of his works (Kitahara 1987: 29.494). Volume 29 contains most of his early folk-style 'poems for reading'; volume 30 has the majority of *shin-min'yō* of the type discussed here. Some of his early folk-style poems were set to music by composers trained in the Western art-music tradition, perhaps starting with 'Jōgashima no ame' in 1913 (see Fukasawa 1993: 68). These settings are not, however, considered *min'yō*, nor do they sound like *min'yō*.

27. For an interesting example of the rise and fall of a local propaganda song – in fact, of two competing songs from the same town, 'Noshiro Kouta' and 'Noshiro Ondo' – see Asahi 1980: 123–4. The adaptation of the text of a local traditional song ('Shimotsui Bushi') in hopes of attracting tourists is described in Takeuchi 1978: 258ff.

28. The *goze* version has converted the original *in* mode on 7 into a *yō* on 6 with upper auxiliary 7 (R8, record 3, side A). Remember that the *goze*'s repertoire contained many popular songs as well as old and new folk songs.

29. It may be hypothesized that the new breed of Romantic poet felt the need for more room for self-expression. Also, advances in transportation and communication meant that the Japanese of the early twentieth century were inundated with ever more new information, verbal and otherwise; perhaps people thus became accustomed – even addicted – to longer, denser verses.

30. Similar observations on this and other points can be made regarding the folk-style poems of several European Romantics, with their refrain-like sections; cf. 'The Sands of Dee' and 'The Three Fishers' by Charles Kingsley (1819–75) or 'The Echoing Green' by William Blake (1757–1827). Both Europeans and Japanese also often give their verses parallel syntactic and thematic structures uncommon in true folk song lyrics.

31. This is a common trend worldwide, due to factors such as Westernization and increased leisure time. Manuel notes (1989a, 1989b) that the pitch sense of flamenco singers in Spain has become more precise due to audience expectations.

32. My sample consists of twenty-seven scores from Machida 1933 plus twenty-four songs recorded in the LP set R57 (partially re-issued on R58).

33. The modification of Western harmonic language for use in modal musics deserves more scholarly attention (see e.g. Pennanen 1997; Manuel 1989b).

34. The various approaches listed here do not seem to occur in early Western attempts at harmonizing pentatonic melodies, where the usual approach is to determine a single tonic, a 'key', and harmonize in usual Western language (e.g. Polak 1905).

35. The Three Songs of Tsugaru ('Tsugaru Jongara Bushi', 'Tsugaru Ohara Bushi' and 'Tsugaru Yosare Bushi') are now among the best-loved *min'yō*, with no remaining aura of low social status. Moreover, later in his career Narita chose as his accompanist the outstanding Takahashi Chikuzan – precisely one of the 'blind beggars' he had formerly eschewed.

36. For details of Gotō's life, career and contributions, see NMMM: 58ff., Takeuchi 1973: 213ff, 1974: 68ff, 1981: 249ff, among many other sources.

37. NHK = Nihon Hōsō Kyōkai, Japan Broadcasting Corporation.

38. In fact, it is still a common venue. Around 1980 I was honoured to accompany Asari Miki on shamisen at a spa near Narita Airport; the audience, primarily elderly, wore yukata as they relaxed between dips in the radon-rich waters.

39. An earlier version had been launched in 1946. See Takeuchi 1969: 18–9; 1981: 17.

40. Takeuchi does not mention Fujimoto by name, since he is being somewhat disapproving of Fujimoto's aesthetic judgment in arranging accompaniments and influencing vocal styles. For the identification of Fujimoto as well as other information, I am grateful to Maruyama Shinobu, who was involved in the show's production after 1955.

41. Its early history is described in Kikuchi 1980. Note that there is no historical connection with the short-lived group of the same name formed in 1928 (§3.4.2).

42. My principal source is Masui 1980, a selective compilation of data on musical tastes and activities from various sources between the 1920s and 1978. He cites surveys such as NHK 1980: 456–8, which reports musical preferences of over 32,000 people throughout Japan. Since his bibliographic citations are often incomplete, I have referred to his reprinted tables rather than trying to trace down all the primary sources. Further information in English on musical tastes in the early twentieth century can be found scattered through Komiya 1956: 387–448, 491–507.

43. *Naniwa-bushi* is generally absent from recent surveys, as its popularity has steadily faded. In the 1978 survey (Table 4.2 below), it runs a distant third to folk song (15% vs. 46%) even among its principal remaining audience, people over fifty-five. The decline of *naniwa-bushi*, *gidayū*, and *biwa* recitations at the expense of popular song and *min'yō* is usually attributed to length: the modern attention span can supposedly no longer encompass a lengthy narrative vocal form. Surely another cause is competition from television, cinema and novels, the modern narrative media.

44. The 1949 survey lumped *min'yō* with *zokuyō*. Since *zokuyō* generally patterns like *min'yō* except at a lower percentage, it is doubtful that the combining has added more than a few percentage points to the figure for *min'yō* alone. The higher figure for 1953 presumably marks the effect of the first post-war *min'yō* boom, triggered by the expansion of the broadcast media.

CHAPTER 4

The Modern Urban
Folk Song World

4.1 Introduction

By the 1960s, Japanese folk song had become primarily an urban phenomenon. Most renowned regional performers had shifted their activity bases
to Tokyo or other large cities. Formal performance occasions were predominantly urban affairs. *Min'yō* had also become a commodity and an industry:
the broadcast media, record companies, newspaper companies, publishers all
had a considerable stake in the *min'yō* world. Tokyo and Osaka now offered
potential professionals sufficient economic opportunity to tempt them to
forsake the life of the travelling trouper.

Min'yō activity in the urban centres differs vastly from the picture of music
life in the traditional village painted in Chapter 2 (though the two are not
always clearly separable). Let us now consider the urban *min'yō* world in its
full flower, in the years since approximately 1960. Though events throughout these years are described, the focus is particularly on 1977–81, the years
of my most intensive fieldwork, which coincided with a '*min'yō* boom' of
major proportions and established the patterns that continue with little sub-
stantive change until today. Chapter 7 provides an overview of the most
important recent developments.

4.2 Social parameters of musical preferences

A look at post-war patterns of musical tastes will help orient the subsequent
discussion. The American Patia Isaku wrote of her experiences with *min'yō*
in the 1960s–70s: 'Almost every Japanese I've ever met – in Tokyo, New York,
Los Angeles; on the street, in bars, on trains – has enjoyed talking about
folk song' (1981: ix). Possibly her own palpable passion for the subject
carried her interlocutors along. My own experience, however, in countless

conversations since 1977, has been that a solid and ever-increasing proportion of Japanese have virtually no interest at all in the topic; persistent questioning elicits only embarrassment or a few grudging, unenthusiastic comments.

Most Japanese I interact with regularly during my *min'yō* fieldwork are fans – but only because I seek such people out. Conversely, many Westerners interact primarily with highly Westernized Japanese, who are the least likely to profess any interest in or respect for the genre. Each of us is liable to generalize to the entire populace and misrepresent the diversity of viewpoints.

Japanese often misunderstand the distribution of musical tastes in their own country – just as an American rock music fanatic might doubt that more than a tiny proportion of young people liked opera. In 1989 a minor Japanese composer (Western-style) gave a lecture at his embassy in London, entitled '36,000 Days of Music in Japan'. Aided by a Japanese soprano and a piano, he took us through what he saw as the world of Japanese music since the onset of Meiji Westernization. Virtually all the music discussed was the product of Japanese composers with an overwhelming preference for and training in Western music. Touching briefly on *min'yō*, he claimed that 'nobody' (*sic*) likes it, then proceeded to imitate what was clearly intended as a very bad *min'yō* voice. (Doubtless he could not have imitated a good one.) When I informed him that recent surveys had revealed that over 40 per cent of Japanese enjoyed listening to *min'yō*, a figure far greater than those enjoying Western classical music, he simply refused to believe it. Such blinkered opinions are easy to come by.[1]

Similarly, the novelist Dazai Osamu's 1944 travelogue *Return to Tsugaru* virtually ignores what must have been a fairly abundant folk music life in his home region even in the latter war years: village singing, the excitement of itinerant performers, and so forth. He even derides the bit he does mention (93–4) – and while he's at it, insults *gidayū* as 'insignificant' (13) and exposes a small-town hospital head's insincere fawning over Western classical music (54). Perhaps he is simply anti-music in general, but he is typical of one segment of Japan.

To some extent one can correlate the musical attitudes and behaviour of individual Japanese with sociocultural or demographic attributes such as age, residence, occupation and education. Less easily measured but equally important is family background, including parental musical tastes. Seeking similar correlations for 'traditional Japan' in Chapter 2 required reliance on indirect evidence of various kinds. In §3.6, however, we noted the availability of national public opinion surveys since the 1920s. Focusing now on more recent decades, let us note some patterns emerging from these surveys. We begin with the 1970s.

Consider first the effect of age. As noted in §3.6, surveys of adults throughout the twentieth century found traditional Japanese music ('folk' or otherwise) consistently more popular among older people, with the reverse largely true for Western and Westernized genres. In 1971, for example, people were asked to indicate *any* of fifteen categories of music they enjoyed listening to (Table 4.1). *Min'yō* was chosen by 31 per cent of people in their twenties and 69 per cent of people in their fifties. For the same two age groups, the figure for Western-style *fōku songu* showed a decline with age from 50 per cent to 16 per cent and the popularity of symphonic music fell slightly from 15 per cent to 12 per cent.[2] In 1978, over 32,000 people were asked to name a single favourite music from a list of eight categories (Table 4.2). *Min'yō* was by far the most popular genre among those over fifty-five but generated little enthusiasm among those under thirty-five. Note that gender is not a significant variable as regards *min'yō*. (The anomalous category *enka* is discussed separately below.)

One possible interpretation of this pattern is that *min'yō* is steadily losing popularity over the years, so that members of the older generation show more interest in it because they were raised in a time when its popularity

Table 4.1. Musical preferences and age, 1971

	national total	men 20-29	men 50-59	women 20-29	women 50-59
sankyoku	5	3	6	5	8
Bunraku (*gidayū*)	2	1	2	3	7
nagauta etc. (longer shamisen song genres)	4	2	7	3	8
kouta/hauta/zokkyoku	8	2	23	6	18
min'yō	44	31	71	30	67
enka and Japanese-style *kayōkyoku*	53	56	52	50	58
Western-style ('pops') *kayōkyoku*	20	33	2	37	3
other *kayōkyoku* (e.g. *fōku songu*-style)	38	46	12	55	20
popular/chanson/latin/tango etc.	30	56	14	59	8
jazz	12	25	2	25	3
symphonic music	15	14	14	16	10
opera	3	2	1	2	2

Respondents were asked which of fifteen categories of music they enjoyed listening to; twelve are shown here. Multiple answers were permitted; mean score per genre for the five categories of person shown was respectively 16, 19, 15, 20, 15. Data from Masui 1980: 166, which was based on a survey by NHK.

Table 4.2. Musical preferences and age, 1978

	nat'l total	men					women				
		16-	26-	36-	46-	56+	16-	26-	36-	46-	56+
hōgaku	2	1	0	0	2	3	1	2	1	3	5
rōkyoku	5	0	2	4	7	17	0	1	1	5	12
min'yō	24	2	11	23	35	46	4	12	24	36	47
enka-style *kayōkyoku*	31	16	44	45	36	21	13	34	39	31	20
Western-style *kayōkyoku*	5	13	5	2	1	1	16	8	3	2	2
popular [chansons etc.]	16	27	23	13	6	2	30	30	17	9	2
rock/other new musics	6	30	4	1	0	0	25	3	1	1	0
Western classical	8	6	7	8	9	5	7	9	12	11	6
other	1	4	2	1	0	1	3	1	1	0	1
don't like music	2	1	2	2	2	3	0	1	1	2	3

Respondents were asked to choose a single favourite from the eight genres listed. Total 100% for each age bracket. 16– = age 16–25, and so forth; 56+ includes all those over 56. Data from Masui 1980: 169, which was based on a survey by NHK. 'No response': 1–3%.

was higher as a whole. Available surveys are not sufficiently comparable to permit a definite decision on this interpretation, but comparison with §3.6 suggests that *min'yō*'s audience share held remarkably steady from the 1930s to the 1970s. The other interpretation is that each individual develops an increased liking for *min'yō* with age. This is supported by the statements of many elderly fans today. Even if today's youngest generation follows this pattern, I doubt that the increase will be as large.

Tables 4.1–2 shed light on other factors correlated with musical taste. The 1978 survey was also tabulated by prefecture of residence (Masui 1980: 170), revealing that tastes also correlate with urban/rural and centre/periphery dichotomies. *Min'yō* is most popular in northeast Japan and along the Japan Sea coast of Honshū; Akita leads with 42 per cent. Three of the four lowest figures, from 17 per cent to 19 per cent, come from the three foremost urban centres: Tokyo, Osaka and Kyoto (see also ibid.: 167).[3] Western Japan in general gives low figures, especially in prefectures bordering the Inland Sea, which have always interacted more closely with the centre than have the Japan Sea prefectures. The same geographical pattern emerged from several other questions in the survey unrelated to music: residents of the northeast and the Japan Sea coast scored high on identification with locality, participation in local festivals, and self-consciousness about local dialect (NHK 1980: 366–7, 435–40). My own interviews, however, make it clear that, aside from current residence, one's native place also has an important effect on preferences. Thus within Tokyo interest in *min'yō* is much higher among recent in-migrants than native Tokyoites.

The 1971 survey was also tabulated by occupation (Masui 1980: 167), yielding these percentages of people who enjoy listening to *min'yō*: 74 per cent of farmers, 59 per cent of independent small entrepreneurs,[4] 50 per cent each of housewives and blue collar, 36 per cent of white collar,[5] and 12 per cent of children and students. The pattern is almost exactly reversed for Western popular and classical genres (omitting children). In no occupational category, however, do any genres other than popular song outstrip *min'yō*.

Finally, tabulating the same results by education (ibid.) reveals a strong inverse correlation between years of schooling and appreciation of *min'yō*: 66 per cent of middle-school graduates, 39 per cent of high-school graduates, and 33 per cent of college graduates enjoy it. Among children and current students, the figure is 12 per cent. Once again, the opposite pattern holds true for Western genres. Since formal musical education in Japan is highly Western-oriented, this is expected.

These four variables (age, occupation, education, native place/residence) are all themselves partially covariant. Due to increasing urbanization, members of today's oldest generation are more likely than their descendants to have been reared in the countryside and to have left school early to work on the family land or to begin an apprenticeship in a trade. Also, small entrepreneurs, urban or rural, usually depend greatly on family labour and thus often remove their children from school after the compulsory period. They also tend to prefer to train their children on the job, scorning formal education. Blue collar workers are more likely than white collars to have been raised in the countryside. Finally, young educated urbanites tend to be the most exposed to Western culture and to interact more with Westerners in their work or travels; thus they also tend to conform more to foreign values, including musical tastes.

Might we speak of two polar personality types: 'modernizing' (or 'innovative') and 'traditional' (or 'conservative')? The problem is that individuals who are relatively innovative with regard to some spheres of culture may be conservative with regard to others. For example, many accept modern fashions and industrial or agricultural innovations while showing a preference for tradition in *min'yō* performance.[6]

Here we consider merely tendencies, of course: the audience at a *min'yō* concert are not all elderly farmers. For one thing, the age structure of Japan's population is weighted towards the bottom, partially negating the effect of the *min'yō* age curve.[7] Also, we are not describing active *participation* in *min'yō* culture, only tastes; other economic and geographic considerations help determine actual behaviour. Participation is considered later, in discussing particular activity spheres. For now, let us continue with tastes.

The most popular genre in both surveys is *enka* or Japanese-style *kayōkyoku* (§§1.7.2). The age distribution of *enka* fans, however, peaks at around forty (Table 4.2). Young and old respectively prefer non-Japanese-style pops and *min'yō* to *enka*. Musical factors contribute to the distaste of the young for *enka*: as with *min'yō*, their melodies and vocal styles are too 'Japanese', too 'old-fashioned'. Most elderly people do not actively dislike *enka*, they simply prefer *min'yō*.[8]

Appendix 1.3 includes several *enka* which refer to *min'yō* in their lyrics and sometimes in their music (songs F to N). In all of these, a *min'yō* from home provides solace to the lonely, rootless protagonist. In *enka*, urban migrants can wallow in self-pity, or occasionally show bluff resilience; *min'yō* – and sometimes *enka* aided by *min'yō* – tend to take one away from the negativity of the city, back to an idealized rural world. We return to this in §§6.2 and 6.6.3.

I have located no comparable recent surveys of musical taste. One 1999 survey pertaining to concert-going (Geinō Bunka Jōhō Sentā 1999: 176) implies that *min'yō* has fallen well behind Western classical music in popularity, but the nature of the categories hinders interpretation. The debate continues in Chapter 7.

4.3 Attitudes towards *min'yō*

4.3.1 Negative attitudes

Now that we know *who* likes *min'yō*, we must ask *why*. Actually, it is far easier to find out 'why not'. In 1971, 87 per cent of Japan's teenagers and 69 per cent of people in their twenties professed not to like *min'yō* (Masui 1980: 166). Conversations with such people found these the most commonly given reasons for their antipathy:

(1) '*Min'yō* are old-fashioned (*furukusai*).' Among the young, *furukusai* is a strong pejorative. The music strikes them as dated, and the texts deal with situations possibly relevant to their grandparents but not to them. Folk singers wear kimono; young people wear jeans. The sound of the shamisen is not the sound of the guitar.

(2) 'I can't understand (*wakaranai*).' This seems directed at the *min'yō* world as a whole, but, if pressed, speakers usually pinpoint the lyrics as the main problem. There is some obscure dialect in *min'yō* and, as with folk song everywhere, numerous lexically comprehensible passages whose overall meaning has however been lost in transmission at some stage. But often the speaker seems not even to have tried to understand. The same person may express a preference for current Japanese pop songs – not noted for the clarity of their semantic content – or for English-language rock songs whose meaning may elude even the native speaker. Thus the claim of *wakaranai* reflects primarily a lack of motivation. True *min'yō* fans sing

with gusto or pathos verses whose exact meaning they may not comprehend; some can quote scholarly hypotheses on the intended sense.

(3)   'They're too difficult (*muzukashii*).' This comes from people of all ages,
       particularly those who do not actively dislike *min'yō* but are slightly
       embarrassed to admit (to a foreigner, at least) that they cannot perform
       them. The perception of *min'yō* as difficult to sing is also usual, indeed
       a point of pride, among those who do sing them. It is the ornamen-
       tation (*kobushi*) which is considered particularly difficult. In fact,
       trained Western-style vocalists who do not enjoy listening to *min'yō* may
       nevertheless comment admiringly on the impressive technical skill of
       professional folk singers.

(4)   'They're obscene (*hiwai*).' This opinion has now virtually vanished, but
       thirty years ago it emerged from a broad range of observers cross-cutting
       occupational and residential lines. Such criticisms were often fuelled by
       the social behaviour accompanying *min'yō* performance – especially the
       raucous bibulousness of some urban *min'yō* bars (see §4.7) and the rela-
       tive sexual freedom of traditional village festivals. The image of bawdiness
       is one with which teachers and performers frequently had to contend in
       striving to make *min'yō* a worthy and respectable genre. Two strategies
       were adopted: to suppress the performance of lyrics with erotic content,
       or to justify the eroticism as reflecting an idealized pastoralist state
       of grace. The former strategy was favoured by singers, the latter more
       commonly by scholars. Both strategies have succeeded.

(5)   'They're uncouth (*gehin*).' This, too, comes from a wide range of
       people, sometimes reflecting class or status consciousness. The speaker
       is likely to be a partisan of either Western or Japanese classical music;
       within the latter category, the music of choice may be as elevated as
       gagaku (court music) or as demi-mondaine as *kouta*. It is to overcome
       the objection of couthlessness that *min'yō* teachers pursue dignification,
       primarily by modelling the organization of their professional activities
       on the *iemoto* system characteristic of the classical arts.

Two anecdotes are apposite. Sugita Akiko (b. ca. 1920) was raised in a
farming village in Tochigi Prefecture, north of Tokyo, and loved singing
min'yō. She eventually married the head of the main branch of a large and
prosperous family in a distant city (having met him while employed as a
folk singer in a night club). After her husband died in 1973, she sought
solace by taking lessons in *min'yō* – something her husband would never
have allowed, for 'he was a serious businessman'. Soon, responding to
requests from neighbourhood friends, she set up a small weekly *min'yō* classroom in her home, which I also attended (Fig. 4.1). Her husband's family
remonstrated with her: *min'yō* was *gehin*, and it would be very bad form
(*kakkō warui*) for one of her social standing to teach it. Could she not pursue a more dignified genre, such as Noh chanting, or *kouta*, or *shigin* (singing

Chinese-style poetry)? She retorted (probably borrowing the words of her teacher) that *min'yō* was the true music of Japan, intimately related to the lives of the masses (*minshū no naka ni tokekonda uta*); nor could it be called *gehin*, since even upper-class women and company presidents were taking lessons in it. Despite their continued objections, she persisted in teaching. Within a couple of years she had won her relatives over, aided by the ongoing dignification of the *min'yō* world. It was particularly the fact that one could earn proficiency certificates in *min'yō* just as in the classical genres – the fact that there were standards – that convinced them. By 1978, two of her husband's siblings had begun to study *min'yō*. (Pers. comm. 1980.)

At a *kouta* recital in Tokyo, I met a young *kouta* teacher from Akita and her elderly male patron, a successful entrepreneur from Fukushima. Both claimed to enjoy *min'yō* (Akita and Fukushima being renowned for their songs). He assured me that she was quite skilled at Akita folk songs but too shy to sing them. I offered to take them to a *min'yō* bar run by an Akita singer, where she would have the opportunity to sing with a good accompanist. They accepted eagerly, never having visited a *min'yō* bar before. Typically, this bar had an amplification system which completely overpowered the scale of the room and somewhat distorted the singers' voices. After several guests had taken turns singing in the robust *min'yō* style, the young teacher sang her song: 'Kiyo Bushi', an Akita song reasonably suited to her small *kouta* voice. Even with the microphone, and with the respectful silence accorded a new guest, she could hardly be heard. It was clear that the visitors from the world of *kouta* had not enjoyed the ambience, nor had they seemed to enjoy the performances by the other singers, some of whom were professionals. My guests were too polite to say so, but the word *gehin* surely occurred to them – perhaps with a semantic shading closer to 'inelegant' than to 'uncouth'. Although *kouta* and *min'yō* are linked tenuously via the geisha and share part of their fan base, the aesthetics of the two are far apart.

It is to reach people with negative opinions such as these that the *min'yō* recording and broadcast industries have tried to modernize their product, as we shall see below.

4.3.2 Positive attitudes

Conversely, what sort of explanations do people give for their attraction to *min'yō*? Some of these reasons relate to passive enjoyment, others to the performance experience. Interestingly, many people started studying or performing *min'yō* of their own volition, having made a positive choice, even while claiming *not* to enjoy it. Thus I have asked some folk song students why they like *min'yō* and been told, 'I don't.' Most of these voluntary but unenthusiastic students eventually develop into serious aficionados: exposure is everything. Some children are forced by parents to take lessons, often quitting at the earliest opportunity. Judging by the patterns of preference by age,

Fig. 0.3 Tanaka Yoshio, with the author and his wife, in Tanaka's home classroom, December 2000. Photo Tanaka Yoshishō, used by permission.

Fig. 1.1 Musicians for Bon dance 'Nikkō Waraku Odori'. Instruments: *shinobue* flute, *kane* hand-gong, with *taiko* drum behind. Photo David Hughes, 1980.

Fig. 2.1 Travelling folk musicians with shamisen, from the woodblock print 'Futagawa', one of Hiroshige's series *Fifty-three Stages of the Tōkaidō* (1833).

Fig. 2.2 An *ocha-kai* in Iwasaki, Iwate Pref., 1988. Photo David Hughes.

Fig. 2.3 The author with Kikuchi Kantarō (right) at Chaguchagu Umakko festival, 198
Photo Katō Toshio, used by permission.

Fig. 3.1 The author and his wife on the television programme *Honmono wa dare da*, 1979, awaiting their cue with the other musicians. Typical stage instrumentation and clothing, though singing while playing shamisen, as the author is doing, is rare in 'stage' *min'yō*.

Fig. 3.2 'Dojō-zukui' (mudfish-scooping) dance delights an audience in Iwate, 1979. See also Foreword. Photo Gina Barnes.

Fig. 4.1 *Min'yō* class taught by Sugita Akiko, 1978. Photo David Hughes.

Fig. 4.2 Folk song bar Yoshiwa in Osaka, with typical ensemble: *taiko* (behind screen to reduce volume), shakuhachi, two shamisen. The singer, Dezaki Tayo II, is a professional, but customers also may sing with the 'house band'. Tanaka Yoshio is to the author's left. Photo Gina Barnes, 1978.

Fig. 4.3 Bon dance in Shinodayama, 1978. Photo David Hughes.

Fig. 4.4 Tokyo visitors receive tuition from the Iso Bushi Hozonkai, 1980. Photo David Hughes.

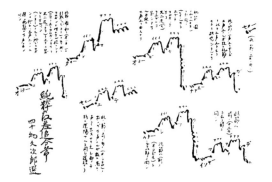

Fig. 4.5 Aimono Hisajirō's notation of 'Esashi Oiwake', ca. 1909 (from Esashi 1982: 105).

Fig. 4.8 Notation for trill as learned by Endō Sayuri from her teacher.

Fig. 4.6 Present-day official notation of the 'Esashi Oiwake Kai'.

ka- mo-   me

Fig. 4.7 Official notation of 'Esashi Oiwake' (first 6 seconds) compared with sonagrams of the singing of Aosaka Mitsuru (*top*; from R36) and Sasaki Motoharu (*bottom*; from R10); staff notation is spaced to align with Aosaka's sonagram.

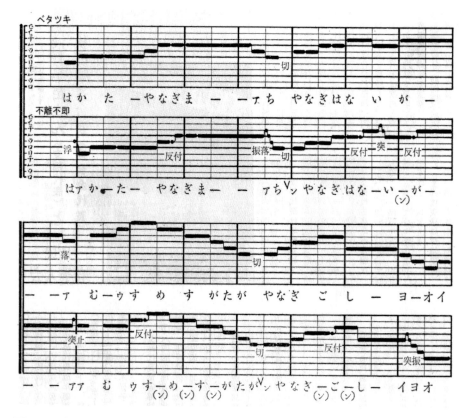

Fig. 4.9 Shibata Takasue's notation for 'Saitara Bushi', comparing simple and fully ornamented versions (from MB 1984.9: 55, used by permission).

Fig. 4.10 Customer sings at folk song bar Oiwake, 2006. Photo David Hughes.

Fig. 4.11 Kanazawa Akiko in jeans, ca. 1979. Photo David Hughes.

Fig. 5.1 Bouchi Uta Hozonkai educational performance, Sagamihara, May 1979. Lead sing is at left. Photo David Hughes.

Fig. 5.2 'Sanko Bushi' lesson, with Senda Kanbei (*middle*) teaching the author, 1979. Photo Gina Barnes.

Fig. 5.3 'Esashi Oiwake' class for visitors at Esashi Oiwake Kaikan, 1988. Photo David Hughes.

Fig. 5.4 *Min'yō* group being televised, Kuryūzawa, 1979. Photo David Hughes.

Fig. 5.5 *Shishi odori* being televised, Kuryūzawa, 1979. Photo David Hughes.

Fig. 7.1 Students at Hamochi High School (Akadomari Branch), Sado Island, practice 'Aikawa Ondo', 2003. Photo David Hughes.

Fig. 7.2 Uchida Akari, age thirteen months, sings at Kotobuki, 2000. Photo David Hughes.

Fig. 7.3 Uchida Miyune, Akari and Mai (*left to right*) practise *taiko*, singing and shamisen at Kotobuki, 2006. Photo David Hughes.

some of these may develop a love for *min'yō* later in life, just as Western adults may regret having abandoned childhood piano lessons. Many other students, of course, started precisely because they liked *min'yō*. In any case, the question of why one likes *min'yō* is often bound up with the question of why one began taking lessons. Here are some case studies:

(1) 'I grew up hearing *min'yō* at home, so I just naturally got to like it.' Children of *min'yō* enthusiasts are much more likely to become fans than are other children. This is often a slow-ripening fondness, emerging perhaps in the late teens. Such people rarely offer more detailed explanations: they have just 'naturally' (*shizen ni*) grown to like *min'yō*.

(2) 'There was a *min'yō* teacher in the neighbourhood, so my parents sent me for lessons.' Even parents who are not *min'yō* aficionados might do this, now that a) folk song has become respectable and b) lesson-taking (*okeiko-goto*) of all types is popular. This path to involvement has become much more common in recent decades with the growth in the number of teachers. It is also primarily an urban path: formal teaching is still uncommon in the countryside.

(3) 'Some friends/relatives were taking lessons, so I started too.' This operates at all age levels and is often a mere attempt to be sociable. Ambivalence may remain. One small-time professional singer had begun lessons at age ten, at her grandmother's urging. Asked in 2000, at the age of thirty-one, whether she liked *min'yō*, she replied, 'I don't dislike it' (*kiraku wa nai*), the equivalent of the lukewarm English 'It's not bad.' When I pressed, 'But do you LIKE it?', she replied unconvincingly, 'I like it a lot' (*daisuki*).

(4) 'I found that I could do the typical *min'yō* ornaments (*kobushi*).' *Kobushi* are considered so difficult that an ability to sing them can be a powerful incentive even without a fondness for *min'yō*. This reason was given to me by a seventeen-year-old boy in 1979 and in the same year by a 47-year-old professional singer; each had made the discovery in his mid-teens.

(5) 'I needed to learn a song to sing at parties.' This is a surprisingly common reason for beginning lessons. Most Japanese organizations hold year's-end parties (*bōnenkai*) or year-opening parties (*shinnenkai*). At these and certain other festive occasions, all present are pressed to take a turn performing. Overwhelmingly these days one sings a popular song; *min'yō*, however, are also appreciated. Since it is easier to find lessons in *min'yō* than in popular song, a person embarrassed at being unable to offer up a decent performance might begin lessons with the aim of learning just one song well. But they rarely stop after one song.

(6) Increasingly today, and far more so than when I began my *min'yō* fieldwork in 1977, young adults may become involved with *min'yō* in a search for their personal identity as Japanese. This is still a relatively rare factor, but it lay behind, for example, the *fōku songu* star Okabayashi

Nobuyasu's invention of his *min'yō*-tinged *en'yatotto* style (§§1.7.1, 7.4.4). Further examples appear occasionally below.

Aside from these reasons, we should mention the positive evaluations which may emerge later in one's experience with the genre. Many people tell me confidently: 'There are no bad people [*akunin wa inai*] among folk singers.' This is a sort of stock phrase frequently used of other music and arts genres as well – by their practitioners. Further questioning reveals the opinion that the very process of striving to learn *min'yō* demands extreme self-discipline: one either develops it or has it from the beginning, but either way a folk singer requires a strength of character incompatible with a life of crime. (Research correlating the pursuit of *min'yō* lessons with a clean criminal record, however, remains to be done.) As the *min'yō* teacher and *tsūjin* Otowa Jun'ichirō put it: 'Folk song builds people.' This view is obviously at odds with the traditional view of many that folk singers were wastrels (§§2.4.2, 3.4.4). Evaluating such opinions requires close attention to the backgrounds and motivations of the speakers.[9]

4.3.3 Some opinions from Iwate

To put meat on the bones of these simple evaluations, I conducted surveys of adults and schoolchildren in the area around Kitakami City, Iwate Prefecture in northern Japan, in 1988. This region has a strong tradition and wide variety of folk performing arts (*minzoku geinō*) and a relatively rich *min'yō* heritage. Although Chapters 4 and 5 focus respectively on city and countryside, this region is relevant to both chapters. The children in the two Kitakami City schools surveyed had relatively more experience of rural lifeways than do Tokyoites; the Waga and Ezuriko schools were in primarily farming communities adjoining the city. The survey results are relevant also to the discussion of music education in §7.5.

The adults' survey differed in detail from that for schoolchildren. The adults were gathered at a senior citizens' event in Iwasaki, a village rich in folklore. One question asked respondents to list the names of 'three to four *min'yō*'. The twenty-four adults collectively listed thirty-eight songs, all of which are indeed *min'yō*. Almost all songs were from Iwate or its immediate neighbouring prefectures; but the youngest 'adult', age sixteen, named only two simple songs, both from far away, which are often taught in school music classes ('Kokiriko Bushi', 'Itsuki no Komoriuta'). All were *min'yō* which would be known to serious folk song fans throughout Japan. Only three of the twenty-four, however, listed 'Sansa Shigure', a famous *min'yō* born not far from this region which is often sung at weddings and other auspicious occasions.

All this is interesting in the light of the next question, which asked which of five specific common local folk songs they had ever sung. These were all functional songs for paddy weeding, celebrations and earth-tamping; of these, only 'Sansa Shigure' would be known to outsiders. The two youngest

Table 4.3. Kitakami area survey results (percentage of positive responses)

	Waga Primary age 10–11 n=45	Kitakami South Primary age 10–11 n=39	Ezuriko Middle age 12–13 n=30	Kitakami South Middle age 12–13 n=34	adults age 16,19, 28, 41–74 n=24
opinions on *min'yō*:					
like	13	18	10	6	71
fun	11	23	13	12	50
nostalgic	7	18	3	12	21
hard to sing	47	38	40	50	29
hard to understand	51	56	47	65	13
dislike	40	23	67	24	0
boring	53	28	67	21	4
old-fashioned	49	18	43	21	0
ever sung a *min'yō*?	13	3	10	32	92
ever danced your local Bon dance?	51	5	50	50	–

(sixteen and nineteen) had sung none of these, but nineteen of the other twenty-two had sung at least one, and all nineteen had sung 'Sansa Shigure'. Why, then, did only three people list 'Sansa Shigure' in answer to the previous question? My best guess is that this is the most dignified of the songs and thus not always considered a 'folk' song.

As further questions revealed, in general these adults had sung quite a few *min'yō*: only two claimed never to have sung any. This contrasts sharply with the schoolchildren: only 14 per cent had sung one. Doubtless this difference in experience accounts largely for the replies when I asked respondents which of eight terms they associated with *min'yō*: 'I like them/fun/nostalgic/ hard to sing' and so forth. None of the adults disliked *min'yō* or found them old-fashioned, whereas around a third of the children did (a figure which would have been higher in Tokyo or Osaka). However, a one-off experience of singing a *min'yō* is not enough to give one a taste for it – possibly quite the contrary: the school at which the most children had sung a *min'yō* was the one where the fewest claimed to like *min'yō*. But the results are more complex than we can go into here: many other variables come into play.

Interpreting the children's statements about their involvement in *min'yō* is complicated by their varying understanding of this term. When asked to name 'two or three *min'yō*' and then any that they had sung, the replies included a number of *enka* (including 'Sake Yo' three times), several old primary-school songs of the *shōgaku shōka* variety, the famous 1890s Western-influenced composition 'Kōjō no Tsuki' ('Moon over the Ruined Castle'), and a few other items that adults would not consider *min'yō*. Thus the number of children who have actually sung a *min'yō* should perhaps be reduced even further. Still, many had sung or at least were familiar with 'real' *min'yō*. By far the most frequent were 'Kokiriko Bushi' and 'Sōran Bushi', both often included in school music classes (performance or appreciation) but neither local to this region, and 'Chaguchagu Umakko', a 'new folk song' associated with, but not sung at, the festival of the same name from a nearby city (§2.5.3).

These surveys make clear the diversity of views about and experiences of *min'yō* even in one tiny region. Although we can safely generalize that adults are much more involved in *min'yō* than are schoolchildren, much else depends on individuals' situations: whether a parent is a *min'yō* fan, whether the local community has an active Bon dance with a local song, and so forth.

To concretize these various observations, here is an edited excerpt of an interview I had with three twelve-year-old first-year students at Kitakami South Middle School (20 August 1988):

(What do you do in music class?) The teacher plunks on the piano, we sing and play *fue* [i.e. recorders].

(What kind of songs?) Hmmm . . .

(Old (*mukashi*) or new?) A few old ones: 'Sakura', 'Kōjō no Tsuki', and those ones that are labelled Ministry of Education something [i.e. *Monbushō shōka*, from official primary-school songbooks]. Oh yeah, like 'Hana'. [Not the 1970s composition by the Okinawan Kina Shōkichi (§7.3), but a school song from 1900.]

(Any *min'yō*?) Hmmm, I don't think so. [Student 3 tentatively sings first three syllables of Iwate *min'yō* 'Sawauchi Jinku', then stops in embarrassment, fearing it is not a *min'yō* after all. Then she says:] How about 'Kokiriko Bushi'? [St. 2:] It's not a *min'yō*, is it?

(How can you tell if a song is a *min'yō* or not?) [St. 3:] If it has 'Bushi' in the title! [We all laugh.]

(Have you heard any Iwate *min'yō*?) [An adult suggests 'Sotoyama Bushi', but they ignore this.] [St. 3:] 'Chaguchagu Umakko' (§2.5.3)? Oh, it's probably not a *min'yō*. How about 'Sawauchi Something-or-other' that [St. 2] did as a two-part chorus in 4th grade? [St. 2:] Oh yeah – but it was 'arranged' to be easier; the teacher said it wasn't *min'yō*-like [*min'yō-ppoi*] in the arranged version. [They can't recall having heard any *min'yō* live, on radio etc.]

(How about Bon dance songs?) We did 'Sansa Odori' in school starting in 2nd grade, but not the song, just the dance. Bon songs around here now are all strange (*hen*).

(How so?) Strange words – *Tsuki ga deta deta* ('The moon has come out') – hard to understand. [This is the opening of the famous dance song 'Tankō

Bushi' (Fukuoka Pref.), which virtually every Japanese has danced, usually at O-Bon. The lyrics are perfectly understandable.]

(How about pop songs – you understand all those?) [St. 2:] No, but at least the *melodies* aren't strange. *Min'yō* are strange in words *and* music.

4.4 Who are the professionals?

4.4.1 Numbers and geography

The '*min'yō* world' centres around the activities of its professionals: performers and teachers. By 'performers' I mean those individuals who frequently are paid to perform in public.

With increasing specialization, almost all performers today are known publicly for one of the five basic skills: solo singing, background vocals (*hayashi-kotoba*), shamisen, shakuhachi (and *shinobue*), or percussion (*narimono*). (Dancers are excluded from this discussion.) This contrasts with the more fluid pre-war situation noted in §3.4.2. Drums and other percussion were originally played by whoever was free at the time; only from the late 1940s did full-time *narimono* specialists begin to appear (perhaps starting with Minami Sankoma; see §4.4.2). Singing backing vocals also began to become a specialist skill from perhaps the 1960s, when certain women whose solo careers had stalled were diverted into this role (e.g. Shirase Haruko, Nishida Kazue).

Regional specializations are also recognized (§4.6). Certain singers are associated primarily with songs of their home region; some shamisen players also specialize, Tsugaru-jamisen being the prime example.

Most solo singers and a few accompanists are under contract to one or another recording company. The majority of performers are also teachers (*sensei, shishō*); in fact, the bulk of their income probably derives from teaching. Many teachers, however, rarely or never perform publicly except in recitals of their own or related *kai*.

The approximate population of professional singers is deducible from the number of artists under contract to the principal recording companies. In 1983 the fifteen major companies dealing with *min'yō* had a total of 291 musicians (170 men, 121 women), over 90 per cent of whom were solo singers. This figure would be far lower today, as *min'yō* recordings sell less well now.[10]

As a legacy of the factors mentioned in §3.4.4, the *min'yō* world is still dominated by performers from northern Japan. Among the 291 contracted performers, of 236 whose native place is known, 153 (65 per cent) are from the six prefectures of Tōhoku (see Map 2) or from Hokkaidō, which contain only about 18 per cent of Japan's population. In *per capita* terms, a northerner was over eight times as likely to be a folk singer. An average of twenty-two people come from each of these seven prefectures, another twenty from

Tokyo, and an average of less than two from the other thity-nine prefectures. This trend is abating gradually among the younger generation, as folk singing becomes a recognized and respected endeavour nationwide – and as artists of rural origin, having relocated to the cities, produce offspring who follow in their footsteps.

Despite the dominance of the north, over 70 per cent of professionals were by 1983 living within commuting distance of Tokyo. This included many of the early stars who travelled with the *min'yō* troupes (Asari Miki, Hamada Kiichi I, Kon Jūzō). Simply put, Tokyo is where the action is: television, record companies, concert opportunities, teachers, potential students – and by-employment if one's career is slow to develop. Some, like Hokkaidō's Sasaki Motoharu, maintain an office or small apartment in Tokyo but spend most of their time back home. Sasaki opened his Tokyo 'office' (with a single secretary) around 1979 as he began to receive an increasing amount of work there due to the latest *min'yō* boom. (He sometimes teaches over the telephone from Hokkaidō.) Suzuki Masao II (b. 1937), throughout his decades-long career, continued to live in the Fukushima countryside because he preferred the pace and flavour of life there – but he could reach Tokyo in a few hours in his dashing sports car, or even faster by bullet train, and did so often. Osaka, Japan's second largest city, forms a subsidiary centre for the *min'yō* business: nearly 10 per cent of professionals lived within its commuting belt in 1983. Osaka resembles Tokyo in that the majority of its most active and visible performers around 1980 were from distant Tōhoku (e.g. Umewaka Baichō, Yamaguchi Kōgetsu, Tanaka Yoshio, Tsuji Seihō).

Gender is an insignificant factor in recruitment of professionals. As noted in §2.4.1, in *min'yō* performance, traditionally and today, few gender constraints are encountered, except that the shakuhachi and (since the same musicians play both) the *shinobue* transverse flute are played virtually exclusively by men; Tsugaru-jamisen still has many more male practitioners, being considered rather macho, but this is changing rapidly. However, men tend to occupy the higher positions in the recording and broadcast business as it pertains to *min'yō*.

4.4.2 Recruitment

Motivations for turning professional have been many and varied. For the older generation from northern Japan (see §3.4.4), several factors operated: the precedent of the *goze*; long winters when little work could be done; economic hardship on non-inheriting children; the presence of Gotō Tōsui at Sendai Broadcasting, etc. Even the younger singers from the north absorbed this self-perpetuating environment. Still, all but the youngest generations likely had to overcome family resistance, since the profession of *geinin* ('performing artist') was traditionally low on the prestige scale. Happily, parents would now rarely be embarrassed if their child were to become a *min'yō kashu* (though they would despair of the economic prospects).

Here are some representative mini-case histories of professionals who chose their calling after the late 1950s. These are based on interviews with each artist (1979–81 except where noted) plus any sources cited.

(1) Harada Naoyuki, born in 1942 in a small agricultural town in Fukushima, had visions in his youth of becoming a choral director; he even took lessons in German *Lieder*. Harada was uninterested in folk song – until he finally yielded to the temptation of the impressive prizes offered at local *min'yō* contests. At age sixteen, he learned a song, entered a contest and won. The vocal ornaments (*kobushi*) seemed to come easily to him, and his new-found skill brought him considerable attention. The social approval and surprising pecuniary benefits led him to continue, almost in spite of himself. By the age of nineteen he had become a live-in student of a renowned teacher in Miyagi Prefecture, and his future career was decided. By 1979, he had over 4,000 students and was Japan's most popular male folk singer. Purists often decry his voice as too 'pretty', not 'earthy' enough. Harada attributes this to his early musical training and defends his style stoutly as fitting for modern Japan.

(2) Kanazawa Akiko (b.1955) is the daughter of a *min'yō* teacher from Tsugaru. She herself was born and raised in the Tokyo commuter belt, yet – unlike Harada – was exposed to *min'yō* almost daily. It was her father's wish that she would someday succeed him as head of his school, but she did not enjoy singing and did not like *min'yō*. However, like Harada, she showed an aptitude for *kobushi* and was soon hooked by the approbation of those around her. At fifteen she won the grand prize in the national contest of the Nihon Min'yō Kyōkai. She soon learned to love *min'yō*, to relish the challenge of learning new songs and styles, and to enjoy relating to her audience. In 1980 she was Japan's best-paid folk singer, charging – and receiving – an average of ¥1,500,000 per appearance for major stage shows (Katō Toshio, pers. comm.).

(3) Honjō Hidetarō (b.1945) was raised in Itako, a small town in Ibaragi Prefecture with a famous geisha district which survives as a major tourist attraction. His was not a musical family, but from early childhood, 'for some reason' (*nan to naku*), he was much drawn to geisha songs. When he asked to begin taking shamisen lessons, his father refused because of the instrument's associations with *goze* and geisha. Hidetarō nevertheless managed to arrange lessons with an ex-geisha at age nine. She taught her voracious pupil several shamisen-vocal styles which geisha performed: *hauta, kouta, min'yō, kiyomoto, tokiwazu*. Family resistance continued at first – his father broke the boy's shamisen in two – but Honjō's perseverance and obvious talent convinced his family to send him to Tokyo at thirteen as a live-in pupil of Fujimoto Hideo, the premier teacher of such styles (§4.5.1). He has kept up his original interest in the entire range of geisha styles and prefers the *ozashiki* type of *min'yō*

to the high-decibel music of northern Japan. Honjō teaches both singing and shamisen but focuses more on the latter in performance. (See MB: 9.40–3.) In recent years, he has also been a leader in seeking new directions for the *min'yō* world, as described in Chapter 7.

(4) Tanaka Yoshio (b.1941) was raised near the farming town of Misawa, eastern Aomori Prefecture, the last of ten children of a farming family (five died in infancy). An American air base was established there after 1945, and as a child Tanaka was as much attracted to the popular music emanating from the American-oriented bars as to the folk song and dance of his community. Unlike Kanazawa Akiko, there were no folk song enthusiasts in his family. Unlike Honjō's home town, there was no prominent tradition of performance in his village: *min'yō* were heard mainly at parties and at the occasional song-and-dance contest at festival time. Because those parties involved considerable drinking, he was told to shun *min'yō* as 'vulgar' (*gehin*). Unlike Harada, he did not develop a taste for the Western-style choral music of the public schools. This was partly because he left school at fifteen to work at home, like most other pupils in this economically depressed region, but also because Aomori was farther than Fukushima from the urban centres of modern culture. Moving to Tokyo at the age of twenty-one, then on to Osaka at twenty-three to live with a brother, he found work in various construction firms. Osaka was lonely for a young man from the north; he missed the food and the dialect and was made to feel like a hick. Gradually the songs from back home emerged as the most effective cure for homesickness: though he had not consciously learned a single local *min'yō*, he recognized many northern songs and found them consolingly familiar. When he and other northerners would gather to drink and sing, they praised his voice and asked that he teach them. Eventually he set up a class at his company, taking lessons himself at the same time from a nearby teacher. Within a few years he had gathered a large number of students and begun to succeed at *min'yō* contests. In 1971 he quit the company and embarked on a full-time music career. With the help of a loan of ¥20 million, he set up his own school (the Yoshiwa-kai) and opened the folk song bar (*min'yō sakaba*) Yoshiwa in 1974 (Fig. 4.2). By 1977, student numbers had stabilized at well over 300. He is equally active today.

It is worth noting that Tanaka's daughter Kimiko (b. 1969) followed in her father's footsteps, studying with him from age four and later with Tōdō Teruaki (see below). Many examples of such genetic continuity pop up throughout this book.

(5) Tōdō Teruaki (b.1942) is one of the few successful and well-known professionals from southwestern Japan. Raised in the small rural town of Kurume in Fukuoka Prefecture, son of a professional *naniwa-bushi* shamisen player, he learned several *naniwa-bushi* as a child. Since this genre has so much in common stylistically with both *enka* and popular *min'yō*, he soon developed a taste for these as well. *Naniwa-bushi*, however, was rapidly

losing popularity by then (§3.6), so Tōdō's singing activities came to focus on the shorter song genres. The modern *min'yō* world was only just beginning in Kyushu, and most urban singers chose to sing northern songs rather than local ones. However, it was a local *sake*-making song that won Tōdō the second prize in the NHK national contest – his springboard to Tokyo and a career. In 1961 he won the Nihon Min'yō Kyōkai national contest, but this time he sang a song from central Japan. (See MB: 4.40–3.) In general, he prefers Kyushu songs, having come to feel it his mission to keep them alive.

(6) Kosugi Makiko (b. ca. 1940) was raised in the town of Koshiji in Niigata Prefecture. At the Bon season she used to hear and enjoy performances of *naniwa-bushi* at the local temple; she, like Tōdō, was led to *min'yō* via *naniwa-bushi*. But Koshiji had also been until recently a centre of *goze* activity. Whenever Makiko sang, her parents would say: 'Stop acting like a *goze*!' She used to sneak off to a nearby town to hear *min'yō* concerts. In her late teens, to avoid an unwanted arranged marriage, she fled to Tokyo. Eventually working her way into the *min'yō* world, she ended up, like Honjō, as a live-in pupil (*uchi-deshi*) of Fujimoto Hideo. (See MB: 3.42–5.)

(7) Kamiya Miwako (b.1956) was raised in Yokohama by parents who had no involvement with *min'yō*. When she demonstrated a childhood aptitude for picking up songs of any type, a family friend urged the parents to recognize this skill and start her on music lessons. Since the friend was a *min'yō* enthusiast, eight-year-old Miwako was sent to study *min'yō* and soon grew to love them. However, at the age of twelve she asked to quit lessons because the children at school mocked her strange musical taste. (Yokohama considers itself a very stylish, modern town.) After graduating from high school, however, she resumed lessons and in 1978 signed a contract with CBS-Sony. Kamiya's preference runs to *ozashiki-uta* and *shin-min'yō* more than to vigorous work songs.

(8) Let us take one example of the 'minor' specialists (percussion, winds, *hayashi*). Minami Sankoma (b. 1916) was, she says, the first specialist player of *min'yō* percussion (*narimono*; pers. comm. 1980). During a small *min'yō* boom in Tokyo around 1946–7, at first there were no taiko specialists. She says this was because nobody wanted to take the time to learn, so the drum parts were just ad-libbed. Probably drumming was simply considered easy enough not to require special training. In any case, her singing teacher urged her strongly to become a drumming specialist. Taking the hint as to her singing prospects, she did so. Now virtually all recordings and broadcasts employ specialists, although a low-budget touring group will still generally share out the drumming among those not singing at the moment. Around 1980 the most sought-after specialists, who captured a goodly share of recording and television work, were Sankoma's student Minami Komasaburō and his two daughters, Harukoma and Narukoma. Today (under the new family name Bihō) this 'school' is still favoured by *min'yō* producers.

(9) Takahashi Yūjirō (b. 1934) is known primarily as one of the leading Tsugaru-jamisen players and as a teacher. Of all the artists listed here, he has perhaps held tightest to rural elements even while functioning as a creative modern urban professional. He was born in Kakunodate Town in Akita into a family of serious amateur performers, featuring his father's shamisen, his mother's singing, his brother's festival *shinobue* playing and his older sisters' dancing. At seventeen, while training as a carpenter, he took up his father's shamisen, and three years later he was playing *min'yō* on radio. He also studied folk shakuhachi and the *shinobue* and dancing of his local festival.

At about the age of nineteen, he heard a touring *min'yō* troupe performing at the local Shinto shrine; captivated by the skill – and the formal kimono the performers wore – he immediately resolved to become a professional. About this time he was also bewitched by the artistry of Mihashi Michiya (see below). By 1955, he was living and learning in the Ranman *min'yō* club in Tokyo, whose star singer was the renowned Hamada Kiichi I, with whom he toured from 1957. Like other early touring pros, but more so, Takahashi became proficient on a range of instruments: not only on the above but also *kokyū* fiddle and percussion. His Min'yūkai school, founded in 1967, now has over 1,000 members. In 1987 he created the Kaze ensemble (see §7.3), which has performed in some two dozen countries. (Pers. comm. over many years.)

(10) For an example bridging the pre-war and post-war periods, consider the career of Dezaki Tayo II (Fig. 4.2; legal name Murakami Mitsue). She was born around 1915 in the Tsugaru region of Aomori but lived in the fish-market area of Tokyo from 1944. A talented singer from a poor household, she saw singing as a way out of poverty. She started formal lessons in Tsugaru songs with the first-generation Dezaki Tayo at the age of ten, and at sixteen she made her first commercial recording. At seventeen she became a live-in student (*uchideshi*) of Tayo(ko) I; she was the nineteenth and last to do so, the rate of turnover reflecting her teacher's harsh and demanding nature. She spent six years in Tayo's house, the last three as a stage performer, and eventually succeeded to the professional name. (The renowned 'Esashi Oiwake' singer Hamada Kiichi I also spent a year with Tayo I to learn Tsugaru songs, which were fast becoming indispensable to the professional. This reflects on the regionality of certain styles: one should learn them from a native; see §4.6.1.) Marriage led Tayo II into a happy retirement for twenty years, but her husband's bankruptcy forced her back onstage as a house singer at a *min'yō* bar, and she resumed her recording career. When we met around 1978, her voice was in decline, and she supplemented her family's income by teaching *min'yō* at a local community centre and performing at minor events. After several decades in Tokyo, she still preferred to hang around with people from the northeast. (See also the anecdote about her in the Foreword.)

(11) Moving up to the post-Beatles generation, consider Kinoshita Shin'ichi (b. 1965), billed as the 'king of Tsugaru-jamisen'. Sometimes sporting a slightly punkish orange-dyed hairdo and performing in various

non-traditional garb, he made this tradition attractive to a wider and younger audience, inspiring performers such as the Yoshida Brothers (Yoshida Kyôdai) and Agatsuma Hiromitsu. The core of his repertoire is solo arrangements of traditional Tsugaru tunes, albeit played with incredible technique and improvisatory imagination. But he also performs with a range of instrumentalists at different times (rarely with traditional singers), including various Japanese instruments, jazz guitar, Hungarian gypsy violin, Turkish musicians, symphony orchestra, rock band – what he calls 'Tsugaru fusion'. But in all of these collaborations, he says, he stays true to traditional style.

He was born in Wakayama Prefecture, not far from Osaka, in 1965. His parents were active folk singers, and he absorbed many songs as a child. His conversion to shamisen occurred at the age of ten, at the Bon dance in his father's home town of Shinodayama, south of Osaka. As hundreds of people danced all night to the ballad 'Shinodayama Bon Uta' (see §4.6.2, Fig. 4.3), his father was among the musicians on the high tower. Young Shin'ichi tried to clamber up to join him – but was stopped because he could not play shamisen. Miffed, he began to learn shamisen from his father immediately thereafter, eventually focusing on Tsugaru style.

At the age of fifteen he went to Tokyo to play shamisen as his father sang in a national contest. While there, they visited a min'yō bar/restaurant, where several young people performed while working as waiters and waitresses. Shin'ichi decided on the spot to follow such a career, but his father forced him to finish high school first. Immediately after graduation, he left for Tokyo to pursue his dream. Kinoshita won a national Tsugaru-jamisen contest in both 1986 and 1987 – and the rest is history. Until the age of twenty or so, he had no interest in any other music, not even the pop styles his friends enjoyed; few children today could sustain such a single-minded focus on traditional music. (Pers. comm., 26 June 2003 and October 2004.)

(12) Finally, consider the stories of the six young members of the Tsugaru-jamisen group DADAN, as related to me in May 2001. The ensemble is led by Ishii Shūgen (b. ca. 1960), who has recorded with Kinoshita. All members are from Kyushu's Miyazaki Prefecture, far from Tsugaru. A concert in Miyazaki in the early 1990s by Fujita Jun'ichi, a renowned player from Hokkaido, was a conversion experience for Ishii and his father: both began studying Tsugaru-jamisen immediately. Until then Ishii had been a rock guitarist. Shida Mitsuyoshi likewise had no traditional music links before hearing the same concert and making the same decision. Nakamura Masafumi's father played classical shakuhachi, but he himself was immune to traditional music until Ishii and Shida dragged him into Tsugaru-jamisen. (These three longtime friends were all born in 1960–61.) Uemura Nami (b. 1981) was forced to study shamisen (non-folk) by her mother from age four, but only came to enjoy it much later, eventually catching the Tsugaru bug. Urahama Mihoko decided at age nine that she wanted to learn various instruments, so began to study shamisen (again due to a family link), accordion and another

Western instrument; Tsugaru-jamisen came later. Finally, Uenozono Kenji, who sometimes plays African djembe drum with DADAN, provides an example to remind us of other possible choices. Lacking any family musical role models, he joined the school band only to avoid athletics, was put on drums due to perceived non-musicality, and soon got hooked – but has never been tempted into folk *taiko*, whether traditional or modern Kōdō-influenced style. (Further recent examples of recruitment are found in §7.7.)

Thus, recruitment to the profession in the post-war period follows diverse paths. Certain trends, however, distinguish the situation today from the pre-war period.

(1) Most importantly, 'folk singer' (*min'yō kashu*) is now a perfectly respectable profession. Kamiya Miwako struggled with schoolmates' opinions of *min'yō* not as disreputable but as old-fashioned. Her parents, despite having no interest themselves, nonetheless encouraged her to take lessons.

(2) It is now common to take formal lessons as part of one's development, most often in a large city.

(3) The profession of geisha, which yielded several of the early recording artists, is essentially defunct as a breeding ground for *min'yō kashu*. There are, however, still many performing geisha. They turn up frequently on television *min'yō* shows, particularly due to the influence of Fujimoto Hideo and Honjō Hidetarō in programme planning.

(4) Although some early pros got their start by success in contests, this has become an increasingly common route as national contests have proliferated.

(5) Record companies and the NHK broadcasting company now hold regular auditions in a quest for new talent, or otherwise actively seek out performers. Tanaka Yoshio and Kamiya Miwako followed the audition route in part.

(6) Finally, members of the youngest generation of professionals have been under the constant influence of the media, particularly the broadcast and recording industries. They may well have found their role models in this indirect fashion, whereas the oldest generation was much more influenced by live performances by *goze*, *min'yō* troupes and so forth. The first post-war *min'yō* boom, during the 1950s, was fuelled primarily by the broadcast and recording industries, culminating with the emergence of Mihashi Michiya as a national star around 1955. Yamamoto Kenji (b.1943) was raised in Tsugaru under the constant stimulus of folk song, but he is one of several current professionals who credit Mihashi's appearance on the scene with their decision to seek a career as a *min'yō kashu*. The broad reach of the media has been crucial in expanding the recruitment area for folk singers beyond northern Japan to the whole country.

This certainly does not exhaust the possible paths by which one comes to a career in folk song. Thus Ōba Itaru's first serious exposure to *min'yō* came as a student in the early 1970s when he joined Nihon University's Min'yō Kenkyūkai (Folk Song Study Club).

Significantly, escape from poverty is now very rarely a stimulus to a singing career in a prosperous Japan. This leads us to consider income sources.

4.4.3 Sources of income

The modern urban folk singer has a wide range of possible employment opportunities. Individuals may draw on several of these at once. The principal sources of income are as follows.

(1) Teaching is potentially the most stable and secure source. Through utilizing the model of the *iemoto* ('headmaster') system, it is possible to build up a network of students who will one day pass on to you a portion of their earnings from their own students. Post-1960s' growth in leisure activities means that ever more people are involved in 'lesson-taking' (*okeiko-goto*) of all types. Since Japanese students tend to be very loyal (as long as the teacher takes his/her job seriously), teaching is a steady income source amidst fluctuating possibilities for paid performance opportunities.

Most new students are attracted via contact with existing students. However, traditionally a teacher advertises by hanging out a *kanban*, a small plaque giving one's name and specialty. Students will be attracted by a *geimei* ('art name') derived from a renowned performer/teacher. For example, Fujimoto Hideyasu will immediately be recognized as having received an art name from the Fujimoto Hideo 'school' (*ryū*). Some also teach at various 'leisure centres' and 'culture centres' (§4.5.3).

Tuition fees vary greatly with the reputation, philosophy and needs of the teacher, as well as with the income level of the neighbourhood. A well-known performer can command a large fee from students he or she hardly ever sees. Around 1980, Nara's Sugita Akiko, teaching for the love of *min'yō* rather than as a living, was only charging ¥500 per month for weekly lessons, while some professionals charged ¥10,000 or more.

(2) Appearances on television (and to a lesser extent radio) can be a singificant income source for a small coterie of leading professionals, although the pay is much lower than for stage shows. Around 1980 Kanazawa Akiko, who could command over ¥1 million for a stage appearance, was getting about ¥50,000 for television work; lower-level accompanists might have received ¥7,000–10,000. During the 1977–81 boom years, several *min'yō* shows were broadcast each week. The number has declined drastically since then, but the fees have kept up with inflation, and the overall benefits are sufficient that some occasionally neglect teaching responsibilities for television work, usually with mild embarrassment. Harada Naoyuki expressed regret that his sudden emergence as a major media figure in 1978 had by 1980 prevented him from

accomplishing his self-imposed goal of meeting each of his 4,000-odd students at least once a year (*sic!*). The students, on the other hand, basked in the glow of their prominent teacher. Since the *iemoto* system allows you to consider your teacher's teacher your own teacher, a customer at a *min'yō* bar in Kyushu may tell you proudly that he is Harada's student although they have never met.

(3) Recording is, again, lucrative only for the top stars. When a singer is first contracted to a record company, the company will foot the bill for a debut album. To cover costs, the company must sell somewhere around 3,000 copies. If sales are low, subsequent recordings may depend on the artist's willingness to subsidize costs – for example, by buying 1,000 copies at cost. In general, albums are moneymakers only for singers with a large number of students or a mass following.

(4) Appearing as a guest performer at recitals may be profitable for the top stars. This is one case where television exposure can be helpful. In 1977, Kanazawa Akiko performed at my Osaka teacher's recital for a mere ¥10,000 plus expenses; a year later, after the astonishing success of the new folk song show *Min'yō o anata ni*, her fee was 100 times higher. For most, however, guest appearances are on an exchange basis with colleagues. Fees from such exchanges cancel each other out, but the net effect of having several guest artists at your yearly recital will be to bring in more paying audience members (including students of the various guests), enhance your prestige and increase your student numbers, thus generating income.

(5) Operating a *min'yō* bar (§4.7) can be profitable if the right factors conspire: prime location, talented 'house band', good atmosphere, big-name owner. For a few years during the 1977–81 boom, these bars were almost guaranteed to turn a profit; since 1981, most have fallen on hard times and many have closed. Oiwake in Tokyo's Asakusa is one of the most successful today.

Success breeds success: the most popular singers find many other opportunities to expand their incomes. Television commercials occasionally feature folk song. Around 1980 the Bon dance song 'Aizu Bandai-san' poured out of the television to advertise the Aizu district's *sake*; the singer was Ōtsuka Fumio, who was born across the mountains from Aizu but had gained renown for his version of the song.

Let us now look in detail at the operation of some of these institutions which provide a living for *min'yō kashu*. We will be concerned less with how they generate income than how they affect musical behaviour.

4.5 Formal teaching of folk song

4.5.1 The iemoto system

Teaching folk song as a profession is a twentieth-century phenomenon whose development was part and parcel of the 'classicization' of *min'yō*. In developing a pedagogy, teachers turned most naturally to the model of the traditional urban performing arts. The intermediaries between these two streams were the geisha, certain influential *tsūjin*, and individuals like Gotō Tōsui, all of whom had studied arts transmitted within the framework of the *iemoto* system.

The *iemoto seido*, possibly translated as the 'househead system', is a common structure for transmission of traditional arts (and some less traditional). It is much discussed by observers of the arts world: some denounce it as a feudal relic, while others acknowledge its exploitative nature but credit it with helping many arts survive to the present in relatively unsullied form. Much besides art is at stake. In recent years, prominent headmasters have frequently been cited for evading taxes on the huge amounts of unreported income from indirect payments from students. In 1980 a traditional dance student, Hanayagi Genshū, stabbed her headmistress in an act of protest against the *iemoto* system.

The system is closely modelled on the structure of the traditional Japanese household (*ie*), where all authority resided in the househead (*iemoto*). Members of an *ie* are largely related by blood or marriage, but official or unofficial adoption is also common. In particular, a family without a suitable male heir will often arrange to absorb an unrelated male, by adoption or by marrying him to a daughter; in either case, he will replace his own family name with that of his new household. The frequently autocratic exercise of the head's authority has survived in the arts world.

The *iemoto* system is in essence a guild system: students are apprentices learning a skill (*waza*) which for some of them will provide a livelihood. It differs from a tradespersons' guild, however, in the sharp distinction between the minority of students who hope to acquire a marketable skill and the many more who are simply seeking a bit of 'culture' or pursuing a hobby. On the other hand, it differs from, for example, piano teaching in the West most obviously in two features: the familistic, fictive-kinship nature of the school's structure, and the high fees paid by students when receiving certificates of proficiency.

Its typical form is as follows. A 'school' or 'sub-school' (*ryū, ryūha, kai* etc.) of a certain art is headed by an *iemoto* (*sōke, kaishu,* etc.), a 'head' in whom resides ultimate authority in all matters – artistic, financial, personal – pertaining to the group. Long-time students (usually but not always talented) may become teachers under the *iemoto*, and in a large school their students may in turn form a third stratum of teachers. Students progress through several levels of instruction, receiving (for a fee) a licence as each level is completed. Often students must purchase materials (notation, books by the *iemoto*, etc.) at rates profitable to the head. There may be a minimum required amount of time (more precisely, of lesson fees) before one can progress to the next level. Despite the obvious economic justifications for such a system, there is a more deep-rooted and 'pure' motive also at work:

Japanese teachers of all genres of traditional arts stress the need to progress slowly, moving ahead only after thoroughly mastering each stage. (This attitude is weakening gradually.) Nothing of value can be learned quickly. Similar observations have been made concerning other cultures.

Simultaneously with or at the level just below receiving a teaching licence, a student may (for a fee often well over £1,000) be granted an 'art name' (*geimei*) – a stage name – and thus become a *natori* or 'name-taker'. This name will include part of the teacher's own *geimei*. The most widespread practice is to receive the family name and the first part of the personal name, so that the *natori* of Fujimoto Hideo will become Fujimoto Hidenari, Fujimoto Hidekazu and so forth. The successor as head receives the entire name along with a generational designation. Around 1980 the ailing folk singer Izumo Ainosuke II passed his name on to a student whom he considered to best embody the requisite combination of talent, loyalty and administrative ability. The younger Ainosuke was thereafter, and for many years after his teacher's death, generally called *sandaime(-san)*, '(Mr) Third Generation'.

Even those starting their own school may reflect a link with their teacher. When Honjō Hidetarō broke away from Fujimoto Hideo's school, he wished to use his own family name but to keep the Hide- element of his teacher's given name; permission was grudgingly granted. Another leading Fujimoto student first taught for many years as Fujimoto Hidenari before his renown allowed him at age forty-three to take the more independent name Chifuji Kōzō, retaining the Fuji element only.

There is a difficulty in applying the *iemoto* system to the *min'yō* world: it is based on the assumption of a 'limited good', a product – a skill – that is in short supply and/or difficult to learn and thus not readily obtained without expert guidance. With the professionalization of *min'yō* teaching, it is clearly in the teachers' interests to maintain that *min'yō* cannot be successfully learned in any other way than through formal lessons. Moreover, to have a product to sell, teachers must preserve the art form intact (or seem to do so), maintaining the characteristic style of the school. To wit, there must be a right and a wrong way to perform, and the teacher is the conservator of the right way. It is of course possible in the age of recording to learn any number of *min'yō* without a teacher (indeed, many teachers themselves do this). Also, given the tradition of 'stealing the art' from other performers (§2.5.2), one might have wondered whether the *iemoto* system could catch on in the *min'yō* world.

In fact, however, it has. The group emphasis in Japanese society is so strong that most Japanese seem to enjoy (or at least feel most comfortable) being part of a well-structured corporate group with a strong, respected head. One point of taking lessons, from this viewpoint, is to receive some concrete token of achievement. Even after a one-day folk dance workshop sponsored by the Nihon Fōku Dansu Renmei ('National [international-style] Folk Dance

Federation of Japan'), participants received Certificates of Completion. Thus, although it is possible to learn songs from recordings, most Japanese prefer to pay the fees and receive the licences and eventually a cherished 'art name'. Kikuchi Tanshige explained (8 November 2000) that he was teaching without calling himself an *iemoto* or establishing a *ryūha*, but he found this disappointed his adult students (though not teenagers), who all wanted to belong to some *ryū-ha* or other. Dance teacher Yoshizawa Anna said the same (7 December 2006); she eventually yielded and now issues *geimei*.

A more serious problem, one would think, is that *min'yō*, unlike, say, koto music, was too variable to be transmitted by a system such as this. If each singer performs a particular local song somewhat differently, and – more importantly – if a single singer shows considerable variation in repeated performances of a single song, then which version does one teach?

Min'yō teachers recognize the existence of multiple versions of most songs. Influenced by the *iemoto* model, they tend to consider variation to exist between individuals or schools but not between a single teacher's successive performances. Thus they inevitably tell their students to imitate them exactly; only after the model provided by the teacher's version has been learned note-for-note, ornament-for-ornament, may pupils begin to find their own 'characteristic flavour' (*mochiaji*).

Since the concept of invariance in *min'yō* performance is a recent phenomenon, many teachers have not (yet) developed stable versions of most songs. In §3.3.3 we learned that the attempt to standardize 'Esashi Oiwake' had little effect initially; now, however, singers aim to repeat it almost identically every time, down to the number of ups-and-downs in a trill. Few other *min'yō* have yet undergone this degree of standardization; the ideology, however, is one of invariance. (See the discussion of melodic variation in §2.5.3, and notations of 'Esashi Oiwake' in §4.5.2.)

Once, learning the accompaniment for 'Tsugaru Ohara Bushi' from a leading performer of Tsugaru-jamisen, I came to my lesson having learned the piece note-for-note from my recording of the previous week's lesson. (I had even notated it.) My teacher, however, said that I had it wrong and taught me a slightly different version. This is a common experience in *min'yō* classes. It seems that, in identifying their teaching methods with those of the classical teachers, many teachers do not recognize how easily variation can creep in.

Variation may be minimal – for shamisen, perhaps merely the difference between playing a certain pair of notes in equal or unequal durations at several points in the piece. Yet this is more variation than is allowed in, say, *nagauta* or most other shamisen lyric genres. In the traditional village, such variation would have gone unremarked; today, it is upsetting to a teacher who sees invariance as a positive virtue.

Such variation bothers teachers today also because most of them are trying to modernize, to 'rationalize' their teaching methods. Here are some examples of such attempts. Almost all teachers now accept or encourage the use of recording devices to accelerate learning. Notation is common now for shamisen, though less so for singing because of the difficulty in notating the all-important vocal ornaments. (But see §4.5.2 below.) Books on how to learn *min'yō* are becoming frequent (early examples being Ozawa 1978; Takeuchi 1983b). Some teachers now try to teach generalized points of music theory. Thus Fujimoto Hideo suggested that there are differences in the ratios of duration of two-note pairs in shamisen accompaniments: for 'Hachinohe Kouta' the ratio is 1:1; for 'Chōja no Yama', 3:2; for 'Sado Okesa' **(CD3)**, 2:1; for 'Sōran Bushi' **(CD29)**, 4:1; for 'Nikkō Waraku Odori', 5:1, etc. (MB 1979.4: 30–1). I do not know whether his students have found this helpful (the degree of precision is dubious), but such mathematical teaching methods are becoming frequent. Kyōgoku Toshinori, a northerner teaching in Kyoto, has for decades often used the piano to pick out song melodies for his students, believing that this would obviate problems of deviant pitch. (Primarily a shamisen player, he mistrusts his control of vocal pitch.)

One Tsugaru-jamisen teacher in Tokyo, hoping to correct the wayward rhythms of one student, in desperation had him play to the accompaniment of an electronic 'rhythm box', which was playing a samba rhythm! For many Tsugaru pieces in steady 2/4 metre, such as 'Tsugaru Jongara Bushi', this would have fit the traditional metre (if not rhythm) adequately. In this case, however, the piece in question was 'Tsugaru Aiya Bushi', whose rhythm features three beats of slightly unequal duration per measure, with agogic accent on an off-beat (§1.6.1, cf. **CD4**). A student who managed to copy the rhythm box would produce a totally new 'Tsugaru Aiya Bushi'. The teacher himself plays in the traditional rhythm, undisturbed by electronics.

Despite such modernizing or Westernizing elements, the basic teaching method for *min'yō* is unchanged from that for classical musics in traditional times. Sitting face-to-face, the teacher provides a model which the student imitates. They begin at the start of a piece and progress slowly and cumulatively towards the end. The main difference from a century ago may simply be that folk song is now subjected (in theory) to the same demands of invariance encountered in the traditional classical genres – reflecting the 'classicization' of *min'yō*.

This rote approach is nearly universal where *min'yō* is taught formally; it extends also to many 'preservation societies' (*hozonkai*; see §5.4.4) around the country. In 1980 I attended a teaching session of the Iso Bushi Preservation Society in Ibaragi Prefecture (§5.4.4). A busload of us had come up from Tokyo for a crash course in singing 'Iso Bushi' (Fig. 4.4). The first singer to stand before the teacher was made to repeat one tiny phrase over and over until the teacher was satisfied – or exhausted **(CD33)**. This is the normal way one learns the fine ornaments (*kobushi*) that are the lifeblood of *min'yō*: just keep imitating until your teacher is happy.

However, verbal or graphic aids are also used. In one lesson Sugita Akiko of Nara instructed students as follows: Mr O's *kobushi*, which should be quick and sharp, have become *yuri* (slower, smoother vibratos) and are too loud: he must be more subtle. Even his actual *uki* and *yuri* are too loud and too frequent. She drew a series of crenellations to show Ms K that her *yuri* were too square and sharp, then drew a wavy line to show the desired smoothness. My own rendition of 'Otachizake' is too ornamented. I must also extend the phrase ends longer, then immediately start the next phrase – that's the trick (*kotsu*) of that particular song: a long breath has no flavour (*aji*). Indeed, the main term used in the *min'yō* world to evaluate a performance is the simple word *aji*: 'It just hasn't got flavour' (*Nan to naku aji ga nai*). (See also Matsukawa's comments on appropriate ornamentation in §1.6.4. For more examples of graphic aids, see the next section.)

Two other forces encouraging invariance or standardization are discernable. One is the trend towards performing in large ensembles, mostly for shamisen rather than singing. At a student recital, the teacher tries to give all students an opportunity to sing a solo, but there is not time for each shamisen student to play alone, especially as student numbers have increased. (Except in Tsugaru-style pieces, the shamisen is far less important to participants than the singing, so a solo slot is less coveted.) It has therefore become common to arrange medleys of *min'yō* as instrumentals for massed unison shamisen. With thirty to fifty players, strict unison or two-part arrangements become much preferable to multiple heterophony. The other force is the rise of the concours. Since accompanists are usually provided by the organizers, it is important that a standard vocal melody be learned so as not to confuse the musicians. (These two tendencies together have resulted in the addition of a choral (unison) division in many competitions, so that all students of one *kai* may compete as a group.) We shall see in §§4.8.3 and 4.9 that judges at competitions also tend to penalize divergence from the most common version of a song.

We conclude this section with a brief discussion of Fujimoto Hideo (1923–2006). His name has arisen several times already, as his impact on the modern *min'yō* world has been immense.[11] His *min'yō* 'school' is called the Fujimoto-kai. But with his wider musical interests, he created in western Tokyo a teaching institution called the Nihon Min'yō Kayō Gakuin, perhaps to be translated Japan Folk Song and Other-types-of-song Academy! (Various non-folk shamisen-accompanied vocal genres were also taught.) This academy had by 1984 had more than 300,000 students mainly through a correspondence course, reaching as far as San Francisco and Brazil (pers. comm. from his son, 1984), so his influence has continued through his myriad students. His career and artistic philosophy are described in his own words in his autobiography (Fujimoto 1978). Aside from interacting with him often at performances, I interviewed him formally at his school in 1984.

Like his renowned student Honjō Hidetarō, Fujimoto studied various classical shamisen-accompanied genres from early childhood. Through genres such as *kouta* and *zokkyoku*, with their folk song links, and through increasing commercial demand, he eventually became involved in the world of *min'yō* as well. With the launch of the radio programme *Min'yō okuni jiman* ('Folk Song, Pride of the Provinces') in 1952, he became the producers' major contact for locating singers and accompanists (§3.5).

Even in 1984, however, with *min'yō* having achieved full respectability as an art form, Fujimoto stated bluntly that he was only teaching *min'yō* as a stepping-stone to the classical shamisen-vocal genres which he valued much more highly. This dismissive attitude, from which he never wavered, was reflected in various aspects of his teaching and has impacted on many of his students (see end of §5.6 and §6.6). And yet his recitals showed a pleasing diversity of content. His 1978 autobiography lists the contents of his school's four major recitals from 1964 to 1977 (pp. 275ff.). Aside from *min'yō* and various shamisen/vocal genres, we find: a segment featuring performers from six other Asian countries; various pieces for traditional instruments derived from or inspired by *min'yō*; a musical voyage from the Meiji period to today, including *min'yō*, *enka*, early popular songs and so forth; a segment by the Young Folkers, a vocal ensemble of teenage *min'yō* singers; a commissioned piece for *gagaku* court ensemble and shamisen; and a segment of *shin-min'yō* (which feature frequently throughout the series).

One of Fujimoto's major contributions was the production of the standard notation collection for *min'yō* shamisen, which leads us to our next topic.

4.5.2 Musical notation

Although the lyrics to many songs that we now call *min'yō*, including lengthy ballads, had often been written down and even sold, the first musical notations of *min'yō* date, for all practical purposes, from the early twentieth century. Here we concentrate on notations intended for teaching, rather than the numerous scholarly collections.

The first folk song notated for teaching purposes was apparently 'Esashi Oiwake' (§3.3). During the first decade of the twentieth century, the Esashi singer Aimono Hisajirō produced the vocal notation shown in Fig. 4.5. This was the springboard for the subsequent development of the distinctive if diverse family of notations for this particular song (examples in Kiuchi 1979: 103–8 or Hughes 1985: 329). No specific model for Aimono's original is known, though there are similarities to certain Buddhist vocal notations. Intriguingly, each phrase of the song, to be sung in one breath, is shown as a continuous undulating line, proceeding horizontally from left to right, with abrupt wiggles to show abrupt ornaments. By 1928, influence from Western notation led Hamada Shōkaku to superimpose these undulations upon a sort of staff of sixteen horizontal lines, though showing only relative pitch (Kiuchi 1979: 105–6).

The official notation of the Esashi Oiwake Kai [Association] today has only a six-line staff (Fig. 4.6). Phrases 3 and 4 are repeated with different lyrics as phrases 6 and 7. Melodic direction is accurately indicated with one or two exceptions, but without indicating specific pitches. Duration is similarly indicated only approximately, by horizontal spacing. Where this notation excels is in showing ornamentation neumatically. At the bottom are shown the eight named ornaments (or melodic motives) which constitute virtually the entire song. Each ornament is consistently performed at each occurrence. Teachers generally display a gigantic version of this notation in front of the student(s) and follow the melody with a pointer (Fig. 5.3).

Sonagrams reveal how well this notation conveys the structure of this particular song and how narrow is the range of permitted variation. Figure 4.7 shows the first few seconds (three syllables) in official notation, juxtaposed with the fundamental frequency (i.e. the melody) and the next harmonic from sonagrams of performances by Aosaka Mitsuru **(CD2)** and Sasaki Motoharu **(CD28)**, two of the most famous and respected singers. A Western transcription of most of the first phrase is given as Example 4.1, with notes spaced to show approximate relative duration.

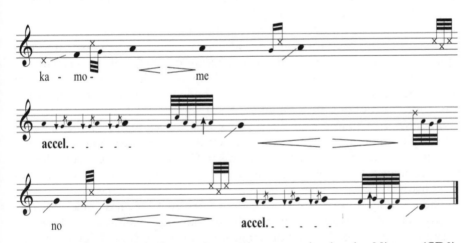

Ex. 4.1 'Esashi Oiwake', first 11.6 seconds as sung by Aosaka Mitsuru (CD2); transposed up a minor second and spaced to show duration at ca. 3cm/second

Aosaka and Sasaki are in striking agreement, but subtle differences at three points help the listener distinguish their styles. First, Aosaka's *setsudo* (Figure 4.7, point 1) leading to the first *momi* is much more violent. Second, Sasaki's *momi* (the downward trill at point 2) is very regular and smooth, whereas Aosaka rests longer on the upper pitch than the lower one and also accelerates slightly but noticeably. Third, although their *hon-sukuri* (point 3)

are virtually identical, Aosaka makes a slight break at its end. In general
Aosaka, the fisherman, sings in a 'rougher' style than Sasaki, the professional
folk singer.

Sasaki sings according to the 'rules' on this particular instructional recording: his *momi* has exactly three downward inflections, as required by the
judges at the annual contest (of whom he is often one). But when he sings
in concert or for non-instructional recordings, he tends to add two or three
extra inflections, as well as extending the phrase-ends from four to as many
as seven inflections. Such extension of ornamentation is characteristic of
professionals' more elaborate treatment of most folk songs. Sasaki thus copes
with the conflicting demands of the local community and his national
record-buying audience through compartmentalization, singing and teaching two slightly but crucially different versions. The modern consumer often
values virtuosity more highly than a spurious authenticity.

I know of no other local song with its own teaching notation system,
though it has probably happened someplace given the combined influences
of Esashi and the West. However, some teachers use graphic aids to illustrate
ornamentation (such as Sugita Akiko, previous section). Endō Sayuri (b.
1969; pers.comm. December 2000), of Osaka's Kotobuki *min'yō* bar, said
that her teacher taught her to 'trill' (*mawasu*) partly by drawing a series of
loops from left to right (Fig. 4.8). These loops, however, had to be supplemented by demonstration and by verbal description, which she recalls as follows: Sing slowly from the stomach, adding strength (*chikara*) as you return
to the main pitch (at the top of the loop) from one below it. This is why the
right-hand, upward-bound side of the loop is thicker. (This description
nearly matches my own perception of the phenomenon: add volume as the
pitch bottoms out and then begins to rise.)

Students also may create their own partial notations for some song or
other by writing idiosyncratic squiggles on lyrics sheets to indicate where a
particular ornament occurs; two students in Fig. 4.1 are looking at such self-
made squiggles. I have observed this in other cultures as well: it seems somewhat instinctive.

The monthly magazine *Min'yō Bunka*, born in 1978, has since the early
1980s carried notations each month for singing, shamisen, shakuhachi,
backup singing and dance. For song, the composer Shibata Takasue provided for many years a monthly feature, 'Konkūru hisshō-hō' – 'How to win
a concours'. He devised a notation, including a staff of variable numbers of
lines, derived from that for 'Esashi Oiwake' (Fig. 4.9). His is, however, more
accurate and detailed: each line represents a specific relative pitch and is
headed by the name of the corresponding shakuhachi pitch; those staff lines
corresponding to open shamisen strings (if shamisen is used) are thicker;
precise pitches of ornaments are shown; and ornaments are named (his own
system mostly deriving from folk or classical terms). In each article, the simpler upper staff represents more or less the tune played by shakuhachi or

shamisen, or what you should sing for choral unison when your teacher says, 'Don't ornament too much' (*Amari goro o mawasanai de*), or what you should teach a beginner. The lower staff represents skilled singers – with better chances at contests, of course. The accompanying text explains numerous singing techniques. (This feature has now been replaced by a similar one by Chifuji Kōzō.)

Shibata's articles are fascinating, but space only allows summarizing the information from two successive and contrasting ones. His disquisition upon the lullaby from Kyūshū, 'Hakata Komori Uta' (Fig. 4.9; MB 1984.8: 51–3), opens with a saying common in the *min'yō-kai*: 'For songs from western Japan, it's *ma* [rhythm, timing of notes], for northeastern songs it's *goro* [ornamentation]'. The focus here is thus on *ma*. The simpler version in Fig. 4.9 begins 5 | 6 6 | −1 22 | 2 − | −1 6 | . . . . (Underlining = eighth-note; double underlining = sixteenth-note; plain = quarter-note.) But a good singer will diverge from the regular beat of the shamisen, often delaying arrival on a syllable and/or pitch, as shown in the lower version (compare the placement of the lyrics shown beneath the two versions). This is what is called *tsukazu hanarezu*, 'neither attached nor separated', and it requires a good sense of *ma*. It is particularly characteristic of songs transmitted by the geisha or similar women of Japan's teahouses who have played such a role in *min'yō*, and it shows influence from other genres they may have studied such as *nagauta* and *kouta*.

Turning a month later to 'Saitara Bushi' of Miyagi Prefecture (MB 1984.9: 53–4) – a northeastern song transmitted among boatmen – Shibata begins by quoting the saying: 'The easier a song is, the more difficult you should consider it.' On the surface, this song does seem easy, which is why it is often found in school music books. Shibata advises that the onbeats should be sung strongly as if pulling on an oar, the offbeats softly as if push-ing the oar back; the vocal part follows the steady beat, eschewing western Japan's *tsukazu hanarezu*. He then defines his various ornaments: *soritsuke* requires sliding ('scooping') up to the main pitch from below, etc. His *saka-mawashi* 'reverse trill' is unique to this prefecture, he claims, so using it for Miyagi songs will increase your chances in a contest. Finally, he explains how to convert a phrase 3 17 to the five-note ornament 343 [triplet] 17: for the second through fifth notes respectively, raise soft palate, return it to original position, lower Adam's apple, further lower Adam's apple. (This matches my personal perception.) Shibata's articles constitute an excellent introduction to *min'yō* ornamentation and technique, going well beyond what you would be told overtly by a teacher.

Instrumental notation is far more common than vocal. Most *min'yō* shamisen notation uses the *bunkafu* tablature developed for the classical gen-res, in which numbers indicating fingering positions are written on three lines representing the strings (Malm & Hughes 2001b; Malm 2000 appen-dix). Fujimoto Hideo's collection of several hundred accompaniments

(1962–; frequently re-issued) is widely used by all levels of performer, creating considerable standardization. Fujimoto not only regularized pre-existing parts while eliminating variation, he also created accompaniments for many songs which had lacked them or altered pre-existing parts (§5.6). His former student Chifuji Kōzō has now similarly produced his own such notations for over 900 *min'yō*. (Earlier, Takahashi Chikuzan had created the first shamisen parts for many Tsugaru songs, at the urging of Narita Unchiku, but these were not notated and did not lead to standardization.)

Finally let us acknowledge the numerous scholarly collections showing songs in Western staff notation. Even now when all Japanese have been exposed to staff notation in school, virtually no *min'yō* aficionados use these. The main exceptions are Western-instrument arrangers of *min'yō*, who are rarely involved with the genre otherwise (e.g. Ishikawa Akira, §6.4), and school music teachers. It is for schoolteachers that the Nihon Min'yō Kyōkai is now producing copious staff notations (Kikuchi Tanshige pers. comm. 8 November 2000). A minor but interesting exception is noted in §4.6.2 below.

4.5.3 Culture Centres

In §4.4.3 we mentioned 'culture centres' (*bunka sentā*, but by the year 2000 mostly called by the 'English' name *karuchā sentā*) or 'leisure centres' (*rejā sentā*) as sources of income for *min'yō* teachers. These centres are a recent phenomenon, dating from the 1970s (Moriya 1984). *Min'yō* is often included among their offerings. Teaching tends to be in classes, with singing mostly in choral unison; more serious (or well-off) aspirants would prefer to study at the teacher's private classroom (which is usually in his/her home or *min'yō* bar), allowing more individual attention.

But culture centres are an increasing force in *min'yō* teaching, suggesting that *min'yō* is now seen as an art or craft on a par with the other courses offered. Let us consider the offerings at two such places.

The Japan Broadcasting Company Culture Centre (NHK Bunka Sentā) opened in April 1979. At that time, their 'hobby courses' (*shumi kōza*), charging fees of ¥4–6,000 a month, were listed in this order and separated into subsections: a) tea ceremony (two 'schools'), flower arranging (three schools), calligraphy (brush or penmanship), character carving, rubbings; b) Western painting, drawing, *Nihonga* (Japanese-style painting), brush-painting, woodblock printing, silk-screening; c) knitting, European crocheting, 'art flower', 'flower design', embroidery, European needlepoint, patchwork quilts, Saga brocade, kimono sashcord knotting, kimono wearing; d) leatherwork, rattanwork, paper crafts, lacquering, metal carving, wood carving, Kamakura carving; e) koto (two schools), *nagauta* (two schools), *kouta* (two schools), Noh singing and dancing (two schools), *kyōgen* farce, Japanese classical dance (two schools), *jiuta-mai* (another type of classical dance), shakuhachi, **min'yō (Ōtsuka Fumio and Kosugi Makiko, teachers)**; f) Western music: chorus for Beethoven's Ninth Symphony, guitar, flute, and others 'planned'; g) *tanka, haiku, senryū* (three traditional poetry genres); h) *go*, Japanese chess (*shō-gi*), Western chess, bridge; i) gardening.

Min'yō thus was the last of the Japanese music genres listed but preceded all Western music genres.

NHK also offers 'health classes' (*kenkō kōza*): Zen meditation, Ogasawara-school traditional etiquette, yoga, Chinese Taichi, various exercise types, social dance and Western folk dance. Notice that Japanese classical dance was listed among the cultural 'hobbies', while Western folk dance was relegated to 'health'. (Japanese folk dance was not offered.)[12]

b) The Tokyo Culture Centre (Tōkyō Bunka Sentā), in August 1979, offered a similar but more varied programme (e.g. language courses). Music and dance courses were: Noh singing and dancing; koto; shakuhachi; Noh *kotsuzumi* drum; *nagauta* singing and shamisen; *kouta* singing and shamisen; **min'yō (including *hauta*) and shamisen (Kawasaki Chieko and co-teachers)**; Japanese classical dance; Japanese folk dance (Nishizaki school, see §7.4, item 4); ballet; modern dance; social dance; modern dance as calisthenics; women's fun chorus; classical guitar; children's modern dance; children's ballet. A few comparative fees: *min'yō* ¥4,000 a month; same for social dance and women's fun chorus; slightly more for the 'classical' Japanese genres; ballet and modern dance ¥12,000. Once again *min'yō* was listed last of the traditional musics but before any Western genres; likewise, Japanese folk dance followed Japanese classical dance but preceded Western dance (which, however, cost more). Including *hauta* within *min'yō* is unusual but stylistically conceivable.

4.6 The repertoire

4.6.1 Eastern songs, western songs

Min'yō teachers and performers can often be divided on the basis of repertoire. Some focus on the songs of a particular region; others are generalists and will teach any song requested by their students.

We found in Chapter 2 that the traditional 'folk' were not musical purists. All songs were *uta*. If regional styles developed, it was not because of an exclusivist intent on the part of the local residents but simply the result of geography and limits on travel. When developments in transportation and communication brought access to more songs, people accepted them gladly (§3.4): songs spread in a flash nationwide. Still, although songs spread, the associated performance styles might not. Features such as vocal timbre and rhythmic sense have moved more slowly.

It is difficult to define general regional styles because of the diversity within each area (village vs. town, parlour song voice vs. work song voice, etc.), but singers and scholars do often claim a stylistic distinction between 'eastern songs' (*higashi no uta*) and 'western songs' (*nishi no uta*). 'Eastern' in this case refers primarily to Hokkaido and the six prefectures of the Tō-hoku (lit. 'northeast') region (Aomori, Akita, Iwate, Yamagata, Miyagi, Fukushima). This style is sometimes also called 'northern' or 'northeastern'. The northern/eastern/northeastern style is conceived of as full-throated, with jagged ornamentation and with the mouth opened wide laterally on the vowel sound 'ah'. The western style is often equated with more sedate parlour songs, with a more rounded, close-mouthed 'aw' sound for the vowel *a*. Put differently, eastern style is generally conceived of as more *hade* (flashy), western style as more *jimi* (restrained). Shamisen accompaniment follows suit.

Congruence of style and region is far from perfect. Indeed, Machida (1933) opined: 'Local colour in old folk songs . . . is certainly not to be found in scales or rhythm but rather in regional pronunciation and accent.' (See also Etchūya Shisaburō's comments on dialect pronunciation and 'Esashi Oiwake', §3.3.3.) Still, the differences are often instantly recognizable, and professionals and amateurs alike speak frequently of this basic east-west split (see title of recording R27). Some professional singers stay within one style: Yamamoto Kenji focuses on songs of his home region of Tsugaru and the neighbouring Nanbu region (i.e. Aomori and Iwate prefectures). Others consciously set out to master both styles. Kanazawa Akiko achieved fame singing northern songs, but during the late 1970s she was taking lessons with one teacher of Tōhoku style and one of western style, aiming to become a compleat performer. Such regional eclecticism is becoming the norm.

Whatever the stylistic reality, geography itself may assume significance in relation to regional identity. For example, from around 1980 the Zen-Kansai Min'yō Kyōkai, an umbrella association of *min'yō* 'schools' headquartered in Osaka but representing much of western Japan, split its annual competition into two Divisions: Western Songs and Eastern Songs. The intention, I would guess, was twofold: to overcome the moderate tendency of judges to favour the flashy, highly ornamented northeastern songs, and simultaneously to encourage more contestants to choose songs from the region covered by the association.

It remains to ascertain where the musical boundary is drawn between east and west in most people's minds. Often 'west' seems to include anything west of Tōhoku, thus including even Niigata and the Tokyo area – which are clearly eastern in a geographical sense.

What is indisputable is that eastern songs still dominate the *min'yō* world as they have since its inception. This may originally have resulted from the predominance of northeasterners among early professionals (§3.4.4) and is certainly encouraged by their continuing predominance today (§4.4.1). The preference for eastern songs, however, is found equally today among amateurs from all parts of the country, although the west is gaining. Evidence can been seen in the songs chosen for performance at contests (excluding of course single-song contests such as that for 'Esashi Oiwake').

Consider the annual national contest (Zenkoku Taikai) of the Nihon Min'yō Kyōkai, Japan's largest *min'yō* association. Kikuchi (1980: 268–82) lists the winning songs for each category from 1951 through 1979. Of performances of 179 songs (including repeats) whose origin I could identify, fully 78 per cent (140) are from the six Tōhoku prefectures or Hokkaido; only 22 per cent (39) are from further west, mostly from the middle of the main island. From 1970 to 1977, only one song from the sixteen westernmost prefectures of the main islands (excluding Okinawa: Tottori, Okayama and westwards) was among the winners: 'Yasugi Bushi', which appeared twice.

In 1978–9, however, three Kyushu songs appeared among the winners a total of five times. Did this herald a slight expansion of choice? I examined the winners' songs from 1990–99 (Kikuchi 2000: 446–57) and found that the trend to Tōhoku dominance is still present but decidedly weaker. Of ninety-six performances (forty-one different songs) by prize-winners, 64 per cent were from the seven northernmost prefectures, 36 per cent from elsewhere. Surprisingly, now twenty-eight of the thirty-five non-northeastern winning entries were from the sixteen westernmost prefectures, and almost all of these songs were performed by local singers. (Two songs from Miyazaki, 'Kariboshikiri Uta' (original version) and 'Hyūga Kobiki Uta', were performed twelve and seven times respectively.) Indeed, by the 1990s singers were overwhelmingly singing songs from their home areas. Notably, one winner in 1998 was from Tokunoshima in the Amami archipelago, playing *sanshin* – another significant step in accepting the very different traditions of the Ryukyus. In terms of the forty-one different songs sung (excluding repeats), twenty-seven (66 per cent) were from the northeast. The percentages were approximately the same even for the organization's annual 'Tokyo Contest' (Tōkyō Taikai), which is for entrants from the central part of Japan, except that songs from the central prefectures outstripped the sixteen westernmost ones, fifteen performances to ten; the northeast still accounted for 68 per cent of seventy-nine performances.

Pending further investigation, I hypothesise that this increase in western representation springs from the overall expansion in interest in and exposure to *min'yō* triggered by the late-1970s boom, combined with a conscious intention by the Nihon Min'yō Kyōkai to overcome northern dominance (e.g. through encouraging entrants from all of its regional branches).

Surprisingly, 'Esashi Oiwake' and 'Yasugi Bushi', two of the most famous *min'yō*, appeared only three times in total at the National Contest from 1990–99. Doubtless the best singers of these songs prefer to enter the prestigious single-song contests (§5.5).

A sobering reminder of northern dominance, however, emerges from the Nihon Min'yō Fesutibaru (Festival). Launched in 1988 by the Nihon Min'yō Kyōkai, supported by the government's Cultural Affairs Agency,

NHK and others, this televised contest features the grand-prize winners from a selection of other *min'yō* contests, both multi-song (as above) and single-song. From 1988–99, eleven of the twelve winners of this contest sang songs from only four northern provinces: Akita (five), Aomori (four), Iwate (one) and Hokkaido (one). The only other winner was the singer from Tokunoshima mentioned above, in 1999.

One tradition which by its very name is regional is Tsugaru-jamisen (§§2.5.3, 7.3, etc). As with 'Esashi Oiwake', local Tsugaru residents strive to maintain their claim as the possessors, masters and arbiters of the art, with two renowned (and rival) annual national contests held for many years in the district (one is now discontinued). And yet this flashy, improvisational instrumental tradition boasts practitioners of all levels from throughout Japan (e.g. Wakayama's Kinoshita Shin'ichi and Miyazaki's DADAN, §4.4.2). Since 1998, the Nihon Min'yō Kyōkai has run a national Tsugaru-jamisen Konkūru Zenkoku Taikai contest-cum-festival in Tokyo, competing with the Tsugaru-based events. Soon this tradition will no more belong to Tsugaru than Chopin's music does to Poland.

4.6.2 Repertoire expansion

One of the most striking developments in the post-war *min'yō* world is the tremendous increase in the number of songs familiar to any one individual. In §2.3, discussing the nature of the folk song repertoire of a traditional community or individual, we concluded that few people would have known more than a few dozen folk songs, nor as many as a hundred of any type of song. But by 1979 the professional singer Harada Naoyuki proudly claimed to me a repertoire of over 600 songs. Even an average *min'yō* student today may well be able to sing more songs (whether *min'yō* or otherwise) than an early professional could in the 1930s. This trend is not limited to *min'yō*, nor to Japan. It results from the same set of factors as in many other industrialized countries: availability of audio equipment and commercial recordings; availability of printed resources; adoption of diverse local elements into a common national culture; increased leisure time; the rise of professionalism; and so forth. The spread of *min'yō* in Japan has also benefited from factors less prominent in some other countries, including strong government encouragement and financial support, and the patronage of several wealthy corporations such as newspaper and television companies and the Kinkan Drug Company (§4.8.3).

Individual repertoire expansion has occurred for various reasons and in various ways. Obviously, as in traditional times, some singers simply enjoy learning new songs, while others take pride in the size of their repertoire. But recent times have seen new factors and methods leading to repertoire growth.

For example, the motivation might now come not from within but from one's students. Tanaka Yoshio, raised in the north, now teaches in Osaka to students primarily from several parts of western Japan. With the currently fashionable stress on learning songs from one's home prefecture, he may receive a request to teach a Kyūshū song to a recent migrant from Kyūshū, an Osaka-area song to another student, and a northern song to another. An Edo-period *nagauta* teacher might have resisted a student's attempt to decide the order of learning pieces, as would a koto teacher today, but most modern *min'yō* teachers strive to accommodate such desires.

Pressures to expand repertoires also come from recording and broadcasting companies, driven by the sense that fans only wish to hear so many versions of a specific song. However well loved and comfortably familiar may be a song such as 'Aizu Bandai-san' or 'Esashi Oiwake', after hearing ten versions (nearly identical) on record and twenty performances on radio and television, you may have had enough – or so the companies believe, and not without some justification. They take two basic approaches to the problem. First, they commission the creation of 'new folk songs' (*shin-min'yō*; see §§3.4.3, 6.3–4). However, such 'new folk songs' today are invariably used only for dancing, via recordings played over loudspeakers, and are virtually never sung at recitals or contests nor taught to students. Thus they do not expand the working, sung repertoire significantly.

Another way to generate new 'product' is to locate little-known local songs. The influence of the scholarly community has helped to make this an important source of material for today's performers. One speaks of *hakkutsu min'yō* – 'excavated songs'. Excavation contributes more to the growth of the actual performing repertoire than does composition of *shin-min'yō*. Record companies may encourage their contracted recording artists to search out local songs, or they may consult researchers for advice. Under the urging of Columbia Records during the 1970s, Tanaka Yoshio added many Osaka-area songs to his repertoire. Tanaka noted that the only songs from his first album that were ever played on the radio were those rarely recorded Osaka songs that he had 'excavated' at the urging of his Columbia producer; after all, he said ruefully, there were so many excellent recordings of the more standard repertoire. Thus both the companies and the performers have reason to excavate.

Opinions divide over the handling of excavated material. We shall see in Chapter 5 that local residents, while proud to have their songs adopted by professionals, frequently object to the inevitable re-arranging these songs undergo in the transfer to commercial use. The professional community usually retort that the village versions are impossible to sing (or at least to market) in the form they were collected: rhythms must be regularized, pitches pinned down, and of course an attractive accompaniment must be provided.

As one example, let us follow the course of an Osaka-area Bon-dance song, a *kudoki* (extended ballad) now known as 'Shinodayama Bon Uta' (Fig. 4.3). Soliciting the help of a local researcher to find some 'unknown' local songs,

Tanaka Yoshio visited the 'village' of Shinodayama (by then on the edge of the urban sprawl) and took a recording of this song. Like many little-known *min'yō*, the two halves of its melody were quite similar, especially at the beginning (**CD34;** Ex. 4.2). Tanaka, with the consent (or the urging, depending on whom one believes) of his producer at Columbia, altered the beginning of the second phrase, starting a seventh lower, to add variety. It was this version that appeared on Tanaka's first album (R25). (The lyrics were also truncated to produce a four-minute recording.) However, some Shinodayama residents had become his students, and Tanaka came to feel remorse at having tampered with the revered local product, saying simply, 'My version wasn't very good; it was a mistake.' He now teaches the original version.

Ex. 4.2 'Shinodayama Bon Uta', local version

Another source of new material is as yet extremely rarely utilized: the printed scholarly collection. Scholarly collections of notation have been invaluable resources for the folk revivalists of the West, but professional Japanese performers rarely learn a melody (as opposed to additional verses) from such a source. In Tokyo in 1980, Sasaki Kazuo and Kawasaki Chieko from Akita Prefecture gave a miniseries of quasi-scholarly recitals of Akita songs. Sasaki (then in his thirties) turned to the Western-style transcriptions in the *Nihon min'yō taikan* Tōhoku volume (NMT vol.2) to expand his Akita repertoire with some lesser-known songs. Providing the appropriate ornamentation and other stylistic features himself was no problem since he was 'of the tradition'.

Although the professional's repertoire may now be huge, and a typical student might be able to sing along with fifty songs and recognize 200 or more, a student may actually only receive instruction on a handful of songs during the course of a year. Often a single song is the focus of most attention, as it is being prepared for performance at a concours. The Japanese willingness to devote so much time and energy to three or four minutes of music is consonant with various cultural emphases such as miniaturizing and attention to detail.

Local traditions may likewise still focus on a small number of songs. 'Yasugi Bushi' was so popular in the Shimane/Tottori border area, and deemed so representative of the region, that local teachers rarely taught anything else until around 1970 (Matsue Tōru and Izumo Ainosuke III, pers. comm.). §5.4 reveals a similarly narrow focus within local preservation societies.

Finally, note that the expansion of the collective *min'yō* repertoire is accomplished differently from that of the popular song repertoire. Popular songs are newly created in the centre by professional songwriters and disseminated via the broadcast media. While *shin-min'yō* are also largely created in the centre, they are disseminated principally through local groups (in the case of songs with local content), through national folk dance organizations or through the Japan Recreation Association. However, almost nobody ever learns to perform them. The most common method of obtaining new *min'yō* material – excavation – is much less important in the pop song world.

4.6.3 Repertoire expansion: a case study

Two other Osaka-area songs excavated by Tanaka Yoshio were first commercially recorded by him on record R26 in 1980: the rice-harvesting song 'Shinodayama Inekari Uta' and the foundation-pounding song 'Hoshida Tsuchiuchi Uta'. He first heard these on a field recording of two elderly singers received from the scholar Migita Isao. Tanaka's initial plan was to fill his side of this LP with songs for which he was already well admired. Since the B side was to be sung by me as the 'strange foreigner' in the *min'yō* world, I often discussed the content with Tanaka, my teacher. Forgetting whatever scholarly objectivity I might have possessed, I asked him whether he might not consider including a couple of new pieces from Migita's tape. By then I had devised a shamisen accompaniment to the foundation-pounding song, as a sort of academic exercise.

Eventually Tanaka did indeed decide to include these two songs, seemingly out of a combination of a sense of local obligation and the commercial likelihood that once again only the least-known songs on this album would ever be broadcast. He modified my shamisen accompaniment, and for the free-rhythm rice-harvesting song he left it to his shakuhachi player to devise a simple introduction and interlude as usual. The foundation-pounding song would be expected to have had a chorus of some sort originally, but as with so many field recordings, Migita had recorded a single elderly man, thus missing any *hayashi-kotoba*. Tanaka was left to devise his own based on experience of similar songs. (As with most professionals, Tanaka saw no need to re-locate the original singer for further information.)

By the time Tanaka recorded these two songs again on cassette R27, his interpretations had elaborated somewhat. He had added a bar to the shamisen part, some *kakegoe* (under local influence), and for the free-rhythm song he had slowed the tempo and increased the melisma, a common development as such songs metamorphose from amateur to professional.

4.7 The folk song bar

The *min'yō sakaba*, or 'folk song bar', is a prime locus for *min'yō* performance in urban Japan. It is difficult to count such establishments, since they are rarely listed separately in telephone directories. Around 1980, at the height of the boom, there were eight to ten prominent ones each in Tokyo and Osaka (now more like three or four), with one or two in the various regional cities. (See Appendix 2 for a list plus some websites with photos.)

In the broad sense, this term could include all bars and restaurants whose owners encourage the performance or broadcasting of *min'yō*. A few merely play recordings. After the early 1980s some bars installed *karaoke* systems so customers can sing *min'yō* (and perhaps popular songs) to recorded accompaniment. Some bars have a shamisen or shakuhachi hanging on the wall for use by customers or by the owner in a slack moment.

The numbers in the first paragraph, however, refer to *min'yō sakaba* in a narrower sense. The distinctive feature of these true *min'yō* bars is that customers take turns singing to the accompaniment of the 'house band', always of the standard type described in §3.4.2 (Fig. 4.2).

The typical *min'yō sakaba* is run by a professional teacher, usually an *iemoto*, who gives lessons there during the day and socializes with customers and performs in the evenings. The accompanists, who may double as waiters and waitresses, may be students of the teacher or outsiders hired on a regular or seasonal basis. They will also perform when the customers are not singing. In this way, these bars are a major training ground for incipient *min'yō* professionals. Many customers will also sing (Fig. 4.10), and the few who can play the shamisen or shakuhachi may take a turn as accompanist. *Teodori* 'hand dances' of the Tsugaru region may also be included. Customers' performance standards range from sublime to ineffably painful.

The term 'bar' may mislead as to size and layout. The average *min'yō* bar will hold thirty to sixty customers, who generally sit on the floor at low tables in traditional Japanese style and buy dinner or light snacks as well as drinks. A stage a few inches high at one end of the room has chairs for the instrumentalists, a couple of Japanese drums – and at centre stage, the inevitable microphone. Professional singers could easily be heard over the somewhat rowdy crowd that tends to populate these bars, but most customers need amplification, at least on weekends when the bar is crowded. However, the volume is *always* excessive regardless of crowd size. The microphone is an important attraction for most customers, giving the amateur a feeling of power, of professionalism. After all, every folk or pop singer one sees sings to a microphone. There is also, however, the fact that noise and hurly-burly are to most Japanese important elements in socializing. How much more enjoyable to be part of a clamouring, jostling crowd than to sit with a few friends in relative silence in a sparsely populated area. This is perhaps partly a legacy of rural life where the yearly festivals and occasional drinking parties were rare chances to cut loose. The adjective *nigiyaka* describes such a boisterous atmosphere. (The image of a Japanese sitting alone in Zen-like tranquility in a garden or temple is also accurate, but that is another face of Japan.) At any rate, high amplification seems to add to regular customers' enjoyment. The thrill of participation at *min'yō* bars certainly contributed to the growth of student numbers.

The *min'yō* bar is a post-war urban phenomenon. The earliest formal ones appeared in the early 1950s in Tokyo's Asakusa area, a major centre of popular entertainment since the Edo period. Kabuki, shamisen musics of various sorts, urban festivals and the mass-oriented Asakusa Opera of the twentieth century all flourished here. Thus it was a natural locus for the first *min'yō* bars.

Several veterans have told me that the first *min'yō* bar was probably Yomogi in Okachimachi, not far from Asakusa, established in 1951–2. It was a small bar with counter service only; a drum hanging from the ceiling could be played from behind the bar, and a microphone could be slid along a clothesline above the counter. Floor-seating bars begun within a decade in this general area included Obako, Ranman, Ringo-jaya, Kokeshi, Oiwake, Hideko, Jinku and Shichi-go-san. By 1958 the phenomenon was familiar enough that the famous *min'yō* and *enka* singer Mihashi Michiya could record an *enka* entitled 'Min'yō Sakaba'. In the 1960s there were dozens in Tokyo; by 1980, perhaps ten survived; today only Oiwake (established November 1957), Hideko (recently revived but short on customers) and Midori (started in 1963) remain in central Tokyo.

Their appearance in the early 1950s may be linked with at least three developments. First, a media-induced *min'yō* 'boom' started up around that time (§3.5.3). Second, the 'Singing Voices coffeehouse' (*utagoe kissa*) movement had just begun (§6.5.1): young folk, mostly university students, gathered to sing together from printed songbooks of international folk songs and other popular songs, although very rarely Japanese *min'yō*. This apparently provided one model for *min'yō sakaba*. Third, rural residents were once again pouring into the cities after several years of urban depopulation due to the war. Scorned as country bumpkins with funny accents, they often met with others from the countryside in bars, and one way to overcome homesickness was to sing songs from home.

The early clubs were not always run by *min'yō* professionals. Often a restaurateur or bar owner merely sought to increase business (as a British

pub owner may encourage a weekly Irish music session to attract customers). The manager of the Tokyo's Hakutsuru (in Kinshi-chō) converted
his large working-class bar to a *min'yō sakaba* around 1963 out of desperation as trade was dwindling; the move was a success, he told me in 1980. But
he never did particularly become a *min'yō* fan, and by 1988 Hakutsuru had
abandoned *min'yō* for *karaoke*.

The *min'yō* bar in Japan differs from its nearest functional analogues in the
West – the amateur 'open nights' at US coffee houses and British folk clubs
– in several crucial ways. First, the repertoire of the performers is restricted
by tacit understanding to *min'yō*, with occasional steps across the borderline
into *zokkyoku*, a type of geisha-party song with close historical and stylistic
relations to folk song. At a Western folk club, 'folk songs' may dominate the
evening, but these are often recent compositions (whereas 'new folk songs'
are rarely heard in Japanese bars), and one may also hear on occasion a
Baroque flute piece, a prose folk-tale, a Beatles song, an Elizabethan lute
solo and so forth (personal observations; see also Mackinnon 1994: 48).
Even the traditional songs may feature a wide range of instruments. Such
eclecticism is unknown in the *min'yō sakaba*. For example, although younger
min'yō fans may enjoy Western-style folk and rock, these will never be heard
in a *min'yō sakaba*. (It would be easy to keep an acoustic guitar on hand, but
this virtually never happens.)

Western-style folk and rock are separated from *min'yō* by a wide stylistic
and social gulf. The majority of *min'yō* aficionados actively dislike rock; some
enjoy *fōku songu* while others do not. (Age is an important factor.) *Enka* is
the bridge, in a way. Stylistically, the vocal quality, melodic ornamentation
and scale structure of *enka* are much closer to *min'yō* than are other Western-
influenced popular song genres (§1.7.2). Also, there is an image of both *enka*
and *min'yō* as very *shominteki*, of the people, the 'masses'. In this sense, the
self-image of *enka* lovers closely parallels that of American country music
fans: they believe that these songs are truer to life than other popular song,
dealing with the real-life problems and concerns of the working people. One
now-defunct 300-seat *min'yō sakaba* in Tokyo, Shichi-go-san, aspiring to a
larger audience of banqueters, actually alternated sets by a small *enka* band
and the house *min'yō* band, the folk singers occasionally accompanied by the
enka band. (Most good *min'yō* singers, by the way, are also reasonably good
at *enka*, but the reverse definitely is not true.)

Second, at a Western folk club there is no 'house band', and not only
solo performers but groups are common. In the modern urban Japanese
tradition, there is virtually always a single singer who carries the melody
alone, standing at the microphone, front stage centre, house band and
chorus behind. There is in Japan no equivalent to the 'session' (usually
Irish music) of many pubs in the British Isles, where musicians gather once
a week to jam, seated in a corner and facing each other, perhaps being paid
in beer.

Third, the Western 'folk revival' encompasses two quite different approaches to traditional material. On one hand, new old songs are unearthed and performed as 'authentically' as possible, often without accompaniment. (As in Japan, such songs become ever harder to find.) On the other, individual performers may devise complex arrangements of traditional songs, striving to produce their own unique version. At the *min'yō sakaba*, however, and in the urban *min'yō* world in general, unaccompanied singing is almost unthinkable: the audience does not care for folkloric reconstructions. Modern *min'yō* performance absolutely requires accompaniment (aside from performances by preservation societies). One is thus constrained from singing a rare song, because the house musicians cannot provide accompaniment. Similarly, complex new arrangements are eschewed – partly because the band cannot accompany those either. There is more room for creative arrangements in concert situations, which allow for rehearsal.

Such factors make an evening at a *min'yō sakaba* comfortingly predictable. Most customers are regulars who have sung the same song(s) often there before. Students find a valuable chance to sing with live accompaniment (as opposed to *karaoke* at home), in preparation for participation in contests. At Hideko in the 1980s, you could even watch a videotape of your performance later.

As with the *enka karaoke* bar, the *min'yō sakaba* provides each customer with a chance to be a star for three minutes. In a *karaoke* club, however, most people aside from close friends ignore the current singer, who is probably seated on a barstool or plush chair, or standing, microphone in hand, reading lyrics from a video monitor. In a *min'yō* bar, the other customers are comparatively attentive and supportive and can be relied upon to provide a chorus. This difference in atmosphere reflects the different nature of *enka* and *min'yō*, noted in §1.7.2.

Min'yō sakaba have dwindled in number since the peak of the boom (see Appendix 2 for addresses of a few traditional-style ones in major cities). One reason is simply the greater profitability of *karaoke* clubs. *Karaoke* began its own 'boom' around 1978 and went into a brief decline a few years later. However, the amazing advances in technology since then – video monitors, instant pitch adjustment to match any singer's needs, electronic scoring machines that rate each singer – have brought it back to the fore. Some *min'yō* bars have either converted 100 per cent to *karaoke* or now mix live *min'yō* performance with *enka* or pops *karaoke*. Most sets of *enka karaoke* recordings will include a few of the better-known *min'yō*, but the accompaniment is generally on Western instruments in Western-style arrangements.

One Osaka *min'yō* teacher converted his bar to *karaoke* in the mid-1980s: straw *tatami* mats were replaced by plush red carpet, wood panelling gave way to velvet-look walls, shamisen wall-racks disappeared, lights were dimmed. The several vivacious kimono-clad musician-waitresses gave way to a couple of self-conscious young women in sexy dresses who would lay a hand on a man's thigh and look embarrassed to be there. The bar became what is generally called a 'cabaret' (*kyabarē*), where drinks, the chance to sing a song and conversation with female employees are all more expensive than anything at a *min'yō* bar. The change was motivated purely financially: no need to serve low-profit dinners or pay a large staff of musicians. But the teacher and his family soon regretted the decision. As his wife remarked, 'something important' had been lost in the process. For example, their daughter, then in her mid-teens, had come to the bar every evening since age nine or so to play drum or sing choruses; now she was not even allowed to enter the bar during working hours. This teacher seemed to have lost some of his enthusiasm for his art and his profession. The business was no longer fun to him and his wife, just a way to 'put food on the table', she said. His students had dwindled from around 500 in 1981 to 200 by 1988; my impression is that this decline is only partly due to the countrywide post-boom contraction in *min'yō* student numbers, but is more the result of his own diminishing interest. The club has now closed altogether, though the teacher has since recaptured his passion for *min'yō*.

While *min'yō sakaba* featuring 'mainland' *min'yō* have declined precipitously, the number of bars and restaurants in Tokyo and Osaka featuring live Okinawan *min'yō* has grown with the Okinawan music 'boom' since the 1990s (§7.3 and Appendix 2).

4.8 The role of the media and the recording industry

4.8.1 Television and radio

We have seen that television in particular can provide a valuable income source for the top rank of *min'yō* performers. Television is also often credited with triggering the latest boom in 1978, via the bi-weekly show *Min'yō o anata ni* ('Folk song to you'), launched on NHK-TV in spring of that year.[13] The producers intended it to attract people of all ages and backgrounds to *min'yō*. To that end, in a 45-minute programme, they provided a mix of kimonos and blue jeans, shamisen and Western orchestras, *min'yō* old and new, celebrity guests from outside the *min'yō* world who would talk about their favourite *min'yō*, and so forth. As one of the producers put it to me, they hoped to bring *min'yō* into the mainstream of Japanese life again, to show that it could fit in. The programme was a huge success, and within a year there were several regular *min'yō* shows on the air waves. As a percentage of total music broadcasting, it was not much, but certainly *min'yō* suddenly seemed to be everywhere.

Much of the show's success can be traced to the co-stars, Kanazawa Akiko and Harada Naoyuki, mentioned frequently above (§4.4.2). Both were young, physically attractive, visibly modern, had engaging personalities and superb voices, and quickly became wealthy through this television exposure. Kanazawa's predilection for tight-fitting blue jeans provided a nickname for this entire 'boom': *jii-pan min'yō*, 'jeans folk song' (Fig. 4.11).

Purists frequently lambasted both stars for lacking the earthy (*tsuchikusai*), folksy, somewhat rough-edged vocal quality which some consider the only appropriate style for *min'yō*. Harada's voice definitely retains some of the smoothness of his *bel canto* days, and sometimes he would accompany himself on acoustic guitar, but his ornamentation is authentically folk-style, and not all traditional voices were rough-edged. In Kanazawa's case, this criticism strikes me more as mere jealousy **(CD35)**.

Min'yō professionals reported an upsurge in student numbers, perform-ance opportunities, *min'yō sakaba* attendance and so forth during the two years following the start of this programme. It is my impression, confirmed by some teachers, that while the boom did succeed in attracting some new young fans, most of the expansion was in the upper end of the age scale. The audience at a Kanazawa Akiko recital I attended was heavily weighted in favour of people above middle age.[14]

It is debatable whether NHK's aim of re-linking *min'yō* with daily life in people's minds succeeded. Negative evidence might lie in the decrease in *min'yō* broadcasts since a peak around 1981, as well as the closing of many *min'yō* bars. On the other hand, overall student numbers have reportedly declined only slightly after more than two decades.

Only one of the six or seven principal members of the production staff of the programme *Min'yō o anata ni* had a serious interest in *min'yō*. This was partly intentional, to prevent the show from catering exclusively for existing *min'yō* fans – preaching to the converted. However, it also reflects typical Japanese business practice: employees are shifted to different divisions within a company every three years or so. By the time I left Japan in 1981, the entire original 1978 production staff of the programme had been trans-ferred to other duties. Thus even if a novice producer of such a programme develops an understanding for *min'yō* over the years, he is likely to be replaced by another novice before that knowledge serves much purpose. This practically guarantees the occasional miscarriage of justice in presenting traditional performers. For one 1979 show, the producers brought up from Osaka an elderly man renowned for his rendition of the old riverboat song 'Sanjukkoku-bune Funauta', a languid free-rhythm melody appropriate for floating downstream. When he sang through it in rehearsal, the first verse took close to two minutes. Time is money in television, and besides, he was an amateur chosen only to add flavour and authenticity rather than for aesthetic reasons; so he was asked to sing only the first half of the verse. Not on your life, he responded: the song would lose its meaning and its heart. After extensive negotiation, he agreed to try to sing it faster. For the final taping, in an apparent fit of pique, he raced through the song at nearly double speed, totally destroying its original character. The song was destroyed, but the point was made. An amateur performer can afford to thumb his nose at the producers in this way, but professionals lack such leeway. The professional singer Ōtsuka Fumio told me that he and other performers felt powerless in the face of the television industry, forced to acquiesce to producers' demands.

The producers were ever striving to make the programme (and thus presumably *min'yō*) attractive to a wider public. In this quest, they often arranged somewhat farcical interludes involving people not normally known as *min'yō* fans. The operatic baritone Okamoto Takao, age approximately forty, returned to live in Japan in 1979 after more than fifteen years in Europe. He was invited to appear on the programme and undergo instruction in the singing of 'Tsugaru Yamauta', a highly ornamented, difficult free-rhythm *min'yō*. He then was made to turn the tables, instructing his teacher in the singing of 'O Sole Mio'. By the respective standards of *min'yō* and *bel canto*, the results of both attempts must be adjudged horrible. Okamoto's ringing baritone impressed the assembled folk singers with its power. Their general reaction, however, can be summarized as: 'That's a great voice – but it's not *min'yō*.' For his part, folk singer Satō Toshiaki, who served as Okamoto's 'teacher', rendered 'O Sole Mio' in a style so replete with folk timbre and ornamentation that his colleagues dubbed it 'O Sole *Min'yō*'.

Okamoto, never previously interested in *min'yō*, was apparently quite proud of his performance. He had a simple explanation for his 'skill' despite his lifelong training in Western vocal style: 'After all, I was born and raised in Japan.' Many Japanese would agree that being born in Japan is a necessary but not sufficient condition for being able to sing *min'yō*.

Audience reaction to such skits was not uniformly supportive. Producer Y. Takagi told me in 1984 that they frequently received phone calls or letters angrily demanding that the producers stop wasting valuable time that could be devoted to true *min'yō*. Many observers felt that the shows were perverting 'pure' *min'yō* by turning it all into 'show biz'; such people were glad to see these shows fade away. (See also Figs 5.4–5.)

4.8.2 *The record companies*

We traced the earlier history of *min'yō* recordings in §3.4. Table 4.4 shows a gradual growth in the number of recordings issued from 1965 to 1980.

As mentioned in §4.6, the record companies have been one force for the digging up of local songs. However, these songs are rarely presented as found: the perception is that hardly anyone will buy a field recording. During the LP era, the only major commercially issued sets of field recordings of *min'yō* were items R1, R3 and R22. Nor would those have existed either but for the yearly national Arts Festival, whose prizes for the most significant recordings incentivize scholarly recordings. Nor did they sell well, apparently. An occasional performance by 'local volunteers' (*jimoto yūshi*) is

Table 4.4. New releases of *min'yō* recordings, 1965–80

	45rpm	%	33rpm	%	cassette	%	companies
1980	170	6	236	7	255	5	20–22
1979	271	10	291	7	275	7	20–22
1978	373	14	300	7	129	4	20–22
1977	300	10	231	6	120	5	20–22
1976	169	7	262	6	118	5	20–22
1975	327	15	230	6	–	–	16
1974	130	8	147	4	–	–	16
1970	369	15	118	5	–	–	10
1965	190	10	36	3	–	–	8

The above figures represent new issues for the year in question; percentages are of all domestic new issues. Sales figures were not available. SOURCE: Publications of the Japan Record Association (Nihon Rekōdo Kyōkai): NRK 1981, and photocopies of relevant pages from earlier publications, kindly provided by the Association.

included in large sampler sets of so-called *genchi rokuon* ('field recordings') from different areas of Japan; all other tracks are performed by local professionals or semi-pros.

In the CD era, and with the general diversification of music genres and recording formats, the issue has become more complicated. Some early field recordings have been re-issued and some new recordings made. At the same time, Japan Victor (JVC), for example, once a major producer of recordings by urban professionals, no longer issues such recordings. They have spun off a separate educational foundation to issue recordings of cultural or academic value, and they also continue to issue recordings on a commission basis for dance teachers and the like. Kawabata (1991: Table 4) provides a snapshot of new releases by Japanese artists in 1990. Some sample figures, totalling analogue and digital media, singles and albums: *enka* 2,410, pops 2,400, 'new music' (a soft pop genre) 3,625, Western classical music 424, 'folk song and traditional music' 535. This is a sharp drop from an average 787 releases for *min'yō* alone in 1978–80, over 7 per cent of all domestic releases.

Those in charge of *min'yō* recording sessions and decisions on repertoire are often specialists in traditional classical music or theatre (Kabuki, Noh) or otherwise less than sympathetic to rural-style *min'yō*; Fujimoto Hideo dominated at King Records. This contributes to the continued classicization of *min'yō* in subtle ways, including choice of accompanists. The major exceptions were those recordings made under the guidance of Machida Kashō or Takeuchi Tsutomu, scholars who tended (though not exclusively) to favour local performers and seek authenticity. For a fascinating insight into record companies' marketing strategies, see Appendix 3.

4.8.3 Other private companies

Aside from the broadcast and recording industries, certain individual companies not directly connected with the music business have also contributed to *min'yō* activity. The two most prominent examples have been the Kinkan Company and Sankei Shinbun newspaper.

Kinkan is best known as the producer of an insect-bite salve. Its second claim to fame is that from 1961 until 1993 it sponsored a weekly television show, *Shiroto min'yō meijin-sen* (Amateur Folk Song Championship Battle), in which six amateurs competed before a panel of expert judges and a huge national audience of viewers. A beloved feature of the show was that the final few minutes were devoted to performances by audience members. One after another, they stepped up to the microphone, announced their song, then began to sing to the accompaniment of the 'house musicians'. A dull clunk of a gong rudely interrupted the worst singers, but a good performer had a chance of being invited to compete formally in a subsequent show.

The judges on the show around 1980 included: scholars such as Kojima Tomiko, Misumi Haruo and Machida Kashō; veteran singers such as Satō Matsuko (1909–98); and representatives of the television and recording industries. The opinions of such respected figures, heard across the land for more than three decades, were a major force in the dissemination of attitudes towards performance among amateurs. Two themes arose frequently in their remarks. First, professional singer Satō Matsuko in particular could rarely resist correcting particular melodic passages, thus contributing to the idea of a single 'right way' to sing a given song. Her occasional half-hearted comment that 'There is *that* way of singing it, too, I suppose' could not vitiate the effect of her initial remark. (Trained from childhood in classical shamisen styles, she was later a student of Fujimoto Hideo and often reflected his influence.) Second, all judges seemed to favour contestants who sang songs from their own home area. This was clear in their comments ('You're not from Akita? I didn't think so.') as well as in the divergence between their voting and the results of the studio audience poll: the audience enjoyed a good performance regardless of geographical considerations. It is my unprovable impression that the judges were swayed by this local identity issue even when it did not affect the performance.

Kinkan's involvement in *min'yō* stems directly from its founder, Yamazaki Eiji (1895–1988), who sat in the front row of the audience for almost every broadcast for twenty-seven years until his death. He was, simply, a lover of folk song.

Sankei Shinbun, based in Osaka, has since 1966 sponsored a yearly *min'yō* contest (now with six preliminary contests in the Osaka area) and frequently lends its name (though little of its money) to concerts and student recitals. Although partly an advertising ploy, it also (according to the company official in charge of *min'yō* activities in 1978) reflected the sincere belief of a former company president that *min'yō* could contribute to Japan's spiritual revival in the post-war years. Kinkan's Yamazaki gave the same motivation for his company's sponsorship of *min'yō*-related events (NMMM: 216–7). This theme is encountered frequently (§5.4).

We should note also the appearance of various monthly magazines devoted to *min'yō*. The three main ones, all emerging from the late 1970s boom, are *Min'yō Bunka* (MB in the bibliography; produced by the Sankei Shinbun newspaper company), *Gekkan Min'yō* and *Min'yō Shunjū*. These carry a wide range of articles: biographies of performers, events listings and reviews, feature articles on particular songs or dances, performance notations (§4.5.2) etc. *Min'yō* in all three titles is written in *hiragana* rather than Chinese characters, allowing the word to signify both song and dance (see Chapter 1, note 12). The more recent *Hōgaku Janaru*, which covers all genres of traditional Japanese music including their contemporary and fusion guises, also carries listings of many *min'yō* events and broadcasts. Finally, there is *Bachi-Bachi*, launched in 2004, whose title plays on the homophony of the words *bachi* meaning shamisen plectrum and taiko stick. It caters for fans of the two most popular genres of traditional music: Tsugaru-jamisen, and *wadaiko*, the large neo-traditional drum ensembles inspired by Kodō.

4.9 Urban *min'yō* contests

In §3.5 we described the success of NHK's amateur national *min'yō* contests, broadcast from 1948. Several other national contests emerged subsequently. At the start of the boom in 1977–8, the five most important were the NHK contest itself, the twice-yearly competitions held by the two rival groups Nihon Min'yō Kyōkai and Nihon Kyōdo Min'yō Kyōkai, the Sankei Shinbun contest just mentioned, and the Yomiuri Television contest launched in 1977. Major record companies such as Japan Columbia also held contests. The Kinkan competition continued to be televised on Saturdays. Smaller-scale monthly competitions were sometimes held in *min'yō* bars. Even more such contests exist today. At all of these, contestants from anywhere (even from abroad) can, in theory, choose to sing any *min'yō*, hence I call these 'multi-song contests'. These may be held on a national, prefectural or even occasionally a city level.

Meanwhile, single-song contests sprang up from Hokkaido to the southern tip of the Ryukyus. These aimed to encourage the performance of one cherished local song – and also to attract tourist revenue and build local pride. We return to these local single-song contests in §5.5, when discussing regional as opposed to big-city *min'yō* life.

What effects do these contests have on performance and transmission? The principal effects may be exactly those described in the previous section with reference to the Kinkan programme. For major national competitions, there is strong support from the judges for those who sing songs from their home prefecture. Second, there is a tendency to penalize singers who perform a familiar song in an original way: they will be said to have 'quirks' (*kuse*). There is a fine, highly subjective line between developing a personal style – a positive thing – and quirks. The safest approach is obviously to avoid any original interpretation at all. This situation, common to virtually all modern competitions aside from those for Tsugaru-jamisen, is in diametric opposition to the sorts of contests mentioned in §3.4.1, where individuality was prized.[15]

Sugita Akiko of Nara had a teacher (Otowa Jun'ichirō) who encouraged his pupils to find their own style as soon as possible; to him, 'heart' was more important than form. Under his influence, Sugita often taught versions of well-known *min'yō* which departed from the most familiar recorded performances. Once, however, a student asked if she would instead teach him the 'usual' version of a certain song, to avoid confusing the accompanists and judges at a contest; she did.

Competition fever also encourages students to work on a single song for up to an entire year or longer. Although this may be in keeping with traditional Japanese approaches to art, it is certainly not in keeping with traditional folk song performance. In ways such as these, competitions contribute to the classicization of *min'yō*.

The benefits of contests for participants and sponsors are varied and complex. Winning a major competition is a common springboard to professionalism, as we have seen. For most singers the stakes are not so high: a contest, aside from its social aspects, simply provides a focus or goal for one's efforts. Some see it as a chance to gain useful feedback from judges. Sponsors' motivations are also diverse, as exemplified above.

Attention to song contests cross-culturally is badly needed, for judges' opinions and values generally seem to exert an untoward and often unremarked influence on singing style. (*The World of Music* 45.1 (2003), a special issue entitled *Contesting tradition: cross-cultural studies of musical competition*, makes an excellent start.) Let us mention two cases. Collinson (1966: 30–1) reported that publishers of notation for Scots songs 'for the concert platform or competition festival' often reversed the rhythmic values of the 'Scots snap' (sixteenth note followed by a dotted eighth), considering the reversed form more tasteful. 'Competitors, who may have inherited their own orally transmitted versions of the songs, are forced to sing against their instincts the refined versions of the book, or lose marks.' Who are these judges?

Blankenhorn (1987: 10–12) reported that the judges at Ireland's Oireachtas festival of Gaelic song must be recruited from 'outside the [sean-nós] tradition they presume to judge', since insiders are loath to pass judgement upon their fellows. The adjudicators tend to be 'people with degrees in music and so forth', who seemingly have no doubt that their value judgments are appropriate to this tradition alien to them. Their call for 'expression' and praise of 'ornamentation' has led to longer performances with more mannered ornamentation, to dramatic concluding rallentandos in place of the more traditional quasi-spoken final phrase, to a devaluing of the less flowery Donegal tradition at the expense of Connemara, and so forth.

A rather different case is described from personal experience by Janet Fargion (pers. comm. ca. 1989). In apartheid times, judges for the all-night contests of *isicathamiya* choral singing in the Black townships of South Africa were generally White outsiders, since they could be assumed not to know any of the competitors and thus to be objective and above bribery. Meanwhile, back in Japan, a somewhat reverse situation: During the boom years around 1980, Misumi Haruo, one of the Kinkan judges mentioned above, was head of the Performing Arts Division of the Tokyo National Research Institute for Cultural Properties and as such perhaps Japan's most respected authority on folk performing arts. He was often asked to serve as judge at local contests, including the 'Esashi Oiwake' annual concours. He admitted freely, however, that he and his fellow Tokyo-based researchers generally feel incompetent to distinguish the fine points of local style. Fortunately, he said, the 'Esashi Oiwake' concours organizers set his mind at rest: they never took his scores into consideration anyway! The same is probably true whenever I judge at a contest.

The Nihon Min'yō Kyōkai's national Tsugaru-jamisen contest, held in Tokyo each April since 1998, is a throwback to the old Tokyo-based 'Esashi Oiwake' contests: a single-tune contest held not in the home region but in the urban centre of Japan. All contestants must improvise on 'Tsugaru Jongara Bushi'. Although the performances may diverge far from the original vocal melody that informs these improvisations, there is still a clear vocabulary of motifs and techniques that define the style. One (foreign) performer at the 1998 contest was technically quite skilled but somehow, to my ears, not playing in the same style as the rest: too many unfamilar phrases arose, standard techniques were underused, tempo was slightly hurried, and power was lacking. I asked the judge sitting next to me for his opinion, and he said, 'Skilful, but it isn't Tsugaru-jamisen.'

4.10 Summary

This chapter examined the *min'yō* world as it stands in the present day in the principal cities of Japan. The urban condition contributes certain features to *min'yō* performance and transmission. For example, performances are on a larger scale, in terms of numbers both of audience and of performers. Teachers also have more students, more professional opportunities and higher incomes than in the countryside. The urban setting also brings together diverse regional styles, so that one individual may learn to perform songs from all over Japan. Nevertheless, the *min'yō* world still depends greatly on personalized, affective links as embodied in the *iemoto* ('headmaster') system.

Musical preferences can be correlated with certain sociocultural attributes. 1) Throughout the past half-century, increasing age seems to lead to an increased fondness for *min'yō* (and for traditional Japanese music in general). 2) *Min'yō* are most popular in 'peripheral Japan' (in the northeast and along the Japan Sea coast) and least popular in the large cities. In the cities, they are most popular with recent in-migrants. 3) In terms of occupation, *min'yō* are most popular with farmers, then among small entrepreneurs (mostly urban); students show the lowest interest, followed by white-collar workers. 4) Among adults, those with the least amount of formal education most enjoy *min'yō*.

By those who do not enjoy them, *min'yō* are perceived as old-fashioned, difficult to understand and to perform, obscene and/or uncouth. People who are involved with *min'yō* usually became so because of childhood exposure; because a friend convinced them to take lessons; because they found that the difficult vocal ornaments came easily to them; because they needed a song to sing at parties; or because of a search for their identity as Japanese.

The majority of 'star' performers and teachers still come from Tōhoku and Hokkaido, although most of those with recording contracts have settled near Tokyo, where employment opportunities are most numerous.

As folk singing has at last become a generally respected profession, methods of recruitment have changed from fifty years ago. The younger generation of singers have mostly had formal lessons; were often born in a large city; may have first been exposed to *min'yō* through the media and recordings; and may have gotten their start through contests or formal auditions.

Teaching is the largest source of income for most professionals: since the 1960s a 'leisure boom' has provided a large and affluent pool of potential students. The trends cited in Chapter 3 continue today – for example, the stress on invariance and standardization. In general, teaching methods have been 'rationalized', partly in pursuit of the ideal of invariance, but apparently also due to an attraction to prestigious modern gadgetry such as tape recorders.

Min'yō students and teachers alike have huge repertoires when compared with fifty years ago. Despite some regional specialization, the trend is toward singing songs from all parts of Japan. The repertoire as a whole is growing steadily via the 'excavation' of pre-existing local songs. New compositions are rarely sung, being intended principally as recorded dance accompaniment.

At *min'yō* bars, at concerts, in broadcasts and in nearly all commercial recordings, *min'yō* are sung with instrumental accompaniment, in 'stage' versions. The activities of preservation societies and others who attempt to perform in traditional village style have little appeal for the vast majority of *min'yō* fans.

The impact of urban multi-song contests, with their panels of influential and highly judgemental judges, has led to increasing standardization but has also provided a stimulus to students.

NOTES

1. His views are, alas, enshrined in a book: Hattori 1996, reviewed in Hughes 1997.
2. Figures obtained by averaging those for men and women in each age bracket.
3. This might seem to challenge my claim that most folk singing now takes place in cities. However, I include regional cities such as Aomori, Akita and Morioka. Also, I am speaking of activity, not tastes: in modern rural Japan, appreciation of *min'yō* is relatively passive, while urban enthusiasts are more likely to take lessons, enter contests and so forth.
4. Japanese scholars call this category *jieigyō(-sha)*, 'self-employed'. It includes the head of a small shop or factory with only a few employees; a carpenter or gardener; the owner-driver of an independent taxicab; etc.
5. Although many scholars now consider the white/blue-collar distinction less important than the size of the firm for which one works, the reverse is largely true in this survey. The notion of social class as such seems less useful here than a characterization by occupation.
6. NHK 1980: 1351–68 is an interesting attempt to define the features of *shominsei*— the quality of the common people, the masses — as distinct from upper-class or intellectual value orientations. As the chart on p. 1357 shows, the correlation among features is suggestive but not compelling.
7. The median age in 1980 was thity years six months. Only 18 per cent of the population was over fifty-five (EOJ: 6.223). Both figures have risen rapidly since then, however.
8. This preference pattern is one of many that may be changing in recent years, although comparable surveys are not available. Just as there are now many sixty-year-old Rolling Stones fans (and Rolling Stones!) in the West, while few existed in the 1970s, so in Japan *enka* and even Western-style pop and folk musics may now be taking their audience with them as they age.
9. Beliefs in the moral efficacy of singing also appear elsewhere: Slobin (1993: 6) cites an old German saying, 'Where people are singing rest easy, since bad people sing no songs.' But the opposite view is also common.
10. A list of artists by company is found in NMMM: 219–44. The following figures are also tabulated from this source
11. Isaku (1981) dubbed him Fujimoto Shūjō, misreading the characters for his given name.
12. In 1978 Yamamoto Riyo of Nara, a teacher of both traditional and Western-style folk dance, claimed significant health benefits for Japanese folk dance: it had relieved a friend's chronic back and shoulder pains. 'Classical Japanese dance won't do that, absolutely,' she noted.

13. Actually, the boom had already begun. In October 1977 a certain record company issued a 24-page in-house booklet for their sales personnel, suggesting strategies for selling a new set of *min'yō* records (see Appendix 3). Its opening sentence was: 'There's a *min'yō* boom!' So NHK may have been reacting to rather than creating a boom.

14. A growth in youthful involvement in *min'yō* can be gathered from the 50 per cent increase in entrants in the children's division of the Kyōmin concours in 1979 (MB 1979.10: 53). This is surely due in large part to conscious efforts to attract younger students. Many teachers and contests have started 'children's divisions'.

15. My comments derive from observation of several dozen contests, at some of which I also served as a judge. See also the valuable Takeuchi 1985.

CHAPTER 5

THE MODERN COUNTRYSIDE AND THE PERFORMING ARTS

5.1 Introduction

In this chapter we leave the big cities to examine the state of the performing arts in modern peripheral Japan. Choosing the word 'peripheral' – in a geographical rather than evaluative sense – in preference to 'rural' reminds us that the regional towns and smaller cities often share features with the villages which are not found in the urban professional performing arts world. In this sense, they are part of the countryside and often fall within the scope of this chapter.

Despite the inroads of Western-style popular culture into the countryside, the traditional folk performing arts often remain strong, vital and important to the residents. Many traditions are even healthier than they were during the 1930s and 1940s, when economic depression and wartime travail sapped their vigour.

In particular, we will consider the role of the performing arts in strengthening local identity. Strictly speaking, the performing arts can fulfil this same role in cities such as Tokyo and Osaka. However, when, for example, a folk song or dance is used in the city to create a sense of neighbourhood identity and unity, this is often called *furusato-zukuri* – creating a *furusato*, an 'old village' or home town. The traditional rural hamlet, such as described in Chapter 2, is taken as the model for ideal social interaction even in urban neighbourhoods. These traditional values and lifeways are generally felt to survive in the modern village as well. Let us therefore take the modern hamlet as our point of departure, returning in Chapter 6 to urban and suburban *furusato-zukuri*.

5.2 Hamlet identity and local rivalries

In Chapter 2, describing musical activities in traditional rural Japan, we considered the hamlet (*buraku*) as the most significant unit. We also noted, however, that the social network of the average villager has been gradually expanding since the late nineteenth century (§2.1). Now most residents may exit the hamlet daily for school or work, leaving behind a daytime populace consisting principally of housewives, small children and the elderly. Political, economic, educational, social and cultural institutions are now also mostly organized on the basis, not of the hamlet, but of the modern 'village' (*mura* or -*son*) of several thousand residents. For example, the *mura*-wide Young Men's Association (*seinenkai* or *seinendan*) has replaced the hamlet *waka-monogumi* described in §2.5. Such consolidation is often necessitated by a dwindling of interest and/or appropriate population base within each hamlet, so that only a village-size organization can muster a viable membership. The ongoing political mergers noted in §2.1 both reflect and stimulate increasing contacts with neighbouring communities. The modern villager is also more involved than his ancestors with the national culture – through television and other media, the education system, travel, politics and a shared consumer culture, among other factors.

The hamlet is, nonetheless, still a significant social unit. It often serves as an important sub-unit of higher-level associations, and is frequently the unit of identification for the local performing arts. Ritual, festival and social activities often take place at the level of the local Shinto shrine community, which, despite government-mandated shrine mergers during the Meiji period, is still often of hamlet or sub-hamlet size.

That consciousness of hamlet unity can still be a potent force even amidst the ongoing enlargement of political units is illustrated by this typical sequence of events. The village of Yanagawa near Kitakami City, southern Iwate Prefecture, is famous for its version of the Deer Dance (*shishi odori*), a *minzoku geinō* widespread in that region. Until the mid-1970s, the team's performers were all from one hamlet, Kuryūzawa. Then, however, the group's leader, encouraged by outside demand, embarked on an attempt 1) to spread the Yanagawa style by teaching it to groups in neighbouring villages and 2) to recruit performers for the Yanagawa group from other hamlets within the village. (Apparently it had long been called the 'Yanagawa Deer Dance' even when all performers were from Kuryūzawa, since the name Yanagawa was more recognizable to outsiders than Kuryūzawa.) With reference to the first point, a few Kuryūzawa (and other Yanagawa) residents were upset about allowing other villages to learn the local style, but most were flattered that their style had become so prestigious; in fact, scholars often speak of performances by the borrowing villages as belonging to the Yanagawa-*ryū* ('school', 'lineage'). (At another level, locals have long called their style Kanatsu-ryū, a name which acknowledges its founding in nearby northern

Miyagi Prefecture around 1810.) On the second point, some Kuryūzawans were also upset that performers were being recruited for the Yanagawa team itself from outside their hamlet. (The loudest complainers were the members of the original team.) By 1980, when I first made contact, the leader's son had been manipulated into the position of spokesman for this lobby, so father and son were hardly on speaking terms. In 1981, there were two eight-man teams within the village: one led by the son, consisting only of Kuryū zawa residents, the other led by the father and including men from other Yanagawa hamlets. For various reasons including population attrition – Kuryūzawa had dwindled from seventy to forty households since the war amidst general rural depopulation – the 'pure' Kuryūzawa team could rarely field a full complement of eight dancers, and in any case the pan-Yanagawa team was considered far more skilful. With the father's death in late 1981, the son became the official leader of both factions. Returning in 1993, however, I found that the father's group was now led by the head of the Board of Education of Ezashi City, within which Yanagawa had been incorporated as a neighbourhood, under the name Ezashi Yanagawa Kanatsu-ryū Shishi Odori.[1] By 2006, Ezashi itself had become a mere ward (ku) of the new Ōshū City, but the group still performed under its 1993 name and listed Yanagawa as its 'place of transmission' (denshōchi) on a prefectural website,[2] thus maintaining its village link. The son, however, now runs a separate, apparently geographically non-specific non-profit organization called the Kanatsu-ryu Shishi Odori Shinkōkai, to 'promote/encourage' (shinkō) and preserve this style.[3] The name Kuryūzawa is no longer mentioned in either case.

This story highlights two common and interrelated themes in the modern rural performing arts. First, the hamlet and some larger political unit are often in rivalry for control of the art and its associated performing rights. Second, there is ambivalence and lack of unanimity within a hamlet as to whether the art should be taught to outsiders: pride that outsiders would want to perform the local art, but fear that those outsiders might then surpass the locals in skill or renown. In any case, rural depopulation often necessitates a geographic expansion of the membership base.[4]

Rivalries and jealousies arise especially when significant outside attention is involved. Chances to perform for tourists, to travel to Tokyo to appear on television or at the National Theatre, to receive substantial payment for appearing at large hotels or wedding receptions – competition for such opportunities sharpens rivalries. Thus, in the same hamlet of Kuryūzawa, there is no contention regarding the performance of the Lion Dance (shishi-mai) for the yearly Fire Prevention Festival (hibuse-matsuri), since this less spectacular event is purely for local consumption. Each spring, a sacred wooden lion's head is taken from storage at the village shrine and carried to each building in the village for a fire prevention ritual. There is some dancing in the forecourt, the throwing of sake on the roof, and in the case of a new or partially rebuilt house, a more elaborate rite in the parlour. The group includes about six dancers, three or four musicians, and a couple of hamlet dignitaries to record the donations which each house is expected to make. When I made the rounds with the group in 1980, the dancers included a single adult plus four boys aged seven to twelve. I asked the boys how they had come to be involved in the event. 'For money!' they chimed in chorus: their parents were paying them to participate. Also, there was the fact that they were given sweets and refreshments at each house they visited. Village tradition was not a motivating factor for them.

One musician was from another hamlet. Although several other hamlets in the village had a similar rite, his did not. He had been delegated to participate by the Yanagawa Agricultural Cooperative, of which he was an employee. Agricultural cooperatives are one of many modern pan-village organizations which may inherit some of the social responsibilities once fulfilled by the Young Men's Association. The Cooperative considered it part of its mission to aid the survival of important traditions in individual hamlets. As we walked around the hamlet, along the paddy paths between houses, the employee practised his part under the tutelage of the senior musician. None of the residents I spoke with seemed bothered that an outsider should join the *hibuse* group – except insofar as his presence reflected a decline in commitment within the hamlet itself. The Fire Prevention Festival was a local ritual, not a public performance to be judged on artistic grounds. There was no sense of rivalry with other hamlets. This is not to say that all participants considered the ritual element paramount: even some adults seemed to value the experience primarily as a chance to dance, play and drink.

These examples are from the realm of *minzoku geinō*, but similar comments could be offered regarding folk song. The farming hamlet of Nishi-Mochida, Shimane Prefecture, is now incorporated into Matsue City but retains much of its pre-modern character. This region boasts a widespread song type called 'Sanko Bushi'. With the increased media attention on *min'yō* since the 1960s, some residents of Nishi-Mochida came to feel that *their* version of 'Sanko Bushi' had been overlooked by singers and scholars despite its superiority to other versions. To remedy this, a Sanko Bushi Preservation Society was formed in 1976 (§5.4.4), both to ensure the song's survival (for it was on the verge of dying out) and to make it known to a wider public. When I visited in 1979, the members asked me to introduce the song to some of my acquaintances among professional folk singers in Tokyo; they particularly hoped that Kanazawa Akiko might be interested. (I tried.)

Opportunities for outside recognition have increased dramatically in recent decades, and local rivalries over performing arts have intensified in response. It may be not merely a matter of local pride but of potential tangible benefits: performance fees, chances to travel, increased tourist revenue, possible government designation as an Important Intangible Cultural Property and so forth. (See for example §5.5 concerning nationwide single-song contests.)

5.3 Performing arts in the villages and towns

With changes in opportunities for performance as well as in the purposes of the performances, it is not surprising that the social organization of transmission has also changed. Young Men's Associations (now called *seinendan*) still play a role in organizing events in many areas, but their potential is weakened by the fact that membership is now voluntary. They are often helped, however, by Housewives' Associations (*fujinkai*), which did not exist in pre-modern times. These often arrange classes for their members, which may include koto or *min'yō* lessons – but without the social class implications of former times (§2.2.2). Post-war land reforms and general prosperity have vastly reduced class consciousness in most rural areas.

In Fujimi-chō, a formerly rural district now part of Nara City, in 1978 the annual Bon dance was being sponsored jointly by the district's Young Men's and Housewives' Associations. These groups saw to the constructing of the musicians' tower, hired the musicians (from nearby Osaka) and arranged a practice session with a local dance teacher, which about a dozen members attended. The Young Men's Association members bemoaned the poor participation rate of the district's men in their organization. Many local men commute to Osaka for work, leaving little free time to participate in such a local group. Facing diminished membership, the Association often cooperates with its counterpart in an adjacent neighbourhood. The Bon dance that year was an unqualified success, serving its traditional social functions. Some participants suggested, however, that the dance's ritual significance was somewhat diminished by holding it, not on the official date of Bon, but on the nearest weekend to ensure maximum attendance – now a common practice throughout Japan.

Increased opportunities for tourist-oriented performance have had an interesting effect on the *yamabushi kagura* of Ōtsugunai (§2.2.2). By 1981, Sasaki Kaneshige was saying that the troupe rarely performed anymore at the hamlet's fall festival, its original *raison d'être*: since they perform so often each year, often in tourism contexts, nobody would be interested in watching yet another performance. I wondered later whether 'nobody' referred also to the gods for whom the *kagura* was originally intended. However, the troupe still performs at Hayachine Shrine, a major regional religious site, in alternation (and competition) with the troupe from nearby Take. (See Thornbury 1997: 110–12.)

Schoolteachers are increasingly finding uses for local music and dance. For examples, see the discussion of music education in §7.5.

In the towns of peripheral Japan, we may encounter features recalling the *min'yō* world in Tokyo and Osaka, including folk song bars and professional teachers. These are not sufficiently distinct from those discussed in the previous chapter to merit detailed description. The major difference is that teachers in peripheral towns are almost certainly locally born and have in their repertoires many songs from their own prefecture.

A large percentage of traditional rural performance events today are conducted under the aegis of so-called preservation societies. It is to these that we now turn our attention.

5.4 Preservation societies

5.4.1 The origins of preservationism

The twentieth century in Japan saw the emergence of a type of organization known as the *hozonkai* – literally, 'preservation society'. Though existing in various fields, they are primarily a feature of the world of performing arts, particularly the folk performing arts. In the realm of folk song, these *hozonkai* are almost all small local groups, and the majority of them are dedicated to 'preserving' only one local song, with or without a dance. That song's title ordinarily forms part of the group's name.

One might assume that *hozonkai* in the performing arts represent a defensive reaction against the encroachments of Western culture – an attempt to preserve the traditional arts in the face of the overwhelming emphasis in the school system and the media on Western music to the exclusion of Japanese music. Government officials charged with preserving the traditional arts often give this reason for encouraging *hozonkai* formation. Members, however, virtually never mention this, nor do *hozonkai* charters make explicit reference to it. To the members, the 'enemy' (if any) is not the West but modern society in general, the ravages of time, and perhaps the traditional performing arts of other communities which are competing for public recognition.

Compare the situation in, say, the USA. 1) The United States does have many performing groups or organizations for the replication of earlier styles, as well as organizations which sponsor performances by traditional artists. The word 'preservation', however, rarely graces their titles: they have names like the New Lost City Ramblers, the Friends of Old Time Music, the Country Dance Society, etc.[5] Whether this is merely a matter of choice of words or whether there is a deeper significance will be discussed below. 2) No US group would be devoted to only one song or dance: there is no 'Sail Away Ladies' Society. 3) Most importantly, the song (or complex of songs) preserved by a *hozonkai* is from a specific local community. Despite increasing geographic mobility and cultural homogenization, the Japanese identification of people and songs with their original home areas is still very strong. In the USA, the average resident of most states could not even name a local folk song, let alone sing one. Many Americans identify with their home areas primarily through sports teams.

The notion of preservation with reference to traditional performing arts is not limited to Japan, of course: it is encountered in many if not most developing countries. It is my impression, however, that in most countries such organized 'preservation' is at the urging and under the control of the national or state government, whereas in Japan *hozonkai* are generally born of private initiative (although frequently with governmental prodding as described below). National initiatives now may also be stimulated by UNESCO's Masterpieces of the Oral and Intangible Heritage of Humanity programme, which ironically is based on Japan's own national policy of designating Important Intangible Cultural Properties (Jūyō Mukei Bunkazai). But in Japan itself, at least for the 'folk' (*minzoku*) category, local initiative is paramount (see further §5.6).

In Japan, one might assume, ritual songs would be preserved naturally through traditional organizations such as Young Men's Associations and shrine guilds (§2.5.1): *hozonkai* should hardly be necessary. It would seem also that the positive value traditionally placed on textual improvisation in non-ritual songs, where lyrics were frequently altered to suit new tastes and situations, is antithetical to the notion of preservation. In fact, however, both ritual and non-ritual songs are today widely performed and transmitted by *hozonkai*.

5.4.2 The birth of the hozonkai notion

The first groups calling themselves *hozonkai* apparently date from the late Meiji period. Of course, Japan had long had organizations to perpetuate various performing arts: the government *gagaku* (court music) bureau from the seventh century; the Blind People's Guild (*tōdō*), from the fourteenth to the nineteenth centuries the main public purveyor of *heike-biwa*, koto and *jiuta* shamisen music; the village-level organizations mentioned above for transmitting ceremonial and dance music; and the *iemoto* system for most classical arts. Each differs in important details from the typical *hozonkai*, but collectively they demonstrate a tendency for Japanese arts to be transmitted by highly organized groups.

We must consider the shifting moods of Meiji to pinpoint the reasons for the rise of *hozonkai* at that time. We have noted (§§1.5, 3.3.2) the Meiji government's initial wish to Westernize, followed by a swing back towards respect for tradition after 1890. The initial devaluation of tradition extended to the plastic arts as well: a period of government indifference toward the arts (there were more 'important' matters in the rush to modernize) and antagonism towards Buddhism resulted in the loss or decay of many important art treasures. In 1897, as the climate shifted towards the traditional, the government passed the first law protecting art treasures, the 'Old Shrine and Temple Preservation Law' (Koshaji Hozon Hō; see Bunkachō 1972: 13), and several temple and shrine *hozonkai* quickly emerged – with some government financial support (Tateyama 1910: 691f.). The word *hozon* thus seems to have signalled first the preservation of tangible objects – sculptures and buildings. Indeed, one can at least imagine 'preserving' such objects in a relatively unaltered state.

The concept was then broadened to apply to performing arts. At this point, doubts arise. It might be considered reasonable to attempt to preserve with minimal changes certain types of ritual or classical music, but it is when the concept is extended to village song that we must examine closely its validity and effects.

5.4.3 The first folk song preservation societies

Two of the earliest *hozonkai* for folk song were organized at about the same time.[6] A *hozonkai* was formed in the town of Yasugi, Shimane Prefecture, in 1911 to preserve and spread the correct version of the local song 'Yasugi Bushi'. Far to the north, in the town of Esashi in Hokkaido, an Oiwake Bushi Hozonkai arose around this time, founded for the same purpose (§3.3). These two set the tone for the activities of many current *hozonkai*.

According to the Yasugi Bushi Hozonkai's 1979 yearbook (Yasugi 1979), during the 1870s the region saw a tremendous influx of former samurai who had lost their positions after the 1868 Meiji restoration. As a result, local tea-houses and pleasure palaces did a booming trade, and the geisha were swept along in a wave of vulgarity which led them to alter their performances of 'Yasugi Bushi' for the worse. Apparently this means that they were singing some rather bawdy lyrics. 'Yasugi Bushi' continued to be performed in 'ambiguous' (*aimai*) forms until 1911, when a group of concerned citizens decided to rescue the original 'correct/authentic' (*seichō*) version and formed the Seichō Yasugi Bushi Hozonkai.

In §3.3 we noted a similar chain of development in Esashi: an attempt by concerned citizens to recapture the 'original' version of the increasingly respected local song. This contributed to the formation of several rival organizations, each claiming to transmit the most 'authentic' version. At least one was called a *hozonkai*: the Oiwake Bushi Hozonkai, created through the urging of local Viscount Shinagawa Yaichi to save the song from 'decay' (Yokota 1920). The common element in the statements of purpose by the 'Yasugi Bushi' and 'Esashi Oiwake' preservation movements was the desire to rescue these songs from the women of the teahouses and recirculate the 'correct' version. (Note that no reference was made to the threat of *Western* music. Nor was any thought given to rescuing the women themselves, many of whom had basically been sold into prostitution.) This seems a case of moral judgements influencing aesthetic prejudices. Associating with geisha had long been considered deleterious to the warrior spirit; now, under the influence of Western values, it was also increasingly thought immoral. Thus the high-minded individuals (predominantly men) who organized these early *hozonkai* stressed their preference for more masculine, less feminine styles.

The same attitude crops up in some later *hozonkai*: the Iso Bushi Hozonkai was founded in 1947 partly to rescue 'Iso Bushi' from the geisha parlour and restore its masculinity as a sea song (Iso 1979: 1). Many *hozonkai*, however, have precisely the opposite effect. The boat-rowing song 'Kaigara Bushi' of Tottori Prefecture was adapted in 1932–3 to be performed by the women of a local spa as a publicity song, to increase tourism. The Kaigara Bushi Hozonkai currently preserves this version – although a rival Motouta Kaigara Bushi Hozonkai later sprang up nearby to preserve the 'original' (*motouta*) rowing song (Machida & Asano 1960: 283, 288).

Another factor in the birth of these first *hozonkai* was the model provided by the teaching structure for most traditional classical genres: the *iemoto* system (§4.5). Many *hozonkai* founders had studied such genres and doubtless hoped to give their local songs the same aura of prestige adhering to such systematic transmission. A major difference between the *iemoto* system and *hozonkai* is the profit motive. It is very strong in the former: students pay large fees to receive certificates representing different levels of proficiency. Some *hozonkai* issue such certificates, but as incentives rather than for profit.

Pre-war *hozonkai* were, however, uncommon. Before the notion had become widespread, the Japanese were hit by both the worldwide depression and increasing militarism, with negative effects on the performing arts (§3.5). Many early *hozonkai* and other *min'yō* organizations lapsed during this period. A new 'Esashi Oiwake' *hozonkai* (called simply Esashi Oiwake Kai) was formed in 1957; the song's continued renown was such that by 1977 the *hozonkai* boasted seventy-five branches with 2800 members throughout Japan, rising to 122 and 4400 by 1988 through the effect of the *min'yō* boom and settling at 155 and 4000 as of 2007. The Yasugi Bushi Hozonkai in 1977 had forty-six branches with 3800 members, increasing to sixty-six and 4000 by 2007. In both cases, the number of branches has increased dramatically while total membership has held fairly constant. These are exceptional figures for *hozonkai*, reflecting the ongoing popularity of these two songs as well as their early starts on organization building. Almost all other *hozonkai* draw members primarily from the local community. The Esashi Oiwake Kai, though, has branches in Brazil, Hawaii, and three cities in California, whose members are nearly all of Japanese descent. Its activities include holding the annual national contest and its ten regional preliminaries, licensing teachers, grading singers outside of the contest as well, running study sessions amd seminars, and in recent years – in common with almost all *min'yō* organizations – teaching as volunteers in the schools in an attempt to interest the young and counteract the ageing trend in the *min'yō* world.

5.4.4 Post-war examples

Moving to the post-war era, with the term *hozonkai* being widely heard, it has been adopted by organizations of diverse types. In some cities, for example, a professional *min'yō* teacher may form a *hozonkai* to cover the songs of an entire prefecture – or even the whole country, as with the Japanese Folk Song Preservation Society (Nihon Min'yō Hozonkai) in Osaka. These are not, however, generally considered typical *hozonkai* but rather *aikōkai*, where *aikō* means love or affection (*aikōsha* = aficionado). In its narrower sense, the word *hozonkai* conjures up a relatively clear image: a small organization of elderly amateurs in a village or regional town, clinging conservatively to a local song and/or dance tradition, transmitting it in a form unsuitable for modern urban tastes. This is how urban enthusiasts usually characterize *hozonkai*. However, most people would recognize the following diverse set of examples as legitimate 'typical' *hozonkai*.

(1) Sakamoto Odori Hozonkai, Sakamoto Village, Nara Prefecture. In this tiny mountain village a Bon dance is held every August, and relatives of villagers return from their jobs or schooling in the cities to dance all night. The term Sakamoto Odori ('Sakamoto Dance(s)') applies collectively to the fifteen or so local Bon dance songs, each having a specific name as well. The songs are performed by about three singers in alternation, accompanied only by a large drum. Actually, said the leading singer in 1979, although the name of the group is printed on his name card, there isn't really any *hozonkai* – no membership system, dues, or constitution as for larger *hozonkai*. During and immediately after the Second World War, Bon dances throughout Japan had been scaled down or suspended for political, economic and emotional reasons; in Sakamoto, after the war some local leaders strove to resuscitate their dance, with guidance from a man born in 1886. This effort was so successful that by 1979 there seemed no need to speak of *hozon*. When the villagers are called upon to perform their dances on a city stage, they identify themselves as a *hozonkai*. They are not, however, particularly interested in spreading their dances: they dance primarily for themselves. Change is generally resisted: when a professional shamisen player from Osaka (the nearest large city) wanted to add an accompaniment to two of the songs for a stage appearance, she was allowed to play offstage – virtually inaudibly – in the wings. (Japanese politesse and/or local power relations apparently precluded rejecting her offer altogether.) However, several new verses have been written in recent decades by the principal singers. It is also recognized that some of the dances are less than a century old.

The direct stimulus for the formation of a *hozonkai* came from outside. Around 1960, 'some folk song researcher' (apparently Machida Kashō) came to the village to record the songs. He opined that the villagers should form a *hozonkai*, and, the Japanese being ever sensitive to the opinion of prestigious people, they did. We will return to this matter of direct outside stimulus later.

Why do the young people come home to dance at O-Bon? 'It's fun / It's a chance to see my family and friends / After all, it's my *furusato*.' Around 1980, two sisters in their twenties who were living and working in Osaka would get together there occasionally to practise the dances: it helped them cope with the loneliness of big-city life, they said, as did coming home at O-Bon. Some *hozonkai* members also point to the value of the dances in 'unifying the village'. Since the war the village has suffered severe depopulation and the construction of a dam which necessitated considerable relocation. 'Sakamoto Odori' is one mechanism for preserving identity when faced with such challenges.

(2) Bouchi Uta Hozonkai, Sagamihara City, Kanagawa Prefecture. Here too, there was not really an organized *hozonkai* when I visited in May 1979. 'Bouchi Uta' is, however, a work song, a barley threshing song. Most early *min'yō hozonkai* preserved dance songs or widely popular songs; only after the war did pure work songs commonly spawn *hozonkai*. Since manual barley threshing had been unnecessary since the 1920s, this song had seemingly died a natural death until revived by a man who heard it in 1959 from his 86-year-old uncle. Amidst a general revival of interest in local tradition, he gathered some two dozen elders who knew the song, and they began to perform it at local functions – complete with threshing (Fig. 5.1). The singers were almost all over fifty, most over sixty. They were united by memories of their youth, when their parents threshed barley to make a living. Only a few of these individuals had done so – including two of the principal singers, both eighty-three years old – but the song was well known to all of them and evoked an era now remembered as simpler and more comforting.

Efforts by the city Board of Education to propagate the song via the schools had failed. The song is probably too simple by modern standards to be appreciated as pure music by today's youth, nor do they comprehend the original social context of the song. The Board also made a strategic error when producing a recording for school use. The *hozonkai*'s public performances are lively and spirited, the song joyous **(CD16)**. The recorded rendering, however, is slow, almost lugubrious in tempo, tending towards the intervals of the sad-sounding *miyako-bushi* mode, and without the lively sounds of threshing **(CD36)**. It conveys none of the joy of the live version. This may be attributed to at least three factors: the singers were in a studio, not actually threshing; the lead singer, granted that honour because it was he who had revived the song (and maybe because, as a doctor, he held high social status), was perhaps imitating his aged uncle's lonely, nostalgia-tinged singing; and the lead singer had never actually threshed barley and so had little conception of the typical mood.

In any case, the participating elders value their experience highly, for several reasons. Two in particular recur frequently in other *hozonkai* as well. First, participation is an enjoyable social activity. Second, it gives them a feeling of self-worth, of the validation of their life experiences: participation reaffirms the value of traditional lifeways which are rapidly being redefined by the young as 'old-fashioned'. This point was made explicit by one member: 'Young folks today haven't experienced suffering (*kurō*). We [elders] know what it's like to do manual labour, and the experience is valuable in building good human beings (*ningen-zukuri*).' This statement does not refer specifically to the accompanying song, but members of *hozonkai* frequently invoke the value of song study in building character.

Drawing strength from their collective memories, these elderly folk no longer can be made to feel antiquated and irrelevant by the pace of modern life: they take pride in possessing experience, skills and knowledge which today's youth can never have. Their agricultural past is invaluable in a very direct and relevant way: if you are not from a farming household, they say, you'll never capture the spirit of this song.

(3) Kichiseikai, Kichijōji City, Tokyo. We met this group briefly in §2.5.2. The word *hozonkai* does not appear in this group's name, but the members use it freely in their discussion of their activities.

Traditionally, construction work in Japanese cities was done by firemen, since they had plenty of spare time between fires and were experienced at climbing about in the skeletons of buildings. The term *tobi* designated workers in both professions. Until the early twentieth century, songs known as *kiyari* were used by the *tobi* of the Kantō region to coordinate the rhythmic work of foundation pounding (earth tamping) for new buildings. With mechanization these songs have retreated to the realm of ceremony and nostalgia. The members of this group are construction workers who – consciously clinging to a revered tradition – double as volunteer firemen, supplementing the municipal force when necessary. Any *tobi* who doesn't know *kiyari*, they feel, should be ashamed; since most modern construction workers fail to share this view, it was necessary for these advocates to form a *hozonkai*. Around 1980 the fifteen or so members met several times a month to practise their songs, which they perform on festive and ceremonial occasions.[7] The members, feeling that context is important, took pains to describe to me the traditional methods of foundation pounding and urged me to visit the exhibition of these methods on display at a local museum.

To keep the rhythm of the songs, each member strikes the floor with a short but heavy wooden rod to imitate the rise and fall of the foundation-pounding pole. Thus the imitation of the work itself is more abstract than with the barley threshing *hozonkai* – although the latter usually thresh only for public performances, not for practice.[8]

(4) Nikkō Waraku Odori, Nikkō City, Tochigi Prefecture. Most *hozonkai* are formed either by groups of private citizens (usually encouraged or later supported by local governments) or by a Chamber of Commerce hoping to attract trade. Here is a rare exception. The copper refining plant of the Furukawa Electric Company, in the city of Nikkō, has sponsored a dance at O-Bon annually since 1914, to the song 'Nikkō Waraku Odori'. It was originally created by order of the plant manager, to increase company morale and friendship among employees,[9] and secondarily to commemorate the company's founding day and a 1913 inspection-visit by the emperor (Takeuchi 1978: 101ff.). It is maintained by a special department of the company. It is most pointedly *not* a publicity venture, according to company officials in 1980. The dances and music **(CD37)**, based on local Bon dances, have been transmitted intact since 1914, although about fifteen new 'official' verses are now selected each year from entries submitted by employees.

The company tries without success to discourage the town's high-school students who persist in making up their own unofficial dance steps, but these new steps pose no threat to the three official steps danced by the adults, since the students revert to orthodoxy in adulthood. When I asked one girl why most of the teens just jogged around the tower in a circle, thrusting their fists upward rhythmically while shouting, she said, 'It's an ancient custom' (*Mukashi kara no shūkan desu*). 'Ancient' is the standard translation of *mukashi*, but the Japanese tend to use the word with little regard for time depth – in this case, at most seventy years. Using the word seems a sort of magic wand to bestow authenticity.

This dance-song is popular throughout Japan and is frequently recorded by city singers, almost always with shamisen added to the original percussion and flutes; such external events are considered irrelevant by the company. The dance is open to the public, and thousands of dancers come from far and wide, but – unusually – the town tourist office has no official connection with the event. Instead, there is a separate 'Waraku Odori' dance held in the town centre, trading on the success of the Company's dance.

(5) Gujō Odori Hozonkai, Gujō Hachiman City, Gifu Prefecture. This town has been an important pilgrimage site for centuries, and its local Bon dance, 'Gujō Odori', has long attracted visitors from great distances. Since the 1960s, the dance has been held for up to sixty nights each summer, at different sites around the town, and advertisements throughout Japan encourage tourists to come to participate.[10] My wife and I did so in 1978. While dancing around the musicians' tower in front of the rail station, we were pulled from the circle by a *hozonkai* official and led to a small office. There, two men at desks issued certificates of proficiency to those of us who had been 'selected' from the crowd. What the dance meant to the locals (aside from tourist trade), I cannot say, but we outsiders were rather touched by this little ceremony.

This *hozonkai* now performs ten dance songs, called collectively 'Gujō Odori' – 'Dances of Gujō'. In 1923 only two of these were being performed as Bon dances; two more had been added by 1940; a further five local songs were added around the time of the group's formation in the early 1950s (Asano 1983: 169); and another has also crept in. As always, things are preserved at a specific moment in time – in this case, more or less the 1950s. The *hozonkai* now also sometimes holds the dances in Tokyo, where young and old dance while Gujō's tourist agency does publicity.

(6) Iso Bushi Hozonkai, Nakaminato Town, Ibaragi Prefecture, was formed in 1947 by the shakuhachi player Tanii Hōdō (1899–1973) for three purposes: to honour the Japanese war dead, to rally the depressed spirits of the post-war Japanese, and to return 'Iso Bushi' to its original nature as a sea song and deliver it from the geisha. The group's activities continue to have a highly moral tone, reflecting the founder's belief that effort devoted to mastering a difficult and valuable song such as 'Iso Bushi' will pay dividends in building

character. Thus, for example, in 1972 they performed at a juvenile detention home. Related to this attitude, when a group of us from Tokyo came to Ibaragi for the first national 'Iso Bushi' contest in 1980, our leader, a member of the Preservation Society, took us to Tanii's gravestone, where we all sang 'Iso Bushi' to soothe his spirit.

It remains conjectural whether 'Iso Bushi' was ever a 'sea song' at all. Regardless, Tanii did alter the song to differentiate it from the geisha version. It is his new version whose preservation is the society's object, as with the Kaigara Bushi Hozonkai mentioned in the preceding section.

This organization, despite its name, also has come secondarily to perform and transmit other local songs; however, like all 'true' *hozonkai*, it restricts its choices to songs from the immediate vicinity. Its stated aim is to 'preserve, propagate, and develop (*hatten*)' these songs. According to the leader in 1980, development does not imply any changes in the music, only continued efforts to improve one's imitation of the model provided by the teacher(s).

The founder of this *hozonkai* also in 1956 rearranged the fishnet-tightening song 'Aminoshi Uta' for performance at a local folk arts festival. A *hozonkai* soon formed to preserve this new version at the expense of the original. Examples such as these clarify that *hozonkai* do not necessarily prevent a song's further evolution. To alter a *hozonkai* song, you can simply form your own new *hozonkai*, perhaps prefacing the word 'authentic/correct melody' (*seichō*) or 'original song' (*motouta*) to the title.

(7) Sanko Bushi & Kanehori Odori Hozonkai, Nishi-Mochida, Matsue City, Shimane Prefecture. This group was introduced briefly in §5.2. 'Sanko Bushi' is a close relative or ancestor of the renowned 'Yasugi Bushi' (§5.4.3). Senda Kanbei (b. ca. 1896) and his son summarized the situation for me in 1979. In the 1920s, before a *hozonkai* existed, Senda and a friend created a 'Gold-digging Dance' ('Kanehori Odori') to the accompaniment of 'Sanko Bushi'. Senda had studied shamisen in his spare time and was conversant with Kabuki music and *naniwa-bushi*; he typified the artistic aspirations of a middle-class farmer of this district. They then trained youths from their hamlet and others to perform around the district – for fun and fame, not for profit. Typically they performed as part of a whole evening of entertainment, which might also feature Kabuki dance and recitations of *naniwa-bushi* ('for the old folks'; it was already losing popularity among the young).

Typically, the song and dance ceased to be performed during World War II. They were, however, revived by the village Young Men's Association as a tool to alleviate post-war depression – but soon lapsed again for lack of interest. In 1976 another revival occurred, and the *hozonkai* was formed with some fifty members and support from the Matsue City Board of Education. Senda was the primary teacher during all of these periods.

The tradition of holding variety performances (*engeikai*), indoors or out, on temporary or permanent stages is still far from rare in villages around Japan (although rarer since the advent of television). Indeed, when I visited

Nishi-Mochida in 1979 to study 'Sanko Bushi' for two days with Senda and his Hozonkai (Fig. 5.2), the second evening was given over to such a performance. I demonstrated my minimal skills at singing the song, and my wife and I were asked to offer various other items of our choice (Japanese and Western), sandwiched in among other traditional entertainments.

(8) A story spanning the pre-war and post-war periods concerns the song known to most *min'yō* fans as 'Etchū Owara Bushi' but locally simply called 'Owara'. In 1919, with this song from Toyama Prefecture gaining renown elsewhere, local aficionados formed the Owara Research Association (Owara Kenkyūkai). When a member's performance won the first national contest of the Nihon Min'yō Kyōkai in 1928 (§3.4.3.1), the group capitalized on this success and staked their local claim by adding in 1929 not one but two place-names to their title: Etchū Yatsuo Min'yō Owara Hozonkai, the Etchū [Province] Yatsuo [Town] Folk Song 'Owara' Preservation Society. In 1951, those two place-names were replaced by one, the modern prefectural name: Toyama-ken Min'yō Owara Hozonkai. Finally, in early 2007, the two place-names deleted in 1951 were re-inserted, giving a total of three: Toyama-ken Min'yō Etchū Yatsuo Owara Hozonkai. According to Mr Shimabayashi, the *hozonkai* member who told me about this latest change (18 July 2007), its main intention is to heighten awareness of the unique character of Etchū as a region – the pre-modern provincial name Etchū evoking a sense of tradition lacking in the prefectural name. It is no coincidence that the *hozonkai* is now reached via the Toyama City Tourist Association. If one phones that office and is put on hold, the music heard may be an electronic version of 'Home on the Range' or Foster's 'Camptown Races', which I suppose is preferable to a similar rendition of 'Owara'. Many other *hozonkai* are now also based in local government tourism sections, reflecting *min'yō*'s recognized pulling power. This is further considered in the next section.

(9) Meguro Ginza Ondo Hozonkai, Meguro Ward, Tokyo. Since perhaps the late 1960s, as a partial cure for the alienation of city life, there has been a movement to try to replicate in urban neighbourhoods the sense of community characteristic of rural hamlets – in effect, to manufacture a *furusato* (further discussed in §6.2). In the neighbourhood centred on the Meguro Ginza shopping street in western Tokyo (named after the posh Ginza shopping area of central Tokyo), some 132 women who had been studying folk dances together came to feel a need for their own local dance. They located a recording from around 1930 of a 'new folk song' written in praise of Meguro Ward as a whole. It was perceived, however, as having three short-comings: it was too slow, it didn't mention the Meguro Ginza shopping street, and the song was 'old-fashioned'! A new song was obviously necessary. Thus a fresh text was chosen through a contest, and new music was commissioned from a neighbourhood pop-song composer. A professional folk singer was hired to record it and a professional choreographer to choreograph it for use as the local Bon dance. In summer 1979, the new song and

dance, 'Meguro Ginza Ondo', were unveiled at a ceremony in the shopping street. In December 1979, less than six months after their new song had been born, the shop-owners formed a *hozonkai*. Its titular head was a resident famous actor. Its stated goals: to pass the song on to the next generation, and to contribute to a 'brighter town' (MB 1980.3: 56).

Note that this song was apparently *not* created as a publicity vehicle. As with 'Suzaka Kouta', the song which triggered the publicity-song boom of the 1920s (§3.4.3.1), or 'Nikkō Waraku Odori' (see above), the propaganda was directed first and foremost at the community itself, whether factory or urban neighbourhood, to create solidarity and pride. The decision to form a *hozonkai* perhaps reflected an awareness of the role of more traditional *hozonkai* in building a sense of community. In this sense, 'Meguro Ginza Ondo', as a local song, was a reasonable candidate for a *hozonkai*, whereas most other recent *shin-min'yō* would not be, since they lack a geographical focus (as we shall see in §6.4). On the other hand, perhaps the *hozonkai* structure was simply the most obvious and available model for the modern transmission of a lone song and dance (see below).

With these examples as points of reference, we can confirm our earlier characterization of the features common to most *hozonkai*.

(1) They are locally-based organizations for preserving local songs. They generally identify themselves with a particular village, town or section of a city.
(2) They are amateur groups with no thought of pecuniary benefit. There are occasional exceptions, however. The Gōshū Ondo Hozonkai of Shiga Prefecture, although born of local pride, by the mid-1980s also served as a booking agency to provide singers for Bon dances, tourist entertainment and other events. This is perhaps inevitable in cases where, as with 'Gōshū Ondo', a song is popular over a large region.
(3) They tend toward conservatism, resisting change in music, lyrics, dances, costumes, etc. – but with exceptions. When change does occur, the *hozonkai* will want to be in control of it. This is one point at which clashes may arise between *hozonkai* and urban professional performers.
(4) The members are often very old. Many *hozonkai* were formed in the 1950s or 1960s in an attempt to revive village traditions which had lapsed during the 1930s and 1940s. The teachers thus tended to be quite elderly. As noted in §5.2, it is difficult to generate enthusiasm among the younger generation for local folk songs. It is far easier to attract them when a lively dance is involved.
(5) Members commonly hope that their beloved song(s) will achieve national prominence. Many *hozonkai* charters stress the duty to strive to propagate and diffuse (*fukyū*) the song. More than once, when visiting with the members of a *hozonkai* for a little-known song, I have been asked to encourage my acquaintances among urban professionals to adopt the song, guaranteeing it a wide currency. At the same time, members

frequently complain about the way professional singers inevitably alter their songs in some way. This dilemma is discussed in §5.6.

Another perspective on these matters emerges when one asks individual members why they joined the organization. The most common reasons are as follows.

(1) They feel they must contribute to the preservation of their *local* tradition. The word 'local' emerges again; it is a matter of their village *against* the rest of Japan – not against the West. (Village pressure sometimes forces people to join.) This reason is least often given by the younger generation, but it is becoming more common as more young folk are moving back from the cities to their rural homes (the 'U-turn phenomenon' mentioned in §5.6).
(2) Without conscious thought about 'tradition', they join because the song links them with their youth, now remembered fondly, and with what now seems like the simpler, more romantic life of the past. Less consciously in most cases, participation serves to validate their life experiences in the face of apathy or disrespect by the young.
(3) They join because it is fun (*tanoshii*). This is the most common reason given by younger members, and perhaps the only motive that will keep the music truly alive. Even this motivation, however, is no guarantee of creativity: many singers of 'Esashi Oiwake' began to sing because it was a challenge, and fun, to try to sing this difficult song exactly as taught.

Clearly the effects of *hozonkai* activities on folk song transmission are varied. In the case of 'Iso Bushi' and 'Esashi Oiwake', the teaching methods ensure little change even in the smallest details of performance. This is further guaranteed by the National Competitions held annually by both groups (§5.5): the judges penalize divergence from the norm, musically or textually. By contrast, the Preservation Societies for 'Etchū Owara Bushi' (see Takami 1981) and 'Yasugi Bushi' actually encourage individual creativity. Smaller *hozonkai*, like the Sakamoto and Bouchi groups, generally pay little attention to such concerns: they do not hold contests, nor judge, nor issue proficiency licences. There is variation among individual performances by different singers or even by the same singer, whether intentionally or accidentally.

Still, the nature of a *hozonkai* is basically conservative. Even 'Yasugi Bushi' cannot be varied beyond certain (or rather, uncertain) limits without ceasing to be 'Yasugi Bushi'. Furthermore, certain songs have been designated as Important Intangible (Folk) Cultural Properties by federal or local governments, from which moment their alteration is generally considered officially forbidden. Certainly the trend in recent decades is away from improvisation: influence from both traditional classical music and Western music has valorized correctness and relative invariance. And yet we have seen several examples of innovation at odds with the seemingly intransigent word 'preservation'. Some people even state that it is necessary to change a song in order to preserve it. Whey then do such groups call themselves 'preservation societies'?

Originally, as described above, the notion of *hozon* seems to have been associated with the plastic arts, gradually transferring less appropriately into the performing arts. Today, groups often adopt the appellation with little concern for the lexical meaning of the term. It is not a word consciously pulled out of a dictionary to describe a group's philosophy, but one floating freely through Japanese society in association with a particular type of organization, to be adopted by groups who perceive their activities as similar to those organizations.

There is one other major factor promoting the use of this term: local and national governments actively encourage it. This is discussed in §5.6.[11]

5.5 Local single-song contests

A phenomenon linked to *hozonkai* is the proliferation of local single-song contests. In Chapters 3 and 4 we learned that contests devoted solely to versions of 'Oiwake Bushi', or even to 'Esashi Oiwake' alone, were held in Esashi, in Tokyo and elsewhere early in the twentieth century; that multi-song contests were held in various parts of Japan after 1920, although 'Esashi Oiwake' still often predominated even in the 1930s; that national-level *min'yō* contests became common starting in 1948 with the NHK national radio competition, which included a *min'yō* division; that current national contests are sponsored by the media and major *min'yō* organizations.

The word 'national' above refers to contests in which *min'yō* from all over Japan could be sung. In this section we focus on what I am calling 'local single-song contests'; though contestants from anywhere (even from abroad) may enter, these are 'local' because they are held in the putative native place of the single song which all contestants must perform. They are generally called *zenkoku taikai*, 'national contests', but distinguished from multi-song contests by a single song's title preceding those two words.

The late 1970s *min'yō* boom triggered a sudden and amazing proliferation of such local contests, on the model of those for 'Esashi Oiwake' and 'Yasugi Bushi'. Researcher Kojima Tomiko had counted over one hundred by 1988 (pers. comm.), as opposed to a handful before the boom. The list of eighty-three single-song contests in Table 5.1 below, shown in descending order of longevity, was compiled from a wide range of sources. Several dozen less publicized contests have surely been missed. The ordinal numbers shown apply to the 2007 contests; the 'Yasugi Bushi' contest began in some form before the Second World War, but *hozonkai* officials are not sure of the date and so do not affix a number.

Most contests award prizes only for singing, but a few include a dance section, and the 'Yasugi Bushi' contest additionally rewards the best performers of shamisen, drums (uniquely for *min'yō*, the *kotsuzumi* and *ōtsuzumi* are

Table 5.1. Single-song national contests

??th Yasugi Bushi	22nd Nanbu Ushioi Uta
60th Etchū Owara	22nd Oki Shigesa Bushi
57th [Jōhana] Mugiya Bushi	21st Shanshan Uma Dōchū Uta
45th Esashi Oiwake	21st Otachizake
29th Komuro Bushi	21st Izumozaki Okesa
28th Iso Bushi	20th Hyūga Kobiki Uta
26th Tōkamachi Kouta	20th Akita Funakata Bushi
25th Seichō Kariboshi-kiri Uta	20th Shizuoka Chakkiri Bushi
25th Sawauchi Jinku	19th Tankai Bushi
25th Sansa Shigure	19th Noto Mugiya Bushi
25th Mogamigawa Funauta	19th Nanbu Tawaratsumi Uta
25th Ajigasawa Jinku	19th Dōnan Kudoki [Bushi]
24th Yame Chaya Uta	19th Akita Obako [Bushi]
24th Tokachi Umauta	18th Sōma Nagareyama
24th Seichō Mogamigawa Funauta	18th Seichō Echigo Oiwake
	18th Nanbu Uma no Uta
24th Honjō Oiwake	18th Iwamuro Jinku
24th Echigo Oiwake	18th Akita Oiwake
23rd Yamanaka Bushi	17th Kahoku Chayama Uta
23rd Shinjō Bushi	17th Ishikarigawa Nagashi Bushi
23rd Owase Bushi	
23rd Nikkō Yamauta	17th Enkoro Bushi
23rd Hietsuki Bushi	17th Chōja no Yama
23rd Hakone Magouta	16th Suzuka Magouta
23rd Aki no Yamauta	16th Shirahama Ondo
23rd Aizu Bandai-san	16th Okazaki Gomangoku
22nd Sotoyama Bushi	16th Nagaoka Jinku
22nd Shimotsui Bushi	15th Yodogawa Sanjukkoku-bune Funauta
22nd Obonai Bushi	

(continued)

Table 5.1. Continued

15th Komoro Magouta	10th Seichō Hakata Bushi
15th Hyūga Taue Uta	10th Kesenzaka
15th Kinu no Sendō Uta	10th Kariboshi-kiri Uta (Nasu Bushi)
15th Hokkai Bon Uta	
14th Tsugaru Yamauta	9th Ryōtsu Jinku
14th Seichō Yoneyama Jinku	9th Hakata Bushi
13th Ashio Sekitō Bushi	7th Sado Okesa
12th Tabaruzaka	7th Misaki Jinku & Danchone Bushi
12th Sasayama Kobiki Uta	7th Nanbu Yoshare
12th Kumagawa Funauta	5th Iyo Bushi
12th Akita Ohara Bushi	
12th Akita Kusakari Uta	4th O-Natsu Seijūrō (Sugegasa Bushi)
11th Akita Magouta	3rd Nanbu Umakata Bushi
10th [Sano no] Koina Funauta	1st Natsu no Yamauta

used, and uniquely in Japanese music, they are played by one musician!). Many now have divisons for different age groups.

Three of these contests are for *shin-min'yō*, for three of the few 'new folk songs' that have effectively become traditional: 'Tōkamachi Kouta', 'Chakkiri Bushi' and 'Shirahama Ondo'.

The 'Esashi Oiwake' National Contest, long the most prominent single-song concours, has been held annually in Esashi since 1963, following on from various predecessors. In Esashi, one Saturday in September 1988, I watched 246 contestants each sing a single verse of 'Esashi Oiwake'; on Sunday the highest-rated fifty returned to vie for the national championship. They had been selected from among the 4,400 members of the Esashi Oiwake Kai's 122 branches all over Japan. Most had practiced for years at a local branch, with a teacher pointing out their mistakes on a gigantic copy of the official notation (Fig. 5.3). Instructional tapes are also available (e.g. R10, R36). For the twenty-sixth straight year since the contest's inception, the winner was from Hokkaido (sixteen from Esashi), to the consternation of the organizers, who feared accusations of parochialism or prejudice. To their relief, the streak was broken the next year with a winner from Iwate, but only two winners since then have been from outside Hokkaido (both from Akita). (A gender note: Only four of the first twenty-three winners were women, but fifteen of the next twenty-one.)[12]

Let us now contrast the natures of the contests associated with several famous songs, each organized by its local preservation society. In the case of 'Iso Bushi' and 'Esashi Oiwake' (whose contests I have attended), the teaching methods approved by the organizing bodies minimize change even in the smallest details of performance. Reflecting this, at the contest the judges penalize divergence from the norm. (Until the mid-1980s, judges in Esashi used a stopwatch to ensure that the verse lasted about 2'20'; ridicule forced abandonment of this practice.) This philosophy extends even to the texts: although there are dozens of verses to 'Iso Bushi', whose content does not require them to be sung in any fixed order, in fact well over 90 per cent of the contestants in the first competition in 1980 sang the same verse. Try to imagine listening, over an eight-hour period, to 227 people singing one verse each as similarly as possible, 220 of whom sing the same words:

Iso de meisho wa Ōarai-sama yo / matsu ga miemasu honobono to
Iso's famous site is Ōarai Shrine; / the pine tree is visible faintly, in the distance.

The 'Esashi Oiwake' competition shows only slightly more textual variety.

The 'Yasugi Bushi' National Contest differs greatly (Izumo Ainosuke III, pers. comm.). More scope is given to creativity: singers may win points and attract interest according to how they improvise on the basic melody. The accompanists vary their parts and must match the timing of the singer. Even greater encouragement of creativity is found in singing 'Etchū Owara Bushi' (see Takami 1981). The 'Sawauchi Jinku' contest, while not stressing creativity and improvisation *per se*, allows varied interpretations of any of three quite different versions of the song.

Sasaki Motoharu and Izumo Ainosuke III, leading exponents of 'Esashi Oiwake' and 'Yasugi Bushi' respectively, met for the first time during a 1980 concert tour of northern Japan, for which I was a guest performer. When I drew them into conversation about the different degrees of creativity expected at their respective contests, they were startled to discover the contrast: both took as natural the situation most familiar to them. In fact, however, the relative invariance expected for 'Esashi Oiwake' is now much more typical.

As single-song contests have proliferated, rivalries between communities recall Esashi's early days as well as the rivalries of *hozonkai* (see §5.4.3, '(Motouta) Kaigara Bushi'). In 1983 a national contest for the renowned boatmen's song 'Mogamigawa Funauta' was begun in Higashine City in Yamagata. The following year, nearby Ōe Town began its own contest for the same song, asserting its primacy by prefixing the word 'Authentic' (*seichō*) to its contest's title (*Gekkan Min'yō* Sept 1988: 38–9). Similarly, Nishi-Niigata City (Niigata Pref.) began its contest for 'Echigo Oiwake' (a relative of 'Esashi Oiwake') in 1984; six years later, Kashiwazaki City launched its own contest for 'Seichō Echigo Oiwake'.

In such cases, local pride is as important a stimulus for establishing contests as is attracting tourists, but the latter is also generally a clearly acknowledged aim. Ōe's town website states: 'The Seichō Mogamigawa Funauta National Contest [is intended to] transmit the *seichō* to future generations, and to increase the fame of Ōe Town.' The rival Higashine contest's purpose, says the city Tourism and Commerce Association, is: 'through "Mogamigawa Funauta", to introduce Higashine City nationwide, and to encourage singing of *min'yō* '.[13] In 2004 Himeji City (Hyōgo Pref.) launched the 'O-Natsu Seijūrō (Sugegasa Bushi)' concours; already attracting hordes of visitors to see perhaps Japan's most famous castle, surely Himeji was motivated partly by local pride.

But such contests and the resultant publicity can indeed have a major impact on tourism. Esashi does quite well by its song. Although the annual contest fills the hotels, perhaps more important is the Esashi Oiwake Kaikan, a municipal museum established in 1982. Visitors can hear recordings of famous past singers, watch live performances, see dioramas of the town's history, even have a lesson and receive a certificate of achievement. During the late 1980s, visitors to the museum numbered 50–60,000 annually. Had the participants in the 1909 meeting (§3.3.3) been able to foresee this development, they would have been delighted. By 2006, the number had dropped to a still significant 27,000 (pers. comm. from Mr Odajima of the museum office, 23 July 2007).

Many contest titles prefix a local place-name, especially for songs whose titles lack one. The prefecture name Shizuoka has been added in front of 'Chakkiri Bushi'; likewise, 'Shigesa Bushi' has acquired a prefix, Oki, the island which claims it. Those two songs are famous enough that the only purpose of adding the prefix must be local pride. Some contests have added such prefixes only belatedly. Toyama's famous 'Mugiya Bushi' has boasted a contest since 1951, but after the host town Jōhana was merged into the new, obscurely named Nanto City in 2004, with its identity hidden rather far down the new city's website, the prefix 'Jōhana' was added. We see here also a reaction to the recent nationwide rash of municipal mergers which are raising worries about local identity (Chapter 2, note 2). The 'Koina Funauta' contest (Tochigi Pref.) recently added the prefix Sano: that city, formed through mergers in 1943, was further enlarged in 2005, a fact celebrated by this addition.

But let us remember that most such contests were created by aficionados, not bureaucrats. Though Fukuoka City is the locus for national contests for both 'Hakata Bushi' and 'Seichō Hakata Bushi', the spokesperson for the two events was adamant (18 July 2007) that there are absolutely no links with tourism: both are sponsored by local *min'yō* groups for the purpose of finding the best singers of these songs. She noted their link with the Nihon Min'yō Kyōkai, whose aims centre purely around *min'yō*; their website makes no mention of tourism.

The 'Etchū Owara Bushi' contest is indeed now a tourist event, having been absorbed into Toyama City's 'Toyama Matsuri', a non-traditional festival. The

46th Matsuri in August 2006 included the 59th national contest, though limited to a half-day in duration – far shorter than other contests.[14] This is partly because local singers often prefer the less official, less publicized competition held just after the conclusion of the 'Kaze no Bon' festival that attracts some 200,000 people during the first three days of September. After those three days of street-dancing and singing, after the tourists have left, the locals may sing for themselves. (See also Takami 1981.)

Over the years, the structure of such contests has often evolved. In 1988, the 'Esashi Oiwake' contest was simply a two-day event featuring 246 undifferentiated contestants. In 2006 it spanned three days; the main contest had 223 entrants, but the 10th contest for the 'mature' (*jukunen*, over age sixty-five) had 127 and the 10th children's contest (through middle school) had fifty – a total of 400 competitors.

Ironically, the national contest for 'Sado Okesa' – one of Japan's best-known *min'yō* since the 1930s, which appears on nearly all sampler recordings and has inspired dozens of *enka* – began only in 2001. Nakamura Shigetoshi, head in 2003 of the Tatsunami-kai, the primary preservation society for 'Sado Okesa', felt that the contest was begun out of rivalry with a song of lesser prestige from the other side of Sado Island, 'Ryōtsu Jinku', whose own contest had been launched in 1999. Somehow, he said, they just never thought of it earlier (pers. comm. 3 September 2003). But Murata Mamoru (pers. comm. 22 May 2007) says that a previous attempt at a national 'Sado Okesa' contest was launched 'about thirty years ago', foundering after a few years. It collapsed, he feels, because any tourist could enter for a fee, regardless of skill, and thus good singers shunned the event. Not listed above, since it is not strictly a single-song contest, is the Zenkoku Okesa Taikai held in Niigata City, whose entrants may sing any of the hundred or more different 'Okesa' around Japan, including 'Sado Okesa', 'Izumozaki Okesa' and so forth.[15]

5.6 City vs. country

We noted above that it is now difficult to draw a line between rural and urban Japan in terms of values and aspirations. Television in particular has united all Japanese in a common culture with common expectations. Still, differences remain. The villages and small towns still preserve a sense of community, of neighbourhood. This was not uncommon in urban areas as well in the Edo period but is much weaker in large cities today. Also, outside of the big cities there is a weaker tendency to dress in the latest fashions; this is less an economic matter, it seems to me, than a sense of appropriateness to the mood of the place and to the work that one does. (This is changing rapidly, however.)

To alleviate urban overcrowding, the government has since the 1960s been encouraging migration back to the countryside. To make it attractive, they have stressed the virtues of rural life and of maintaining a sense of local identity. Phrases put in the service of this movement include *chihō no jidai* ('the age of the countryside'), *chiiki shakai* ('regional society') and of course *furusato* ('home town') (see further §6.2 and Robertson 1991). Attempts to make such out-migration attractive by encouraging the growth of local industry have only partly succeeded. Nevertheless, there has been a definite increase in the number of rural-born young people who, after a stay in one of the core cities for education or employment, decide to return to their home areas (the so-called U-turn phenomenon, *yū-tān genshō*) or to other rural areas (J-turn, *jē-tān*). The 1990s brought the I-turn phenomenon, urban natives abandoning their homes for the countryside. Talking to such migrants reveals that the decision was motivated in most cases by a preference for the human and natural environments of the periphery over those of the core. Local songs, dances and festivals are often cited by returnees as among the attractions of the countryside – further evidence of their continued significance in local identity.

Ever since the first professional folk singers appeared, the locals have been ambivalent towards them.[16] Residents of Esashi were proud to have their local song admired elsewhere, but many were upset when non-local performers achieved acclaim for singing 'Esashi Oiwake'. Local expressions of regret that after twenty-six years nobody from outside Hokkaido had ever won the national contest (previous section) were not always sincere. The battle between hamlet and village factions for control of the Deer Dance in Yanagawa (§5.2) is paralleled by the tension between local residents and urban professionals over *min'yō*. One early example involved Kouta Katsutarō, the first nationally famous folk-singing geisha (§3.4.1). Raised in Niigata Prefecture, she often recorded Niigata songs during the 1930s, gaining them national recognition. One of these was 'Sado Okesa'. By the time she recorded it, a preservation society on Sado Island maintained what it considered the standard version, suitable for group dancing; this featured a repeated flute melody independent of the vocal melody, and a full-bodied 'outdoor' vocal style **(CD3)**. Katsutarō had learned a somewhat different version in a geisha house; her performance used the small, geisha voice and gentle *kouta*-style shamisen accompaniment. When her recording became a nationwide hit, the *hozonkai* protested vigorously in the media that her version was incorrect. They even accused her of betraying her own home town. Katsutarō responded politely that she had every respect for the local version but saw no harm in offering her own variant.

It is not unusual today for professional singers to be thus rebuked upon returning to their old homes. Ōtsuka Fumio from Yamagata had made the local song 'Daikoku Mai' one of his standard numbers by 1980, but was sad to receive frequent local criticism that he had changed the song. Since there were already several versions locally, Ōtsuka explained he was bound to offend somebody even if he had copied one particular performance of one local version exactly. This is one defense commonly offered by professionals:

which version should they have chosen? Also, they complain that even a single *hozonkai* version is impossible to copy: it shows variation from performance to performance, because amateurs' lesser musical skills undermine their attempts at exact preservation. Since today's younger professionals have Western-influenced senses of pitch and rhythm, they tend to assume that local deviations from Western intervals or isochronous metres are errors due to the limitations of amateur singers and thus should not be imitated. Fortunately for the professionals, only a small minority of local residents make such complaints. (See also Chapter 1, note 26.)

Harada Naoyuki is one of many who desires a clear division between *min'yō* as music and as folklore. The latter should be left to the locals, to *hozonkai*, while professionals such as himself should be free to adopt a style intended for 'appreciation' (*kanshō*) without trying to be 'folksy' (*tsuchikusai*). He believes, in any case, that *hozonkai* do not succeed in preserving songs unchanged. The version of 'Iso Bushi' that he learned from the late Tanii Hōdō is different, he feels, from the one transmitted today by the *hozonkai* Tanii founded. Recall also Sasaki Motoharu's maintenance of a distinction of local and professional ways of singing 'Esashi Oiwake' (§4.5.2).

Since most urban professionals now perform *min'yō* from all over, rural styles are inevitably homogenized in the city to some degree. Dialect was an early casualty. After decades of emphasis on diffusing the standard language (as exemplified by NHK broadcasters), even some local-born people have difficulty singing in dialect. Even if they could, the near unintelligibility to outsiders of dialects from regions like Tsugaru and Kagoshima would limit diffusion of the songs. Around 1980, Yamamoto Kenji was one of the few younger singers on national television to maintain Tsugaru pronunciation, but this was partly a calculated decision to give him a unique selling point. The judges at contests and on the Kinkan show (§§4.8–9) look fondly on those who sing in dialect, but it is a losing battle. The locals themselves, insofar as they accept the migration of their songs to the city, likewise see little point in having outsiders try to imitate their dialect – since it would get mangled as much as a Texan would mangle Highland Scots. At the first 'Iso Bushi' national contest, one singer had a thick Tsugaru accent. The first word of the song, *iso*, sounded like *uso* in his pronunciation (meaning 'a lie' in standard language), but the judges still awarded him a prize. His friends, however, joked that he had sung not 'Iso Bushi' but 'Uso Bushi' – 'False Song'.

There are of course songs like 'Otemoyan' and 'Imogara Bokuto' which preserve dialect grammar and lexical items, sometimes for conscious effect, and countless songs contain occasional local expressions. These will generally be sung as transmitted. Lexical items are maintained; only pronunciation is not usually imitated.

The twentieth century also saw a tendency towards slight homogenization of styles of vocal ornamentation, tone colour and instrumental accompaniment. The early dominance of the *min'yō* world by northern performers encouraged a taste for flashier shamisen accompaniments and more dynamic vocal style.[17]

Thus, despite some local resistance, regional differences are fading in the city, in folk song as in other spheres of culture. People still, however, speak with conviction about personality differences among natives of different regions. This is usually called *kenjinsei* ('prefectural character'). Even in 1772, the song collection *Sanga chōchūka* was divided by provinces (*kuni*), with a brief description of local character before most sections (Sasano 1956: 301, 320, etc.). The characteristics attributed today are not consistent, but here are some examples: Tsugaru people express their minds, Nanbu people are close-mouthed, Kōchi people are heavy drinkers, Ibaragi people seem calm but can explode suddenly, Gunma women work hard and rule the roost, Fukuoka people are self-centred. Such traits are said to be reflected in the songs as well: Akita songs are sunny, Nanbu songs are dark and depressed. Accurate or not, such generalizations are occasionally invoked by teachers or judges as prescriptive criteria: 'It's an Akita song, so you must sing it with more liveliness.'

Another aspect of rural–urban interaction is the influence of agents of the scholarly community and the Cultural Affairs Agency (Bunkachō) of the Ministry of Education. In this case, rather than the locals trying to control change in the centre, it is the centre which is attempting to impose limits on local change. The mechanism of control is the coveted designation of Important Intangible Folk Cultural Property (the approved translation of Jūyō Mukei Minzoku Bunkazai), issued by the Cultural Affairs Agency to *minzoku geinō*: 237 had been so designated as of November 2005, with two or three added each year. No *min'yō* are designated just as songs: the handful included are all part of a larger designated event, e.g. the Bon dance songs collectively called 'Gujō Odori' or the rice-transplanting ritual songs of Hiroshima's Aki district.[18] Similar honours, more likely to include 'pure' *min'yō*, are offered by prefectural and local governments (ca. 1,600 and 5–6,000 designations respectively, according to Miyata Shigeyuki, 4 July 2007). At first the designation would be given to only one of a closely related family of performing arts, which led to fierce competition. To prevent such competition, the designation is now often shared among a group of tradition-bearing hamlets. One stipulation of designation was that the art must thenceforth remain immutable, which obviously led to conservatism in performance; this has been rethought due to an increasing distaste among scholars for mere preservationism, but change is still discouraged. Aside from tangible benefits (the right to apply for matching funds to maintain instruments or costumes, training of successors, etc.), the honour is such that the kind of possessiveness seen in the case of the Yanagawa Deer Dance may be accentuated.[19]

In Iwate in 1980, I heard a tale which demonstrates the potency of this governmental designation. A scholar from Tokyo visited a certain hamlet to reearch the history of the local Devil Sword Dance (*oni kenbai*), for this hamlet was purported to have the longest record of unbroken transmission. If this transmission could be proven, it would become a powerful factor in the Cultural Affairs Agency's decision on designation. While the scholar was there, a representative of a neighbouring hamlet suddenly appeared with a scroll which he said had recently been found in the attic of an old farmhouse. According to the scroll, *his* hamlet's Devil Sword Dance tradition was in fact the oldest of all. The scholar looked over the scroll, said 'That's interesting,' and went on with his research on the original hamlet's transmission. The person who told me this story is convinced that the scroll was a fake and that the scholar knew it. Whether it was a fake or not, my informant's belief in its spuriousness reflects the cutthroat competition which sometimes arises. (*Oni kenbai* received the coveted designation only in 1994, but it was applied to the entire local tradition rather than to the version of a specific village. Sasamori 1981 reports a similar case.)

Locals do not, however, always accord such respect to scholars from the city. Recall that the 'Esashi Oiwake' contest organizers invited prestigious urban-based scholars to serve as judges – but then disregarded their marks (§4.9).

To conclude, we return once again to Fujimoto Hideo (see end of §4.5.2). Despite teaching many of the most famous professional singers, and producing a collection of several hundred *min'yō* shamisen accompaniments widely used by professionals and amateurs alike, he preferred his *min'yō* classicized. Thus his student Harada Naoyuki told me of Fujimoto's insistence that the syllabic nasal in the word *han'ya* in the famous 'Kagoshima Han'ya Bushi' should be sung as *m* (as in many classical shamisen-vocal genres) rather than as the nasalized vowel found in speech and in all rural singing styles. Fujimoto confirmed this to me, saying that it was inelegant to leave your mouth open while producing a nasal, and also that a well-articulated *m* provided a much clearer rhythmic pulse (which is true). Virtually no local folk singer does this, however, as field recordings reveal. Fujimoto did accept my suggestion that the more rural *min'yō* should be sung as in the villages, that is, with the mouth wide open for the vowel *a*; for parlour *min'yō*, though, he expected a more closed mouth yielding a sound like 'aw', as in classical genres.

Fujimoto also felt free to re-arrange pre-existing local shamisen accompaniments without compunction. In the case of some northeastern pieces, he went so far as to change the tuning, which could create a startlingly different chordal drone effect. Thus 'Tawaratsumi Uta' (Aomori Pref.) was locally performed in *niagari* tuning, but he changed it to *honchōshi* because, he told me around 1980, this was the logically 'correct' tuning according to classical shamisen traditions. In his opinion, the locals were just wrong. Few professionals outside his own school have followed his lead.

Such an attitude extended to other instruments as well. Fujimoto was in charge of accompaniment for the contestants on the weekly Kinkan *min'yō* television show (§4.8.3); the percussionists and other musicians were answerable to him. When a local master of 'Shinodayama Bon Uta' (Osaka Pref.; §4.6.2) was to sing it as a contestant around 1978, he found, to his dismay and confusion, that the *taiko* player at the preliminary contest was playing a part totally unrelated to the local one. At his request, I sent my transcription of the correct part to the musicians in hopes that they might play it for the televised finals. For whatever reasons – aesthetic judgement, lack of time, distrust of the foreign scholar – they stuck to their earlier version.

All of this is to say that many professional folk musicians have a limited interest in tradition and authenticity. There is, they feel, no point in following local practice if the local versions lack quality by their self-imposed standards. Let the locals preserve their versions: leave professional performance to the professionals.

5.7 Tradition, identity, authenticity

Terms such as tradition and authenticity have featured frequently above. An entire book or chapter could usefully be devoted to these concepts and their usage in the *min'yō* world, along with other terms such as identity and nostalgia, but space does not permit. Here I consider these concepts only briefly with reference specifically to *min'yō*, neglecting the growing body of literature on them worldwide. Note that all four of the concepts mentioned attract more conscious attention now simply because of the greater pace and scope of change in the modern era.[20]

Moeran wrote in 1981 that the Japanese were 'going through a phase of what has been called a 'tradition cult' (*dentō sūhai*), of which governmental designation of Important Cultural Properties was just one aspect (1981: 36). But Japan has always worshipped tradition, even before the word was in common use. This 'tradition cult' will surely continue to be important in the foreseeable future, precisely because of its role in balancing the negative effects of modernization on social organization and life-style.

Many urban Japanese, partly through the mediation of the folklorist Yanagita Kunio (§1.3) and subsequent like-minded scholars, consider the essence of traditional Japan to reside in rural society. Even in 1979, by which time only a small minority of the populace was engaged in agriculture, the respected folklorist Tanigawa Ken'ichi could insist: '[T]o understand Japan, it is essential to understand the world view of . . . the most representative Japanese . . . farmers, fishers, hunters and artisans' (1979: 2). This belief forms a keystone in the debates about *nihonjin-ron*, 'theories of Japaneseness'.

Among *min'yō* performers, pursuit of tradition takes various forms. The professional singer Ozawa Chigetsu (b. 1926) is from Saitama Prefecture, until recently a famous barley-growing district. Ozawa felt that he would only really get to the heart of a barley-threshing song if he gained some experience growing barley. To that end, he and some friends were planning in 1979 to cultivate a small field and follow the crop from ploughing to threshing. This sort of attitude is a direct outgrowth of the folklorists' stress on authenticity and on *min'yō* as a part of daily life. Similarly, in §1.7.1 we found that the *fōku songu* 'god' Okabayashi Nobuyasu spent a spell as a rice farmer in order to re-orient his career towards a more traditional ethos partaking of aspects of *min'yō*.[21]

A rather different example is seen in the performance of a dance and song called 'Kokiriko (Bushi)' in Toyama Prefecture. It survives in an area supposedly settled by fleeing Heike warriors, the losers in the epic battles of the twelfth century. (Many villages claim such origins, although proof is elusive.) Some time in the twentieth century the local preservation society, apparently seeking to buttress this claim, adopted costumes in the style of the twelfth century. This has now become an 'invented tradition', and many local people believe this performance style to be a direct inheritance from ancient times. This is disproved by drawings and descriptions of the dance from the years around 1800 (*Kikan Hōgaku* 1977). Traditions can form with startling rapidity in Japan, as seen in some of the *hozonkai* described in §5.4.

These conscious attempts to reforge the link between a song and its former sociohistorical context should be distinguished from the case of Itō Moyo (§2.3). When singing a paddy-weeding song, even on stage, she would go through the motions of weed-pulling; otherwise, she said, she couldn't get into the rhythm. Despite Itō's professed respect for tradition, she was not searching for a 'traditional' experience which she had never had, as Ozawa Chigetsu was, nor for authenticity for its own sake. To her, the weeding song retained powerful and necessary links with its traditional context, familiar to her through personal experience; to neglect that context would impoverish the song. On the other hand, she did actively seek out such experiences because of her love of such songs.

A desire for authenticity informs Sasaki Motoharu's choice of his stage version of the work song 'Sōran Bushi' (R31 under title 'Okiage Sōran Bushi'). He feels that all versions should begin with the vocable ē, to reflect the original need to coordinate the start of the work action (pers. comm. September 1988). And yet almost no professionals follow this practice, nor do most *hozonkai* versions.

Consider finally Kabasawa Yoshikatsu (1899–1977). As a child in Gumma Prefecture, he often worked as a pack-horse driver (*umakata*), absorbing the song now known as 'Jōshū Magouta', 'Horse-driver's Song from Jōshū'. Later he studied *min'yō* formally with various renowned teachers. As the first and primary purveyor of 'Jōshū Magouta' in the *min'yō* world, Kabasawa became a stickler for authenticity, as various incidents reveal (Takeuchi Tsutomu, pers. comm.). Around 1965, he became incensed with a *min'yō* percussionist whose job it was to shake the horse-bells (*suzu*) to accompany the song, giving the illusion that a horse was present: the performer could not capture the correct timing (*ma*). Kabasawa therefore stepped out the correct rhythm with his feet for the player to follow. His sense of authenticity perhaps led him to extremes, as when he stipulated (says Takeuchi) that the pellet inside each bell must roll exactly 2.5 times per shake. When making a studio recording, he held both the bells and a horse's bridle (devoid of horse), and for further inspiration looked at a photo of a horse and driver on a mountain road. Late in his career – and long after he had last actually worked as a horse-driver – he recorded the song with a real horse (perhaps at Takeuchi's urging); between lines of the song (and the horse's neighs), he can be heard encouraging and soothing the animal **(CD21)**.

Tradition and personal identity are sometimes explicitly linked. In §4.3.2 we listed some of the reasons why people start studying *min'yō*. Another reason occasionally offered is: 'Because I'm Japanese.' The speaker may continue: 'and *min'yō* is a traditional Japanese music'. This explanation is more frequent among young adults, who through some turn of events may suddenly come one day to fear for their identity. They may then seek it in *min'yō* (or certain other traditional arts). After performing in public in Japan, I was occasionally contacted by perfect strangers who would announce their embarrassment that they, although Japanese, could not sing *min'yō* – 'our traditional music' – as well as I. They would often then promise to start learning immediately. (Of course, I don't know whether they did.) A fundamental tenet held with pride by most Japanese (though waning with globalization) is that no foreigner can ever master the intricacies of the 'unique' Japanese culture; thus a foreigner's progress at one of the traditional arts may occasionally act as a stimulus to native participation.

A town official in Kitakami City (Iwate Pref.) introduced a stage performance of the local Deer Dance (*shishi odori*) in 1980: 'When I hear the cymbals and drum [of the "Deer Dance"], in my heart I remember what I had forgotten: Ah, I'm a Japanese after all (*ā nihonjin da nā*).'

Nonetheless, tradition, Japanese identity, nostalgia and local pride are only occasionally primary factors in stimulating participation in traditional performing arts. In interviews with several dozen young performers (ages approximately ten to thirty) of the Devil Sword Dance (*oni kenbai*) and Deer Dance genres of Iwate around 1979, only one mentioned respect for tradition as his prime motivation; all others cited the lack of other entertainments in their villages and the fun of getting together with friends.

Turning to authenticity: Japanese social scientists, and even some *min'yō* fans, may use the English word in Japanese pronunciation (*ōsentishitii*) and discuss the concept much as Western scholars do. One native equivalent is *shōshin shōmei*, 'the real thing, the genuine article', as in *shōshin shōmei no baka*, 'a confirmed fool', but this is a scholarly Sinate term. The native word *honmono* meaning 'real thing' is used in casual speech. In the *min'yō* world, the terms most employed are specifically musical: the native *motouta*, 'original song', and the Sinate *seichō*, 'correct melody' (§§1.5, 3.3.3, 3.4.3.1, 5.4.3–5, Appendix 3).

As seen above, often *seichō* is just a word to mobilize when claiming the superiority of your version of a song over a rival's. But the term is not limited to unaccompanied work songs and the like. 'Kariboshi-kiri Uta' (Miyazaki Pref.), a grass-harvesting song in the *miyako-bushi* mode, was selected for teaching to all third-year middle school students in the early 1970s (§7.5). In its home district, the *miyako-bushi*-mode version was paralleled by another in the *ritsu* mode (or indeed with intervals intermediate between the two). By the 1980s this *ritsu* variant had also become widely appreciated in the *min'yō* world. To distinguish it from the earlier-known version, its title often prefixed the word 'Seichō' or changed 'Uta' to 'Motouta'. It was thus called when sung in the 1990s Nihon Min'yō Kyōkai national contests (§4.6.1), and since 1983 it is this version that has been the subject of a local single-song contest. There is no real evidence that the *ritsu* version is the older one, but, as so often, the variant that surfaces second is able to appropriate the magic words *seichō* 'authentic' and *motouta* 'original song'. Perhaps the singer who made this version familiar was hoping to claim an advantage. The way these terms are used reveals that authenticity is positively valued, whatever the problems in defining and proving it. Perhaps in the future some newly discovered *min'yō* will launch a pre-emptive strike by using one of these terms from the beginning, before any variant exists!

Interestingly, both versions of 'Kariboshi-kiri Uta' are today virtually never heard without shakuhachi accompaniment. This deviation from the original work context does not reduce the 'authenticity' of the *ritsu* version: it is an authenticity of melody, not of overall performance practice. By contrast, those Japanese who use the English term 'authenticity' in discussions of *min'yō* tend to be less concerned with which version of a song is older but focus more on factors such as context, function, instrumentation and vocal quality (preferring the folksy *tsuchikusai* voice). These are the people who are likely to complain that there are no real *min'yō* anymore. They bemoan the relocation of both folk song and *minzoku geinō* to the stage and the resultant accommodations made to the audience.

Television companies also strive, on occasion, to present a simulacrum of authenticity. In 1979 in Kuryūzawa, Iwate Prefecture (§5.2), a local television crew placed a group of *min'yō* performers, fully dressed in formal stage garb, incongruously in front of a barn, with a row of daffodils conveniently re-located (Fig. 5.4). Then they spread a team of *shishi odori* dancers up along a terraced agricultural hillside, again with daffodils in place, and again inappropriately (Fig. 5.5). Authentic or not, the result is somehow more enjoyable than a studio shot.

5.8 Summary

This chapter has dealt with folk song in modern 'peripheral' Japan. Even as the villager's social and economic universe expands, folk song and the folk performing arts still play an important role in creating and supporting community identity. Indeed, this role may even have been intensified by modernization. Rivalries may now occur between the hamlet and the larger administrative village or town in which it is contained, sometimes expressed in the organization of folk performance. Also, there is continuing ambivalence about artistic relations with the outside (as seen with 'Esashi Oiwake' in Chapter 3): villagers are proud when a local song is adopted by the urban professionals but bitter when the urban version then attracts more attention than the local version. Thus, outside interest often incites local concern as well.

The distinction between elite music and community music, raised in Chapter 2, has less significance in the modern village, partly because class consciousness in general has diminished with Japan's rising prosperity. Housewives' Associations may sponsor music lessons for members, including both koto music and *min'yō* without discrimination.

The Young Men's Associations may still sponsor Bon dances, and some ceremonial music and dance is still in the hands of Shrine Guilds. However, the most distinctive and significant organs of folk music transmission in the modern villages are preservation societies (*hozonkai*). Chiefly a post-war phenomenon, *hozonkai* are almost all small local amateur groups, often dedicated to 'preserving' a single local song or *minzoku geinō*, with a very high median age of membership. Traditional performance practice is largely maintained, in conscious opposition to urban *min'yō* trends. Older members in particular find in *hozonkai* participation an important way of validating their life experiences: the group reaffirms the value of traditional lifeways which have been redefined as 'old-fashioned' by the young. *Hozonkai* generally resist changes in the songs they transmit, although there is considerable variation in their degree of success. Sometimes a group will even maintain the necessity of introducing changes in a song and its performance precisely to facilitate its preservation. *Hozonkai* also often organize locally-held national contests for the single song they 'preserve'; local government sees these as of touristic and publicity value.

Despite a general homogenization of Japanese culture via the media and education, there are still conflicts between city and country over matters of cultural style, including the performance of *min'yō*. But the conflict is often really about control and possession rather than stylistic preferences *per se*. In general, local musical and linguistic differences are fading from the *min'yō* world, especially in the city. However, some teachers and scholars do stress the importance of singing songs from one's own region in order to be fully able to capture the intended style. The coveted governmental designation Important Intangible Cultural Property is used as a lever to encourage maintenance of traditional styles in the countryside.

Concepts such as tradition, authenticity and identity are often invoked by villagers, urban professionals, scholars, officials and interested amateurs in evaluating *min'yō*.

NOTES

1. Ezashi is now officially pronounced Esashi, though written with different characters than the Hokkaido home of 'Esashi Oiwake'.

2. www.bunka.pref.iwate.jp/dentou/kyodo/list/sisi.html

3. www.pref.iwate.jp/~hp2518/kakubu/chiiki/chiikidukuri/jouhousite/jirei/bunnk-ageijutu/kanaturyuu/kanaturyu.html

4. Thus in Okinawa City the Bon dances locally called *eisā* are transmitted proudly within rival neighbourhoods, but for example the Sonda group, under that neighbourhood name, accepts members from anywhere to maintain its strength.

5. Exceptions include the Preservation Hall Jazz Band and the Society for the Preservation of Barber Shop Quartet Singing in America (SPBSQSA). There are doubtless also exceptions to the generalizations that follow among unified ethnic minority communities in the United States.

6. I have found no studies tracing the history of the *hozonkai* phenomenon; one must research each organization separately. Therefore, this is not a thorough survey. I have discovered only one *hozonkai* predating the two groups described just below: the Aikawa Ondo Hozonkai on Sado Island (Niigata Pref.), which was formed in 1909 but died within two years (Kikuchi 1980: 58). A Kiso Bushi Hozonkai existed by 1920 (Takeuchi 1974: 69).

7. At a house-raising ceremony I attended, a representative of the construction company (not from this *hozonkai*) sang 'Kiyari Kuzushi', a popular geisha-style adaptation of a true *kiyari*. When I related this to the *hozonkai* members, they nodded ruefully.

8. Collinson reported (1966: 69) that, though the waulking of cloth had died out in the Hebrides decades earlier, the waulking songs often survive, preserved by groups of women young and old as a social activity. Since the 1920s in some villages, a growing consciousness of the songs' folkloric value has also stimulated performance. To keep the rhythm, the women imitate the motions of waulking, using scarves or pieces of cloth (but eschewing the animal urine originally used in treating the cloth).

9. The notion of a certain dance or music being 'imposed from above' as a simple form of social control is common in Japanese folk music history. For example, during the early eighteenth century, the administrator of what is now the Tokyo region encouraged the spread of the festival music *kasai-bayashi* to prevent the growth of juvenile delinquency – to 'keep the kids off the streets.' As one incentive, local representatives were selected to parade before the shogun as part of the Kanda Festival (Honda 1964: 19). As noted in §3.4.3.1, some observers also feel that 'new folk songs' such as the textile factory song 'Suzaka Kouta' were commissioned by the 'bosses' to keep the workers docile.

10. Down to thirty-one nights in 2007 (www.gujohachiman.com/kanko/gujo_odori_e.htm).

11. Bohlman's distinction between the 'small-group canon' and the 'mediated canon' (1988: 111ff) might apply here. The 'small group' is 'a buttress of continued differentiation within modernized societies. Thus, its canon may well emerge as a response to modernization and as a means of emphasizing more intimate cultural expression . . .' (ibid.: 112). This could apply to *hozonkai*. The 'mediated canon' (ibid.: 114) might correspond to the nationwide *min'yō* world (although Bohlman's examples have more cultural and ethnic diversity).

12. Statistical information gathered from www.hokkaido-esashi.jp.

13. www.town.oe.yamagata.jp/event/funautataikai/index.html, and www.yamagatakanko.com/cgi/event.cgi?m=9&a=&id=410

14. The festival itself also had the sub-title 'Yosakoi Toyama'; see §7.4.2 regarding the spread and localization of 'Yosakoi' festivals.

15. Sado as a whole knows the drawing power of its *min'yō*. The Hotel Hirane in Sado's Hiranesaki hot springs area has lyrics to four local songs printed on their chopsticks wrappers: 'Sado Okesa', 'Aikawa Ondo', 'Aikawa Jinku' and 'Senkoba Okesa'. Similar devices occur in many tourist regions.

16. The phenomena discussed in this section remind us of the urban–rural struggle for control of *jarocho* music in Mexico (Stigberg 1978), to cite one of many possible parallels.

17. Kakinoki Gorō has used the melograph to try to demonstrate concretely the differences between northern and western ornamentation (*kobushi*). Such efforts will eventually yield very interesting results, although the value of his 1981 article (and versions of it) is limited by using only two informants who are likely atypical.

18. For a list to 1995, see Thornbury 1997 appendix; fuller details appear, mostly in Japanese, on the website of the Ministry of Education (www.mext.go.jp).

19. Note that 'folk' intangible properties are distinguished from non-folk (e.g. Kabuki) by insertion of the word *minzoku*. All folk designations are given to groups, whereas most non-folk go to individuals, so-called Human National Treasures.

20. Discussions of these concepts with specific reference to Japan, though not to *min'yō*, can be found in Ivy 1995 and in many chapters of Vlastos 1998.

21. Parallels abound elsewhere as well. Pete Seeger, mid-twentieth-century left-wing US folk singer, strove to overcome his upper-class background through his clothes and language, even moving from New York City to the countryside and building a log cabin (Filene 2000: 201ff.).

CHAPTER 6

AT THE EDGES OF THE 'FOLK SONG WORLD'

□

6.1 Introduction

Chapters 4 and 5 described the principal activities and values relating to the performance of traditional folk song in present-day Japan. We saw that the urban professional singing tradition is basically conservative in its choice of material, so that few recent 'new folk songs' are taught to students, heard at contests, or featured on television programmes (further confirmed below). The 'home town' tradition represented primarily by the activities of preservation societies is likewise conservative at heart, with occasional exceptions. True, classical composers have sometimes drawn on *min'yō*, and a few pop or *fōku* singers have performed new arrangements, as indeed have some *min'yō* singers, but these activities are seen as on the fringes or beyond the edges of the *min'yō-kai* (folk song world).

We have also introduced the role of folk song in maintaining community identity and creating self-esteem. Through local performing arts traditions, sociogeographical communities are reaffirmed. In some cases, as with the elderly barley threshers of the Bouchi Uta Hozonkai (§5.4.4), groups of individuals within a community can validate collectively their life experiences in the face of a modern society that seems to have rejected their traditions. People lost in the anomie of urban society, denied even the comfort of the sense of belonging that accrues from employment in a large modern business firm, may discover the joys of membership in a *min'yō* school, with its familistic structure.

In the above cases, even when the national media are involved, the frame of reference is decidedly narrow geographically. The founders of the Bouchi Uta Hozonkai, for example, were concerned with preserving a *local* tradition. Although the threat to that tradition was occasionally identified in universal terms – one *hozonkai* official defined it precisely as 'modernization' (*gendaika*)

– the real 'enemy', the target of their activities, was the growing lack of interest within the local community itself and among the younger generation in particular. As reiterated often above, it is very rare for anyone aside from scholars and the occasional folk song teacher to single out Westernization as a problem to be dealt with.

At the same time, Japan today is a modern nation-state solidly ensconced in the international community. It would thus be surprising if the local folk world was not at some stage directly affected by two new reference communities: Japan and the world. We have had many glimpses of this in earlier chapters: in the role of *min'yō* in tourism (mostly domestic), the often national (but rarely international) reach of the broadcast and recording industries' involvement with *min'yō*, and so forth.

In the present chapter we examine several disparate examples in which folk song, quintessentially a local phenomenon, takes on wider resonances, whether through the political concerns of central government, the needs of new communities, the commercial interests of the recording companies, the ideological stance of international socialism, or the steadily Westernizing (if rarely globalizing) musical tastes of today's Japanese. Distinguishing some of these from topics described in other chapters is largely a presentational convenience: amidst much overlapping, lines can rarely be clearly drawn.

6.2 *Min'yō*, *furusato* and nostalgia

The word *furusato* – 'old village', implying one's 'old country home' – has been encountered frequently throughout this book, indeed featuring in our opening quotation. That this word carries a deep emotional resonance is both cause and result of its frequent employment by social philosophers, politicians, authors, poets, lyricists, recording companies and the media in general. But the *concept* and its emotional dimensions would have arisen in the twentieth century even without the *word*. Nostalgia for rural lifeways perhaps never actually experienced, and for ways of relating to other people that are quite different from those in the modern city, is surely an inevitable product of rapid urbanization for many people. But Japan, more than most modernizing countries, has, shall we say, wallowed in this nostalgia, drawing various kinds of strength and value from it, often (and of most interest to us) with reference to *min'yō* and *minzoku geinō*. Let us then begin this chapter with a general discussion of *furusato*. This will consist more of a series of citations, anecdotes and mini-case studies than a developed narrative.[1]

Furusato is a native Japanese word, usually written in the *hiragana* phonetic syllabary, and thus has stronger nativist resonances than its Sino-Japanese ideographic synonym *kokyō* (故郷), which is however often read *furusato*, ignoring its official pronunciation.[2] By around 1900 *furusato* was beginning to assume its current significance as a symbol of pre-modern, pre-Western, quintessentially Japanese lifeways, to be held up as both a moral model and a nostalgic comfort. In the *furusato*, human relations are assumed to have been ideal and thus a perfect model for building an 'imagined community' (Anderson 1983) at any level: local community, city, prefecture, the nation (even the world?). The ideal model *furusato* is not any specific place.

One significant early use was in the song 'Furusato' (written 故郷), composed for the sixth volume of government-issued books of 'primary-school songs' (*shōgaku shōka*) (1914). Since every child in Japan sang such songs, they became nostalgic and remain so today; this one still appears often in government-approved music textbooks. Its lyrics (by Takano Tatsuyuki, also a collector of *min'yō* texts) employ the somewhat stiff literary Japanese favoured for educational songs, yet its contents evoke the *furusato* that every child must imagine: 'I used to chase rabbits on that mountain / I used to catch small carp in that river / I still dream of it / It's hard to forget one's *furusato*.' The music is in a major key in 3/4 metre: even by 1914, for the sort of Westernized composers employed to produce songs for an over-Westernized school system, these musical features were felt to capture idyllic, nostalgic emotions better than traditional musical elements.

In 1933, we learned in §3.4.3.1, the literary critic Kobayashi Hideo claimed that the nostalgia of Tokyo natives like himself for a *furusato* was misplaced, since the imagined village harmony had never existed. Yet he felt that literature and 'new folk songs' might nonetheless create such a convincing image of that fictional world that comfort could be drawn from those art forms. (Indeed, it might be safer to take comfort from such depictions and avoid the disillusionment of living in an actual village!) Pre-war *shin-min'yō* fulfilled this function; in the next two sections we will find that more recent *shin-min'yō* aim to do the same, with the *furusato* now often not identified via a particular local place-name in a song's title but expanded to encompass all of Japan.

In 1977, the record-sales manual quoted in Appendix 3 linked *min'yō* directly with singers from the *furusato*: 'Recently . . . the worship of artificial, mechanically produced things is fading, and a yearning for natural and human things has begun to blossom. Against this background, the songs of villagers (*furusato-bito*) – *min'yō* – have suddenly been re-assessed and a "boom" has developed' (Anon. 1977).

It must be stressed that not all Japanese have accepted the pressure to feel a hankering for some real or imagined *furusato* (perhaps because they have not been involved with *min'yō*!), but the trope is well recognized even by those who resist its power. The 1995 Japanese animated film *Mimi o Sumaseba* (*Whisper of the Heart*), based on a comic book story of the same title, has as its theme song John Denver's US hit 'Take Me Home, Country Roads', which also appears in the film in Japanese translation under the title 'Kokyō ni Kaeritai' ('I Want to Go Back to My *Kokyō*'). The fourteen-year-old heroine, Shizuku, jokes with a friend about changing 'country roads' to 'concrete roads' to reflect modern reality in the Tama 'new town' where they live in the Tokyo suburbs. An on-line study guide, in Japanese and computer-generated English, devotes over a thousand words to discussing 'What does "home town" mean for Shizuku?'[3] This quotes her as saying that, while her father's *furusato* is in distant Niigata, she has only this new town with no tradition and no distinctive culture. The anonymous author of the study guide predicts that, given rapid technological and social change, in ten years Shizuku will see *furusato* in temporal rather than regional terms: not as some specific location but as a lost or fading way of life. (*Min'yō* apparently does not figure in this film, which I have not yet seen.)

In §5.6, we noted government efforts since the 1960s to encourage relocation to the depopulating countryside, linked to phrases such as *chihō no jidai* ('the age of the countryside'), *chiiki shakai* ('regional society') and of course *furusato* ('home town'). Local songs, dances and festivals are seen as important tools in this process. Thus in 1992 the so-called 'Festival Law' (O-matsuri Hō) was enacted, sponsored by five ministries for their varied purposes – tourism, preservationism, economic growth, population shift, etc. (see Thornbury 1997: 67–74 for details). The law promoted not only local performing arts but the contexts and customs associated with them. Among other things, it created a Folk Performing Arts Promotion Centre (Chiiki Dentō Geinō Katsuyō Sentā) in Tokyo, funded primarily by the travel and tourism industry; this sponsors various festival performances in urban venues, where local products are also touted. Many scholars resent such 'touristification' of the performing arts, but local communities see the benefits. So do most individual Japanese: in the words of Marilyn Ivy (1995: 12–3):

> Through the powers of mass-mediated dissemination and spectatorship, a revived [or indeed new – DWH] folk festival . . . not only becomes a local representation of a cultural world where such festivity had its place but also becomes generically representative, [reminding] Japanese of what such festivals . . . used to signify. At the same time it consoles them with what still undeniably lives . . . .

The Cultural Affairs Agency (Bunkachō) has also established what its website translates as a Programme to Revitalize Hometown Cultures (Furusato Bunka Saikyō Jigyō). Through local Boards of Education, they will offer financial and other support to groups aiming at 'preserving and developing traditional culture', including of course performance-related groups.[4]

The word *furusato* continues to pop up in discussions of music, and not only of *min'yō*. The nineteen-year-old Western-style pop singer Teshima Aoi from Fukuoka City, appearing on the television programme *Daimei no nai ongakukai* (*Nameless Concert*, 13 May 07), explained: 'The *furusato* is a gentle (*yasashii*) thing, so one sings gently.' She was referring to songs with obvious links to any *furusato*, not necessarily her own.

Among such songs, of course, are *enka* (see §§1.7.2, 4.2). Do *enka* rival *min'yō* as 'the heart's home town'? For some *enka* and for many people, yes. These are songs strongly associated with rural-to-urban migrants, but the link to the *furusato* is often made via referencing *min'yō*, allowing the protagonist to escape for a moment the problems of the city (see §4.2). Christine Yano addresses this directly in her 1994 paper 'Longing for *furusato*: the shaping of nostalgia in Japanese popular *enka* songs' (see also Yano 2002). She focuses on the *enka* 'Bōkyō Jonkara', where *bōkyō* means 'longing for the *furusato*' and 'Jonkara' refers to 'Tsugaru Jongara [Jonkara] Bushi'. Three other 'Bōkyō' songs (one with the same title as this one) are translated in Appendix 1.3.I, K, L. Mita Munesuke, in a 1977 lecture, noted that *enka* were particularly rich in themes of migrant workers 'longing for the relatives they left in their home towns, and vice versa'. He further argued that the *furusato* 'used to be sung about as [a concrete] object of nostalgia until the early 1960s, after which it became a more abstract object of yearnings conceived by new citizens', who were often newly settled migrant workers.[5]

Can *fōku songu* (§1.7.1) also be 'the heart's home town'? Rarely: these tend to relate to modern life and general values, not to the *furusato* wherever it might be. The book *Uta no furusato* ('The home town of song'; Asahi 1980) contains sixty-two songs with links to northern Japan. These include only three *min'yō* and three *shin-min'yō*, presumably because the local connections of such songs are too obvious to need inclusion in such a book. There are many *enka*, other popular songs recent and old, *dōyō* art songs for children, but – though it is hard to be sure – only one definite *fōku songu*.

There are many valuable studies in English of *furusato*-ism, nostalgia, the related nativist discourse and other matters, but these are so well written and deal so tangentially with music that I will not summarize them but simply recommend: Gluck 1985; Robertson 1988 and 1991; Ivy 1995; and Vlastos (ed.) 1998, in which at least eight chapters are relevant. All of these point to important Japanese-language studies. Robertson 1991: ch.1 and 1998 are useful compact introductions to the issues, reminding us again that the nostalgia for *furusato* is often misplaced, given that personal relations in a village were not as rosy as the current image would have it. She also introduces us to terms such as 'Furusato Japan' (the government's idea that the entire country can be unified under traditional human values) and *furusato-mura* ('old-village villages', which are real villages aiming to reverse local decline through nostalgia-based tourism). Thornbury 1997 starts from *minzoku geinō* but addresses many of the issues listed above. Dodd 2005 focuses on the *furusato* in modern Japanese literature.

Even today, with *min'yō* less prominent in general, identification with home may well include a local folk song. The *Pelican Club Europe* monthly magazine, issued in England for UK-based Japanese, often contains a report on one of the many Prefectural Residents' Associations (*kenjinkai*) uniting people in England linked to that home prefecture. In July 2004, the focus was Fukuoka (p. 18): 'The image of Fukuoka held by outsiders [and by residents] varies with age: Muhōmatsu [famous fictitious rickshaw man, known from an early movie whose climactic scene has him beating the drum at a Bon dance]; the Genkai seacoast; Tenjin-sama [famous nineteenth-century courtier]; "Kuroda Bushi" [a *min'yō*]; the Daiei Hawks professional baseball team.'

Throughout this book, I have stressed the strong Japanese sense of local identity. And yet Kären Wigen could claim: 'By any comparative standard, modern Japanese regionalism is undeniably weak. [F]or all the fuss over its local festivals and folk arts, modern Japan lacks the "vigorous particularism of the provinces" [quoting Braudel] still evident across much of Europe' (1998: 235–6). True in many ways; for example, there have been no separatist movements or battles for recognition of local languages as for example in Basque or Catalan Spain (except to the tiniest extent in Okinawa). And yet, there *is* a great deal of 'fuss' over local festivals and performing arts. Japan is highly unified ethnically and now linguistically, which may indeed be precisely why there is all this fuss. What may seem like fairly small cultural differences among the different regions and sub-regions of Japan are intentionally magnified in the interests of identity. This is a well-known process to cultural anthropologists and sociologists.[6]

6.3 *Min'yō* and community-building

The previous section dealt with *furusato* mainly as a nostalgic link to an imagined idyllic countryside, with or without specific geographical referents, and possibly including one's original urban childhood home. But the concept has also been mobilized in the interests of creating a sense of community and tradition where none exists. This is in the formation of new communities: suburban commuter-belt 'new towns', urban apartment complexes, regional cities and towns newly enlarged by mergers, and so forth. It is in such cases that we typically encounter the expression *furusato-zukuri*, '*furusato*-building'. Related but distinct is *machi-zukuri*, 'neighbourhood-building', involving more clearly structured citizens' movements and civic action to improve urban life while also creating a sense of neighbourhood (see Sorensen & Funck 2007). In both cases, *min'yō* often have a role to play, though these usually, like the communities they represent, need to be newly constructed. A 'new folk song' (*shin-min'yō*), almost certainly with a dance, can help create the desired image of sunny, forward-looking communality and encourage residents to unite to improve living conditions. Such songs share with the pre-war *shin-min'yō* of §3.4.3 the linkage to a specific place identified in the title; the main difference is that these newer *shin-min'yō* are generally more specifically aimed at 'making' a community rather than just advertising it for tourism.

We met one such song in §5.4.4: 'Meguro Ginza Ondo', written and choreographed in 1979 to enhance solidarity and pride and contribute to a 'brighter town' in the neighbourhood around the Meguro Ginza shopping street in Tokyo.

Since the mid-1970s, with the spread of the *machi-zukuri* and *furusato-zukuri* concepts, there has been a nationwide wave of composing 'citizens' songs', where 'citizen' translates *shimin* for cities and *chōmin* for towns, and 'song' is *ondo*, implying a folk-dance song. (*Chō* and *machi* are respectively the Sino-Japanese and native Japanese words for 'town' as well as for a neighbourhood within a large city.) Given the uniformity of the titles, I assume that the national government provided a stimulus. Consider 'Shibata Chōmin Ondo' (Miyagi Pref.), composed in 1976.[7] Miyazaki Norio's lyrics recall the earliest *shin-min'yō*, each verse mixing lines of 7 and 5 moras with semantically empty *min'yō*-like *kakegoe* and *hayashi-kotoba*: an opening drawn-out *hā*, an interjected *hora hora hora*, and a repeated refrain: 'With "Shibata Ondo", *haitone haitone*.' (The word *chōmin* is part of the official title but omitted in casual reference.) The ten verses are (unusually for such songs) in heavy literary-style Japanese, very un-*min'yō*-like but recalling those often moralistic *shōgaku shōka* school songs. The content, however, is specifically local, naming many local places, prominent natural features and the feudal clan that once ruled the region. But several key words remind us of the more general desire to create or retain that idealized spirit of the old village: *furusato*, *machi-zukuri*, *natsukashisa* (nostalgia), *mukashi* (the [good] old days). A few snippets of text: 'The road runs straight ahead, just for you / It's a [powerful] sentiment, *machi-zukuri* . . . As we compete to use our skills, shouting the *hayashi* loudly / All hands joining in . . . In that girl's cheeks too, tomorrow's dream / That dream is a [guiding] flame – our desire will not be extinguished . . . How nostalgic!' The melody differs from the pre-war *shin-min'yō* but follows the main trend in *enka* in using the so-called pentatonic minor plus accidentals (§§1.7.2, 3.4.3.3).

Another *chōmin ondo* in the same spirit is 'Miyashiro Ondo' (Saitama Pref.), composed in 1985.[8] Its refrain is: 'Dance, form a circle, "Miyashiro Ondo" / Call out the *hayashi: yoi yoi yoi toko*' (nice, nice, nice place). Its lyrics, by Sekine Toneo, are posted on the web, allowing a common type of written-language pun unique to Japanese and of course impossible in orally transmitted songs: writing a Chinese loan word with its Sino-Japanese ideographic characters but adding *furigana*, a phonetic indication that it should be pronounced as a native Japanese word of the same meaning – or sometimes, to interesting effect, a different meaning. Thus in the phrase *yume no machi*, 'town of dreams', Sekine wrote *yume* not with the Chinese character for 'dream' but with two characters meaning 'future', hence conveying a sort of double meaning: that this town will realize its dreams in a bright future. He also wrote *toshi* 都市, a Sino-Japanese word for 'city, metropolis', but indicated the pronunciation *machi*, the native word for 'town' or for a somewhat cohesive urban neighbourhood. *Machi* has a much more comforting, intimate ring than *toshi*, implying a more traditional, resident-friendly locale than the anonymous modern big city. (Hence the term *machi-zukuri* is much more 'human' than *toshi kaihatsu*, 'urban development', or *toshi keikaku*, 'city planning'.) Sekine also wrote *shiseki*, 'historical site' (e.g. an old castle, archaeological site, etc.) but indicated the pronunciation *mukashi*, that native word meaning 'ancient, the old days': he asks us to visit historical sites = think back to the good old days.

These sample lyrics from the two songs reveal three features common in 'new folk songs' since the 1970s: (1) Native Japanese words are more comforting and folksy than 'hard' Sinate ones. (2) As revealed by the frequent use of the words *mukashi* and *furusato*, the past provides comfort in an impersonal present. (3) And we can dream of a better future. This last point in particular distinguishes these recent *shin-min'yō* from traditional *min'yō*, which almost never look beyond tomorrow.

These neo-folkish *ondo* work well as dance songs for enlivening and uniting residents. But new communities also need more formal songs for group singing at certain types of ceremony, perhaps accompanied by brass band or other purely Western-style ensemble, and never for dancing. While the new *ondo* tend to use the pentatonic major or minor, aiming for a traditional feel, these more formal songs are mostly in normal Western style. In contrast to the folksy term *ondo*, they will be marked by the character 歌, a more neutral term for song, pronounced *ka* in formal Sino-Japanese compounds but *uta* when a warmer nativist feel is wanted. Their standard title format is place-name followed by 'Chōka/Shika', 'Chōminka/Shiminka' or 'Chōmin/ Shimin no Uta'. Many newly-emerging communities will have both a 'citizens' *ondo*' and a 'citizens' *uta/-ka*'.[9]

6.4 The newest 'New Folk Songs' and (inter-)national identity[10]

6.4.1 Introduction

In §3.4.3 we described the 'New Folk Song' movement of the 1920s and 1930s, which, in effect, produced advertising jingles for towns, spas and factories throughout Japan, while also serving the interests of local pride. The lyrics and musical modes were not far from traditional style. The movement died a quiet death with the need to produce militaristic songs during the Second World War and in the face of competition from the newborn *kayō kyoku* genre of popular urban song. But some examples of this local praise song (*gotōchi songu*) type have appeared since the war. Possibly best known is 'Shirahama Ondo', written in 1965 (Appendix 1.1.R; notated in Hughes 1991: 45). It is a rare case of a locally-focused *shin-min'yō* which is widely sung by *min'yō* aficionados. In 1977, it became the only *shin-min'yō* among 275 songs sung by any of the winners at the annual national contest of the Nihon Min'yō Kyōkai during the years I examined (1951–79, 1990–99). (Recordings of several others were played for dance accompaniment.)

Meanwhile, we saw in the preceding section that similar locally-focused *min'yō*-influenced songs have been produced in recent decades in the service of *furusato-zukuri* and *machi-zukuri*. These, however, have tended to replace traditional modes with the Western-influenced fusion modes, the pentatonic minor and major. Their lyrics also take a more progressive stance, touting a bright future available if all residents pull together in the (supposedly) traditional way.

Songs of this 'citizens' *ondo*' type are, by definition, almost never heard beyond the local community; their role is political, social and psychological more than commercial. They are rarely called *shin-min'yō*. And yet they form a sort of typological bridge to an important and interesting new type of *shin-min'yō* which emerged at about the same time, the 1970s. These are songs which seek to identify with 'modern Japan' as a whole rather than with local communities. One term sometimes used to refer to such songs is (*zenkoku*) *sō-odori*, '(national) mass dances'. As the term suggests, these are all dance songs. Reflecting this characteristic, their titles commonly contain the words *odori* ('dance') or *ondo* ('dance song', in this case), rather than *kouta* ('little song') as found in many pre-war *shin-min'yō*. These 'mass dance' songs share many other features as well.

First, as to use, they are from the beginning intended for dancing rather than singing. Unlike their pre-war predecessors, these newest *shin-min'yō* have almost never been sung except during recording sessions: they exist mainly as 45-rpm records and now as CD singles. The primary users are dance teachers and their students; every recording comes with detailed choreographic drawings.

The considerable demand for new releases of this type is fuelled partly by a new post-war view of dancing – that it is good for one's health. Organizations like the National Recreation Association of Japan (Nihon Rekurieshon Kyō kai, founded 1947) and the National Folk Dance Federation of Japan (Nihon Fōku Dansu Renmei) promote dance as an important element contributing to both social and physical well-being. As their names imply, these two groups were modelled on Western organizations; at first, therefore, they favoured Western folk dances such as the Virginia Reel. To young post-war Japanese, these foreign dances bore none of the 'old-fashioned' image clinging to most Bon dances. Gradually, however, perhaps to satisfy the more traditional-minded middle-aged women who joined these groups in increasing numbers for health and social reasons, a need was recognized for dances which had the same 'modern' (i.e. Western or international) feeling as, say, the Virginia Reel but were more Japanese. One result is this *sō-odori* category of *shin-min'yō*. The modernity resides more in the songs than the choreography.[11]

Since the onset of the 'leisure boom' in the late 1960s, many a village and urban neighbourhood has a small weekly folk dance class populated almost exclusively by women over age forty. The teacher may hold a certificate from one of the two above-mentioned organizations, or from a less internation-ally-minded group such as the All-Japan Folk Dance Teachers Federation (Zen-Nihon Min'yō Shidōsha Renmei). Note the distinction between the words *fōku dansu* '(international) folk dance' and *min'yō* 民踊 '(Japanese) folk dance', paralleling that between *fōku songu* and *min'yō* 民謡 (§1.7). The homophonous words *min'yō* meaning 'folk song' and 'folk dance' are distin-guished in writing; to avoid confusion, some now prefer the term *minbu* 民舞 for '(Japanese) folk dance'. To win an advanced certificate from the National Folk Dance Federation of Japan, a teacher must be able to teach both for-eign and Japanese dances. Usually, however, the two styles are not taught together. At *minbu* classes, students may dance simplified choreographies to traditional folk songs set to dance-orchestra arrangements, along with mod-ern *sō-odori*. In urban areas, there will be public dances several times a year (including the O-Bon season) at which these records will be played. Sometimes the dances are held in a public shopping area or a shrine com-pound, sometimes in the courtyard of a large apartment complex as a way of promoting amity among the residents. Instead of live musicians, we now much more commonly encounter a stereo, perhaps accompanied by one large drum. Many *sō-odori* were commissioned directly by national organi-zations such as the above, or by major national recording companies, which accounts in part for their non-local character.

It is interesting that the emergence of these new, pan-Japanese-cum-international *shin-min'yō* should overlap temporally with the phenomenal growth in popularity of traditional *min'yō* from the late 1970s. Although contributing to the climate for the creation of *shin-min'yō*, that '*min'yō* boom' focused on the performance of *traditional* songs, if often in somewhat modified form. The stylistic gulf between traditional *min'yō* and the newer *shin-min'yō* is quite wide. Still, a typical Sunday all-day student recital might alternate segments of *min'yō* sung live by the pupils of a singing teacher, on the one hand, with sets of *shin-min'yō* dances by the pupils of a dance teacher, performed to recordings.

Despite this separate-but-equal coexistence on the Sunday stage, *shin-min'yō* have until now largely been ignored by the professional *min'yō* singers (except when they are paid to record them!) and by amateurs as well. They have few of the qualities that attract people to traditional song. They do, however, serve their purpose in setting a lively mood for dancing. And at least one younger professional singer (Kamiya Miwako, b. 1956) felt in 1979 that such songs represent the wave of the future, 'just what the modern generation needs' (pers. comm.).

Only time will tell whether she was right. Dances to *shin-min'yō* continue to be popular for Bon dancing today. At recitals, however, they are increas-ingly being replaced by a genre often called *buyō-kayō* or *kayō-buyō* ('dance songs' or 'dances to song'). These are solo or small-group dances set to *enka*-like pop songs which often have traditional or folksy themes. Falling between traditional classical dance (*buyō*) and the new folk dances, they have the advantage over the former of being shorter, more accessible and not requiring expensive costumes, and over the latter of being slightly more challenging and allowing one to dance a solo. (See also §7.4.)

Let us now consider the characteristics of the lyrics and music of these 'new *shin-min'yō*'.

6.4.2 Lyrics

There is a striking contrast between the lyrics of the early *shin-min'yō* of the 1920s and 1930s and the new ones of the 1970s and 1980s. The former largely resemble traditional lyrics in content and form, except for being slightly more precious than traditional songs, somewhat wordier, using varied repetition, and never failing to include at least one verse of local praise.

Fifty years later, the nature of the lyrics of newly-composed *shin-min'yō*, like Japan itself, had changed radically. For one thing, the textual density has increased even further as the information revolution continues, but this is a minor point. More important is the fact that, whereas the lyricists of the 1920s still focused on the local community, by the late 1970s the Japanese had long since expanded their frame of reference to encompass all of Japan and even the world. Also, economic success had brought the word 'progress' into everyone's consciousness. A whole new vocabulary of key words redolent of modernistic optimism creeps into the songs. Peace, hope, world, spring, young, prosperity, future, tomorrow, cheerful, dream – such words recur again and again, with semantic tinges related to the future. Some lyrics refer to the communal holding of hands by the dancers (e.g. Appendix 1.2.M), a choreographic feature found in many Western-style folk dances but never in Japanese folk dances – even the new ones whose lyrics mention it! Whereas most earlier songs had titles containing the local place-name, the newest wave have titles like 'The Happiness Song', 'The Peace Song', 'The Blue Skies Song', 'The Cherry Blossom Song' and so forth (App. 1.2). These changes were gradual. 'Shirahama Ondo' of 1965, for example, has a transitional nature (Appendix 1.1.P): we find global, modern, optimistic words and images in the first two verses, while the last two verses are very traditional. But the songs from 1977–81 shown in Appendix 1.2 are quite consistently 'modern' and universalistic, even while retaining the image of the *furusato* as the ideal in many cases; subsequent songs continue this pattern.[12]

One can notice, however, a certain ambivalence in many of these texts: the vision of the Japanese as citizens of the world is tempered by the continuing belief in the primacy of identification with Japan and her traditional cultural values. The opening verse of 'Shōwa Ondo' (Appendix 1.2.A), for example, grandly trumpets: 'All nations of the earth are neighbours'; but by verse 4 the emphasis has shifted: 'This is the country where we were born and raised'. The final verse of 'Dai-Tōkyō Ondo' (Appendix 1.2.I; **CD38**) pictures the

Japanese as travelling happily to 'the ends of the earth' (with no imperialist overtones) yet speaks proudly of 'the aspirations of Japanese Culture'. Such lyrics are an accurate reflection of the ambivalence of the modern Japanese and presumably also of other peoples caught up in the twin waves of Westernization and modernization.

Despite the extent of their 'modern' content, these latest *shin-min'yō* lyrics are still distinct from those of both Western-style popular songs and *enka*. *Enka*, quintessentially the songs of the recent rural-to-urban migrants, resemble American country-western ballads or blues in their focus on the problems of the individual adapting to modern city life; they speak of love, drink, loneliness, homesickness, occasionally with macho defiance, often with resignation. The *shin-min'yō* texts speak always of community, although now rarely the rural community. *Enka* texts cater to self-pity, or at least self-absorption, and address the (often imaginary) present situation, while 'new folk song' lyrics paint a hoped-for and expected future.

For completeness' sake, let us mention again that songs with a narrow local orientation continue to be made, in small quantities. An interesting example, 'Meguro Ginza Ondo', is discussed in §5.4.4 above. 'Dai-Tōkyō Ondo' (Appendix 1.2.I) is not strictly speaking a 'local praise song', because Tokyo is considered the shared national capital city of all Japanese.

6.4.3 Music

The sociocultural changes reflected in the evolution of *shin-min'yō* lyrics have wrought similar effects on the music. The style of pentatonic harmonization of early *shin-min'yō*, described in §3.4.3.3 above, is still often used today – but only for orchestral accompaniments to traditional *min'yō*. Example 6.1 shows part of a harmonization of the traditional dance song 'Kiso Bushi' by Ishikawa Akira, a thoroughly Western arranger who told me around 1979 that the 'secret' to harmonizing *min'yō* was 'sus4' (in Japanese: *sasu-foa*), the unresolved suspended 4th chords mentioned in §3.4.3.3. Modern *shin-min'yō*, however, have changed in modal structure and thus require a different harmonization. Let us trace these modal changes.

We saw in §3.4.3.3 that the same composers who imitated folk pentatonic modes for their 'new folk songs' in the 1920s were using a different pentatonic style for popular songs. Some popular songs were indistinguishable melodically from Western songs, but the subset known as *nihonchō kayō kyoku* ('Japanese-mode popular songs') or more recently as *enka* used the pentatonic major and pentatonic minor, which in terms of pitches are the *yō* mode on 1 and the *in* mode on 6 respectively. These two modes, exceedingly rare in traditional song and early *shin-min'yō*, still dominate in the *enka* genre. An important advantage of melodies in these two modes is that they can be harmonized nearly like normal Western major and minor tunes.

Ex. 6.1 Ishikawa Akira's arrangement of 'Kiso Bushi', excerpt (adapted from Fujine 1979)

The strength of the modern preference for the pentatonic major and minor can be seen in the *enka* 'Rōkyoku Okesa', which quotes a passage from the traditional folk song 'Sado Okesa'. The original flute part which ends the piece (**CD3**), in the *in* or *ritsu* mode, cadences on 7 (in the *in* mode, this would be 1764 367, alternating quarter- and eighth-notes), but in the *enka* version two notes are added to resolve to a cadence on 6 (1764 3671 6), where 6 is the 'tonic' of the pentatonic minor.

The vast majority of *shin-min'yō* of the 1970s and 1980s employ these two modes, very occasionally veering into heptatonicism or chromaticism for awhile. Given the modern, often Western-looking content of their lyrics, it is fitting that these songs should also be harmonized Western-style. Given the optimistic nature of their lyrics noted above, it is also not surprising that the pentatonic major predominates – as opposed to the more sentimental and self-pitying *enka*, which favour the pentatonic minor. Through continuous exposure to Western music, most Japanese ears have come to perceive both *yō* on 6 and the *in* modes in general as sounding minor and thus somewhat sad by comparison with *yō* on 1.

Still, this conversion of tastes is only partial. Compare, for example, 'Shōwa Ondo' (Ex. 6.2), in the pentatonic major, with 'Aozora Ondo' (Ex. 6.3), in the pentatonic minor: the latter's lyrics are no less happy and opti-mistic. (But see the note to Appendix 1.2.K.) The modal difference between these two songs is paralleled by another diagnostic feature: 'Shōwa Ondo' is performed by two professional folk singers (a man and a woman), 'Aozora Ondo' by a male *enka* singer. This triggers the observation that the modern *shin-min'yō* in the *in* scale are more likely to be in *enka* vocal style. In con-trast to *min'yō*, *enka* tend to be sung in a lower tessitura, using a voice richer in overtones, with a different style of vibrato and ornamentation. When *enka* singers such as Kitajima Saburō and Sen Masao sing *min'yō*, they tend to retain their *enka* vocal style. Conversely, singers trained in *min'yō* who also perform *enka* are likely to sing the latter closer to *min'yō* style (e.g. Hosokawa Takashi, Nagayama Yōko).

Modern *shin-min'yō* share several other musical features. Most are sung in octave unison by a male and female folk singer – something which in the vast majority of traditional dance songs occurs only on the refrains, when everyone joins in with the soloist. This feature of *sō-odori* songs (also occasionally found in the earlier 'new folk songs') may represent a compromise between traditional solo singing and the desire to include symbolically a larger public in the performance event. The voice quality is usually a toned-down version of the *min'yō* voice, less piercing and using less ornamentation; this too is clearly a compromise with 'modern' tastes. Text setting is largely syllabic, with more syllables per minute than formerly. Metre is usually 6/8, which the modern audience seems to consider more lively (*hazunde iru*) than 2/4. The rhythmic structure of a bar of 6/8 is almost always a lilting quarter-eighth-quarter-eighth, just as in traditional song (§1.6.1) and earlier

Ex. 6.2 'Shōwa Ondo', excerpt (transcribed from Victor 45rpm MV3023A)

Ex. 6.3 'Aozora Ondo', excerpt (transcribed from Toshiba 45 rpm TP17121B)

shin-min'yō, but the tempo varies less, centring near 52 bars per minute – suitable for the typical choreographic style for *shin-min'yō*. Instrumental ensembles are larger and even more Westernized: standard accompaniment is something between a Western big band and small dance orchestra, including a traditional flute or shamisen less often than in the 1920s and 1930s. Most recordings do, however, include a large festival drum, playing the same sort of rhythmic phrases as at many traditional ancestral Bon dances.

In conclusion, it can be seen that the evolution of 'new folk songs' during this century reflects accurately, both musically and textually, the changing views of many Japanese concerning their cultural identity and their place in Japan and the world. Just as the lyrics of recent *shin-min'yō* combine a global perspective with a Japanese heart, so the music combines traditional pentatonicism (or pentacentrism) with ever more Western modality and harmony. Further research is needed, however: Is it only the record companies and their conservatoire-trained composer-arrangers who find joy in these

Westernized products, who take pride in their own ability to incorporate the prestigious Western musical style? Why does nobody sing these songs? Is there any evidence that Kamiya Miwako was right in claiming that *shin-min'yō* represent the wave of the future?

A case study: Oshio Satomi (pers. comm.) reported that in 1996 several different songs were being used for Bon dancing in her town of Ichikawa (Chiba Pref.) in the Tokyo commuter belt. This was a small farming village until perhaps the 1960s. No traditional Bon-dance song has survived. Instead, residents dance to recordings of: 'Ichikawa Ondo', a local-praise *shin-min'yō* of recent vintage but of the older type in terms of text emphasis (hence presumably a 'citizens' song'); 'Heisei Ondo', a national 'new "new folk song" ' created since the start of the Heisei era (1989); and several of the nationally popular traditional Bon-dance songs such as 'Tankō Bushi' (the 'coal-miner's dance' from Fukuoka Prefecture, now widely danced outside Japan as well) and 'Hokkai Bon Uta'. The two *shin-min'yō* were the least popular with the dancers – not necessarily for musical reasons or out of purism, but because their choreographies were more difficult than the others. The point is, though, that two contrasting types of *shin-min'yō* share the dance plaza with various other songs. This is very typical of the current situation.

6.5 Folk music and international socialism: Warabiza

6.5.1 History of Warabiza

Considering the important role of 'folk' song throughout the last century in labour and protest movements in the USA in particular, it is interesting to compare the situation in Japan. I will suggest that *min'yō* is unsuitable for development as a vehicle for protest in present-day Japan, for both musical and historical reasons.

We noted in §2.2.4 the striking absence in documented traditional *min'yō* of lyrics of overt protest. This has not prevented the adoption of folk music and dance as a 'weapon' by some Japanese representatives of the international socialist movement. Such cases, however, are exceedingly rare. The most prominent exemplars of this practice are the Warabiza troupe.

Warabiza have never been part of the so-called 'folk song world' (*min'yō-kai*): they do not appear on television folk programs or as guests at live folk song concerts. At their beginning in 1947, they belonged to the active leftist performing arts movement. By the 1980s, however, their ideology had evolved somewhat, and today it would be more accurate to call them social activists. Let us trace their history.

Their prime mover, both ideologically and musically, was Hara Tarō (1904–88). He detailed the history of the group in the book *In search of Japanese song* (Hara 1971).[13] Demobilized from the imperial forces in 1947, the young Hara went to work for a petroleum company; having already joined the labour movement, he was active in unionizing and in forming communist cells at his firm. He was also a member of a leftist choral group. In July 1948 the Artists' Council of the Japanese Communist Party held a public meeting, inspiring Hara to become a musical activist.

Attempts to establish a proletarian music movement for agitprop purposes had been suppressed in the 1930s,[14] but the political environment was more receptive in the heady atmosphere of post-war democracy. With two like-minded friends, Hara was soon performing for union groups and for day labourers during their rest breaks. As Warabiza's English-language website puts it, 'Hara would play folk songs on the accordion while the other two would sing and dance for the weary people who had lost so much during the war. This experience left a profound impression on the young troupe, and solidified its commitment to using folk traditions to create a positive contribution to society.'[15] Hara turned to folk material because in his view it was the music of labourers, commoners, the masses.

Early post-war leftist music trends in Japan were strongly influenced by repatriates from Soviet Siberia, by the Chinese revolution and the Korean War. The internationalist element was stressed, and Soviet songs were especially popular. This tendency continued well into the 1960s within the Utagoe ('Singing Voice') Movement. This movement started up immediately after the war with the formation of small choral 'circles', and continued with the establishment after about 1954 of numerous 'Utagoe tea houses' (*utagoe kissa*) in major cities, where young folk (mostly college students) would gather to sing together from printed songbooks.[16] (See §4.7 for the importance of these clubs as models for folk song bars.)

I examined the songs in three lyric books printed apparently in the mid-1960s by the Utagoe club Tomoshibi in Tokyo. According to an afterword, these contain at least four types of song: songs of nostalgia for one's *furusato* (a typically Japanese sentiment, as we have seen, but also encountered in songs of Stephen Foster included in these books); songs to evoke happiness; songs expressing hopes for peace; and songs of anger for the downtrodden post-war mother country (in that order). Of 133 pieces whose origin I could identify, fifty-four were Japanese (thirteen *min'yō*, forty-one composed songs), twenty-six were Soviet (fourteen folk songs), fifteen from the United States (mostly 'folk songs'), twenty-seven European, four Chinese, four Korean; the remaining identifiable items were 'The Internationale', the International Students League Song, and 'The Banana Boat Song'. All items but the last one were sung in Japanese. These were not revolutionary song sessions but comradely social events, as may be gathered by a sampling of titles: 'Comrades'; 'My Home Village is my Mother'; 'Cherry Pink and Apple Blossom White'; 'Bluebells of Scotland'; 'O Sole Mio'; 'Carry Me Back to Old Virginny'; 'I've Been Working on the Railroad'; and several songs by Stephen Foster. Less than 10 per cent of the repertoire were *min'yō*, and even these few were rarely sung. Two other such collections, obtained by William Malm, followed the same trends and contained only twenty *min'yō* out of 227 songs and four out of seventy-six respectively (Ongaku Sentā 1971; Seki 1965). (Thanks to Haruko Uryū Laurie for lending me her songbooks and reminiscences. Tomoshibi, after a long lapse, re-opened around 1999.)

Hara himself followed the internationalist trend at first, being somewhat sceptical of the use of traditional Japanese material. Although he felt it his mission to create a new Japanese musical culture with roots in the traditional music of the labouring class, he had also seen how composers claiming to be creating 'Japanese-style' music had put themselves at the service of militant nationalism during the war years. Nevertheless, he gradually came to feel that traditional material could be utilized, adapted and extended in a positive way to contribute to a badly-needed post-war rebirth of Japanese pride, whereas European-style songs were unlikely to have this effect.

Hara never intended to eliminate non-Japanese elements from the repertoire, simply to place the emphasis on native material. In fact, from 1948 to 1952 his group was named Umitsubame (Petrel), after a poem by Gorky. A typical performance in 1951 started with foreign – though hardly revolutionary – songs such as 'Jeanie with the Light Brown Hair' and the Korean folk song 'Toraji', and finished with *min'yō* such as 'Chichibu Ondo'.

In 1953, their membership gradually expanding, the troupe settled in the spacious farming village of Tazawako in the mountains of Akita Prefecture, generally considered the prefecture richest in folk song. Since then they have devoted themselves to several tasks simultaneously: learning traditional folk songs and dances, creating a new 'people's music' from traditional roots, and developing a repertoire of people's dramas incorporating such music. (Note that their move to the countryside already distinguished them from the strongly urban mainstream of the proletarian arts movement.) By 1980 they had over 300 members living communally at their Akita headquarters.

When they shared the stage in their early days, it was usually with other Japanese socialist performers or People's Artists from other socialist countries. Most often they performed alone, taking their message to small schools and community halls throughout Japan, or to union gatherings and protest rallies. Their first overseas performances, in 1963, were in China, North Korea and North Vietnam; in 1989 they visited the Soviet Union (in its last days), East Germany (ditto), France and Italy. Since then they have toured more widely and with less emphasis on socialist countries and socialism itself.

The name Warabiza, 'Bracken Troupe', was chosen to express the group's intimate links with their home base in the bracken-covered mountains of Akita (Hara 1971: 1.80). The troupe's official name also includes the modifier Minzoku Kabudan, 'Ethnic Song and Dance Group'. Actually, *minzoku* (民族) is ambiguous in this context. Given the ideological orientation of the troupe, one might choose the translation 'People's' rather than 'Ethnic'. In everyday use, however, *minzoku* has slightly different overtones than *jinmin*

(人民); Chinese *renmin*, as in 'People's Republic'): it carries suggestions of '(our) race, (our) nation, Japaneseness'.[17]

This does not mean that Warabiza soon abandoned the class struggle to align themselves with the slightly resurgent nationalist trend in Japan. Instead, the shift toward *min'yō* is a result of the troupe's changed perception of the nature of tradition among leftists. Folk song, once seen as a relic of feudalistic thinking, came to be considered an extremely powerful mechanism for triggering the Japanese people's ethnic consciousness in order to unite them for the struggle for freedom from outside (i.e. American) domination. Before true internationalism could be pursued, it was felt, Japan must first regain its own independence by, among other things, abrogating the US-Japan Joint Security Treaty of 1960; before this could be accomplished, the Japanese people must regain a sense of self. Folk song and dance were only tools to that end: 'the form is nationalist, the content is socialist' (Hara 1971: 2.197, quoting Mao Zedong).[18] The members perceived further confirmation of the correctness of their approach in the positive audience response to their 1963 overseas performances. At an international gathering of socialist youth groups some years earlier, the Japanese representatives had been criticized because all of their home-grown socialist songs had 'European-style' melodies (Hara 1971: 1.247). The success of Warabiza's folk material led Hara to conclude: 'Because it belongs to the masses, it's national; and to the degree that something is national, it is international' (Hara 1971: 2.200).

I attended a Warabiza concert in 1978, a typical one for that period, in the community hall of a small town in rural Nara Prefecture. The first half was devoted to traditional material with no unifying theme, drawn from several regions of Japan; perhaps this native material was intended to unify the audience's ethnic consciousness, so that the message of the second part of the programme could be received. The second part, mostly accompanied by taped internationalist music played on Western instruments, featured Chinese-style socialist-realist drama set in a modern-day farming village, with healthy, bright-eyed, educated youths triumphing over older, rather degenerate-looking capitalist landlords and developers. At moments the 'peasants' would burst into traditional song or dance. These two disparate parts were both skilfully and energetically performed and well received.

Superficial class-warfare dramas seem now, however, to have fallen from their repertoire. Now traditional items or arrangements thereof may be paired with musicals (*myūjikaru*) of a still socially meaningful but more whimsical sort. The 1995 flyer for one such play, 'Oga no Onimaru', promises Akita dialect, costumes based on ancient times, and live performances of 'children's songs, lullabies, Dixieland jazz, flamenco, Akita *min'yō*, etc.' Both Dixieland and flamenco originate, of course, from oppressed minorities.

There are now five sub-troupes, one of which focuses on such musicals, another performing only traditional pieces, another items for children (pers. comm. from member Jin Shizuka, 1997, still confirmed by the website

www.warabi.jp). They give over 1,000 performances each year. What is now
called Tazawako Art Village has a 650-seat theatre, hotel, hot spring resort
and other facilities, including a Folk Arts Research Centre with recordings
or videos of 150,000 *min'yō* and 5,000 folk dances. The website further
explains the troupe's philosophy and aims, still solidly based in helping
humanity but without a touch of the earlier leftist-activist language. For
example:

> Warabiza uses Japanese traditions to shed light on various aspects of modern
> humanity [and] focuses on positive potential in human (*sic*) and presents this
> image of happiness and cooperation to as many people as possible. . . .
> Warabiza's purpose is to depict human dignity and love. . . . 10,000 school chil-
> dren visit its village each year. They not only experience traditional Japanese
> folk dances and music . . . but with the co-operation of 700 local farmers, they
> also learn how to grow the rice. Most of these children have never experienced
> farming before. . . . This is something Warabiza feels is important to correct,
> since Japan has traditionally held rice farming at the centre of its spiritual and
> cultural life. In over fifty years of activities, Warabiza has been guided by three
> defining principles: (1) to stay rooted in the essential human experience, (2) to
> join tradition with modernity, and (3) (quoting Zeami, the founder of Noh
> Theater) to express the charm of common people.

Warabiza received prizes from Akita Prefecture in 1988 and the Ministry
of Education in 1994 for their contributions to the arts and to regional culture respectively.

6.5.2 Warabiza's interpretation of folk material

Some idea of the Warabiza's attitude towards traditional material during
Hara's heyday can be gathered by his remarks about three *minzoku geinō*
widespread in southern Iwate Prefecture. Whatever the origin of the Devil
Sword Dance (*oni kenbai*), the important question for Hara is how such a
samurai-flavoured dance took root among the farming villages of central
Iwate. It is, he writes, probably connected with the long history of peasant
uprisings in this chronically famine-stricken region under the Tokugawa
shogunate (Hara 1971: 2.23). *Hinako kenbai*, a dance for young girls, is
thought to honour a high-ranking Buddhist priest who showed concern
and compassion for the peasants. To Hara, this shows how the peasants, 'in
the midst of their lonely struggle, had come to respect deeply this person
of another class who aided them in it' (ibid.). He notes that the Deer
Dance (*shishi odori*) contains depictions of 'courtship between buck and doe,
of fights between bucks, the triumph of love' and so forth; this can be viewed
as an example of 'the peasants, trapped in the fetters of feudalism, expressing their human desires through the medium of the deer' (ibid.: 23–4).

Also typical are Hara's remarks on the following verse from the song 'Akita Jinku':

> jinku odoraba sanju ga sakari / sanju sugireba sono ko ga odoru
> If you dance *jinku*, age thirty is the peak; / when you pass thirty, your children will dance.

Hara sees here the symbolic expression of 'the life of woman'. The joys and excitement of youth pass in an instant; the 'old, unfeeling conventions send her into a marriage where her dreams and hopes are broken', accompanied by hard labour and mental stress. And the energy to bear up lasts only until the age of thirty (ibid.: 10–11). A more orthodox interpretation would doubtless stress the physical demands of dancing, the role of dance in courting, the responsibilities of adulthood, and other factors favouring withdrawal from the dance plaza at around that age.

Finally, it is somewhat surprising to see that Hara includes in his songbook the eminently feudal 'Chōja no Yama' ('The Rich Man's Mountain') without tendering any remarks of social criticism (Hara 1976: 72). Its first verse congratulates the local landowner on the discovery of gold in his mountain, wishing him well for generations to come. Hara says no more than that. (This song is discussed in §2.2.1.)

By 1986, Hara had mellowed slightly: 'I interpreted the folk performing arts . . . in Iwate . . . as the example of farmers' heroic cries for emancipation [and similar cases]. I still think that the interpretation of each subject was correct. But . . . I may have reached dogmatic conclusions' (Hara 1989: 8). Two years before his death, he now saw the folk performing arts as arising from the excitement generated by human respect, cooperation and love towards life. This was still, of course, an internationalist perspective.

6.5.3 Creative activities of the early Warabiza

The Warabiza continually stress the importance of their creative activities. In addition to simply transmitting traditional music and dance, they aim to create a new national performing art which by definition must draw on traditional forms, especially on the arts of the masses. Their recent 'musicals' were discussed above; here we consider some of the earlier works. With reference to folk song, some idea of their approach can be gleaned from an examination of their publication, *Japanese folk song choral collection* (Hara 1976). Volume 1 contains twenty-eight traditional *min'yō* arranged for two to four voices, thirteen transcriptions of unharmonized *min'yō*, and eleven 'new compositions'. The lyrics of the forty-one traditional pieces are unaltered; the musical arrangements draw heavily on European triadic harmony, but with some of the Japanizing features found in *shin-min'yō* arrangements in general, such as frequent use of unresolved 'suspended fourth' and open 5th chords (§3.4.3.3). Strangely, none of these forty-one lyrics seems to express any protest or class consciousness, although Hara could have found such *min'yō* if he had tried.

The eleven new compositions typify the troupe's principles of tradition-based creativity. Musically, traditional features have been largely disregarded. To mention the most obvious features: (1) none of the melodies adheres to common Japanese folk scales (although two come close); (2) all are harmonized in slightly Japanized Western style; (3) non-traditional syncopations abound. Traditional features that do appear include: (1) frequent passages of pentatonicism; (2) avoidance of triple metre; and (3) occasional use of *min'yō*-style 'nonsense' choruses (*hayashi-kotoba*). (Some of their compositions not included in that book, however, do make use of folk scales.)

The lyrics themselves are varied in style, but none would be mistaken for *min'yō*. Only one of the eleven songs consistently uses the most prevalent Japanese poetic line-lengths of 5 and 7 syllables; none uses the dominant folk metre, 7–7–7–5. Some sample lyrics:

(1) 'Girl with Red Hands': My big red hands make beautiful things in abundance. Although roughened, they're valuable hands. Let's all say in a big voice: I'm the girl with red hands. (Spoken over a hummed background:) Rubbing my frostbitten little hands, as if singing a lullaby, my mother prayed: 'Turn into pretty white hands, not like her mother's cracked and wrinkled ones, but soft and gentle hands which can grab happiness.' But as the little girl grew, her hands became red and powerful. The frostbite healed, but the hands didn't turn white as my mother had prayed. But these hands, taking a lively deep breath, can make their own happiness. (Sung:) These hands of mine have a dream. They will hold tight to proper loving feelings. Big, strong hands. Let's all say in a sunny voice: I'm the girl with red hands.

Hara remarks that the singer could be any factory girl, singing of her 'hopes and convictions' (1976: 78). (Interestingly, Hara did not include any 'industrial' folk songs in his collection.)

(2) 'When Transplanting is Over': The frogs are calling! Transplanting is over! Mama is in her room, sewing clothes for me. Mama, mama, I'll rub your sore shoulders for you. (ibid.: 82)

(3) 'Bravely Advance': Link arms, throw out your chests, sing your own song and bravely advance! Standing at the head of your people (*minzoku*), bravely advance. From this will be born a marvellous Japan. Young folk! Young folk! Young folk! (ibid.: 84)

(4) 'Spring': The wind on the river is still chilly, but the blizzard has fled to the mountain depths. When Mr Sun smiles behind the clouds, the spring we've been waiting for has come. (ibid.: 94)

(5) 'Harvest': Grab the rice sheaves firmly and slice them off in one breath. I won't even stop for lunch today – gotta work a little harder. The waves of

grain roll quietly in the autumn breeze; red dragonflies flit around my hat . . . We sure are busy from dawn to dusk: negotiations with the town office, preparations for migrant work. Young farmers, whose collective strength has built this village, let's always stand tough together. (ibid.: 110)

One notes the occurrence in these lyrics of certain evocative key words rarely found in the same senses in traditional *min'yō*: happiness, dream, sunny (in the social sense), marvellous, youth. These are not simply adopted in imitation of the similar energetic optimism encountered in the songs of post-revolutionary China. Rather, such words recur in certain other types of Japanese songs since the optimistic 1960s, in particular the new type of non-local *shin-min'yō* (§6.4) and other songs linked with the Japan Recreation Association and similar internationalist but non-socialist organizations. They are part of the spirit of the times. Other key phrases are more specifically socialist: bravely advance, collective strength, stand tough together.

6.5.4 The impact of Warabiza

Warabiza's achievements are impressive, and their message is an important one to which folk music and dance seem well suited, especially when fused with an appropriate modernity. Yet it is fair to say that the early, more specifically socialist Warabiza had little overt political effect. Why should this be so? A fundamental problem was that the non-socialist members of their audiences likely did not interpret the traditional songs and dances in the same way that Hara did. Aside from general ideological messages, it is also apparent that traditional folk song and dance do not today generate quite the unifying effect envisioned by the troupe's members. Moreover, the troupe's efforts at creating a widely accepted new Japanese 'people's music' did not succeed.

This failure stemmed from many sources. *Min'yō* fans, though perhaps attracted by the traditional aspects of a Warabiza performance, are relatively conservative musically and therefore unlikely to appreciate Hara's choral pieces; they also tend to be older and less likely to be politically mobilized by lyrics which continually stress the leading role of youth. On the other hand, pseudo-traditional melodies hold little attraction for the highly Westernized young. (Recall that less than 10 per cent of the songs in the Utagoe songbooks were *min'yō*.) Perhaps the major factor is simply that socialism as a whole lost momentum in Japan (notwithstanding the startling ascension of a Socialist prime minister in 1994) due to the unprecedented national prosperity. Younger Japanese in particular are, by and large, still too well-fed to follow the socialist call.

On the other hand, Warabiza are well known, not for their political stance, but for their belief in the importance of learning traditional music and dance 'in the field' (*genchi de*), directly from the local practitioners. In this they have had a significant impact. One of their members left to found the Ondeko-za *taiko* group on Sado Island, which metamorphosed into Kodō and the phenomenon now called *wadaiko*. Media coverage of Warabiza's activities seems generally to focus on the artistic side, ignoring their ideology; most descriptions in the *min'yō*-related literature do likewise (e.g. Asano 1983: 545–6; NMZ: 2.153). But their less overt political stance – their basic humanity – comes through powerfully and surely has a significant impact on the 10,000 children who visit Tazawako annually.

6.6 *Min'yō* meets other musics

The interaction of *min'yō* with other genres and styles of music has figured often in our narrative. We have noted the important role of *min'yō* in *enka*, as well as the impact of Western music on *shin-min'yō*. This section introduces a number of cases of such interaction, most of which involve hybridization or what in today's world would be called fusion. Most but not all examples involve Western music.

In the global age, cross-genre and cross-cultural fusions have of course increased rapidly. The events listing for traditional Japanese music in the July 2006 issue of *Hōgaku Jānaru* magazine, covering only a six-week period, included combinations of instruments such as the following: Tsugaru-jamisen and koto; the same two plus violin or Chinese *erhu*; *wadaiko*, koto and the transverse flutes of Noh and Kabuki; shakuhachi and *shō* (mouth-organ of *gagaku*); *shō* with Chinese *pipa* and *erhu*; shakuhachi and contra-bass; shakuhachi, Bunraku shamisen, keyboard, bass, Western drum kit; koto and cello; Japanese transverse flutes, Indian tabla, violin and *taiko*; and yet others. It would be surprising if *min'yō* were not involved in this trend.

6.6.1 *Min'yō* and other Japanese traditional genres

We begin by considering the fusion of *min'yō* with other traditional native genres. The two most prominent figures in this endeavour have been Fujimoto Hideo and his former student Honjō Hidetarō (§§4.4.2, 4.5.1). Each came to *min'yō* from a background in several classical shamisen-vocal genres of the Kabuki and geisha worlds.

Honjō, like his teacher but more so, has explored various new directions for shamisen-centred music. He creates purely instrumental arrangements of folk melodies, or new compositions evoking folk scenes, with titles linked to places famed for specific *min'yō*, such as 'Awa no Uzushio' (The Whirlpools of Awa) and 'Yuki no Yamanaka' (Snowy Yamanaka). Honjō has named this genre *risōgaku* 俚奏楽 (literally 'village/rural performance music', but possibly also intending a pun on *risō* meaning 'ideal'). Pieces may draw on several traditional instruments, not only those common in *min'yō*. The CD with Honjō's book-length statement of his philosophy (Honjō 2006) includes the *risōgaku* 'Tōri-ame' (Passing Showers), which depicts a musical evening in the pleasure quarters of Itako in his home region. Following Honjō's preference for fairly sedate music, it resembles less a *min'yō* than a gentle geisha song as interpreted on the Kabuki stage, but with a second vocal line at some points. (Recording R69 contains more *risōgaku*.)

Risōgaku, born around 1980, has not found a major audience among *min'yō* fans; they would generally rather listen to songs they might imagine themselves singing, whereas Honjō's lovely pieces tend to be through-composed and relatively complex, depending heavily on elaborate instrumentation. But Honjō as aiming for an audience beyond the *min'yō* world, and in this age of fusion, he might find it. He performed two major *risōgaku* concerts in Tokyo in July 2006.

Overall, *min'yō* is not mixing much with other traditional genres today. Classical shakuhachi and koto masters sometimes make and teach arrangements of or fantasias on *min'yō*, but the number of such pieces is small, and they tend to be considered suitable for non-advanced performers.

6.6.2 Min'yō arranged as popular songs

The impact of Western popular music styles on Japan, already a factor in early *shin-min'yō*, increased manyfold during the Occupation (1945–52). The occupying forces, mostly young American males interested in jazz and pop, provided a significant new body of patrons whose tastes must be catered for. Then during the 1950s, Mihashi Michiya (§4.4.2) was leading a *min'yō* boom, often singing with Western dance-orchestra accompaniment while also making his mark as an *enka* singer. Though *min'yō* contests and *hozonkai* continued to demand 'traditional' performances, a populace raised under the hegemonic power of Western music was likely also to enjoy performances fusing East and West. Many popular singers have since issued recordings of *min'yō* in Western-style arrangements. Let us consider four cases only: Eri Chiemi, the Peanuts, Akai Tori and Hosono Haruomi.

Eri Chiemi (1937–82) debuted in 1952 with her version of Patti Page's 'Tennessee Waltz'. Though Eri was generally called a 'jazz singer', her subsequent repertoire drew on American popular songs, *enka*, lively geisha songs and – on ten LPs – *min'yō*, all in Western-style arrangements.[19] Her 1958 LP *Chiemi no min'yōshū* (King 10' LP, LKF-1011) included seven well-known *min'yō* and one *zokkyoku*. She was backed by the Tokyo Cuban Boys (and on later *min'yō* albums by the Tropical Melodians, the Six Lemons and others). The recording of 'Otemoyan' (available on recording R71) features some brief tap-dance interludes by performers from Eri's stage show. Her section of the liner notes tells her fans:

We Japanese cannot think about our lives or songs without including *nihon min'yō*. I think this is because *min'yō* are the only songs truly born and nurtured within the daily lives of our ancestors. The most familiar to us among this large number of Japanese *min'yō* have almost all been sung and recorded by various people in various forms, so I decided to try singing, in my own style 'as I felt them', seven songs. . . . I was determined, in making this LP, to retain the flavour of the original songs while also matching them in a lively way to the vigorous (*hageshii*) tempo of our modern lives.

Then the Tokyo Cuban Boys' arranger, Naitō Norimi, explains:

A word in reply to a criticism we sometimes hear: that this sort of attempt ruins the original goodness of Japanese *min'yō*. Some people may feel that multi-layered harmony and a powerful brass section 'destroy the naive beauty of *min'yō*'. But our aim is elsewhere [not clearly explained – DWH]. This is also why we did not use shamisen, koto or other Japanese instruments. We hope that this album will be widely enjoyed even by those who are not so-called jazz fans [e.g. *min'yō* fans? – DWH].

So Eri and her arranger are (like Honjō Hidetarō and his *risōgaku*) aiming confidently at an audience for *min'yō* beyond the *min'yō* world – and Eri's successful career says that they found it. Audio samples of Eri's output are at www.neowing.co.jp/detailview.html?KEY=KICX-3467; tracks 3 and 4 are *min'yō*. She was never considered a *min'yō kashu* ('folk singer'), but her love for *min'yō* helped keep the genre in the public ear. Her vocal style was typical of most *enka* singers who tackled *min'yō*: her ornamentation (on the relatively unchallenging songs she chose) was somewhere between *min'yō* and *enka*, and her pitch level and volume were both lower than in stage *min'yō* style.

The Peanuts (*Za Pīnattsu*) are the singing twins Itō Yumi and Emi, born in 1941. Though their performing career extended only from 1959 to 1975, their popularity continues to this day. Like Eri Chiemi, their repertoire was diverse: it encompassed Japanese-composed non-*enka* pop songs, Western popular songs, and, from the very beginning of their career, arrangements of *min'yō*. Like Eri, they often favoured Latin-style arrangements. Like Eri, some tracks the Peanuts labelled *min'yō* would not be called such by aficionados or scholars but were of a related style or mood. Their vocal style was even further from *min'yō* style than was Eri's, but their clever two-part vocal harmonies were a unique contribution.

Sometimes they altered the title of a *min'yō* to remind that their version was special: 'Chakkiri Bushi' became 'Chakkiri Cha Cha Cha' (included on recording R71); 'Otemoyan' became 'Batten Batten Battenten', reflecting the *hayashi*-like repetition of a single distinctive local-dialect word meaning 'but'.

In his notes to the 1998 CD re-issue of their 1970 LP of *min'yō* (R70), music critic Kurosawa Susumu comments:

Since the moment of their debut in 1959, the Peanuts have always included *nihon min'yō* abundantly in their repertoire. . . . Thinking back on it now, one wonders, 'What was that all about?', but at the time we listened with no sense of strangeness or unnaturalness. After all, popular singers (*popyurā shingā*) were often made (*yaraseru*) to sing Japanese-style (*nihon-chō*) tunes. However, some intellectuals (*shikisha*) didn't like this. In 1959 . . . a critic wrote bitingly: 'It is meaningless to make the Peanuts sing "Chakkiri Bushi". It would be different if the song had first been made jazzier.'

The implication of that last comment seems to be that *min'yō* lose their meaning when sung by non-specialists; I would rather say that the meaning changes. But also, Kurosawa claims that many singers were forced to sing *nihon-chō* tunes, which implies *min'yō* or pentacentric *enka* as opposed to the more purely Western pop style. Maybe so, but in the case of Eri and the Peanuts the decision was all theirs, and heartfelt at that.

Now to Akai Tori, a *fōku songu* group. As Western-style *fōku songu* settled into Japan in the 1960s (§1.7.1), so some musicians added guitar chords and vocal harmonies to extant *min'yō*. They did this only very rarely, and seemingly could find ways to harmonize only the simplest tunes with the most regular metres. Thus in 1971 Akai Tori recorded a version of a hitherto unremarked lullaby from the Kyoto area, 'Takeda no Komoriuta'; accompaniment consisted of two guitars and cello, with the slightly irregular metre of the original smoothed out to suit 'Western' tastes. This was a nationwide hit on the pop charts, now known and liked even by most *min'yō* fans.[20] But as noted in §1.7.1, *min'yō* and *fōku songu* remain far apart.

Hosono Haruomi (b. 1947) first achieved fame as a member of the techno-funk trio Yellow Magic Orchestra; now he is well known on the World Music scene, drawing on and often fusing techno, funk, Latin, ambient and many other styles. Though not involved in the *min'yō* world, Hosono opened his 1989 album *omni Sight Seeing* (R42) with a track called 'Esashi', which is none other than an arrangement of our old friend 'Esashi Oiwake' (§3.3). In the notes (p. 6), Hosono explains:

> In 1988, watching a song contest on TV, I saw a fourteen-year-old girl from Esashi sing this song. Since then I haven't been able to forget the vocal ornamentation (*kobushi*). At last I located her, Kimura Kasumi, and recorded her *a cappella*. Later, through the help of Honjō Hidetarō, a major figure in the *min'yō* world [see above], I had the [*min'yō*] veterans Kawasaki Masako and Honjō Masaya overdub the *hayashi*. [T]he style heard here is that of a requiem (*chinkonka*).

Perhaps Hosono couldn't forget the girl's singing, but he managed to limit her performance to less than two minutes out of a forty-eight-minute CD, and to submerge her under an intrusive accompaniment of synthesizer, accordion and Turkish kanūn! No other Japanese elements merited inclusion in this album. It is also diagnostic that Hosono heard this song as some sort of requiem, obviously not grasping the song's original atmospherics. Still, by placing this traditional-based track at the very beginning of his album, he is making a statement: 'I am Japanese (sort of).' Unlike Eri Chiemi and the Peanuts, Hosono otherwise virtually ignores *min'yō*, though he often draws on Okinawan music. To him, it seems, *min'yō* are exotic; to Eri and the Peanuts, they seem to have been much more familiar.

There have been literally hundreds of arrangements of *min'yō* in various popular music styles, sometimes as instrumentals, especially in the immediate post-war decades. One might find 'Sōran Bushi', one of the best-known *min'yō*, in versions with titles like 'Sōran Rumba', 'Sōran Mambo' and 'Sōran Cha Cha Cha'.[21] In more recent decades, rock guitar bands might tackle Tsugaru-jamisen riffs.

6.6.3 Min'yō referenced in enka

Enka, so often representing the viewpoint of homesick urban migrants, find in *min'yō* a convenient tool to evoke the *furusato*. The referencing of a *min'yō* may be via quoting any or all of its title, lyrics and melody. And that reference may be clear and logical or instead very tangential. Here are three contrasting examples of *enka* that reference 'Sōran Bushi'; lyrics are given in Appendix 1.

In 'Sōran Wataridori' (Ex. 6.4; text: Appendix 1.3.G), the singer has left his beloved Esashi in Hokkaidō. To soothe his homesickness, he joins in with 'Sōran Bushi', a song of the Hokkaidō herring fisheries, as soon as anyone starts playing the shamisen accompaniment (whether in a *min'yō* bar or perhaps on a recording). In this *enka* he sings the first part of the first line of the folk song's chorus. The *min'yō*'s full title is not given, but any Japanese who hears the word *sōran* will think of that song.[22]

In 'Sōran Jingi' (Appendix 1.3.H), the singer introduces himself: 'I was born in Hokkaidō, renowned as the home of "Sōran Bushi".' That Hokkaidō's fame rests on 'Sōran Bushi' recalls yet again the power of *min'yō* to symbolize

Ex. 6.4 'Sōran Wataridori', excerpt (adapted from Natsu n.d.: 2.138)

locality. The melody of the original *min'yō* is quoted only briefly in the instrumental break after verse 1: just naming the song is enough to trigger a host of images. 'Sōran Bushi' evokes instantly the herring fisheries and the migrant workers who find their way to them, then vanish to who knows where. One can imagine the protagonist having to leave his Hokkaidō home as the fisheries collapsed, to seek work elsewhere. He can't go home to his *furusato*: surely his woman hasn't waited for him. Such potential images enhance the meaning of the actual *enka* lyrics.

'Sōran Koiuta' (Appendix 1.3.M) is the song of a woman disappointed in love. It quotes the lyrics to the chorus of 'Sōran Bushi', but not the melody, nor is the song itself directly mentioned, nor even any specific places; nor could a woman have done the work associated with the original work song. Mention of a seagull recalls the *min'yō*'s most famous verse: 'If you ask the seagull, 'Have the herring arrived?' / [It replies] 'I'm just a migratory bird; ask the waves.' Our singer too is like the seagull, doomed to be a migratory bird. This *enka*'s elusive, impressionistic lyrics use a *min'yō* connection to call up certain motifs: nostalgia for fading rural lifeways, the *furusato* – anyone's *furusato* – as a comforting place to go to nurse a broken heart.

Thus a well-known folk song can trigger images of place or mood via even the slightest reference: the title, a snatch of melody, a few words of the chorus. In these three songs, 'Sōran Bushi' seems to represent respectively homesickness, pride and a lonely love life, among other possibilities.

The other *enka* translated in Appendix 1.3 that reference *min'yō* (songs F-N) confirm the approaches of the above three. The one exception is song J, 'Hanagasa Tsukiyo', which is not an *enka* but a dance-song of the type called *min'yō-kayō* ('folk song-pop song'). It incorporates a bit of melody and lyrics from the famous Bon-dance song 'Hanagasa Ondo'. Choreography for a new dance is included in the record jacket: as with the recent *shin-min'yō* of §6.4, the focus is more on the dance than the song. Here a *min'yō* is quoted to give a happy feeling, different from most *enka*.

Occasionally an *enka* will feature a longer segment of a *min'yō*, embedded within or between verses. One such is 'Okesa Funauta' (1957), a typical *enka* about a collapsed love affair: its two verses are separated by a traditional-style rendition of a verse of the *min'yō* 'Sado Okesa'. The singer was Mihashi Michiya, skilled at both genres.

6.6.4 Min'yō and Western classical music

Composers trained in the Western classical tradition worldwide have drawn on local folk material in their works; Japan is no different. And as elsewhere, this material is utilized in diverse ways. Since Western music journals often deal with such Japanese composers, I will simply give a few examples here without musical analysis (Herd 2008 is a good starting point for sources). I have also been unable to delve into composers' motivations.[23]

Min'yō being at heart vocal music, a starting point for many composers or performers is to arrange one or more songs for a Western-style chorus or vocalist. When the Kyushu University Mixed Chorus held its first concert in 1964, they decided, as their website puts it, to *min'yō arēnji de sutāto*, 'start with *min'yō* arrangements' as the core.[24] Alongside choral works by Schumann, Schubert and Mozart, a choral suite by a Japanese composer, and arrangements of American, French, Italian and Russian folk songs, they performed (no arranger mentioned) five well-known *min'yō* (one being from Kyūshū, though from a different prefecture). The next year's concert included a suite of five songs from Tsugaru (again anonymously arranged), along with Italian madrigals and other works. *Min'yō* featured almost annually for the first decade or so but have been rare in recent years, for whatever reason.

On the composing side, the renowned Mamiya Michio (b. 1929) was one of four founders of the Yagi no Kai composers' group in 1953, who pledged 'to devote themselves to the creation of a truly national music' (Herd 2007). This came as Japan, recovering from the war, was striving to rebuild self-confidence and national pride. Mamiya approached this aim most obviously via arrangements of *min'yō*, some of which have been sung by the above-named chorus. His vocal works include (giving only a translation of the titles) 'Six Japanese *Min'yō* for Cello and Piano', 'Four Japanese *Min'yō* for Women's Chorus', 'Japanese *Min'yō* Collection, Vols. 1–6 (for soprano or baritone and piano)', and 'Twelve Inventions Based on Japanese *Min'yō* (for mixed chorus)', this last intentionally featuring songs from all over Japan. Mamiya tended to set songs unfamiliar to the urban *min'yō* scene; one such was 'Oboko Iwai Uta' (Aomori Pref.), traditionally sung on the seventh night after the birth of a child.

Many other composers have followed this route of arranging existing songs, sometimes in instrumental versions. Others have taken the next step, using the originals only as points of departure, as in Kiyose Yasuji's 'Fantasia on a Japanese Folk Theme' ('Nihon min'yō no shudai ni yoru gensōkyoku', 1939) and Mamiya's 'Inventions'.

A yet further step is to draw on traditional style without reference to a specific original *min'yō*. Actually, this approach had been taken already around 1920 by Japan's first famous Western-style composer, Yamada Kōsaku (1886–1965), introduced in §1.2 as composer of the Schumann-derived song 'Akatonbo'. After three years in Berlin, he turned his attention in 1918–9 to the study of Japanese music. In Herd's words (2008):

He began to integrate diatonic harmonies with the more dissonant quartal and hexachordal harmonies which he preferred for his quasi-pentatonic melodies. ... classical forms studied in Germany were replaced by freer structures. For many of his piano and orchestral works, Yamada preferred a sparse, linear structure imitative of traditional Japanese solo and ensemble music. Vocal works composed after 1920 freely imitate the melodic flow, phrase structure and vocal range of Japanese folk songs.

We conclude by considering 'Oiwake Bushi Kō' ('Thoughts on "Oiwake Bushi" ') by Shibata Minao (1916–96). Written in 1973, this work takes the song 'Shinano Oiwake' and develops it into a complex theatrical experience. Like Yamada, Shibata aimed for a style appropriate to but not directly imitative of such free-rhythm songs. But he also had the conductor flash random signals to different sections, who would thus combine differently for each performance. And those sections include: a male chorus singing 'Shinano Oiwake' and variants; an improvisatory male chorus; a female chorus singing a variant as might have been heard from the women of the teahouses; a female chorus producing tone clusters derived from the pitches used in the melody plus their overtones; one shakuhachi player; and last but not least, a woman speed-reading passages from Uehara Rokushirō's 1895 study of Japanese scales and modes, even as the men's and women's choruses sing a painful semitone apart.

To my knowledge, no classical composer has yet written a piece or made an arrangement intended to be *sung* by a *min'yō* singer. Some performances may involve imitation of *min'yō* vocal style, but most will be sung in *bel canto*, much as would the arrangements of British folk song by Benjamin Britten for the tenor Peter Pears.

The activities described in this section are indeed on the edges, at best, of the *min'yō* world. Honjō's *risōgaku* is unlikely to be heard at any concert that does not involve him directly; a *min'yō* recital will not feature a pianist, a mixed chorus, an *enka* singer (with rare exceptions), a *fōku shingā* or a rock band. And yet each of these activities in its own way contributes to the perpetuation of Japanese folk song, and the typical *min'yō* aficionado will most likely enjoy folk-influenced *enka* and the Peanuts.

In §§6.6.2–4 I have been writing about people with whom I have had no contact. Because of their liminal position in the folk song world, I have not made time or space to explore their motivations or trace their life histories. But so far as I can tell, their motivations and stimuli for interacting with *min'yō* cover nearly the same range as those in the *min'yō-kai*: love of the music; a sense of identity as a Japanese and possibly a related sense of obligation; local links to particular songs; in some cases, hopes of profit; and so forth. Perhaps only two main motivations are missing: continuing a family tradition; and enjoying the social side of learning and performing *min'yō*.

6.7 Summary

Previous chapters revealed that present-day aficionados of *min'yō* are highly conservative in their choice of material, nearly ignoring recently composed 'new folk songs'. It was also noted that, while folk song often serves in establishing community identity and group membership, the frame of reference is decidedly narrow and local. In the present chapter, we have examined approaches to *min'yō* which defy these generalizations and which position *min'yō* in a larger musical context. In these cases, the frame of reference is no longer the small local in-group or community, but the entire nation or even the world.

(1) Rampant urbanization and rural depopulation fuelled the rise of nostalgia for the life-style of the old home village, the *furusato*, with its sup-posedly simpler, kinder ways of living and stronger sense of community. Even urban-reared Japanese may share this idealized (and often inaccurate) view of rural life. Central and local governments have encouraged such *furusato*-ism in hopes that many urbanites will relocate to and thus re-invigorate shrinking rural communities. Meanwhile, 'new towns', suburbs and urban neighbour-hoods often seek to establish *furusato* values in building a sense of community – *furusato-zukuri* or *machi-zukuri*. Such new communities often create a 'cit-izens' *ondo*', a *shin-min'yō* for group dancing, whose lyrics stress the virtues of that community and the bright future that awaits it if all residents pitch in. These 'citizens' *ondo*' are remarkably similar throughout Japan.

Linking songs with place, we might propose a simple typology. There are songs about activities occurring in your native place from the perspective that you are living there, which includes most *min'yō* and most of the 'citizens' *ondo*'; songs encouraging others to value and visit your native place, which is most early *shin-min'yō* (§3.4.3); songs about missing your home, which includes many *enka*; and songs about being part of the much wider new local community called Japan (perhaps extending to the whole world), which are most of the 'new "new folk songs"' since the 1970s.

(2) Those new *shin-min'yō* of recent decades are much more internation-alist and 'modern' than their predecessors. As the *shin-min'yō* of the 1920s and 1930s were often intended to raise spirits and group consciousness within factories or small communities, those of today often have lyrics clearly expressing a modern, optimistic, internationalist spirit. To further suit mod-ern, Westernized Japan, the following trends appear in these new songs: melodies are chiefly in the *yō* mode on 1, now perceived as similar to the happy, Western major mode and thus called by scholars the pentatonic major; accompaniment is by Western instruments with Japanese festival drumming; and vocals are by a male and female in octave unison, suggest-ing heightened sociability. Such songs are virtually never sung at *min'yō* gatherings: once recorded, they are heard only through loudspeakers as accompaniment for public dancing. Since such dancing has become increas-ingly popular, however, the recordings do sell reasonably well – but to dancers, not to singers.

(3) The Warabiza is a performing troupe founded in 1948 by committed Japanese international socialists, which soon recognized the importance of traditional Japanese folk material for reaching and uniting its audiences: before throwing off Western domination and uniting the world community,

it was first necessary to help the Japanese regain a sense of self. Folk song and dance were considered the most suitable tools, because they 'belong to the masses'. A typical Warabiza concert of the 1970s mixed music and dance of several types, including: faithfully transmitted traditional pieces; new compositions in a style mixing *min'yō* and Western musical features; and new compositions in an international socialist style but with Japanese lyrics. A problem is that the traditional and modern portions of their concerts do not generally appeal to the same people. Most people think of them merely as a group which performs folk material rather than as a political troupe. However, their aims remain optimistic and worthy: through the folk performing arts, 'to depict human dignity and love', to encourage mutual respect, happiness and cooperation.

(4) Those at the heart of the *min'yō* world overwhelmingly maintain its traditionalist core, with modest moves (e.g. by Honjō Hidetarō) to bring elements of *min'yō* into creative contact with other Japanese traditional genres. But many other Japanese find wider musical uses for *min'yō*: arrangements in Western popular styles ('Chakkiri Cha Cha Cha'), or even in world music fusion mode (Hosono's 'Esashi'); multifarious uses in *enka*; inspiration for Western-style classical composers, and so forth. These activities, however much enjoyed, remain on the fringes of the *min'yō* world.

NOTES

1. Nostalgia for one's actual home rather than an imagined one is of course common throughout history worldwide. In Japan, the eighth-century *Kojiki* chronicle records that the famous military leader Yamato Takeru, homesick on his deathbed, sang several *kuni-shinobi-uta* 思国歌, 'songs of longing for home' (Philippi 1969: 248–9).

2. The element *kyō* also forms part of the Sinate word for nostalgia, *kyōshū*, 'grieving for home'. The other two main words for nostalgia are the native *natsukashisa* and the loan-word *nosutarujī*, each imparting a different flavour.

3. Japanese: www.asahi-net.or.jp/~hn7y-mur/mimisuma/mimilink02.htm#book5; English: . . . mimilink02e.htm#book5

4. 210.137.20.12/geijutsu_bunka/chiikibunka/shinkou/sisaku/furusato/index.html

5. 'The mental structure of the contemporary Japanese' (Japan Foundation, Tokyo, 9 June), as summarized in a supplement to the *Japan Studies Center News* 2.2 (July 1977).

6. Variants on *furusato*-ism worldwide deserve comparative study. For example, in the United States, a magazine article entitled 'The new burb is a village' (Adler 1994) begins: 'Remember the sweet little town you wished you'd grown up in? A few planners say you can still have it.' This is 'the New Urbanism', a term which puts the focus on the city (or the suburbs), not the village. As summarized by Adler, the advantages of bringing the village to the city relate not to social relations, as for Japan, but to spatial ones: shops and the train station are 'within walking distance'; you can visit a friend 'on foot or by bicycle'. Convenience, not community, is the prime goal.

7. See www.town.shibata.miyagi.jp/reiki_int/reiki_honbun/ac21600041.html for lyrics and staff notation.

8. See www2.town.miyashiro.saitama.jp/reiki_int/reiki_honbun/ae38600081.html.
9. E.g. www.town.haga.tochigi.jp/townoffice/soumu/reiki/reiki3/reiki_honbun/ae125 00061.html, www.town.miyako.lg.jp/machi/kouhou/News/info03.jsp, www.city-awa.jp/gappei/parts/kyoutei1800.pdf. Robertson 1991: 46, 51–2, 57–8, 92, 103, 181–2 discusses three songs put in the service of 'building' the Tokyo suburb of Kodaira.
10. This section and §3.4.3 are an expansion, revision and re-arrangement of Hughes 1991.
11. Similar pseudo-traditional dances had been created for many of the pre-war *shin-min'yō* as well. For virtually all dances to *shin-min'yō*, the choreography is kept very simple, using the same basic gestural vocabulary over and over, as an aid to dissemination. True folk dances are much more varied.
12. One example of a traditional image (remembering that these are dance songs) is that references to the full moon still occur in many songs, even though Bon dances are now rarely held on the full-moon night but instead on a convenient weekend evening.
13. My summary of the troupe's early history comes principally from Hara 1971, vol. 1, ch. 1 (for *min'yō*, see especially pp. 14–9), supplemented by their website www.warabi.jp.
14. For a history of proletarian music movements in Japan, with guidance to the Japanese-language sources, see Malm 1984. See also the discussion of 'Taishō Democracy' and *shin-min'yō* in §3.4.2.
15. www.warabi.jp/english/index.html
16. Details: www.asahi.com/english/lifestyle/TKY200410230107.html
17. This is true despite its use by scholars in the words *minzokugaku* ('ethnology'), *minzoku ongaku* ('ethnomusicology'), etc.
18. Charles Seeger used almost identical words in the USA in the 1930s, arguing that 'proletarian music' must be 'national in form' but 'revolutionary in content' (quoted in Denisoff 1983: 101). American communists of that period decided to rely on traditional rural music to attract urban workers into the organization, drawing on 'native folk consciousness' to build class solidarity, rather than trying to create a new form of workers' music (Denisoff 1971). Veteran British folk singer and activist song-writer Ewan MacColl (1915–1989) took a similar stance after the 1950s (Watson 1983: ch.10; Woods 1979: 57). On the other hand, his brother-in-law, Pete Seeger (son of Charles), maintained his strongly internationalist repertoire and travel itinerary.
19. Most of her LP output is listed at www.geocities.jp/chiemi_eri/chiemi_sub3-lp_list.htm; clicking on an album title may lead to the original album notes including Eri's comments. Heartfelt thanks to Gerry McGoldrick for originally steering me to Eri's output.
20. See Mori & Spector 2000 concerning the song's later partial banning from broadcasting due to 'problems' arising from its origin in an 'untouchable' village.
21. For alphabetized lists of post-war popular song titles, see www.geocities.jp/rojin1937.
22. The tune can be heard in synthesized form at http://8.pro.tok2.com/~susa26/natumero/36–40/souran.html.
23. Many Japanese composers have also drawn on non-folk genres such as Noh, gagaku, Buddhist chant and so forth, and/or written contemporary pieces for koto, shakuhachi and other traditional instruments.
24. See www.d1.dion.ne.jp/~yosek/kyukon/teien.html.

CHAPTER 7

JAPANESE FOLK
SONG: RETROSPECT,
CIRCUMSPECT, PROSPECT

7.1 Introduction

This book has traced the development of Japanese folk song from traditional times up to the present day, in the context of extensive urbanization, modernization, Westernization and globalization. Before about 1890, folk song was more or less a natural adjunct to daily life, rarely an object of reflection or research. After 1890, various forces conspired to make it a discrete, consciously recognized and (eventually) respected category of Japanese culture, under the name *min'yō*, as detailed in Chapter 3 in particular.

In modern Japan, folk song can be seen as existing in two polar forms, although there are of course many shades in between. At one pole is the world of the urban specialists, with the accent on professionalism, virtuosity, entertainment and profit; authenticity is a secondary consideration. At the other pole, village groups of amateurs maintain traditional performance styles for their own enjoyment as well as in the interests of identity and 'tradition'. The distance between the two is mediated in various ways. For example, the scholarly community plays a major role in setting the values of both camps; television ensures that each is aware of the activities of the other; movement between town and country is freer than in the past; and the rural-urban divide has shrunk physically with urban sprawl, citification of villages and so forth. (See Chapters 4 and 5.)

In both the urban professional and the amateur setting, the approach to folk material is largely conservative. The folklorists' admiration for orally transmitted culture threw the spotlight on folk song as an object of value in itself – which paradoxically was one factor leading to the eventual freezing of many songs at a particular stage in their history, in defiance of the oral process. The government's preservationist approach to the designation of Important Intangible Cultural Properties has had a similar effect, even if usually indirectly. Among professional singers, a major factor contributing to conservatism in the form of standardization was the attempt to upgrade the image of folk song through classicization – the adoption of conventions of transmission and performance characteristic of the more prestigious traditional classical arts (for example, the *iemoto* system) and of Western classical music (notation in particular). Eventually the availability of recordings became a mild force for standardization, but the diversity of those recordings has mitigated the effect of this factor. Standardization as a virtue is still too recent in the *min'yō* world overall to have eliminated variation, though its impact is growing. Most urban teachers consider standardization both necessary at the teaching level and admirable on ideological grounds.

One might suggest that *min'yō* is now a classical genre in the eyes of professional teachers but a potentially popular genre from the viewpoint of the broadcast and recording industries. These industries, searching for new products and wider audiences, strive to dress up familiar songs in novel garb, or commission the composition and recording of 'new folk songs'. These efforts have had remarkably little effect on teachers and little more on public modes of performance.

In sum, *min'yō* has become a major, named category of Japanese music. As recently as 1971, over 40 per cent of the adult population of this highly modernized country said they enjoyed listening to *min'yō* (Table 4.1), and in 1978 it was still the second favourite musical genre overall, after *enka* (Table 4.2). It continues to retain a reasonable 'audience share' by finding new roles to play. In the villages it has become much more important as a force for local identity than in the traditional past – for, as we have seen, modernization of transportation and communication actually increased the need to establish such an identity. For urbanites, *min'yō* may provide an antidote to the more dehumanizing aspects of urbanization and modernization, helping to build a community. In serving these functions, *min'yō* are often difficult to separate from *minzoku geinō* as a whole.

Still, the decline in *min'yō* aficionados is indisputable. My first teacher, Tanaka Yoshio, when asked in 2007 what the major change had been in the *min'yō* world since I met him thirty years earlier, asnwered in a single word: *kōreika* – ageing. Mr Odajima, head of the Esashi Oiwake Kaikan museum office, said the same (23 July 2007): the ageing trend makes it difficult to rear successors (*kōkeisha*) to this important cultural heritage. The youngest generation has been far less receptive to this genre than in the past. There are, however, some signs of revival, as many *min'yō* musicians now do voluntary outreach work in the school system with some success, and the Nihon Min'yō Kyōkai is making major efforts in reaching the young (see next section).[1]

Table 7.1 summarizes a 1999 survey which, although structured differently from those of Chapter 4, gives some hints as to current preferences. In terms of structure, the lack of a breakdown by age is disappointing, as is the lumping of *min'yō* with other Japanese traditional musics (*junhōgaku*), which may have misled some respondents.[2] Note that the terms 'pops, rock, fusion, easy listening, classic(al)' were all written as English in the Japanese phonetic *katakana* syllabary. Domestic pop and rock is overwhelmingly sung in Japanese (with a heavy dose of often dubious English). The meaning of *minzoku ongaku* is surely unclear to most Japanese; it might be taken to indicate 'folkloric music' of any culture, probably signifies domestic *minzoku geinō* to many, but might even be taken to include Okinawan folk song (discussed below). The misleadingly named pair *dōyō* ('children's songs') and *nihon no uta* ('songs of Japan') probably indicates the repertoire of Western-influenced art songs produced since the 1890s (including the famous 'Kōjō no Tsuki' and 'Akatonbo'), which are widely sung with Western harmonies by choruses throughout Japan, plus a few traditional tunes such as 'Sakura'. Despite the shortcomings in the nature of this survey, it is clear that *min'yō* has fallen well behind most other genres, and my experience suggests that age is still a factor: the youngest generation have little overt interest in the genre, except in the instrumental form of the Tsugaru-jamisen tradition. On the other hand, if indeed only 9 per cent of the populace enjoy *min'yō*, that is still some 11 to 12 million people!

Having traced in detail a century's evolution of folk song in Japan, we are now in a position to take a broader perspective. This final chapter has a

Table 7.1. Musical preferences, 1999

pops/rock (domestic)	33
pops/rock (foreign)	29
kayōkyoku/enka	26
fusion	14
easy listening	7
classical [Western-style]	22
minzoku ongaku	11
dōyō/nihon no uta	11
nihon min'yō/junhōgaku	9

Respondents were asked which of ten categories of music interested them. Multiple answers were permitted. I have omitted one category and rounded to the nearest percent. Data from Geinō Bunka Jōhō Sentā 1999: 176.

number of purposes. One, returning to some of the issues raised in the opening chapter, is to try to draw some conclusions with reference to the interaction of forces such as modernization and tradition. Finally, a glance into a crystal ball will attempt to foresee the future of *min'yō*. But let us begin by examining certain recent trends which indicate changes in attitude towards the performance and significance of traditional rural song.

7.2 The Nihon Min'yō Kyōkai as exemplar of recent trends

We begin with the Nihon Min'yō Kyōkai – Nichimin for short – the single most influential *min'yō* organization, with over 40,000 members (§3.5). Founded in 1950, they now boast an impressive headquarters in Shinagawa, southwest Tokyo, with a library, concert hall, teaching facilities and offices. (See Appendix 2 for contact details.) Their website (www.nichimin.or.jp) lists their major aim as 'preserving, teaching and spreading folk song and dance, thus contributing to the improvement of Japanese culture'. More concretely, they will do this through: research and dissemination; fieldwork, recording and transcription; 'excavation' of songs and dances; publication; and performance.

Nichimin's public activities have proliferated in the past two decades, and a survey of these will reveal most recent trends in the *min'yō-kai*. From the beginning, they have run Japan's most prestigious multi-song national contest. This is now titled the Min'yō Minbu Zenkoku Taikai and held over four days each October. Including the recent word *minbu* clarifies that dance is now a major element. Choosing the word *taikai*, 'grand meeting, convention, etc.' in preference to one of the words meaning 'contest' is appropriate as the event now also includes diverse non-competitive elements reflecting the growth in Nichimin's concerns. Still, the contest is central.

Nichimin now also conducts over fifty regional *taikai* to cater for its local branches. Since 1988 they have also run the Nihon Min'yō Fesutibaru (Festival), a contest among grand-prize winners from many other *min'yō* contests (§4.6.1); this serves the excellent purpose of crossing over among many more parochial events. Of most interest to us, however, are the three recently established annual events that capture current trends.

(1) The Tsugaru-jamisen Konkūru Zenkoku Taikai, held in Tokyo, was launched in 1998 as this genre's popularity soared (see §4.9 and next section).

(2) In response to the ageing dilemma mentioned above, a separate national contest-cum-festival for children, the Min'yō Minbu Shōnen Shōjo Zenkoku Taikai, began in 1999. Primary- and middle-school children are divided into three age-groups for the singing contest, but united into one group for each of the dance, group song and group instrumental sections. There are regional preliminaries for entrants to the song contest. Further activities aimed at children are described below.

(3) In April 2006, in collaboration with the Yomiuri Shinbun newspaper's Tokyo office and *Hōgaku Jānaru* magazine, Nichimin made its greatest leap away from the *min'yō* world, launching a contest for mixed ensembles of Japanese and Western (or presumably other) instruments (Wayō Gakki Gurūpu Kontesuto). The prizes include an electric shamisen. Even the title's use of the English words 'group contest' targets a growing constituency, the fusion-loving young. Fusion of native and foreign instruments has burgeoned, as is evident in the selective concert listings cited from *Hōgaku Jānaru* in §6.6 and from further examples below. In this contest, the Japanese instruments need not be from the *min'yō* world. Choice of clothes is also free, allowing for the latest shredded jeans or, like, whatever. As the new national curriculum mandating experience of traditional instruments in middle schools takes full effect (§7.5), this contest should loom ever larger. (Photos of the children's and mixed-instrument contests are on the web at www.nichimin.or.jp/info/info-tai.html#5.)

Some other activities are less visible to the general *min'yō* public. These include activities relating to two of the greatest needs in the *min'yō* world today: the training of the young and the expansion of the repertoire.

Since 1988, as an antidote to the ageing of the *min'yō* populace, Nichimin have conducted special activities for children, which since 1997 have been under the aegis of their Seishōnenbu (Youth Division). First they established a 'club' to train children in song and dance (Shōnen Shōjo Min'yō Minbu Ikusei Kurabu). But as this title was considerably too long and formal for today's youth, the club was replaced in 1996 by Utae•mon (歌え・もん), a club for children through middle school. Since 1998, graduates of Utaemon can join the new group WA•KA; writing its name in romanization is again calculated (correctly) to appeal to the young. Under these two names, monthly training sessions in singing, shamisen, shakuhachi, taiko, 'etc.' are held at the Kyōkai's headquarters in Shinagawa, Tokyo.[3]

Since 1998 the Youth Division have also been running sessions in primary and middle schools, mostly near their headquarters but, with increasing demand, often much further away. They also hold educational 'mini-live' performances to introduce instruments, culminating in students learning the simple *min'yō* 'Kokiriko Bushi' on vocals and taiko.

For several years the Research Division (Kenkyūbu), in response to the perception that the same old songs keep getting sung, has encouraged expansion of the repertoire via soliciting submissions of *hakkutsu min'yō* and *shinsaku min'yō*. Successful applicants in either category will receive a 'small token of gratitude', and their songs will be performed at the Zenkoku Taikai.

Hakkutsu min'yō, 'excavated songs' (§4.6.2), are here defined as those that, having died out or nearly so, are targeted for revival; entrants must submit documentation, including the song's original function and context. *Shinsaku min'yō*, 'newly composed *min'yō*', must be one's own work and so far uncirculated. They must 'incorporate a region's local colour, lifeways, industry, tourist sites, etc.', thus being 'suitable (*fusawashii*) as *min'yō*'. Applicants must send a demo on cassette to the Research Division, along with the lyrics, performers' names, and (if any) the choreography and photos of the costumes. Only traditional instruments (*hōgakki*) may be used. We have now met three terms for newly composed songs in a *min'yō* vein: Machida's term *sōsaku min'yō* (§1.3); the most common term, *shin-min'yō*; and now *shinsaku min'yō*. Nichimin's definition, however, is quite narrow and traditionalist and would exclude many of the newer *shin-min'yō* of §6.4, as well as any performance featuring Western instruments. I have not yet been able to examine any of these *shinsaku min'yō*.

Nichimin also, at eight locations around Japan, holds qualifying exams for teachers (*shidōsha*) for song, dance and instruments, assigning university-type titles depending on how many of the specified pieces are well taught as part of the exam (e.g. five pieces to be a Professor).

7.3 *Min'yō* meets Tsugaru-jamisen, *wadaiko* and Okinawan music

For many young Japanese today – indeed, even for young foreigners who have stayed in Japan – the only 'traditional' musics that interest them may be Tsugaru-jamisen, Okinawan music and *wadaiko* ('Japanese drums'). Even older Japanese may prioritize these as representatives of Japanese culture. Around 1999, a Japanese friend working in London had the task of bringing together the upper echelons of certain Japanese and British companies for social occasions. He told me that two of the Japanese executives suggested that Japanese culture should be introduced via music, in particular Okinawan music and Tsugaru-jamisen. (Yasutaka Jun'ichi, pers. comm. 1999.)

In a sense, this section continues from §6.6, which looked at the interaction of *min'yō* with other genres. The difference is that the three genres named here are closer to the core of the *min'yō* world. Honjō's *risōgaku* (§6.6.1) could perhaps have gone here as well.

Let us start with Tsugaru-jamisen, which is clearly a part of the *min'yō-kai* and thus has already been mentioned several times (§§2.5.3, 4.6.1, etc.). The person most responsible for bringing this genre to prominence nationwide was the charismatic Takahashi Chikuzan (§2.4.6, Groemer 1999), through his recordings and his one-man shows at the 'Jean-Jean'/Jan-Jan music club in Tokyo's Shibuya. Recent years have seen a huge boom among the young, led by musicians from outside Tsugaru such as Kinoshita Shin'ichi (§4.4.2) and the Yoshida Kyōdai (Yoshida Brothers). Rather in the fashion of British violinist Nigel Kennedy, Kinoshita and the Yoshidas appeal to the young not only through their incredible musicianship and technique but through their punk hairdos and eclectic dress sense and through their eager embracing of fusion with other musics. Kinoshita, for example, has jammed or recorded with Turkish musicians, a gypsy violinist, rock musicians, a Chinese *erhu* player and others.

Other reasons for this genre's popularity are shared with *wadaiko*: a powerful beat recalling aspects of rock music, and – since these are instrumental genres – the fact that the young are not required to make potentially embarrassing attempts at singing seemingly old-fashioned lyrics in a difficult traditional style. Japan's guitar-playing youth are ready to tackle Tsugaru-jamisen in a way that singers of pop music and *fōku songu* are definitely not prepared for *min'yō*.

The genre appeals to all ages. Tickets for the Nihon Min'yō Kyōkai's first national Tsugaru-jamisen contest in 1998 (see previous section) cost ¥3,000–5,000, yet Tokyo's large Hibiya Kōkaidō hall was nearly full. The age range of both competitors and audience was impressively wide, though the young predominate among the entrants. There are separate sections for primary and middle school competitors. Interestingly, although this used to be considered a rather macho genre, in 2007 eight of the seventeen prize-winners in the general division were women, with a similar proportion among the school groups.

Late 2004 saw the release of the feature film *Overdrive* [*Ōbādoraibu*], a fantasy tale of a young urban guitarist who through magical means ends up in Tsugaru learning Tsugaru-jamisen, and then wins a national contest. Kinoshita Shin'ichi plays himself as the contest emcee, and other Tsugaru-jamisen greats also appear.

The opening scene of *Overdrive* features a rap sequence with shamisen. Such eclecticism is a major feature of the Tsugaru-jamisen phenomenon. The instrument often takes the role of a lead guitar. Some varied if less than compelling samples of guitar-type shamisen are on the website of the group Shah, featuring Kudō Takeshi on shamisen (shah.gozaru.jp/music.html). The track 'SATO' aims to tempt us with the *furusato* image, beginning with the lyrics 'Recalling the song(s) of the *furusato*'. But the shamisen is submerged under a standard pop-rock piece (hmm, where is this *furusato*?). Things get interesting, if painfully so, when a sample is introduced of Tokyo-area *matsuribayashi* festival flute and drums, but with no rhythmic connection with the other instruments and with every fourth beat or so mysteriously deleted. The notes (on that website) to their first album claim that their music is 'not *min'yō* or pops or such a category, but places importance on music's mass appeal (*taishūsei*)'. (Meanwhile, from the 1960s Terauchi Takeshi and the Blue Jeans, a Ventures-type rock guitar group, recorded instrumental versions of *min'yō* with Terauchi's guitar often imitating Tsugaru-jamisen, as on the album *Tsugaru Jongara* (R72).)

A more successful example of fusion, or at least one with a clearer role for Tsugaru-jamisen, is any album by Agatsuma Hiromitsu. His 2001 debut CD, *Agatsuma* (R76), won a national record prize. He is the lead shamisenist in the animated film *Nitabō* (*Nitaboh*, 2004), the story of the eponymous blind supposed founder of the genre in the late nineteenth century. What all the prominent Tsugaru fusionists have in common is that they have won one or more of the national Tsugaru-jamisen contests, playing in a purely traditional style; many of them, such as Agatsuma, include both traditional and fusion in their albums and concerts. But virtually none of them (Kudō being an exception) perform with singers of Tsugaru *min'yō*, even though this genre grew out of song accompaniment. The older generation of Tsugaru-jamisen performers such as Takahashi Yūjirō and Sawada Katsuaki also experiment with fusion, but they are still wonderful accompanists for singers.

In Tokyo, you can hear some incredible Tsugaru-jamisen at the Oiwake folk song bar, where several superb young players trade solos but also accompany singers (Appendix 2).

Wadaiko and Okinawan music are further from the heart of the *min'yō-kai* than is Tsugaru-jamisen. *Wadaiko* (often called in English merely 'taiko') has been developed since the 1960s most prominently by the group Ondekoza and its descendant Kodō, whose concerts around the globe have made this genre the chief representative of Japanese music for many people. It involves 'orchestras' of Japanese stick-drums of varying sizes, shapes and timbres, combined in ways they never were in the past, playing purely instrumental pieces (perhaps joined by hand-gongs, bamboo flutes and often now Tsugaru-jamisen) in highly complex and virtuosic arrangements. Via new compositions, fusion with non-Japanese instruments is now common as well. The sound can be deafening, and the larger drums reverberate in the pit of one's stomach much as do the drum and bass of a modern Western DJ club. Aside from this feature congenial to young urban Japanese, *wadaiko* also provides a sense of contact with tradition that does not, however, require any embarrassing attempts at 'traditional'-style singing. Given all this, it is not surprising that the use of larger and more numerous drums has become one aspect of the broadening of *min'yō* style for a few performers. *Wadaiko* groups have sprung up throughout Europe and the Americas, and youth in other Asian countries have been spurred to develop their own neotraditional drum ensembles, often imitating but partly indigenizing the stage style of Kodō (e.g. the Korean group Dulsori).

Wadaiko groups are occasionally included in *min'yō* concerts and recitals. As noted earlier, the monthly magazine *Bachi-Bachi* now caters specifically for fans of Tsugaru-jamisen and *wadaiko*, as if the two's audiences were the same.

Okinawan music has also become popular among young people in 'mainland' (*naichi*) Japan and to some degree abroad as well.[4] For mainlanders, Okinawa is the most accessible and comfortable 'foreign' culture. Okinawan language, music, dance, clothing – all are related to those of the mainland, yet sharply different. Instead of the shamisen, we find its ancestor, the snake-skin-membrane *sanshin*. Thus most mainlanders hold a romantic, exotic, 'orientalist' image of Okinawa. It is also seen as a subtropical paradise of sea, sun and sand, which since the 1970s has led to its folk songs, especially its 'new folk songs', often being proudly called *shimauta*, 'island songs', rather than *min'yō*.

Okinawan folk song in particular has several advantages over mainland folk song from the viewpoint of young Japanese. First, coming in effect from another culture, it is not tarred with the negative associations – 'rural', 'old-fashioned', 'my grandfather's music' – that distance mainland *min'yō* from most young people; on the contrary, it is 'exotic' and novel while still in a sense belonging to 'our' culture. Second, the two predominant Okinawan musical modes (C (D) E F G B C (Koizumi's 'Ryūkyū mode') and C D E G A C) both strike the ear as similar to a Western major mode. As with the pentatonic major favoured by Japanese composers of *shin-min'yō*, these modes are easier to harmonize and also both sound relatively familiar to Westernized ears – a useful selling point in the modern era. Third, Okinawans have continued to create successful and popular new songs in the style of their traditional folk songs, thus avoiding the slightly artificial feel of mainland *shin-min'yō*. Fourth, the swinging dance style known as *kachāshī*, accompanied by frantic *sanshin* plucking, vigorous drumming and synco-pated piercing whistling, is relatively congenial to a generation raised on MTV and pulsating disco. Fifth, Okinawa has spawned a number of fusion artists who have managed to hold tight to Okinawan musical elements while adding Western pop and rock elements; Kina Shōkichi (Shoukichi Kina; recording R51) and the Nēnēs (recording R54) in particular have achieved fame outside Okinawa.

Spurred by various combinations of the factors listed above, mainland pop artists began to latch onto Okinawan music. Rock groups such as The Boom (with their hit song 'Shimauta'; R47), Shang Shang Typhoon and Soul Flower Union (R55) have featured Okinawa-derived elements in their music.

A very few mainland *min'yō* musicians have also attempted to perform Okinawan songs; Honjō Hidetarō had included one in a recital already by 1980, playing *sanshin* while singing. Some of the young musicians of the Oiwake *min'yō sakaba* in Tokyo can provide accompaniment (on Tsugaru-jamisen!) to a handful of Okinawan songs if an audience member wishes.

In August 1999, the Virgin and HMV superstores in Tokyo's trendy Shibuya district each stocked around 150 different CDs of Okinawan music, but only ten or so of mainland *min'yō*; even in Hiroshima I found a similar imbalance. By contrast, Miyata Records in Asakusa, a small shop specializing in traditional Japanese music (see Appendix 2), held some 190 CDs of main-land *min'yō*, including thirty of Tsugaru-jamisen, and some seventy from Okinawa. Miyata attracts a very different type of client from the superstores.

The integration of Ryukyuan culture (this term includes both Okinawa Prefecture and the Amami archipelago of Kagoshima Prefecture) into Japan in recent decades has impacted on the traditional *min'yō* world in one important way: as a factor in national contests. Performers from the Okinawan and Amami traditions now sometimes participate. Okinawa may still be excluded on the grounds of constituting a separate music culture, though Kikuchi Tankyō, head of the Nihon Min'yō Kyōkai, admitted that he felt this was, strictly speaking, wrong (pers. comm. 8 November 2000). The islands of Amami, however, are politically part of Kagoshima Prefecture, whose 'mainland' sectors teem with standard-style *min'yō*, and this makes it difficult to exclude Amami performers despite their unique vocal style, use of the *sanshin*, and other differences from the rest of Japan.

But questions arise when a Ryukyuan performer wins the contest. A woman from Tokunoshima won the spring 1999 national contest of the Nihon Min'yō Kyōkai. This earned her the right to participate in the Japan Folk Song Festival [Nihon Min'yō Fesutibaru] that August, against twenty-nine other winners of various national contests (mostly of the single-song variety). She won again. The judge who announced the winner felt obliged to assure all present that the panel had not been swayed by exoticism, by the cultural uniqueness or novelty of this one performer and her song. Having watched the contest on television, I am dubious: technically she was far from the best, too far to win purely on the grounds of, say, expressiveness or singing on key. (Most judges at such contests are drawn from outside the *min'yō* world, though having a strong interest.) In any case, around that time many in the folk song world did feel that Ryukyuan performers have an unfair advantage due to their uniqueness. After all, judges must get bored with hearing the same well-worn songs over and over, year after year. Given that 'new folk songs' virtually never catch on among singers, and that any significant re-arranging of a traditional song would be unacceptable in a contest, the only possible novelty is either in 'excavating' obscure local songs, or in adding the Ryukyus. The debate will doubtless continue.[5]

Some recent young ensembles combine *min'yō* with all three of these recently popularized styles, *wadaiko*, Tsugaru-jamisen and Okinawan music, and even with other, non-Japanese traditions. One such is the self-styled 'neo-*min'yō*' group Chanchiki, whose fusion album *Gokuraku* (R73; samples on website www.chanchiki.com) exemplifies the new directions young Japanese may take. Their English website explains their justificatory philosophy:

> As the band 'Chanchiki' places itself in the world of Minyo [which] seems like losing inherent energy, they are one of few bands that are making a new departure . . . to restore the balance between tradition and creation. Featuring traditional singing and playing with Japanese instruments, updating the aspect of rhythm by adding a variety of percussion and freely grooving electric bass, they have incorporated Rock, Jazz, Funk, Boogie, Caribbean, Latin, African music,

and etc. On the other hand, they have visited the places where Minyo songs were born, engaged in active exchanges with local musicians, and conducted field research. They are always conscious of respect for the root of Minyo in the conduct of composition.

This is 'neo-*min'yō*' partly because some traditional elements are disregarded in the interests of gaining a new audience for folk songs. I am not so sure about the 'traditional singing': the lead singer, who has won at least one national *min'yō* contest, seems to have dropped most *min'yō* ornamentation and gone for a smoother pop-style voice. And their version of the rowing song 'Funakogi Nagashi Uta' is at such a breakneck tempo that surely the boatmen would have heart attacks. But the members do stress the importance of connecting to the local roots of *min'yō*.

7.4 Other recent developments

Other miscellaneous recent developments can only be noted in passing. Here are several which will have to stand as representatives of all.

7.4.1 Evolved purists

Some mainland, mainstream *min'yō* performers sought a way to attract a younger audience by moving towards pop music, though with less reliance on electricity. Two of Japan's leading folk shamisen players, Honjō Hidetarō and Takahashi Yūjirō, made minor moves in that direction. (See §4.4.2 for their biographies and §6.6.1 for yet another face of Honjō.)

During the 1980s, with encouragement from NHK and others and on the model of his teacher Fujimoto Hideo's Young Folkers (§4.5.1), Honjō took several young perfomers interested in *min'yō* under his wing, successively creating two short-lived ensembles, Jinjin and Toichinsa (Young Min'yō). Their performances often mixed traditional elements with acoustic guitars, Western clothing and the like.

Takahashi Yūjirō similarly sought to involve young people in the *min'yō* world, by meeting them halfway. In 1987 he formed the group Kaze ('Winds'), whose concerts centre around some fifteen Tsugaru-jamisen players, often playing in unison, along with the other standard *min'yō* instruments. Most numbers are performed as instrumentals. According to Nakatsubo Isao, their agent (for this is big business), the group regularly draws full houses at large regional concert halls – proof of their popularity and impact. In Kawaguchi City on 18 April 1998 they filled a 2,000-seat hall and delivered an exciting, well-received performance which I attended. By my estimate, however, 80 per cent of the audience were over age fifty, and 80 per cent were women. This is the same general demographic – middle-aged to elderly women – which supports most traditional art forms, from Kabuki and Noh to koto to flower arranging. Many of the men or younger folks in attendance seemed to be accompanying such women. We shall return to this depressing reality in the final section.

With a young audience in mind, the concert included an extensive 'American Medley' featuring Tsugaru-jamisen arrangements of, among other songs, Elvis Presley's 'Heartbreak Hotel'. This was well received despite the unpromising demographics. No Western instruments were involved.

Honjō (b. 1945) and Takahashi (b. 1934) were both raised in an environment of traditional music far from the big city and relatively isolated from the influences of the growing world behemoth, rock'n'roll. Most of their early musical activity was in the traditional vein, and much of it still is. One might thus call Honjō and Takahashi 'evolved purists'.[6]

In which case Itō Takio (known as Takio) would then be a much further evolved purist. Born in Hokkaidō in 1950, he was exposed to folk song before he could walk, particularly via his father. As he explained in the liner notes to his 1988 'crossover' album, *Takio* (R40): 'When I was small, the first song I sang, I am told, was "Sōran Bushi", familiar from my dad's chorus of *sōran sōran sōran*. . . . When dad drank, the first thing to come out was this "Sōran Bushi" ' (p. 4). By age ten he was singing in local *min'yō* bars, and a few years later he had begun a career as a typical *min'yō kashu*, often singing with a travelling troupe.[7]

But as with most Japanese of his generation, he had also absorbed a taste for 'modern', 'Western' popular music (and a dislike for the formality of the *iemoto* system that increasingly dominated *min'yō* transmission). In 1985 he organized the Takio Band to provide versions of *min'yō* that could unite his disparate musical worlds. The album *Takio* came emblazoned with the following slogan: 'exciting the blood of the [Japanese] race, that's Takio!' (*minzoku no chi no sawagi, kore ga TAKIO da*). The nine tracks on the album are all traditional folk songs. In his 4-page statement of philosophy (liner notes pp. 4–7; written in a free-flowing, sometimes elusive style), he states: 'On this album, I have tried to confront head-on (*butsukeru*), without reserve, the songs I've hitherto been singing in the environment in which I was born' (*ima made umareta kankyō no naka de utatte kita*).

'Hitherto' is a key word here. On this album, he wanted to bring these songs into new environments and interpret them afresh. In the main, he hewed fairly close to traditional style: he sings in a perfectly standard *min'yō* voice (although with more dynamic variation), the modes are traditional (save one chromatic shamisen motif), Western harmony is not employed, and accompaniments include the standard instruments of modern 'stage' *min'yō*. But the accompaniment is not quite as 'standard' as this would suggest: the only shamisen are a pair of vigorous, powerful Tsugaru-jamisen; the two shakuhachi sometimes improvise independently of one another, as never done traditionally; and the percussion is primarily of the *wadaiko* style popularized by Kodō, mentioned above, using gigantic deep-voiced barrel drums not heard with standard 'stage' *min'yō*. Finally, some tracks employ Western electronic drum-pads or keyboards, the latter sometimes providing a deep bass drone. The result is a thickening of texture and volume, an extension of range, a couple of unusual rhythms in the accompaniment, overall a hard-driving, up-tempo sound – but in the final analysis no major deviation from the timbres and forms of traditional folk song. Somewhat more of a departure are his striking variations of tempo and dynamics within a single song, his passages of breathy voice, and his occasional melodic flexibility.

A year earlier, on the 1987 CD *Takio Jinc* (R39), Takio had again recorded a set of traditional *min'yō*, but this time accompanied only by piano, marimba, subtle percussion and *wadaiko* (a single drummer). Many songs are nearly whispered, and the accompaniment is spare and haunting, sometimes jazzy, only one musician on some tracks, again generally eschewing Western chordal harmony. The likely audience for this CD was somewhat different from the CD *Takio*.

As early as 1985, renowned *min'yō* scholar Misumi Haruo opined that, amidst the decline of the folk song boom, Takio was 'reheating the cooled-off *min'yō* world' (MB 1985.7: 20). Still, as of the late 1990s some of my 'traditional' professional *min'yō* friends felt that Takio's impact had been minimal: few people, they claimed, had been drawn into the world of *min'yō* through his recordings. One professional dismissed him as merely 'different' (*betsu*), having nothing to do with their world. There is plenty of evidence that such views are erroneous. Takai Tadahito, editor of the monthly *Min'yō Bunka*, told me in August 1999 that to the populace in general (*ippan no hito*), 'folk singer = Itō Takio' (*min'yō kashu ikōru Itō Takio*). When in that same month I took one of Japan's leading popular music scholars to his first 'folk song bar', he announced to the assembled *min'yō* fans that his only direct experience of the genre was through Takio's albums, which he admired greatly. It was in recognition of Takio's role in (re-)popularizing *min'yō* among the younger generation that he received in 1997 a Distinguished Service Award from the Nihon Min'yō Kyōkai.

Takio's biggest impact has been through his various recordings of 'Sōran Bushi'. The long, complex version (over seven minutes) on the CD *Takio* begins slowly and then jumps to a frantic disco-tempo. It features the above-mentioned two independent shakuhachi, two often independent Tsugaru-jamisen, *wadaiko*, melodic variation, major changes in tempo and dynamics, and a repeated sequence of shouted call-and-response *hayashi: a dokkoisho dokkoisho* (*a dokkoisho dokkoisho*) *a sōran sōran* (*sōran sōran*). Most of his other versions omit the slow introduction and jump straight to the up-tempo disco-feel section; they also include some rock instruments. Similar changes are encountered under our next topic, the recent evolution of festival music and dance.

7.4.2 Evolved festivals

Festivals (*matsuri*) in Japan have diversified over the years. On an August Saturday in Kōenji on the west side of Tokyo, you can join over half a million people enjoying an 'Awa Odori' festival (begun in 1957), with traditionally dressed teams totalling over 5,000 dancers and musicians moving through the streets in a processional Bon dance originally from Tokushima Prefecture on Shikoku; or on the other side of town you can be among the half-million spectators at the Asakusa Samba Festival (begun in 1981), most of the dancers being Japanese, the women rather more scantily clad than their 'Awa Odori' counterparts. The popularity of these two events is about equal, though the 'Awa Odori' festival continues on Sunday with a similar turnout.

Or you could experience samba and Bon dancing as part of a single event. Each August since 1962, the city of Kitakami in Iwate Prefecture has held the Michinoku Geinō Matsuri, uniting *minzoku geinō* groups from all parts of the northeast (§4.3.3; 121 groups in 2007). In the early years the opening parade featured the major participating groups, including the musicians and drum- and hand-dancers of the nicely complex local Bon dance 'Sansa Odori'. Later was added a *shin-min'yō* with simple accompanying dance: 'Kitakami Odense' ('Welcome to Kitakami', using a local dialect word). Then in the mid-1990s, to increase interest among the younger generation, for a while the centrepiece of the parade became . . . the samba! Members of a Brazilian samba school, including Japanese students, came from Tokyo to dance to the vibrant sounds of Rio. This was well received. East and West co-existed without obvious tension. Such mixtures are not only recent: a television programme I caught around 1980 noted that the 1937 Sado Island Mining Festival featured not only traditional folk music and theatre, including the famous local *min'yō* 'Sado Okesa', but also a Western 1920s-style 'flapper'.

In contrast to such peaceful but separate co-existence, one festival tradition merges East and West directly, through fusion: The Yosakoi Matsuri and its myriad local offshoots. Since 1954 Kōchi City on Shikoku Island has held this festival each August, now lasting four days, whose main feature is the competition among teams of young dancers (192 teams in 2007; see www.yosakoi.com) all dancing to arrangements of the *shin-min'yō* 'Yosakoi Naruko Odori'. This massive street event was inspired by the 'Awa Odori' of neighbouring Tokushima, which attracted so many tourists that Kōchi saw possibilities as well, especially for a more 'modern' festival. The Yosakoi Matsuri captures the liberation and licence of traditional *matsuri* but extends this by allowing creative costuming and musical arrangements. One of the few rules is that all dancers must carry the wooden clappers called *naruko*, originally used to scare away birds from freshly seeded rice paddies; otherwise each team is free to create its own costumes, choreography and music.

The website notes: 'Costumes worn . . . vary from traditional Happi and Kimono to modern ones. Also modern music like Rock n' Roll, Samba, Club (Disco) Music and *Enka* . . . have become popular now, as well as the traditional [*sic* – since 1954] Yosakoi music.'

This sort of event was so appealing to young Japan that at least 200 descendants have sprung up around the country. These have localized titles, e.g. Yosakoi Toyama, using the local prefectural name, or the Yosakoi Okesa Matsuri on Sado Island, whose title refers to the famous local 'Okesa' tune family of *min'yō*. There is even a version in Kōchi's sister city Surabaya in Indonesia. All require dancers to use *naruko*, but otherwise each festival specifies that each team's music must quote in some way a *min'yō* from the locality.

The spread from Kōchi apparently began with the launch of the Yosakoi Sōran Matsuri in Sapporo, Hokkaidō's main city, in 1992 (see www.yosanet.com/yosakoi/foreign/en/). The idea came from several local university students, who had visited the Kōchi festival in 1991 and hit upon 'Sōran Bushi' as the most instantly identifiable musical symbol of Hokkaidō. Now, watched by 2 million spectators, as many as 400 teams and 45,000 dancers take part over five days in June, including many from outside Hokkaidō and guest teams from the parent Yosakoi Festival. The main rule is that each team's music must include, in some form, the local *min'yō* 'Sōran Bushi'. At festival's end, professional folk singers perform the standard 'Sōran Bushi'. The website records that the 2005 festival generated over UK£120 million in revenue for local businesses.

Musical accompaniments tend to feature a synthesized disco feel, with plenty of *min'yō*-like shouts (*kakegoe*) from the dancers. Crown Records has been issuing CDs of each year's best songs from the Yosakoi Sōran Matsuri; let us introduce one track from the 1999 festival (R60), 'Yosakoi Sōran' by the Mitsuishi Naruko Kai team. The track begins with an *a cappella* doo-wop chorus: 'Dooo-wah didit dooo-wah!' This is joined by a full rock band with funk bass, then a refrain in English: 'Mitsuishi ladies' – the dancers are young women from Mitsuishi Town. Then a male rock voice joins, singing the first verse of 'Sōran Bushi' ('Have the herring come? . . .') in Japanese, but in a drawl imitative of Mick Jagger imitating American blues singers, and culminating in the English line, 'Gotta keep on movin' on!'

The various websites mentioned in this subsection contain photos of dancers, of whom the vast majority are young females. Choreographies are often too demanding for older women, but they have their own dance world, to which we now turn.[8]

7.4.3 Folk dance

I have barely touched on the world of folk-related dance. Folk songs accompany the traditional community Bon dances and various, often largely improvised, party dances, while 'new folk songs' are almost always created along with a newly choreographed group dance. From the 1970s, *min'yō* concerts and television shows often presented newly arranged or completely newly created 'stage' dances to accompany songs, performed by the choreographer and a few of her students. The dancers smiled constantly, mostly towards the audience, in the manner favoured by most of the modern world's 'folkloric' dance troupes. The teacher herself wore a contrasting costume and occupied the centre. A handful of teachers dominated in this sphere, most prominent being Nishizaki Midori.

These teachers tended to come from the world of classical Japanese dance (*nihon buyō*); as they turned to folk dance, more for commercial reasons than out of personal preference, they brought with them many of the aesthetic and attitudinal values from that world, much as Fujimoto Hideo had done for folk song. The more elaborate new choreographies, verging on classical dance style, might be called *min'yō-buyō*, 'folk song dances'. Later, from around 1980, such teachers began to create dances suitable for accompaniment by *enka*, called *buyō-kayō* or *kayō-buyō*. The terms *buyō-kayō* and *kayō-buyō* seem to differ only in emphasizing the song or the dance respectively.

The presence of the element *buyō* in each of these terms indicates the influence of classical dance on the overall style, but this has to be bent to the mood of the text and music of the accompanying song – *min'yō* or *enka* (=*kayō*). Four elements unite these three genres and make them attractive for amateur dancers in today's busy world: they are shorter (perhaps three or four minutes long), simpler and often of somewhat lighter mood than classical dance; and crucially, they are often solos, giving the dancer a chance to be the star rather than just one of a unison group in a Bon dance. Any of these dance types might be included in a recital of either classical dance or folk song.

We noted in Chapter 1 that the word *min'yō* can also mean 'folk dance' if the character *yō* 踊 meaning 'dance' replaces its homophone 謡 meaning 'song'. In careful use today, it seems that the term *min'yō* 民踊 is restricted to newly choreographed dances, while traditional dances are referred to as *minbu* 民舞, using the element *bu* of *buyō* (Yoshizawa Anna, pers. comm. 1 December 2006).

7.4.4 A fōku shingā approaches min'yō

In §6.6.2 and elsewhere, we have discussed arrangements of *min'yō* by artists in other genres, including the *fōku* group Akai Tori. But Okabayashi Nobuyasu (§1.7.1) took another approach.[9] On overseas concert tours in the mid-1980s, this Western-style guitar-plucking *fōku shingā* was challenged by various Korean and British folk musicians to produce something more Japanese. He decided the answer must lie in *min'yō*, which had never interested him until then.

He thought of two widely-known work songs that should brim with the requisite energy: the herring-netting song 'Sōran Bushi' and the boat-rowing song 'Saitara Bushi'. But mechanization meant that the original work rhythms survived, barely, only in versions by preservation societies, which seemed to him 'old-fashioned' (*mukashi no mon*): he was seeking the living rhythms of today's daily life. He rejected the idea of singing 'Sōran Bushi' as it was: since it is not used now for catching herring, 'we' (*bokutachi*) are unable to 'put our hearts' (*kokoro o komete*) into singing or dancing such music. (One wonders whether he had heard Takio's version.)

So he decided to try to compose 'music for now' (*ima no ongaku*) using tradition as a base. He created a style of strongly rhythmic *fōku songu* he called *en'yatotto* after the vocable of 'Saitara Bushi' originally chanted by the rowers. (His compositions never quoted music or text directly from existing *min'yō*.) Two prime examples are 'Kazeuta' and 'Ran no Funauta' (R74). Both are in the *yō* mode on 6, backed by Western harmonies on guitar and other *fōku* instruments; both feature shakuhachi, and 'Ran no Funauta' adds Tsugaru-jamisen and *wadaiko*. 'Kazeuta' has a chorus of typical *min'yō* *hayashi-kotoba: yansa no ē yoiya makasho*; on 'Ran no Funauta', a 'boat song', Okabayashi trades macho shouts of *sōrya sōrya* with a male chorus.

Although I enjoy both of these songs, it is difficult for me to hear how their rhythms are linked to 'today's daily life' any more than are those of 'Sōran Bushi' or 'Saitara Bushi'. But Okabayashi does seem to have found a style that combines *min'yō* and *fōku songu* in interesting ways.

7.4.5 Kikusuimaru and boundaries

As a final case study, consider Kawachiya Kikusuimaru's 1991 album *Happy* (R46). As indicated by the stage name he received from his teacher, he was trained as a singer of 'Kawachi Ondo'. This is a Bon-dance ballad genre that arose in the Kawachi region around Osaka, in which a single melody is used for a number of long ballad texts. In the cover photograph, Kikusuimaru poses in kimono, beside the Bon-dance *taiko* that traditionally joins the shamisen in accompanying 'Kawachi Ondo'. He sings throughout in the distinctive vocal timbre of this particular narrative genre (basically a *min'yō* voice but lower-pitched, with prominent overtones). The album, though, is more eclectic than all this might suggest. Of seven tracks, only the last is in traditional 'Kawachi Ondo' style, with shamisen, *taiko* and *hayashi-kotoba* unison choral response – plus guitar and electric bass. (Track 4 is 'Hana', composed by Kina Shōkichi – the Okinawan fascination continues!) 'Kawachi Ondo' also forms a sort of stylistic bridge, both musically and textually, between folk song and *enka*; the vocal timbre in particular is close to *enka*. Meanwhile, the album is also situated solidly in the World Music arena: some tracks were recorded in Jakarta and Singapore, with the participation of local musicians and their instruments; some feature 'Jamaican rap'. The lyrics address the concerns of young Japanese. One track is entitled 'Furītā' ('freeter'), a word derived from English 'free-lance' and indicating someone who is not tied into the ethos of corporate Japan that ideally links an employee with a single company for life – an ideal that has increasingly become a fiction since the burst of the economic 'bubble' in 1992.

Artists like Kikusuimaru blur the neat boundaries between genres. Is he a folk singer, a pop singer, or something else? Fortunately, this question only seriously vexes record shops and the more pedantic academics. But it does pose a challenge to the relatively monolithic nature of the 'folk song world' described in previous chapters. As mentioned above, the artists introduced in this section have had little effect – so far – on the activities of the typical *min'yō* teacher, student or performer (as has also been true of the *shin-min'yō* discussed in §§3.4.3 and 6.3–4). Urban *min'yō* classrooms and rural preservation societies will continue in the same vein for years to come. Even Takahashi Yūjirō and Honjō Hidetarō will presumably continue to teach and perform traditional-style *min'yō* – for love as well as for money – even as they explore new approaches and seek new audiences.

7.5 Tradition and music education

Let me start this section with a verbal snapshot.

> The music classroom of a primary school in northern Japan, on a Tuesday evening in 1988. Thirty-odd housewives sit at the desks; under each desktop is a small electronic keyboard. K-sensei, the school's principal and music teacher, conducts the Iwasaki Village Housewives' Chorus once a week, at the fervent request of the Housewives' Association. Sensei sits at the piano and leads them through some vocal exercises. Then they launch into 'Edelweiss' from *The Sound of Music*, sung in Japanese. On the wall are portraits of Brahms, Schubert, Wagner.
>
> After an hour of Western-style choral music (some of it composed by Japanese), Sensei asks the foreign visitor to say a few words of appreciation. Not renowned for his tact, the foreign visitor struggles to find a nice way to express his somewhat narrow-minded, pig-headed opinion: 'Why are all you Japanese singing these puerile Western melodies, especially since you are fortunate enough to live in Iwate, a region particularly rich in wonderful folk songs? We Westerners know too little about the rest of the world's music; you Japanese know too little about your own. Don't you know any local songs?'
>
> After I manage to say it a little more politely than that, Sensei, ever courteous, acknowledges the correctness of my view and leads the group in their one 'local' song. It is a Western-style setting of a poem in local dialect by a renowned local poet of recent vintage, Miyazawa Kenji. [Hughes 1990: 11; slightly altered]

We have here a mismatch between what a *min'yō* fan might consider a 'local' song and what other Japanese might. Although the setting for this event was a music classroom and the teacher was the school principal, the singers in this case were not school students. Still, the musical tastes of these house-wives were partly formed in their school days, in music classes. How has Japanese school education approached *min'yō* and other traditional genres?[10]

National guidelines on school music curriculum matters are set by the Ministry of Education, although teachers are free to determine the actual content of instruction to accord with local resources and conditions. Since the Second World War, revised National Curricula have been promulgated in 1947, 1951, 1958, 1969, 1977, 1990 and 1999, each being put into effect a few years later.

Until 1969 the Ministry had never seen fit to make Japanese traditional music a standard part of the curriculum, aside from a bit of guided listening unreinforced by any hands-on (or mouth-open) experience. The origins of this lacuna are clear enough: the Meiji-period policy of 'catching up' with the West, formulated while in the throes of a national inferiority complex (§1.5).

During the recent decades of prosperity, the attitude of the Ministry of Education has changed somewhat. For several years after 1972 (in accor-dance with the 1969 National Curriculum), middle school students were to be taught actually to *perform* a single *min'yō* each year – the first time that any Japanese music performance had ever been built into the curriculum. The three songs chosen ('Kokiriko Bushi', 'Saitara Bushi' and 'Kariboshi-kiri Uta' in that order) progressed from very simple to moderately difficult, from relatively syllabic to highly ornamented, from a simple 2/4 metre to a more challenging free rhythm. Alas, even this minimal traditional content was soon dropped from the performance curriculum, since even the simplest *min'yō* proved too daunting for the vast majority of school music teachers who had to teach them.[11]

This is hardly surprising given a teacher training syllabus that had prepared them not at all for teaching *any* genre of traditional music. Nor are most school music teachers even interested in traditional music, though this is rapidly changing. The situation parallels that in, among other countries, England, where an increasing official emphasis on 'multicultural' music education in recent years is running ahead of the teaching provision: most teachers lack either the motivation, the knowledge, the resources or – when they do have some skills – the confidence to teach about 'other' musics. In Japan, oddly, 'other' musics include Japanese music. The system of teacher training tends to be self-perpetuating.

Kikuchi Tanshige told me (8 November 2000) that his wife was in middle school during those years. She remembers her female music teacher singing the cowherding song 'Nanbu Ushioi Uta' in *bel canto*, leading the students to think, 'Strange stuff, folk song' (*Hen da, min'yō wa*).

But the Ministry of Education had truly turned an important corner. Realizing the futility of mandating instruction in any traditional Japanese music performance given inadequate human resources (the teachers), they nonetheless increased the overall emphasis on traditional genres in the curriculum, leaving scope for performance where local conditions permitted. A full treatment of subsequent developments merits a separate study; only aspects directly relevant to *min'yō* are considered here.

Given Japan's tens of millions of *min'yō* fans, surely most school districts could count among their residents a competent teacher of folk song performance? Indeed they could. And there are often as well teachers of other traditional genres and instruments – koto, shakuhachi, various shamisen styles, Noh singing – not to mention various traditional dance styles. Therefore, if school music teachers cannot teach these styles and are not willing to learn, why do they not call on someone who can?

I asked these questions of several school music teachers in southern Iwate Prefecture in 1988 and in Sapporo (Hokkaidō Pref.) in 1989. The responses were in general strikingly uniform.

The first justification can be paraphrased as: 'Japanese traditional music is becoming an alien music (*ikoku no ongaku*) to the students, so we don't teach it.' The blame was being passed on to the students. This seems a novel way to determine a school curriculum. Had I been given the option, at the age of twelve, of determining the content of my classes, I would now know considerably less about math, science, geography and literature and rather more about baseball, cowboys and rock guitar. These teachers had, of course, precisely reversed the causality: It is not taught, so it is becoming an alien music.

As soon as I raised this argument, the teachers generally wilted in guilty acknowledgement and moved on to justification number 2: 'But in Japan, you know, traditional music is transmitted in its own exclusivist "schools" (*ryūha*); if we select a teacher of, say, Ikuta-school koto, then the rival Yamada school will be offended.' This problem, too, insofar as it exists at all, has been solved at institutions such as Tokyo University of Fine Arts and Music by, for example, alternating teachers every few years or simply ignoring the issue, but there could be other solutions.

A third excuse then followed: 'But these local teachers do not have any qualifications.' To which one can only retort: Who is it who is unqualified? A degree from a Japanese teacher-training music college awarded to someone who is unable to teach any style of Japanese music seems to me less of a qualification than is an advanced certificate from a school of traditional music under the *iemoto* system.

Teachers trained only in Western-style music cannot, of course, afford to admit that there is an important part of the curriculum that they are unqualified to teach, for that would imply that they should share their job – and salary – with another. Indeed, the uniformity of the responses leads to the suspicion that these arguments were supplied to teachers, perhaps via a professional journal, as part of a defence of the *status quo*.

Notice that none of these three justifications requires teachers to take a stand on the absolute or comparative value of traditional music. But most will eventually admit that they find, say, *min'yō* vastly inferior to the music of Mozart, or Wagner, or whichever style they most adore. Some will simply say that it is not worthy of being taught. One teacher sympathetic to traditional music revealed that, when the Kitakami-area teachers met periodically to discuss overall curriculum policy, traditional music was simply ignored: discussion centred around such questions as the relative merits of Classic vs. Romantic music. In reality, even when taught, most traditional performing arts – folk or classical – are banished from the music class and treated as are sports or other extracurricular activities.

Still, some individual teachers do make the effort to expose students to traditional music, including performance, as part of the actual music class (see e.g. Pecore 2000). This obviously requires them to first learn the art themselves. Some may by chance have been raised in an environment conducive to traditional music; others are late converts, for whatever reasons. One high school band teacher in southern Iwate, at about the age of thirty-five in the early 1980s, began taking shakuhachi lessons on the side. He had come to feel that as a Japanese he *must* expose his students to traditional music, and the shakuhachi was the instrument that most appealed to him. (He was primarily a brass player.) He confessed in 1988 that his skills were still woefully inadequate, yet he felt that his students would pick up an important message from seeing his enthusiasm and determination. He played for them often and began to teach those who were willing.

Here are some examples, all from the 1980s, where particular schools or districts had found it possible and indeed valuable to make time for traditional folk performing arts.

(1) The Yasugi City High School (Shimane Pref.) had, in 1980, for several years been teaching its graduating students to sing 'Yasugi Bushi', telling them that they would be glad of it someday. Classroom response was less than enthusiastic at first, but apparently several graduates have reported that they found the effort worthwhile. It is almost automatic, at a year's-end party or other large-scale social event, that a person from Yasugi will be asked to sing the local 'famous product'; thus the school's foresight has saved many a graduate from embarrassment in Osaka or Tokyo (Matsue Tōru, pers. comm.). 'Esashi Oiwake' was being put to similar use in its home town, and with similar success, when I visited in 1988.

(2) In 1980, the music of the 'Deer Dance' of Yanagawa (§5.2) was being played on cassette to provide the rhythm for exercise during gym class at the village primary school; some students were asking that the dance itself be taught.

(3) In the village of Iwasaki (Waga City, Iwate Pref.), as of 1988 all students at the primary school were being required to take classes in the music and/or dance of the Devil Sword Dance (*oni kenbai*). Following the traditional learning method, dancers sing the syllables of the drum part

(*den suko den* . . .) to the flute melody to keep their place. The national
fame of this vigorous and impressive masked dance is one reason that the
students tended to participate enthusiastically; another is that they would
most likely be able to perform it at the yearly Festival of Northern
Performing Arts (Michinoku Geinō Matsuri) in nearby Kitakami City,
watched by thousands of spectators from far and wide. The adult version
of the dance, transmitted in several nearby hamlets, is 'officially' restricted
to male performers, but girls join in at Iwasaki Primary School.

This tuition was the initiative of the school principal, K-sensei – the same
individual who was directing the Western-style Iwasaki Village Housewives'
Chorus described at the start of this section. He required all teachers (most
of whom hailed from elsewhere) to learn this music and dance in order to
teach the students. To cope with a low budget, he made the flutes himself
from grey plastic plumbing pipe. Thus he has shown what can be accomplished when the will is there.

The impact of such efforts still remains to be gauged. A preliminary
discussion, based on surveys of school students, was offered in §4.3.3.

A truly exciting change was included in the 1999 National Curriculum,
which began to be taught in April 2002. As part of an overall increase in
teaching about Japan's traditional culture (which some see however as
reflecting a resurgence of right-wing nationalism), from now on, all middle
school students are to be given some practical experience of playing at least
one traditional Japanese instrument. This time the government, learning
from the failed attempts to require the teaching of *min'yō* in the 1970s, has
striven to ensure the availability of trained teachers as well as reasonably
priced instruments, teaching materials and so forth. The focus this time is on
instrumental rather than vocal music, so the effect on the folk song world
cannot be predicted with confidence. Initial results are encouraging, helped
no doubt by a separate growth in the use of traditional instruments in fusion
music of various sorts (see §§6.6, 7.3–4).

The choice of instrument(s) is left to each school. Unfortunately, so is the
actual amount of time devoted to these: in some cases less than a few hours over
three years. Furthermore, all that is required is that students 'experience' an
instrument first-hand: true performance teaching is rare. As one (anonymous)
teacher told me disparagingly in June 2007, this could amount to nothing more
than a teacher briefly demonstrating a koto, then leaving the students to try
composing a koto piece with a title such as 'Spring Flowers' during the next
thirty minutes – with virtually no further guidance. This reflects the increased
emphasis on creative activities, an antidote to a century of rote learning.

Fortunately, the new National Curriculum also created a new time slot for
'integrated study' (*sōgō gakushū*). Its intention, in large part, is to allow each
school to bring in local culture in an integrated fashion, relating to the community. Combining this, the traditional instrument requirement, and the

longstanding trend to encourage after-school 'club activities' (*kurabu katsudō, bukatsu*), in some schools the amount of traditional musical activity has increased dramatically. Here are two examples related to *min'yō*.[12]

Sado Island (Niigata Pref.) has been cited several times already for its strong *min'yō* tradition as well as being the base of the Kodō *wadaiko* group. No surprise, then, to learn that many schools there – primary, middle, high – have been teaching either *min'yō* or *wadaiko* or both for over a decade. (Other instruments may also be taught: one school was loaned ten koto by a music education professor as part of his research.) Instructors are usually local musicians rather than school music teachers; most are volunteers, though a budget for expenses may be available. The focus is on local *min'yō* such as 'Sado Okesa' and 'Aikawa Ondo'. If there is a local Bon-dance song, students may learn that as well. For 'Aikawa Ondo', student groups usually learn song, shamisen, dance and drum (Fig. 7.1); 'Sado Okesa' adds flute as well.

Okinawa is somewhat of a special case, as we discussed in §7.3, in that its *min'yō* tradition has continued to develop, has fused easily with Western influences, and has maintained wide popularity among both young and old. The *sanshin*, the ancestor of the shamisen and a badge of Okinawan identity, is widely played. Gradually since the 1990s, many schools at all levels have begun to include some teaching of performance of *sanshin* and associated songs. The repertoire generally includes only fairly simple pieces, but chosen from a wide repertoire: folk songs, songs from the old Okinawan court repertoire, 'Twinkle Twinkle Little Star' sung in Japanese, and perhaps one of the Okinawan-pop-fusion songs by the group Begin that are now popular throughout Japan. *Sanshin* are donated by local residents (most houses have one or more) or purchased cheaply. In middle schools, this is the common response to the National Curriculum requirement on instruments. Okinawa's distinctive regional culture is a source of great local pride, and in fact virtually no other Japanese traditional music is taught in the schools there.

An additional incentive or reward for learning, as for the Devil Sword Dance in Iwate mentioned above, is the chance to perform in public. All schools and school districts have sports days, culture festivals and so forth where such performances might be offered. There is also, each August, an annual week-long National High School Culture Festival, which includes sections for brass bands, drama, Japanese chess and so forth, plus two days devoted to local *minzoku geinō*. High schools from both Sado and Okinawa are virtually always included.

7.6 Modernization, Westernization and tradition

In §1.1 we introduced some approaches to the concepts of modernization and Westernization. Let us now see to what extent these general concepts are useful in understanding developments in the world of Japanese folk song.

Now that we have come to the point of actually applying these concepts, it will first be necessary to define them with more precision. I find myself encouraged by the Japanese data to distinguish two types of modernization as well as two types of Westernization.

Pragmatic modernization (abbreviated **PM**) will refer to changes resulting from (1) increased access to new approaches to problems, combined with (2) an increased ability to foresee the possible advantages of new approaches and a concomitant willingness to try them. These 'approaches' could include technological innovations, techniques, values, new models for social relations, etc. An increased confidence in predicting the effects of new approaches is in part an indirect result of the spread of mechanization and the harnessing of inanimate energy sources – two factors involved in many definitions of modernization. Increased efficiency is often one goal of pragmatic modernization. The use of the tape recorder for learning *min'yō* is one example, even if the results of its adoption can be regarded as either positive or negative.

Ideological modernization (**IM**) will designate the relatively conscious pursuit of modernity itself by people who are familiar with the concept and who consider modernization (*gendaika*) a desirable goal for reasons of prestige or self-image. I mean this to encompass cases where a 'modern' device or technique may be adopted without a clear expectation of its suitability for the task at hand but partly or chiefly because one wishes to be thought 'modern' (*modān*, using the English word). IM is itself an outgrowth of PM, but treating it separately may prove enlightening.

Ideological Westernization (**IW**) covers only those cases where elements of Western culture are borrowed or imitated primarily because of the prestige accorded Western culture as a whole. This resembles IM, except that the borrower is assumed to have had a particular geographical or cultural unit in mind (the United States, France, the West) rather than the more universal concept of modernity.

Assimilative Westernization (**AW**), a subtype of IW, corresponds to Nettl's characterization (§1.1): the borrower's intention is to make a portion of the host system a part of the Western system. This would be the case if, for example, a Japanese hoped that Noh music would be fully accepted by Europeans as a genre of *European* classical music if only certain key European traits were adopted.

Distinguishing these four processes in an actual case requires determining the intentions of the actor. This is obviously problematic, especially since people are often not aware of their own intentions. Did the person who first used the lined staff in notating 'Esashi Oiwake', or the shamisen teacher who employed an electronic 'rhythm box', make a considered, rational choice based on potential increased efficiency of transmission (PM) or rather simply wish to be thought 'modern' (IM) or 'Westernized' (IW)? If we decide on either IM or IW, we run the risk of being considered patronizing.

Nonetheless, specification of intention must be crucial in defining these processes. The alternatives – for example, to assume Westernization whenever a trait found in Japan can be shown to have existed first in 'the West' – are obviously unpalatable.

Let us single out two other features which, although they may occur in the absence of modernization, are also among its most important outgrowths: **urbanization (U)** and the growth of **leisure (L)**. Each has important and distinctive effects on musical life.

Now let us list the most noticeable developments in folk song performance and transmission in Japan since the late nineteenth century and then try to attribute each to one or more of the above 'causes' (PM, IM, IW, AW, U, L). When a development represents the interaction of one of these causes with a strong element of **traditional culture**, we will indicate this by the letter **T**. The letters are listed after each development in approximate order of importance. (We could add yet another factor, globalization, but we shall refrain.)[13]

adoption of the concept of 'folk song' (*min'yō*): IW, AW (for some people), U, L, T
rural songs flourish in city: U, T, ?L
more elaborate accompaniments (on traditional instruments): PM, T, L, ?IW
increased virtuosity (e.g. in ornamentation): L, T
use of notation: PM, T, sometimes IM or IW
professional teaching: T, U, L, PM, IM
issuing of licences: T, L, U?
professional performing: T, U, L, PM
proliferation of contests: T, L, PM, U, ?IW
large ensemble performances: U, L, PM, IW
specialization: PM, U, L, T
decreased bawdiness: IM, IW
min'yō study as moral education: T, ?
standardization (melodic and textual) replaces improvisation: L, PM, IM, IW, T
loss of class implications: PM, U
pursuit of dignification: T, PM, ?IW
larger individual repertoires: L, PM, U
fading of dialect in lyrics: U, PM, IM
less singing while working: PM
increase in stage/public performance: L, U
focus on solo singer: T, IW, ?PM
possible increased use in local identity: PM, T
standardization of intonation: L, T, PM, IW
recordings as source of repertoire: PM
birth of preservation societies: PM, L, U, ?T
birth of folk song bars: U, L, T
use of pentatonic major and minor in 'new folk songs': IW, ?PM, T
harmonized orchestral accompaniments in 'new folk songs': IW, ?AW
increased academic attention to *min'yā*: U, L, IW, ?T

These attributions are obviously subjective. Nevertheless, the point is clear: it is rarely safe to attribute any one development to any single cause. For example, the *iemoto* ('headmaster') system of teaching comes to *min'yō* from the world of traditional classical arts and might thus be considered to represent merely the extension of tradition; its adoption, however, was facilitated by factors U, L, PM and probably IM. The move toward stage performance (often professional) might seem an example of PM, but even in earlier times folk performing arts were often 'presentational' (e.g. Tsugaru *te-odori* hand dances, many *minzoku geinō*), so again this may be merely the extension of a traditional category. Even the adoption of the pentatonic major as the principal mode in recent *shin-min'yō* is not to be attributed solely to conscious imitation of the West (IW). The writers of these recent *shin-min'yō* were raised in a Japan which had already experienced more than a half-century of European-based school music education. Japan's adoption of the European model during the Meiji period can perhaps be attributed to IW, but it might also be seen as an inevitable result of PM in the context of traditional attitudes (T) concerning the importance of music to a nation's overall development. Whatever the situation in the Meiji period, by the 1970s the pentatonic major may be said to have become traditional in Japan – i.e. only partly identified as Western or foreign.

Note that Assimilative Westernization, which corresponds to Nettl's definition of Westernization, is virtually unknown in the *min'yō* world. It is unlikely that there can be more than a handful of Japanese who hope to see *min'yō* – or any other traditional Japanese music – become 'part of the Western system' of music. This is particularly true of *min'yō*, which is seen as quintessentially Japanese, even by those who consider it to represent a provincial or backward aspect of Japanese culture unsuitable for international exposure. The Japanese perceive a close link between 'Japaneseness' and *min'yō*.

We can then offer the following conclusions: (1) Discussions of musical change must avoid the use of blanket terms such as Westernization, no matter how narrowly defined, unless detailed examples are given. (2) It is almost always badly misleading to speak even informally of a single 'cause': we must recognize the interaction of several causes or facilitating factors of differing strength. (3) What looks like the Westernization of a culture over the course of a century may not be Westernization in the short run or for a particular individual.

Having just summarized the most noticeable changes in folk song performance and transmission, let us also note some features which have remained relatively unaltered from traditional times. In doing so, we can disregard most *shin-min'yō* since they are virtually never performed at folk song events and are rarely accepted by performers and fans as *min'yō*. The surviving traditional elements are:

pentatonic scales
textual content (if we ignore bowdlerization)
no vocal harmony
vocal style (timbre and ornamentation) (by and large)
accompaniment limited to shamisen, shakuhachi, *shinobue* and percussion
association of each song with a particular region

Why have these particular features been maintained? My experiences suggest that most Japanese would treat vocal style, instrumentation and textual content as the three fundamental features of *min'yō*. Vocal style in particular is frequently cited as the most distinctive feature of folk song (see the anecdote about the opera singer in §4.8.1). Pentatonicism is less often mentioned, perhaps because it is too specialized a concept to pass the lips of most people; as a trait of *min'yō*, it seems to be maintained instinctively by performers and intentionally by most composers of *shin-min'yō*. As for vocal harmony, its absence may well be due to the basic incompatibility of most traditional Japanese melodies and Western functional harmony; vocal monophony may then be a 'central trait' only by default rather than by conscious consensus. Finally, most people expect a *min'yō* to have a 'home town' or belong to a particular prefecture (a traditional element even further emphasized by the *furusato-zukuri* movement of recent decades).

In calling these the 'fundamental features' or (using Nettl's term) the 'central traits' of *min'yō*, I am thus relying partly on expressed native opinion and partly on the very fact that they have survived. By virtue of their survival, all six of these traits would seem to be more central to the conception of *min'yō*, whether consciously or otherwise, than the traits which were shown in the earlier list to have undergone change. But is the concept of 'central traits' useful if we can only discover such traits after the fact? Can we predict which features of musical performance and transmission are most likely to change?[14]

Comparing the lists of changed and unchanged features, it is apparent that musical features are on the whole less subject to alteration than extramusical ones. Even the shift toward standardized intonation approximating Western diatonic intervals is not a fundamental change but just the selection of one of the many traditional possibilities for intonation. Similarly, increased virtuosity and more elaborate accompaniments represent quantitative rather than qualitative change. We might hypothesize, then, that extramusical features will in general prove more mutable than musical ones. This will have implications for the indigenous conceptualization of the defining features of a given genre. Thus we might expect that a song performed in the appropriate style, with a suitable text and an attribution of locality, will be accepted as a *min'yō* even if performed in an evening gown at Carnegie Hall, whereas a Puccini aria sung in a bel canto style will fail to qualify even if the performer is wearing peasant garb and weeding the rice paddy. We must make a distinction between a song and the performance of that song, as demonstrated also by the opera anecdote mentioned above.

The exact fate of musical features will vary in different cultures, depending for example on the possibilities for syncretism or hybridization. *Min'yō* intonation has stabilized partly because of the existence of a prestigious foreign model which corresponded to one of the traditionally possible intonation patterns; vocal timbre and ornamentation have remained relatively unaffected because the gulf between Japanese and Western styles is too great for influence to occur.

Much more comparative work is needed, however. For example, Manuel (1989a), describing recent developments in the performance practice of flamenco in Andalusia, noted that pitch sense was becoming ever more exact, due to the expectations of an increasingly demanding audience; he also chose the term 'dignification' to describe for flamenco the same process observed in the Japanese folk song world. Are similar forces operating in these two music cultures?

7.7 The future of *min'yō*: beyond identity and tradition

As the new millennium dawned (from a Japanese perspective), on 3 January 2001, NHK television broadcast a special, *Haru wa Medetaya: Sore Ike Min'yō*. Many of the major artists of the *min'yō* boom years around 1980 were still playing a prominent role and thus appeared on this programme: Harada Naoyuki, Ōtsuka Fumio, Hayasaka Mitsue, Yamamoto Kenji and others. But they were joined by a number of much younger artists who rarely grace the *min'yō* stage, and of nineteen numbers, almost all traditional songs, only a handful were performed in something close to traditional style. As usual, NHK sought to reach a broad audience through diversity. Here are few of the more interesting items:

Teams from the Yosakoi Matsuri and Yosakoi Sōran Matsuri (§7.4.2) opened the show; three young woman sang 'Mogamigawa Funauta' in beautiful three-part harmony, in traditional *min'yō* voices; the punk band Straight performed 'Akita Nikata Bushi'; the female emcee changed from kimono to cocktail dress and sang 'Sotoyama Bushi' with piano, adding a bit of scat singing; two young girls demonstrated briefly the 'Sōran Bushi' dance they had learned for their primary school athletic meet; Jadranka Stojaković, a Bosnian pop singer living in Japan since 1988, sang a bit of *min'yō* with her acoustic guitar and opined that world folk songs (N.B. not just Japanese ones) have a special 'cosmic energy'.

The announcers solicited opinions about what it was that was important in *min'yō* and what must be done in the future. Creativity and individuality were recurring themes. Asked for suggestions for those coming to *min'yō* in the twenty-first century, Harada Naoyuki stressed that performers must 'express their indivuality' (*kosei o dasu*); Hayasaka Mitsue advised the young not to be caught up in formalism (*katachi ni torawareru*); Ōtsuka Fumio said that young folks should trust their instincts and look for creative ways to bring to life (*ikasu*) traditional *min'yō*. Kinoshita Shin'ichi, who launched the Tsugaru fusion phenomenon, performed a new composition with a Chinese erhu player, and called for the development of an orchestra of international folk instruments (*minzoku gakki no ōkesutora*). Kazu, leader of the punk band Straight, said he hoped his example would lead other young people to *min'yō*; he himself wants to search for the heart (*kokoro*) of *min'yō*. Finally, young *kyōgen* actor Izumi Motoya, now a TV personality, related that he had heard 'Kuroda Bushi' sung in its home town of Hakata and was very moved by this connection of a song with its *furusato*. As if to support this traditionalist statement and re-emphasize the roots of *min'yō*, the final four items took us back to conservatism and to the 1970s, as elder masters Ōtsuka, Hayasaka and Harada sang standard 'stage' *min'yō*.

One must realize, of course, that on such a self-congratulatory special programme, nobody is likely to express negative opinions about the genre or its future. But the emphasis on creativity was compelling. Just as the word 'preservation' (*hozon*) is being pushed aside in favour of 'safeguarding' (*hogo*) in discussions of intangible cultural heritage, with the realization that preservation can imply mummification, so those in the *min'yō-kai* realize that the future of their world may depend on avoiding over-conservatism and finding new directions.

The programme was followed by a short advertisement for an opera and ballet special later that night.

In preceding chapters we have often given a functional explanation for one factor leading to the survival and development of *min'yō*, namely, the role of this genre in the formation and maintenance of identity in a rapidly changing society. Elderly rural residents find that joint participation in preservation societies reaffirms their life experiences and thus raises their self-esteem. New urban migrants turn to songs from their home regions to recapture their identities amidst the sea of superior strangers. Newly formed neighbourhoods often feel the need for a 'new folk song' to create a sense of community. Urban residents of longer standing may join a *min'yō* class in order to find a group to belong to outside the family – an important need in a society which puts so much stress on belonging, and one which *min'yō* with its communal orientation is particularly well qualified to fill. Increasingly, participation in *min'yō* contributes to one's sense of identity as a Japanese: it is a uniquely Japanese form of music, often considered uniquely difficult for foreigners and thus a symbol of the superiority of Japanese culture.

Folk song is not, however, the only element of Japanese culture which contributes to identity; someday its importance in this respect may be usurped. What else does the future hold for *min'yō*? Will it lose these social functions but come to be appreciated purely as a form of classical music? Will Japan become so international-minded that the sorts of identity conveyed by *min'yō* will actually be rejected? Will *min'yō* survive only in pop-fusion or other new modes?

Such matters do worry some Japanese observers of the *min'yō* scene. There is widespread agreement among scholars that folk song must not be allowed to become a form of classical song, losing its spontaneity and individual variation. Performers, though, rarely agree entirely with this view: the influence of the prestige associated with traditional classical music has been overwhelming. There seems little doubt that *min'yō*, both as taught in the cities and as 'preserved' in the villages, will become increasingly standardized and that methods of transmission will continue to reduce the amount of deviation from the model. The genre *min'yō* will surely continue to exist, but it will indeed become more and more a type of 'art song' (*geijutsu kayō*).

Even amid classicization, one feature that is likely to continue to distinguish *min'yō* from many other leisure-time music pursuits (piano, koto, *utai*, etc.) is the emphasis on community, on group performance. Even students of *nagauta*, the Kabuki dance music which can involve well over a dozen performers, rarely get a chance during their lessons to perform with anyone but their teacher. *Min'yō* students often accompany each other on instruments or provide a backup chorus – indeed, the entire clientele at a folk song bar may join in your performance. Thus *min'yō* is a highly communal and participatory music, whether you are on stage or in the audience.

Some scholars would even challenge the value of such performance as this. Misumi Haruo, for example (pers. comm. 1981), spoke of 'robot *min'yō*': a singer these days stands rigid, expressionless and self-absorbed before a microphone. How communal or participatory can such an experience really be? Despite appearances, however, it is my impression that these singers generally value the experience of singing very highly in both social and personal terms. Adorno claimed that mass media and mechanical reproduction lead to the loss of non-professional musical initiative, that there is no room for amateurs among the petty bourgeoisie (1976: 6). As a statement of a general tendency, this may be acceptable. *Min'yō*, however, provides a clear exception. In auditoriums and gymnasiums throughout Japan on any Sunday afternoon, or in the folk song bars on any evening – and even on television every weekend – amateur members of the bourgeoisie (petty or otherwise) are singing their hearts out. In the countryside, groups of villagers gather to practise cherished local songs, dances and dramas. In all cases, the experience is embedded in a social environment marked by cameraderie and mutual supportiveness, a sense of being engaged in a common endeavour. Individual initiative or creativity *per se* may be low, but this is not to be blamed totally on mechanization: Japan has long discouraged these traits. (See also Keil 1984 regarding the humanizing of mechanical means of musical reproduction in Japan.)

The value of *min'yō* camaraderie, particularly as the population ages, is stressed in the *shin-min'yō* 'Bokenai Ondo' from 1997 (on CD R75). The lyrics by Hori Keiji tell us:

uta ya odori o narau hito / nakama ga iru hito bokemasen . . . / boketaku nai hito utaimashō
    People who study song and dance / And have a circle of friends will not grow senile . . . / Those who don't want to get senile, let's sing!

It is often assumed that repertoires of traditional music are shrinking throughout the non-Western world in the face of international pop music. In Japan at least, the matter is not so simple. It is true that the total number of independent *min'yō* which are being sung somewhere in Japan will diminish as the years pass. However, many individuals will be able to sing or at least recognize far more *min'yō* than ever before. In other words, the country's shared, common repertoire is growing as more and more local songs are 'excavated' and brought to the public ear via the media.

The nationwide Emergency Folk Song Survey of the 1980s (see §1.1) was intended partly to bring more buried songs to the public's attention. Local researchers tape-recorded 2,548 songs in Aichi alone – a prefecture thought to be poor in folk song (Hoshino 1981: 13–4). This came as quite a revelation to the scholarly community (not to mention the residents of Aichi!): previous estimates at the prefectural level were from 300 to 700 songs (Takeuchi 1981: 26). However, the figure of 2,548 actually represents individual recorded performances: many of the songs are close relatives or indeed versions of the same song or tune family. The same is true for Niigata, where 3,686 performances were recorded. By contrast, Saitama Prefecture researchers found only some 280 songs (MB 1985.3: 80), which suggests considerable variation in methods of counting and in collectors' efforts as well as in the actual number of song species. In any event, there is as yet no shortage of folk songs in Japan.

In sum, it is clear that *min'yō* will play a role in the future, although the nature of that role is less clear. Presumably, as more and more people are raised in urban environments, *min'yō* will lose some of their significance as carriers of rural traditions and values. When that happens, it will mean that the Japanese themselves have lost their home towns, their *furusato*. Until then, folk song will continue to be the heart's home town.

7.8 A few final vignettes

We finish with a few snapshots of young Japanese interacting with *min'yō*.

First, let us return to the concert by Takahashi Yūjirō's group Kaze on 18 April 1998. Next to me sat a 23-year-old woman. Stylishly dressed in European fashion, she had come, not out of any interest in the music, but merely to support her mother, who was performing. She, like 'all' her friends, preferred what she called *futsū no poppusu* – 'the usual pop'. She did appear to enjoy the concert, but seemed unlikely to suddenly decide to follow in her mother's footsteps.

Her mother, Katakura Yukiji, born in 1944 in a small town in Ibaragi, had started experimenting with her grandmother's shamisen at the age of three, and at six was taking lessons in the shamisen of *nagauta* and *hauta* with a neighbourhood geisha. Later, bewitched by the 'gypsy'-like sound of Tsugaru-jamisen (interestingly, flamenco guitar was her point of reference), she began lessons with Takahashi Yūjirō; within two months she was recording with him. She also developed her talents in folk singing and dancing, in a desire to be a compleat *min'yō* artist.

Two other members of Kaze, men in their mid-twenties, had come to the group by paths divergent from hers yet strikingly parallel to each other. Their fathers were folk shamisen performers and teachers. In childhood both boys enjoyed this music and even began to learn shamisen. By their teens, however, they had abandoned shamisen for rock guitar due to peer pressure, this being the music beloved of all their friends. Later, though, both returned to the shamisen, but specifically to Tsugaru-jamisen, because it was the most energetically powerful (*hageshii*) and lively style, suitable to their generation's tastes. One of them expressed regret at having to perform such simple, dull folk songs as 'Kokiriko Bushi' (so simple that it was the first *min'yō* I myself chose to learn from recordings before going to Japan), and having to learn to sing as well, but both agreed that such was necessary for becoming a successful professional.

Whatever their experiences of traditional music in the bosom of the family, the three young folks got precious little support for their tastes from the outside world. And yet who knows exactly why the 23-year-old woman, raised in a family awash in traditional music, never moved into that world at all, and why the two young men left the *min'yō* world but then returned. (They did both say that they had tried rock guitar but saw no future in it.)

These lingering questions lead to our next snapshot. On an evening in April 1998 I visited Kotobuki, the pre-eminent surviving folk song bar in Osaka, located in Taishō Ward (see Appendix 2). As usual, the walls were hung with folk song paraphernalia, including posters advertising concerts, recordings and so forth. A stack of shamisen cases lay at the back of the small performing platform: the instruments are used for lessons during the day. One by one the customers took their turns on stage, singing and/or playing as others supported them with choruses or simply with sympathetic ears. They – we – sang into a microphone that was totally unnecessary in the small room. The club was owned and primarily staffed by the Uchida family. Thirty-something Uchida Minoru showed off the Tsugaru-jamisen skills that he taught during the day (and used in the rock-fusion band Joppari, named after a common dialect word describing the spunkiness and energy of Tsugaru music); his wife sang, drummed and played shamisen, his father played shakuhachi, his mother sang. Finally a tiny girl, who had been rolling around on the tatami-mat floor, eating an ice cream bar, playing with toys and generally acting like a tiny girl, made her way to centre stage. The microphone was lowered, and incredibly she burst into song.

Uchida Mai, all of three years old, was accompanied by her father on shamisen, her mother on drums and her grandfather on shakuhachi. She was tackling a very challenging song from the far north, 'Dōnan Kudoki'. Her demeanour seemed disengaged, yet her voice was loud and confident, the lengthy lyrics perfectly recalled, and she clearly basked in the kudos from the customers. Her pitch wavered, and she imagined rather than executed most of the ornaments (much as I myself do, alas . . .). But it was a truly moving moment.

Visiting Kotobuki again in November 2000, I was delighted to find that Mai, now six, had added other songs to her repertoire, some very difficult. She also played drums on several songs, concentrating diligently, guided by other staff.

How did Mai get her start? Probably in a similar way to her younger sister Akari. Still just past her first birthday and not yet able to talk, in 2000 Akari was held up to the microphone by her aunt, who sang a song while Akari did her best to keep up, happily emitting occasional syllables which, while linguistically inscrutable, seemed to be roughly on pitch (Fig. 7.2).

In July 2006, I paid another visit. Mai, now eleven, was a mature singer with a trophy to her credit from a young people's *min'yō* contest, and a skilled Tsugaru-jamisen player. Akari, seven, was also impressive. They were now joined by their cousin Miyune, age twenty-five months, who could sing choruses, drum (somewhat unsteadily but with commitment and with help from her relatives) and even dance with the other girls (Fig. 7.3). All three children, like their parents, were absorbing a love and talent for *min'yō* from a nurturing familial and social environment.

Kotobuki boasts another young singer, Kayō Eri. Born in 1982 and raised nearby by her Okinawan immigrant parents, she might have been expected to be found at one of Taishō Ward's several Okinawan folk song clubs rather than at its only mainland Japanese club. (Some 20,000 of Taishō's 80,000 inhabitants are of Okinawan descent.) But when Eri was three, for reasons unknown, her mother brought her to Kotobuki. Somehow the music, or perhaps the human environment, 'grabbed' her. Although her mother sometimes sang Okinawan songs around the house, Eri cannot sing any Okinawan *min'yō* except 'Asadoya Yunta', which has Japanese lyrics and is familiar to most Japanese. Had her mother taken her instead to a local Okinawan *min'yō sakaba*, her life might have followed a different path. On the same night in November 2000 that I visited Kotobuki, I also looked in on Haisai, an Okinawan club next to Taishō station whose performers were Isa Hikaru, her daughter Tae – and Tae's daughter, two weeks short of her second birthday, banging enthusiastically on a pair of small drums. A return visit in 2006 suggests that she may become the Uchida Mai of the local Okinawan folk world.

But back to eleven-year-old Uchida Mai. As she grows up, she is finding that the vast majority of her friends have no interest in this music; under their relentless apathy, she may turn her back on this world for a time, like the young men of Kaze. What could these old songs of the far north, singing of a land and a life she has never known, offer her? Will she embrace other musics, originally from far lands, and become a singer in a rock or salsa band? Will she, like many other young Japanese, instead be bewitched by Okinawan music or *wadaiko*? And will she too, like the young men of Kaze, come home to *min'yō*?

NOTES

1. On Saturdays and Sundays from about 6.30 to 9am, a dozen or more retirees gather near the entrance to Ueno Zoo in Tokyo to sing and play *min'yō* for their own enjoyment.

2. The term *junhōgaku* has recently largely replaced *hōgaku* to refer to 'pure' traditional genres, since *hōgaku*, 'national music', is now used in record shops to mark Japanese pop genres, as opposed to *yōgaku*, 'foreign/Western music' for Western pop and rock.

3. Writing WA•KA in semantically neutral romanization allows a complex pun: *waka* meaning 'young'; and *wa* 'Japan' but also 'harmony' plus *ka* 'song'. (No reference was intended to old court poems called *waka*.) As for Utae•mon, a connection to the popular cartoon character Doraemon can be intuited.

4. Despite my translation, *naichi* includes all islands except the Ryūkyū archipelago.

5. Adjudicatory susceptibility to certain kinds of uniqueness is not new. Around 1979 the winner of one national contest was a man who sang an obscure local hunting song while in full traditional hunter's dress, unaccompanied. He had in fact never worn such clothes for hunting, but I have no doubt that this ploy helped him to his victory. There has been no movement to include Ainu songs in the *min'yō* world. Whereas Ryukyuan culture shares linguistic roots and many elements of musical style with the mainland, Ainu culture shares neither.

6. The bass shamisen deserves mention here. Chifuji Kōzō, a leading accompanist for non-Tōhoku songs, has occasionally (e.g. in performance with Honjō Hidetarō) employed a slightly larger shamisen tuned about an octave below standard, to expand the pitch range downward. Such an instrument was invented in the 1920s for use in New Japanese Music (*shin-nihon-ongaku*), under Western influence, but never took hold (Katsumura 1996). Chifuji uses it mostly to duplicate the basic shamisen part an octave below, often at a lower melodic density. Takahashi Yūjirō has since explored its use as a melodic instrument (R67). It is rarely used.

7. See his website www008.upp.so-net.ne.jp/takio, which is one source for this section and also leads to a brief English profile.

8. A related phenomenon: Since the late 1970s young Tokyoites have gathered on Sunday afternoons in Yoyogi Park near Harajuku Station to dance to recorded Western-style pop songs. *Min'yō* do not feature, but the dancers often dance in unison groups, sometimes shouting *kakegoe* such as *sore sore*, almost as if this were a

Bon dance. Try Googling 'Takenoko-zoku'; the phenomenon of that name has ended, but other groups continue in styles such as rockabilly.

9. Sources: Nagira 1995: 35, 53–4, and the television special *Kankoku: tamashi no rizumu o motomete* (NHK BS2, ca. 1997; tape supplied by Takahashi Miki).

10. For good English-language treatments of the question, see Ogawa 1994, Machida 1956, Murao & Wilkins 2001, Pecore 2000.

11. Articles introducing these three songs were included in a 1977 issue of *Kikan Hōgaku*, a journal generally devoted to traditional classical music genres. They formed part of a 43-page special section on *min'yō*, intended to be a 'school teaching resource'. Ironically, by 1977 this policy had already been found unworkable.

12. What follows is based on conversations with education officials, teachers, students and others as well as in-school observations during visits in 2003 and 2007.

13. We also refrain from considering several other concepts mentioned by Nettl, Kartomi and others, such as consolidation, intensification and peaceful co-existence.

14. In typologizing musical change, Blacking, Nettl and Kartomi do not offer precise hypotheses as to the conditions leading to a particular type of change, but they suggest certain tendencies. I shall not repeat those here.

TEXTS OF *SHIN-MIN'YŌ* AND RELATED POPULAR SONGS

The three sections of this appendix contain my translations of the texts of *shin-min'yō* from the 1920s to 1970, *shin-min'yō* from 1977 to 1981, and popular songs with a significant relation to folk song, respectively. The distinction between categories is fuzzy in some cases. Occasional verses have been omitted, as have almost all extra-metrical vocables (*hayashi-kotoba*). The last entry of each heading shows the poetic metre of the text (ignoring vocables and repeated lines) and the scale structure (*miyako-bushi* is abbreviated as *miyako-b*). Many phrases italicized in the texts below are onomatopoeic or other mood-setting words, including dialect used for effect. The songs given here are discussed particularly in §§3.4.3, 6.4 and 6.6.3 above.

1.1 Older *shin-min'yō*

The heading for each song gives: title; prefecture; sources for lyrics and/or tune; date of publication; lyricist; composer; poetic metre; mode. Abbreviations for sources: NMD=Asano 1983; OK=Okuni 1976; YA=Yamamoto 1970; FU=Fujimoto 1962– (with volume number); MI=Mikado 1977; NMJ=Nakai et al. 1972; Osa=Osada 1976a. Entries are ordered approximately by date of publication. All songs with lyrics by Nakayama Shinpei are recorded on R57 and R58 (except 'Sakaide Kouta', absent from R58).

A. 'Suzaka Kouta' (Nagano; MI 2.125, NMJ 192, FU6, YA 136, OK 121; 1924, Noguchi Ujō/Nakayama Shinpei) (7775; *yō* on 6 w. upper neighbour 7)

1. The moon is peeking out over the mountain; / Who is it waiting for, or keeping waiting?
2. It's not waiting for anyone, nor keeping anyone waiting; / It's come to see *you*, you cutie!

3. You, you cutie, in Suzaka Town – / Do you like Suzaka and that moon?
4. The moon comes and looks down on the factory, / Thinking of whom?
5. Thinking of whom, my friend(s)? / *Hororo hororo*, the night deepens.
6. *Hororo hororo*, the moon / Keeps guard over Suzaka Town, never sleeping.

Notes: Commissioned by a local textile mill. Intended not as publicity but to replace the bawdy songs favoured by the thousands of employes (all women). The intention was partly to give the workers pride in their factory. The song spread throughout the country despite the initially possessive attitude of the company president. This was the song that set off the publicity song boom. (Cf. Kojima 1970:18–9.) Verse 4, the only one that mentions the factory, is omitted from some sources; as with 'Hachinohe Kouta' (song J below), the publicity verses survive poorly.

B. 'Chakkiri Bushi' (Shizuoka; MI 2.148, FU2, YA 141; 1928, Kitahara Hakushū/ Machida Kashō) (metre unclear; complex mix of *yō* and *miyako-b*; 2/4)

1. Among songs, it's 'Chakkiri Bushi'; / Among men, it's Jirōchō; / Among flowers, it's the orange blossom – / In summer, the orange blossom / And the scent of tea. / CH.: *Chakkiri chakkiri chakkiri yo!* / 'The frogs're callin' – / It's gonna rain, y'all!'
2. Tea mountain, tea district, / Tea gardens – / Hey, won't you come with me? / Come on now, won't you come with me / To pick tea? (CH.)
3. Look, look at the mountains – / At that hat-shaped cloud! / Hey, why don't you wear it, / Why don't you wear it today, / Your sedge hat? (CH.)
4. Fine weather, / Gentle breeze, / And the tea-gathering scissors, / The scissors in your hand, / Make a nice sound: (CH.) /

(More verses in YA.)
Notes: 'Chakkiri' literally means 'tea-cutting', and Shizuoka is famous for its tea, but the word is being used here primarily for its sound: the sound of the tea-leaf gatherers' scissors (verse 4). This was intended as a geisha song, not a pseudo-work song. It was commissioned by the prefectural railway to increase tourism. The chorus uses local dialect. The melody is a complex mix of *yō* and *miyako-bushi*, partly betraying the composer's expertise at traditional shamisen genres. Along with 'Hachinohe Kouta', this is one of the few tourism songs that is still sung regularly at *min'yō* events. Jirōchō was a famous Edo-period gangster boss from Shizuoka, a sort of Robin Hood figure and the hero of many *naniwa-bushi* narratives.

C. 'Jōshū Kouta' (Gunma; MI 2.106, NMJ 179, FU6, OK 245, NMD 265; 1929, Noguchi Ujō/Nakayama Shinpei) (7775, 7775; *yō* on 6; 2/4)

1. The winds come down from Mt. Akagi, / Blowing the butterflies around. / Well, well, warbler on Mt Myōgi, / Wake us for the morning grass-cutting.
2. Even the water boiling up from the Kusatsu hot springs / Turns misty at the sadness of parting. / Well, well, cross mountains, cross river valleys: / Shima [placename] is a world apart.

3.　The Akagi azalea lives on Mt Akagi, / The firefly in the daytime lives in the grass. / Well, well, for skiing it's the ski-jump at Akagi – / The snow that falls here won't melt when you walk on it.

4.　(<NMJ) From Mt Haruna the clouds stretch out their legs / And make rain at Ikaho [a hot spring town] too. / Well, well, even to Maebashi and Takasaki / The rains come *gorori pikari*.

Notes: More humorous than most of Noguchi's lyrics; it is said that at first the locals thought he was making fun of them (why?).

D. 'Tōkamachi Kouta' (Niigata; MI 2:177, FU6, YA 128, NMJ 234, NMD 348, OK 243; 1929, Nagai Hakubi/Nakayama Shinpei) (7775,75; *miyako-b* on 3; 2/4 or 6/8)

1.　The Echigo region boasts many famous products, especially / Akashi crepe-cloth and snow-white skin. / Wear it and you'll never let it go, it's so wonderful.

2.　How do young girls pass the height of their youth? / Buried in snow, sitting at their looms, / Still half a year before they flower.

3.　Telling tales around the hearth on a snow-deep night – / I won't let you go home; / It's okay even if it piles up 5 or 10 feet.

4.　The gentle sound of snowflakes against the window pane – / Hearing it, I can't fall asleep, all night long. / How wretched – the snow is too bright.

5.　If someone comes, slip into a side-street: / You can hide in the tunnels of snow – / The secret paths, the detours of love.

Notes: Commissioned to advertise the local crêpe-cloth.

E. 'Niigata Kouta' (Niigata; MI 2.197, FU6, NMJ 256; 1929, Kitahara Hakushū /Machida Kashō) (7775; *miyako-b*)

1.　Niigata, City of Water, with 8,008 rivers, / Going down through 10,000 generations, the long bridge. / CH.: Beat away on the fulling block barrel: / A ship has entered the harbour, too.

2.　If only for a day, I'd like to be / A pine tree on Mt Hakusan, rustling in the wind. (CH.)

3.　Even though Matsubara is full of prying eyes, / I go to the horse races by horse. (CH.)

4.　Even the Milky Way is cold when it's hazy; / How much colder out on the rough seas, at Sado Island.

Notes: Commissioned to commemorate the 1929 replacement of Niigata City's largest bridge, Bandai Bridge, with a concrete one.

F. 'Misasa Kouta' (Tottori; NMZ 4.160, MI 2.235, FU6, OK 171; 1927, Noguchi Ujō/Nakayama Shinpei) (7775; *yō* on 6 w. upper neighbour 7)

1.　When you part in tears, even the sky clouds over; / When it clouds over, it rains at Misasa.

2. Yunokami Spa in Misasa – you should go with a friend; / If you go alone, they won't let you sleep and they won't let you leave.
3. Everyone's talking about Misasa. / I wish there were a bridge to love.
4. Along the river in Misasa, the spring peeper cries, / Calling its loved one: 'I love you, I love you.' / CODA: Next time you're in Izumo, come to see me again. / If you come [to town] but don't visit me, that's mean. / In that case, I'll come chasing after you.

(Three more verses in OK.)
Notes: Written after Noguchi visited this famous radon hot spring. This is the pioneer of the *(shin-)onsen* ((new) hot spring) *kouta* genre (cf. also 'Iizaka Kouta', song G below). The coda is of a kind common in lively *ozashiki-uta* of western Japan, except that this one is set to a melody rather than spoken rhythmically.

G. 'Iizaka Kouta' (Fukushima; MI 2.27, FU6, OK 242, NMJ 40; ca. 1930, Saijō Yaso/Nakayama Shinpei) (7775; *miyako-b* on 7)

1. On the Northern Road of love, hiding from prying eyes, / In the steam of the stylish hot springs at Iizaka. / CH.: Well, then, come along, come to visit, / Come around to Iizaka.
2. Is that a spring peeper crying or is that her? / Parting tonight at Tozuna Bridge. (CH.)
3. Where are you going, carrying your lunch? / I'm going to the river banks to fish for sweetfish. (CH.)
4. Shall I go on to Matsushima? Shall I go back to Tokyo? / I like it right here, in the baths at Iizaka. (CH.)

Notes: One of the many hot-springs *kouta* from that period (cf. 'Misasa Kouta' above); meant to be sung by local geisha in a parlour setting. The first verse contains three untranslatable puns on local place names. Each verse begins with a drawn-out note on the syllable *hā*, a common feature in traditional folk songs; this device (sometimes with a different vocable) is used in many *shin-min'yō* as well.

H. 'Sakaide Kouta' (Kagawa; NMZ 4.251, YA 209, OK 182, NMJ 154; ca.1930, Saijō Yaso/Nakayama Shinpei) (7775; *miyako-b* on 7 and 3)

1. I was raised in Sakaide, by the harbour; / I don't mind the winds and waves of love.
2. If you marry a salt master, / You may not see him in the daylight for days on end.
3. In Sakaide in Sanuki, when morning rolls in, / Sanuki's Mt Fuji is veiled in tears.
4. The beach is covered with salt fields, with a thousand smoke columns rising; / Out on the sea, departing steamers pour out black smoke.
5. The Inland Sea seems wide, but it's small – / From Mt Iino you can see it all at a glance.
6. Seki(?) Island has no cherry blossoms, / But in the spring it's awash with cherry-bream.

7.   As numerous as the waves are the Konpira pilgrims; / Today, too, they pass through Sakaide.

Notes: A famous salt-field region since the seventeenth century.

I. 'Gion Kouta' (Kyoto; NMZ 4.67, FU6, OK 157, Osa 225; 1930, Nagata Mikihiko/Sasa Kōka) ((75)X4, 77; *miyako-b* with one *yō* accidental; 2/4)

1.   The moon hangs hazily over the Eastern Mountains; / In the bonfires of a cloudy night, / The scarlet cherry blossoms set one's dreams drifting – / A painfully recalled love, a long kimono sleeve. / CH.: Gion is so dear, obi dangling down.
2.   In summer, the evenings are cool along the river bank; / Black hair lapping at the white collar, faintly seen, / Eyes clouded by tears, lip-rouge scarlet, / Burning all aflame, Daimonji. (CH.)
3.   The waters vanish from the Kamo River floodplain. / The sobbing rapids, the sound of the [temple] bell, / A withered willow and the autumn wind, / Crying again tonight, all through the night. (CH.)
4.   The snow falls gently against the window; / The lovers meet, tête-a-tête, / In the flickering lantern light in the wee hours: / A pillow for two, the plovers along the river. (CH.)

Notes: Theme song from a movie about an apprentice geisha in the Gion district of Kyoto. Original record's A side had shamisen accompaniment, B side had orchestra. This is considered a *shin-min'yō* by many people, as is the lyricist's similar effort, 'Tenryū Kudareba' (see below). The lyrics are loaded with vocabulary and literary devices of the kind found in cultivated poetry, rather than in popular and folk song. Note the 'four seasons' progression. Daimonji is a festival involving the setting afire of patches of grass in the form of giant Chinese characters on the mountainsides surrounding Kyoto.

J. 'Hachinohe Kouta' (Iwate; NMZ 2.72, MI 1.182, YA 27, OK 21, FU1; 1931, Hoshihama Ōhaku/Gotō Tōsui) (777775; *yō* on 6; 2/4)

1.   Singing goes on 'til dawn at the harbour of seagulls. / The boats head out to the south and north. / Point Same is hidden in sea-spray.
2.   When the ships dock at the misty wharf, / White wings are dyed by the setting sun; / Who are the seagulls waiting for?
3.   Dropping anchor in the wispy fog, / You can see the flickering scarlet lights – / Shall we go to dear old Harbour Bridge?
4.   The snow powders down on the wind from Mt Hakusan. / If you go skating at Nagane rink, / There are figures dancing in the moonlight.
5.   In the mountain sunlight, the rice is in blossom; / Dance, girls, dance 'Ōshimako Odori'. / A 20,000-*koku* castle town, village of chrysanthemums.

Notes: Commissioned to commemorate a harbour opening. The tune, by Gotō Tō-sui, is based on the Akita folk song 'Obonai Bushi' (according to Gotō; see NMJ). Verses 4 and 5 are now rarely sung, perhaps because they seem too blatantly tourist-oriented by comparison with the first three verses.

K. '(Tsugaru) Waiha Bushi' (Aomori; NMZ 2.77, FU5, NMD; 1932, Narita Unchiku) (7775; *yō* on 6; 6/8)

1. Rice and apples are the lifeblood of Tsugaru; / Harvest them, grow them, for the sake of the country.
2. In my home region we're especially proud of / The mountain pilgrimage and *baka-nuri* / OR: The *nebuta* floats, and their flutes and drums.
3. You can't disguise your Tsugaru dialect: / *waiha, donden, budzimageda*.
4. Tsugaru women – I guess it's the apples – / Their colour is beautiful and they taste great.
5. People from Tsugaru may talk poorly, / But you'll see, if you meet them, that they're dead honest.

Notes: Written by homesick Unchiku during his travels; tune based somewhat on 'Etchū Owara Bushi', according to Unchiku. *Waiha* means something like 'wow!'

L. 'Tōkyō Ondo' (Tokyo; Osa 239, FU6, OK 241; 1932–3, Saijō Yaso/Nakayama Shinpei) (7775; *miyako-b* on 7; 6/8)

1. If you're going to dance, / [Make it] 'Tōkyō Ondo', / Right in the centre / Of the flowering capital.
2. For cherry blossoms it's Ueno, / For willows it's Ginza, / For the moon it's the Sumida River, / Riding in a roofed boat.
3. To the west, Mt Fuji, / To the east, Mt Tsukuba; / The girl doing the singing / Is right in the middle.
4. They flow in and out, / Out and in, / Prosperous Tokyo's / Waves of people.

Notes: Tokyo's Hibiya entertainment district was losing customers to Ginza. The owners of the various enterprises in Hibiya, mostly country-born males, felt that a Bon dance might bring people running as it would in a village. Via Japan Victor, they commissioned a song called 'Marunouchi Ondo' (Marunouchi being the district containing Hibiya). The 1932 dance was so successful that Victor had Saijō change the lyrics to include all of Tokyo, then re-released the song the following summer. It has been a popular Bon dance song throughout Japan ever since.

M. 'Tenryū Kudareba' ('Going Down the Tenryū [River]') (Nagano; MI 2.172, FU6, YA 136, OK 121, NMJ 232; 1933, Nagata Mikihiko/Nakayama Shinpei) (7775; *miyako-b* on 7; 6/8)

1. Going down the Tenryū River, you'll get soaked by the spray; / Azaleas in bloom, and a rainbow bridge.
2. (<NMJ) Ina has cleared up, the crimson clouds; / Going downriver tomorrow, I'll need a hat.
3. The wisteria cords holding the raft together – / Even if only *they* are severed, it'll be upsetting to the Married Rocks.

Notes: Originally considered more of a popular song, but soon became a *shin-min'yō*. In fact, variant texts have developed, so it's now a 'real' folk song.

N. 'Miyagino Bon-uta' (Miyagi; MI 2.238, NMZ 2.118, 143, FU1, NMD; 1949, Watanabe Hakō/Satō Chōsuke) (7775; *yō* on 6; 2/4)

1. The sparrow rests so gracefully in the bamboo; / The skilful dancer rests in your eye.
2. Old and young, all come out to dance – / The moon is so special in Miyagino.
3. The moon peeks out and lights up the dance-ground, / And lights up the faces of the dancers.
4. When, tired from dancing, they slip from the circle, / It's always by twos.
5. When people start saying that you're a good dancer, / You're happy but embarrassed.
6. The singer's voice echos off the mountains, / Even warbling cheerfully as far as Mt. Aoba.

(Four other verses in MI, three in NMZ, some thirty altogether.)
Notes: Miyagi folks wanted their own Bon dance – they had been borrowing one from Fukushima. It's now treated as a traditional song and dance. Folk singer Oonishi Tamako from Iwate did the choreography; her husband, Takeda Chūichiro, a folk song scholar, made an arrangement for Western instruments.

O. 'Hokkai Tairyō Bushi' ('Hokkaido Great Catch Song') (Hokkaido; NMZ 2.423, MI 1.194, FU4; 1953, Matsumoto Issei/Sudō Takashiro) (7775; *yō* on 2 w. upper neighbour 7; 2/4)

1. In the spring, prosperity springs from the sea: / Squid, salmon, trout and herring-boats.
2. Herring are everywhere! The sailors on the beach / Are more excited than when they're waiting for their girlfriends.
3. After a big catch, the dancing is lively too; / Old ladies and young girls [dance] merrily.
4. Rejoice, mama! What shall I buy you? / This year was a great herring catch along the beach.
5. A hard-working man raised in a fishing town – / That's who I'll give my daughter to, with a dowry.

Notes: The composer Sudō, a folk song teacher, drew on fishing songs from various parts of Japan for elements of tune and text. When it proved popular, he revised the melody, gave it a title, and asked Matsumoto to create new lyrics.

P. 'Imogara Bokuto' ('Clumsy Oaf') (Miyazaki; NMZ 5.103, 113, MI 2.33, FU10; 1955, see below) (7775×2; *yō* on 6; 6/8)

1. My back is sore from clearing the fields; / These foggy spring days sure are long. / When it's time for my five cups of bedtime / *shōchū* [=rotgut *sake*], / I wish I had a wife to serve it to me. / CH.: I got one! I got one! [Me,] the clumsy oaf: / A good bride, a 'Hyūga pumpkin'. / Holy smoke, I've really done it now!

2. With rape-flowers decorating the saddle, we rattle along, / Around seven inlets [to Udo Shrine], with a red horse-blanket, / My pretty bride riding on the Jingle-jingle Horse. / This year there'll be two of us to do the rice planting. (CH.)
3. The seeds have multiplied 10,000-fold, the weather's perfect – / What a great harvest season! / Drink up the celebratory *sake*, / And the wife can wear her long kimono for once. (CH.)
4. Wow – is that snow on Kirishima Island? / My hands're sure sore from cutting radishes. / Next year I'll be somebody's father already – / Can't go complaining about being sore anymore. (CH.)

Notes: For Miyazaki City's 30th Anniversary, a *shin-min'yō* lyrics contest was held; Kurogi Junkichi's lyrics were revised by Kurogi Kiyosugi and Nakamura Jihei. But it contained too much dialect to make a national recording, so Victor Records reworked it, leaving only a few words of dialect. Junkichi's original entry, called 'Nosan Bushi', was recorded by King Records around 1974. The original lyrics were completely in local dialect, translatable roughly as follows:

P'. 'Nosan Bushi' (NMZ 5.113; 1955, Kurogi Junkichi)

1. On Mt Osuzu, a spring mist; / Exhausted from clearing the forest, / I take a bit of bedtime *sake* and hit the hay. / I want a wife too. / CH.: If you don't get one soon, you'll soon be an old man. / You're the only one without a wife.

Q. 'Shin Gōshū Ondo' (Shiga; NMZ 4.56; 1957–8, no lyricist given)
Standard traditional-style folk song lyrics, except for occasional lines such as: 'The textile factories are known throughout the world.'
Notes: 'New Gōshū Ondo'. This is one of many twentieth-century songs with titles of the form 'Shin – -', which are revisions or new arrangements of traditional songs. 'Gōshū Ondo' is a Bon-dance song so popular that its singers are often hired to perform in neighbouring prefectures at the Bon season. Its original lyrics consisted predominantly of long adventure and love ballads (*kudoki*), but in 1957 in Yōkaichi City, Shiga Pref., a contest was held to produce some new lyrics in praise of the region (cf. Fukao 1971:36, 136). The members of the Gōshū Ondo Hozonkai have adopted this version as well; it is frequently accompanied by electric guitar.

R. 'Shirahama Ondo' (Chiba; MI 2.111, FU6, NMJ 184; 1965, Namioka Ryūji)
(7775, 7775; *ritsu* on 5 and 2; 2/4)

1. Come on, everybody, let's dance – / The dance song is so fine down on the beach. / If you dance, both your body and the world around you become sunny; / [N.B. 'world' here does not mean the whole world, just the / immediate surroundings.] / Tomorrow too, a cheerful smiling face.
2. Shirahama in Chiba is a nice place to live: / Even in mid-winter the rape-flowers bloom; / In summer a cool breeze blows in off the ocean; / Napping under a pine, you can dream your dreams.
3. If you call across to Ōshima Island from Nojima Point, / The Ōshima girls will come out and beckon. / In sympathy, Mt Mihara [on Ōshima] also burns: / 'I miss you, I miss you', it belches out smoke.

4. The harbour at Iwame, with its old-fashioned charm; / Now a young woman sits there, thinking of love, / Writing the name of her man in the sand – / When the waves erase it, she writes it again.

Notes: This song was written by a local resident without a commission from any tourist-minded organization. Local praise songs are still being written, with or without commissions. Interestingly, this one is in the *ritsu* mode, which is extremely rare in *shin-min'yō*.

1.2 *Shin-min'yō* from 1977 to 1981

The heading for each song gives: title; record co.; sponsoring orgzn. (if any) in brackets; date of release; lyricist/composer; poetic metre; mode; musical metre. Abbreviations: Victor=Japan Victor; Toshiba=Toshiba; CBS=CBS Sony; Columbia=Japan Columbia; ZMSR=Zen-Nihon Min'yō Shidōsha Renmei [All-Japan Folk Dance Teachers League]; TMR=Tōkyō-to Min'yō Renmei [Tokyo Metropolitan Folk Dance League]; NFR=Nihon Fōku Dansu Renmei [Japan Folk Dance League]; ZBR=Zen-Nihon Buyō Renmei [All-Japan Traditional Dance League]. Songs are in no particular order.

A. 'Shōwa Ondo' ('Shōwa Song') (Victor [ZMSR, TMR]; 1981, Yoshikawa Shizuo /Yoshida Masashi) (75×4; penta. major; 6/8)

1. Living on this round earth, / It's a bad habit to be a ceremonious square. / All nations of the earth are neighbours – / Even space travel is not a dream. / CH.: Flowering Japan, flowering Japan, *sano yoi yoi* / With 'Shōwa Ondo', *yoyoi no yoyoi no sano yoi yoi.*
2. Through Meiji, Taisho, up through Shōwa, / The whole family is all smiles, / [Remembering] those days, those times, those events – / Bitter suffering, too – all old tales now. (CH.)
3. Obligation and human feelings are two sides of a coin; / To be of service to each other is the way of the world. / Even (such) old ideas are fresh – / That's why life is so interesting. (CH.)
4. Mt Fuji, cherry blossoms, you and I, / And all those unforgettable moments. / This is the country where we were born and raised – / Let's all keep the lamp of hope burning! (CH.)

Notes: Shōwa is the period from 1926 to 1989. Note the shift from the universalist first verse to the Japan-centred chorus and later verses.

B. 'Dai-Shōwa Ondo' ('Great Shōwa Ondo') (Toshiba [ZMSR]; 1981, Kaneko Tomoji/Rikuō? Takashi) (7, 7775, 77; CH: 7(775); penta. major; 6/8)

1. Auspicious, auspicious! / Three generations in one family living in the Shōwa period, / Beaten by rain and storm; / Japan grows into a springtime of peace, / Her dreams expanding – / CH.: With 'Shōwa Ondo', with 'Shōwa Ondo', let the flower bloom!

2. Auspicious, auspicious! / Chrysanthemums flourish, the morning sun rises; / Cultural progress is the result / Of years of sweat and labour. / Young lives! (CH.)
3. Auspicious, auspicious! / Peace on earth, living in Shōwa, / Blood flaming in our willing hearts. / World peace, too – (CH.)

Notes: The first line (*medeta medeta ya*) is a standard opener in congratulatory folk songs.

C. 'Ginza Burabura Odori' ('Ginza Strolling Dance') (Victor [ZMSR, TMR]; 1981, Ida Seiichi/Yoshida Masashi) (7775; major; 6/8)

1. In the morning, mist; in the evening, neon lights. / Budding in your dreams, the willow of love. / CH.: 1st ward, 2nd ward, 3rd ward, / Love you [*rabu yū*], stroll with you [*bura yū*], / strolling along, / Strolling through the eight wards of Ginza.
2. There's that *kan-kan* girl from the old days, / In a smashing wine-coloured dress. / CH.: 2nd ward, 3rd ward, 4th ward, / etc.
3. Shall we dance to rock music, or join the *kiyari*? / You look good in a happi-coat too. / CH.: 3rd ward, 4th ward, 5th ward, / etc.
4. Strolling in the gentle Ginza-tinted breeze, / A 'top-mode' [high-fashion] young lady. / CH.: 4th ward, 5th ward, 6th ward, / etc.
5. Among the poplars on Namiki Avenue, / The two swallows enjoy each others' company / CH.: 5th ward, 6th ward, 7th ward, / etc.

Notes: Ginza was Tokyo's major shopping and entertainment district at the time of this song. There are foreign loan-words in every verse: neon, wine colour, can-can, rock, top-mode, poplar, love you. '*Kan-kan* girl' refers to a 1949 hit song about a modish post-war Ginza girl.

D. 'Aozora Ondo' ('Blue Skies Song') (Toshiba [ZMSR]; 1981, Nikaidō Susumu/ Oka Chiaki) (7775, 7777; penta. minor; 6/8)

1. In the Japanese skies, where dreams make flowers bloom, / Voices echo to the west and east. / If you clap your hands, your heart dances too; / The wind blows fresh, with the Blue Skies Ondo. / CH.: Come on, everyone, do 'Aozora Ondo'.
2. In the Japanese skies, clouds are scudding; / The flower-fresh smiling faces light up the dance circle. / You and I, in our hearts, / Today and tomorrow, have 'Aozora Ondo'. (CH.)
3. In the Japanese skies, whether it's sunny or cloudy, / The bell of hope will ring tomorrow too. / Our feet moving together, shoulders in line, / In healthy spirits, we dance 'Aozora Ondo'. (CH.)
4. In the Japanese skies, flowers are blooming! / There's a song that'll make you forget your troubles. / Old and young, let's dance together, / With cheerful voices, to 'Aozora Ondo'. (CH.)

Notes: Recorded version was sung by a solo male voice in *enka* vocal style, suitable to the pentatonic minor used here but atypical of most *shin-min'yō* of this period (see §6.4.3).

E. 'Wakashū-daiko' ('Young Folks' Drum') (King; 1981, Isobe Takeo/Komachi Akira) (7777, 7775; penta. major; 6/8)

1. In cherry-blossom Japan, from end to end, / Start beating it out, the 'Young Folks' Drum'. / Surrounding the tower, raising our voices, / Let's sing at tonight's Bon dance.
2. The skilful drumming draws us, pulls us, / Beats in our breasts, the 'Young Folks' Drum'. / Joining in the lively chorus by imitating the others, / Let's all flower, flower, burst into flower!
3. Nice patterns dyed on the backs of our matching jackets, / Who are we waiting to meet, [playing] the 'Young Folks' Drum'. / In a lively Edo-style costume, / Drumming as if to reach the heavens!
4. The moon is round, and so is the ring of dancers – / All in a circle, to the 'Young Folks' Drum'. / Hands pointing, hands flowering, all joined by the smiling faces – / Let's dance at tonight's Bon dance.

Notes: Typically for Japanese, there are no subjects or pronouns to tell us who the actors are: I, you, we, they, he, she . . .; this vagueness actually allows the song to include everyone.

F. 'Nippon Hanjō Ondo' ('Japan Prosperity Song') (King; 1981, Tanaka Yukio/ Sakurada Seiichi) (9575, 7777, 75; yō on 6; 6/8)

1. Summer has come, *yakkorasatto*, / Bringing along its dancing buddies of an evening, / 'We're all lined up' – that girl, this girl, / Around the tower, 'Prosperity Song'. / Eye meets eye – how happy!
2. The rice has come, *zakkuriko to*, / Bringing along an autumn harvest and a song. / If the sparrows want some, let them stuff themselves. / This year's a bumper crop – look at any storehouse: / Rice bags piled high – how happy!
3. The waves have come, *zanburiko to*, / Bringing along ships with full-catch banners. / The harbour is alive with silver-scaled fish – / Seagulls, won't you dance with us? / Dawn on the sea – how happy!
4. The people have come, *dossariko to*, / With their cries of prosperous businesses. / Wherever you look, the flowers of smiling faces. / From early morning, the streets are full of spirit – / Such a lively mood – how happy!
5. The dance has come, *dokkoisa to*, / Bringing along gongs, drums and drumsticks. / In stylish yukatas, clap your hands: / All of Japan, from north to south, / Is joined by this song – how happy!

Notes: The parallel structure of the first two lines of each verse is very untraditional, but frequent in *shin-min'yō*.

G. 'Omatsuri Ondo' ('Festival Song') (Victor; 1977, Yoshikawa Shizuo/Yoshida Masashi) (7775; penta. major; 6/8)

1. The song comes flowing, the drums resound; / The heart is floating, the spirit soars. / CH.: To 'Omatsuri Ondo', *shashan to na* / *Shashan to, shashan to, yoi, yoi, yoi.*

2. That stylish girl carrying the portable shrine – / She's even prettier wearing that light makeup. (CH.)
3. Joining hands with childhood friends – / Who could ever forget these faces? (CH.)
4. Sing the song sunnily, dance the dance flashily, / And live every day happily. (CH.)
5. Everyone's smiling at a Japanese festival – / 100 million flowers dancing together. (CH.)

Notes: Despite the lyrics of verse 3, this dance does not involve joining hands; virtually no Japanese *min'yō* or *shin-min'yō* does. Holding hands is simply a modern Western image of friendly interaction.

H. 'Furusato-bayashi' ('Home-town Dance Music') (Victor; 1977, Yoshikawa Shizuo/Yoshida Masashi) (7775,7577; penta. minor; 6/8)

1. The plum and cherry blossoms, when seen in one's native place, / Why are their colours and fragrance different [from elsewhere]? / The mountains, the rivers are unchanged, / Mother, sister, brother are all fine. / CH.: Born and raised with 'Furusato-bayashi', / The dancers too become flowers – / Form a circle, become flowers!
2. The Bumper Year Drum celebrates the harvest; / Excited by the flute music, the red dragonfly / Must have been drinking – such a red face! / And the pretty rainbow still carries a dream. (CH.)
3. It's a hazily moonlit night; the yukatas are fragrant. / No matter how you hide behind your fan, / I recognize my childhood friend immediately – / That's it! That voice, that way of laughing! (CH.)
4. Around the hearth, [drinking] the fondly remembered local *sake*. / There's the nursemaid that used to watch over me. / Look at that cute kid – / Waving and saying 'hello, hello' [in English].

I. 'Dai-Tōkyō Ondo' ('Great Tokyo Song') (King, etc. [Tokyo Channel 12 TV]; 1979, Takita Tsuneharu/Endō Minoru) (7777, 75, ??, 75; penta. major; 6/8)

1. People form a circle, the circle becomes a flower; / The lingering fragrance of Edo is faintly caught / And flowers again in every heart. / CH.: Tokyo, Tokyo, Great Tokyo – / Let's bloom and make it bloom / Forever after, forever after.
2. With a fervent wish for a happy tomorrow – / The growing subways, the express-ways – / Blow all our cares away. / CH.: Tokyo, Tokyo, Great Tokyo – / Look! Even the Sumida River is running clear!
3. You can see Mt Fuji and Mt Tsukuba. / Of old it was Musashino, now it's all New Towns. / In the forest of buildings, a song comes bubbling up. / CH.: Tokyo, Tokyo, Great Tokyo – / The moon, with a smiling face, says 'Good evening'.
4. The dream spreads to the south and west, / Riding on the aspirations of Japanese Culture. / Even today, by air or by sea, / CH.: Tokyo, Tokyo, Great Tokyo – / We're on our way to the ends of the earth!

Notes: In 1979, Tokyo Channel 12 sponsored a prize competition for lyrics for a song reflecting Tokyo's modernity, to replace the 1930s hit dance tune 'Tōkyō Ondo' (see previous section). They then contracted to have it recorded by twelve different record companies and launched a campaign to make it 'the Bon-dance song of the year'. They succeeded.

J. 'Furusato-dayori' ('News from Home') (King; 1979, Yokoi Hiroshi/Hosokawa Jun'ichi) (7777, 7775; penta. minor & *miyako-b* on 7; 6/8)

1. Accompanied by a spray of mountain cherry blossoms, / A letter from you arrived again today. / If I had my way, like a skylark / I'd fly back to my home town. / CH.: Truly the old home town is great, isn't it?
2. Two strangers become happy friends / When they hear the charming beachside drumming. / Dancing 'til they drop, shoulder to shoulder – / Unforgettable, under the pine trees. (CH.)
3. To lovers, even the moon's light / Is too bright along the wooded path. / Recalling that night and our vow so sweet, / I can still hear the insects singing. (CH.)
4. If I can live with you from now on, / Why should that cold north wind bother me? / We can quit our clumsy posturing, throw it in the fire, / And drink of each other as we watch the snow fall. (CH.)

Notes: The same lyricist wrote 'Bōkyō Jonkara' (song 1.3.I). This is a borderline *shin-min'yō* and might also be called a *buyō-kayō*. Its narrow focus – a pair of lovers – sets it apart from the other songs in this section.

K. 'Shiawase Ondo' ('Happiness Song') (Victor [ZMSR]; 1980, Yoshikawa Shizuo/Tokuchi Masanobu) (7785, 7575; penta. minor; 6/8)

1. The heart has springtimes with flowers blooming, / But it also has autumns with falling leaves. / Say 'I'll do it! I'll live! I'll fight on!' / If you beat your breast, a song will come out. / CH.: Amiably, smiling, cheerfully, / To 'Shiawase Ondo', / *Shan to, shashan to,* cheerfully.
2. However upset you are, there's nothing to do but go on. / Throw away those feelings and get up on your feet again. / Don't defeat yourself – / [Follow] that rainbow to the hope of tomorrow. (CH.)
3. A cheerful household is one full of warm relations, / Brimming over with healthy spirits. / The wide world is ever wider, / And everywhere a spring breeze blows. (CH.)

Notes: Slightly unusual for its period in using the pentatonic minor despite the particularly strong emphasis on happiness implied by the title. Perhaps this relates to the lyrics, which suggest that one must fight through frequent adversity. – Another song of the same title was recorded in 1997 by its composers, the brothers Maekawa Hitoshi and Hiroshi (Teichiku CD TEDA-10406). It too was intended for dancing and has many of the typical 'new "new folk song" ' elements: happy, optimistic lyrics, bouncy 6/8 metre, *kakegoe* (*a sore* etc.), and (synthesized?) *shamisen* and (imitated?)

Japanese drum. But it is in the pentatonic minor and sung in voices closer to *enka* than *min'yō* by artists associated with the former genre.

L. 'Oppeke Odori' ('Oppeke Dance') (Victor [ZMSR]; 1980, Yoshikawa Shizuo/Tokuchi Masanobu) (7775, 7777; *yō* on 6 (and 2); 2/4)
CH.: *Oppekepeppo peppoppo, katchikichinton chintonton*

1. My distant native place – I miss it so; / The colour of the moon over the apartment complex. (CH.) / Those home-town praise songs – / Sing one for me, dear mother. (CH.)
2. Fireworks overhead, and lovers down here / Are on fire along the beautiful Sumida River. (CH.) / Even the stubbornest heart will be softened / By the stylish sounds of the downtown shamisen. (CH.)
3. Hills: Nogi Hill, Persimmon Tree Hill, / Kagura Hill with its swaying red lanterns. (CH.) / In life you've got to climb some hills / And suffer – or else you haven't tasted life. (CH.)

Notes: 'Oppekepe' was a popular song of the middle Meiji period, ridiculing the indiscriminate adoption of Western fashions; it was pro-modernization but anti-Westernization (cf. Osada 1976a: 50; Malm 1971; a recording from 1900 is on CD R35). Aside from the first half of the chorus, it has nothing in common with the new song except perhaps a certain sense of the need to persevere in the face of adversity.

M. 'Notte Notte Ondo' ('Get-the-Spirit Song') (CBS [ZBR]; 1979, Yoshioka Osamu/Yamamoto Naozumi) (??; major w. penta. major as core; 6/8)

1. Form a circle! / (Form it, a circle!) [Many other refrains throughout] / Dancing makes you 'happi', all in the middle of your youth. / I'll bet I can fly! (2X) I'm flying! (2X) / Flying happily, round and round. / Even the squarest heart turns round. / CH.: Grandpa, Grandma, get the spirit! / Father, mother, get the spirit! / You two lovers, get the spirit! / You too, stranger, get the spirit!
2. Trying to fly, but can't? / Try stamping the ground with your feet. / I'll bet you'll get the spirit! (2X) You've got the spirit! (2X) / When you get it, you float along lightly. / Even a chubby person like you can get it. / CH.: Superman, get the spirit! / Beethoven, get the spirit! / Invisible Man, get the spirit! / Kurama Devils, get the spirit!
3. A thousand gather and hold hands – / The touch is gentle and warm. / Hello, hello; thank you, thank you. / The dance soon fades; your troubles soon fade, too. / CH.: [same as first verse chorus]

Notes: As for the previous song, despite the lyrics of verse 3, this dance does not involve holding hands.

N. 'Shiki Ranman' ('Four Seasons in Full Bloom') (CBS [ZBR]; 1979, Yoshioka Osamu/Yamamoto Naozumi) (7585, 7575; penta. major; 6/8)

1. Springtime: beneath the cherry blossoms, / Drinking and viewing the blossoms from our little mat. / When you get drunk, your true feelings come out; / That's fine – a blizzard of blossoms. / CH.: Right now, all Japan is in the height of spring. (2X)
2. Summer: hydrangeas and sudden showers; / Sheltering together under the eaves – / Do we want the rain to stop or not? / The soaking heightens the flowers' colour [and our passions]. / CH.: Right now, all Japan is in the height of summer. (2X)
3. Autumn: the fall colours, and hot *sake* / Warming the palm of the hand. / Where are you going, migrating bird? / O sorrowful, changeable heart! / CH.: Right now, all Japan is in the height of autumn. (2X)
4. Winter: waiting for spring and the prosperity-plant, / And the arrival of a happy season. / Carrying each other, helping each other – / A flower-calendar of human kindness. / CH.: Right now, all Japan is in the height of flower [NB: not winter]. (2X)

Notes: The word 'flower' occurs in the same position in the last line of each verse – a structural device unknown in this form in traditional song. Similar parallellism in many *shin-min'yō*. The 'prosperity-plant' (*fukujusō*) is a flower cultivated as a New Year's plant.

O. 'Wakakusa Ondo' ('Young Sprout Song') (Columbia [ZMSR]; 1981, Maki Yoshimi/Fukuhara Tsuneo) (??; *yō* on 6 w. upper neighbour 7; 2/4)

1. Hey, let's dance! / Children of wind, children of spring, children of green, / Blow softly through the town, *yoi yoi yoi yoi!* / Clap hands to 'Wakakusa Ondo' – / That's it – all the plants have put out sprouts.
2. Hey, let's dance! / Children of wind, children of summer, children of green, / To the sparkling sea, *sui sui sui sui!* / Double your hopes with 'Wakakusa Ondo' – / I'll split my tears with you.
3. Hey, let's dance! / Children of wind, children of autumn, children of green, / To the distant sky, *gun gun gun gun!* / Have a dream and go for it with 'Wakakusa Ondo' – / Right in the middle of your youth!

Notes: Notice that this song, like the previous one, finds winter a less congenial season than the others.

P. 'Furusato Bon Uta' (Columbia [ZMSR]; 1981, Noguchi Kensaku/Kai ?Harufumi) (7's, 5's, 8's; penta. minor; 6/8)

1. (CH.: Bon song, love song, red lanterns, Bon dance.) / The waves beat a solo along the beach; / Stars fall along the beach, as the bonfires burn; / The seagulls flying high dance too.
2. (CH.: *Shan shan*, clap your hands, *chonchon to ne*.) The moon is round, a protective spirit; / When the wind blows through the forest boughs, / The fireflies, making love, dance too.
3. The matching yukatas are dyed with indigo [=*ai*=love]; / All hands move together, the fans flutter; / You and I dance too.

Q. 'Nippon Hanami Odori' ('Japan Flower-viewing Dance') (Columbia [NFR, ZMSR]; 1979, Oka Toshio/Ichikawa Shosuke) (7775, 7775; *yō* on 6 w. upper neighbour 7; 2/4)

1. It's spring; a spring breeze is blowing, / And the Japan archipelago is in full bloom. / It's spring; the whole world / Is in full bloom with the 'Flower-viewing Dance'. / CH.: The cherries have bloomed, bloomed . . .
2. A man's heart is like a cherry blossom, / Bearing up through the cold, blooming in spring. / A woman's heart too is like the cherry blossom, / Blooming in the heart of you, her loved one.

1.3 *Min'yō*-connected popular songs, old and new

The heading for each song gives: title; record co. (for recent releases) and/or printed source (for older songs); date of publication; lyricist and composer. Abbreviation not yet explained: Natsu=Natsu n.d.

A. 'Sendō Kouta' ('Song of the Boatman') (Osa 93; 1921, Noguchi Ujō/Nakayama Shinpei) (7575, 7575; penta. minor; 2/4)

1. I am a withered eulalia on the riverside; / You, too, are a withered eulalia. / Both of us are, in this world, / Nothing but flowerless, withered eulalias.
2. Whether we live or die, the water / Won't change its flow – right, friend? / You and I might as well spend our lives / As captains on the Tone River.
3. The withered rushes are illumined / By the moon of Itako Dejima. / From now on I'll spend my life / As a captain on the Tone River.

Notes: Like the other pre-war songs in this section, it was written by major figures in the *shin-min'yō* movement. Eight different recorded versions were released during 1922–23. This was supposedly the first widely popular song in the 'pentatonic minor' scale, which is now (still) the dominant scale of *enka*. The third verse refers to a famous eighteenth-century popular song, 'Itako Bushi', which speaks of flowers blooming among the rushes at Itako Dejima, bringing a note of optimism to this song. Its overall textual mood, however, is much too pessimistic to resemble traditional folk song: even Buddhist-tinged folk verses about the impermanence of all things are less morbid than the first two verses here. See Nakamura 1991:265–6 for the song's history.

B. 'Habu no Minato' ('Habu Harbour') (Osa 100; 1923, Noguchi Ujō/Nakayama Shinpei) (777775; penta. minor; 2/4)

1. The cormorant on the beach returns to roost at sunset. / In Habu harbour, the sun sets. / Will tomorrow's weather be calm, I wonder?
2. The boats are bustling with preparations for departure; / The island women live by the Sacred Fire; / What is in their hearts as they wait?
3. We live in poverty on this island. / Messages come from Ito [on the mainland] by mail / And from Shimoda [on the mainland] on the wind.

4.   It's a salt wind that blows down from the Sacred Fire; / When the boats depart, the island women / Cry as they untie the hawsers.

Notes: Habu is the harbour of Ōshima, a volcanic island in the sea 20 km off the Izu Peninsula. The Sacred Fire refers to the island's volcanic nature. The lyrics show occasional parallels with the island's best-known *min'yō*, 'Ōshima Bushi'. The melody is a mixture of the *miyako-bushi* mode and the Western minor mode. 'Habu no Minato' was recorded in 1928 and was such a hit that several of the writers and singers of the 'New Folk Song' movement became more involved in the nascent popular song world (Kojima 1970:25; see also Nakamura 1991:267).

C. 'Defune no Minato' ('Harbour of Departing Boats') (Osa 218; 1925, Shigure Otowa/Nakayama Shinpei) ((7777) × 2; *yō* on 6, w. 7 substit. for 1 occasionally; 2/4)

1.   Bouncing, bouncing over the waves, / One, two, three oars, eight oars to make her fly. / Suddenly, there it is – the whale's waterspout; / Beyond the waterspout, the morning sun is dancing.
2.   *Essa, essa, essa,* the arms that row / Are strong as iron. That iron / Is challenged by the waves. The waves come pounding, / Pounding, pounding, the waves come pounding.

Notes: The recording, released in 1928, sold well over 100,000 copies. The lyricist was describing the activities in his home-town harbour in Hokkaido. The tune is mostly in *yō* on 6, but the occasional substitution of 7 for 1 gives it a momentary sense of modulation to another *yō* mode.

D. 'Shima no Musume' ('Island Girl') (Osa 110, 237; 1934, Nagata Mikihiko/Sasaki Shun'ichi) (775, 775; penta. minor; 2/4)

1.   Raised on an island, a sixteen-year-old girl / Gets to thinking about love. / Far from prying eyes, / A night of fleeting love.
2.   Out on the stormy seas, a wind from the mountains – / A wind of parting. / Her lover, a sailor, will return no more / From beneath the waves.
3.   The lamps are extinguished on the island; / On the beach, a plover. / Don't cry for me – / I'm just a wretched abandoned boat.
4.   He must be cold, sleeping every night / In his watery bed. / The snowflakes fall; crying at dawn, / The plover on the beach.

Notes: Sung by geisha Kouta Katsutarō in a purely traditional vocal style, this song triggered the wave of geisha pop singers. The original first verse, shown here, was found too explicitly suggestive by the censors, who forced its alteration. The record sold over a half-million copies in 1932. Each verse begins with a long melisma on the syllable *ha*, a feature which derived from Katsutaro's hit recording of the *min'yō* 'Sado Okesa'. The introductory *ha* subsequently became a common feature of folk-style *kayōkyoku* as of many 'new folk songs'.

E. 'Sendō Kawaiya' ('The Boatman is So Dear') (Osa 115; 1935, Takahashi Kikutarō /Furuseki Hiroshi) (7775; *yō* on 6; 2/4)

1. In dreams we are lovers, /moistened by the sea wind, the night wind; / The boatman is so dear to me, sleeping on the waves.
2. Although a thousand miles apart, our thoughts are one: / We look up at the same moon in the night sky.
3. When I sleep alone, my pillow is even wetter. / At least I'd like to show him my dream.

Notes: Text by a folk song researcher/poet; a popular song to be sung '*min'yō* style'. It was sung in a *geisha-min'yō* voice by Otomaru – a housewife who sang under a geisha-like name to take advantage of the 1930s boom in geisha pop singers (Katsutarō, Ichimaru etc.). The words 'wet' and 'moist(en)' are used, as usual, as synonyms for sexual relations as well as to imply the falling of tears.

F. 'Tsuki no Okesa-bune' ('The Okesa Boat on a Moonlit Night') (Natsu 2:150; 1956, Ishimoto Miyuki/Hirakawa Hideo) (7775, 77775; penta. minor; 2/4)

1. The moon is full, the dance is 'Okesa'; / 'To Sado, to Sado', even the waves call. / The oar-handles of love are soaked by the spray: / In my thoughts [I travel] the 49 leagues, stealing to meet you, / Stealing to meet you, on the Okesa boat.
2. When we are far apart, the nights of waiting are long; / When we meet, they're too short, the island nights. / Hearing the dance music, / Carried by the waves of a blue moonlight night, / On a blue moonlight night, the Okesa boat.
3. When you're in love, you try to avoid prying eyes. / You and I are both plovers on the beach; / Our dreams and feelings melt into one. / Despite our parting, it's a never-fading memory, / A never-fading memory: the Okesa boat.

Notes: As in the previous song (by the same lyricist), a local folk song (here, 'Sado Okesa') takes one back home – on the imaginary Okesa boat to the island of Sado. On the word *okesa* in the last line, the melody recalls the well-known opening bars of the folk song.

G. 'Sōran Wataridori' ('Soran Migratory Bird') (Columbia; Natsu 2:138; 1961, Ishimoto Miyuki/Endō Minoru) (7577, 7777, CH.; penta. major; 2/4)

1. I've crossed the Tsugaru Straits [leaving Hokkaidō], / An orphaned swallow without a roost. / I miss Esashi, I miss the herring fisheries; / When the shamisen plays, I join in with feeling: / CH.: '*Yāren sōran sōran sōran*' / Singing '*Sōran*'; oh, I'm a migrating bird.
2. Although I miss my home harbour, / My dreams can't reach that far, to the northern skies. / I hide my suffering behind a winsome smile. / How many mountains and rivers have I crossed in this world? (CH.)

Notes: The fishermen's song 'Sōran Bushi' here evokes and symbolizes the singer's beloved, distant home, Esashi in Hokkaidō. A bit of the folk song's refrain (words and melody) is incorporated into the chorus. The song is sung in the pentatonic major, the choice of a major tonality indicating that the protagonist is resigned to, indeed happily wedded to, her endless travels and her homesickness. Although women were not allowed on the herring boats, this song was popularized by the twin sisters Komadori Shimai from Hokkaidō.

H. 'Sōran Jingi' ('Sōran Self-Introduction') (Crown; Natsu 1:147; 1964, Handa Kōkichi/Narita Takeo) (7777×3, 7775×2; penta. major; 2/4)

1. I was born in Hokkaidō, / Renowned as the home of 'Sōran Bushi'. / Strolling past the bars on the back streets, / In this man's self-introduction are imbued / Pride and stubbornness, hard work and suffering. . . .
3. I was born and raised in the fisheries, / Salt spray in my face, among the silver scales of the herring. / That woman I loved, surely she won't have waited for me – / Rumour has it she's married another man. / Right, I'll forget her and get on with my life.

Notes: Notice that Hokkaidō is made famous only by 'Sōran Bushi', showing the importance of *min'yō* in symbolizing local identity. 'Sōran Bushi' can also evoke instantly the herring fisheries and the migrant workers who find their way to them, then vanish to who knows where. One can imagine the protagonist having to leave his Hokkaidō home as the fisheries collapsed, to seek work elsewhere. A *jingi* is a stylized self-introduction, a personal history recitation often associated in the public mind with *yakuza* or gamblers. The melody of the original folk song is quoted only briefly after the first verse. But it too uses the pentatonic major, and for similar reasons: 'pride and stubbornness' require a macho heartiness in the face of suffering. Compare further 'Sōran Koiuta' (song M below).

I. 'Bōkyō Jonkara' ('Jonkara Homesickness') (CBS Sony; 1979, Yokoi Hiroshi/??) (7775, 7775, 885; penta. minor; 2/4)

1. After working at the bar, you turn out the light / And sing 'Jonkara', the song from back home; / I can feel your sorrow when I hear your voice. / That village where the apple blossoms bloom – / You and I, the two of us, / Let's go home, let's go home.
2. The hopes I carried with me when I left my native place – / Why has the city wind disrupted them? / She always comforts my bitter heart, / My mother with her Tsugaru dialect – / You and I, the two of us, / Let's go home, let's go home.
3. On the overnight train, let's throw our tears out the window – / Morning is near, and our home-town sky. / Winter is fierce in the Tsugaru blizzards, / But one can dream of a new beginning. / You and I, the two of us, / Let's live together, let's live together.

Notes: Originally written for and recorded by Sasaki Shin'ichi, the son of Tsugaruya Suwako II (b. 1913); she was a former touring professional singer who had released a recording of the folk song 'Tsugaru Jongara Bushi' as early as 1933. 'Tsugaru Jongara (Jonkara) Bushi' is a favorite song from the Tsugaru district and one of the best-known *min'yō*; hearing it might indeed make a former resident homesick. (The same lyricist also wrote 'Furusato-Dayori' (song 1.2.J above).) A later song of the same title is discussed in Yano 1994 (see also Groemer 1999: 68). Indeed, numerous *enka* have titles beginning with the word 'bōkyō' – nostalgia for home (see K and L below).

J. 'Hanagasa Tsukiyo' ('Flower Hat Moonlit Night') (Toshiba; ca. 1980, Suzuki Hiroshi/Yamanaka Hiroshi) (7575 [insert] 7775; *yō* on 6; 6/8)

1. I danced with the moon at my back, / In my red-and-white spotted kimono. / 'I don't wear my flower-hat just for appearance . . .' / We'll never part, the two of us – / I wonder if the waxing moon knows.
2. I can't tell you that I love you, but / At the night festival we can rub shoulders. / 'Even the moon plays around at night; all the more . . .' / As the young couple drifts off into the shadows, / The moon also stealthily slips behind the clouds.
3. When the singing is in our local dialect / And we all dance in a circle, what fun! / 'How auspicious – the young pine's branches . . .' / What I remember from those festive nights / Is the distant sound of music under the shining moon.

Notes: A *min'yō-kayō* ('folk song-popular song'), incorporating a bit of melody and lyrics from the famous *min'yō* 'Hanagasa Ondo', which accompanies a hat dance. Choreography for a new hat dance is included in the record jacket.

K. 'Bōkyō Sakaba' ('Homesick Tavern') (1981, Satomura Ryūichi/Sakurada Seiichi) ((77, 75)×2; penta. minor; 2/4)

1. A drunkard like my old man, / I never wanted to become one, but I did. / When I'm drunk, 'Ushioi Uta' / comes out of my mouth, on a night like this: *interlude* (first two lines of 'Nanbu Ushioi Uta'): Although it's the countryside, / the province of Nanbu . . .
2. Shredded by the wind, the hem of the door curtain . . . / The train whistle's lonely cry, heading north – / when it calls to me, how painful: that girl's image / flutters before me through the *sake*.
3. Drowning in *sake*, I'm emaciated, wasting away. / I send a dream back home as a souvenir. / Up north, is it time for sleet or winter showers? / I'm desperately worried about my mother.

Notes: *Minyō*-like interjections (*yo*, *hāyai*) punctuate each verse. Unlike the same lyricist's 'Bōkyō Esashi' (L below), this song actually inserts a passage of a folk song, the 'Nanbu Cowherd's Song'. In verse 3, 'back home' translates the word *kuni*, written in the lyrics books with *kokyō*, which is also read as *furusato*.

L. 'Bōkyō Esashi' ('Homesick for Esashi') (King cassette K10H-20004; ca. 1988, Satomura Ryūichi/Kanō Gendai]) ((77)×4, 75; penta. minor; 2/4)

1. Borne on the wind, the night train's whistle – / Hearing it reminds me of my dear home. / I recall it, but I still can't go home. / When I drown my pain in *sake*, / Spilling from my lips comes a song from home. . . .
3. Even a migratory bird, a thousand *ri* away, / Thinks 'I miss Esashi' and comes flying. / The north must be having blizzards about now. / No way 'Oiwake Bushi' can reach that far. / Those rosy clouds seem to be calling me.

Notes: Performed by the famous *min'yō* and *enka* singer Mihashi Michiya (§§3.4.4, 4.4.2). 'Esashi Oiwake', though not quoted directly, is so famous among *enka* fans, and Mihashi's folk song roots so well known, that no quotation is necessary: a title which links Esashi and homesickness guarantees that the song would have evoked 'Esashi Oiwake' in the listener's mind even without the mention in the penultimate line. The phrase 'song from home' translates *kuni no uta*, with *kuni* again being written as *kokyō* (see notes to previous song).

M. 'Sōran Koiuta' ('Sōran Love Song') (Columbia cassette COSA-990; 1996, Sakai Tomoo/Yamaguchi Hiroshi) (7775, 7575; 7777, *yāren* etc.; penta. minor; 2/4)

1. The coastal train line stretches northward; / Through the train's window, the fishing fires [to attract fish for night fishing], / Distant, sad, along the way, / A face is reflected [in the window], then is gone. / As if to cut off the lingering flame of love, / Breaking the waves, heard from afar: / *'Yāren sōran yāren sōran sōran'*, / The seagull's lonely journey.
2. (omitted here: incomprehensible to me!)
3. The lonely steam whistle pierces my body, / At the desolate harbour I step down from the train. / Today I'll stroll along the seashore / And let the wind blow me clean. / Nameless fishing boats here and there, / Chasing a vanished past, a destiny: / *Yāren sōran yāren sōran sōran*, / The seagull's tearful journey.

Notes: The lyrics to the chorus to 'Sōran Bushi' are quoted, but not the melody, nor is the song itself directly referred to. This elusive, impressionistic lyric uses its *min'yō* connection to call up certain motifs: nostalgia for fading rural lifeways, the *furusato* – anyone's *furusato* – as a comforting place to go to nurse a broken heart. The singer who popularized this song, Kagawa Noriko, is also a skilled *min'yō* singer.

N. 'Okesa Koiuta' ('Okesa Love Song') (Teichiku cassette 10SH-136; ca. 1998, Satomura Ryūichi/?Gen Tetsuya) (7775, 777775; penta. minor; 2/4; quotation from 'Sado Okesa': *hā* 77; *miyako-b* on 7; 6/8)

1. Borne by the wind perhaps, the sound of festival music – / Hearing it, I miss my *furusato*. / I may cry, but I can't move back home: / I'll sing 'Okesa' and bear up/reminisce again tonight. / Sado [Island] is 49 leagues across the waves. // *'Hā, Ogi Harbour, when the evening lights go on . . .'*
2. Worse than the snow that falls on the island cape / Is the bitter, cold city wind. / I've known love, I've known *sake*; / Now, with tales of heartbreak as my souvenir, / The [train's] steam whistle shakes my village heart.
3. The night train arrives at the break of dawn; / I change to a boat and return home. / The lights of Ryōtsu harbour rend my heart. / Today too, on a sea of urban tears / I'll weave dreams of brocade.

Notes: Yet again a folk song takes the singer home. The fifth line quotes a snippet of the original lyrics to 'Sado Okesa' but is sung with typical *enka* timbre and melody. The following line (after //), after a slight pause, is both a textual and a melodic quotation, sung in *min'yō* style; its cadence on what Westerners would hear as the supertonic is accompanied by a dominant sus4 chord (see §3.4.3). In line 4, the verb *shinobu* triggers two homophonous concepts which in some strange way seem to overlap in the Japanese mind: 'to recall, remember, reminisce, wallow in nostalgia', and 'to bear, endure, put up with (suffering, pain, etc.)'. The piece ends on a minor triad on the tonic (6), but then a guitar plays one phrase of the *shamisen* accompaniment to 'Sado Okesa', ending on 7.

ADDRESSES RELATED TO *MIN'YŌ*

1) Main *min'yō sakaba* (folk song bars) in Tokyo

The *min'yō sakaba* listed open by 6pm or so but are primarily active from about 7.30 to 11.00, heating up as the evening progresses. Best nights are usually Friday and Saturday. Customers may sing at any of these.

Oiwake [a.k.a. Asakusa Oiwake] 追分, Nishi-Asakusa 3–28–11, Taitō-ku, Tokyo; tel. (03) 3844–6283. On Kototoi-dōri, west of Kokusai-dōri; Iriya station (exit 2, 10-min. walk). 40-minute shows at 7, 9, 10.30pm (¥2,000 cover), though times may slip. Closed Monday (or Tues if Mon is 19th). On 19th of month, 6–9pm, special guest concert with 5-course meal and all you can drink, ¥7,500. www.oiwake.info

Midori みどり, Asakusa 5–13–4, Taitō-ku, Tokyo; tel. (03) 3875–5681 / 3874–1330. On Hanazono-dōri, east of Kokusai-dōri; Iriya station (exit 2, 10-min. walk). Closed Tuesday? Komatsu Midori and other senior musicians from Akita lead the way.

Tokiwa ときわ, Minami-Tokiwadai 1–18–2, Itabashi-ku, Tokyo; tel. (03) 5966–8879. Tokiwadai (Tōbu-Tōjō Line) south exit (3-min. walk). Closed Tuesday. Website www16.ocn.ne.jp/~m-tokiwa/index.htm shows performances.

Yosakoi よさこい, Edogawa 5–32–27, Edogawa-ku, Tokyo; tel. (03) ??. Closed Monday. Opened September 2005.

Hideko 秀子, Asakusa 2–11–1, Taitō-ku, Tokyo; tel. (03) 3845–0727. Just east of Kokusai-dōri, from Matsuya shop; Tawaramachi station (7-min. walk). Closed which night? Hikage Yūko from Akita sings when customers demand, but *karaoke* may dominate.

Others listed at www.ne.jp/asahi/hooki/koko/syami/sake/002.html.

2) Main *min'yō sakaba* (folk song bars) in the Osaka area

Kotobuki ことぶき, Izuo 1–5–7, Taishō-ku, Osaka; tel. (06) 6553–2886. 5-min. walk on main street south of Taishō station. Closed Mon. Three generations of the Uchida family perform: Hōsen and wife, their son Minoru and wife Endō Sayuri, granddaughters Mai (b.'94) and Akari (b.'99). But Mai and Akari may only perform during school holidays.

Sanraku 三楽, Naniwa-machi 4–19, Kita-ku, Osaka; tel. (06) 6371–1483. Call for information.

Misuji みすじ, Jinai-chō [寺内町] 2–5–19. Moriguchi-shi, Osaka; tel. (06) 6991–3922. By west exit of Keihan Moriguchi-shi station. Closed which night? Run by Saitō Isao and Sayoko, husband and wife from Akita.

3) Umbrella organizations of *min'yō* groups

Nihon Min'yō Kyōkai: Minami-Shinagawa 6–8–20, Shinagawa-ku, Tokyo 140; tel. (03) 3471–8888; www.nichimin.or.jp. Their building, the Nihon Min'yō Kaikan, has a good-sized reference collection and hosts many activities.

Nihon Kyōdo Min'yō Kyōkai: Hon-Komagome 6–24–3, Bunkyō-ku, Tokyo 113; tel. (03) 3947–1363; www.kyomin.jp. A much smaller office, no reference collection. There are many smaller local organizations as well.

4) Record shops

Miyata Records: Asakusa 1–31–7, Taitō-ku, Tokyo; tel. (03) 3841–0409. Probably the largest stock of *min'yō* CDs (in 2000, ca. 200, of which thirty are Tsugaru-jamisen); ca. seventy Okinawa CDs; also good holdings of all traditional genres, *wadaiko*, neo-traditional dance instruction videos etc. – Branch, not seen, at Asakusa 1–1–12; tel. (03) 3843–8988.

The large general record shops tend to have ca. ten to twenty CDs of *min'yō* – virtually all regional collections and generally by professionals – plus 100+ CDs of Okinawan music and a smattering of other traditional genres.

5) Further events information

Min'yō Bunka みんよう文化, tel. (03) 5283–7511. Monthly magazine in Japanese; information about events, publications, people; notations of songs, accompaniments. Web page www.sankei-kaihatsu.co.jp/minyou.

Hōgaku Jānaru [*Hougaku Journal*] 邦楽ジャーナル, tel. (03) 3360–1329. Monthly; in Japanese; information about traditional Japanese music events, publications, etc; not much about *min'yō*. Japanese-language home page: www.zipangu.com/HJ/

Bachi-Bachi バチバチ tel. (03) tel. (03) 3360–1329. Monthly; in Japanese; information mostly about Tsugaru-jamisen and *wadaiko*. Produced by *Hōgaku Jānaru*.

Japan National Tourist Organization, Tourist Information Center (TIC). Produces English-language lists of festivals, folk performing arts events, etc. (Check for dates of Gujō Odori, Etchū Owara Kaze no Bon, etc.) Offices in Tokyo (tel. (03) 3201–3331), Kyoto, at Narita and Kansai Airports, and in many major cities abroad.

Occasional concerts are announced in the English-language newspapers.

6) Okinawan *min'yō sakaba* and information in Tokyo and Osaka

Many of the 100-plus Okinawan restaurants and bars in Tokyo and the smaller number in Osaka will provide live music nightly if anyone asks or if a customer performs (a *sanshin* is always available). The following are among those that have frequent formal performances.

Shimauta Rakuen, Roppongi 7–14–10–4F, Minato-ku, Tokyo; tel. (03) 3470–2310. Northwest corner of Roppongi crossing; Roppongi station (30-second walk). Varied live music about twice a week; phone for schedule.

Tubarāma, Kabuki-chō 1–3–15 (1st floor, Za Katerina Building), Shinjuku-ku, Tokyo; tel. (03) 3200–4639. On Kuyakusho-dōri, north of Shinjuku Ward Office (Kuyakusho); Shinjuku station (6-min. walk). Oyamori Takashi and Miyara Kimiko sing.

Chunjun, Shikanjima 2–7–4, Konohana-ku, Osaka; tel (06) 6468–0725; closed Wednesday. Chidoribashi station (2-min. walk). Three shows from around 7.30.

Haisai, Sangen'ya-higashi 1–4–6, Taishō-ku, Osaka; tel. (06) 6555–9807; closed Monday & Tuesday. North side of Taishō station. Three generations of women of the Isa family perform, Hikaru, Tae and Rena (b. 1998), though less often since opening a second club in Higashi-Ōsaka City (tel. 06–6726–8131).

Uruma Goten, Minami-Okajima 2–7–27, Taishō-ku, Osaka; tel. (06) 6555–8111; closed Monday. Taxi or bus from Taishō station. Large and vibrant. Two to three shows from around 7.30; singers include Kawakami Kiyomitsu.

For others in or near Osaka, see gkabudan.ivt.org/~sanshin-w/minyousakaba.html and kiyora34.ti-da.net/c90732.html.

For further information about Okinawan music activities throughout Japan, contact Ginza Washita Shop, Ginza 1–3–9, Chūō-ku, Tokyo; tel. (03) 3535–6991; near Yūrakuchō, Nishi-Ginza stations (another branch near Ueno station). The Washita Shop in Osaka provides similar information.

A Marketing Guide for

Min'yō Recordings

◉

In 1977, a certain Japanese recording company produced a document to provide guidance for salespeople in marketing a boxed set of eighteen LPs with booklets. The front cover advises: 'Handle with care' (*toriatsukai chūi*); clearly the company preferred to keep its sales strategies secret, so though I came by this document fairly, I will hide the company's identity to avoid upset. This was titled *Guidebook for sales of XX* (*XX hanbai no tebiki*), *XX* being the title of the LP set. The Preface's anonymous author was a *min'yō* researcher also involved in record production.

There are seven LPs of 'genre poems' (*fūbutsushi*, not poems but sonic descriptions of local customs, lifeways, festivals, etc.) and eleven of *min'yō*. The 'genre poem' LPs are arranged regionally, with narration linking recorded examples. This approach, we are told, has a tourism-related 'Discover Japan' mood to it. Recordings include: festivals and drumming traditions; local tour bus guides, auctioneers, street vendors; boat and locomotive whistles; streetcars, jets, horsedrawn carriages; rapids, straits, waterfalls; swordsmiths; seagulls and monkeys; hot spring resorts; wind chimes, temple and church bells. These genre poem LPs also include some folk songs – but usually as field recordings of unaccompanied amateurs (often preservation societies), whereas the same song by a (semi-)professional singer with standard modern *min'yō* accompaniment may occur on the *min'yō* LPs. In the latter, not all singers are from the region whose song(s) they are performing; most are contracted to the company in question.

[Direct translation of excerpts, with my square-bracketed comments added:]

PREFACE: There's a folk song boom! (*Min'yō būmu da!*). These days, on Sundays, virtually without fail, in gymnasiums and community halls, old (and young) [note the brackets!] men and women, clad in kimonos ..., gather in large numbers. Accompanied by shamisen, shakuhachi and drums, with two or three backup singers behind, they stand in the middle of the stage, face the microphone and sing a *min'yō*. Afterwards they receive a bouquet of flowers, bow to the audience and disappear. This three-minute pattern repeats without pause from 9 am to 9 pm. [The singers are mostly amateurs.]

Meanwhile, . . . record companies release a total of some forty *min'yō* records – LPs and singles – each month. . . . Moreover, folk song is regularly being included in music education in primary and middle schools [but see my §7.5]. . . .

This is the first time in our country's history that *min'yō* has been spotlighted to such an extent. Why has it begun to attract so much attention?

The era of reconsidering good things. . . . What we call *min'yō* is one of the rich treasures we Japanese have received from our ancestors. Moreover, it is not something for a handful of the ruling class, but an entertainment for the . . . masses. In the midst of the rapid Westernization of the Meiji period and the shock of [a high] economic growth rate, the living environment of the masses changed: the base provided by the communal society centred in farming and mountain villages was destroyed. This was also the source of the tendency to look down on ancient Japanese things (*nihon korai no mono*).

Recently, however, the worship of artificial, mechanically produced things is fading, and a yearning for natural and human things has begun to blossom. Against this background, the songs of villagers (*furusato-bito*) – *min'yō* – have suddenly been re-assessed and a 'boom' has developed.

Middle and upper age groups lead the way, young folks watch and wait. A common saying in the folk song world these days is, 'The love of *min'yō* begins at thirty-seven'. Indeed, most *min'yō* fans are middle-aged or older. Long ago (actually, the Edo period), it wasn't like this. As revealed by the folk song lyrics 'I'll marry a girl who can sing well', young folks were also actively involved. Why have *min'yō* become the property of the older generations?

1) There are few [non-*min'yō*] songs for older folks to sing. Although the past ten to fifteen years have seen a flood of hit songs aimed at young folks, songs appealing to their elders have been remarkably scarce. Some compensation is offered by so-called *natsumero* [nostalgic melody] *enka*, but songs are needed which offer more chance for empathy (*kyō kan*).

2) *Min'yō* were the hit songs of their youth. [A]mong the hit songs of the record and broadcast industries from about 1945–65 were many *min'yō*. Moreover, these were songs performed by 'authentic folk singers' (*seichō min'yō kashu* [e.g. Mihashi Michiya]). To older folks, these constituted significant 'revival hits' (*ribaibaru hitto*) of the beloved songs of their youth.

For these reasons, *min'yō* fans tend to be older. A remarkable recent trend, however, has seen the success of younger singers and the continuing increase in the number of younger pupils in *min'yō* classrooms.

The desire for 'authenticity' (*seichō*). This age group is rarely impressed by performers in flashy kimonos (or young 'talents' in miniskirts) who merely dress like professionals. Since *min'yō* was born from the daily life of the people, they feel, a good singer must convey a sense of [local] life and customs as well as sympathy (*ninjō*). This is the desire for authenticity. 'Authenticity' may be rephrased as 'the orthodox style of folk song' (*seitō ha min'yō*). This phrase refers to local songs performed, not in a 'pop' style, but with the melody and ornamentation recognized as legitimate by the local people. . . . It's not enough for a song merely to be old.

[Next follow two dictionary definitions of *min'yō*, a listing of Takeuchi Tsutomu's four great elements of *min'yō* (occupation, purpose, place and movement), and four short sections entitled 'The trend of searching for "roots" ' (*rūtsu = genryū*), 'There are various sounds in the *furusato*', 'The history of *min'yō* in mass communication' and 'The *min'yō* world and national contests'.]

[From here on, the translation is a paraphrase only, except for phrases contained in quotation marks.]

p. 5: Four rival recording sets are listed, each with over 200 songs. Whereas most singers in those sets are 'of the previous era' (*ichijidai-mae*), this set's chief advantage is its use of 'present-day first-rank singers' (*genzai dai-issen no jitsuryoku kashu*).

pp. 21–24: 'Towards the selling of *XX*', by Direct Marketing Operations Dept., Sales Promotion Section:

This product's aim: 'to pioneer a new "user stratum", a new market', to 'create new demand'. Targeted age group: 30+ = 50.4% of the population.

Analysis of consumers of *min'yō* products: **Gender:** 58% male, 42% female [no source]. **Age:** Japan Record Society study [undated]: buyers of *min'yō* records: age 10–19, 3%; 20–29, 11%; 30–39, 35%; 40–49, 31%; 50+, 19%. [Total 100%; people over fifty probably buy less because they already have a decent collection and the repertoire is extremely stable.] Compare Sumiya record store chain study of buyers of all records: 0–9, 0.5%; 10–19 45%; 20–29, 42%; 30–39, 7%; 40+, 5%. Since over-thirties (50.4% of population) only buy 12% of all records, they represent a huge potential demand – especially in an ageing society!

NHK-TV's *Furusato no uta-matsuri* (*Home Town Song Festival*) in 1973 had a regular audience of around 15 million [when the population was ca. 120 million]!! Considering that not all *min'yō* fans watched, the **potential demand stratum** should be ca. 20 million, i.e. a third of the over-thirties.

We estimate the solid base of *min'yō* fans at 4 million – the 1/30th of the population who are actually taking lessons (source: Ministry of Trade and Industry, Leisure Development Centre 1977 statistics for 'Estimated hobby population'). (The full listing: flower arranging 10 million people; *min'yō* 4m; guitar 4m; tea ceremony 4m; *nagauta* 3.5m; Japanese dance 3m; piano 1.6m; *koto/shamisen* 1.5m.) Also, one mustn't forget all the folk dance groups (*min'yō o shu to shita buyō no kai*).

Another survey asked 5,000 people what hobbies they wanted to pursue in the future (Bureau of Economic Planning, Citizens' Lifestyle Office, ed. (no date given) *Recreation in daily life* (*Kurashi no naka no rekuriēshon*)). Of over twenty categories, those who put *min'yō* first = age 30–39, 2%; 40–49, 3%; 50–59, 5%; 60+, 3%. That's 2 million people! . . .

Various caveats concerning salesmanship: 1) The chief target must be the 'potential demand stratum' – not existing practitioners such as students in a *min'yō* or folk dance class. The latter, unlike in the classical Japanese arts, do not buy directly from or under the influence of a teacher. [Actually, now they may.] Given the genre poem section, it's best to target the potential stratum within [local] schools, government offices and industry [as opposed to what – farmers & fishers?].

2) The target shouldn't be too rigidly narrow: given the 'live/field recording mania' among the young, one can imagine a pattern: 'genre poems for the son, folk songs for the father'. [This mania, driven by technology and a thirst for 'tradition', is manifested in the equipment-toting hordes who jostle with spectators and participants at traditional events.]

3) Points to remember when approaching a *min'yō* or folk dance class for sales: Many are tied to other record companies, so approach with caution.

In sum, it's best to focus mainly on beginners and amateurs.

BIBLIOGRAPHY

⊡

Useful bibliographies of works relating to Japanese folk song are: 1) Nakai et al. 1972: 363–92, which lists works from 1868 on, with brief descriptions of the most significant; 2) NMZ 5: 187–210, which lists books from the Edo period as well; and 3) NMMM 43–54, the most complete list for works from all periods up to mid-1983. Each important work is discussed in a separate entry in Asano 1983. Many items are given brief annotations in English in Isaku 1981.

When no author or editor is listed in the publication, a substitute designation has been devised (cf. NMZ above); this is used for citations in the text and occurs in the author slot in square brackets below.

Translations of Japanese titles are supplied in square brackets. For multi-volume works, e.g. Mikado 1977: 2.50 means page 50 of volume 2 of Mikado 1977.

There are now many useful websites for *min'yō*, though almost exclusively in Japanese. The Japanese version of Wikipedia has a good entry on *min'yō*, with sub-entries on many of the older musicians mentioned in this book and on the more famous songs, though some of the sub-entries do not yet exist. See:

http://ja.wikipedia.org/wiki/%E6%B0%91%E8%AC%A1

A few items below are not referred to in the main text but are included here for potential interest.

Adler, Jerry (1994) 'The new burb is a village'. *Newsweek International* 26 December 1959.

Adorno, Theodor W. (1976) *Introduction to the sociology of music*. New York: Seabury Press.

Anderson, Benedict (1983) *Imagined communities: reflections on the origin and spread of nationalism*. New York: Schocken.

Andō, Yoshinori & Sagara, Taeko (1969) 'Pitch intonation of koto-music'. In *Nomura Yoshio sensei kanreki kinen ronbunshū*, 25–39. Tokyo: Ongaku no Tomo Sha. [in English]

Anon. (1977) *Furusato no kokoro: min'yō to fūbutsushi* ['Guidebook for sales of The Heart of the Home Town: folk songs and genre poems']. CBS Sony Family Club.

Aoki, Keiichirō (1974) *Yonaoshi no uta [Millennial songs]*. Tokyo: Sanseidō.

Aoki, Michiko Y. & Dardess, Margaret B., ed. (1981) *As the Japanese see it: past and present*. Honolulu: University of Hawaii Press.

Appadurai, Arjun (1996) 'Disjuncture and difference in the global cultural economy'. In his *Modernity at large: cultural dimensions of globalization*, 27–42. Minneapolis: Univ. of Minnesota Press.

Arai, Tsuneyasu (1958) *Geinō shūdan [Performing groups]*. Tokyo: Heibonsha.

Asahi Shinbun Tsūshinbu (1980) *Uta no furusato: michinoku o tazunete [Homeland of song: a visit to the far north]*. Tokyo: Daiichi Hōki.

Asano, Kenji, ed. (1961) *Zoku Nihon kayō shūsei [Further collection of Japanese song]*, vols. 3–4. Tokyo: Tōkyōdō.

—— (1966) *Nihon no min'yō [Japanese folk song]*. Tokyo: Iwanami Shoten.

——, ed. (1983) *Nihon min'yō daijiten [Great dictionary of Japanese folk song]*. Tokyo: Yūzankaku.

Ashkenazi, Michael (1993) *Matsuri*. Univ. of Hawaii Press.

Aston, W.G., ed. (1972) *Nihongi: chronicles of Japan from the earliest times to A.D. 697*. Tokyo: Tuttle.

[Awaji] (1825) *Awaji nōka [Awaji farmers' songs]*.

Bailey, Jackson H. (1991) *Ordinary people, extraordinary lives: political and economic change in a Tohoku village*. Univ. of Hawaii Press.

Beardsley, Richard K. (1965) *Cultural anthropology: prehistoric and contemporary aspects*. New York: McGraw-Hill.

——, Hall, J.W., et al. (1959) *Village Japan*. Univ. of Chicago Press.

Bennett, John W. (1967) *Japanese economic growth: background for social change*. Princeton Univ. Press.

Berger, Donald P. (1969) *Folk songs of Japanese children*. Rutland, Vt./Tokyo: Tuttle.

—— (1972) *Folk songs of Japan*. New York: Oak Publications.

—— (1991) *Shoka and doyo: songs of an educational policy and a children's song movement of Japan, 1910–1926*. PhD thesis, Kent State Univ. UMI, 1995.

—— & Hughes, David W. (2001) 'Japan, II,5. Shakuhachi'. In Sadie & Tyrrell 2001: 12. 831–6. London: Macmillan.

Bernier, Bernard (1975) *Breaking the cosmic circle: religion in a Japanese village*. Ithaca: Cornell Univ. China-Japan Program.

Blacker, Carmen (1975) *The catalpa bow: a study of shamanistic practices in Japan*. London: George Allen and Unwin.

Blacking, John (1977) 'Some problems of theory and method in the study of musical change'. *Yearbook of the Intrntl. Folk Music Council* 9: 1–26.

Blankenhorn, Virginia (1987) 'The Connemara sean-nós since the gramophone'. *ICTM UK Chapter Bulletin* 18: 6–16.

Bock, Felicia G. (1948) 'Elements in the development of Japanese folk song'. *Western Folklore* 7.4: 356–69.

—— (1949) 'Songs of Japanese workers.' *Western Folklore* 8.1: 202–18.

Bohlman, Philip V. (1988) *The study of folk music in the modern world*. Bloomington: Indiana Univ. Press.

Bonneau, Georges (1933) *L'expression poétique dans le folklore japonais*. Paris: Musée Guimet.

Boyes, Georgina (1993) *The imagined village: culture, ideology and the English Folk Revival*. Manchester: Manchester Univ. Press.

Britton, Dorothy Guyver (1969) *20 folk songs of Japan.* Tokyo: Nihon Hoso Shuppan Kyokai.

Bronson, Bertrand (1969) *Mrs. Brown and the ballad.* Univ. of California Press.

Broughton, Simon & Ellingham, Mark, eds (2000) *Rough Guide to World Music: Vol. 1: Africa, Europe & The Middle East; vol 2: Latin and North America, the Caribbean, Asia & the Pacific.* London: Rough Guides.

Brown, Keith (1966) 'Dozoku and the ideology of descent in rural Japan'. *American Anthropology* 68: 1129–51.

Bunkachō=Cultural Affairs Bureau, ed. (1972) *Bunkazai tokuhon [Cultural properties reader].* Tokyo: Daiichi Hōki.

Burstow, Henry (1911) *Reminiscences of Horsham.* Horsham: Free Christian Church Book Society.

Clunies Ross, Margaret & Wild, Stephen A. (1984) 'Formal performance: the relations of music, text and dance in Arnhem Land clan songs'. *Ethnomusicology* 28.2: 209–35.

Collinson, Francis (1966) *Traditional and national music of Scotland.* London: Routledge and Kegan Paul.

Coplan, David (1978) *Go to my town, Cape Coast! The social history of Ghanaian Highlife.* Univ. of Illinois Press.

Cornell, John B. (1964) 'Dozoku: an example of evolution and transition in Japanese village society'. *Comparative Studies in Society and History* 6: 449–80.

—— & Smith, Robert J. (1956) *Two Japanese villages.* Univ. of Michigan Press.

Crawcour, E.S. (1963) 'Changes in Japanese commerce in the Tokugawa period'. *Journal of Asian Studies* 22.4:

Crihfield, Liza (1979) *Ko-uta: 'little songs' of the geisha world.* Tokyo/Rutland, Vt.: Tuttle.

Dalby, Liza (1983) *Geisha.* Univ. of California Press.

Davis, Winston (1976) 'Parish guilds and political culture in village Japan'. *Journal of Asian Studies* 36.1: 25–36.

Dazai, Osamu (1985/1944) *Return to Tsugaru.* Trans. J. Westerhoven. Tokyo: Kodansha.

Dazai, Shundai (1976) *Dokugo [Solitary words].*

de Ferranti, Hugh (1996) 'Music and text in biwa narrative: the zatō-biwa tradition of Kyūshū'. PhD thesis, Sydney Univ.

Denisoff, R. Serge (1971) *Great day coming: folk music and the American Left.* Univ. of Illinois Press.

—— ed. (1983) *Sing a song of social significance.* Bowling Green Univ. Popular Press.

Dizer, William H. (1951) 'The Hakata Niwaka: a study in Japanese folk drama'. *Univ. of Michigan Center for Japanese Studies Occasional Papers* 1: 74–101.

Dodd, Stephen (2005) *Writing home: representations of the native place in modern Japanese literature.* Harvard Univ. Press.

Dore, Ronald P. (1958) *City life in Japan: a study of a Tokyo ward.* Univ. of California Press.

—— (1959) *Land reform in Japan.* Oxford Univ. Press.

—— (1965) *Education in Tokugawa Japan.* London: Routledge & Kegan Paul.

——, ed. (1967) *Aspects of social change in modern Japan.* Princeton Univ. Press.

Dunn, Ginette (1980) *The fellowship of song: popular singing traditions in East Suffolk.* London: Croom Helm.

El-Shawan, Salwa (1984) 'Traditional Arab music ensembles in Egypt since 1967: "The continuity of tradition within a contemporary framework"?' *Ethnomusicology* 28.2: 271–88.

Elbourne, Roger (1975) 'The question of definition'. *Yearbook of the International Folk Music Council* 7: 9–29.

—— (1980) *Music and tradition in early industrial Lancashire 1780–1840.* Woodbridge, Suffolk: D.S. Brewer.

Embree, John F. (1939) *Suye Mura: a Japanese village.* Univ. of Chicago Press.

—— (1944) *Japanese peasant songs.* Philadelphia: American Folklore Society.

[EOJ] (1983) *Kodansha Encyclopedia of Japan.* Tokyo: Kōdansha.

Eppstein, Ury (1994) *The beginnings of Western music in Meiji era Japan.* Lampeter: Mellen.

Esashi Oiwake Kai='Esashi Oiwake' Association, ed. (1982) *Esashi Oiwake ['Esashi Oiwake'].* Esashi: Esashi Oiwake Kai.

Fargion, Janet Topp (1993) 'The role of women in *taarab* in Zanzibar: an historical examination of a process of "Africanisation"'. *The World of Music* 35.2: 109–25.

Feld, Steven (1990 [1982]) *Sound and sentiment*, 2nd ed. Univ. of Pennsylvania Press.

Filene, Benjamin (2000) *Romancing the folk: public memory & American roots music.* Univ. of North Carolina Press.

Foard, James H. (1982) 'The boundaries of compassion: Buddhism and national tradition in Japanese pilgrimage'. *Journal of Asian Studies* 41.2: 231–51.

Foreman, Kelly (in press) *The gei of geisha.* Aldershot, UK: Ashgate.

Frith, Simon (1981) ' "The magic that can set you free": the ideology of folk and the myth of the rock community'. *Popular Music* 1: 159–68.

Fritsch, Ingrid (1992) 'The social organization of *goze* in Japan: blind female musicians on the road'. *CHIME* 5: 58–64.

—— (1996) *Japans blinde Sänger im Schutz der Gottheit Myoon Benzaiten.* Munich: Iudicium.

Fujie, Linda (1986) *Matsuri-bayashi of Tokyo: the role of supporting organizations in traditional music.* PhD thesis, Columbia Univ. Ann Arbor: UMI.

—— (1992) 'East Asia/Japan'. In Jeff Todd Titon (ed.) *Worlds of music*, 318–75. New York: Schirmer. 2nd ed.

Fujii, Tomoaki, ed. (1985) *Nihon ongaku to geinō no genryū [The sources of Japanese music and performing arts].* Tokyo.

Fujimoto, Hideo (1962–) *Shamisen bunkafu Fujimoto Hideo min'yō senshū [Fujimoto Hideo's folk song selection in shamisen bunkafu notation].* Tokyo: Hōgakusha.

—— (1978) *Misuji hitosuji [One life devoted to three strings].* Tokyo: Nihon Min'yō Kayō Gakuin.

Fujine, Iwao (1979) *Min'yō o anata ni [Folk song for you].* Tokyo: Nihon Hōsō Shuppan Kyōkai.

Fujisawa, Morihiko (1932) *Nihon min'yō kenkyū [Research on Japanese folk song].* Tokyo: Rokubunkan.

Fujita, Tokutarō (1940) *Nihon min'yōron [Thesis on Japanese folk song].* Tokyo: Banrikaku.

Fukao, Toranosuke (1971) *Gōshū Ondo ['Goshu Ondo'].* Kyoto: Shirakawa Shoin.

Fukasawa, Margaret B. (1993) *Kitahara Hakushū: his life and poetry.* Ithaca: Cornell East Asia Series.

Fukazawa, Shichirō (1956) *Narayama Bushi kō [Thoughts on 'Song of Narayama']*. Tokyo: Shinchōsha.

Gammon, Vic (1984) ' "Not appreciated in Worthing?" Class expression and popular song texts in mid-nineteenth-century Britain'. *Popular Music* 4: 5–24.

Gamō, Masao (1981) *The traditional social structure of Japan and changes in it.* Tenterden, England: Paul Norbury.

Gamō, Mitsuko (1983) *Sōga no ongakuteki kenkyū [Musical research on sōga]*. Tokyo: Ongaku-no-tomo Sha.

Gamō, Satoaki (1986) 'Several aspects of enka singing style: comparison using melograph . . .' In Henshū-iinkai (ed.) 1986: 385–409.

Geinō Bunka Jōhō Senta [Performing Arts Culture Information Centre], ed. (1999) *Geinō hakusho 1999 ['Performing arts data book 1999']*. Tokyo: Geidankyō Shuppanbu.

Gerstle, C. Andrew (1989) 'Flowers of Edo: Kabuki and its patrons'. In C. Andrew Gerstle (ed.) *eighteenth century Japan*, 33–50. Sydney: Allen & Unwin.

Giddens, Anthony (1990) *The consequences of modernity.* Cambridge: Polity Press.

Gillan, Matthew (2004) *Multiple identities in Yaeyaman folk music.* PhD thesis, SOAS, Univ. of London.

Gluck, Carol (1985) *Japan's modern myths: ideology in the late Meiji period.* Princeton Univ. Press.

Greenway, John (1953) *American folksongs of protest.* Univ. of Pennsylvania Press.

Groemer, Gerald (1993) 'Tsugaru-jamisen ni okeru sokkyô ensôteki yôso no bunseki [An analysis of improvisational elements in Tsugaru-jamisen]'. *Tōyō Ongaku Kenkyū* 57: 41–61.

—— (1994a) 'Fifteen years of folk song collection in Japan: reports and recordings of the "Emergency Folk Song Survey" '. *Asian Folklore Studies* 53.2: 199–209.

—— (1994b) 'Singing the news: *yomiuri* in Japan during the Edo and Meiji periods'. *Harvard Journal of Asian Studies* 54.1: 233–61.

—— (1995) 'Edo's "Tin Pan Alley": authors and publishers of Japanese popular song during the Tokugawa period'. *Asian Music* 27.1: 1–36.

—— (1996) 'Dodoitsubô Senka and the *yose* of Edo'. *Monumenta Nipponica* 51.2: 171–87.

—— (1999) *The spirit of Tsugaru: blind musicians, Tsugaru-jamisen, and the folk music of northern Japan, with the autobiography of Takahashi Chikuzan.* Warren, Michigan: Harmonie Park Press.

—— (2001) 'Japanese folk music'. In Robert Provine et al. (eds) *Garland Encyclopedia of World Music: East Asia: China, Japan, and Korea*, 599–606. New York: Garland.

—— (2007) *Goze to goze-uta no kenkyū [Research on goze and their songs].* Nagoya: Nagoya Daigaku Shuppankai.

—— (2008) 'Popular music before the Meiji period'. In Tokita & Hughes 2008, chapter 11.

Hall, John W. (1970) *Japan: from prehistory to modern times.* New York: Dell.

—— & Jansen, Marius B., ed. (1968) *Studies in the institutional history of early modern Japan.* Princeton Univ. Press.

Hara, Tarō, ed. (1971) *Nihon no uta o motomete [In search of Japanese song].* Tokyo: Miraisha.

——, ed. (1976) *Nihon min'yō gasshō shū, 1 [Japanese folk song choral collection, vol. 1]*. Tokyo: Iizuka Shoten.

—— (1989) 'Folk tradition as ploof [*sic*] of human development'. *Warabi-za Today* 1: 8–9.

Harada, Tomohiko (1963) *Genroku bunka [Genroku era culture]*. Tokyo: Iwanami Shoten.

Hashimoto, Katsuhiko (1985) *Senro kōshū no uta ga kikoeta [I heard the songs of the railroad workers]*. Tokyo: JICC Shuppankyoku.

Hattori, Koh-ichi (1996) *36,000 days of Japanese music*. Southfield, Michigan: Pacific Vision.

Hattori, Ryūtarō, ed. (1966) *Traditional folk songs of Japan*. Tokyo: Ongaku-no-tomo Sha.

—— (1967) *Min'yō no furusato: Meiji no uta o tazunete [Homeland of folk song: visiting the songs of the Meiji era]*. Tokyo: Asahi Shinbunsha.

—— (1973) *Nihon min'yō no tabi [Japanese folk song travels]*. Tokyo: Kawade Shobō Shinsha.

——, ed. (1974) *Japanese folk songs with piano accompaniment*, 8th ed. Tokyo: Japan Times.

Hattori, Tomoji (1959) *Nihon no min'yō [Japanese folk song]*. Tokyo: San'ichi Shobō.

Hayakawa, Kōtarō, ed. (1924) *Nomi-gun min'yō shū [Collection of folk songs from Nomi county]*. Tokyo: Kyōdo Kenkyūsha.

Hearn, Lafcadio (1894) 'Three popular ballads'. *Transactions of the Asiatic Society of Japan* 22: 285–336. (Reprinted as Appendix (pp. 327–88) in L. Hearn, *Kokoro: hints and echoes of Japanese inner life* (Boston: Houghton Mifflin, 1896/repr. Tokyo: Tuttle, 1972.)

Henshū-iinkai, ed. (1986) *Shominzoku no oto [The sounds of various peoples]*. Tokyo: Ongaku-no-Tomo Sha.

Herd, Judith Ann (1984) 'Trends and taste in Japanese popular music: a case-study of the 1982 Yamaha World Popular Music Festival'. *Popular Music* 4: 75–96.

—— (2008) 'Western-influenced "classical" music in Japan'. In Tokita and Hughes 2008, chapter 16.

Hetherington, Kevin (1998) *Expressions of identity: space, performance, politics*. London: Sage.

Higuchi, Akira (1989) 'Kindai no min'yō no bunrui (Yanagita Kunio no bunruian made)' [Modern *min'yō* classification (prior to Yanagita Kunio's schema)]. In Kojima (ed.) 1989: 23–5.

—— et al. (1986) 'Kyōto no min'yō' [Folk songs of Kyoto]'. In Henshū-iinkai (ed.) 1986: 191–236.

Hijiya-Kirschnereit, Irmela (1981) *The concepts of tradition in modern Japanese literature*. Tenterden, England: Paul Norbury.

Hiramatsu, Morihiko & Ijiri, Kazuo (1991) 'Local culture on a global scale'. *Japan Echo* 18.1: 72–6.

Hirano, Kenji, Kamisangō, Yūkō, et al., ed. (1989) *Nihon ongaku daijiten [Encyclopedia of Japanese music]*. Tokyo: Heibonsha.

Hobsbawm, Eric J. (1983) *Introduction: Inventing traditions*. Cambridge Univ. Press.

—— & Ranger, Terence O., ed. (1983) *The invention of tradition*. Cambridge Univ. Press.

Hoff, Frank (1971) *The genial seed: a Japanese song cycle.* New York: Mushinsha-Grossman.

—— (1978) *Song, dance, storytelling: aspects of the performing arts in Japan.* Ithaca: China-Japan Program, Cornell Univ.

—— (1981) 'City and country: song and the performing arts in sixteenth-century Japan'. In George Elison & Bardwell L. Smith (eds) *Warlords, artists, and commoners: Japan in the sixteenth century,* 133–62, 313–9. Univ. Press of Hawaii.

Hōgaku Jānaru ['Monthly Music Magazine Hougaku Journal']. See www.hogaku.com for details.

Honda, Yasuji (1964) *Edo no kagura to matsuribayashi [Kagura and festival music of Edo].* Notes to LP of same name, Victor SJ3004.

—— (1974) 'Yamabushi kagura and bangaku: performance in the Japanese Middle Ages and contemporary folk performance'. *Educational Theatre Journal* 26.2: 192–208.

—— (1998 [1975]) *Nihon no minzoku ongaku [Japanese folkloric music].* Tokyo: Japan Victor. – Booklets with recordings R15.

Honjō, Hidetarō (2006) *Shamisen-gatari [Shamisen narrative].* With CD. Kyoto: Tankōsha.

Horiuchi, Keizō (1977) *Teihon Nihon no gunka [A manual of Japanese military songs].* Tokyo: Jitsugyō no Nihonsha.

Hoshino, Hiroshi (1981) 'Min'yō chōsa no hōkoku [Report on the folk song survey]'. *Gekkan Bunkazai* 216: 11–5.

—— & Yoshika, Hideo, eds (2006) *Nihon no matsuri bunka jiten [Dictionary of Japan's festival culture].* Tokyo: Tōkyō Shoseki.

Hosokawa, Shūhei (1999) 'Soy Sauce Music: Haruomi Hosono and Japanese self-Orientalism'. In Philip Hayward (ed.) *Widening the horizon: exoticism in post-war popular music,* 114–44 (ch. 5) + bibl. Sydney/London: John Libbey & Co.

—— (2000) 'Odoru nashonarizumu: "Tōkyō Ondo" no wa to yagura' [Dancing nationalism: the circle and tower of 'Tōkyō Ondo']. *Ex Musica,* 'pre-publication' issue: 6–19.

Howard, Keith (1999) 'Minyo in Korea: songs of the people and songs for the people'. *Asian Music* 30.2: 1–37.

—— (2001) '[Korea:] Contemporary genres'. In Provine et al. 2001: 951–74.

Hsu, Francis (1975) *Iemoto: the heart of Japan.* New York: Schenkman.

Hughes, David W. (1980) 'Sato-kagura: old Edo lives in modern Tokyo'. In *The Fifth Festival of Asian Arts,* 93–5. Hong Kong: The Urban Council.

—— (1981a) 'Japanese folk song preservation societies: their history and nature'. In *Proceedings of the 4th International Symposium on the Conservation and Restoration of Cultural Property,* 29–45. Tokyo: National Research Institute of Cultural Properties.

—— (1981b) 'Hauta, utazawa, kouta and zokkyoku'. In *1000 years of Japanese classical music,* 121–5. Tokyo: Kōdansha.

—— (1983a) 'Ryukyu music'. In *Kodansha Encyclopedia of Japan.* Tokyo: Kōdansha.

—— (1983b) Review of Donald Philippi, *Songs of gods, songs of humans. Ethnomusicology* 27.3: 562–4.

—— (1985) *The heart's home town: traditional folk song in modern Japan.* PhD thesis, Univ. of Michigan. Ann Arbor: UMI, 1986.

—— (1990) 'Japanese folk song today: visits to the heart's home town'. *Japan Foundation Newsletter* 7.3: 9–13.

—— (1991) 'Japanese "new folk songs", old and new'. *Asian Music* 22.1: 1–49.

—— (1992) ' "Esashi Oiwake" and the beginnings of modern Japanese folk song'. *The World of Music* 34.1: 35–56.

—— (1993) 'Japan'. In Helen Myers (ed.) *The New Grove handbooks in musicology: Ethnomusicology, vol. 2: Historical and regional studies*, 345–63. New York/London: Norton/Macmillan.

—— (1997) Review of K. Hattori 1996. *British Journal for Ethnomusicology* 6: 191–5.

—— (2001) ' "Sōran Bushi": the many lives of a Japanese folk song.' *CHIME* 14/15: 31–47.

—— (2008) 'Folk music: from local to national to global'. In Tokita & Hughes 2008, chapter 12.

[IFMC] (1955) 'Proceedings of the 7th Conference of the International Folk Music Council, Sao Paulo, 16–22 August 1954'. *Jnl. Intrntl. Folk Music Council* 7: 6–46.

Ichikawa, Nobutsugu (1969) 'Takada-goze no seikatsu to kayō [The life-style and songs of the goze of Takada]'. *Minzoku Geinō* 35: 25–32, 58.

Ikeda, Yasaburō & Miyao, Shigeo (1961) *Min'yō rekishi sanpo [A walk through folk song history]*. Tokyo: Kawade Shobō Shinsha.

Ikema, Hiroyuki (1981) *Folk dances of Japan*. Tokyo: National Recreation Association of Japan.

Imano, Ensuke (1958) *Shokugyō shūdan II [Occupational groups II]*. Tokyo: Heibonsha.

Isaku, Patia (1973) *An introduction to Japanese folk song*. PhD thesis, Wesleyan Univ. Ann Arbor: UMI.

—— (1981) *Mountain storm, pine breeze: folk song in Japan*. Univ. of Arizona Press.

Ishino, Iwao (1953) 'The oyabun-kobun: a Japanese ritual kinship institution'. *American Anthropologist* 55: 695–707.

[Iso] (1979) *Iso Bushi ['Iso Bushi']*. Ōarai, Ibaragi Pref.: Ibaragi-ken Min'yō Iso Bushi Hozonkai Honbu.

Itō, Naoki, ed. (1912) *Nihon Chikuonki monku zenshū [Compendium of lyrics from Nihon Chikuonki Co.]*. Tokyo: Nihon Chikuonki Monku Zenshū Hakkōsho.

Ivy, Marilyn (1995) *Discourses of the vanishing: modernity, phantasm, Japan*. Univ. of Chicago Press.

Iwate-ken Kyōiku Iinkai, ed. (1965) *Iwate-ken no min'yō [Folk songs of Iwate prefecture]*. Morioka: Iwate Bunkazai Aigo Kyōkai.

Jimukyoku, Itabashi-ku Kyōiku-iinkai (1971) *Itabashi no kyōdo geinō ta-asobi [Ta-asobi, local performing art of Itabashi]*. Tokyo: Itabashi Ward Board of Education.

Johnson, Erwin H. (1967) *Status change in hamlet structure accompanying modernization*. Princeton Univ. Press.

Johnson, Henry (2006) 'Tsugaru shamisen: from region to nation (and beyond) and back again'. *Asian Music* 37: 75–100.

Johnson, Irmgard (1982) 'The role of amateur participants in the arts of No in contemporary Japan'. *Asian Music* 13.2: 115–33.

Kakinoki, Gorō (1975) 'Music analysis of a traditional song: Meaning and function of "kobushi".' *Ongakugaku* 21.2: 78–88.

—— (1980) 'Nihon *min'yō* ni mirareru chiikiteki ongaku yōshiki [Regional musical styles in Japanese folk song]'. *Geinō no Kagaku* 11: 1–29.

—— (1982) 'Kariboshikiri Uta no hikaku bunseki [Comparative analysis of "Kariboshikiri Uta"]'. In Tōyō Ongaku Gakkai (ed.) *Nihon no onkai*, 97–121. Tokyo: Ongaku no Tomo Sha.

Kalland, Arne (1981) *Shingu: a study of a Japanese fishing community*. London: Curzon Press.

Kamishima, Jiro & Ito, Mikiharu, ed. (1973) *Shinpojiumu Yanagita Kunio*. Tokyo: Nihon Hōsō Shuppan Kyōkai.

Kanai, Kiyomitsu (1979) *Minzoku geinō to kayō no kenkyū [Research on folk performing arts and song]*. Tokyo: Tōkyō Bijutsu.

Karpeles, Maud (1973) *An introduction to English folk song*. Oxford Univ. Press.

Kartomi, Margaret (1981) 'The processes and results of musical culture contact'. *Ethnomusicology* 25.2:227–49.

Kata, Kōji (1975) *Uta no Shōwa-shi [History of song in the Shōwa era]*. Tokyo: Jiji Tsū-shinsha.

Katō, Bunzō (1980) *Min'yō saijiki: kurashi no bunkashi [Folk song calendar: cultural history of daily life]*. Tokyo: Aoki Shoten.

Kato, Hidetoshi, ed. (1959) *Japanese popular culture: studies in mass communication and cultural change*. Rutland, Vt./Tokyo: Tuttle.

Katō, Tōgiku (1962) *Yamagata min'yō [Folk songs of Yamagata]*. Yamagata: Nihon Min'yō Tōgiku Kai (private printing).

Katsumura, Jinko (1986) 'Some innovations in musical instruments of Japan during the 1920's'. *Yearbook for Traditional Music* 18: 157–72.

Kawabata, Shigeru (1991) 'The Japanese record industry'. *Popular Music* 10.3: 327–45.

Kawachi, Kaname (1979) *Hitotsu Hirosaki no Yone bāsan: mukashi-uta ga yomigaeru [Granny Yone of Hirosaki: the resurrection of songs past]*. Tokyo: Ongaku-no-tomo Sha.

Kawada, Minoru (1993) *The origin of ethnography in Japan: Yanagita Kunio and his times*. London: Kegan Paul International.

[KDJ] (1992) *Kokushi daijiten [Encyclopaedia of Japanese history]*. Tokyo: Yoshikawa Kōbunkan.

Keil, Charles (1984) 'Music mediated and live in Japan'. *Ethnomusicology* 28.1: 91–6. Repr. in Charles Keil & Stephen Feld (1994) *Music grooves* (Chicago Univ. Press).

Kikkawa, Eishi (1965) *Nihon ongaku no rekishi [History of Japanese music]*. Osaka: Sōgensha.

Kikuchi, Takuzō, ed. (1980) *Nihon Min'yō Kyōkai shi [History of the Japan Folk Song Association]*. Tokyo: Nihon Min'yō Kyōkai. (Revised most recently in 2000, ed. Kikuchi Tankyō.)

Kikuchi, Tankyō, ed. (2000) see Kikuchi, Takuzō (1980)

Kikuchi, Yuko (2004) *Japanese modernisation and mingei theory: cultural nationalism and oriental Orientalism*. London: RoutledgeCurzon.

Kimura, Shigetoshi (1981) 'Min'yō no kashi: sono denpa to teichaku [Folk song lyrics: their diffusion and acceptance]'. *Gekkan Bunkazai* 216: 28–32.

Kindaichi, Haruhiko (1967) *Kayō no senritsu to kashi no akusento [Song melody and textual accent]*. Tokyo: Tōkyōdō.

—— & Anzai, Aiko (1977) *Nihon no shōka (jō): Meiji hen [Japanese shōka songs, vol. 1: Meiji]*. Tokyo: Kōdansha.

Kirby, R.J. (1900) 'Dazai on Japanese music'. *Transactions of the Asiatic Society of Japan* 28: 46–58.

Kitahara, Hakushū (1927) *Nihon min'yō sakka shū [Japanese folk song writers' collection]*. Tokyo: Dainippon Yūbenkai.

—— (1941) *Hakushū shikashū [Hakushū poetry anthology]*. Tokyo: Kawade Shobō.

—— (1987) *Hakushū zenshū [Hakushū complete anthology]*. Tokyo: Iwanami Shoten.

Kitahara, Michio (1966) 'Kayokyoku: an example of syncretism involving scale and mode'. *Ethnomusicology* 10.3: 271–84.

Kitano, Seiichi (1959) *Oyakata-kokata [Oyakata-kokata]*. Tokyo: Heibonsha.

Kiuchi, Hiroshi (1979) *Kita no hatō ni utau: 'Esashi oiwake' monogatari [Singing to the northern waves: the story of 'Esashi Oiwake']*. Tokyo: Kōdansha.

Knight, John (1993) 'Rural kokusaika? Foreign motifs and village revival in Japan'. *Japan Forum* 5.2: 203–16.

Kobayashi, Hideo (1933) 'Furusato o ushinatta bungaku' [The literature which has lost its *furusato*]. *Bungei Shunjū*, May 1933.

Kodera, Yukichi (1935) *Nihon min'yō jiten [Dictionary of Japanese folk song]*. Tokyo: Mibu Shoin.

Koizumi, Fumio (1958) *Nihon dentō ongaku no kenkyū, 1 [Research in Japanese traditional music, 1]*. Tokyo: Ongaku-no-tomo Sha.

—— (1965) 'Towards a systematization of Japanese folk-song'. *Studia Musicologica* 7: 309–13.

—— (1968) *Nihongo no ongakusei: gengo to ongaku no sōgō kankei [The musicality of the Japanese language: the relationship between speech and music]*. Tokyo: Japan Victor.

——, ed. (1969) *Warabe-uta no kenkyū ['Game songs of Japanese children: report of a group-study on warabeuta of Tokyo in 1961']*. Tokyo: Warabe-uta no Kenkyū Kenkō.

—— (1973) *Nihon ongaku no onkai to senpō [Scale and mode in Japanese music]*. Tokyo: Ongaku-no-tomo Sha.

—— (1977) 'Musical scales in Japanese music'. In F. Koizumi et al. (eds) *Asian musics in an Asian perspective*, 73–9. Tokyo: Heibonsha.

—— (1984a) *Kayōkyoku no kōzō [The structure of popular song]*. Tokyo:

—— (1984b) *Nihon dentō ongaku no kenkyū, 2: rizumu [Research in Japanese traditional music, 2: rhythm]*. Tokyo: Ongaku-no-tomo Sha.

Koizumi, Fumio & Hughes, David W. (2001) 'Japan, VII. Folk music'. In Sadie & Tyrrell 2001: 12. 871–6. London: Macmillan.

Koizumi, Fumio; Tokumaru, Yoshihiko, et al., ed. (1977) *Asian musics in an Asian perspective*. Tokyo: Heibonsha.

Kojima, Tomiko (1967) 'Dokusha e no tebiki [Readers' guide]'. In Tōyō Ongaku Gakkai (ed.) *Nihon no min'yō to minzoku geinō* [Japanese folk song and folk performing arts], 11–24. Tokyo: Tōyō Ongaku Gakkai.

—— (1970) 'Shin-min'yō undō no ongakushiteki igi [The music-historical significance of the *shin-min'yō* movement]'. *Engekigaku* 11: 1–29.

—— (1983) 'Nihon no fūdo to ongaku: hi-inasaku kōminteki yōso o megutte, sono ni [Japanese climate and music: on elements of non-rice-growing agricultural people, part 2]'. *Jinrui no kagaku* 36: 167–98.

——, ed. (1989) *Min'yō no bunruihō to sono dētabēsu-ka ni kansuru sōgōteki kenkyū [Collective research on the classification and data-basing of min'yō]*. Sakura: Kokuritsu Rekishi Minzoku Hakubutsukan.

—— (1991) 'Gendai shakai to min'yō' [Modern society and *min'yō*]. In T. Fujii (ed.) *Gendai to ongaku [Modern times and music].* Tokyo: Tōkyō Shoseki.

—— (1992) 'Tsugaru min'yō no denshō – Tairadate-mura o chūshin ni ['Transmission of folk songs in Tsugaru District, Aomori Prefecture – centering around folk songs of Tairadate Village']'. *Bull. National Museum of Japanese History* 43: 63–78.

Komiya, Toyotaka, ed. (1956) *Japanese music and drama in the Meiji era.* Tokyo: Ōbunsha.

Kornhauser, David (1976) *Urban Japan: its foundations and growth.* London: Longman.

Kosaka, Masaaki, ed. (1958) *Japanese thought in the Meiji era.* Tokyo: Pan-Pacific Press.

Koschmann, J. Victor; Oiwa, Keibō, et al., ed. (1985) *International perspectives on Yanagita Kunio and Japanese folklore studies.* Ithaca: Cornell East Asia Series.

Koshiba, Harumi (1977) *Atobe no odori-nembutsu.* Tokyo: Heibonsha.

Kubo, Ken'o (1960) *Minami-nihon min'yō kyokushū [Anthology of folk song melodies from southern Japan].* Tokyo: Ongaku-no-tomo Sha.

Kumakura, Isao (1981) 'The iemoto system in Japanese society'. *Japan Foundation Newsletter* 9.4: 1–7.

Kurabayashi, Yoshimasa & Matsuda, Yoshiro (1988) *Economic and social aspects of the performing arts in Japan: symphony orchestras and opera.* Tokyo: Kinokuniya.

Kuramitsu, Toshio (1976) *Tsugaru-jamisen [The shamisen music of Tsugaru].* Tokyo: Rippu Shobō.

Kurata, Yoshihiro (1979) *Nihon rekōdo bunkashi [Cultural history of Japanese records].* Tokyo: Tokyo Shoseki.

Lancashire, Terence (1998) 'Music for the gods: musical transmission and change in Iwami *kagura*'. *Asian Music* 29.1: 87–123.

Lee, Edward (1982) *Folksong and music hall.* London: Routledge & Kegan Paul.

Lloyd, A.L. (1944) *The singing Englishman.* London: Workers' Music Association.

—— (1967) *Folk song in England.* London: Lawrence & Wishart.

Lord, Albert (1960) *The singer of tales.* Harvard Univ. Press.

Mabuchi, Usaburō (1971) 'Denshō senritsu no nendai kettei ni tsuite [Concerning the determination of the date of traditionally transmitted melodies]'. *Osaka Kyō-iku Daigaku Kiyō* 20.1: 129–38.

Machida, Kashō (1933) *Nihon shin-min'yō kyokushū [Tune collection of Japanese new folk songs].* Tokyo: Shunjusha.

—— (1956) 'The use of traditional music in music education'. In Komiya Toyotaka (ed.) *Japanese music and drama in the Meiji era,* 365–70. Tokyo: Ōbunsha.

—— (1964) *Nihon rōsaku min'yō shūsei [Collection of Japanese work songs].* Tokyo: Japan Victor. – Booklet with recording R1.

—— (1971) *Min'yō [Folk song].* Tokyo: Shōgakkan.

—— (1976) *Nihon no min'yō [Japanese folk song].* Tokyo: Shōgakkan.

—— & Asano, Kenji (1960) *Nihon min'yō shū [Collection of Japanese folk song].* Tokyo: Iwanami Shoten.

—— & Asano, Kenji (1968) *Warabe-uta: Nihon no denshō dōyō [Warabe-uta: traditional children's songs of Japan].* Tokyo: Iwanami Shoten.

Mackinnon, Niall (1994) *The British folk scene: musical performance and social identity.* Buckingham, UK: Open University Press.

Makino, Eizō (1964) 'Daimokutate no senritsu kōzō ni tsuite ['The melodical construction of Daimokutate']'. *Nara Gakugei University Bulletin (Humanities and Social Sciences)* 12: 56–69.

Makita, Shigeru (1973) 'World authority on folklore: Yanagita Kunio'. *Japan Quarterly* 20: 283–93.

Maliangkay, Roald (1999) *Handling the intangible: the protection of folksong traditions in Korea.* PhD thesis, SOAS, Univ. of London.

Malm, William P. (1971) 'The modern music of Meiji Japan'. In Donald Shively (ed.) *Tradition and modernization in Japanese culture.* Princeton Univ. Press.

—— (1975) 'Shoden: a study in Tokyo festival music'. *Yearbook of the Intrntl. Folk Music Council* 7: 44–66.

—— (1984) 'A century of proletarian music in Japan'. *Transactions of the Asiatic Society of Japan, 3rd series* 19: 173–96.

—— (2000) *Japanese traditional music and musical instruments.* With CD. Tokyo: Kodansha.

—— & Hughes, David W. (2001a) 'Japan, II,6. Shamisen'. In Sadie & Tyrrell 2001: 12. 836–9. London: Macmillan.

—— & Hughes, David W. (2001b) 'Japan, III. Notation systems'. In Sadie & Tyrrell 2001: 12. 842–50. London: Macmillan.

Manuel, Peter (1988) *Popular musics of the non-Western world.* Oxford Univ. Press.

—— (1989a) 'Andalusian, gypsy, and class identity in the contemporary flamenco complex'. *Ethnomusicology* 33.1: 47–65.

—— (1989b) 'Modal harmony in Andalusian, Eastern European, and Turkish syncretic musics.' *Yearbook for Traditional Music* 21: 70–94.

Maring, Joel M. & Maring, Lillian (1997) 'Japanese erotic folksong: from shunka to karaoke'. *Asian Music* 28.2: 27–49.

Maruyama, Shinobu (1981) 'Min'yō no genba kara no shōgen [On-the-spot witness to folk song]'. *Gekkan Bunkazai* 216: 22–7.

Masui, Keiji (1980) *Dētā, ongaku, Nippon [Data, music, Japan].* Tokyo: Min'on Ongaku Shiryōkan.

Matsuhara, Iwao (1927) *Minyo: folk-songs of Japan.* Tokyo: Shinseidō.

Matsukawa, Jirō (1934) *Zenkoku kyōdo min'yō shū [Countrywide collection of local folk songs].* Osaka: Kōjinsha.

Matsumoto, Shinhachirō (1965) *Min'yō no rekishi [The history of folk song].* Tokyo: Sekkasha.

May, Elizabeth (1963) *The influence of the Meiji period on Japanese children's music.* Univ. of California Press.

[MB] (1978–) *Gekkan: Min'yō Bunka [Monthly: Folk Song/Dance Culture].* Cited by year and month.

McCann, David R. (1979) *Arirang: the national folksong of Korea.* Honolulu: Center for Korean Studies, Univ. of Hawaii.

Middleton, Richard (1981) 'Editor's introduction to Volume 1'. *Popular Music* 1: 3–7.

—— & Horn, David (1981) 'Preface'. *Popular Music* 1: 1–2.

Migita, C.I. (Isao) (1970) *The first folk song book of Nippon.* Tokyo: Kawai Gakufu.

Mikado, Tenpū (1977) *Nihon min'yō zenshū [Complete collection of Japanese folk songs].* Tokyo: Shinfonii Gakkiten.

Miki, Nyōhō (1939) *Hokkaidō riyō Seichō Oiwake Bushi [Hokkaido folk song 'Authentic Oiwake Bushi'].* Sapporo: Kinmondō Shoten.

Minami, Hiroshi (1959) *A content analysis of post-war Japanese popular songs.* Rutland, Vt./Tokyo: Tuttle.

Misumi, Haruo (1976) *Min'yō to geinō [Folk song and the performing arts].* Tokyo: Heibonsha.

Mitamura, Engyō (1926) *Kawaraban no hayariuta [Popular song broadsides].* Tokyo: Shun'yōdō.

Mitsui, Toru (1983) 'Japan in Japan: notes on an aspect of the popular music record industry in Japan'. *Popular Music* 3: 107–20.

—— (1984) 'Chronological list of popular music books published in Japan from January 1981 to September 1983'. *Popular Music* 4: 366–76.

Miyao, Shigeo (1976) *Min'yō to odori no saijiki [Calendar of folk song and dance].* Tokyo: Heibonsha.

Miyata, Teru (1974) *Furusato no kokoro [The heart of the home town].* Tokyo: Noberu Shobō.

Miyazaki, Takashi (1999a) *Miyata Ureho shiryō: Shōwa shoki no kakeuta shūshū nōto [Miyata Ureho's materials: notes on an early Shōwa kakeuta collection].* Self-published.

Miyazaki, Takashi (1999b) 'Kanazawa Hachimangū dentō kakeuta' [Kanazawa Hachiman Shrine traditional *kakeuta*]. Unpublished programme notes.

Miyazaki, Takashi (1999c) 'Dai-47-kai Zenken Kakeuta Taikai' [47th Prefecture-wide *Kakeuta* Contest]. Unpublished programme notes.

Moeran, Brian D. (1981) *Tradition, the past and the ever-changing present in a pottery village.* Tenterden, England: Paul Norbury.

Mori, Masato (1999) 'Tatta hitori ga shikaketa matsuri – Sapporo "Yosakoi Sōran Matsuri" ' ['Yosakoi-Soran Festival originated from the idea of a university student']. *Toshi Mondai* 90.8 (special issue, *Toshi no matsuri ['Festival and urban community']*), pp. 39–51. (Journal of Tokyo Institute for Municipal Research)

Mori, Tatsuya & Spector, Dave (2000) *Hōsō kinshika [Songs forbidden for broadcast].* Osaka: Kaihō Shuppansha.

Morigaki, Jirō (1960) *Rekōdo to gojūnen [Fifty years with records].* Tokyo: Kawade Shobō.

Moriya, Takeshi (1984) *The history of Japanese civilization through aesthetic pursuits.* Senri, Japan: National Museum of Ethnology.

Morris-Suzuki, Tessa (1995) 'The invention and re-invention of "Japanese culture"'. *Journal of Asian Studies* 54.3: 759–80.

Motegi, Kiyoko (1999) *Sake o tsukuru uta no hanashi [Tales of sake-making songs].* Keijō Village, Niigata Pref.

Murao, Tadahiro & Wilkins, Bernadette (2001) 'Japan'. In David J. Hargreaves & Adrian C. North (eds) *Musical development and learning: the international perspective.* London: Continuum.

Nagai, Michio & Bennett, John W. (1953) 'Summary and analysis of T. Kawashima's Familial Structure of Japanese Society'. *Southwestern Journal of Anthropology* 9: 239–50.

Nagatsuka, Takashi (1989 [1912]) *The soil.* Trans. Ann Waswo. Univ. of California Press.

Nagira, Ken'ichi (1995) *Nihon fōku shiteki taizen [Personal compendium of Japanese 'folk'].* Tokyo: Chikuma Shobō.

Nakai, Kōjirō, Maruyama, Shinobu, et al. (1972) *Nihon min'yō jiten [Dictionary of Japanese folk song]*. Tokyo: Tōkyōdō.

——, Nishitsunoi, Masahiro, et al. (1981) *Minzoku geinō jiten [Dictionary of folk performing arts]*. Tokyo: Tōkyōdō.

Nakamura, Tōyō (1991) 'Early pop song writers and their backgrounds'. *Popular Music* 10.3: 263–82.

Nakane, Chie (1967) *Kinship and economic organization in rural Japan*. London: Athlone Press.

Nakano, Mitsutoshi (1989) 'The role of traditional aesthetics'. In C. Andrew Gerstle (ed.) *eighteenth century Japan: culture and society*, 124–31. Sydney: Allen & Unwin.

Narita, Mamoru (1978) *Bon-odori kudoki [Bon-dance ballads]*. Tokyo: Ōfūsha.

[Natsu] (n.d.) *Natsumero 500-kyoku [500 nostalgic melodies]*. Tokyo: Tōkyō Gakufu.

Nettl, Bruno, ed. (1978a) *Eight urban musical cultures: tradition and change*. Univ. of Illinois Press.

—— (1978b) 'Persian classical music in Tehran: the processes of change'. In Bruno Nettl (ed.) *Eight urban musical cultures: tradition and change*, 146–185. Univ. of Illinois Press.

—— (1983) *The study of ethnomusicology: twenty-nine issues and concepts*. Univ. of Illinois Press.

—— (1985) *The Western impact on world music: change, adaptation, and survival*. New York: Schirmer.

Neuman, Daniel M. (1978) *Gharanas: the rise of musical 'houses' in Delhi and neighboring cities*. Univ. of Illinois Press.

[NFDR] (1977) *Shidō no tebiki [Guidance for teachers]*. Tokyo: Nihon Fōku Dansu Renmei [National Folk Dance Federation of Japan].

NHK=Japan Broadcasting Co. (1979) *Seichō min'yō: furusato no uta [Authentic folk songs: songs from back home]*. Tokyo: NHK Service Center.

NHK Hōsō Yoron Chōsasho (1980) *NHK yoron chōsa shiryōshū: shiryō to bunseki (55-nenban) [NHK public opinion survey report: data and analysis (1980)]*. Tokyo: NHK Service Center.

Nihon Fōkuroa Kyōkai=Japan Folklore Society (1977) *1978 Nihon min'yō tokuhon [1978 Japan folk song/dance reader]*. Tokyo: Ōfūsha.

Nihon Min'yō Kyōkai (2000) *Schedule 2001*. Tokyo: Nihon Min'yō Kyōkai.

Niijima, Shigeru (1968) *Soba no uta [Buckwheat songs]*. Tokyo: Tōkyō Bijutsu.

Nishikawa, Rinnosuke (1934) *Min'yō no tsukurikata [How to make folk songs]*. Tokyo: Seikōkan Shoten.

Nishio, Jirōhei & Yazawa, Tamotsu (1985) *Nihon no kakumeika [Japanese revolutionary songs]*, rev. ed. (Orig. 1974.) Tokyo: Isseisha.

Nishitsunoi, Masahiro (1976) *Minzoku geinō [Folk performing arts]*. Tokyo: Shōgakkan.

Nishiyama, Matsunosuke (1959) *Iemoto no kenkyū [Research on iemoto]*. Tokyo: Azekura Shobō.

—— (1964) *Edo bunka to chihō bunka [Edo culture and regional culture]*. Tokyo: Iwanami Shoten.

—— (1971) *Iemoto monogatari [Tales of iemoto]*. Tokyo: Shūei Shuppan.

—— (1997) *Edo culture: daily life and diversions in urban Japan, 1600–1868*. Transl. Gerald Groemer. Univ. of Hawai'i Press.

[NKD] (1972ff) *Nihon kokugo daijiten [Great dictionary of the Japanese language]*. Tokyo: Shōgakukan.

[NMGJ] (1976) *Nihon minzoku geinō jiten [Dictionary of Japanese folk performing arts]*. Tokyo: Daiichi Hōki.

[NMMM] (1983) *Nihon min'yō min'yō meikan [Directory of Japanese folk song and dance]*. Tokyo: Nihon Denshō Geinō Bunka Shinkōkai.

[NMT] NHK=Japan Broadcasting Co., ed. (1944–88) *Nihon min'yō taikan [Conspectus of Japanese folk song]*. Tokyo: Nihon Hōsō Shuppan Kyōkai. – 9 vols.; re-issued 1992–4, with 90 CDs.

[NMZGT] (1958) *Nihon minzokugaku taikei [Overview of Japanese folklore]*. Tokyo: Heibonsha.

[NMZ] (1975) *Nihon min'yō zenshū [Compendium of Japanese folk song]*. Tokyo: Heibonsha.

[NOD] (1989) Hirano, Kenji et al. (eds) *Nihon ongaku daijiten [Encyclopaedia of Japanese music]*. Tokyo: Heibonsha.

Norbeck, Edward (1953) 'Age-grading in Japan'. *American Anthropologist* 55: 373–84.

—— (1954) *Takashima: a Japanese fishing community*. Univ. of Utah Press.

—— (1978) *Country to city: the urbanization of a Japanese hamlet*. Salt Lake City: Univ. of Utah Press.

[NRK] (1981) *Shōwa 55-nen rekōdo seisan no zenbō [Overview of record production in 1980]*. Tokyo: Nihon Rekōdo Kyōkai.

[Ochiai] (1980) *Ochiai chōshi: minzoku hen [Ochiai town history: folkways volume]*. Ochiai, Okayama Pref.: Ochiai-chō.

[ODJ] (1982) *Ongaku daijiten ['Encyclopaedia musica']*. Tokyo: Heibonsha.

Ogawa, Hisao (1979) *Amami min'yō shi [Amami folk song]*. Tokyo: Hōsei Univ. Press.

—— (1984) *Min'yō no shima no seikatsushi [Life on the 'island of folk song']*. Kyoto: PHP Kenkyūjo.

Ogawa, Masafumi (1994) 'Japanese traditional music and school music education'. *Philosophy of Music Education Review* 2.1: 25–36.

Ōhashi, Shunnō (1974) *Odori-nenbutsu [Dancing nenbutsu]*. Tokyo: Daizō Shuppan.

Okada, Maki (1991) 'Musical characteristics of enka'. *Popular Music* 10.3: 283–303.

Okinawa Bijutsu Zenshū Kankō Iinkai, ed. (1989) *Arts of Okinawa*. Naha, Japan: Okinawa Times.

[Okuni] (1976) *Okuni meguri Nihon min'yō zenshū [Touring the country: Japanese folk song compendium]*. Tokyo: Shinkō Gakufu.

O'Neill, P.G., ed. (1981) *Tradition and modern Japan*. Tenterden, England: Paul Norbury.

Ongaku Sentā, ed. (1971) *Utagoe kashū [Utagoe song collection]*. Tokyo: Ongaku Sentā.

Ongaku Zasshi=Music Magazine (1891) Unsigned article on p.9 of 25 September issue.

Ono, Hideo (1960) *Kawaraban monogatari [The story of the broadsides]*. Tokyo: Yūzankaku.

Ōnuki, Toshiko (1989) 'Kindai izen no min'yō bunrui' [Pre-modern classifications of *min'yō*]. In Kojima (ed.) 1989: 17–22.

Ortolani, Benito (1969) 'Iemoto'. *Japan Quarterly* 1969: 297–307.

Osabe, Hideo (1974) *Tsugaru Yosare Bushi ['Tsugaru Yosare Bushi']*. Tokyo: Kadokawa Shoten.

Osada, Kyōji (1976a) *Meiji Taishō Shōwa ryūkōka 140-kyoku shū [Collection of 140 Meiji, Taishō and Shōwa period popular songs].* Tokyo: Zen'on Gakufu.

—— (1976b) *Shōwa hayariuta hiwa [Secret tales of Shōwa-period popular songs].* Tokyo: Doremi Gakufu.

Ōtsuki, Miyoshi (1983) *Yagi Bushi kō [Thoughts on 'Yagi Bushi'].* Ōta, Gumma Pref.: Gendai Shobō.

Ōyama, Mahito (1977) *Watashi wa goze: Sugimoto Kikue kōden [I am a goze: the oral reminiscences of Sugimoto Kikue].* Tokyo: Ongaku-no-tomo Sha.

Ozawa, Chigetsu (1978) *Min'yō o hajimeru hito no tame ni [For those starting to learn folk song].* Tokyo: Ikeda Shoten.

Ozawa, Shōichi (1999 [1971]) *Dokyumento: Nihon no hōrōgei [Itinerant arts of Japan].* Tokyo: Japan Victor. – Booklets for recording R14.

Pecore, Joanna T. (2000) 'Bridging contexts, transforming music: the case of elementary school teacher Chihara Yoshio'. *Ethnomusicology* 44.1: 120–36.

Pegg, Carole (1984) 'Factors affecting the musical choices of audiences in East Suffolk, England'. *Popular Music* 4: 51–73.

Peluse, Michael S. (2005) 'Not your grandfather's music: Tsugaru shamisen blurs the lines between "folk," "traditional", and "pop"'. *Asian Music* 36: 57–80.

Pennanen, Risto Pekka (1997) 'The development of chordal harmony in Greek rebetika and laika music, 1930s to 1960s'. *British Journal of Ethnomusicology* 6: 65–116.

Philippi, Donald L., ed. (1969) *Kojiki.* Princeton Univ. Press.

Picken, Laurence (1968) Review of U. Reinhard, *Vor seinen Hausern eine Weide . . . Jnl. Interntl. Folk Music Council* 20: 75–7.

Plath, David (1964) *The after hours.* Univ. of California Press.

Polak, A.J. (1905) *Die Harmonisierung indischer, türkischer und japanischer Melodien [Harmonisation of Indian, Turkish and Japanese melodies].* Leipzig: Breitkopf & Härtel.

Potter, John (2003) *The power of Okinawa: roots music from the Ryukyus.* Kobe, Japan: S.U. Press.

Provine, Robert C. et al., eds (2001) *Garland encyclopedia of world music, vol. 7: East Asia.* New York: Garland.

Rausch, Anthony (2006) 'The *Heisei Dai Gappei*: a case study for understanding the municipal mergers of the Heisei era'. *Japan Forum* 18.1: 133–56.

Read, Cathleen & Locke, David (1983) 'An analysis of the Yamada-ryu sokyoku iemoto system'. *Hogaku* 1.1: 20–52.

Reader, Ian (1987) 'From asceticism to the package tour: the pilgrim's progress in Japan'. *Religion* 17.2: 133–48.

—— (1991) *Religion in contemporary Japan.* University of Hawaii Press (1990, Macmillan).

—— (1993) *Japanese religions: past and present.* London: Curzon Press.

—— & Walter, Tony, eds (1993) *Pilgrimage in popular culture.* Basingstoke: Macmillan.

Redfield, Robert & Singer, Milton (1954) 'The cultural role of cities'. *Economic Development and Cultural Change* 3.1: 53–73.

Rice, Timothy (1994) *May it fill your soul: experiencing Bulgarian music.* Univ. of Chicago Press.

Riddle, Ronald (1978) *Music clubs and ensembles in San Francisco's Chinese community*. Univ. of Illinois Press.

—— (1983) *Flying dragons, flowing streams: music in the life of San Francisco's Chinese*. Westport, CT: Greenwood Press.

Robertson, Jennifer (1988) 'Furusato Japan: the culture and politics of nostalgia'. *International Journal of Politics, Culture and Society* 1.4: 494–578.

—— (1991) *Native and newcomer: making and remaking a Japanese city*. Univ. of California Press.

—— (1998) 'It takes a village: internationalization and nostalgia in postwar Japan'. In Vlastos 1998: 110–29.

Rodnitzky, Jerome L. (1976) *Minstrels of the dawn: the folk-protest singer as a cultural hero*. Chicago: Nelson-Hall.

Rohlen, Thomas P. (1974) *For harmony and strength: Japanese white-collar organization in anthropological perspective*. Univ. of California Press.

Sadie, Stanley, ed. (1984) *New Grove dictionary of musical instruments*. New York/London: Macmillan.

—— & Tyrrell, John, eds (2001) *New Grove dictionary of music and musicians*, 2nd ed. New York/London: Macmillan.

Saitō, Shinji (1975) *Echigo goze nikki [Diary of an Echigo goze]*. Tokyo: Kawade Shobō Shinsha.

Sanbe, Masaichirō (1974) *Nihon dōyō zenshū [Complete collection of Japanese children's songs]*. Tokyo: Ongaku-no-tomo Sha.

[Sanga] (1772) *Sanga chōchūka [Mountain home, bird and insect songs]*.

Sasamori, Takefusa (1981) 'The preservation and development of the performing art of Tsugaru'. In *Proceedings of the 4th International Symposium on the Conservation and Restoration of Cultural Property*. Tokyo: National Research Institute of Cultural Properties.

Sasano, Ken, ed. (1956) *Kinsei kayōshū [Song collection of the Early Modern era]*. Tokyo: Asahi Shinbunsha.

Satō, Kunihiro, ed. (1987) *Etchūya Shisaburō-ō ryakuden [Brief biography of Etchūya Shisaburō]*. Sapporo: (private).

Satō, Sōnosuke (1946) *Min'yō no kenkyū [Folk song research]*. Tokyo: Bunka Shobō.

Schafer, R. Murray (1968) *The new soundscape*. Toronto: Berandol.

Schimmelpenninck, Antoinet (1997) *Chinese folk songs and folk singers: Shan'ge traditions in southern Jiangsu*. Leiden: CHIME Foundation.

Seeger, Charles (1966) *The folkness of the non-folk and the nonfolkness of the folk*. Hatboro, PA: Folklore Associates.

Seigle, Cecilia Segawa (1993) *Yoshiwara: the glittering world of the Japanese courtesan*. Univ. of Hawaii Press.

Seki, Akiko, ed. (1965) *Seinen kashū daikyūhen [Youth song collection, vol. 9]*. Tokyo: Ongaku Sentā.

Seshaiah, Sreenivasaiah (1980) *Land reform and social change in a Japanese village*. Bangalore: Shiny Publications.

Sharp, Cecil (1954 [1907]) *English folk song: some conclusions*, 3rd ed., revised by Maud Karpeles. London: Methuen.

Shibata, Minao (1978) *Ongaku no gaikotsu no hanashi [The skeletal structure of music]*. Tokyo: Ongaku no Tomo Sha.

Shibusawa, Keizo, ed. (1958) *Japanese society in the Meiji era*. Tokyo: Ōbunsha.

Shijō, M. (1988) ' "Kochae-bushi" and ballads'. *Minzoku Ongaku* 3.1/2: 10–20.

Shimazaki, Minoru (1953) 'Geinō shakai to iemoto seidō [The performing arts world and the iemoto system]'. *Shakaigaku Hyōron* 3: 131–56, 4: 101–34.

Shively, Donald H. (1955) 'Bakufu versus Kabuki'. *Harvard Journal of Asiatic Studies* 18: 326–56.

—— (1971) 'The Japanization of the middle Meiji'. In Donald Shively (ed.) *Tradition and modernization in Japanese culture*. Princeton Univ. Press.

Signell, Karl (1976) 'The modernization process in two oriental music cultures: Turkish and Japanese'. *Asian Music* 7.2: 72–102.

Slobin, Mark (1993) *Subcultural sounds: micromusics of the West*. Wesleyan Univ. Press.

Smith, Patrick (1994) 'Inner Japan'. *National Geographic* Sept 1994: 65–95.

Smith, Robert J. (1976) 'A Japanese community and its anthropologist'. *Journal of Japanese Studies* 2.2: 209–23.

Smith, Thomas C. (1952) 'The Japanese village in the seventeenth century'. *Journal of Economic History* 12.1: 1–20.

—— (1959) *The agrarian origins of modern Japan*. Stanford Univ. Press.

—— (1977) *Nakahara: family farming and population in a Japanese village, 1717–1830*. Stanford Univ. Press.

Soeda, Tomomichi (1966) *Nihon shunka kō [Thoughts on Japanese erotic songs]*. Tokyo: Kōbunsha.

—— (1967) *Enkashi no seikatsu [Life style of the enka singers]*. Tokyo: Yūzankaku.

Song, Bang-song (1980a) *Source readings in Korean music*. Seoul: Korean National Commission for UNESCO.

—— (1980b) *Music*. Univ. Press of Hawaii.

Sonobe, Saburō (1962) *Nihon minshū kayō-shi kō [Thoughts on the history of Japanese popular song]*. Tokyo: Asahi Shinbunsha.

Sonoda, Minoru (1975) 'The traditional festival in urban society'. *Japanese Journal of Religious Studies* 2.2/3: 103–35.

Sorensen, André & Funck, Carolin, eds (2007) *Living cities in Japan: citizens' movements, machizukuri and local environments*. London: Routledge.

Steven, Rob (1983) *Classes in contemporary Japan*. Cambridge Univ. Press.

Stigberg, David K. (1978) 'Jarocho, Tropical, and "pop": aspects of musical life in Veracruz, 1971–72'. In Nettl 1978a: 260–95.

Stokes, Martin, ed. (1994) *Ethnicity, identity and music: the musical construction of place*. Oxford: Berg.

Suda, Naoyuki; Daijō, Kazuo; & Rausch, Anthony (1998) *The birth of Tsugaru shamisen music: the origin and development of a Japanese folk performing art*. Aomori: Aomori Univ. Press.

Sugae, Masumi (1967) *Sugae Masumi yūranki, 4 [Chronicle of the excursions of Sugae Masumi, vol. 4]*. Tokyo: Heibonsha.

Suppan, Wolfgang (1976) 'Research on folk music in Austria since 1800'. *Yearbook of the Intrntl. Folk Music Council* 8: 117–29.

Takahashi, Chikuzan (1975) *Jiden Tsugaru-jamisen hitori-tabi. [Autobiography: lonely travels with Tsugaru-jamisen]*. Tokyo: Shinshokan. (Transl. and annotated in Groemer 1999.)

Takahashi, Hideo (1989) 'Min'yō Kinkyū Chōsa to min'yō bunrui' [The Emergency Folk Song Survey and *min'yō* classification]. In Kojima (ed.) 1989: 26–30.

Takahashi, Kikutarō (1960) *Nihon min'yō no tabi, jōkan [Japanese folk song travels, vol. 1]*. Tokyo: Daini Shobō.

Takami, Tomiko (1981) 'Methods of learning folk music and their influence on the music itself: the case of "Etchu Owara Bushi"'. In *Proceedings of the 4th International Symposium on the Conservation and Restoration of Cultural Property*. Tokyo: National Research Institute of Cultural Properties.

Takano, Tatsuyuki (1928) *Nihon kayō shūsei [Collection of Japanese song]*. Tokyo: Shunjūsha.

Takeda, Akimichi & Okudo, Sanae (1971) 'Senritsu-kōzō no tōkeiteki bunseki: rokushū no Kariboshi-kiri Uta o taishō to shite' [Statistical analysis of melodic structure, based on six versions of 'Kariboshi-kiri Uta']. *Musashino Ongaku Daigaku Kenkyū Kiyō* 5: 29–50.

Takeuchi, Tsutomu (1969) *Uta no furusato: Nihon no min'yō o tazunete [Homeland of song: in quest of Japanese folk song]*. Tokyo: Ongaku-no-tomo Sha.

—— (1973a) *Nihon no min'yō [Japanese folk song]*. Tokyo: Nihon Hōsō Shuppan Kyōkai.

—— (1973b) *Shinpo Kodaiji: min'yō no koseki shirabe [Shinpo Kodaiji: a folk song genealogy]*. Tokyo: Kinseisha.

—— (1974) *Min'yō ni ikiru: Machida Kashō hachijūhachi-nen no ashiato [Living for folk song: Machida Kashō, 88 years of activity]*. Tokyo: Horupu Rekōdo.

—— (1976) *Min'yō no ruten to kōryū [The migration of folk songs]*. Tokyo: Heibonsha.

—— (1978) *Min'yō no furusato o iku: watashi no saishū techō [Going to the homeland of folk song: my collecting notebook]*. Tokyo: Ongaku-no-tomo Sha.

—— (1980) *Oiwake Bushi: Shinano kara Esashi made ['Oiwake Bushi': from Shinano to Esashi]*. Tokyo: Sanseidō.

—— (1981) *Min'yō: sono hassei to hensen [Folk song: its development and transformation]*. Tokyo: Kadokawa Shoten.

—— (1982) *Min'yō no kokoro [The heart of folk song]*. Tokyo: Tōken Shuppan. [Re-issued 1993.]

—— (1983a) *Min'yō no kokoro 2 [The heart of folk song, vol. 2]*. Tokyo: Tōken Shuppan.

—— (1983b) *Min'yō no kokoro 3: min'yō okeiko techō [The heart of folk song, vol. 3: Notes on min'yō lessons]*. Tokyo: Tōken Shuppan.

—— (1983c) *Zoku min'yō no furusato o iku: watashi no saishū techō (zoku) [Going to the homeland of folk song: my collecting notebook (continued)]*. Tokyo: Ongaku-no-tomo Sha.

—— (1984) *Min'yō no kokoro 4 [The heart of folk song, vol. 4]*. Tokyo: Tōken Shuppan.

—— (1985) *Min'yō no kokoro 5: min'yō no konkūru techō [The heart of folk song, vol. 5: Notes on min'yō contests]*. Tokyo: Tōken Shuppan. [Re-issued 1996 under the subtitle alone.]

—— (1986) *Min'yō no kokoro 6 [The heart of folk song, vol. 6x]*. Tokyo: Tōken Shuppan.

—— (1989) *Min'yō techō [Folk song notebook]*. Tokyo: Shinshindō.

—— (1992) *Min'yō no kokoro 7: min'yō no koe-zukuri techō [The heart of folk song, vol. 7: Notes on the min'yō voice]*. Tokyo: Tōken Shuppan.

—— (1995) *Min'yō no kokoro 8: min'yō no kobushi techō [The heart of folk song, vol. 8: Notes on min'yō ornamentation]*. Tokyo: Tōken Shuppan.

—— (2002a) *Jongara to Echigo goze ['Jongara' and the Echigo goze]*. Tokyo: Hon'ami Shoten.

—— (2002b) *Haiya, Okesa to sengokubune ['Haiya', 'Okesa' and the freight ships]*. Tokyo: Hon'ami Shoten.

—— (2003) *Oiwake to shukuba/minato no onnatachi ['Oiwake' and the women of the highway towns and harbours]*. Tokyo: Hon'ami Shoten.

—— (2004a) *Tōkyō no nōmin to ikada-shi [Tokyo's farmers and raftsmen]*. Tokyo: Hon'ami Shoten.

—— (2004b) *Tōkyō no ryōshi to sendo [Tokyo's fishers and boatsmen]*. Tokyo: Hon'ami Shoten.

—— (2006) *Taue-uta to nihonjin [Rice-planting songs and the Japanese]*. Tokyo: Hon'ami Shoten.

Tanaka, Eiichi (1969) *Furusato no taue-uta [Rice-planting songs of the home village]*. Matsue: Imai Shoten.

Tanigawa, Ken'ichi (1979) 'Ancient Japanese folk beliefs about death'. *Center News* (Japan Foundation, Tokyo), July 1979: 2–6.

Tansman, Alan M. (1996) 'Mournful tears and *sake*: the postwar myth of Misora Hibari'. In John W. Treat (ed.) *Contemporary Japan and popular culture*, 103–33. Richmond, UK: Curzon.

Tateyama, Zennoshin (1910) *Heike ongaku-shi [History of Heike music]*. Tokyo: Tōkyō Insatsu.

Teruoka, Yasutaka (1989) 'The pleasure quarters and Tokugawa culture'. In C. Andrew Gerstle (ed.) *Eighteenth century Japan*, 3–32. Sydney: Allen & Unwin.

Teruya, Rinsuke (1998) *Terurin jiden [Autobiography of Terurin]*. Tokyo: Misuzu Shobō.

Thompson, Robin (2001) 'Japan, VIII,1. The Ryukyus'. In Sadie & Tyrrell 2001: 12.877–82. London: Macmillan.

—— (2008) 'The music of Ryukyu'. In Tokita & Hughes 2008, chapter 13.

Thornbury, Barbara E. (1997) *The folk performing arts: traditional culture in contemporary Japan*. Albany: State University of New York Press.

Tokita, Alison M. (1996) 'Mode and scale, modulation and tuning in Japanese shamisen music: the case of *kiyomoto* narrative'. *Ethnomusicology* 40.1: 1–34.

—— & Hughes, David W. (2008) *Ashgate research companion to Japanese music*. With CD. Aldershot, UK: Ashgate.

Tokyo Academy of Music (1888) *Collection of Japanese koto music*. Tokyo: Department of Education.

Tōyō Ongaku Gakkai, ed. (1967) *Nihon no min'yō to minzoku geinō [Japanese folk song and folk performing arts]*. Tokyo: Ongaku-no-tomo Sha.

Trevor-Roper, Hugh (1983) *The invention of tradition: the Highland tradition of Scotland*. Cambridge Univ. Press.

Tsuge, Gen'ichi (1986) *Japanese music: an annotated bibliography*. New York: Heinrichshofen.

Tsukitani, Tsuneko (2008) 'The *shakuhachi* and its music'. In Tokita & Hughes 2008, chapter 7.

Tuohy, Sue (1988) *Imagining the Chinese tradition: the case of hua'er songs, festivals, and scholarship*. PhD dissertation, Indiana Univ. Ann Arbor: UMI, 1990.

—— (1999) 'The social life of genre: the dynamics of folksong in China'. *Asian Music* 30.2: 39–86.

Uchida, Ruriko (1978) *Taue-bayashi no kenkyū [Research on rice-planting music]*. Tokyo: Ongaku-no-tomo Sha.

—— (1983) *Amami min'yō to sono shūhen [Amami folk songs and their surroundings]*. Tokyo: Yūzankaku.

Uehara, Rokushirō (1895) *Zokugaku senritsu kō [Thoughts on Japanese popular melodies]*. Tokyo: Iwanami Bunko.

Uyehara, Yukuo (1949) *Songs for children sung in Japan*. Tokyo: Hokuseido.

Varner, Richard E. (1977) 'The organized peasant: the wakamonogumi in the Edo period'. *Monumenta Nipponica* 32.4: 459–83.

Vlastos, Stephen, ed. (1998) *Mirror of modernity: invented traditions of modern Japan*. Univ. of California Press.

Wade, Bonnie C. (2005) *Music in Japan: experiencing music, expressing culture*. With CD. Oxford Univ. Press.

Wakamori, Tarō (1958) *Shinkō shūdan [Religious groups]*. Tokyo: Heibonsha.

Ware, Naomi (1978) *Popular music and African identity in Freetown, Sierra Leone*. Univ. of Illinois Press.

Waswo, Ann (1977) *Japanese landlords: the decline of a rural elite*. Univ. of California Press.

Waterhouse, David (1975) 'Hogaku preserved (II)'. *Recorded Sound* 57/58: 408–26.

Watson, Ian (1983) *Song and democratic culture in Britain: an approach to popular culture in social movements*. Beckenham, Kent: Croom Helm.

Wigen, Kären (1998) 'Constructing Shinano: the invention of a neo-traditional region'. In Vlastos (ed.) 1998: 229–42.

Wilgus, D.K. (1959) *Anglo-American folksong scholarship since 1898*. Rutgers Univ. Press.

Williams, Henry B. (1974) 'Shinto-sponsored theatre, the farmers' Kabuki'. *Educational Theatre Journal* 26.2: 175–82.

Williams, Raymond (1983) *Keywords: a vocabulary of culture and society*. London: Fontana Paperbacks.

Wiora, Walter (1949) 'Concerning the conception of authentic folk music'. *Jnl. Intrntl. Folk Music Council* 1: 14–9.

—— (1972) 'How old is the concept "folk song"?' *Yearbook of the International Folk Music Council* 3.

Yamada, Norio (1962) *Nanbu ushioi uta [The 'Nanbu Cowherding Song']*.

Yamamoto, Kichizō (1988) *Kutsuwa no oto ga zazameite: katari no bungei kō [The horse's bridle jingles: thoughts on the textual art of narrative]*. Tokyo: Heibonsha.

Yamamoto, Yoshiki, ed. (1970) *Nihon no min'yō [Japanese folk songs]*. Tokyo: Kin'ensha.

Yanagita, Kunio (1940) *Min'yō oboegaki [Notes on folk song]*. Tokyo: Sōgensha.

—— (1954a) *Studies in fishing village life*. Lexington: Kentucky Microcards.

—— (1954b) *Studies in mountain village life*. Lexington: Kentucky Microcards.

—— (1957) *Japanese manners and customs in the Meiji era*. Tokyo: Ōbunsha.

Yano, Christine (1994) 'Longing for *furusato*: the shaping of nostalgia in Japanese popular *enka* songs'. In *Proceedings of the 5th Annual PhD Kenkyukai Conference on Japanese Studies*. Tokyo: International House of Japan.

—— (2002) *Tears of longing: nostalgia and the nation in Japanese popular song*. Harvard University Asia Center.

—— & Hosokawa, Shūhei (2008) 'Popular music in modern'. In Tokita & Hughes 2008, chapter 15.

Yasugi Bushi Hozonkai (1979) *Yasugi Bushi ['Yasugi Bushi']*. Yasugi: Yasugi Bushi Hozonkai Office (City Hall).

Yokota, Setsudō (1920) *Oiwake Bushi monogatari [The tale of 'Oiwake Bushi']*. Tokyo: Yasufuku Tsūshinsha.

Yoshida, Teigo (1964) 'Social conflict and cohesion in a Japanese rural community'. *Ethnology* 3.3: 219–31.

Yuasa, Chikusanjin (1926) *Kouta kenkyū [Kouta research]*. Tokyo: Arusu.

AUDIO-VIDEOGRAPHY

□

The following is a selective list of useful or representative recordings relating to Japanese folk song, including CDs, VHS video tapes, long-playing phonodiscs and commercial cassette tapes. Not all of the items listed are actually referred to in the text. Most of the LPs have been discontinued, including the valuable anthologies R1, R20, R21 and R22, but some may be re-issued as CDs, and others are available second-hand via the internet.

R1: *Nihon rōsaku min'yō shūsei* [Collection of Japanese work songs]. 6 LPs, Japan Victor JV158–163. Various artists. 1964.

R2: *Nihon no min'yō* [Japanese folk songs]. 10 LPs, Nippon Columbia AL4118–4127. Various artists.

R3: *Min'yō genryū-kō: Esashi Oiwake to Sado Okesa* [Thoughts on folk song genealogies: 'Esashi Oiwake' and 'Sado Okesa']. 4 LPs, Nippon Columbia AL5047–5050. 1965.

R4: *Seichō min'yō: Furusato no uta* [Authentic folk songs: Songs from back home]. NHK Service Center JK 3161–3172 (12 records). Various artists. 1979.

R5: *Nihon jūdan zenkoku min'yō daizenshū* [Collection of folk songs from the length and breadth of Japan]. 2 LPs, Polydor MN9039–9040. Various artists. No date.

R6: *Aizō ketteiban: Nihon min'yō daizenshū* [Treasured definitive recordings: Compendium of Japanese folk songs]. 20 LPs, Nippon Columbia FB7031–7050. Various artists. 1980.

R7: *Hizō SP-ban fukkoku: Nihon no min'yō* [Re-recording of treasured 78s: Folk songs of Japan]. 4 LPs, Nippon Columbia FX7021–7024. Various artists. 1984.

R8: *Echigo no goze-uta* [*Goze* songs of Echigo]. 3 LPs, CBS/Sony SODZ1-3. Two groups of *goze* from Niigata. 1973.

R9: *Echigo goze no uta* [Songs of the Echigo *goze*]. 4 LPs, Nippon Columbia FZ7011–7014. One group of *goze* from Niigata. 1975.

R10: *Esashi Oiwake osarai kyōshitsu* ['Esashi Oiwake' classroom]. Cassette, Akita City: Fujio Kikaku (no number). Sasaki Motoharu. ?1979.

R11: *Esashi Oiwake: omoide no meijinshū* ['Esashi Oiwake': memorable performances by great artists]. Cassette tape accompanying the book Esashi 1982. Various artists.

R12: *Esashi Oiwake meienshū (Eien no SP meiban shiriizu 9)* [Collection of great performances of 'Esashi Oiwake' (Immortal Famous 78-rpm Recordings Series, No. 9)]. LP, Japan Victor SJX1309. Various artists. 1984.

R13: *Esashi Oiwake kyōenshu: rekidai yūshōsha kenzen shūroku 1–20dai* ['Esashi Oiwake' competition collection: complete record of successive winners 1–20]. 2 cassettes, Pony 35P8129, 1–2. Various artists. 1983.

R14: *Dokyumento: Nihon no hōrōgei* [Document: Itinerant arts of Japan]. 7 CDs, Victor VICG60231–7. Various artists. 1999. [Orig. 7 LPs, SJX2051–7, 1971.]

R15: *Fukkoku: Nihon no minzoku ongaku* [Re-issue: Japanese folkloric music]. 36 CDs, Victor VZCG-8006–41. Various artists. 1998. [Orig. 39 LPs, SJL2166–2204 (*Nihon no minzoku ongaku*), 1975–6.]

R16: *Columbia World Library: Japan, the Ryukyus and Formosa*. LP, Columbia. Various artists.

R17: *Folk music of Japan*. CD, Smithsonian Folkways F4429. Various artists. 19??. (Orig. LP, Folkways FE4429, 1952)

R18: *Traditional folk songs of Japan*. 2 CDs, Smithsonian Folkways F4534. Various artists. 19??. (Orig. 2 LPs, Folkways FE4543, 1961)

R19: *Traditional folk dances of Japan*. CD, Smithsonian Folkways F4356. Various artists. 19??. (Orig. LP, *Traditional dances of Japan*, Folkways FE4356, 1959)

R20: *Nihon koten ongaku taikei* ['1000 years of Japanese classical music']. 74 LPs from various labels, published by Kodansha. A few *min'yō* in vol. 8. 1980–81.

R21: *Hōgaku taikei* [Japanese classical music compendium]. 26 LPs, Chikuma Shobō. *Min'yō* and *minzoku geino* in vol. 12.

R22: *Tōkyō no koyō* [Old songs of Tokyo]. LP set, Nippon Columbia. Various artists. 1964.

R23: *Orijināru-ban ni yoru Meiji Taishō Shōwa Nihon ryūkōka no ayumi* [Japanese popular songs of the Meiji, Taisho and Showa periods, reproduced from the original recordings]. 10 LPs, Columbia ADM1001–1010. Various artists. 1970.

R24: *Gottan [Gottan (wooden shamisen)]*. LP, CBS/Sony 25AG247. Aratake Tami. 1978.

R25: *Tanaka Yoshio ohako min'yō-shū* [Tanaka Yoshio's best folk song collection]. LP, Nippon Columbia FW7265. 1976.

R26: *Min'yō & min'yō: Tanaka Yoshio/David Hughes* [Folk song folk song: Tanaka Yoshio/David Hughes]. LP, Nippon Columbia FZ7128. 1980.

R27: *Tanaka Yoshio: min'yō no miryoku (nishi no uta o utau)* [Tanaka Yoshio: the charm of folk song (singing songs from western Japan)]. Cassette, Nippon Columbia CAY9053. 1983.

R28: *Wakai min'yō: Kanazawa Akiko Tsugaru o utau* [Young folk song: Kanazawa Akiko sings Tsugaru]. LP, Japan Victor SJV6098. 1977.

R29: *Harada Naoyuki risaitaru* [Harada Naoyuki recital]. Double LP, Polydor 33MF8203–4. Harada and others. 1980.

R30: *Tsugaru-jamisen meijinshū* [Collection of great Tsugaru shamisen players]. LP, King SKM111. 1972.

R31: *Japanese work songs*. CD, King KICH 2023. 1991. Notes (but not lyrics) in English.

R32: *Japanese dance music*. CD, King KICH 2022. 1991. Notes (but not lyrics) in English.

R33: *Music of Japanese festivals*. CD, King KICH 2028. 1991. Notes (but not lyrics) in English.

R34: *Jam session of Tsugaru-shamisen*. CD, King KICH 2024. 1991. Notes (but not lyrics) in English.

R35: *Yomigaeru 'Oppekepe'* ['Oppekepe' revived]. CD, EMI TOCG-5432. 1997. (Orig. 1900.)

R36: *Esashi Oiwake no utaikata* [How to sing 'Esashi Oiwake']. Cassette, Esashi: Ōseikai. Aosaka Mitsuru. No date.

R37: *Min'yō: folk song from Japan: Takahashi Yūjirō and friends*. CD, Nimbus NI 5618. 1999.

R38: *Ōita-ken no min'yō: furusato no shigoto-uta* [Ōita Prefecture folk songs: work songs of the *furusato*]. 2 VHS videos, 41-page lyrics booklet; Ōita Prefecture Board of Education. 1997.

R39: *Takio Jinc* (Itō Takio). CD, CBS/Sony 32DH 544. 1987.

R40: *Takio* (The Takio Band). CD, CBS/Sony 32DH 5123. 1988. Deleted but re-issued in 2001 under title *Takio: Sōran Bushi*.

R41: *Ondo* (Itō Takio & Takio Band). CD, Vap VPCC-80501. 1997.

R42: *omni Sight Seeing* (Hosono Haruomi). CD, Epic/Sony 28.8P–5258. 1989.

R43: *Paraiso* (Harry Hosono and the Yellow Magic Band). CD, Alfa ALCA-9068. 1978.

R44: *Neo Geo* (Sakamoto Ryūichi). CD, Epic 46994. 1991.

R45: *Beauty* (Sakamoto Ryūichi). CD, Virgin 86132 CD. 1990.

R46: *Happy* (Kawachiya Kikusuimaru). CD, Rackyo Records PCCY-00261. 1991.

R47: The Boom: 'Shimauta' [Island song], CD single, Sony SRDL3590 (1992); also on 1992 CD albums *Shishunki* [Diary of thinking of spring/youth] (SRCL2280) and *The Boom* (SRCL2471).

R48: *Music of Okinawa*. CD, King KICH 2025. 1991.

R49: *Music of Yaeyama and Miyako*. CD, King KICH 2026. 1991.

R50: *Yomigaeru Okinawa no utagoe* [Nostalgic singing voices of Okinawa]. 4 CDs, Columbia COCF-10551 to –4. 1993. – Condensed re-issue of LP set *Okinawa ongaku sōran*.

R51: *Shoukichi Kina and Champloose: the music power from Okinawa*. CD, Ace Records CDORBD 072. 1991.

R52: *The Rough Guide to the music of Japan*. CD, World Music Network RGNET 1031 CD. 1999.

R53: *Talvin Singh OK*. CD, Island/Omni CID 8075/524 559–2. 1998.

R54: *Ashibi* (Nēnēs). CD, Ki/oon Sony KSC2 48. 1993.

R55: *Soul Flower Union: Ghost Hits 93–96*. CD, Ki/oon Sony KSC2 155. 1996.

R56: *Asyl Ching-dong: Soul Flower Mononoke Summit*. CD, Soul Flower SF-032. 1995.

R57: *Nakayama Shinpei no min'yō* [Folk songs of Nakayama Shinpei]. 2 LPs, Victor. 1967.

R58: *Tōkyō Ondo, Tenryū Kudareba: Nakayama Shinpei no shin-min'yō*. CD, Victor VZCG-124. 1997.

R59: *Echigo sakezukuri-uta no sekai*. CD, Columbia COCF-15050. 1998.

R60: *Dai-8-kai Yosakoi Sōran* [8th Yosakoi Sōran]. CD, Crown CRCN-45592. 1999.

R61: *Zenshū Nihon fukikomi kotohajime* ['1903 First Japanese Recordings by Frederick Gaisberg']. 11 CDs, Toshiba-EMI TOCF 59061 to –71. 2001.

R62: *Kaze no bon: Etchū Owara Bushi no subete* [Kaze no Bon: All about 'Etchū Owara Bushi']. CD, Victor VZCG-122. 1997.

R63: *Genchi rokuon ni yoru Shiiba no min'yō* [Field recordings: Folk songs of Shiiba]. CD, Victor VZCG-8064–5. 1999.

R64: *Gujō no uta* [Songs of Gujō]. CD, Victor VZCG-8062–3. 1999.

R65: *Aihachi: Nagasaki Burabura Bushi.* CD, Victor VICG-60403. 2000.

R66: *Wax-cylinder recordings of Japanese music (1901–1913).* CD, Staatliche Museen zu Berlin BphA-WA1. 2003.

R67: *Nihon no kamisuki uta* [Japanese paper-making songs]. 4 CDs, Camerata CDT 1012 to –15. 1992.

R68: *Oku no yorimichi* [Road to the north]. CD, JVC VZCG-315. 2003.

R69: *Honjoh [Honjō] Hidetarō: Yumeura/Dream Divining.* CD, Tachibana Music TACD 0002. 2000.

R70: *O-kuni jiman da! Pīnattsu* [Pride of the provinces: Peanuts]. CD, King KICX 7007. 1998. [Orig.å LP, 1970.]

R71: *SP-ban sairoku ni yoru hana no sutā arubamu* [Star album of re-issued single recordings], vol. 3. CD, King KICX 3120. 2001.

R72: *Terauchi Takeshi & Blue Jeans: Tsugaru Jongara.* CD, King KICS-8151. 2006.

R73: *Gokuraku: Minzoku Gakudan Chanchiki* [Paradise: Folk music group Chanchiki]. CD, Ripple RIPP-8. 2004.

R74: *Okabayashi Nobuyasu: Kazeuta.* CD, Crown CRCN-20202. 1998.

R75: *Ketteiban bon-odori shū* [Definitive edition: Bon dance collection]. CD, Columbia COCF-14300. 1997.

R76: *Agatsuma Hiromitsu: Agatsuma.* CD, Toshiba TOCT-24615. 2001.

GLOSSARY OF SELECTED TERMS

◼

Brief definitions are given for a selection of Japanese words that occur within the text. Many of these only occur once and thus are unlikely to need looking up, but they are included here so that a read-through of the Glossary might evoke a sense of the vocabulary of the *min'yō* world. Many also occur in the General Index under appropriate headings. Sino-Japanese characters are included in a few cases to prevent ambiguity.

aji: 'flavour', an essential but undefinable element in good *min'yō* performance

ameuri: sweets vendors

angura: 'underground' folk group

anko-iri: 'filled with sweet bean-paste'; a type of sweet bread

atouta: 'aftersong'

bareuta: 'bawdy songs'

bin-zasara: a set of concussion plaques used for percussion

biwa: pear-shaped lute usually used to accompany sung ballads

bon-odori: dances of the Bon festival

bosama: 'priest', but also a common traditional term for a blind male musician

bunka: 'culture'

bunka-fu: 3-line staff teaching notation for shamisen

bunmei: 'civilization'

Bunraku: traditional puppet theatre

buraku: hamlet

bushi: common suffix in folk song titles; derived from *fushi* 'melody'

buyō-kayō: dances to accompany *enka*; also called *kayō-buyō*

chihō-riyō: a 1930s designation for folk song

chō: 'town'; also pronounced *machi*

chōnin: 'townspeople', often implying especially merchants

daikoku-mai: dance of the god Daikoku, performed door-to-door at New Year's

danmono: (among other meanings) long ballads in the repertoire of the *goze*

denshō: (oral) transmission, tradition

dentō: tradition

dodoitsu: a traditional popular song genre which has given its name to the 7-7-7-5 poetic metre

dōrakumono: pleasure-bent carouser

dōyō: 'children's songs', generally composed rather than traditionally evolved and transmitted

Edo sato-kagura: a Tokyo-area shrine masque

enka: popular song genre closely linked with *min'yō*; also called *nihon-chō kayōkyoku*; in Meiji and Taishō periods, a kind of protest song

fōku dansu: international folk dance

fōku no kamisama: 'God of folk' as applied to Okabayashi Nobuyasu

fōku shingā: folk singer'

fōku songu: modern, composed songs in the American tradition of popular folk songs

fue: 'flute'

fūga: 'aesthetic, elegance, refinement'; pronounced *feng'ya* in Chinese

fukyū: 'dissemination'

furusato: native place, home town or community

fuzoku(-uta): court song genre of the Heian period

ga: elegant, refined

gagaku: Japanese court music

geijutsu kayō: 'art song' in the Western sense

geimei: 'artist's name', stage name

geinin: performing artists

gei o nusumu: 'steal the art', a learning philosophy of informal transmission

genchi rokuon: field (as opposed to studio) recording

gendai: 'modern'

gendaika: modernization

gidayū: music of the Bunraku puppet theatre

goeika: Buddhist hymns

gotōchi songu: 'local praise songs'

goze: blind itinerant women musicians

haiku: a poem genre

hakkutsu min'yō: 'excavated folk songs'

haru-tauchi: agricultural ritual performance; also called *ta-asobi*

hauta: short parlour songs with shamisen

hayariuta: popular songs

hayaru: to become popular

hayashi/-bayashi: instrumental accompaniment

hayashi(-kotoba): 'words of encouragement'; a responsorial refrain in leader-chorus folk songs; also called *utabayashi*.

hikyoku: 'secret pieces' taught only to successors

hiradaiko: 'flat drum'; a shallow tacked-head stick-drum

hiwai: 'bawdy'

hōgakki: traditional Japanese instruments

hōgaku: traditional Japanese classical music, but nowadays also applied to pop genres recorded in Japan by Japanese performers

hozon: preservation

hozonkai: 'preservation society'

ie: household

iemoto: head of an artistic 'school' under the 'headmaster/houshead' system

iemoto seido: 'headmaster/houshead system', a pyramidal familistic structure for artistic transmission

iki: 'elegance'

in: (pronounced *yin* in Chinese, as in *yin-yang*) hemitonic pentatonic scale; also called the *miyako-bushi* scale

inaka-bushi: anhemitonic pentatonic scale; also called *min'yō* or *yō* scale

iwai-uta: celebratory or congratulatory songs

jimoto yūshi: 'local volunteers', a common term to designate unnamed performers in a field recording

jun-hōgaku: 'pure/true Japanese music': traditional Japanese music

Kabuki: traditional townspeople's theatre

kagura: Shinto music and dances

kai 会: group, association, society

kakegoe: time-keeping or ornamental calls in folk song

kakuon: 'nuclear tones' according to Koizumi's modal analysis of Japanese music

kane: a hand-gong, also called *surigane* or *atarigane*

kayō-buyō: dances to accompany *enka*; also called *buyō-kayō*

kayōkyoku: commercial popular songs

kenkyū: research

kenkyūkai: research society

kiyari: specialist songs of firemen/construction workers (*tobi*)

kobushi: general term for vocal ornamentation in folk song

kojiki: beggar

kōkeisha: successor

kokiriko: thin bamboo concussion sticks

kokumin kayō: 'citizen's songs'

kokyū: three-stringed spike-fiddle

komusō: mendicant shakuhachi-playing priests

konkūru: competition, concours

koto: 13-string Japanese zither

kotodama: 'word soul'

kōtō denshō: aural/oral transmission

kotsuzumi: a hand-drum of the Noh and Kabuki theatres

kouta: short parlour songs with shamisen

kudoki(-bushi):   long ballads

kyōdo: local

kyōdo geinō: local performing arts

kyōdo min'yō: 'local' folk song in Machida's typology

kyōiku iinkai: a Board of Education

kyōkai: 'association'

kyoku-biki: virtuoso solo in Tsugaru-jamisen

machi: 'town'; also pronounced *chō*

matsuri: festival

min: 'people'; also pronounced *tami*

minbu: 'traditional folk dance'

mingei: 'folk crafts'

min'yō 民謡: 'folk song', specifically of rural origin in Japan

min'yō 民踊: 'choreographed folk dance'

min'yō-buyō 民謡舞踊: 'folk song dances'

min'yō-kai 民謡界: folk song world

min'yō kashu: folk singer

min'yō (onkai):   anhemitonic pentatonic scale; also called *inaka-bushi* or *yō* scale

min'yō sakaba: folk song bar

min'yō taikai: 'folk song meet'; a *min'yō* event sometimes with less of a competitive element than a *konkūru* or *nodojiman*

minken undō: Democratic Rights Movement of Meiji period

minshushugi: 'democracy'

minzoku geinō 民俗芸能: folk performing arts

minzokugaku 民俗学: folklore

minzokugaku 民族学: ethnology

miyako-bushi: hemitonic pentatonic scale; also called the *in* scale

miyaza: Shinto shrine guild

mukashi: ancient; old times

mura: 'village'; also pronounced *son*

nagauta: song type associated with the Kabuki theatre

naniwa-bushi: narrative shamisen genre

narimono: drum and percussion accompaniment

natori: 'name-taker', a student who is awarded the right to adopt a professional name related to that of his/her teacher

natsumero: 'nostalgic melodies', referring particularly to early *enka*; abbreviated from *natsukashii merodii*

nenjū gyōji: calendrical observances

Nihon: Japan

nihon buyō: Japanese classical dance

nihon-chō: 'Japanese-style', particularly with reference to music

nihon-chō kayōkyoku: Japanese-style popular songs, relating to *enka*

Nihon Kyōdo Min'yō Kyōkai: the second largest *min'yō* organization in Japan; abbreviated as Kyōmin

Nihon Min'yō Kyōkai: Japan Folk Song Association, the largest such organization in Japan; abbreviated as Nichimin *nō* (Noh): music-dance-drama developed within the feudal court tradition

nodojiman: singing competition

nōhonshugi: doctrine of agricultural economic centrality

nyū myūjikku: 'New Music'; a 1975 outgrowth of *fōku songu* without social protest

o-bon: Buddhist ancestral festival

odori: dance

odoriuta: 'dance songs'

ondo: common suffix in song titles, especially dance songs

ondo-tori: lead singer in a group singing context

onkai: '(musical) scale'

ōtsuzumi: hand-drum of the Noh and Kabuki theatres

ozashiki-uta: 'parlour songs', often sung by geisha

poppusu: 'pops'

popyurā: 'popular [music]'

rejā būmu: 'leisure boom'

ri: village; also pronounced *sato*

risōgaku 俚奏楽: 'village/rural performance music', a new genre of Honjō Hidetarō's making

ritsu: an anhemitonic pentatonic scale common in *gagaku* and *min'yō*

riyō: lit. 'village song'; local folk song

rōkyoku: (see *naniwa-bushi*)

rōsaku-uta: work songs

ryū(-ha): artistic lineage or school

ryūkōka: popular songs

saibara: court song genre of the Heian period, supposedly derived from folk songs

sake: rice wine

sankyoku: chamber music genre for shamisen, koto and shakuhachi

sanshin: three-stringed plucked lute of Okinawa with snakeskin head

sato: 'village'; also pronounded *ri*

sawagiuta: boisterous songs sung at drinking parties

seichō: 'correct, authentic' (version of song)

seinendan, seinenkai: Young Men's Association

senden: publicity

senpō: '(musical) mode'

sensei: teacher

shakuhachi: end-blown bamboo flute

shamisen/-jamisen: three-stringed Japanese plucked lute

-shi: 'city'

shigoto-uta: work songs

shimedaiko: a laced-head stick drum

shin-min'yō: 'new folk song'

shinnai: An urban shamisen genre

shin-nihon-ongaku: 'New Japanese Music'; compositions for Japanese instruments but using Western musical elements

shinobue: bamboo transverse flute; also called *takebue* or just *fue*

shinsaku min'yō: 'newly composed *min'yō*'

shizen ni: naturally

shōmyō: Buddhist chant

shunka: lit. 'spring song': bawdy songs

soboku (ni): 'naive(ly)', usually meant as a compliment regarding the supposed simplicity of true folk style

soikake: the person who yells *soi*! between lines of the song 'Esashi Oiwake'

sokkyō: improvisation

son: 'village'; also pronounced *mura*

sō-odori: newly choreographed folk-style dance for all to join

sōsaku: 'composed'

sōsaku min'yō: 'composed' folk songs in Machida's typology

suri-zasara: a scraper used for percussion

sui: elegance

ta-asobi: agricultural ritual performance acting out the rice cycle; also called *haru-tauchi*

taikai: 'grand meeting', convention, competition

taiko: a generic term for stick drums

takebue: a bamboo transverse flute; see *shinobue*

takemono: songs accompanied by shakuhachi

tami: '(the) people'; also pronounced *min* in combination

taue: rice transplanting

taue-uta: rice-transplanting songs

te-odori: 'hand-dances'

tokiwazu: an urban shamisen vocal genre of the Kabuki theatre

tsū: in the know, showing connoisseurship

Tsugaru-jamisen: solo shamisen tradition developed in the Tsugaru region

tsuchikusai: 'smelling of the earth', generally a compliment when said of a folk singer's vocal timbre

tsūjin: man-about-town; a habitué of the geisha houses, a connoisseur of traditional arts

tsuzumi: an hourglass-shaped hand-drum

ujiko: Shinto shrine parishioner

uta: song

utabayashi: same as *hayashi(-kotoba)*

utai: Noh theatre singing

wadaiko: general term for the music of large drum ensembles, developing primarily under the influence of the group Kodō

wakamonogumi: Young Men's Associations

warabeuta: children's songs, especially traditionally transmitted ones

yō: (pronounced *yang* in Chinese, as in *yin-yang*) anhemitonic pentatonic scale; also called *min'yō* or *inaka-bushi* scale

yōgaku: 'Western music'

yoimiya: eve of a festival

yomiuri: sellers of song-sheets

yonanuki tan'onkai: 'pentatonic minor' mode

yonanuki chōonkai: 'pentatonic major' mode

yose: 'variety theatre'

yukata: an unlined kimono of cotton, worn as lounge wear, in summer and at festivals

zashiki-uta: see *ozashiki-uta*

(zenkoku) sō-odori: see *sō-odori*

zokkyoku 俗曲: geisha party song

zoku 俗: common, vulgar, popular

zokugaku 俗楽: 'secular music'

zokuyō 俗謡: wide-ranging term for popular song, for folk songs arranged by professionals and so forth

INDEX OF MUSICAL
WORKS

◼

Listed here are all sorts of musical works, both Japanese and Western, that are referred to in the text and Appendices. Ex = Example, F = Figure, T = Table; see Table of Contents for Ex, F and T page numbers.

NOTES TO
ACCOMPANYING CD

□

N.B. (1) Because of space concerns, virtually all tracks below are excerpts. (2) The Index of Musical Works will lead to any text references for these songs. (3) Many of the tracks taken from commercial CDs are re-issues, and the liner notes do not always state the original dates of recording. For example, CD13 below was probably recorded about twenty years earlier than shown. (4) Melodic modes are shown at the end of each entry. Concerning the distinction of *yō* and *ritsu*, see pp. 36–8. Remember that the *miyako-bushi* mode may substitute a *yō* (*inaka-bushi, min'yō*) tetrachord in some passages, that occasional neighbour or passing notes may appear, that *miyako-bushi* and *ritsu* often shade into one another in actual performance, and that classification is difficult and sometimes arbitrary. (5) All tracks taken from commercial recordings are used by permission of the relevant company, who hold the copyright with all rights reserved. Sincere thanks to Fujimoto Soh for his help in licensing some tracks.

CD1: 'Yagi Bushi' (Gunma Pref.). Horigome Genta IV (vocal), Shiina Suketarō (*shinobue*) et al. As usual for this song, the singer chooses a convenient pitch without regard for the pitch of the preceding flute passage. In some songs (e.g. CD7 below) this may even happen when flute and voice co-occur. Percussion sometimes traditionally included empty wooden *sake* barrels, an effect imitated here. This long dance-ballad tells the tale of the famous local gambling boss and Robin Hood figure Kunisada Chūji (1810–50). (Victor CD *Ketteiban: Nihon no min'yō*, VICG-41013–14, 1997.) [*yō* on 2]

CD2: 'Esashi Oiwake' (Hokkaido). Aosaka Mitsuru (vocal). As with track 28, this comes from an instructional cassette. See Fig. 4.7. (Cassette *Esashi Oiwake no utaikata*, n.d. Esashi: Ōseikai.) [*yō* on 6/3]

CD3: 'Sado Okesa' (Niigata Pref.). Murata Bunzō (vocal) et al. (Columbia LP *Aizō ketteiban: Nihon min'yō daizenshū* FB7031–50 (side FB7050A), 1980 (recorded ca. 1929).) [vocal: mix of *miyako-bushi* & *yō*; flute: *yō* on 2/*ritsu*]

CD4: 'Tsugaru Yosare Bushi' (Aomori Pref.). Kikuchi Tetsuo (vocal), Hasegawa Yūji (shamisen) et al. An incredible piece of vocal artistry, partially improvised; other versions of this famous song may sound very different. Note the uneven rhythm of the shamisen part. (Columbia CD *Ketteiban: kore ga Tsugaru min'yō da*, COCF-10981, 1993.) [*yō* on 6 with upper neighbour 7]

CD5: 'Kiso Bushi' (Nagano Pref.). Kiso Bushi Preservation Society, Agematsu-machi, Kiso-gun. Note that the dance-cycle length (marked by clapping) and the song-cycle length of this Bon dance song differ. (Victor CD *Fukkoku: Nihon no minzoku ongaku, Furyū 4*, VZCG-8020, 1998 (recorded 1966).) [*yō* on 5 = *ritsu*]

CD6: 'Itsuki no Komoriuta' (Kumamoto Pref.). Dōsaka Yoshiko (vocal). Before a popular arrangement around 1953 led to a standard stage version, countless variants of this lullaby were sung in the Itsuki region of Kumamoto; this is one of them. (Smithsonian Folkways CD *Traditional folk songs of Japan* (2 CDs), F4534 (original LP 1963); singer is identified only as 'Japanese woman' but is clearly Dōsaka.) [*miyako-bushi* on 6]

CD7: 'Shinjō Hayashida' (Hiroshima Pref.). Local residents of Shinjō. Rice-transplanting song. Notice that the vocals and flutes are melodically independent. (Victor LP *Hōgaku Taikei 12: Kyōdo geinō*, VP-3029, 1972.) [*yō* on 6 with variation]

CD8: 'Akita Nikata Bushi' (Akita). Kikuchi Tomojirō (vocal), Katakura Yukiji (shamisen), Takahashi Yūjirō (shakuhachi). Frantically rhythmic shamisen contrasts with slow-moving but highly ornamented free-rhythm vocal and shakuhachi. (Nimbus CD *Min'yō: folk song from Japan*, NI 5618, 1999.) [*yō* on 6.]

CD9: 'Etchū Owara Bushi' (Toyama Pref.). Kagayama Akira (vocal), Kagayama Akihiro (*kokyū*) et al. (Victor CD *Ketteiban: Nihon no min'yō*, VICG-41013–14, 1997.) [*yō* on 6]

CD10: 'Sakata / Medeta Bushi' (Iwate Pref.). Five elderly residents of Iwasaki gathered for a tea-drinking session, at which songs are sung (see Fig. 2.2). (Recorded by David Hughes [tape 1988.4], 24 July 1988.) [*miyako-bushi* on 3 / *yō* on 3]

CD11: 'Kuzunoha Kowakare' (Niigata Pref.). Sugimoto Kikue (vocal, shamisen) and another singer. Two *goze*, blind female itinerant performers. Sugimoto briefly has to re-adjust her shamisen's tuning in mid-song. (Victor LP *Hōgaku Taikei 12: Kyōdo geinō*, VP-3029, 1972.) [*yō* on 6/3]

CD12: 'Kagoshima Ohara Bushi' (Kagoshima Pref.). Maezono Tomiko (vocal), Ijichi Ayako (shamisen) et al. At 1'12" the lead singer inserts a spoken *hayashi-kotoba* passage in heavy local dialect: *ima kita nisedon yoka nisedon / sōdan kaketara hatchikoso na nisedon*, 'The boy who's just arrived is a good-looking guy / but talk to him and he'll probably run away'. A simple shamisen motif recurs throughout. (Victor CD *Ketteiban: Nihon no min'yō*, VICG-41013–14, 1997.) [*miyako-bushi* on 3]

CD13: 'Yasugi Bushi' (Shimane Pref.). Izumo Ainosuke II (vocal), Adachi Junkichi & Nosaka Suketoshi (shamisen) et al. This is a lively male dance version of this famous song. As usual for 'Yasugi Bushi', two shamisen improvise independent lines. Liner notes credit a player of the *ōtsuzumi* and *kotsuzumi*, which are uniquely played by one performer for this *min'yō*, but none are audible. (Victor CD *Ketteiban: Nihon no min'yō*, VICG-41013–14, 1997.) [*yō* on 6]

CD14: 'Sasa Odori' (Aomori Pref.). Residents of Neshiro, Hachinohe City. A single verse of 26 moras is made to last around a minute through repetition of lyrics. (Victor CD *Fukkoku: Nihon no minzoku ongaku, Furyū* 4, VZCG-8020, 1998 (recorded 1959).) [*yō* on 3]

CD15: 'Yamanaka Bushi' (Ishikawa Pref.). Yonehachi III (vocal), Matsumi & Kikugorō (shamisen). The performers are local geisha. (Victor CD *Ketteiban: Nihon no min'yō*, VICG-41013–14, 1997.) [*yō*]

CD16: 'Bouchi Uta' (Kanagawa Pref.). Bouchi Uta Preservation Society, Sagamihara City. A barley-threshing song recorded with actual threshing, on stage at Sagamihara Shimin Kaikan auditorium (Fig. 5.1). Compare track 37. (Recorded by David Hughes [tape 43], 10 May 1979.) [*ritsu* with shadings of *miyako-bushi*]

CD17: 'Dozuki Uta' (Iwate Pref.). Itō Moyo et al. (Victor LP *Nihon rōsaku min'yō shūsei*, JV158–163, track 242, 1964.) [between *ritsu* and *miyako-bushi*]

CD18: 'Tsukudajima Bon Uta' (Tokyo). Iida Tsuneo (vocal). Bon dance song from Tsukuda Island in Tokyo harbour. (Recorded by David Hughes [tape 44], 14 July 1979.) [*yō* on 2 = *ritsu*]

CD19: 'Ki-oroshi Uta' (tree-felling song) (Miyazaki Pref.). Kuroki Fukuichi (vocal). The mountain god (*yama no kami*) is asked for understanding prior to cutting down a tree. (Victor CD *Genchi rokuon ni yoru Shiiba no min'yō*, VZCG-8064–5, 1994.) [*ritsu*]

CD20: 'Sōran Bushi' (Hokkaido). Yoichi Seinendan [Youg Men's Association, Yoichi City]. Several groups in Hokkaidō continue to try to preserve this herring-fishing song in something like its original form. It is far better known in its arranged version (track 29). (Columbia LP set *Nihon no min'yō*, AL4118–27, 2nd track, 1963 (recorded 1936).) [*yō* on 6]

CD21: 'Jōshū Magouta' [Gunma Pref.] Kabasawa Yoshikatsu (vocal). Kabasawa, searching for authenticity in the studio, recorded this packhorse-driver's song complete with horse. (Victor LP *Nihon rōsaku min'yō shūsei*, JV158–163, track 283, 1964.) [*yō* on 6]

CD22: 'Ondo Funauta' (Hiroshima Pref.). Takayama Norimasa (vocal), Aki Riyū (*shakuhachi*). Once sung by boatmen as they sculled their boats through the narrows along the Inland Sea. Here we have the sound of waves (produced by pebbles rolled in a screened frame) and of the sculling oar for 'authenticity', but also a *shakuhachi* to make it suitable for stage presentation. (Columbia LP set *Nihon no min'yō*, AL4118–27, track 133, 1963.) [*yō* on 6]

CD23: 'Otemoyan' (Kumamoto Pref.). Performed by 'group from Kumamoto prefecture' (no names given). (Smithsonian Folkways CD *Traditional folk songs of Japan* (2 CDs), F4534 (original LPs 1963); song title given as 'songs of Kumamoto'.) [*yō* on 6]

CD24: 'Daikoku Mai' (Tottori Pref.). Performers (vocals, shamisen, taiko, *kokyū*) from Entsūji, Tottori City. Until a century ago this was performed door-to-door at New Year's, with dancing puppets, to bring good fortune via Daikoku, God of Wealth; today it has been incorporated into a local puppet play tradition. (Victor CD *Dokyumento: Nihon no hōrōgei*, VICG60231–7, disc 2, 1999 (recorded 1970).) [*ritsu* on 5]

CD25: 'Akita Daikoku Mai' (Akita Pref.). Kikuchi Tomojirō (vocal), Takahashi Yūjirō (shamisen) et al. Polished stage version of another song about the god Daikoku once sung door-to-door. (Victor cassette *Kikuchi Tomojirō no min'yō*, VCK-1683, 1989.) [*yō* on 2/*ritsu*]

CD26: Foundation-pounding song (*jizuki uta*) (Miyazaki Pref.). Nakase Mamoru, Nakase Mitsuko, Nakase Asue, Nakase Kesayo (vocals). Recorded out of context many years after the last use of this song in an actual work situation. From 0'31–56", the words and tune are clearly derived from 'Ise Ondo', a song spread throughout Japan via pilgrimages to Ise Shrine. At that point the mode shifts from *yō* on 2 (*ritsu*) to somewhere between *miyako-bushi* and *ritsu*. Such a shift within a single song is uncommon, but the imprecision of intermediate pitches during the solo passage is common enough (see p. 36). (Victor CD *Genchi rokuon ni yoru Shiiba no min'yō*, VZCG-8064–5, 1994.)

CD27: 'Kaigara Bushi' (Tottori Pref.). Hamazawa Chōzaburō (vocal) et al. A rowing song of shellfish gatherers fell into disuse, then in the 1930s was converted to an *ozashiki-uta* to attract tourists to the local Hamamura hot springs. Decades later, the singer recorded here met with elderly fishermen in an effort to restore the song's original mood and melody. (Smithsonian Folkways CD *Traditional folk songs of Japan* (2 CDs), F4534 (original LPs 1963); singers are identified only as 'group from Tottori prefecture' but are clearly led by Hamazawa.) [*yō* on 6]

CD28: 'Esashi Oiwake' (Hokkaidō). Sasaki Motoharu (vocal). This performance comes from an instructional tape on which Sasaki is striving to sing precisely the version preferred by the judges at the annual national contest. See Fig. 4.7. (Cassette *Esashi Oiwake osarai kyōshitsu*, no number, n.d. (ca. 1979) Akita: Fujio Kikaku.) [*yō* on 6/3]

CD29: 'Sōran Bushi' (Hokkaidō). Hamada Kiichi I (vocal) et al. This is a typical modern stage version of the song whose earlier form is captured on track 20. (Victor CD *Ketteiban: Nihon no min'yō*, VICG-41013–14, 1997.) [*yō* on 6]

CD30: 'Kuroda Bushi' (Fukuoka Pref.). Mito Yūji (vocal), Victor Orchestra including koto and *kotsuzumi*. An example of Western harmonization of *min'yō*. Koto is used partly to evoke this song's melodic origins in the *gagaku* piece 'Etenraku'; *kotsuzumi* is rare in *min'yō* but is sometimes used for this song, perhaps because it was often sung by local geisha, who also played this drum. The singer is better known as an *enka* performer (as his timbre suggests), but he has a strong interest in *min'yō*, especially in arrangements such as this. As often in the professional world today, he is not a native of the region of this song. (Victor CD *Ketteiban: Nihon no min'yō*, VICG-41013–14, 1997.) [*miyako-bushi* on 3]

CD31: 'Suzaka Kouta' (Nagano Pref.). Satō Chiyoko (vocal) et al; Noguchi Ujō (lyrics), Nakayama Shinpei (music). Note the use of a *shinobue* intentionally in a different key from the other instruments, as often in traditional folk song. (Victor CD *Tōkyō Ondo, Tenryū Kudareba: Nakayama Shinpei no shin-min'yō*, VZCG-124, 1997 (recorded 1928).) [*yō* on 6 w. upper neighbour 7]

CD32: 'Iizaka Kouta' (Fukushima Pref.). Fujimoto Fumikichi (vocal) et al; Saijō Yaso (lyrics), Nakayama Shinpei (music). (Victor CD *Tōkyō Ondo, Tenryū Kudareba: Nakayama Shinpei no shin-min'yō*, VZCG-124, 1997 (recorded 1931).) [*miyako-bushi* on 7]

CD33: 'Iso Bushi' lesson (Ibaragi Pref.). Iso Bushi Preservation Society members with student from Tokyo. An example of how ornamentation is taught: the visitor from Tokyo is made to repeat a short motif over and over (Fig. 4.4). (Recorded by David Hughes [tape 67], March 1980.) [*yō* on 6]

CD34: 'Shinodayama Bon Uta' (Osaka Pref.). Mori Takenobu (vocal) et al. Bon dance with close to 2,000 people dancing (Fig. 4.3). (Recorded by David Hughes [tape 40], 16 August 1978.) [*yō* on 5/2]

CD35: 'Tsugaru Jongara Bushi (shin-bushi)' (Aomori Pref.). Kanazawa Akiko (vocal), Sawada Katsuaki (shamisen) et al. (Victor CD *Nihon ongaku nyūmon*, VZCG-541, 2005.) [*yō* on 6 w. upper neighbour 7]

CD36: 'Bouchi Uta' (Kanagawa Pref.). Bouchi Uta Preservation Society. Studio recording of this barley-threshing song. Compare track 16. (Victor 45rpm disc, PRA-10135-A, n.d. (ca. 1979).) [*miyako-bushi* on 3]

CD37: 'Nikkō Waraku Odori' (Tochigi Pref.). Employees of Furukawa Denkō Company. Bon dance in the company grounds with diverse vocal interjections from perhaps a thousand dancers including busloads of tourists (Fig. 1.1). Fireworks add to the mood. Singers swap after each verse or two; each chooses a pitch without regard for the flutes, which continue throughout. (Recorded by David Hughes [tape 66], 5 August 1979.) [*yō* on 3]

CD38: 'Dai-Tokyo Ondo' (Tokyo). Kanazawa Akiko & Hashi Yukio (vocals); Takita Tsuneharu (lyrics), Endō Minoru (music). Kanazawa the *min'yō* singer and Hashi the *enka* singer meet halfway stylistically, as is fairly typical of the 'new "new folk songs" ' of this period. (Victor CD *Bon odori ketteiban* VZCG-156, 1999; originally 1979.) [pentatonic major]

GENERAL INDEX

▣

(Compiled by Gina L. Barnes)

Indexed here are the main chapters and their endnotes only, not the front matter or (with a few exceptions) the appendices. All song titles mentioned in the chapters or appendices are indexed only in the separate Index of Musical Works, which is also helpful for finding discussions of the songs included on the CD.

A section marker (e.g. §1.6.6) generally indicates the most extensive unified discussion of a topic; these important sections are, however, noted at the end of entry page number sequences. T = Table, Ex = Example, F = Figure; see Table of Contents for their page numbers.

This index is a combination of alphabetical and classified listings; many items are grouped under a common classified heading as indicated by small capitals (e.g. ASSOCIATIONS, AUDIO EQUIPMENT, GOVERNMENT INSTITUTIONS, HISTORICAL EVENTS, MEDIA, MOVEMENTS, MUSEUMS, PERFORMANCE GROUPS, PERFORMANCE VENUES, PERFORMERS, RESEARCH, SCHOLARS, SINGERS, SONG GENRES, SONG TYPES, etc.). So if a term is not listed alphabetically, please look under a logical classified heading for it. An effort has been made to limit the number of Japanese terms as main entries, with English entries given priority. Translations and some Sino-Japanese characters for Japanese terms can be found in the Glossary.